PLANT PHYSIOLOGY

BERNARD S. MEYER

Chairman, Department of Botany and Plant Pathology,
The Ohio State University and Ohio Agricultural
Experiment Station

AND

DONALD B. ANDERSON

Head, Division of Biological Sciences,
Associate Dean of the Graduate School,
North Carolina State College of Agriculture and Engineering

SECOND EDITION—EIGHTH PRINTING

D. VAN NOSTRAND COMPANY, INC.

PRINCETON, NEW JERSEY

TORONTO   LONDON

NEW YORK

D. VAN NOSTRAND COMPANY, INC.
120 Alexander St., Princeton, New Jersey (*Principal office*)
24 West 40 Street, New York 18, New York

D. Van Nostrand Company, Ltd.
358, Kensington High Street, London, W.14, England

D. Van Nostrand Company (Canada), Ltd.
25 Hollinger Road, Toronto 16, Canada

First Published, May 1939

Thirteen Reprintings

Second Edition, August 1952

*Reprinted February 1954,
August 1955, August 1956,
March 1958, May 1959,
August 1961, June 1963*

PRINTED IN THE UNITED STATES OF AMERICA

PREFACE

The widespread classroom and reference use of the first edition of this book has encouraged the authors to prepare this second edition. The revision has been a very thorough one and in many respects this second edition is virtually a new book.

As was true of the previous edition this book can be readily adapted to use with any introductory course in plant physiology based upon prerequisites of general botany and general chemistry. It can be used as the basis for a conventional recitation course or as a background source of information for student reading in connection with lecture-discussion courses. If only certain topics are selected for lecture or laboratory consideration, reading of the intervening chapters should help the student fit the classroom work into a coordinated picture of the science as a whole. Although the presentation is coordinated from chapter to chapter, the book has been planned so that more advanced phases of most topics can be skipped by omitting certain chapters and portions of chapters without materially disrupting the continuity of the discussion. This feature should make the book useful to those teachers who attempt to present a well-rounded course in plant physiology in one quarter or one semester.

While the content, organization and relative emphasis on various topics have undergone some obvious changes, the fundamental objectives of this second edition are virtually the same as those of the first. The authors have attempted to organize a discussion of the fundamental facts and principles of plant physiology which can be included between the covers of a volume of moderate dimensions. It has been our purpose to give some consideration to all topics which would be considered significant by the majority of plant physiologists. We have attempted to present a reasoned evaluation of the data rather than a mass of undigested facts and contradictory interpretations. Most of the discussion is based directly on data selected from the original literature, much of which is presented in tabular or graphical form. This approach is, we believe, consistent with the thesis that data are the source material from which all scientific

concepts arise, yet it recognizes that facts alone may be a barrier to
scientific progress unless fitted into a logical system of ideas. Students
should grasp uncompromisingly the viewpoint that scientific knowledge
is a structure of ideas derived from facts and observations.

Changes in the text from the previous edition are in content, emphasis,
and organization. Modifications in content reflect principally advances in
our knowledge of plant physiology over the last dozen years. Changes in
emphasis and organization are based largely upon the judgments of the
authors, often reinforced or tempered by suggestions from other teachers
of plant physiology. Some condensation has been effected in the early discussion of basic physicochemical principles, because it is our impression
that students are coming into plant physiology courses with a better
background of such concepts than formerly. The chapters on various
aspects of water relations have been somewhat abridged so that greater
emphasis could be placed on metabolic processes and growth, those phases
of plant physiology in which the most rapid advances have been made in
recent years. A chapter on enzymes has been introduced just after the
discussion of water relations, in order to catalyze an understanding of
immediately following chapters on metabolic processes. This chapter
replaces the chapter on digestion which in the first edition was given a
much later position in the book. Also worthy of note is the shifting of the
discussion of respiration to a position ahead of most discussion of metabolic processes. The increasing realization that respiration is the key to
the synthetic as well as degradative processes of metabolism makes its
earlier discussion desirable. The chapters on growth have undergone a
considerable reorganization, one of the principal objectives of which has
been the achievement of a sharper differentiation between vegetative and
reproductive growth, which contrast just as greatly in their physiological
as in their morphological aspects.

The authors are acutely aware that, for most of the students who will
use this textbook, plant physiology is not an end in itself but a tool to
the better understanding of the behavior of plants under natural or, at
most, only partially controlled conditions. Recognition of this situation
accounts for the essentially ecological viewpoint which underlies much
of the discussion. The effects of various factors on different processes,
relations between daily periodicities of plant processes and daily periodicities of environmental factors, and the bearing of seasonal cycles of
environmental factors on seasonal patterns of plant behavior are consequently given a prominent place in the discussion. On the other hand,
consideration of the mechanisms of processes, always ultimately needful
in the explanation of ecological behavior, has also been quite comprehensive. Explanations of many process mechanisms require excursions

into the domain of biochemistry which we have not hesitated to undertake whenever the level of interpretation which seemed desirable required it.

Although less emphasized than in the previous edition, considerable space is devoted to a review and extension of physicochemical principles with which the student of physiology should be familiar. Some of this discussion is essential for the interpretation of plant processes as such; some of it is essential for an understanding of the nature of the physical factors of the environment and the manner in which they influence plant processes. Likewise the structure of organs, tissues, and cells has been described at appropriate places as necessary background information. Structure and process are inseparable and an integrated picture of both is essential for a clear concept of any phase of the physiological activity of plants.

With only a few exceptions each chapter has appended to it a list of discussion questions. These lists are meant to be suggestive and it is recommended that each teacher supplement them with additional questions, of more or less similar purport, but adapted to the interests and background of his own student group. Most of the questions are of the "problem" type, and many of them have been deliberately chosen to extend the classroom discussion to applications which have not been considered in the text. Effective teaching in any science should not only lead to the acquisition by the student of the basic facts, principles, and viewpoints of that science, but should also train him in the use of that science in the interpretation of natural phenomena. The use of properly selected problems as a teaching device should aid the student in making use of the facts and principles of a science as well as learning them.

A large part of the manuscript of this edition has been read critically by Dr. H. T. Scofield of North Carolina State College and by Dr. C. A. Swanson of The Ohio State University. Certain chapters have likewise been critically read by Dr. G. W. Blaydes and Dr. R. C. Burrell of The Ohio State University, by Prof. T. C. Broyer of the University of California and by Dr. C. O. Miller of the University of Wisconsin. We are indebted to all of these readers for their constructive criticisms. Thanks are also due to Grace Townsend Meyer for checking most of the references. Those figures which have been taken from other sources are properly credited in the captions.

BERNARD S. MEYER
DONALD B. ANDERSON

Columbus, Ohio
Raleigh, N. C.
April, 1952

CONTENTS

I

THE FIELD OF PLANT PHYSIOLOGY

In an effort to understand the mechanism of a plant in its entirety, many separate phases of the dynamic activity of plants have been recognized and studied as individual processes. In attempting to interpret these individual processes and their interrelationships, the plant physiologist is confronted with many problems: What is the mechanism by which water, gases, and solutes enter a plant from its environment? How do such substances pass out of a plant into its surroundings? How are foods and other complex organic compounds synthesized in the plant? How are they utilized in the development and maintenance of plants as living systems? What transformations of energy occur within a plant, and what exchanges of energy take place between a plant and its environment? How are water and solutes transported from one part of a plant to another? How are new tissues constructed? How is the development of one organ or tissue coordinated with the development of other organs or tissues? Why does a plant produce only vegetative organs at certain stages in its life cycle and reproductive organs only at other stages? How are individual plant processes and the development of a plant as a whole influenced by environmental conditions? All of these problems and many other related or subsidiary ones lie within the province of the branch of science that is known as plant physiology.

For convenience, the study of plant life is subdivided into various branches such as physiology, morphology, anatomy, ecology, pathology, and genetics. Such a classification is necessarily more or less arbitrary. Neither physiology nor any other phase of plant life can be singled out for study without some consideration of plants from other viewpoints. A particularly intimate interrelationship exists between the structures and processes of plants. Every physiological process is conditioned by the anatomical arrangement of the tissues, and by the size, configuration, and

1

other structural features of the cells in which it occurs. Furthermore, the coordinated development of cells and tissues, *i.e.*, of the plant itself, is a complex of physiological processes. Thus the sciences of plant physiology and plant anatomy merge in the study of plant growth.

Just as different species of plants differ in outward configuration and internal anatomy, so do they also differ in physiology. The world of plants includes a great number of very diverse kinds of organisms that range in size from simple bacterial cells a few microns long to the enormous redwoods of California. Their difference in size, although striking enough, is not as fundamental as another distinction which exists between redwoods and bacteria. The redwoods and all other green plants are able to manufacture their own food, while bacteria (with a very few exceptions) and all other non-green plants must obtain their nourishment from some outside source. The physiology of the green and the non-green plants is therefore basically unlike. This book is essentially a discussion of the physiology of the chlorophyllous (green) plants with the emphasis on the vascular green plants. The physiological processes of the bacteria and fungi have been considered only when they have a direct bearing on the physiology of the green plants.

In general the basic physiology of all vascular green plants is similar. This is not to say, however, that the processes occurring in one kind of green plant are always identical with those occurring in another. The physiology of a tomato plant differs from that of an oak tree in the same sense that the physiology of a horse is different from that of a cat. Many qualitative differences in metabolism are known to exist among plants. Most green plants, for example, synthesize starch, but many do not. Most of the physiological differences among species of green plants are quantitative rather than qualitative. All vascular green plants synthesize chlorophylls *a* and *b*, for example, but the proportions of these two pigments present differ considerably from one species to another. Similarly, under identical soil and climatic conditions, the rates of absorption of water by two kinds of plants may be very different. Even varieties of the same species may differ markedly in their physiological reactions to a given environmental complex. Under the same climatic and soil conditions, for example, some varieties of wheat are markedly cold resistant, while others are not.

The Relation of Physiology to the Physical Sciences.—Formerly the opinion was almost universal that living organisms owe their distinctive properties to the possession of subtle and unknown forces which are peculiar to "living matter." At the present time such "vitalistic" theories find very few advocates. The contrary and now widely held assumption is that living organisms operate in accordance with the same physicochemical principles that hold in the inanimate world. The complexity and elusiveness of living processes are not assumed to result from intangible, unknown varieties of energy, but to the intricateness of the interplay of recognizable physicochemical forces in the complex organized system of the protoplasm.

Adoption of this latter point of view has led to a widespread use of the tools of physics and chemistry in experimental work on plants, and to the interpretation of plant processes in terms of these two sciences. This has led to notable progress in our understanding of the physiology of plants and has permitted the analysis and expression of many physiological relations in quantitative terms.

A knowledge of certain fundamental principles of physics and chemistry is therefore essential to the understanding of physiological processes. For this reason several of the earlier and parts of some of the later chapters in this book are devoted to a brief exposition of certain underlying principles of the physical sciences with which a student of plant physiology should be familiar.

The Relation of Plant Physiology to the Agricultural Sciences.—Green plants are not only the ultimate source of all food but supply the raw materials for many of our basic industries. With the rise of modern industrial civilization both the quantities and kinds of plant products which we utilize have increased rather than decreased. In addition to foods some of the more important raw products obtained from plants are wood, textile fibers, pulp, rubber, vegetable oils, gums, and drugs. Even most of the so-called "synthetic products" of the chemist are not synthetic in the sense that they have been built up from simple inorganic compounds, but only insofar as they represent modifications of naturally occurring plant products.

An industrial civilization not only requires a wide variety of plant products but insists that these products meet certain standards of quality. The successful cultivation of plants has, therefore, become a highly skilled occupation, and the agricultural sciences are rapidly becoming a domain of the specialist. Success in controlling the activities of living plants cannot be achieved without some understanding of the processes which occur within them, and of the effects of environmental conditions upon these processes. The problems of the forester, the fruit grower, the cotton planter, the floriculturist, the grain farmer, and of all others who cultivate plants differ in detail, yet they all have a fundamental similarity in requiring an application of the principles of plant physiology for their solution.

Fundamental investigations in plant physiology have contributed in many ways to improved methods of propagating, cultivating, and harvesting economically important plants, and to methods of handling and storing many plant products. Furthermore, control of the fungous diseases and insect predators of plants often requires application of the principles of plant physiology. Much of the investigational work carried on by scientific agronomists, horticulturists, floriculturists, and foresters actually lies in the field of pure or applied plant physiology, although often it is not formally classed as such.

The last hundred years have witnessed the evolution of the agricultural sciences from largely empirical arts into the realm of applied sciences. More progress has been made in their improvement during this period than during all previous history. In substantial part this development of a scientific approach to the practice of agriculture has come as a result of advances in our knowledge of the physiology of plants.

Plant Physiology as a Science.—The origin of man's first conscious interest in plants long antedates recorded history. Agriculture had already become a highly developed art thousands of years before any experimental study of plant processes began. Consequently, there had grown up a vast body of traditional plant lore which passed orally from father to son, generation after generation. This practical knowledge of plants developed over many centuries as a result of countless, mostly involuntary, trial-and-error experiences and innumerable observations of plant behavior under all kinds of circumstances. Much of this mass of mingled facts and beliefs regarding plants is alive in the consciousness of the common man today. The closer he lives to the soil and the more familiar he is with traditional plant lore, the more they influence his thoughts and actions.

Many of these customarily accepted beliefs are essentially sound and most of them contain elements of truth. Others, however, are entirely erroneous, and not a few are tempered with superstitions, some of which have an unbroken lineage back to the days of witch-doctors and savagery. No reputable botanist has held for generations, for example, that plants obtain their food from the soil, yet this and many other fallacious beliefs are still widely entertained among the general population.

The value of practical information about plants should not be underrated, since its perpetuation in the mind of man permitted the development of agriculture to a high plane as a practical art before any widespread investigation of plants from a scientific point of view was undertaken. Nevertheless, traditional plant lore frequently is not only inadequate, but is riddled with misconceptions, and often suffers from points of view which are inherently stultifying to the acquisition of further knowledge.

The layman, for example, often personifies plants in an attempt to explain their behavior. Man has desires and foresight, and it is often assumed, either consciously or tacitly, that plants are similarly endowed. To many, for example, the statement that "roots grow downward in search of water," or that "stems grow upward in order to reach the light" are accepted as adequate "explanations" of plant behavior. Man's knowledge that water and light are essential to plants is not evidence that plants are similarly aware of these facts. To assume that plants realize their needs and are able to act in conformity with their requirements is equivalent to crediting them with a high order of intelligence. Explanations of plant behavior are commonly encountered in which purposeful action on the part of plants is tacitly or deliberately implied, although there is no justification for the adoption of such a point of view.

Furthermore, the layman seldom pursues his quest for information about plants beyond the stage of observation, while the scientist frequently does. Observation has suggested, for example, that light is necessary for the continued existence of plants. To one who is scientifically minded, either by instinct or training, the obvious next step is to test this postulate experimentally. If the suggested hypothesis is substantiated by experiment it is tentatively accepted as a theory. Theories such as those proposed in explanation of the processes or reactions of plants, together with the experimental results which are considered to support them, are usually published in a scientific journal or monograph and thus exposed to evaluation and further experimental testing by other scientists.

Continued experimentation may lead to substantiation, rejection, or modification of the theory as originally proposed. Modification would undoubtedly be the fate of the hypothesis used as an example, since sooner or later some investigator would find that non-green plants can thrive in the absence of light.

Experiments often raise more questions than they answer. New approaches to the problem under consideration as well as desirable new lines of inquiry are constantly opening up to the alert investigator. In this way experimentation leads to more experimentation, more facts accumulate, and more theories are proposed. Some of the suggested hypotheses are confirmed, others are rejected, and still others are modified. Most of them, sound or fallacious, in turn suggest further observation and experimentation. As a result of such endless and painstaking labors there is slowly built up that vast, complex, and ever-changing body of knowledge which we refer to as a science.

The system of subjecting all hypothetical explanations of natural phenomena to experimentation is the essence of experimental science. Progressive modification of accepted concepts in the light of new experi-

mental findings continually increases the soundness of scientific generalizations. Thus there are incorporated into any science theories and
generalizations in various stages of acceptance. Some stand upon such a
firm substructure of facts that they are accepted by all authorities in
the field. Others, less securely supported by experimental results, are
subscribed to by some but rejected by other workers. Finally, in any
science there are always some theories which are so dubious that they
find only a few advocates. Furthermore, some of the theories now
widely held sooner or later will be discarded or modified as a result of
new findings or as a consequence of different interpretations of facts
already known.

However, not all scientists are always in agreement regarding the interpretation of the same sets of facts. Although this state of affairs is
entirely consistent with the spirit of scientific research, it is frequently
puzzling to students and laymen. Differences of opinion regarding the
hypotheses which suitably explain scientific phenomena are most likely
to arise when experimental data are inadequate. Disagreements regarding the interpretation of experiments and observations are often inevitable steps in the clarification of scientific generalizations. Controversies
usually focus attention upon gaps in our factual information. Frequently, therefore, they are stimulating to research and often lead to a
further enrichment of human knowledge.

Without the knowledge of plant processes which has been slowly accumulated through more than two centuries of observation, experimentation, and critical evaluation by numerous workers in all parts of the
world, this book could never have been written. In spite of the patient
labors of these many workers, vast gaps still exist in our understanding
of the physiology of plants—gaps which are reflected in the necessarily
inadequate treatment of many topics in this book. The future of this
science and all others lies in the hands of the front-line investigators
who wage a continual struggle for the extension of human knowledge.

SUGGESTED FOR COLLATERAL READING

Dampier, W. C. A History of Science. 3rd Ed. The Macmillan Co. New York.
    1946.
Harvey-Gibson, R. J. Outlines of the History of Botany. A. and C. Black. Lon-
    don. 1919.
Nordenskiöld, E. The History of Biology. Translated by L. B. Eyre. Alfred A.
    Knopf, Inc. New York. 1932.
Reed, H. S. A Short History of the Plant Sciences. Chronica Botanica Co. Wal-
    tham, Mass. 1942.
Sachs, J. History of Botany. Translated by H. E. F. Garnsey. Revised by I. B.
    Balfour. Clarendon Press. Oxford. 1906.

II

PROPERTIES OF SOLUTIONS

Water is the most abundant compound present in all physiologically active plant cells. The water which occurs in a liquid state in plant cells invariably contains other substances dissolved in it and usually also contains dispersed particles which are not in true solution. When the particles dispersed throughout the water are within a certain range of sizes the system of water plus particles falls into the category of *colloidal systems*. The complicated dynamics of living systems can be largely interpreted in terms of the physicochemical properties of solutions and colloidal systems, one component of which is water, although it should not be inferred that nonaqueous solutions and colloidal systems are entirely absent in living organisms.

Similarly liquid water never occurs in the pure state in the natural environment of living organisms. The water of streams, lakes, and oceans invariably contains various substances in solution and usually in the form of dispersed particles as well. This is likewise true of the soil water. Even raindrops, the products of natural distillation, contain gases and other solutes which have dissolved in them from the atmosphere.

General Nature of Solutions.—Simple solutions are systems in which one component (the solute) is dispersed throughout the other (the solvent) in the form of molecules or ions. Theoretically the solvent may be a gas, a solid, or a liquid, but solutions in which the solvent is a liquid are by far the most important in living organisms. Except in extremely concentrated solutions the average distance between the solute particles is usually very great relative to their size. Naturally occurring solutions, whether in living organisms or their environment, usually contain a number of different solutes and are often exceedingly complex. Water is the commonest and most important of all solvents both in the in-

7

organic world and in the realm of living organisms. The further discussion will be principally in terms of aqueous solutions.

Solutions of a Gas in a Liquid.—The water present in living organisms usually contains dissolved gases. Those most commonly present are carbon dioxide, oxygen, and nitrogen. Practically all the water in the environment of organisms—in oceans, lakes, streams, soils, and raindrops—also contains these gases in solution, and sometimes others as well.

A given volume of water or any other liquid will hold only a limited quantity of gas in solution at a given temperature. When no more of a certain gas can be dissolved in a liquid it is said to be *saturated* with respect to that gas. Gases vary widely in their solubility in water, but in general fall into two groups: those which are sparingly soluble, and those which are highly soluble. When only a small fraction of a unit volume of a gas will dissolve in a unit volume of water the gas is classified in the sparingly soluble group. When from one to many unit volumes of a gas will dissolve in one unit volume of water it is classified in the highly soluble group.

Oxygen, hydrogen, and nitrogen are familiar examples of gases belonging to the first group, while carbon dioxide, ammonia, and hydrogen chloride are examples of the second. When gases are highly soluble in water it is usually evidence that a chemical reaction takes place between the gas and water. The reactions between water and carbon dioxide and water and ammonia are indicated in the following equations:

$$CO_2 + H_2O \rightleftarrows H_2CO_3$$

$$NH_3 + H_2O \rightleftarrows NH_4OH$$

In a solution of such gases not only are molecules of the gas present, but also molecules of a compound formed by the reaction of the gas with water. The apparently great solubility of gases such as these results from the formation of relatively soluble compounds by the reaction of the gas with the water. The solubilities of some common gases in water are shown in Table 1.

In general, as also shown in Table 1, an increase in temperature decreases the solubility of a gas in a liquid.

Increase in pressure of a gas above a liquid increases the solubility, *i.e.*, the concentration of that gas in the liquid. For sparingly soluble gases the increase in solubility is directly proportional to the increase in pressure ("Law of Henry"). This principle also holds qualitatively, but not quantitatively, for the very soluble gases.

When a mixture of several gases is maintained over water, each dissolves independently and in accordance with the gaseous pressure ("partial pressure") which it exerts against the surface of the water ("Law of Dalton"). This principle holds strictly only for those gases which are slightly soluble in water. For example, about one-fifth of the atmospheric pressure results from the oxygen present. Assuming an atmospheric pressure of 760 mm. Hg (the value at standard conditions), the pressure resulting from the oxygen is equivalent to about 152 mm. Hg. The quantity of oxygen which dissolves in water exposed to the air is the same as that which would dissolve if oxygen only at a pressure of 152 mm. Hg occupied the space over the water.

TABLE I—SOLUBILITY OF SOME COMMON GASES IN WATER AT DIFFERENT TEMPERATURES WHEN THE PRESSURE OF THE GAS IS ONE ATMOSPHERE

Gas	Volume of gas dissolved in one volume of water (reduced to standard conditions)		
	10° C.	20° C.	30° C.
Carbon Dioxide.....................	1.194	0.878	0.665
Oxygen...........................	0.0380	0.0310	0.0261
Nitrogen..........................	0.0186	0.0154	0.0134
Hydrogen.........................	0.0195	0.0182	0.0170

Solutions of a Liquid in a Liquid.—In general, solutions of a liquid in a liquid fall into two classes: those in which the liquids are freely miscible with each other in all proportions, and those in which each liquid reaches a definite point of saturation in the other. Ethanol (ethyl alcohol) and water, for example, mix with each other in all proportions; such a solution is an example of the first mentioned type. Many oily liquids also are miscible with each other in all proportions. A familiar example is the solution of lubricating oil in gasoline. In solutions of this kind the liquid present in excess is usually considered to be the solvent. In a 50 per cent solution of ethanol and water, either liquid could be considered the solvent, or either could be considered the solute.

Ether, chloroform, and many other liquids are sparingly soluble in water. After water and ether, for example, are shaken together in a flask, two distinct layers of liquid separate upon standing. The upper layer consists of the lighter ether, saturated with water, and the lower consists of water saturated with ether. In both layers, however, the concentration of solute present at saturation is small. In the upper layer ether is the solvent, water the solute; the opposite is true of the lower layer.

Solutions of a Solid in a Liquid.—This is by far the most familiar type of solution and in many respects the most important. Substances in the solid state vary greatly in their solubility in water, ranging all the way from those which are virtually insoluble to those which are extremely soluble. There is usually a limit to the amount of any solute which can be dissolved in a given volume of water at a given temperature. When this limiting concentration is reached the solution is said to be *saturated*, following the same terminology used with solutions of gases and liquids in liquids. It is almost impossible to prepare a true saturated solution of any solute unless some of it is also present in the solid state. Under certain conditions, and only when none of the undissolved solid is present, a *super-saturated* solution can be prepared; *i.e.*, a solution in which the concentration of the solute is greater than that in the saturated solution. If a fragment of the solid solute be added to such a solution, the excess solute usually crystallizes out immediately, and the concentration of the solution decreases to that usually present at saturation.

Usually increase in temperature increases the solubility of a solid in a liquid, but there are some exceptions to this principle. The solubility of common salt (NaCl) in water, for example, is only slightly influenced by temperature, whereas the solubility of many calcium compounds is decreased by an increase in the temperature of water.

Methods of Expressing the Composition of Solutions.—If a mol [1] of any soluble compound be dissolved in just enough water to make exactly one liter of solution, the result is a *volume molar* solution. Since the volume of water changes with temperature, it is usual to specify that the solution is to be made up to a liter volume at 20°C. Whenever the word *molar* is used without qualification, this type of solution is meant. Similarly, if half the molar weight or one-tenth the molar weight of a substance be dissolved in enough water to make exactly one liter of solution, the result is a half molar (0.5 M) or tenth molar (0.1 M) solution, respectively, etc. Gram molar weights of all substances contain the same number of molecules. The best estimate to date shows this number to be about 6.02×10^{23} molecules. Hence, one liter of any volume molar solution will contain this number of solute molecules, one milliliter (0.001 liter) will contain one thousandth of this number, and so on. Equal volumes of all solutions of the same volume molarity contain the same number of solute molecules but different numbers of solvent molecules. If a given volume of a volume molar solution be diluted with an equal volume of water, the result is a 0.5 M solution; if a given volume be diluted with nine volumes of water, the result is a 0.1 M solution, etc. Therefore a volume molar solution of any strength may be diluted with water, and the resulting more dilute solution will have a volume molarity in proportion as it has been diluted.

[1] A mol is the molecular weight of a compound in grams.

If a mol of any soluble substance be completely dissolved in 1000 g. of water, the result is a *weight molar* or *molal* solution. Such solutions are used principally in experimental work upon various osmotic phenomena. The addition of a mol of most solids to a liter of water increases the volume of the resulting solution to more than one liter. This increase in volume is called the *solution volume* of the solute. The solution volume of many substances is very small, and for a few it is even negative, *i.e.*, there is a shrinkage in volume when the solute is added to the solvent. On the other hand, the solution volume of some compounds, especially the sugars, is considerable. When a mol of sucrose is added to 1000 g. of water, the resulting solution will have a volume of 1207 cc. at 0°C. Hence the solution volume of a mol of sucrose is 207 ml. The solution volume of a mol of sodium chloride, on the other hand, is only about 18 ml. Since every solute has a different solution volume, it follows that equal volumes of molal solutions of different substances do not contain the same number of either solvent or solute molecules. Dilution of a given volume of a 1 molal solution with an equal volume of water does not result in a 0.5 molal solution because such solutions must be diluted in terms of the volume of solvent present, not in terms of the total volume of the solution.

In physiological work it is often convenient to make up solutions on a percentage basis. Unfortunately not all workers follow the same rules for the preparation of percentage solutions. The simplest and least ambiguous procedure to follow is to make all such solutions strictly on the basis of percentage by weight. A 10 per cent solution of sodium chloride, for example, is made by dissolving 10 g. of sodium chloride in 90 g. of water. Similarly, a 20 per cent solution of acetone is made by mixing 20 g. of acetone with 80 g. of water. Solutions of liquids in liquids, such as the immediately preceding example, are often made up according to percentage by volume. Because of the shrinkage in total volume which often results when two liquids are mixed, however, this is not a very satisfactory procedure.

Electrolytes and Non-Electrolytes.—Some aqueous solutions readily conduct an electric current; others do not. The former are called *electrolytes;* the latter *non-electrolytes.*[2] The solutions of all acids, bases, and salts are electrolytes. Solutions of most organic compounds such as the sugars, alcohols, ketones, and ethers are non-electrolytes.

Passage of an electric current through an electrolyte results in its decomposition. This process is called *electrolysis.* If hydrochloric acid is the electrolyte, for example, hydrogen gas will be liberated at the nega-

---

[2] Strictly speaking the term electrolyte refers only to a *solution* of an ionized substance, but it is also often applied to any *compound* which, when dissolved in water, produces ions. A similar dual usage of the term non-electrolyte also prevails.

tive pole (*cathode*) and chlorine gas will be liberated at the positive pole (*anode*). If electrolysis is continued long enough, eventually all of the hydrochloric acid present in the system will be decomposed into hydrogen gas and chlorine gas.

The occurrence of electrolysis, as well as the unusually large effects of electrolytes on the osmotic pressures of solutions (Chap. VI), has led to an explanation of the behavior of electrolytes in terms of the theory of electrolytic dissociation. This theory was first advanced by the Swedish chemist Arrhenius in 1887. According to the Arrhenius theory, when an electrolyte is dissolved in water some of the molecules *dissociate* into two kinds of particles, one positively charged, the other negatively charged. Each of these particles is called an *ion.* Ions are supposed to be present in a solution whether any electrolysis occurs or not. Two, three, four, or even more ions may be formed from a single molecule. The conduction of an electrical current by an electrolyte is a consequence of the presence of these ions. The dissociation of several typical electrolytes is indicated by the following equations:

$$NaCl \rightleftarrows Na^+ + Cl^-$$

$$CaCl_2 \rightleftarrows Ca^{++} + Cl^- + Cl^-$$

$$Na_2SO_4 \rightleftarrows Na^+ + Na^+ + SO_4^{--}$$

The positively charged ions, which in electrolysis migrate toward the cathode, are called *cations;* the negatively charged ions which migrate toward the anode are called *anions.* A cation may carry one, two, three, or even four positive charges; an anion may carry from one to several negative charges. When an electrolyte dissociates, the number of positive charges carried on the cations is always equal to the number of negative charges carried by the anions.

The Arrhenius theory does not assume complete ionization of all of the solute molecules in an electrolyte but that the molecules are continuously dissociating into ions, while free ions in the solution are continuously reuniting and forming molecules, both processes proceeding at an equal rate whenever an equilibrium condition prevails. An equilibrium of this sort, which is maintained by two opposing processes proceeding at equal rates, is termed a *dynamic equilibrium.* Electrolytes vary greatly in degree of ionization (Table 2). Those in which a large proportion of the molecules are maintained in a dissociated condition are termed "strong" electrolytes; those of which the contrary is true, "weak" electrolytes. "Strong" electrolyte solutions conduct electric currents better than "weak" electrolyte solutions of equal concentration. In general the more dilute a given electrolyte solution the larger the proportion of dissociated molecules present. In extremely dilute solutions ionization is practically complete.

It is probable that many of the so-called non-electrolytes also dissociate very slightly in solution, but the degree of ionization of such compounds is so small that it can be detected only by very refined methods, if at all. Even water, as the subsequent discussion will show, dissociates slightly, producing hydrogen and hydroxyl ions.

The theory of electrolytic dissociation accounts much more satisfactorily for the behavior of weak electrolytes than of strong electrolytes. Furthermore, X-ray studies of the crystals of electrolytes, such as sodium chloride, show them to be composed wholly of ions. For these and other reasons Debye and Hückel (1923) advanced a modification of the original dissociation theory which reconciles otherwise conflicting facts.

TABLE 2—DEGREE OF DISSOCIATION OF NORMAL SOLUTIONS OF SOME
COMMON ELECTROLYTES

Electrolyte	Degree of Dissociation	Electrolyte	Degree of Dissociation
HNO_3	82 per cent	$Ba(OH)_2$	69 per cent
HCl	78	KCl	74
H_2SO_4	51	$BaCl_2$	57
KOH	77	K_2SO_4	59
NaOH	73	$CuSO_4$	22

According to the Debye-Hückel theory all strong electrolytes are completely ionized in solution. The fact that they appear to be only partly ionized is accounted for in terms of interionic attractions. The anions and cations of NaCl, for example, attract each other, and this attraction is so great that a considerable proportion of the ions present become immobilized. Thus there are supposed to be present in the solution both immobile or bound cations and anions, and mobile free cations and anions. The two categories of ions are supposed to be in dynamic equilibrium with each other. The greater the dilution of the solution, the greater the proportion of free to bound ions.

One further aspect of this theory should be mentioned. A bivalent cation such as Ca^{++} carries twice the positive charge carried by a univalent cation such as Na^+. Such bivalent cations attract anions more strongly than univalent cations. Hence, in a solution of $CaCl_2$ there is a larger proportion of immobile ions (equivalent to a smaller degree of ionization) than in a solution of NaCl of equal concentration. In a solution of $CuSO_4$, both ions being bivalent, the proportion of immobile ions is even greater, resulting in a still lower apparent degree of ionization (Table 2).

The consequences of electrolyte behavior as pictured by the Debye-Hückel theory are almost identical with those pictured by the original Arrhenius theory. According to the Debye-Hückel theory the *degree of ionization* of an electrolyte represents the proportion of *free ions* in a solution in contrast to immobile or *bound ions;* according to the Arrhenius theory it represents the proportion of *ions* in contrast to *undissociated molecules.*

Acids, Bases, and Salts.—An acid may be defined as a substance which forms hydrogen ions (H^+) when dissolved in water. Since H^+ is a proton (*i.e.*, a hydrogen atom minus an electron), from another point of view an acid can be considered to be a compound which is a proton donor. For various reasons it is considered unlikely that free protons wander at large in a solution, and there is evidence that each proton (hydrogen ion) becomes loosely attached to a water molecule, becoming a *hydronium* ion (H_3O^+). From this point of view the ionization of an acid represents a reaction with water:

$$HCl + H_2O \rightleftarrows H_3O^+ + Cl^-$$

Although this theory of the ionization of acids is widely accepted, in actual practice the symbol H^+ is still generally used in discussions of acidity and hydrogen ion concentration.

The most common inorganic acids are hydrochloric (HCl), nitric (HNO_3), and sulfuric (H_2SO_4). In living organisms a large group of more complex, but much weaker acids, known as organic acids, play important roles. The "strength" of an acid depends upon its degree of ionization; the greater the proportion of hydrogen ions an acid produces in solution at a given concentration, the "stronger" it is.

A base may be defined as a substance which produces hydroxyl ions (OH^-) when dissolved in water. The characteristic properties of bases result from the hydroxyl ions produced. Some of the commonest bases are sodium hydroxide (NaOH), calcium hydroxide ($Ca(OH)_2$), and potassium hydroxide (KOH). The "strength" of a base, like that of an acid, depends upon its degree of ionization. The greater the proportion of hydroxyl ions a base produces in solution at a given concentration, the "stronger" it is.

A salt may be defined as a compound which has been formed by the union of an anion or anions of an acid with the cation or cations of a base. Salts are formed when an acid and a base are brought together in a solution, as a result of a chemical union between the hydrogen ion(s) of the acid and the hydroxyl ion(s) of the base, forming water. This reaction is called *neutralization.* Following are several examples:

$$HCl + NaOH \rightleftarrows NaCl + H_2O$$

$$H_2SO_4 + 2\ KOH \rightleftarrows K_2SO_4 + 2\ H_2O$$

$$2\ HCl + Ca(OH)_2 \rightleftarrows CaCl_2 + 2\ H_2O$$

Since water is practically undissociated, neutralization reactions go rapidly to completion. The reverse reaction, indicated in the above equations by the arrows pointing to the left, is called *hydrolysis*.

Under certain conditions hydrolytic reactions may proceed at a rapid rate, although in the examples presented above the speed of the reaction toward the left (hydrolysis) is negligible compared with the speed of the reaction toward the right (neutralization).

Normal Solutions.—The concentrations of acids and bases are most commonly expressed in terms of normal solutions. A *normal solution* of an electrolyte contains in a dissolved state per liter of solution at 20°C. a weight of the compound in grams equal to its molar weight divided by its hydrogen equivalent. The *hydrogen equivalent* of a compound is defined as the number of replaceable hydrogen atoms in one molecule, or the number of atoms of hydrogen with which one molecule could react. Thus a normal solution of an acid contains 1.008 g. of replaceable hydrogen per liter; a normal solution of a base 17.008 g. of replaceable hydroxyl per liter. By this system the concentration of any acid, base, or salt can be designated as 0.1 N, 0.5 N, 2 N, etc., as the case may be.

The normality of an acid solution is a measure of its *total acidity, i.e.,* of its concentration in terms of replaceable hydrogen ions. Similarly the normality of a base solution is a measure of its *total basicity.* Since 1.008 g. of replaceable hydrogen represents the same number of ions as 17.008 g. of replaceable hydroxyl, it is evident that equal volumes of acid and base solutions of equal normality will exactly neutralize each other.

Hydrogen Ion Concentration.—The effects of acids upon chemical reactions and upon physicochemical conditions generally in both inorganic systems and in living organisms result principally from the hydrogen ions which they produce when in solution. Some of the most fundamental of physiological phenomena are markedly influenced by the concentration of hydrogen ions in the medium in which they occur. For many purposes, therefore, it is more important to have some sort of a measuring stick of the concentration of hydrogen ions present in a solution than of the total acidity of the solution.

Total acidity, as already noted, is customarily expressed in terms of normality. It is also entirely possible to use the normal system for expressing the concentration of hydrogen ions. A normal solution of hydrochloric acid, for example, behaves as if about 78 per cent of the molecules are dissociated. The term "normal" as used in the preceding sentence refers to total acidity, *i.e.*, to all the ionizable hydrogen whether actually present as ions or combined with anions in the form of molecules. In terms of the hydrogen *ions* present, however, such a solution is only 0.78 N. The term "normal" as used in this latter sense refers only to the *ionized* hydrogen. We may speak, therefore, of a normal solution of hydrogen ions as well as of a normal solution of an acid.

Since no acid ever behaves as if completely dissociated, a normal solution of any acid will always be less than normal when its concentration is expressed in terms of the hydrogen ions present. In order to prepare a normal solution of hydrogen ions it is necessary to make up a solution which is more than normal in terms of total acidity. Such a solution must be of the precise strength and degree of dissociation that exactly 1.008 g. of the ionizable hydrogen present are actually in the dissociated form— as ions—per liter of the solution.

Although hydrogen ion concentration can be readily expressed in terms of normalities, in actual practice this system is not generally used because it is likely to prove cumbersome, especially when it is necessary to refer to the very small concentrations of hydrogen ions usually dealt with in biological problems. The hydrogen ion concentration of a solution is generally defined in terms of its pH value. The pH value bears a simple mathematical relation to the hydrogen ion concentration of a solution in terms of its normality. Because of the practically universal acceptance of this system it is necessary to understand the significance of the term pH and its relation to hydrogen ion concentration expressed in terms of normality.

The relation between pH and hydrogen ion concentration in terms of normality is a logarithmic one (Table 3). The pH of a normal solution of hydrogen ions is 0, of a 0.1 N solution 1, of a 0.01 N solution 2, and so forth. Zero is the logarithm of 1, 1 is the logarithm of 10, 2 is the logarithm of 100, and so forth. The pH value for any solution is the negative of the logarithm of the hydrogen ion concentration in terms of normality. It may also be defined as the logarithm of the number of liters of solution that contains one gram atomic weight of hydrogen ions.

All aqueous solutions as well as pure water contain hydrogen ions in some concentration. Corresponding to the concentration of hydrogen ions is a certain definite concentration of hydroxyl ions. This concentration of hydroxyl ions is indicated in Table 3 as pOH. It can be shown by the principle of mass action that the mathematical product of the concentration of hydroxyl ions and the concentration of hydrogen ions in a solution is a constant. This may be expressed as follows:

$$(H^+) \times (OH^-) = K. \qquad K = 10^{-14} \text{ at } 22°C.$$

TABLE 3—THE RELATION OF pH TO HYDROGEN-ION CONCENTRATION EXPRESSED IN TERMS OF NORMALITY

							Acid Range							Alkaline Range	
H ion concentration in terms of normality	I 10^0	.I 10^{-1}	.0I 10^{-2}	.00I 10^{-3}	.000I 10^{-4}	.0000I 10^{-5}	.00000I 10^{-6}	.... .0000001 10^{-7}	.00000001 10^{-8}	.000000001 10^{-9}	.0000000001 10^{-10}	.00000000001 10^{-11}	.000000000001 10^{-12}	.0000000000001 10^{-13}	.00000000000001 10^{-14}
pH	0	1	2	3	4	5	6	7	8	9	10	11	12	13	14
pOH	14	13	12	11	10	9	8	7	6	5	4	3	2	1	0
OH ion concentration in terms of normality	.00000000000001 10^{-14}	.0000000000001 10^{-13}	.000000000001 10^{-12}	.00000000001 10^{-11}	.0000000001 10^{-10}	.000000001 10^{-9}	.00000001 10^{-8}	.0000001 10^{-7}	.000001 10^{-6}	.00001 10^{-5}	.0001 10^{-4}	.001 10^{-3}	.01 10^{-2}	.1 10^{-1}	I 10^0

Hence, as the pH of a solution is increased, the pOH decreases and *vice-versa*. For example, if the pH increases from 5 to 6, the pOH decreases from 9 to 8.

Furthermore, only at pH 7 can the concentration of hydrogen ions equal the concentration of hydroxyl ions. This is, therefore, the neutral point on the pH scale (at 22°C.) and corresponds to the dissociation of pure water. This pH value represents a dissociation of only one water molecule in approximately every 555,000,000.

Values below 7 on the pH scale represent the acid range, those above 7 the alkaline range of the scale. An "acid" solution is one with a larger concentration of hydrogen ions than hydroxyl ions, while in an "alkaline" solution the reverse is true. The lower the pH value the greater the hydrogen ion concentration of a solution. A pH value of 5 represents ten times the hydrogen ion concentration of a solution with a pH of 6 and one hundred times the hydrogen ion concentration of one with a pH value of 7. This is a consequence of the fact, previously emphasized, that the numbers on the pH scale are related to each other as logarithms and not as ordinary arithmetic numbers.

The hydroxyl ion concentration of a solution could be expressed in pOH units instead of in pH units. For alkaline solutions especially this would seem to be a logical practice. But because of the definite mathematical relationship between the pH and pOH, the pH value alone also defines the pOH value. Hence both the acidity of a solution in terms of H^+ ions and its alkalinity in terms of OH^- ions may be, and customarily are, expressed in terms of pH units.

Table 3 shows only the pH values corresponding to the range between a normal solution in terms of hydrogen ions and a normal solution in terms of hydroxyl ions. It is possible for aqueous solutions to exist which have a pH value of less than 0 (*i.e.*, a minus pH value) or more than 14. A 5 N solution of hydrochloric acid, for example, would have a pH value of a little less than 0; correspondingly a 5 N solution of sodium hydroxide

TABLE 4—pH VALUES OF SOME COMMON ACIDS AND BASES

Acid or Base	Normality	pH
HCl	1.0	0.10
HCl	0.1	1.071
CH_3COOH	1.0	2.366
CH_3COOH	0.1	2.866
NaOH	1.0	14.05
NaOH	0.1	13.07
NH_4OH	1.0	11.77
NH_4OH	0.1	11.27

would have a pH value a little greater than 14. Table 4 gives the pH value for solutions of some common acids and bases.

Buffer Action.—The initial pH value of a 1 N solution of sodium chloride will not differ appreciably from that of the water with which it is made.[3] If, however, 1 ml. of a 1 N hydrochloric acid solution be added to 10 ml. of a 1 N solution of sodium chloride the pH of the resulting mixture will be found to have dropped abruptly to a value of about one. If, on the other hand, a 1 N hydrochloric acid solution be added, 1 ml. at a time, to 10 ml. of a 1 N solution of sodium acetate, it will be found that change in the pH of this solution takes place much more slowly. These facts, as well as the others discussed in this section, are illustrated

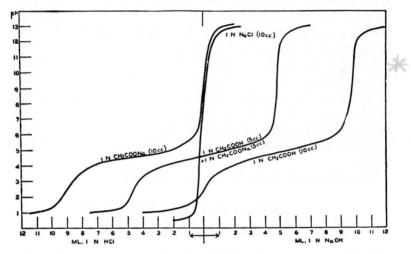

FIG. 1. Curves illustrating buffer action.

graphically in Fig. 1. It is evident that the sodium acetate solution retards in some way changes in pH value upon the addition of an acid while a solution of sodium chloride does not.

Solutions of such compounds as sodium acetate which are relatively resistant to changes in pH resulting from the addition or loss of hydrogen or hydroxyl ions are known as *buffer solutions*, and this property of solutions is called *buffer action*. Solutions such as sodium chloride which show no buffer effect are called *unbuffered solutions*.

If 1 ml. of a 1 N sodium hydroxide solution be added to 10 ml. of a 1 N solution of sodium chloride, a marked increase in pH will occur. If 1 ml. of the same solution be added to 10 ml. of a 1 N solution of sodium

[3] The pH of distilled water when in equilibrium with the carbon dioxide of the atmosphere is about 5.7.

acetate, its pH will also increase markedly. In other words, the sodium acetate solution is buffered against the addition of an acid, but not against the addition of a base. If, on the other hand, 10 ml. of a 1 N solution of acetic acid be substituted for the sodium acetate, it will be found that this solution is strongly buffered against the introduction of hydroxyl ions into the solution. A mixture of equal volumes of molar sodium acetate solution and molar acetic acid solution will exhibit buffer action against both acids and bases over a considerable range of the pH scale.

Different buffer solutions vary greatly in their effectiveness in maintaining pH stability. Some are strongly buffered against acids and weakly buffered against bases; of others the converse is true. The commonest types of buffer systems are those composed of a weak acid plus one of its salts. The sodium acetate-acetic acid buffer system already described is such a system. Practically all of the buffer solutions of importance in living organisms belong to this group.

Buffer action consists essentially in the tying up of free hydrogen or hydroxyl ions nearly as rapidly as they are introduced into the solution by the formation of compounds which are only slightly dissociated. The ensuing change of pH is therefore relatively small in proportion to the volume of acid or base added. As an illustration let us consider once more a solution consisting of both sodium acetate and acetic acid dissolved in water.

These two compounds dissociate as follows:

$$CH_3COONa \rightleftarrows CH_3COO^- + Na^+$$
$$CH_3COOH \rightleftarrows CH_3COO^- + H^+$$

The sodium acetate is strongly dissociated, but the acetic acid will dissociate only slightly, being a weak acid.

Suppose now that a little HCl be added to this solution. This is equivalent to adding H^+ and Cl^- ions and HCl molecules; the latter, however, will dissociate, forming additional ions as rapidly as the H^+ and Cl^- ions already present are bound up in chemical combination. H^+ and CH_3COO^- ions cannot exist side by side in the same solution in appreciable concentrations since CH_3COOH is a poorly dissociated compound. Hence the added H^+ ions are almost all tied up in the formation of CH_3COOH. The Cl^- ions form NaCl with the Na^+ ions which dissociates in the usual way. The result is that there is only a slight increase in the concentration of hydrogen ions in the solution, and hence only a very slight reduction in pH value.

Suppose now that instead of HCl, a little NaOH be added to this solution. This is equivalent to adding Na^+ and OH^- ions and NaOH molecules; the latter, however, will produce additional ions by dissociating as rapidly as the Na^+ and OH^- ions already present are tied up in chemical combination. But OH^- and H^+ ions cannot exist side by side in the same solution in appreciable concentrations since H_2O is only slightly dissociated. Most of the added OH^- ions therefore combine with the H^+ ions produced by the CH_3COOH and form H_2O. More of the CH_3COOH dissociates producing more H^+ ions, which in turn unite with more of the OH^- ions. This continues until practically all of the added OH^- ions are tied up. The Na^+ ions form CH_3COONa with the CH_3COO^- ions which dissociates in the usual way. The final result is that there is only a very slight decrease in the concentration of H^+ ions in the system, and hence only a very slight increase in its pH value.

Any mechanism which will act in such a way as to remove hydrogen or hydroxyl ions from a solution may operate as a buffer system. Other types of buffering are known but they are probably of much less importance in living organisms than the type of chemical mechanism which has just been considered.

SUGGESTED FOR COLLATERAL READING

Britton, H. T. S. *Hydrogen Ions*. 2nd Ed. D. Van Nostrand Co., Inc. New York. 1932.

Clark, W. M. *The Determination of Hydrogen Ions*. 3rd Ed. The Williams & Wilkins Co. Baltimore. 1928.

Clark, W. M. *Topics in Physical Chemistry*. The Williams & Wilkins Co. Baltimore. 1948.

Crafts, A. S., H. B. Currier, and C. R. Stocking. *Water in the Physiology of Plants*. Chronica Botanica Co. Waltham, Mass. 1949.

Dorsey, N. E., Compiler. *Properties of Ordinary Water Substance*. Reinhold Publishing Corp. New York. 1940.

Parkes, G. B. *Mellor's Modern Inorganic Chemistry*. Longmans, Green, and Co. London. 1939.

SELECTED BIBLIOGRAPHY

Barnes, T. C., and T. L. Jahn. Properties of water of biological interest. *Quart. Rev. Biol.* **9**: 292-341. 1934.

Debye, P., and E. Hückel. Zur Theorie der Electrolyte. *Physik. Zeitschr.* **24**: 185-206; 305-325. 1923.

Gortner, R. A. The role of water in the structure and properties of protoplasm. *Ann. Rev. Biochem.* **1**: 21-54. 1932.

Gortner, R. A. Water in its biochemcial relationships. *Ann. Rev. Biochem.* **3**: 1-22. 1934.

DISCUSSION QUESTIONS

1. How would you prepare a 1 molar solution of glucose, of NaCl, of $CaCl_2 \cdot 4H_2O$, of $MgSO_4 \cdot 7H_2O$? One molal solutions of the same compounds?

2. Given a 1 molar solution, how would you prepare 125 cc. of a 0.75 molar solution? Given a 0.5 molar solution, how would you prepare 50 cc. of a 0.225 molar solution?

3. What is the molal concentration of a 20 per cent sucrose solution?

4. When a molal solution of sucrose is prepared by adding 342.2 g. of sucrose to 1000 g. of water, the volume of the resulting solution is 1207 cc. at 0°C. What is its molar concentration?

5. How much water must be added to the 1207 cc. of molal solution (question 4) in order to convert it into a 0.5 molal solution?

6. If 15 cc. of KOH solution requires 17.5 cc. of 1 N HCl solution to neutralize it, what is the normality of the KOH solution?

7. If an electrolyte from which two ions form is 75 per cent dissociated, what will be the per cent of dissolved particles (ions plus molecules) in the solution relative to the number of particles which would be present if no dissociation occurred? Answer the same question for an electrolyte from which three ions form.

8. If the pH of a molar solution of hydrochloric acid is 0.1 and the pH of a molar solution of acetic acid is 2.37, what is the total acidity of each of these solutions?

9. How much greater is the concentration of hydrogen ions in a solution of pH 4 than one of pH 7? One of pH 3 than one of pH 9?

10. Why will an increase in the CO_2 content of water result in an increase in its hydrogen ion concentration?

11. Why will the addition of a base to water decrease the concentration of hydrogen ions present?

III

COLLOIDAL SYSTEMS

Most of the problems that confront the plant physiologist lead ultimately to a consideration of one phase or another of the structure and physicochemical properties of colloidal systems. When reduced to their ultimate tangible mechanism, physiological processes are found either to occur in a colloidal matrix or to be strongly influenced by the colloidal organization of the cells in which they take place. The world of living organisms has, in fact, been molded largely on a colloidal pattern. It is quite impossible, therefore, to obtain any adequate comprehension of physiological processes without a background of facts and principles regarding colloidal systems.

Some of the most important components of the material environment of plants and animals are also essentially colloidal. Most soils contain a considerable proportion of matter in the colloidal or near-colloidal condition, and owe many of their most distinctive properties to this fact. Few streams or bodies of water are entirely free from matter in the colloidal condition. Clouds, fogs, mists, and smoke also represent matter in the colloidal state.

General Nature of Colloidal Systems.—If a little sugar be shaken up in water the crystals soon disappear. The molecules composing the crystals have been separated from each other and dispersed throughout the water forming a solution. Solutions are systems in which *molecules* or *ions* of one substance are dispersed in between the molecules of another substance.

If, instead of sugar, we stir some fine river bottom silt into water, a different sort of a system results. The silt particles do not separate into their constituent molecules, but simply become dispersed throughout the liquid. Such a system is called a *suspension*. The particles in a suspension are large enough to be seen readily under a microscope. Suspensions are not stable systems, because the particles slowly settle out and the two

23

original components become separated within a relatively short period of time.

Similar systems can be prepared by vigorously shaking together two immiscible liquids such as oil and water. Such systems are called *emulsions*. Emulsions are not stable unless there is also present in the system a third component called an *emulsifier*.

Still another type of system consisting of particles dispersed through water can be prepared. If a trace of sulfur be dissolved in a small volume of alcohol which is then poured into a somewhat larger volume of water, a cloudy opalescent liquid will result which is composed of sulfur *particles* dispersed through water. This type of system is intermediate in its properties between solutions and suspensions. The dispersed particles are not molecules, but, as in suspensions, aggregates of molecules. Unlike suspensions, however, such systems are relatively stable, as the particles will remain dispersed throughout the liquid indefinitely. The sulfur-in-water system which has just been described is a simple example of a colloidal system.

Colloidal systems, as the preceding discussion has indicated, are two-phased systems. Unlike solutions, however, the particles of the dispersed phase are not in the molecular or ionic condition, but—with certain exceptions to be noted shortly—are molecular aggregates. One colloidal particle is often composed of hundreds or even thousands of molecules lumped together. The molecular aggregates must not be so large, however, that the particles settle out of the system, as stability is one of the essential attributes of colloidal systems. In general, if the dispersed particles fall within the range of 0.001-0.1 μ in diameter, the system is considered a colloidal system; if larger than this, a suspension or an emulsion; and if smaller, a solution. The individual molecules of some substances (certain dyes, some proteins) are so large as to bring them within the colloidal range of dimensions. Hence molecular dispersions of such substances are simultaneously both solutions and colloidal systems. The limits generally accepted for the range of sizes of colloidal particles have been somewhat arbitrarily set and actually there is no sharp boundary between colloidal systems and suspensions on the one hand, or between colloidal systems and solutions on the other. There is a perfect gradation in properties from one type of system to the next. The properties of suspensions or emulsions in which the suspended particles are of small dimensions approach those of colloidal systems, while the smaller the dispersed particles in a colloidal system the more closely it approaches a solution in its properties.

Particles of suspensions and emulsions can ordinarily be seen under a microscope, but those of colloidal systems cannot. Colloidal particles can be detected, however, under the electron microscope (Chap. IV) or under the ultramicroscope (see later).

Interfacial Area of Colloidal Systems.—The most important properties of colloidal systems are a consequence of the small size of their dispersed particles. As the size of the particles becomes smaller their aggregate surface area becomes greater (Table 5).

TABLE 5—EFFECT OF PROGRESSIVE SUBDIVISION UPON THE SURFACE EXPOSED BY A GIVEN MASS OF MATERIAL

Length of one edge		Number of cubes	Total surface
	1 cm.	1	6 square cm.
	1 mm.	10^3	60 " "
	0.1 mm.	10^6	600 " "
	0.01 mm.	10^9	6000 " "
	1.0 μ	10^{12}	6 square m.
Colloidal	0.1 μ	10^{15}	6c square m.
Range of	0.01 μ	10^{18}	600 " "
Sizes	0.001 μ	10^{21}	6000 " "

As shown in Table 5, the exposed surface of 1 cc. of solid matter, if cut up into cubes 0.001 μ on an edge (the approximate size of the smallest colloidal particles), will be 6000 square meters. This represents an increase of 10,000,000 times over the exposed surface area of a cube 1 cm. on an edge. The contact surfaces between a solid and a liquid or between two immiscible liquids are known as *interfaces*. This term also applies to the contact surfaces between colloidal particles and the liquid in which they are dispersed. The interfacial area of colloidal systems is enormous in proportion to the actual mass of material which is dispersed. Some of the most important properties of colloidal systems are a consequence of their enormous interfacial area.

Adsorption.—Interfaces are characteristically the seat of the phenomenon called *adsorption*. A simple example of adsorption is illustrated in the following experiment. Enough of the dye methylene blue is dissolved in water to make about a 0.05 per cent solution. About 1.0 g. of activated charcoal is then stirred into about 50 ml. of solution. Upon filtering the filtrate is found to be colorless. A little ethanol is now poured over the charcoal on the filter paper and it is found that most, if not all, of the methylene blue redissolves in the alcohol. In the experiment just described the methylene blue molecules were retained, *i.e.*, adsorbed, at the carbon-water interfaces, because the attractive forces between the methylene blue molecules and the carbon molecules are greater than those between the methylene blue molecules and the water molecules. The attraction between the alcohol molecules and the methylene blue molecules, however, is greater than that between the carbon and methylene blue molecules; hence the adsorbed molecules are released when ethanol replaces water as the liquid component of the interface.

Adsorption consists of an interfacial concentrating of molecules such as occurs to those of methylene blue at a carbon-water interface and is a phenomenon of very general occurrence, taking place at all kinds of interfaces. Adsorption of gas molecules at solid-gas interfaces is a common phenomenon. Solutes may be adsorbed at solid-liquid, liquid-liquid, or liquid-gas interfaces. Solvent molecules, such as those of water, also become adsorbed at certain kinds of interfaces. Adsorption is probably of universal occurrence at the interfaces of colloidal systems. In some such systems solute molecules are adsorbed, in others solvent molecules, and in some both solute and solvent molecules.

Molecules of the adsorbing surface usually attract certain atomic groupings in the adsorbed molecules more strongly than others, a fact which results in a more or less regular arrangement of adsorbed molecules at interfacial boundaries. Commonly this orientation of adsorbed molecules results in their closer packing and is an important factor in accounting for their higher concentration in the interface than in the surrounding medium. Adsorbed molecules are not static but exhibit a continuous, although reduced, kinetic activity. Molecules adsorbed at interfaces are in dynamic equilibrium with the molecules of the same species in the body of the system. An adsorption equilibrium is attained when the number of adsorbed molecules passing out of the interface, in a unit of time, is equal to the number passing into the interface. When adsorption occurs from a liquid containing many solutes, as is true of most biological liquids, all solutes are adsorbed to a greater or lesser degree depending upon their specific properties in relation to the adsorbing surface. In general, however, under such conditions no one solute will be adsorbed as completely as if it alone were present.

It is possible, under certain conditions, for equilibria to be established in which one or more components of a system are less concentrated at an interface than in the surrounding medium. Such equilibria are recognized as examples of *negative adsorption*. Negative adsorption is a much less common phenomenon than positive adsorption.

The Biological Significance of Adsorption.—Adsorption phenomena are known to play a manifold role in living organisms, probably being involved in practically all cell activities. Within plant cells many interfaces occur, as at the boundaries between the protoplasm and cell wall, and the nucleus and cytoplasm, at all of which a concentrating of solutes undoubtedly occurs. The adsorption of certain compounds at the cytoplasmic interfaces is generally believed to exert a marked influence on the permeability of the cytoplasm. Imbibitional phenomena, of basic importance in the water relations of plant cells, involve the adsorption of water (Chap. VII). The action of enzymes (Chap. XVI) as well as of other catalysts is generally believed to involve adsorption phenomena. Much information regarding the structure of cells has been gained by the use of dyes which are differentially adsorbed by various constituents of cells. Chromosomes, for example, are so named because they strongly adsorb certain stains.

The Nomenclature of Colloidal Systems.—The word *colloid* is derived from the Greek roots KOLLA (glue) and EIDOS (appearance). Thomas Graham, a prominent early investigator of colloidal phenomena, who did his most important work just after the middle of the nineteenth century, used this term to designate a certain group of substances that seemed to be set apart from other substances by several distinctive properties. When dispersed in water these substances had a slow rate of diffusion and failed to diffuse through membranes of parchment paper. Furthermore, they did not form crystals. He applied the term *crystalloid* to those crystal-forming substances which, when in solution, diffused relatively rapidly and passed readily through parchment membranes. We now know that, strictly speaking, no such distinction can be made; the word *colloid* properly refers to a distinctive *state* of matter and cannot be applied with accuracy to any one class of substances. Theoretically any substance can, by proper manipulation, be brought into the colloidal state, and actually this has been experimentally accomplished for a large number of substances.

Colloidal systems, as has already become evident, are composed of two phases—a continuous phase, and a discontinuous phase—the latter composed of discrete particles, each entirely separated from its fellows by the intervening continuous phase. The continuous phase is commonly called the *dispersion medium,* and the discontinuous phase the *disperse phase.* According to another terminology, applicable however only when the dispersion medium is a liquid, each individual dispersed particle is called a *micelle,* while the continuous phase of the system is called the *intermicellar liquid.*

To Graham, also, we are indebted for the terms *sol* and *gel.* A sol is a colloidal system which possesses the property of fluidity. Such systems can be poured more or less readily from one vessel to another. To the unaided eye they often appear to be true solutions, but examination by means of an ultramicroscope reveals their colloidal nature.

Many sols "set," forming solid, but more or less elastic systems, generally called *gels*. Gelatin desserts, custards, and ordinary household jellies are familiar examples of gels. The change of a sol to gel is called *gelation*. The reverse change, as for example when gelatin is "melted" by the application of heat, is called *solation*. Some authorities use the term "gel" in a generic sense to include systems of the type just described, which they call *jellies*, and another type of colloidal system which they term *coagula*. The white of a hard-boiled egg is typical coagulum.

Sols may be classified into *lyophobic* and *lyophilic* types. In the latter an appreciable affinity exists between the particles of the disperse phase and the dispersion medium; in the former no such affinity is present. When the dispersion medium is water the corresponding terms *hydrophobic* (Gr.: "water-fearing") and *hydrophilic* (Gr.: "water-loving") are employed. This last pair of terms will be used consistently in the following discussion, since from the biological standpoint colloidal systems in which water is the dispersion medium are by far the most important. The affinity between the two phases of a hydrophilic sol manifests itself by *hydration* of the micelles. Hydration is the association of one or more molecules of water with an ion, molecule, or micelle.

Most colloidal systems composed of metallic substances dispersed in water are examples of hydrophobic sols. Gelatin, agar, starch, and gum acacia sols are familiar examples of hydrophilic systems. Protein sols also belong in this group. Actually all possible gradations exist from highly hydrophilic sols to highly hydrophobic sols.

Suspensions.—The general nature of suspensions has already been indicated. Suspensions are not generally regarded as playing a very significant role in living organisms. The particles of suspension size which frequently can be observed in the protoplasm are apparently composed entirely of relatively inert materials. Particles of suspension size are very common in soils, and as such are an important part of the environment of the roots of plants. A consideration of suspensions is also of importance in developing the conception of the structural and dynamic aspects of colloidal systems proper.

Emulsions.—Emulsions are systems in which one liquid is dispersed throughout another with which it is virtually immiscible, the particles of the dispersed liquid exceeding about 0.1 μ in diameter. While other types of emulsions are theoretically possible all such systems encountered in common experience fall naturally into two groups generally known as *oil-in-water* emulsions and *water-in-oil* emulsions. In the former type an oil or some other liquid insoluble in water, or practically so, is dispersed throughout a water dispersion medium. In the latter type the converse is true; the oil or other liquid immiscible with water constitutes the dispersion medium, while small aggregations of water molecules are dispersed through it. The proportions of the components of most emulsions can be varied between wide limits. Emulsions are not generally considered to be true colloidal systems, but, like suspensions, approach them in properties. Emulsions occur commonly in the cells of plants and animals and are generally believed to be essential components of protoplasm. Both water-in-oil and oil-in-water emulsions are known to exist in living cells, but the latter type is more common. When examined under high magnification with a microscope, protoplasm in its grosser aspects often presents the appearance of an emulsion of fats and fat-like substances dispersed through the body of the protoplasm.

Emulsions, with the exception of some very dilute ones, lack stability unless there is also present in the system an *emulsifier*. In the absence of an emulsifier, the two components of an emulsion rapidly separate, the oil, being the component of lower specific gravity, rising to the top. The group of substances classified as emulsifiers is chemically a very heterogeneous one. Some of the best known emulsifiers are the soaps, saponins, various substances which form hydrophilic colloids when dispersed in water (gums, gelatin, etc.), and fine suspensions of certain rather inert materials such as sulfur, carbon, silica, and resin. Emulsions found in living organisms are usually stabilized by proteins.

Hydrophilic and Hydrophobic Sols.—Most of the important differences between hydrophilic and hydrophobic sols result from the hydration of the dispersed particles in systems of the former type. There is no general agreement regarding the exact physicochemical relationship between the micelle and its water of hydration; but only two conceptions have any wide currency. One of these relates this hydration to an actual solution of some of the water in the substance of the micelles (Fig. 2A).

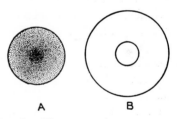

A   B

Fig. 2. Diagrammatic representation of possible relationships between a micelle and its water of hydration: (A) solution of water in the micelle. The proportion of dissolved water present is represented as decreasing toward the center of the micelle. (B) Orientation of the water molecules as a "shell" around the micelle.

A more probable theory, however, holds that no actual solution of the medium in the micelles occurs, but that water molecules are oriented around each dispersed particle forming a "shell" many layers of molecules in thickness (Fig. 2B). It is presumed that the first layer of oriented water molecules is so firmly attached ("adsorbed") to the micelle that it is essentially an integral part of it. The successively enveloping layers of water molecules are also oriented, but with increasing distance from the periphery of the micelle the forces of attraction and orientation progressively decrease. In this zone there is a gradual transition from water molecules which are practically all oriented to those which are completely unoriented. Oriented molecules fit together more closely than unoriented molecules. They are "packed" more closely, just as more bricks can be stacked in a given space if arranged regularly than if tossed in indiscriminately. As a result of this packing the water in these oriented shells has a greater density than that in the bulk of the liquid; in other words, there is an actual contraction in the volume of the liquid associated with the micelles.

The fact that micelles may, under certain conditions, lose their water of hydration very rapidly would seem to favor the latter theory. It is possible, of course, that in some hydrophilic systems the water is actually dissolved in the micelles, that in others it is present only as a shell of oriented molecules, while in still others both of these two suggested modes of hydration may exist.

The important properties of sols will now be summarized, with special attention to differences between the properties of sols of the hydrophilic type and sols of the hydrophobic type.

Filterability.—Sols pass through ordinary filter papers without any appreciable separation of the disperse phase from the dispersion medium by the filter. Since the pores in ordinary filter papers are about 2-5 μ in diameter, and even porcelain filters, such as those widely used in bacteriological work, have pores 0.2-0.6 μ in diameter, it is easy to understand why micelles with diameters in the size range 0.001-0.1 μ pass through.

Special filters have been devised, however, with pores of such a small diameter that the disperse phase can be separated from the dispersion medium by filtering a sol through them. Such filters are known as *ultrafilters*. The process of filtering through such a filter is known as *ultrafiltration*. The most commonly used types of ultrafilters are those made of collodion or gelatin. The size of the pores in such filters can be controlled by the length of time allowed for drying and in other ways. It is possible to prepare ultrafilters with pores of such dimensions that solutes can pass through them, but colloidal micelles cannot.

Tyndall Phenomenon.—Suppose that a clean glass vessel, preferably one with flat, parallel sides, be filled with pure water and held so that a strong pencil of light passes laterally through the vessel. If an observation be made laterally and at right angles to the path of the beam of light, no distinctive trace of its path through the water can be detected. Such a liquid is said to be optically empty. The same will be true if the water in the vessel be replaced by a sugar or salt solution, or in fact, by any true solution.[1] Suppose, however, that the vessel be filled with a hydrophobic sol and observed in the manner just described. The results are strikingly different. The path of the light will be clearly delineated as a cloudy, often opalescent, track through the sol. Even a colloidal system which seems perfectly transparent to the unaided eye will usually show some turbidity when submitted to this test. The intensity of this effect varies greatly with the specific colloidal system, and with the concentration of the disperse phase, but it is universally shown by hydrophobic sols.

The phenomenon just described is called the *Tyndall phenomenon* and results from the scattering or diffraction of light. The difference in the index of refraction between the two phases of the colloidal system is also a factor determining the intensity of the Tyndall effect. The greater this difference, the stronger the effect. Since in the diffraction of light, the short wave lengths (blue end of the spectrum) are bent more than the longer wave lengths, a partial separation of the spectrum results. For this reason a sol with a colorless disperse phase often appears to be pale blue when viewed in the path of a strong beam of light.

Similar Tyndall phenomena are exhibited by hydrophilic sols, but usually the effect is less striking when sols of this type are viewed in the path of a beam of light than the effect observed when hydrophobic sols are employed.

The instrument known as the ultramicroscope is based on the principle of the Tyndall phenomenon. The limit of the resolving power of ordinary microscope is about 0.1 μ. The ultramicroscope can be used for detecting the presence of particles in the size range 0.001 μ to 0.1 μ, *i.e.*, in the colloidal range. It is not possible to observe colloidal particles directly in the ultramicroscope; only the light diffracted from their surfaces can be seen. Neither can any definite image of particles in this small range of sizes be obtained. The ultramicroscope is a microscope which is so arranged that the colloidal system or other material to be examined can be illuminated laterally (*i.e.*, at right angles to the tube of the microscope). This lateral illumination is usually provided by a powerful source of light and a suitable series of condensing and focusing lenses, so arranged that the light is focused to a point within the mount. Under the ultramicroscope the dispersed particles of a hydrophobic sol appear as bright spots of light varying in size and brilliancy. Very little concerning the actual size or shape of the micelles can be determined since each bright spot represents merely the light diffracted by a single particle. It

---

[1] Actually a trace of the light track will usually be perceived even in water or true solutions, because of the presence of contaminating dust particles. In order to prepare a truly optically empty liquid, provision must be made for the removal of such dust particles.

is possible, however, to determine the *number* of particles in a given volume of sol by means of the ultramicroscope. The use of the ultramicroscope consists essentially in an observation of the Tyndall phenomenon in a small volume of a sol under the microscope.

Brownian Movement.—In 1828, the botanist Robert Brown observed through a microscope that pollen grains which were suspended in water showed a rapid oscillatory motion. Brown at first was inclined to attribute this motion to the fact that the pollen grains were alive, but examination of preparations of dead pollen grains and spores showed that they likewise exhibited such a motion. It became evident therefore that this movement was in no way connected with living processes. We now know that any particle up to about 4 or 5 μ in diameter will exhibit this movement when suspended in a liquid. This phenomenon is termed *Brownian movement,* after its discoverer.

Many suspensions in which the particles are within the range of microscopic visibility exhibit Brownian movement. It is clearly shown by many of the smaller species of bacteria when suspended in water. In solid-in-gas colloids, such as tobacco smoke, the dispersed particles show a very vigorous Brownian movement. Particles in the protoplasm of slime molds and certain other species frequently exhibit a Brownian movement which is clearly discernible under the microscope. For particles of a given mass, the smaller their volume the greater the amplitude of their Brownian movement. For particles of equal volume, the less their mass the more vigorously they will exhibit Brownian movement. In general, this phenomenon is exhibited more clearly by the micelles of hydrophobic sols than by those of hydrophilic sols. The viscosity of the liquid phase is also an important factor governing the rapidity with which the dispersed particles move. The more viscous the liquid, the more sluggish the movement of the particles.

Brownian movement is caused by the kinetic activity of the molecules of the solvent. Even the smallest particles in which Brownian movement can be observed are very large in proportion to the size of the solvent molecules which impinge upon them. A particle suspended in a liquid such as water suffers a continual bombardment by the molecules of the liquid. If the particle be relatively large, at any given moment it is bombarded on every side by numerous molecules, moving in all possible directions and at different speeds. The effects of the individual impacts largely counteract each other, however, and there is little or no movement of the particle. If the particle be smaller, however, the results are quite different. At any given moment a much smaller number of water molecules impinge upon the particle. The resulting forces cease to be balanced and the sum total effect of the blows which the particle sustains on some one side are greater than the effect of the blows sustained on any other side. Hence the particle moves. The next moment a greater impetus may be given to the particle from some other direction and the course of its movement is changed. In this way the highly erratic movements of suspended particles, known as Brownian movement, originate. Increase in temperature increases the rate of Brownian movement because of an increase in the kinetic energy of the solvent molecules. This phenomenon is the nearest approach we have to actual visible evidence of the validity of the kinetic theory of matter. It almost brings before our eyes the veritable "dance of the molecules."

Viscosity.—The viscosity of a fluid is its resistance to flow. The more viscous a liquid the less readily it will flow. Glycerine, for example, is much more viscous than water. The viscosity of hydrophobic sols never varies appreciably from that of the dispersion medium—water. Unlike hydrophobic sols the viscosity of hydrophilic sols is usually greater than that of the dispersion medium. The viscosity of hydrophilic sols increases appreciably with increase in the concentration of the sol, but the relation is not a linear one (Fig. 3). The rapid increase in the viscosity of hydrophilic sols with increasing concentration is ascribed to the hydration of the micelles. Increasing the concentration of the disperse phase results in a decrease in the relative amount of free water present because of the association of a larger proportion of the water with the micelles. This reduces the "fluidity" of the sol, hence raises its viscosity.

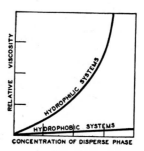

FIG. 3.   Relation of relative viscosity of hydrophilic and hydrophobic sols to the concentration of the disperse phase.

The viscosity of all liquids, including sols, is influenced by temperature. In general, increase in temperature decreases viscosity. In hydrophilic systems this reduction in viscosity with increase in temperature probably results in part from the decrease in viscosity of the medium itself, and in part from the decrease in the hydration of the micelles.

Electrical Properties.—The dispersed particles of all *hydrophobic sols* carry electrical charges. A colloidal system, however, is electrically neutral, because for every charge carried on a micelle an equal charge of opposite value is carried by ions in the dispersion medium. The situation is similar to that in a solution of an electrolyte. Although the individual ions are charged, for every negative charge carried by an anion an equal positive charge is carried by a cation. In some colloidal systems the dispersed particles are negatively charged, in others positively charged, but ordinarily all the dispersed particles in any one system bear a charge of the same sign.

Whatever the origin of the micellar charges they invariably are produced in such a way as to involve the release of ions into the dispersion medium which may therefore be regarded as also being charged. When the micelles are negatively charged, the dispersion medium is positively charged and *vice versa*. Electrostatic attraction therefore exists between the surface charges of a colloidal particle and the ions of opposite charge in the dispersion medium. The result is that surrounding each colloidal particle with its charged surface is a "shell" of ions of opposite charge.

This arrangement of charges at the surface of a micelle is called an *electric double layer*. Similar electric double layers exist also at boundaries between solid surfaces and liquids, as for example along the walls

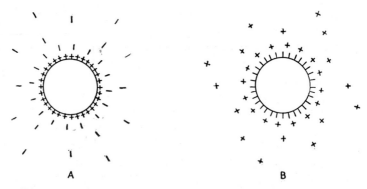

A   B

FIG. 4. Diagrammatic representation of the electric charges around micelles: (A) positively charged, (B) negatively charged.

of a capillary tube. Figure 4 represents the distribution of the electrical charges around two micelles, one positively charged, one negatively charged. The innermost layer of ions in the dispersion medium is probably compactly oriented around the oppositely charged micelle, which is in turn surrounded by progressively more diffuse layers. That is, while most of the ions are close to the charged surface of the micelle, some are farther away; although, with increasing distance from the surface of a micelle, the number of ions associated with that micelle decreases rapidly.

The ions of the double layer are in dynamic equilibrium with undissociated molecules at the periphery of the micelle proper. Anions and cations of the double layer are continually uniting and forming uncharged molecules which become part of the micelle. Contrariwise, molecules at the surface of the micelle are continually dissociating into cations and anions. If the micelle is negatively charged the anions adhere to its surface; if positively charged, the cations. The ions of the opposite charge become part of the outer shell around the micelle.

The presence of this electrical double layer results in a difference of electrical potential between the micelle and the intermicellar liquid. The magnitude of this difference of potential varies with different sols and with the same sol under different conditions.

The usual method of determining the sign of the charge upon the dispersed particles of sols is to observe the direction of their migration in an electrical field. If two electrodes are so arranged as to dip into a hydrophobic sol contained in a suitable vessel, and the electrodes connected with a direct current of proper potential, it will be found that the dispersed particles will move toward one of the poles. By suitable arrangements, using a microscope or ultramicroscope (depending upon the size of the particles), the migration of the particles may be actually watched. In a positively charged ferric hydroxide sol, for example, the micelles will move toward the negatively charged electrode, while in a negatively charged arsenious sulfide sol they will move toward the positively charged pole. This phenomenon is known as _cataphoresis_ or _electrophoresis_.

As a micelle moves under the influence of an electric current only the innermost layer of the electric double layer—the one which determines its electrical charge—clings to the micelle and moves with it. This inner layer slides past the oppositely charged ions of the outer shell of one micelle after another as it moves toward the anode if negatively charged, or toward the cathode if positively charged. Simultaneously ions of the outer layer move toward the opposite pole from the one toward which the micelles migrate. There is a close analogy between this phenomenon and the behavior of the ions of an electrolyte during electrolysis.

The sign of the charge on the dispersed particles of any sol can be determined by cataphoresis. Particles considerably above the colloidal range of dimensions frequently can be shown to exhibit cataphoretic migration. The phenomenon can be demonstrated with bacteria, unicellular algae, and spores. Practically all such small living organisms are negatively charged.

The dispersed particles of hydrophobic sols apparently acquire their charges either by electrolytic dissociation or by adsorption. In some such systems the charges seem to arise as a result of ionization of some of the molecules composing the micelle. The ions released into the dispersion medium become the outer envelope of the double layer, leaving the micelle with a residual and compensating charge of ions of opposite sign. Individual molecules of some substances are large enough to fall within the colloidal range of sizes. The dye Congo Red, which is the sodium salt of a complex organic acid, is an example of such a substance. Dispersed in water this compound produces sodium ions and a colloidal anion, the latter, of course, being negatively charged.

In other systems the electrical charge on the dispersed particles is apparently acquired by adsorption of either the positive or negative ions of an electrolyte, the ion of opposite charge becoming the outer shell of the double layer. Ferric hydroxide sols[2] are normally positively charged. The charge on the micelles of these sols is often ascribed to the adsorption of Fe^{+++} ions of the $FeCl_3$ from which ferric hydroxide sols are usually prepared, the Cl^- ions forming the outer layer around the micelles. Similarly the negative charge of the micelles of arsenious sulfide sols is often ascribed to the adsorption of H_2S which is used in the preparation of this sol. Dissociation of H_2S results in the release of H^+ ions into the dispersion medium leaving the dispersed particles with a residual and compensating negative charge.

Similarly it is believed that some substances acquire an electrical charge by adsorbing hydrogen or hydroxyl ions—more frequently the latter— from their water dispersion medium. Certain inert substances such as cellulose, carbon, quartz, and collodion are believed to become charged in this way. All of these substances acquire a negative charge when in contact with water, indicating that the hydroxyl ions are adsorbed, the hydrogen ions becoming the outer shell of the double layer.

The micelles of some *hydrophilic sols* are charged; those of others are not. As in hydrophobic systems the dispersed particles of different hydrophilic sols acquire their charges in different ways. In some the charges on the particles originate by ionization of some of the surface molecules of the micelles. The electrical charges on the micelles of protein sols arise in this way. In other systems the charges may originate from traces of electrolytes which are present as impurities. This is probably true of agar sols. Such charges may be regarded as similar in their origin to those acquired by adsorption on the micelles of hydrophobic sols, in that the charge is contributed by some compound associated with the substance of which the micelle is composed, and not to that substance itself. Most of the better known hydrophilic sols are negatively charged.

Flocculation.—Since the dispersed particles of any sol are in rapid motion it would seem that repeated collisions would result in a progressive agglomeration of the particles into larger and larger masses which eventually would settle out of the system. Sols, however, are relatively stable systems, and it is important to understand the mechanism by which the stability of such colloidal systems is maintained.

The stability of *hydrophobic sols* is maintained by the charge which

[2] Most investigators believe that the so-called ferric hydroxide sol is actually a sol of hydrated ferric oxide ($Fe_2O_3(H_2O)_x$).

each micelle carries. Although by Brownian movement the dispersed particles are repeatedly brought close together, actual collision seldom occurs because the shells of ions around the micelles are mutually repellent.

Reduction of the charge on the micelles of any hydrophobic sol to the point where there is no difference of electrical potential across the double layer results in agglomeration of the individual particles into flakes of a size which rapidly settle out of the surrounding liquid. This phenomenon is called *flocculation, coagulation* or *precipitation*. The point at which there is no difference of electrical potential across the double layer is known as the *isoelectric point* of the sol. At the isoelectric point the micelles of a sol are, relative to the surrounding medium, completely uncharged. As, by Brownian movement, two such micelles are bought into contiguity they no longer repel each other with sufficient intensity to prevent their agglomeration. By the addition of other micelles such particles rapidly increase in size, soon resulting in flocculation of the sol. Merely reducing the electric charge to a value approaching that of the isoelectric point is sufficient to induce instability and slow flocculation in many sols.

Flocculation is most commonly initiated by the introduction of electrolytes into the system. Very small quantities of an electrolyte are often sufficient to cause the flocculation of a relatively large volume of sol. The important principles regarding the flocculation of hydrophobic sols by electrolytes can be most easily elucidated by a discussion of some of the data in Table 6.

The flocculating effect of an electrolyte is due primarily to the added ion of opposite charge from that borne by the colloidal particle. Thus the As_2S_3 sol may be flocculated by cations such as Na^+, Ca^{++}, or Al^{+++}, while the $Fe(OH)_3$ sol may be flocculated by anions such as Cl^-, NO_3^-, or SO_4^{--}.

Furthermore, the flocculating effect increases with an increase in the valency of the effective ion. The first part of Table 6 shows that the trivalent cation Al^{+++} is more effective in flocculating the negatively charged As_2S_3 sol than the bivalent cations Ca^{++}, Ba^{++} or Mg^{++}, which in turn are much more effective than the univalent cations K^+, Na^+, and Li^+. Similarly the second part of the table shows that the flocculating effect of bivalent anions (SO_4^{--}, $Cr_2O_7^{--}$) upon a positively charged $Fe(OH)_3$ sol is greater than that of univalent anions (Cl^-, NO_3^-).

However, the influence of the valency of an ion upon its flocculating effectiveness does not follow a simple 1 : 2 : 3 arithmetical ratio. It took, as shown in Table 6, about 88 times as much NaCl as $CaCl_2$, and about 7 times as much $CaCl_2$ as $AlCl_3$ to accomplish complete flocculation of the As_2S_3 sol.

TABLE 6 —FLOCCULATING EFFECT OF ELECTROLYTES ON HYDROPHOBIC SOLS   (DATA OF
FREUNDLICH, 1903.) THE CONCENTRATION OF ELECTROLYTES IS THE MINIMUM WHICH
RESULTS IN COMPLETE FLOCCULATION

Negatively charged arsenious sulfide sol. (15.57 millimols As₂S₃ per L.)		Positively charged ferric hydroxide sol. (10.3 millimols Fe(OH)₃ per L.)	
Electrolyte	Concentration (millimols per L.)	Electrolyte	Concentration (millimols per L.)
LiCl	81.5	NaCl	9.25
NaCl	71.2	KCl	9.03
KCl	69.1	KNO₃	11.9
KNO₃	69.8	K₂SO₄	0.204
MgCl₂	1.00	MgSO₄	0.217
MgSO₄	1.13	K₂Cr₂O₇	0.194
BaCl₂	0.964		
Ba(NO₃)₂	0.959		
CaCl₂	0.905		
AlCl₃	0.130		
Al(NO₃)₃	0.137		

In the flocculation of hydrophobic sols the ion of the added electrolyte with a charge of the same sign as that of the micelle is not entirely without effect. The influence of such ions is usually to increase the stability of the system. Precisely stated, therefore, the influence of an electrolyte upon the micelles of a hydrophobic sol is a differential effect between the anions and cations, but the influence of the ion of opposite charge predominates.

Flocculation may also be initiated by introducing into a hydrophobic sol another hydrophobic sol with micelles bearing a charge of opposite sign. If $Fe(OH)_3$ sol be slowly added to an As_2S_3 sol, a point will be reached at which complete flocculation will occur. The particles of the two sols will settle out as an intimate mixture. The same phenomenon occurs when any negatively charged hydrophobic sol is added to any positively charged hydrophobic sol in sufficient quantity, or *vice versa*. This process is called *mutual flocculation*. When this phenomenon occurs the ions of the outer zone of one kind of particle pair off with the oppositely charged ions of the outer shell of the other kind.

The actual mechanism of flocculation of a hydrophobic sol is too complex to be considered in detail in an introductory discussion. The fundamental cause of flocculation, however, is invariably the destruction of the electrical double layer around the micelles. There is a close analogy between the flocculation of a hydrophobic sol and a precipitation reaction of one electrolyte with another. The micelles of hydrophobic sols behave in flocculation phenomena like giant ions bearing numerous charges.

The addition of a small amount of a hydrophilic sol, such as a gelatin or gum arabic sol, to a hydrophobic sol makes flocculation of the latter by electrolytes or micelles of opposite charge difficult or impossible. This effect of a hydrophilic on a hydrophobic sol is termed _protective action_. Protective action is apparently a result of the adsorption of the micelles of the hydrophilic sol around the micelles of the hydrophobic sol. The properties of the sol, therefore, become essentially those of the hydrophilic system. As will be seen shortly, hydrophilic sols are much less easily flocculated by electrolytes than hydrophobic sols, and this is undoubtedly the basis for protective action.

We turn now to the question of the mechanism of the flocculation of _hydrophilic sols_. The micelles of such sols may or may not carry an electrical charge, but whether charged or not such colloidal systems are stable. Hydrophobic sols, as already shown, are stable only when the micelles bear an electrical charge. One of the most important differences between hydrophobic and hydrophilic sols is the possession by the latter of a second stability factor, which in itself is effective in keeping such sols stable for long periods of time. In our previous discussion we have seen that uncharged micelles of hydrophobic sols soon agglomerate and settle out of the dispersion medium. Why do not the uncharged micelles of a hydrophilic sol behave in the same way? The micelles of all hydrophilic sols, it will be remembered, are highly hydrated. Each particle is "cushioned" against impacts with other particles by its enveloping shell of oriented water molecules. Agglomeration of the micelles is thus prevented, and hence even uncharged hydrophilic sols are stable.

The possession of two stability factors by hydrophilic sols complicates the mechanism of flocculation in such systems. The manner in which flocculation of hydrophilic sols may occur can be illustrated by reviewing a simple experiment. The experimental material is a dilute (about 0.1 per cent) sol of agar-agar. Such a sol is perhaps the most typical example of a simple hydrophilic system. If a relatively large volume of alcohol be added to a small portion of such a sol, the micelles lose their water of hydration, and the sol acquires the cloudy, bluish, opalescent appearance typical of many lyophobic sols. In fact, it now _is_ a lyophobic sol and shows all the typical properties of such systems. The alcohol, which is a powerful dehydrating agent, has robbed the micelles of their shells of oriented water molecules. Nevertheless, the sol is still stable, since the micelles retain their original negative charges. Finally, let a drop of a solution of an electrolyte such as $AlCl_3$ be added to the sol. The sol now flocculates almost immediately, since the only remaining stability factor—the electrical charge—has been destroyed by the addition of the electrolyte, and the opalescent cast of the sol disappears.

The stability factors of a hydrophilic sol can also be dissipated in the opposite order. Suppose that the $AlCl_3$ solution first be added to the agar sol until the charges on the micelles are neutralized. Although now at its isoelectric point, unlike hydrophobic systems, the sol does not flocculate. If, however, alcohol now be added to the system, immediate flocculation occurs, because of a dehydration of the micelles, resulting in an elimination of the only remaining stability factor in the system.

Briefly then, in order to flocculate a hydrophilic sol, its micelles must

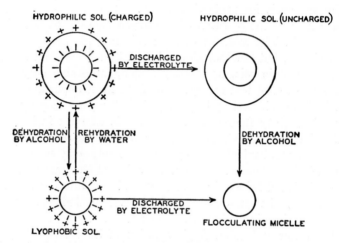

Fig. 5.   Diagrammatic representation of the flocculation of a micelle of a hydrophilic sol.

be both dehydrated and electrically discharged, except in the occasional systems in which micelles are uncharged, in which dehydration alone will suffice. Dehydration alone of a hydrophilic sol with charged micelles results in its conversion into a lyophobic sol.

The interrelationships among the factors involved in the stability and flocculation of hydrophilic sols are shown in Fig. 5 which is self-explanatory.

The addition of relatively large quantities of certain electrolytes to hydrophilic sols will result in their flocculation without any previous removal of the water of hydration of the micelles by means of alcohol or any other dehydrating agent. Only very soluble salts are effective in this way. It is evident that this phenomenon, usually called *"salting out,"* involves a more complicated reaction than that taking place in simple flocculation and must be distinguished from the latter phenomenon. Three salts which are especially suitable for salting out hydrophilic sols are $(NH_4)_2SO_4$, $MgSO_4$, and Na_2SO_4. In these three salts the ions, especially the anions, acquire relatively large quantities of water of hydration. The result of the addition of a very strong solution of such a salt to a hydrophilic sol is a twofold one. A small initial amount of the added electrolyte discharges the micelles. Addition of further increments of an electrolyte eventually brings about dehydration of the micelles because of the great attraction of the added ions for water, and the resultant separation of the dispersed phase out of the system. Salting out, therefore, results in the destruction of both of the stability factors of the system.

Amphoteric Properties of Protein Sols.—Protein sols differ from most others in that the micelles are amphoteric, *i.e.*, they may act either as an acid or as a base. The acid properties of proteins depend upon their —COOH groups; their basic properties upon their —NH_2 groups (Chap. XXVI). Whether the proteins will combine with acids or bases depends principally upon the *p*H of the dispersion medium. In a gelatin sol, for example, in which the *p*H of the medium is above the isoelectric point[3] the —COOH groups of the molecules react with a base such as sodium hydroxide, forming "sodium gelatinate." This compound then dissociates into sodium ions and negatively charged gelatin micelles. If the *p*H of the medium is below the isoelectric point the —NH_2 groups of the gelatin molecules may combine with the molecules of an acid such as HCl forming "gelatin hydrochloride." Dissociation of this compound produces chloride ions and positively charged gelatin micelles.

Like the micelles of other sols, those of proteins are uncharged with respect to the medium at the isoelectric point. Therefore no migration of the micelles occurs if an electric current is passed through a protein sol at its isoelectric point. At *p*H values higher than the isoelectric point protein micelles migrate toward the anode, while at values below the isoelectric point they migrate toward the cathode.

The principles governing the stability and flocculation of a protein sol are similar to those which hold for other hydrophilic sols with the one further complication that protein micelles may be either positively or negatively charged. Protein sols are stable at their isoelectric point because, although uncharged, they possess, like all hydrophilic sols, micelles which are highly hydrated. On either side of the isoelectric point the micelles of a protein sol have the additional stability factor of an electrical charge. Addition of a sufficient quantity of a dehydrating agent such as alcohol to a gelatin sol at its isoelectric point will result, as it does with an uncharged agar sol, in immediate flocculation. If the mi-

[3] The *p*H value of the isoelectric point of gelatin is about 4.7.

celes are charged, however, addition of alcohol will result, not in flocculation, but in the conversion of the system into a lyophobic sol. Addition
of a suitable electrolyte to this sol will result in a discharge of the particles
and their consequent flocculation. These relations are shown diagrammatically for a protein sol in Fig. 6.

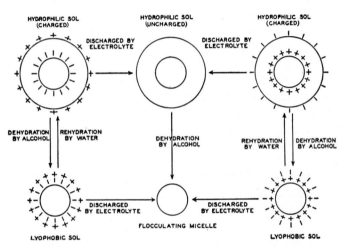

Fig. 6.   Diagrammatic representation of the flocculation of a micelle of a protein
sol.

Properties of Gels.—Under certain conditions most hydrophilic sols
change into gels. Any gelatin sol which is not too dilute, for example,
will "set" upon standing and form a gel. Everyone is familiar with such
gelatin gels, as they appear on the table often as desserts. Other familiar
gels are the agar gels widely used as a medium for the culturing of
bacteria, fungi, and algae, ordinary household "jellies" which are basically pectin gels, and starch gels. The latter also sometimes comes before
our eyes by the dessert route, under the name of corn starch puddings.
Some hydrophilic sols, however, do not ordinarily form gels. This is true
of sols of gum acacia and of some protein sols.

The gel-forming capacity of some substances is very remarkable. A
gelatin sol containing as low a proportion as one part of gelatin to one
hundred of water will usually gelate. Agar gels containing only 0.15 per
cent of agar can be prepared. In such a gel one part of agar has the
property of removing the liquidity from nearly 700 parts of water.

Since gels form from two-phase colloidal systems, it is generally assumed that they also are two-phase systems. In all of the gels which we
shall have occasion to consider, the liquid phase is water, although gels
in which one component is some other liquid are well known. Gels are

usually rigid enough to maintain their shape under the stress of their own weight. This means that they will be molded to the shape of the vessel in which the gelation has occurred and will retain the shape of that vessel after being removed from it.

Two general types of gels are usually recognized: the elastic type, and the nonelastic type. The best-known example of the latter is the silica gel. Elastic gels are the important type biologically. Gelatin-water and agar-water gels are probably the best-known examples of this type of colloidal system. When such a gel dries a gradual and consistent shrinkage in its volume ensues until desiccation is complete. After desiccation the dry matter of the gel will imbibe water (Chap. VII), but no other liquid. Gels in which the liquid phase was other than water will imbibe, after desiccation, only the liquid originally present.

Elastic gels are generally heat reversible. When heated such gels are converted into sols (solation), and when cooled such sols resume their gel condition (gelation). Usually this reversal of state can occur a number of times to a colloidal system without greatly affecting its physical properties when in either the sol or gel condition. The temperatures at which the solation and gelation of a given colloidal system occur are not identical. The processes differ in this respect from the melting and freezing of a solid. For example, a 4 per cent gelatin sol gelates at about 28°C., but the resulting gel must be raised to about 31°C. before solation will occur. For agar gels the temperature spread between gelation and solation is much greater. The former process occurs at approximately 30°C.; the latter at about 70°C. for a 2 per cent gel. The viscosity of a heat reversible sol increases steadily with a decrease in temperature and shows no sudden change as the sol passes into the gel condition.

Solutes diffuse through gels almost as rapidly as through pure water, unless the gels are very concentrated. The diffusion of a solute through a gel is easily demonstrated by a simple experiment. A gelatin sol is allowed to solidify in a test tube which is then inverted in a shallow dish containing a solution of a dye such as methylene blue. Within 24 hr. diffusion of the dye into the gelatin gel can be detected. Because of the fact that there are no convection currents in a gel to complicate the results, this is perhaps the best visual method of demonstrating the diffusion of solutes.

Two equal quantities of an electrolyte, one dispersed in water, the other in a gel of equal volume, will conduct an electric current almost equally well. In other words ionic mobility is apparently as great when the ions are dispersed in a gel as when they are dispersed in pure water.

The velocities of chemical reactions occurring in a gel medium are not appreciably different from the velocities of the same reactions occurring under the same conditions of solute concentration and temperature in a water medium. Neither of the last two general statements are strictly true for very concentrated gels.

The above three properties of gels distinguish them clearly from the solid or amorphous states of matter. These properties must be reconciled with any acceptable theories of the structure of gels.

The Structure of Gels.—Numerous theories of the structure of gels have been advanced, and there are probably elements of truth in most of them since it seems improbable that the molecular structure of all gels is the same. The structure of gels is too fine to be resolved by the microscope, hence most evidence of the structure of gels is indirect.

At the present time the most generally favored hypothesis of gel structure is that both the solid and liquid phases of a gel are continuous. The solid phase is most usually visualized as a meshwork of long, tangled fibrillae of submicroscopic dimensions; the spaces within this interwoven mesh being occupied by the fluid phase. This theory is often called the "brushpile" theory in allusion to the supposed jumble of intermeshing threads of the solid phase. This theory appears to be most acceptable in the light of the known facts regarding the very slight effect of gels upon diffusion, conductivity, and the velocity of chemical reactions. Supporting evidence for this view has also been obtained by examination of gels under the electron microscope (Chap. IV).

Since elastic gels can be readily transformed into hydrophilic sols, and hydrophilic sols into gels, it seems probable that many hydrophilic sols also possess a fibrillar structure. Such a structure is also postulated by many authorities for protoplasm, as later discussion will show.

Hysteresis.—The statement is sometimes encountered that gels possess the faculty of "memory." This statement is not, of course, to be accepted literally. It is merely a way of saying that the previous treatments to which a gel has been subjected have an influence, often marked, upon its behavior, so that in an allegorical sense the gel may be said to "remember" those treatments. This phenomenon of the influence of the previous treatment of a gel upon its behavior is known as *hysteresis*.[4] It is well illustrated by the following experiment of Gortner and Hoffman (1927). Three gelatin gels were prepared containing respectively 10, 20, and 40 g. of gelatin per 100 ml. of water. Strips of these gels of equal rectilinear dimensions and thickness were then dried in a current of warm air until all of them were reduced to a moisture content of about 3.5 per cent. In other words, the three gels were all brought into what would superficially seem to be identical physical conditions. The dried sections were then

---

[4] This use of the term "hysteresis" should not be confused with its common use in another sense in physics and engineering.

placed in distilled water and allowed to imbibe water, weighings being made from time to time. The results are shown in Fig. 7.

In spite of the fact that all three of these gels possessed the same water content when immersed in water their swelling behavior was quite different, depending in each sample on the previous history of the gel. The gel which was originally prepared in the proportion of 10 parts of gelatin to 100 of water swelled the most, followed in order by the one originally prepared in a proportion of 20 parts of gelatin to 100 of water, and finally by the gel originally prepared in a proportion of 40 parts of gelatin to 100 parts of water.

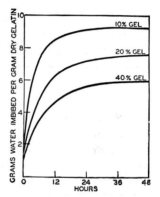

The example cited is just one of the many hysteresis effects which have been recognized in gels. All sorts of factors—mechanical, thermal, electrical, and even the factor of time—may induce such effects in gels. It follows that in experimental work with gels, if results are to be comparable, all the gels used in a given experiment or set of experiments must have had identical previous histories.

FIG. 7. Curves illustrating hysteresis in gelatin gels. Data of Gortner and Hoffman (1927).

Thixotropy.—If a trace of sodium chloride is added to a test tube full of 10 per cent bentonite (a colloidal clay) and shaken vigorously, a colloidal sol will result which will set to a gel after standing a few minutes. By shaking, this gel can be converted to a sol which will again set upon brief standing. The process may be repeated an indefinite number of times. This phenomenon is called *thixotropy*. Protoplasm also exhibits thixotropic reactions. Stirring of the protoplasm or subjection of a cell to pressure can be shown to greatly reduce its viscosity and probably induces gel-to-sol changes. Thixotropic phenomena may therefore play important roles in cellular physiology.

SUGGESTED FOR COLLATERAL READING

Alexander, J. *Colloid Chemistry; Principles and Applications.* 4th Ed. D. Van Nostrand Co., Inc. New York. 1937.

Freundlich, H. *Colloid and Capillary Chemistry.* Translated by H. S. Hatfield. E. P. Dutton & Co., Inc. New York. 1926.

Frey-Wyssling, A. *Submicroscopic Morphology of Protoplasm and Its Derivatives.* Translated by J. J. Hermans and M. Hollander. New York. Elsevier Publishing Co., Inc. 1948.

Gortner, R. A. *Outlines of Biochemistry.* 3rd Ed. Edited by R. A. Gortner, Jr., and W. A. Gortner. John Wiley & Sons, Inc. New York. 1949.

Hartman, R. J. *Colloid Chemistry.* 2nd Ed. Houghton-Mifflin Co. Boston. 1947.

Kruyt, H. R. *Colloids.* Translated by H. S. Van Klooster. John Wiley & Sons,
    Inc. New York. 1927.
Seifriz, W. *Protoplasm.* McGraw-Hill Book Co., Inc. New York. 1936.

SELECTED BIBLIOGRAPHY

Freundlich, H. Über das Ausfallen kolloidaler Lösungen durch Elektrolyte.
    Zeitschr. Phys. Chem. **44:** 129-160. 1903.
Gortner, R. A., and W. F. Hoffman. The imbibition of gelatin dried as a gel and
    as a sol. *Jour. Physical Chem.* **31:** 464-466. 1927.
Seifriz, W. Phase reversal in emulsions and protoplasm. *Amer. Jour. Physiol.* **66:**
    124-139. 1923.
Svedberg, T. Density and hydration in gelatin sols and gels. *Jour. Amer. Chem.
    Soc.* **46:** 2673-2676. 1924.

DISCUSSION QUESTIONS

1. What are the three most outstanding characteristics of colloidal systems in which water is the dispersion medium?

2. How can you find out whether a given organic dye forms a solution or a sol when dispersed in water?

3. The charges on each colloidal micelle are assumed to be balanced by electrostatically equal charges in the dispersion medium. If this is true how can the micelles exhibit cataphoresis?

4. Given an unknown colloidal sol, how would you determine whether it was hydrophilic or hydrophobic? Whether its micelles were positively or negatively charged?

5. List some colloidal systems found in plant cells. List some colloidal systems in the environment which may have important effects on plants.

6. Why do gels not form from hydrophobic sols?

7. The juice expressed from plant tissues usually consists of a mixture of substances in the colloidal state and in true solution. How would you demonstrate this to be true by experimental means?

8. Why do the floating particles of dust in the air which are clearly visible when a beam of light passes through a darkened room become invisible when the room is well lighted?

9. What would be the effect of an increase in temperature upon the rate of adsorption? On the amount of adsorption?

IV

PLANT CELLS

The Structure of Plant Cells.—The typical cell of the higher plants is a tiny compartment enclosed by a tough elastic wall (Fig. 8). The wall of cells consists of two major parts: (1) the *middle lamella* and (2) the *primary wall* (Kerr and Bailey, 1934). *secreted or laid down inside primary wall* In walls of many plant cells a third structural component, the *secondary wall*, is also present. Although some plant cells are known which do not have a well defined cell wall, this structure is so generally present in plant cells as to be considered one of their characteristic features.

Lining the interior of the wall and occupying more or less of the cell cavity is the *protoplasm*. The protoplasm of active cells is a transparent, slightly viscous, granular material that lacks any conspicuous structural background. It is not homogeneous, however, and contains a number of definite structures. One of these, the *nucleus*, is a denser body which is more or less spheroidal in shape and is separated from the remaining protoplasm by a definite membrane, the *nuclear membrane*. Within the membrane surrounding the nucleus are: (1) a clear liquid known as the *nu-*

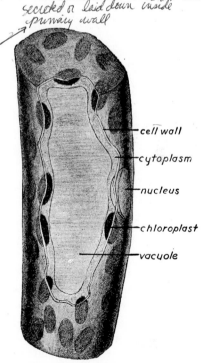

FIG. 8. Diagram in perspective of a palisade cell from the leaf meso-phyll.

cell wall

cytoplasm

nucleus

chloroplast

vacuole

47

clear sap, (2) a delicate network of denser material, the *reticulum,* and (3) one or more small spherical masses of material known as the *nucleolus* or nucleoli.

All of the protoplasm outside of the nucleus of the cell constitutes the *cytoplasm.* In a typical mature plant cell the cytoplasm is present as a thin layer lining the inner surface of the cell wall. The two boundary surfaces of the cytoplasm—that in contact with the cell wall and that in contact with vacuole—are called *cytoplasmic membranes* (Chap. VIII). Imbedded in the cytoplasm are numerous well differentiated bodies known as *plastids.* Plastids are usually centers of certain types of physiological activity. They are commonly classified on the basis of their color into three groups: the *leucoplasts* which are colorless, the *chloroplasts* which contain the green chlorophyll pigments (also yellow pigments), and the *chromoplasts* which contain red or yellow pigments. *Chondriosomes* (mitochrondria), minute rod-like or granular bodies, are also found in the cytoplasm. The significance of these structures is not positively known, although a number of different roles have been ascribed to them.

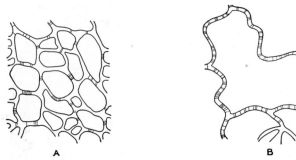

A   B

Fig. 9.   Plasmodesms in cell walls of tobacco: (*A*) in sieve tubes and companion cells, (*B*) in epidermal cells of leaf. Redrawn from Livingston (1935).

Although the cell wall appears to imprison each protoplast and to effectively isolate it from the protoplasm of adjoining cells, actually there is probably a continuation of protoplasm from cell to cell. By certain techniques it can be demonstrated that minute pores extend from cell to cell through the cell walls. These pores often contain cytoplasmic strands which connect the cytoplasms of adjacent cells. These strands are termed *plasmodesms* (Fig. 9). Livingston (1935) has demonstrated the occurrence of plasmodesms in the walls of cells from a number of different tissues of the tobacco plant, and it is generally supposed that they are of widespread if not universal occurrence in the cell walls of higher green plants (Meeuse, 1941).

The bulk of the interior of most mature plant cells is occupied by a

separated by the inner vacuolar membrane; all membranes continuous

single large cavity, the *vacuole,* which is filled with *cell sap.* The cell sap is composed of water in which a great variety of substances are dissolved or colloidally dispersed.

There is no general agreement among cytologists regarding the exact classification of the parts of plant cells. The vacuole, for example, is frequently classified as a part of the protoplasm, because it first appears as minute droplets in the protoplasm of very young cells. Physiologically, however, the vacuole of the mature cell is as distinct an entity as the protoplasm or cell wall, and it is therefore considered as a separate part of the cell in this book. The following classification includes the principal parts of a mature plant cell. A few of these parts, as for example the various kinds of plastids, do not occur in every cell.

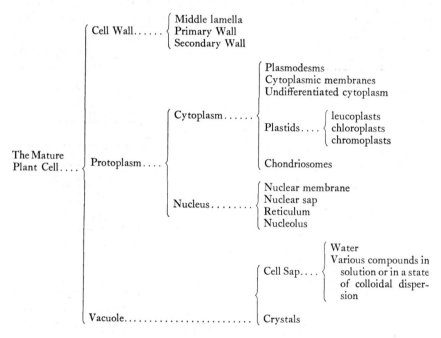

The Mature Plant Cell....

- Cell Wall......
  - Middle lamella
  - Primary Wall
  - Secondary Wall
- Protoplasm....
  - Cytoplasm......
    - Plasmodesms
    - Cytoplasmic membranes
    - Undifferentiated cytoplasm
    - Plastids....
      - leucoplasts
      - chloroplasts
      - chromoplasts
    - Chondriosomes
  - Nucleus........
    - Nuclear membrane
    - Nuclear sap
    - Reticulum
    - Nucleolus
- Vacuole......................
  - Cell Sap....
    - Water
    - Various compounds in solution or in a state of colloidal dispersion
  - Crystals

The Origin and Development of Cells.—As soon as it became clear that all plant and animal tissues were composed of cells, the question of the origin of cells naturally arose. This proved to be a difficult problem for the pioneer investigators, and for many years there was much disagreement over the question. The now universally accepted principle that cells can arise only from pre-existing cells was first demonstrated beyond any reasonable doubt by Nägeli just before the middle of the nineteenth century. In higher plants cell division occurs chiefly in certain restricted regions called *meristems* (Chap. XXIX). The formation of new cells involves not only the division of pre-existing cells, but the subsequent enlargement and maturation of their cell progeny.

The Forms and Sizes of Cells.—All newly formed cells do not differentiate morphologically in the same way. Some elongate parallel to the axis of growth more than in other directions and become the long fiber cells that make up much of the xylem and phloem tissues. These cells commonly develop walls that are greatly thickened. Some cells enlarge about equally in all directions becoming isodiametric cells, the walls of which usually remain thin and flexible. Cells of this type are present in the flesh of apples, melons, potatoes, and in many other parenchymatous tissues.

Plant cells appear to be basically tetrakaidecahedra, *i.e.*, fourteen-sided (Lewis, 1935, 1943), although numerous deviations from this basic pattern exist. Actually this number of cell faces is closely approximated, on the average, in certain relatively undifferentiated plant tissues (Marvin, 1939; Hulbary, 1944, 1948; and others). In some tissues, specifically epidermis cells (Matzke, 1947, 1948) and cortical cells (Hulbary, 1944), the average number of cell faces is characteristically smaller. In general, small cells have fewer faces than larger ones (Marvin, 1944). An almost endless variation in the forms and sizes of cells may be seen in the tissues of any vascular plant. Many different kinds of plant cells are figured and described in greater detail in later chapters.

In size, cells show an even greater range of variability. Relatively few cells in the vascular plants have diameters less than 10 μ or more than 200 μ. The small size of most plant cells may be appreciated from counts that have been made on familiar tissues. An average sized apple leaf contains about 50,000,000 cells; an object 1 square inch in area placed on the surface of many common leaves would cover about a million epidermal cells; a section only 1 mm. in thickness cut very near the tip of a root of the cowpea plant would contain about 128,000 cells. Some cells, however, are very much larger. Many of the cells making up the flesh of a watermelon are large enough to be seen without magnification and have a volume some 350,000 times that of the meristematic cells from which they developed. A cotton fiber is a single cell, and varieties of cotton are grown which produce fibers exceeding 4 cm. in length. The phloem fiber cells of *Boehmeria nivea* are known to reach a length of 55 cm. Such fiber cells have lengths that are many thousand times their diameters.

Origin and Development of the Cell Wall.—In the vascular plants the division of a plant cell is preceded by the division of the nucleus. Nuclear division is a complicated process involving organization of the nuclear reticulum into unit chromosomes, splitting of those chromosomes, separation of the split chromosomes, and finally reconstitution of a daughter nucleus from each set of daughter chromosomes. Just after the final stage ("telophase") of mitosis a membrane develops in the center of the cell and extends its margins until it makes contact on all sides with the existing cell wall, thus forming a septum which separates the protoplasts of the newly formed cells (Fig. 10). There is no evidence that this first membrane, the *middle lamella,* contains cellulose. It seems to be composed largely, if not entirely, of colloidal pectic compounds. As the cell begins

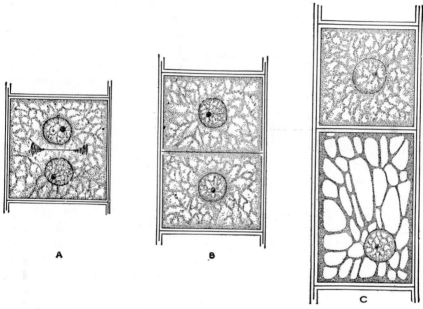

Fig. 10. Diagram illustrating formation of a plant cell wall. (*A*) Cell plate between two daughter nuclei, (*B*) cell plate (middle lamella) completely separating the daughter cells, (*C*) primary wall has been formed on each side of the middle lamella. One of the newly formed cells has undergone considerable enlargement.

to enlarge, a thin layer composed of cellulose and pectic compounds is deposited from the cytoplasm of each young cell on the two surfaces of the middle lamella. This new wall is joined firmly to the existing walls at the sides of the cell so that the protoplast of each daughter cell becomes encased within a continuous wall, the *primary wall,* of cellulose and pectic substances. As long as a cell wall retains a capacity for increase in area and for undergoing reversible changes in thickness it is classed as a primary cell wall. The walls of cambium, parenchyma, and collenchyma cells are all examples of primary cell walls.

After the enlargement of the cell ceases the deposition of cellulose on the inner surface of the primary wall may continue until the wall becomes conspicuously thickened. When this thickening is accompanied by a loss of the capacity for enlargement and a loss of elasticity, the added material is known as the *secondary wall*. In extreme cases secondary walls may increase in thickness until the wall occupies most of the interior of the cell. All cells have a middle lamella and a primary wall, but secondary walls are present only in certain types of cells. Phloem fibers, stone cells, tracheids and wood fibers are typical examples of cells with prominent secondary walls.

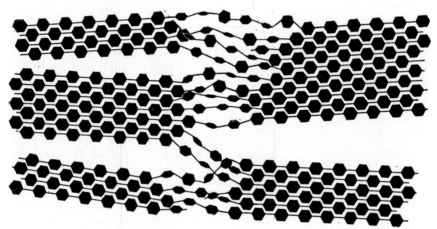

Fig. 11.   Diagram of a small portion of a cellulose micelle, showing crystalline and amorphous cellulose.

Increase in thickness of the wall usually takes place by the addition of definite layers of cellulose or other cell-wall constituents to the inner surface of the existing wall. In most walls these layers are too thin to be detected without swelling or otherwise treating the wall.

The Structure of the Cell Wall.—The structural framework of the plant cell wall is composed of cellulose and the basic unit of this framework is the cellulose molecule. Cellulose molecules are long chains formed by the condensation of many hundred β D-glucose molecules (Chap. XX). Since the length of the chains is not constant, cellulose molecules are not units of definite molecular weight. Many of the cellulose molecules in the walls of living plant cells are long enough to contain at least 5000 glucose residues (a glucose residue is a molecule of β D-glucose minus a molecule of water), whereas others are much shorter.

The geometrical arrangement of the long cellulose molecules in the cell wall has been revealed by studies with the X-ray and polarized light. In certain regions the chain molecules are so closely parallel that they have acquired many of the properties of crystals. In other regions the chain molecules are less perfectly oriented giving rise to what is known as amorphous cellulose. The same cellulose molecule may be a part of a highly crystalline area, pass on into an amorphous region, and then continue on to enter another crystalline zone (Fig. 11). The transition between the crystalline regions (known as micelles or crystallites) and the amorphous areas is not abrupt so the wall is a fabric of very long chain molecules of cellulose which exhibit different degrees of parallelism in different parts of the wall.

Measurement of the X-ray diagrams of some of the natural plant fibers shows that the crystalline regions (micelles) have a rather definite thickness. A single micelle may be considered as rhombus about 5-6 mμ in thickness and at least 60 mμ in length (Heuser, 1944). In terms of cellulose molecules this means that each crystalline micelle is a bundle of some 100-170 parallel molecules and that those portions of the molecule which lie within the micelle consist of at least 120 glucose residues. It is probable that in many cell walls long chain molecules formed by the condensation of other sugars are associated with the cellulose molecules.

The proportions of crystalline and amorphous cellulose in plant cell walls vary within wide limits. In the thickened walls of some plant fibers as much as 90 per cent of the cellulose is crystalline while in the enlarging walls of the young cells the crystalline cellulose makes up only a small proportion of that present. In some young cell walls crystalline cellulose appears to be entirely absent. Since the distinction between the crystalline and amorphous cellulose lies chiefly in the degree of orientation of the molecules it follows that stretching or drying a cell wall will increase, often very greatly, the proportion of crystalline cellulose.

Evidence of various kinds suggests that spaces of submicroscopic size separate the micelles and form an interconnecting system which extends throughout the cellulose framework (Fig. 11, 12B). These spaces range in width from 1 mμ to perhaps 100 mμ and thus constitute relatively enormous channels along which diffusing molecules may penetrate the cellulose portions of the wall. In primary cell walls these spaces are filled with pectic compounds; in woody tissues they are filled with lignin, and in cutinized walls with waxes and cutin. In walls that are almost pure cellulose, such as the secondary wall of cotton fibers, the spaces are filled with water.

The smallest *visible* units of cellulose walls are delicate thread-like strands of fibrils. These fibrils are aggregates of a great many molecules and micelles of cellulose both of which are oriented with their long axes parallel to the long axis of the fibril. In primary walls the fibrils form a fine anastomosing network (Fig. 12A), the meshes of which are filled with colloidal pectic compounds. In secondary walls the fibrils are often grouped into coarser branching strands which wind around the cell in a steep spiral the angle of which may vary in different layers and even in different parts of the same layer (Fig. 13).

The minute details of cell-wall structure have been difficult to fathom because of the limitations imposed by even the finest optical microscopes.

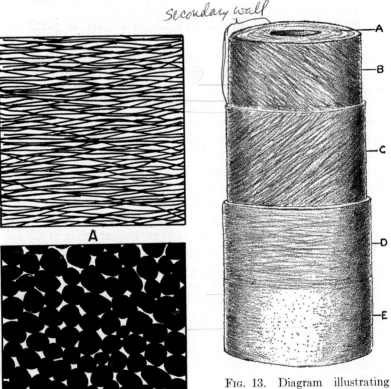

Secondary wall

Fig. 12. Diagrams illustrating submicroscopic structure of primary cell wall. (A) The meshwork of anastomosing cellulose fibrils as seen in surface view. (B) Cross section of a single fibril showing micelles and intermicellar spaces.

Fig. 13. Diagram illustrating the structure of a thickened plant cell wall: (A) inner layers of secondary wall, (B) second layer of the secondary wall, (C) first layer of the secondary wall, (D) cellulose framework of the primary wall, (E) primary wall of cellulose and pectic compounds. Note that the fibrils may be differently oriented in different layers of the same wall.

The limits to the resolving power of an optical microscope are determined by the wave lengths of light used. The shorter the wave length, the greater the resolving power. It follows therefore that, if some method could be found to use wave lengths of radiation considerably shorter than those of the visible spectrum, it would be possible to see or photograph objects that were too small to be visible in the usual compound microscope. Such a method has been developed in the electron microscope. In this instrument beams of electrons are used instead of light, and the

FIG. 14. Electron microscope photograph of a portion of the secondary wall of a ramie fiber showing fibrillar structure of cellulose. (R. W. G. Wyckoff, *Electron Microscopy, Techniques and Applications,* copyright Interscience Publishers, N. Y., London, 1949).

beams are focused magnetically. The wave lengths of the electron beams commonly used are less than one four-thousandth of the length of the shortest wave lengths of the visible spectrum. Because of the very short wave lengths employed in the electron microscope, it is possible to obtain clear images of objects far below the resolving power of the best optical microscopes. Photographs of plant cell walls taken with the electron microscope confirm the general structural patterns that have been deduced from other lines of evidence (Fig. 14).

The Physical Properties of Cell Walls.—The physical properties of primary cell walls differ sharply from those of secondary walls. Primary walls are usually very flexible and elastic. The mesophyll cells of some species, for example, are known to undergo reversible changes in volume of 30 per cent or more as a result of changes in turgor pressure. The great flexibility and elasticity of primary walls are made possible by the large amount of amorphous cellulose in the wall and by the extensive system of intermicellar and interfibrillar spaces which is filled with gelatinous, hydrophilic pectic compounds. The low elasticity, reduced flexibility, and very high tensile strength (comparable to that of spring steel) of secondary walls contrast strongly with the properties just described as being typical of primary walls. The greater stiffness and toughness of secondary walls are caused by the presence of larger quantities of cellulose in the wall and by the high proportion of crystalline cellulose.

Both primary and secondary walls are transparent to wave lengths of the visible spectrum.

Chemical Constituents of Cell Walls.—Cellulose is by far the most abundant compound found in the cell walls of the higher plants. Associated with cellulose in all the primary cell walls of vascular plants are greater or lesser amounts of pectic compounds. Their presence in the middle lamella and in the intermicellar spaces of the primary walls has already been noted. The chemistry of the pectic compounds is discussed in Chap. XX.

Lignin is an important constituent of the walls of most of the cells that make up woody tissues and it also occurs commonly in other thickened walls. The chemical structure of lignin appears to be that of a polyflavone (Bonner, 1950).

Lignin first appears in the middle lamella and primary wall and later can be detected in the secondary wall. When associated with cellulose, lignin is present in the spaces between the micelles and not within the micelles. Lignified walls are usually freely permeable to water and solutes. The tensile strength of lignified cell walls is the same as that of cellulose walls but lignified walls resist compression better than cellulose walls. The increased resistance of lignified walls to compression is explained by the assumption that the presence of lignin in the intermicellar spaces welds the cellulose micelles into a single coherent mass and thus prevents the bending and buckling of the cellulose strands when they are subjected to compression strains.

Cutin is the name applied to the mixture of wax-like materials found on the outer surface of the epidermal cell walls of leaves, stems, fruits, and other organs. These wax-like substances are intimately associated with cellulose and often with pectic substances producing a wall of great structural complexity (Anderson, 1934). Cutinized cell walls are relatively impermeable to water. The presence of cutin in the outer walls of epidermal cells greatly reduces the evaporation of water from the surface of plant tissues.

Suberin is similar in many of its properties to cutin. It constitutes an important part of cork cell walls and it is also found in the walls of a few other types of cells. Most of the surface of perennial plants, aside from the leaves and very young stems is covered with suberized cell walls. Such walls are relatively impermeable to water. The chemistry of both cutin and suberin is discussed in Chap. XXIII.

Hemicelluloses are a poorly defined group of polysaccharides associated with cellulose in plant cell walls. They are not chemically related to cellulose, as the name implies, but possess very different chemical and physical properties. The chemistry and metabolic significance of these substances are discussed in Chap. XX.

Callose is the name given to a carbohydrate found in the perforated septa ("sieve plates") of the sieve tubes. Similar material, presumably of the same chemical composition, has been found in pollen grains and constitutes the inner layer of pollen tubes. It has also been reported as occurring in the fungi. The exact chemical composition of callose is unknown.

Chitin is an amino-hexosan (Chap. XX), common in the exoskeleton of insects, also found in the walls of many fungi and bacteria. It has been reported as being present in the walls of certain algae, but it is unknown in any of the higher plants.

Tannins (Chap. XX) are commonly found in the cell sap, but they also occur in the walls of certain tissues, especially cork and wood cells.

Mucilages (Chap. XX) are common constituents of the outer walls of many water plants and occur also in the outer walls of some seed coats, in glandular hairs, and in other tissues.

Inorganic compounds such as silica and salts of calcium, iron, and other metals are also present in some plant cell walls. None of these inorganic compounds, however, are regarded as essential constituents of the cell wall.

Protoplasm.—In most mature cells of the vascular plants, protoplasm is present only as a thin layer covering the inner surface of the cell walls, but in some cells branching strands of protoplasm also extend across the vacuole. Under high magnification the protoplasm of active cells appears as a colorless fluid, in which are suspended numerous tiny granules and droplets of insoluble materials. These granules frequently exhibit active Brownian movement. The fluid component of protoplasm also is frequently in motion, streaming around the inner surfaces of the cell walls.

Although protoplasm appears to be a simple liquid, no simple liquid could possibly possess the remarkable powers of synthesis, assimilation, reproduction, growth, and sensitivity that characterize the protoplasm of living plant cells. The properties and behavior of protoplasm clearly show that it is not a substance but that it must be regarded as a complex system of substances. This system is dynamic; it is constantly undergoing changes yet at the same time the changes are so regulated and controlled that the system is not disrupted. A cell is alive only so long as the organization of this dynamic protoplasmic system is maintained.

The Chemical Composition of Protoplasm.—Since protoplasm is a dynamic system of substances it is not possible to subject it to chemical analysis without destroying it. In the strict sense, therefore, it is impossible to discover the chemical composition of protoplasm. It is possible, however, to examine the substances present after the protoplasmic system has been destroyed and to determine their chemical composition and relative abundance. A number of such studies have been made.

Water is the chief component of all physiologically active plant protoplasm, usually making up more than 90 per cent of the system. The water content of the protoplasm of dry seeds, on the other hand, may be less than 10 per cent.

Most attempts to determine the chemical composition of plant protoplasm have been made upon species of the myxomycetes (slime molds). At certain stages in their life history these organisms consist of naked masses of labile protoplasm. They are often found "flowing" over rotten logs in damp woods. The fact that the myxomycetes provide relatively large quantities of protoplasm entirely free from cell-wall material has made them a favorite object for chemical analysis. Even in such organisms, however, not all of the constituents of the plant body can be regarded as integral parts of the protoplasm. Distributed throughout the protoplasmic mass are particles of foods and other inert materials which cannot be separated from the protoplasm. The results of a chemical analysis of the dry residue of a myxomycete plasmodium are shown in Table 7.

As shown in this analysis, proteins and other nitrogen-containing compounds constitute the bulk of the organic matter in the plasmodium of this species. Many different varieties of proteins are known to occur in the protoplasm of plant cells. They are compounds of enormous molecular weight (Chap. XXVI) and undoubtedly make up a large proportion of the labile structural framework of the protoplasm.

Lipids (Chap. XXIII) constitute a smaller fraction of the protoplasm than the proteins. Three types of lipids occur in the protoplasm; the true fats (oils), the phosphatides (phospholipids), and the sterols, of which phytosterol is an example. The oils are generally suspended in the protoplasm in the form of minute globules. They are probably more important as food reserves than as actual constituents of the protoplasm. The phospholipids and sterols, on the other hand, are believed to be essential constituents of the protoplasmic system.

The water-soluble carbohydrates and amino acids, present in the plasmodium of this species, are probably almost entirely foods. The inorganic compounds ("mineral matter") in plant cells are chiefly the phosphates, chlorides, sulfates, and carbonates of magnesium, potassium, sodium, and calcium.

TABLE 7 — ANALYSIS OF THE PLASMODIUM OF A MYXOMYCETE RESEMBLING FULIGO VARIANS.
(DATA OF LEPESCHKIN, 1923)

	Percentage of dry weight
A. Water soluble substances, chiefly from vacuoles:	
Monosaccharides..	14.2
Proteins..	2.2
Amino acids, asparagine, etc...............................	24.3
B. Insoluble organic substances, principally constituents of the protoplasm:	
Nucleoproteins	32.3
Nucleic acids...	2.5
Globulin	0.5
Lipoproteins	4.8
Neutral fats..	6.8
Phytosterol...	3.2
Phosphatides..	1.3
Other organic matter......................................	3.5
C. Mineral matter, about half water soluble..................	4.4

An analysis such as that presented in Table 7 is not without value inasmuch as it furnishes some information regarding the kinds and proportions of the compounds present in protoplasm. It supplies no more information regarding the *organization* of protoplasm, however, than a chemical analysis of the ground up debris of a wrecked house would furnish regarding the structure of that house. This point is worthy of emphasis, since with the progress of biology it becomes clearer and clearer that the properties of protoplasm are as much a function of its physiochemical organization as of the specific kinds of compounds present. Although we commonly refer to "protoplasm" as the essential constituent of all living cells, it is evident that there are at least as many different varieties of protoplasm as there are species of plants and animals. All of them, however, are dynamic systems composed of the same types of compounds, and all of them possess a colloidal organization of a complex type.

The Physical Properties of Cytoplasm.—There are enormous difficulties in the way of determining the physical properties of cytoplasm. The cytoplasmic system is so dynamic and so susceptible to change that most experimental procedures are almost certain to alter its physical properties. The magnitude of such induced alterations is usually difficult to estimate, and hence there are often serious discrepancies between the results of different investigators. Certain generalizations, however, seem to have wide application.

1. *Transparency*—Apart from certain pigmented structures, such as chloroplasts, cytoplasm is usually transparent to wave lengths of the visible spectrum.

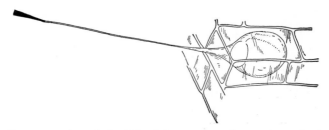

Fig. 15.   Demonstration of the "elastic" property of cytoplasm. Redrawn from Seifriz (1936).

2. *Elasticity*—Cytoplasm appears to combine both elastic and fluid properties to a degree unusual in physical systems. Strands of cytoplasm sufficiently fluid to show protoplasmic streaming behave like elastic threads, and Seifriz (1936) has shown that the cytoplasm of a plant cell may be drawn out into long threads which snap back into the cytoplasmic mass when released (Fig. 15). Cytoplasm is not invariably elastic, however, for sometimes viscous cytoplasm may be more plastic than elastic and highly fluid cytoplasm also may give little evidence of elastic extensibility. The elastic properties which seem so generally present in cytoplasm appear to owe their origin largely to the structure of the protein molecules and micelles which have so important a role in cytoplasmic structures (Moyer, 1942).

3. *Viscosity*—Numerous ingenious methods of measuring the viscosity of cytoplasm have been devised, but the results obtained are not in agreement. The one conclusion which emerges most clearly from all of these studies is that the viscosity of the cytoplasm of living cells may vary within wide limits and with extreme rapidity. It has also been found

that different portions of the undifferentiated cytoplasm of a single living cell possess very different viscosities. Near the surface, cytoplasm is more viscous than in the interior, although according to Scarth (1942) the surface itself is highly fluid. In general, much of the cytoplasm of cells that are physiologically active is very fluid, whereas in dormant cells, such as those of dry seeds, the cytoplasm may be as viscous as a stiff gel. The viscosity of the cytoplasm in active cells may change rapidly as a reaction to mechanical injury or electric shock, to changes in temperature, differences in acidity, and exposure to various chemical compounds. Dehydration increases the viscosity of the cytoplasm and death of the cell results in a marked increase in viscosity.

4. *Immiscibility with Water*—The cytoplasm of cells that are physiologically active is invariably composed predominantly of water, yet when the protoplasts are extruded from such cells into an aqueous medium they do not ordinarily mix with the water. The failure of cytoplasm to become dispersed through the water is largely, if not entirely, a result of the presence of a surface membrane containing fat-like constituents which are insoluble in water. When this surface film is punctured a new membrane quickly forms across the broken surface. If substances are present that prevent the development of this surface film the cytoplasm of active cells readily disperses in the water.

5. *Gelation*—One of the striking properties of the cytoplasmic systems of physiologically active cells is their capacity to undergo reversible sol-gel transformations. In cytoplasm as in physical systems no sharp line of division can be drawn between hydrophilic sols and gels, and every gradation between the two may be found in living cells.

6. *Coagulability*—The cytoplasmic system of most physiologically active cells is destroyed by temperatures of 60°C. or above. Death of plant cells at such temperatures is generally considered to result from a coagulation of some of the proteinaceous constituents of the protoplasm (Chap. XXX). A number of other factors may bring about coagulation of the protoplasm, at least in the cells of certain species. Among these are certain electrolytes, electric currents, freezing, mechanical pressure, supersonic waves, and certain wave lengths of radiant energy (especially ultraviolet radiations, X-rays, and radium radiations).

7. *Electrical Properties*—Numerous attempts have been made to determine the isoelectric point of cytoplasm. It was soon discovered that cytoplasm does not have a definite isoelectric point but rather an isoelectric range. This is doubtless to be explained by the fact that cytoplasm is a complex sol composed of many different proteins, each one of which may possess an isoelectric point different from that of the others. Measurements of the cytoplasm of cells in the root tips of different plants

showed the isoelectric range to be from pH 4.6 to pH 5.0 (Naylor, 1926). These values appear to be representative for cytoplasm in general.

Cytoplasm is usually on the alkaline side of its isoelectric range (see later discussion of the pH of the cytoplasm), and therefore we would expect to find that its constituent micelles are negatively charged. That this is true at least for the visible granules of the cytoplasm of some cells has been shown by Sen (1934). Cataphoretic migration of the granules in the cytoplasm of root hair cells and epidermal cells toward the anode was shown to occur, thus indicating that these particles carry a negative charge. Heilbrunn (1940), on the other hand, has reported finding cytoplasmic inclusions to be positively charged and suggests that the positive charge results from the presence of carbonic acid in the cell. During active photosynthesis, when CO_2 concentrations may be presumed to be low, the charge on the chloroplasts of Elodea cells becomes negative.

The proteins present in the nucleus apparently possess different isoelectric points from those of the cytoplasm. Furthermore, it is probable that some portions of the cytoplasm possess isoelectric points different from those of other parts of the cytoplasm in the same cell.

Cytoplasm contains dissolved electrolytes and would therefore be expected to conduct an electrical current. Brooks (1925) determined the electrical conductivity of the plasmodium of the myxomycete *Biefeldia maxima* and found it to be equivalent to that of a 0.00145 N solution of NaCl, which is a relatively low value. The solution in the moss substrate on which the plasmodium was growing had a conductivity only about one-third as great as that of the plasmodium. Evidence was also found that the conductivity of the protoplasm varies according to the conductivity of the medium with which the cells are in contact.

8. *Streaming*—In many cells the cytoplasm may be seen in active movement. In the simplest cases this movement consists of a rotation of the cytoplasm around the inner surface of the cell wall. Where cytoplasmic strands extend through the vacuole, as in the cells of *Tradescantia* stamen hairs, the circulation of the cytoplasm may become very complex. Rates of cytoplasmic streaming seldom exceed 0.1 mm. per sec. The plastids and the visible granules are carried passively around the cell by the moving cytoplasm. The causes of cytoplasmic streaming (*cyclosis*) are unknown. It is accelerated by increases in temperature up to the point where injury appears and is checked by low temperatures, ceasing at temperatures slightly above the freezing point. Cyclosis is also stopped in the absence of oxygen and by anaesthetics in relatively high concentrations. In dilute concentrations toxic substances such as copper sulfate and narcotics accelerate the streaming movements. Light also appears to increase the rate of streaming under certain conditions

The specific effects of the various factors which influence protoplasmic streaming are reviewed in detail by Seifriz (1943).

9. *Permeability*—The cytoplasm is variably permeable to water and many solutes. Physiologically this is one of its most important properties and is considered in more detail in Chap. VIII.

The Physical Structure of Cytoplasm.—Any satisfactory explanation of the structure of cytoplasm must account not only for its physical properties and for its dynamic behavior, but must also explain how the innumerable diverse physical and chemical reactions characteristic of living cells can occur side by side in the same general medium. The highest magnifications reveal no evidence of any structural background in active cytoplasm, yet its complex activities suggest that it must possess an intricate structural organization. The marked imbibitional capacity of cytoplasm, its stability toward electrolytes, its electrical properties, its coagulability, and its gel-forming capacity all suggest that it is to be classed with the hydrophilic colloids. All modern students of cytoplasm are agreed that it is a hydrophilic colloidal system of extreme complexity and variability.

Elastic gels probably possess a submicroscopic structure of long interlacing fibrillar units which hold a liquid in their irregular interstices (Chap. III). Similar units are believed to be present in many hydrophilic sols. Evidence from a variety of sources suggests that cytoplasm also has a structural background in which such organized units of submicroscopic size play an important role.

Because of the preponderance of proteins and related substances in dried protoplasmic residues, it seems to be a safe assumption that the primary structural framework of cytoplasm is composed of proteins. Protein molecules are long chains of amino acid residues (Chap. XXVI) with many, often complex, side groups. Some kinds of protein molecules exist characteristically in the form of essentially straight chains; others are bent back and fourth upon each other forming globoid units (Moyer, 1942). There is considerable evidence that the configuration of a given protein molecule may change from globoid to linear and *vice-versa*, depending upon the conditions to which it is subjected.

That at least some of the proteins present in the cytoplasm occur as more or less linear molecules or aggregates of such molecules seems extremely probable. To postulate that the basic cytoplasmic structure consists of a three-dimensional network of such interlacing chain molecules with a more fluid phase occupying the interstices among the molecular filaments is entirely consistent with current knowledge regarding the chemical composition and physical properties of cytoplasm. At points of intersection, such interlacing molecules are presumed to be tied together with various types of chemical bonds which may vary in degree of firmness with prevailing conditions. The hydrophilic properties of cytoplasm, its changes in its viscosity, elasticity, and tensile strength, as well as its sometimes rapid sol-gel transformations could all be accounted for on the basis of such a structure.

The Plastids.—All living cells of the higher plants contain prominent cytoplasmic bodies known as *plastids*. These structures are often ellipsoidal in shape and are frequently conspicuous because of the presence of pigments. The color of the pigments in the plastids has been used as the basis for their classification, but this system is highly artificial since a single plastid may be colorless, green, red or yellow at different periods of its existence.

In meristematic and embryonic cells the plastids first appear as tiny granules in the cytoplasm that range in size down to the limit of visibility (Randolph, 1922). These granules gradually enlarge and differentiate until mature plastids are produced. In growing and in mature cells plastids frequently multiply by fission.

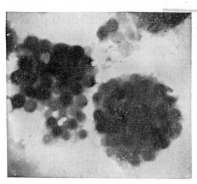

In the algae the chloroplasts exhibit a wide range of size and shape, but in the higher plants they show a remarkable similarity. The mature chloroplast of the higher plants is typically a slightly flattened ovate spheroid with the longer axis ranging between 4 μ and 6 μ in length. The number of chloroplasts present in a cell of a higher plant may range from a few to over a hundred. The number

Fig. 16. Electron microscope photograph of two chloroplasts of spinach showing grana. Photograph from Granick and Porter (1947).

present in a given cell may be quite different at different stages of its development.

Chloroplasts consist basically of a proteinaceous matrix or *stroma* which probably is surrounded by a membrane. The chlorophyll and other pigments are present in small wafer-shaped granules called *grana* which are distributed throughout the stroma (Weier, 1938, 1939 and others). Pigments are distributed throughout the apparently proteinaceous framework structure of each granum. A single chloroplast of spinach contains forty to sixty grana (Fig. 16), each about 0.6 μ in diameter and about one-eighth as thick (Granick and Porter, 1947). Several million chlorophyll molecules could be contained within a single granum.

The chromoplasts contain red or yellow pigments and are frequently very different in size and shape from the chloroplasts. Usually they are very slender spindle-shaped or needle-shaped bodies. They occur both singly and grouped in bundles. The irregular angular outline of these plastids contrasts sharply with the regular curved surface of the chloroplasts. In some species, however, chloroplasts may develop red or yellow pigments and completely lose their green color. The red and yellow colors of some fruits, notably members of the Solanaceae, and some flowers, are caused by chromoplasts.

The colorless leucoplasts are usually present in the cells of meristematic tissues in which they often represent juvenile stages in the development of chloroplasts and chromoplasts. In tissues not exposed to light they remain as colorless plastids and are the structures in which starch grains are formed.

The Nucleus.—The nucleus is a conspicuous spheroidal body which is imbedded in the cytoplasm. In most plant cells the nucleus has a diameter which falls within a range of 5 µ to 25 µ. In the vascular plants there is usually only one nucleus to a cell, although in certain types of cells several may be present. The sieve tube cells are the only well-known example of living cells in the higher plants in which no organized nucleus is present.

The importance of the nucleus centers around the fact that the hereditary potentialities of the cell are determined by the chromosomes which reside in the nucleus. The factors in the chromosomes establish the broad general patterns of growth within which environmental variations occur. It is the chromosomes, for example, which insure that a cotton seed can give rise only to a cotton plant and never under any circumstances to a corn plant or an oak tree. It is clear, therefore, that the nucleus must exert a controlling influence over the physiological processes of the cell, at least insofar as these processes are concerned with the determination of the broad general patterns of growth (Chap. XVI).

The Vacuole.—One of the most characteristic features of a mature plant cell is the presence of a large central vacuole filled with cell sap and entirely surrounded by the cytoplasm.

Meristematic cells in the tips of stems and roots usually contain numerous small vacuoles scattered throughout the cytoplasm. The shape of these vacuoles varies greatly and seems to be determined by the activity of the cytoplasm. In quiescent cytoplasm the small vacuoles are usually spherical, but when the cytoplasm is actively streaming they may assume many different forms. Cambium cells that are actively dividing may contain very large vacuoles (Bailey, 1930). In cambium initials the vacuoles, like those in the meristems of stem and root tips, are not uniform in size or shape, but may be rod-shaped, thread-like, or globular. They may coalesce into a large single vacuole or they may divide into numerous smaller vacuoles. Mature cells, however, whether they arise from primary meristems or from the cambium cells, typically contain one large central vacuole which arises by the increase in size and coalescence of the numerous smaller vacuoles usually present in the meristematic cells.

There is no general agreement as to the method by which vacuoles originate. Three possibilities are recognized: (1) they may arise by the division of pre-existing vacuoles, (2) they may originate *de novo* in the cytoplasm, and (3) they may develop from organized units of the cytoplasm. There is no convincing evidence, however, that the vacuoles of the cells of the vascular plants arise in any way except by the division of pre-existing vacuoles (Zirkle, 1937).

Among the various substances present as solutes in the vacuole are sugars, mineral salts, organic acids (oxalic acid, especially, seems to be of frequent occurrence), amino acids, amides, alkaloids, glycosides, flavones, and anthocyanins. Fats and related compounds often occur in finely emulsified form. Proteins, tannins, mucilages, lipids, and other substances are commonly present in the colloidal state. Crystals of calcium oxalate are also of frequent occurrence in the vacuoles of mature cells.

Hydrogen Ion Concentration of Plant Cells.—The hydration and viscosity of the protoplasm, the permeability of the cytoplasmic membranes, the activity of enzymes, the chemical activity of various ions in the cell, and various other physiological processes and conditions are all influenced more or less by the hydrogen ion concentration of the protoplasm and the cell sap.

Direct measurements of the hydrogen ion concentration of the protoplasm and cell sap have been made by introducing indicator dyes into living cells. By careful manipulation of a micropipette the dyes can be injected into the cytoplasm without penetrating into the vacuole or injected into the vacuole without penetrating into the cytoplasm. Only nontoxic dyes can be injected into living cytoplasm for pH determination, else the results may be invalidated by injury or death of the cytoplasm. Dyes are considered to be nontoxic, or essentially so, if protoplasmic streaming continues in the same way as before the injection. In this manner it is possible to determine the reaction of the cell sap and that of the cytoplasm independently. Results of the microinjection method, when applied to the root hairs of the water plant *Limnobium spongia*, indicated a pH value for the cytoplasm of 6.9 ± 0.2 (Chambers and Kerr, 1932). The cell sap of the same cells was found to be more acid, having a pH of 5.2 ± 0.2.

Indirect measurements of the hydrogen-ion concentration of plant cells are often obtained by expressing the juice from a sample of plant tissue and determining the pH value of the expressed sap. The expressed sap represents a mixture of the liquids from many millions of cells and gives, therefore, only an average value for all of the cells in the tissue under study. Since it is probable that most of the liquid pressed from the sample comes from the vacuoles of the cells, the pH values obtained are considered more typical of the vacuolar solutions than of the cytoplasm. In spite of the obvious limitations of this method, much information of importance has been secured. Extensive studies of plant saps made in this way show that their hydrogen ion concentration usually falls between pH 5.5 and 6.5 (Hurd-Karrer, 1939). The pH value of the cytoplasm of plant cells is higher and appears to be more constant, usually falling between pH 6.8 and 7.0 (Seifriz, 1936). There are many exceptions to these generalizations—the sap of some cells has a much more acid reaction, values as low as pH 0.9 being reported for a species of begonia (Smith and Quirk, 1926). On the other hand, alkaline values have been found in the vacuolar solutions of some species (Haas, 1916).

Buffer Action in Plant Cells.—Both the cytoplasm and cell sap of plant cells are usually buffered. The former, however, as its lesser variability in pH indicates, is usually more strongly buffered than the latter. All the actual information available regarding buffer action is based, however, upon determinations made upon expressed plant saps.

The most important buffer systems in living organisms are those composed of a weak acid and one (or more) of its salts (Chap. 2). Some of the principal acids which are components of plant buffer systems are carbonic, phosphoric, citric, malic, tartaric, and oxalic. The principal base-forming elements present in the salts which may serve as components of buffer systems are sodium, potassium, calcium, and magnesium.

The buffer action of some plant saps is apparently due predominantly, if not almost entirely, to one system. The buffering of lemon juice, for example, can be accounted for almost entirely in terms of the citrate buffer system (Sinclair and Eny, 1946). More commonly, however, a number of different buffer systems are present in a plant sap (Small, 1946).

The Cell in Relation to the Organism.—In this chapter the various parts of plant cells have been considered in some detail, both with regard to their structure and their roles in physiological processes. Cells are commonly referred to as the basic units of plant tissues. Few will quarrel with the idea that cells are units of structure, but it is important to realize that the cells of the higher plants are not isolated physiological units. The minute protoplasmic strands which interconnect all living cells weld them together so that the various tissues of plants are interdependent and are profoundly influenced by one another. The coordination and control of the physiological processes occurring in a plant is clear evidence that such an organism is more than a mere aggregation of genetically equivalent cells and that control of cellular processes resides in the organism as a whole rather than within the individual cells.

SUGGESTED FOR COLLATERAL READING

Bonner, J. *Plant Biochemistry.* Academic Press, Inc. New York. 1950.

Frey-Wyssling, A. *Submicroscopic Morphology of the Protoplasm and Its Derivatives.* Translated by J. J. Hermans and M. Hollander. Elsevier Publishing Co. New York. 1948.

Heilbrunn, L. V. *An Outline of General Physiology.* W. B. Saunders Co. Philadelphia. 1943.

Heuser, E. F. F. *The Chemistry of Cellulose.* John Wiley & Sons, Inc. New York. 1944.

Moulton, F. R., Editor. *The Cell and Protoplasm.* Science Press. Lancaster. 1940.

Seifriz, W., Editor. *The Structure of Protoplasm.* Iowa State College Press. Ames. 1942.

Small, J. *pH and Plants.* D. Van Nostrand Co., Inc. New York. 1946.

SELECTED BIBLIOGRAPHY

Anderson, D. B. The distribution of cutin in the outer epidermal wall of *Clivia nobilis. Ohio Jour. Sci.* **34:** 9-19. 1934.

Anderson, D. B. The structure of the walls of the higher plants. *Bot. Rev.* **1:** 52-76. 1935.

Bailey, I. W. The cambium and its derivative tissues. V. A reconnaissance of the vacuome in living cells. *Zeitschr. Zellf. Mikr. Anat.* **10:** 651-682. 1930.

Brooks, S. C. The electrical conductivity of pure protoplasm. *Jour. Gen. Physiol.* **7:** 327-330. 1925.

Chambers, R., and T. Kerr. Intracellular hydrion concentration studies. *Jour. Cell. and Comp. Physiol.* **2:** 105-119. 1932.

Granick, S., and K. R. Porter. The structure of the spinach chloroplast as interpreted with the electron microscope. *Amer. Jour. Bot.* **34:** 545-550. 1947.

Haas, A. R. The acidity of plant cells as shown by natural indicators. *Jour. Biol. Chem.* **27:** 233-241. 1916.

Heilbrunn, L. V. Protoplasm and colloids. In *The Cell and Protoplasm.* F. R. Moulton, Editor. Science Press. Lancaster. 1940.

Hulbary, R. L. The influence of air spaces on the three-dimensional shapes of cells in *Elodea* stems, and a comparison with pith cells of *Ailanthus. Amer. Jour. Bot.* **31:** 561-580. 1944.

Hulbary, R. L. Three-dimensional cell shape in the tuberous roots of asparagus and in the leaf of *Rhoeo. Amer. Jour. Bot.* **35:** 558-566. 1948.

Hurd-Karrer, Annie M. Hydrogen-ion concentration of leaf juice in relation to environment and plant species. *Amer. Jour. Bot.* **26:** 834-846. 1939.

Kerr, T., and I. W. Bailey. Structure, optical properties and chemical composition of the so-called middle lamella. *Jour. Arnold Arbor.* **15:** 327-349. 1934.

Lepeschkin, W. W. Über die Chemische Zusammensetzung des Protoplasmas des Plasmodiums. *Ber. Deutsch. Bot. Ges.* **41**: 179-187. 1923.

Lewis, F. T. The shape of tracheids in the pine. *Amer. Jour. Bot.* **22**: 741-762. 1935.

Lewis, F. T. A geometric accounting for diverse shapes of 14-hedral cells: the transition from dodecahedra to tetrakaidecahedra. *Amer. Jour. Bot.* **30**: 74-81. 1943.

Livingston, L. G. The nature and distribution of plasmodesmata in the tobacco plant. *Amer. Jour. Bot.* **22**: 75-87. 1935.

Marvin, J. W. Cell shape studies in the pith of *Eupatorium purpureum. Amer. Jour. Bot.* **26**: 487-504. 1939.

Marvin, J. W. Cell shape and cell volume relations in the pith of *Eupatorium perfoliatum* L. *Amer. Jour. Bot.* **31**: 208-218. 1944.

Matzke, E. B. The three-dimensional shape of epidermal cells of *Aloe aristata. Amer. Jour. Bot.* **34**: 182-195. 1947.

Matzke, E. B. The three-dimensional shape of epidermal cells of the apical meristem of *Anacharis densa* (Elodea). *Amer. Jour. Bot.* **35**: 323-332. 1948.

Meeuse, A. D. J. Plasmodesmata. *Bot. Rev.* **7**: 249-262. 1941.

Moyer, L. S. Proteins and protoplasmic structure. In *The Structure of Protoplasm.* W. Seifriz, Editor. Iowa State College Press. Ames. 1942.

Naylor, E. E. The hydrogen-ion concentration and the staining of sections of plant tissue. *Amer. Jour. Bot.* **13**: 265-275. 1926.

Preston, R. D. The molecular structure of cellulose and its biological significance. *Biol. Rev.* **14**: 281-313. 1939.

Randolph, L. F. Cytology of chlorophyll types of maize. *Bot. Gaz.* **73**: 337-375. 1922.

Scarth, G. W. Structural differentiation of cytoplasm. In *The Structure of Protoplasm.* W. Seifriz, Editor. Iowa State College Press. Ames. 1942.

Seifriz, W. *Protoplasm.* McGraw-Hill Book Co., Inc. New York. 1936.

Seifriz, W. The structure of protoplasm. *Bot. Rev.* **1**: 18-36. 1935; **11**: 231-259. 1945.

Seifriz, W. Protoplasmic streaming. *Bot. Rev.* **9**: 49-123. 1943.

Sen, B. The electric charge of the colloid particles of protoplasm. *Ann. Bot.* **48**: 143-151. 1934.

Sinclair, W. B., and D. M. Eny. Stability of the buffer system of lemon juice. *Plant Physiol.* **21**: 522-532. 1946.

Sinnott, E. W., and R. Bloch. Division in vacuolate plant cells. *Amer. Jour. Bot.* **28**: 225-232. 1941.

Smith, E. F., and Agnes J. Quirk. A begonia immune to crowngall: with observations on other immune or semi-immune plants. *Phytopath.* **16**: 491-508. 1926.

Sponsler, O. L., and Jean D. Bath. Molecular structure in protoplasm. In *The Structure of Protoplasm.* W. Seifriz, Editor. Iowa State College Press. Ames. 1942.

Weier, E. The structure of the chloroplast. *Bot. Rev.* **4**: 497-530. 1938.

Weier, E. The microscopic appearance of the chloroplast. *Protoplasma* **32**: 145-152. 1939.

Wyckoff, R. W. G. Visualizing macromolecules and viruses. *Amer. Scientist* **39**: 561-576. 1951.

Zirkle, C. The plant vacuole. *Bot. Rev.* **3**: 1-30. 1937.

DISCUSSION QUESTIONS

1. How would you undertake to ascertain the number of cells in an apple leaf? In a pine needle?

2. In what ways are plant and animal cells alike? Unlike?

3. List some of the phenomena characteristic of colloidal systems which occur in plant cells, citing specific examples.

4. Describe a living green plant cell from a physiological point of view. How will such a description differ from a morphological description of the same cell?

5. How would you undertake to find out whether the interior of a given plant cell was occupied by a vacuole, or by a mass of protoplasm?

6. Using figures given in the text, calculate the volume of a representative plant cell. What assumptions did you make as a basis for your calculation? If this cell shrinks 20 per cent in one dimension, what will its volume be? Twenty per cent in two dimensions? Three dimensions?

7. Do you consider the term "dead protoplasm" a satisfactory one? Explain.

8. Summarize the differences in structure which account for the differences in properties between primary and secondary walls.

V

DIFFUSION

The chemical elements which constitute the bulk of the body of any plant are among the commonest ones on the surface of the earth. They occur in the environment of plants as relatively simple inorganic compounds and enter plants in the form of such compounds. From the relatively small number of compounds which enter it from its environment the green plant fabricates the numerous complex organic compounds which are essential to its continued existence as a living system.

The movement of substances into a plant from its surroundings is accomplished largely by the process known as _diffusion_. Substances enter a plant partly through its aerial organs and partly by way of the root system. From the atmosphere, carbon dioxide and oxygen gases diffuse into plants, principally through the stomates. From the soil, water and the cations and anions of inorganic salts pass into the plant at least partially by diffusion, although other more complex mechanisms are also involved in the entrance of substances into roots.

Similarly the loss of substances from a plant into its environment is accomplished principally by diffusion. Large quantities of water vapor pass out of leaves and other aerial organs of plants into the atmosphere by this process. At times oxygen gas and at times carbon dioxide gas diffuse from plants into the atmosphere. Certain volatile compounds also escape from the aerial organs of many plants by diffusion. Similarly the roots lose carbon dioxide and other compounds into the soil by diffusion.

Likewise some of the movement of substances from one part of a plant to another is accomplished by diffusion. This is true both of the gases which move through the intercellular spaces and the water and solutes which move within the cells. However, much of the translocation of materials from one plant organ to another is accomplished by more com-

71

plicated mechanisms than diffusion. Within any living plant cell diffusion of substances from one part of a cell to another is also continually in progress.

In brief, there are few if any of the physiological processes occurring in plants which do not directly or indirectly involve diffusion phenomena.

Diffusion of Gases.—If a small vial of bromine gas is broken under a bell jar which has previously been evacuated of air, the entire jar quickly becomes filled with the brownish vapor of bromine. The distribution of the bromine gas throughout the bell jar has been accomplished by the kinetic activity of the bromine molecules and is a simple example of the process of diffusion. If the vial of bromine be broken under a bell jar which has not been evacuated of air, the time required for the bromine gas to occupy the bell jar completely will be longer than when diffusion of the gas occurs into a vacuum. Under such conditions the freedom of movement of the bromine molecules is impeded by the presence of molecules of the gases of the air, and the diffusion process is retarded. If the pressure of the air within the bell jar be increased to two atmospheres (which is equivalent to doubling the concentration of all the gases in the jar), the rate of diffusion of the bromine gas through the air would be still less than when the jar was occupied by air at atmospheric pressure.

Many other simple examples of the diffusion of gases might be cited. If a bottle of ammonia, ether, peppermint oil, or of any other readily volatile substance with a characteristic odor be opened indoors, within a very short time the distinctive odor of that substance can be detected in all parts of the room. Such a dispersal of gas molecules is accomplished at least in part by diffusion, although air currents often assist in speeding up such a distribution of molecules. Except in the rare case of diffusion into a vacuum, diffusing molecules move between the molecules of other substances.

The following somewhat fanciful analogy may aid in visualization of the kinetics of the diffusion process in gases. Suppose two adjoining rooms to be connected by a closed double door. Imagine also that one of these rooms contains a large number of tennis balls traveling in various directions along straight pathways at different rates of speed. The average distances between the tennis balls are supposed to be relatively great in proportion to their diameters. Each tennis ball represents a molecule. The individual balls will be constantly bumping into each other and into the walls of the room. Because of the large number of balls present innumerable collisions will occur every second. Each time a ball strikes a wall of the room it will bounce off along a different linear pathway. Similarly, whenever two balls collide, each will be deflected out of its course along a different route, to which it will hold undeviatingly until it is again deflected from its path by another collision. The course of each ball will thus be a zigzag progression through space, each short segment of its path being terminated by a collision which changes its direction. All of the balls do not move at the same speed at any given time, but the speed of each fluctuates from moment to moment as a result of the numerous collisions in which it participates. The average speed of the entire group will remain constant, however, as long as the temperature remains unchanged. As a result of this haphazard mutual buffeting, the tennis balls will remain equally distributed throughout the room.

Suppose now that the double doors connecting the two rooms are thrown open. As a result of their haphazard movement some of the balls close to the door will pass into the empty room. The first ones to do this will travel without interruption until they bump into one of the walls, as their rate of progression will not be impeded by collisions with other molecules. When they hit against one of the walls of the room they will bounce back into its interior along a new pathway. As more and more of the balls pass into the originally empty room their rate of progress becomes slower since the greater their concentration in the room, the greater the number of collisions per unit of time. As soon as any appreciable number of tennis balls has invaded the empty room, as a result of their random movements, some will pass back through the doorway into the room which originally contained all of them. As long, however, as the concentration (number per unit volume) of the tennis balls is greater in one room than in the other their random movements will result in more passing through the door into the room in which their lesser concentration prevails, than in the opposite direction.

In a relatively short time the concentration of tennis balls will have become equal in both rooms. In other words, they have "diffused" from one room into the other. After equality of concentration has been established the number of balls passing through the door in one direction in any interval of time will be exactly equal to the number moving in the opposite direction. When this condition of dynamic equilibrium is attained, diffusion, in the sense the word is used in this discussion, is no longer occurring.

If, in the hypothetical illustration just described, one room were filled with white tennis balls and the other with red tennis balls, diffusion would occur simultaneously in both directions. The red balls would "diffuse" toward the room in which their initial concentration was zero while the white balls would "diffuse" in the opposite direction. At equilibrium the concentration of the white balls would be equal throughout the two rooms, and this would likewise be true of the red balls.

Even after a dynamic equilibrium has been attained in any system, haphazard kinetic activity of the molecules continues. This is sometimes referred to as diffusion, but will not be so considered in this book. The term diffusion will be used only to characterize situations in which there is gain in the number of molecules of a certain kind in one part of a system at the expense of other parts. According to this concept diffusion can occur only when the concentrations of the diffusing substance is not uniform throughout the system, and the process can continue only as long as differences of concentration are maintained.

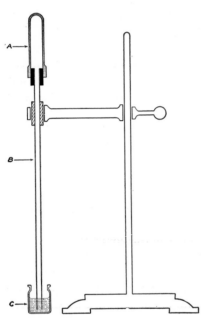

The phenomenon of diffusion is exhibited by the molecules of liquids, solutes, and even solids, as well as by those of gases. Diffusion of ions also occurs, and even colloidal particles diffuse, but only at very slow rates.

Diffusion phenomena should be clearly distinguished from *mass movements*, in which the moving units are not single molecules, but more or less extensive assemblages of molecules. Winds and air currents generally are examples of mass movements of gas molecules. The draft of warm air ascending a chimney is another. All of the phenomena just listed, and many others, result primarily from differences in the density of the gases in various parts of a system. Heavy gases are more strongly attracted by gravitational

Fig. 17. Apparatus for demonstrating the development of pressure during diffusion of gases: (*A*) porous clay cup, (*B*) glass tube, (*C*) vessel of colored water.

forces than light gases. Hence, as in a chimney, cold (relatively heavy) air, displaces hot (relatively light) air, forcing the latter to rise. Similar phenomena on a grand scale are the principal cause of winds and air currents. They are representative of the physical process called *convection*. Such phenomena also occur in liquids. Mass movements of gases and liquids can also be caused in many other ways.

Diffusion Pressure.—That diffusing gases sometimes result in the development of measurable pressures can be readily shown by certain simple experiments. In Fig. 17 is depicted an apparatus which can be used to illustrate a number of aspects of the phenomenon of diffusion of gases. This apparatus consists essentially of a vertically arranged glass tube, to the upper end of which is attached, by means of rubber stopper, a cylindrically shaped porous clay cup. This cylinder is hollow and its thick walls are pierced by numerous minute capillaries. These pores are fine enough to prevent mass movement of gases at any appreciable rate, but the porous clay is not a membrane in the usual sense of the word. The lower end of the vertical glass tubes dips in some colored water. If such a porous clay cylinder, containing air at atmospheric pressure, be enclosed within a bottle containing hydrogen gas, also at atmospheric pressure, a rapid bubbling of gas will occur from the lower end of the tube through the dye solution into which it dips. When the bottle is removed a rapid and sudden rise of liquid up the glass tube will ensue. This is followed by a slow subsidence in the level of the liquid in the glass tube, until it falls to that of the water in the beaker.

The explanation of this sequence of events is as follows. For reasons which are discussed later, the *rate* of diffusion of hydrogen is greater than that of nitrogen or oxygen under comparable conditions. When the porous clay cup is first enclosed within the bottle of hydrogen, rapid diffusion of hydrogen gas occurs through the pores of the cup. This raises the total gas pressure within the cup, since outward diffusion of oxygen and nitrogen occurs at a much slower rate. Hydrogen gas diffuses into the cup in spite of the fact that this results in a greater total pressure inside the cup than in the surrounding atmosphere. The *direction* of the diffusion of the hydrogen gas is controlled entirely by its own differences in concentration and is unaffected by the presence of other gases. The greater gas pressure inside the cup results in the outward bubbling of a mixture of all three gases at the lower end of the vertical glass tube. When the bottle is removed from around the porous clay cup, the direction of the diffusion of hydrogen is reversed, since the concentration of hydrogen gas is now greater inside of the cup. Since, while enclosed in the bottle of hydrogen, some of the nitrogen and oxygen diffused out of the cup and some was lost by the bubbling of gases from the lower end of the glass tube, this rapid outward diffusion of hydrogen results temporarily in a lower total gas pressure inside the cup than that originally present. Hence the solution rises rapidly in the glass tube. Finally, nitrogen and oxygen diffuse slowly inward, because of the reduced concentration of these gases inside of the cup, and the liquid slowly falls in the glass tube to its original level.

That the process of diffusion may result in the development of pressure also can be shown very strikingly by means of another simple experiment. If a pure rubber balloon containing only a little air be suspended in a closed bottle of carbon dioxide gas, it will gradually become distended. Rubber membranes are quite readily permeable to the molecules of carbon dioxide but virtually impermeable to those of oxygen, nitrogen, or other gases of the atmosphere. Since, temperature remaining constant, the pressure exerted by any gas is directly proportional to its concentration (number of molecules per unit volume), it follows that the diffusion of the molecules of gases may be interpreted in terms of the differences in the *partial pressure* (Chap. II) exerted by that gas in different parts of a system. Because of the greater partial pressure of carbon dioxide in the surrounding atmosphere, diffusion of this gas through the walls of the balloon continues until the partial pressure of the carbon dioxide is the same on the two sides of the rubber membrane. Since the initial partial pressure of carbon dioxide inside the balloon was virtually zero, and that in the bottle equivalent to 1 atm., the inward diffusion of carbon dioxide gas results in a considerable distension of the balloon.

In the analysis of diffusion phenomena it is often clarifying to speak of the partial pressure of a gas as its *diffusion pressure*. Solutes and liquids may also be considered to possess a diffusion pressure, although the existence of such a physical quantity is less evident in such systems than in gases. Hence the concept that diffusion is the movement of the molecules of a substance from a region of its greater to a region of its lower diffusion pressure is usually more satisfactory than the interpretation of diffusion phenomena in terms of concentration differences.

Principle of Independent Diffusion.—In the first experiment described in the preceding section it was shown that while one gas (hydrogen) was diffusing in an inward direction through the pores of a clay cylinder, other gases (oxygen and nitrogen) were simultaneously diffusing in an outward direction through the same pores. This exemplifies one of the most important principles governing diffusion phenomena—namely, that the direction in which any substance will diffuse is controlled entirely by its own differences in diffusion pressure, and is not influenced by either the direction or rate of diffusion of other substances in the same system. Hence, in any given system, as, for example, two adjacent plant cells, a number of substances may be diffusing in one direction across the intervening membranes, while simultaneously other compounds may be diffusing in the opposite direction across the same membranes. Each one of these individual substances will diffuse in the direction determined by its own differences in diffusion pressure, and at a speed which is determined by the factors that are influencing the diffusion of that particular substance.

Factors Influencing the Rate of Diffusion of Gases.—1. *Density of the Gas.*—Different gases diffuse at different rates even when influenced by the same set of environmental factors. Hydrogen, for example, diffuses more rapidly than any other gas. The same Thomas Graham who conducted some of the earliest studies on the properties of colloidal systems also was one of the first investigators to study quantitatively the phenomenon of gaseous diffusion. He discovered the principle, often called "Graham's Law of Diffusion," that the relative speeds of diffusion of different gases are inversely proportional to the square roots of their relative densities. By relative density is meant the weight of a given volume of gas as compared with the weight of the same volume of hydrogen.[1] The relative density of oxygen is 16. Hence the rate of diffusion of hydrogen is proportional to $1/\sqrt{1}$ while that of oxygen is proportional to $1/\sqrt{16}$. Hydrogen gas will therefore diffuse four times as rapidly as oxygen gas under the same conditions of temperature and pressure. The relative density of carbon dioxide is 22; hence by similar reasoning it is apparent that hydrogen gas will diffuse nearly five times as rapidly as carbon dioxide gas.

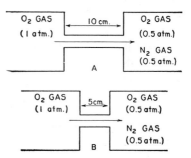

FIG. 18. Diagram illustrating that the length of a diffusion gradient is a factor influencing its steepness.

2. *Temperature.*—Increase in temperature increases the speed of diffusion. This is due, at least in part, to the correlated increase in the kinetic activity of the molecules of the diffusing substance. Actual measurements of the Q_{10} of diffusion[2] generally yield values between 1.2 and 1.3. Such values are characteristic of any purely physical process such as diffusion.

3. *Diffusion-Pressure Gradient.*—The fact that the *direction* of the diffusion of gases is from a region of their greater diffusion pressure to a region of their lesser diffusion pressure has already been emphasized. The *speed* of diffusion is also influenced by differences in diffusion pressure. In general, the greater the difference in diffusion pressures between the two regions, the more rapidly diffusion will occur. The rate of diffusion is influenced, however, not only by the difference in diffusion pressures, but also

[1] Since a molar weight of any gas occupies a volume of 22.4 liters at standard conditions, molar weights of gases are in themselves a measure of the relative density of gases. Since the molar weight of hydrogen (H_2) is 2.016, the relative density of any gas on the basis $H = 1$, is equal to its molar weight divided by 2.016 (usually rounded off to 2).

[2] The Q_{10} of any process—physical, chemical, or physiological—is defined as the number of times that the rate of the process increases with a 10°C. rise in temperature. If the rate of the process is doubled, Q_{10} is 2, etc.

by the distance through which the diffusing molecules must travel. These two factors are components of what may be called the *diffusion-pressure gradient* or *concentration gradient*. This concept may be clarified by a specific illustration, such as that depicted in Fig. 18. In both parts, *A* and *B*, of this diagram, oxygen is represented as diffusing from a region in which its diffusion pressure is maintained at 760 mm. Hg (atmospheric pressure) into a region in which its diffusion pressure it just half as great. The length of the connecting tube is, however, just twice as great in *A* as in *B*. Under the conditions postulated the rate of diffusion from the region of greater diffusion pressure to the other will be just twice as rapid in *B* as in *A*. The diffusion-pressure gradient is equivalent to the differ-ence in the diffusion pressures between the delivering and receiving ends of the diffusion system divided by the length of the distance between. The greater or "steeper" this gradient the more rapidly diffusion will occur. The steeper the gradient, the more rapid the change in diffusion pressure per unit of length along the axis of the diffusion gradient. The steepness of a diffusion-pressure gradient may be changed by varying either factor, the difference in diffusion pressures, or the length of the gradient.

4. *Concentration of the Medium through Which Diffusion Occurs.*— In general the more concentrated the medium, *i.e.*, the more molecules per unit volume in the medium through which the diffusing molecules must pass, the slower the rate of diffusion. Bromine gas, shown earlier in this chapter, diffuses more rapidly through a vacuum than through air.

Diffusion of Solutes.—The molecules or ions of a solute possess suffi-cient kinetic energy to move from place to place within the limits of a solution. The simplest method of demonstrating the diffusion of a solute is to introduce a crystal of copper sulfate, or some other compound which is colored when in solution, into the bottom of a tall glass cylinder filled with water. The cylinder should then be placed in an environment of equable temperature where it will be free from disturbance. The diffusion of the molecules or the ions which pass into solution in the water can be followed by the slow change in color of the water. One of the most strik-ing facts illustrated in such experiments is the extremely slow rate of diffusion of solutes through water. This results partly from the fact that in such an experiment the steepness of the diffusion gradient decreases with time, but principally from the fact that the densely packed mole-cules of the liquid enormously impede the diffusion of the dissolved molecules or ions.

The true rate of diffusion of solutes is probably even less than the rates indicated in such experiments, because in all such setups convec-tion currents may develop in the water and aid in the distribution of the solute throughout the body of the liquid. The diffusion of solutes is often demonstrated by employing a gel rather than a liquid as the medium into which diffusion occurs (Chap. III). Such a technique avoids errors introduced by the development of convection currents.

The *direction* of the diffusion of any solute occurs in accordance with its own differences in diffusion pressure, regardless of the rate or direction of diffusion of other solutes in the same system. The *rate* of diffusion of solute particles is governed by principles essentially similar to those which control the rate of diffusion of gases and is controlled by the following factors:

1. *Size and Mass of the Diffusing Particle.*—Small molecules or ions diffuse more rapidly than large ones. A hydrogen ion, for example, diffuses many times more rapidly than a glucose molecule. Similarly, highly hydrated ions diffuse more slowly than those which have fewer water molecules bound to them, since the association of water of hydration with a molecule or ion in effect increases its size. The mass of the particle will also be a factor influencing the speed of its diffusion. As between two particles of the same size, but different masses, the heavier particle will diffuse more slowly.

2. *Temperature.*—The kinetic activity, and hence the rate of diffusion of solute molecules, increases with increase in temperature.

3. *Diffusion Gradient.*—The steeper the diffusion gradient, the more rapidly solute particles diffuse.

4. *Solubility.*—In general, the more soluble a substance is in a liquid, the more rapidly it will diffuse through that liquid. This influence of solubility upon diffusion rates can be interpreted principally in terms of its effect upon the diffusion gradient, since obviously steeper gradients can be built up if the solute is very soluble in the liquid than if it is only slightly soluble.

SUGGESTED FOR COLLATERAL READING

Parkes, G. B. *Mellor's Modern Inorganic Chemistry.* Longmans, Green & Co. London. 1939.

SELECTED BIBLIOGRAPHY

Meyer, B. S. A critical evaluation of the terminology of diffusion phenomena. *Plant Physiol.* **20:** 142-164. 1945.

DISCUSSION QUESTIONS

1. Why, in an experiment in which copper sulfate crystals are placed in the bottom of a tall cylinder of water, does the steepness of the diffusion-pressure gradient decrease with time?

2. If, in the rubber balloon experiment described in the text, the initial pressure of carbon dioxide outside the balloon is 1 atm., what will be the approximate pressure of carbon dioxide inside the balloon at equilibrium? Outside the balloon?

3. How can the carbon dioxide exert a pressure against the inside walls of the rubber balloon (question 2) when rubber is permeable to carbon dioxide?

4. If a porous clay cup arranged as in Fig. 17 is surrounded with a bottle containing pure carbon dioxide, the water in the tube rises. If the cylinder is first dipped in water, however, and then surrounded by a bottle containing carbon dioxide, gas slowly bubbles out of the lower end of the vertical tube. Explain.

5. Two containers of equal volume, A and B, are connected with a short length of tubing which is closed with a stopcock. Describe what will happen if the stopcock is opened under the following conditions: (1) A contains CO_2 at 1 atm. pressure and B contains H_2 at 1 atm. pressure. (2) A contains one volume of CO_2; B contains 1.5 volumes of CO_2, but the pressure in A equals that in B because of its higher temperature. (3) A and B each contain CO_2 at 1 atm. pressure when the stopcock is opened. The temperature in A is then lowered 10°C. (4) A contains one volume of O_2 and two volumes of CO_2; B contains two volumes of O_2 and one volume of CO_2.

VI

OSMOSIS AND OSMOTIC PRESSURE

Like gases and solutes, liquids exhibit diffusion phenomena. If, for example, water is brought into contact with another liquid such as ether, with which it is only slightly miscible, a slow diffusion of water molecules into the ether will occur. Simultaneously a slow diffusion of the molecules of the ether will take place into the water. Such diffusion will continue until the two liquids are mutually saturated.

Osmosis.—This is by far the most familiar process involving the diffusion of liquids. An understanding of the dynamics of this process and of the significance of the physical quantity termed osmotic pressure is essential to an interpretation of the water relations of plant cells and tissues.

Let us first consider an experiment arranged as in Fig. 19. A sac-like membrane of collodion is completely filled with a strong sucrose solution and immersed in a beaker of water. The top of the sac is tightly plugged with a rubber stopper. The collodion membrane is prepared so that it is permeable to water, but impermeable or practically so to sucrose; in other words, it is *differentially permeable*. It is also slightly elastic.

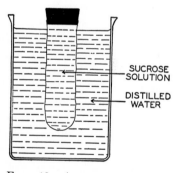

FIG. 19. Apparatus for the demonstration of osmosis through a collodion membrane.

After a short time the originally limp sac becomes rigidly distended. This is a result of the diffusion of water through the collodion membrane into the interior of the sac. Such a diffusion of water is an example of *osmosis*. The pressure developed as a result of the entrance of water prevails throughout the solution and is also exerted against the inside wall

81

of the membrane. If the membrane is virtually impermeable to the solute, eventually the entire system will come to equilibrium, after which there will be no further increase in the volume of water inside of the membrane.

When the movement of the solvent is referred to in discussing osmosis it is always the net movement which is meant. Solvent molecules will always be moving across the membrane in both directions, but, except when an equilibrium has been attained, more molecules will move per unit of time in one direction than in the other. As will be shown in the later discussion this net movement is always from the region of the greater diffusion pressure of the solvent molecules to the region of their lesser diffusion pressure. The maintenance of the diffusion-pressure gradient of the liquid in most osmotic phenomena is made possible by the relative impermeability of the membrane to the molecules of solutes. If the membrane were permeable to the solute particles, they would diffuse outward across the membrane, while the molecules of the solvent were diffusing in the opposite direction; this would be another example of the principle of independent diffusion.

Osmosis, the diffusion of a *solvent* (*not* a solution) across a differentially permeable membrane, may be regarded as a special case of diffusion. Osmosis occurs whenever two solutions with a common solvent, in which the diffusion pressures of the solvent are different, are separated by a membrane more permeable to the solvent than to the solutes. In living organisms water is the only important solvent which moves by osmosis, hence the following discussion of this process will be in terms of water and aqueous solutions.

Diffusion of the molecules or ions of a solute through a membrane is also a common phenomenon but occurs independently of the diffusion of the solvent molecules, in accordance with differences in the diffusion pressure of the solute, and seldom in amounts which are proportional to the diffusion of the solvent. The term "osmosis" is sometimes applied to such a diffusion of a solute across a membrane; likewise it is sometimes applied to the diffusion of a gas across a membrane. Historical considerations, however, give priority to osmosis as a term for the diffusion of a solvent across a membrane. Furthermore, certain aspects of this phenomenon are so distinctive that it is convenient to have a distinguishing term for it.

Membranes and Permeability.—The distinctive aspects of osmosis as compared with other diffusion processes result largely from the presence of the differentially permeable membrane. The concept of permeability is inseparable from the idea of a membrane. Permeability is a property of the membrane, not of the substance which diffuses through it. Thin layers or sheets of many different kinds of substances, such as rubber, parchment paper, collodion, cellophane, gelatin, and copper ferrocyanide, may serve as membranes.

Some membranes are impermeable to all, or virtually all, substances; others allow all or most substances to diffuse through them with little impediment. Many biologically important membranes are of the type known as *differentially permeable*. Such membranes allow some substances to pass through them much more readily than others. They may be, and often are, impermeable or virtually so to some substances, while others diffuse through them quite freely. Alternative but less desirable terms for *differentially permeable* are *semi-permeable* and *selectively permeable*.

The simplest kinds of membranes are essentially molecular sieves. The pores of a given membrane of this type are such that micelles, molecules and ions below a certain size can diffuse through them, while those exceeding this size cannot pass through. Membranes of collodion, parchment paper, and copper ferrocyanide owe their differential permeability largely to their sieve-like properties.

Some membranes are differentially permeable because certain substances are more soluble in them than others. The rubber balloon experiment described in Chap. V furnishes

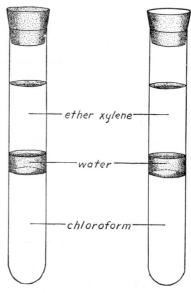

Fig. 20. Experimental arrangement for demonstrating the differential permeability of a water membrane.

an example of such a membrane. Carbon dioxide gas is much more soluble in rubber than oxygen or nitrogen, hence a rubber membrane is much more permeable to carbon dioxide gas than to either of the other two.

Another example of a membrane of this type in operation can be seen in an experiment set up as in Fig. 20. A thin layer of water is introduced on top of a layer of chloroform in a test tube, the tube nearly filled with ether, and stoppered. A second tube is prepared in the same way except that xylene is substituted for the ether. After several days it will be observed that the level of the water layer in the first tube has risen, while in the second tube it has fallen, although the distance through which the layer moves is not as great in the second tube. In the first tube ether is osmosing through the water *membrane* more rapidly than the chloroform; hence the volume of liquid below the membrane is increasing and the layer of water rises. In the second tube chloroform osmoses through the water membrane more rapidly than the xylene; hence the water layer falls in the tube. Much less chloroform osmoses in a given time through the water layer in the second tube than does ether in the first tube. Of these three compounds, ether is the most soluble in water, chloroform next most soluble, and xylene least soluble. Permeability of the water membrane to these three compounds is clearly correlated with their solubility in water.

Diffusion Pressure of Liquids.—Like a gas, water or any other liquid may be considered to possess a diffusion pressure (Haldane, 1918), although the existence of such a physical quantity in liquids becomes apparent only under certain conditions as, for example, when a solvent and a solution are separated by a differentially permeable membrane. Diffusion pressure is the cause of diffusion, not its result. Just as gases have a pressure, whether or not any diffusion is occurring, so do liquids and solutes have a diffusion pressure, whether or not any diffusion is occurring.

The only two factors which influence the diffusion pressure of pure water are pressure and temperature. If pressure is imposed on water, as by a piston in a closed system, or by the confining effects of the walls of a closed osmometer or plant cell when the volume of the enclosed water is expanding as a result of osmosis, the diffusion pressure of the confined water increases by the amount of the imposed pressure. If the imposed pressure is 8 atm., for example, the diffusion pressure of the water increases by 8 atm. Correspondingly, if water is subjected to a "negative pressure" (tension), its diffusion pressure decreases by the amount of the negative pressure. The effect of the imposed pressure on the diffusion pressure of the liquid is quantitatively the same whether the liquid is pure, or whether solutes are present.

Although the diffusion pressure of a liquid is also theoretically affected by temperature, it is usually not necessary to consider this effect in evaluating the mechanism of the diffusion of water in plants (Chap. VIII).

In an aqueous solution, however, the diffusion pressure of the water is influenced by still another factor, the proportion of solute particles (ions plus molecules) to solvent molecules. The greater this proportion, the less the diffusion pressure of the water. Within a wide range of concentrations (see later) of the solute molecules or ions, the diminution in diffusion pressure is closely proportional to the ratio of solute particles to solvent molecules.

Ideally all diffusion phenomena, including osmosis, should be interpreted on the basis of differences in diffusion pressures. Diffusion phenomena in gases can be readily analyzed in this way because gas pressures can usually be ascertained. The exact magnitudes of the diffusion pressures of liquids, on the other hand, cannot readily be measured. Hence use of this physical concept in the quantitative interpretation of the diffusion of liquids is not feasible. It is usually possible, however, to measure quantitatively the amount by which the diffusion pressure of the water in a given solution is less than that of pure water at the same temperature and under atmospheric pressure. This quantity is called the *diffusion-pressure deficit* or *pressure deficit* (Meyer, 1945) and can be used in the interpretation of osmosis and other diffusion phenomena in which water molecules participate, even if we do not know the exact magnitude of the diffusion pressure of water. In this indirect manner it is possible to use the concept of diffusion pressure in the analysis of diffusion phenomena in liquids.

Osmotic Pressure.—This term was originally employed to designate the maximum pressure which develops in a solution enclosed within an osmometer under certain ideal conditions. An *osmometer* is an apparatus for measuring the magnitude of osmotic pressures. If a manometer or pressure gauge were inserted through the stopper of an apparatus set up as in Fig. 19, the arrangement would serve as a crude osmometer. Most precise measurements of osmotic pressures (Pfeffer, 1877; Morse, 1914; Berkeley and Hartley, 1916; Frazer, 1931) have been made with osmometers constructed of cylindrically-shaped porous clay cups (Fig. 21) in the pores of which have been precipitated differentially permeable membranes of cupric ferrocyanide. The pressure developed is measured with a sensitive mercury manometer or in other ways. The necessary ideal conditions, only attained under rigorous experimental conditions, are that the membrane be permeable only to the solvent, that it be

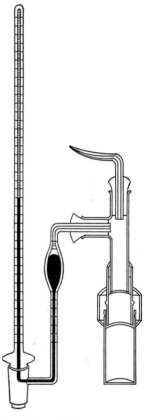

FIG. 21. Pfeffer's osmometer (shown in sectional view) with attached closed manometer for measuring the pressure developed. The lower part of the osmometer is a porous clay cup in the walls of which have been precipitated a differentially permeable membrane of copper ferrocyanide.

immersed in the pure solvent, and that the pressure equilibrium be attained without any appreciable dilution of the enclosed solution. The temperature of the experimental setup must also be controlled and recorded, as the osmotic pressure of a solution is in part a function of its temperature.

The term "osmotic pressure" can be more usefully employed as an index of certain properties of a solution, rather than as a designation for an actual pressure which is attained only under certain seldom realized conditions. In part such a usage is a derivative one from the original usage described in the preceding paragraph. For example, a molal solution of sucrose standing in a beaker may be designated as having an osmotic pressure of 27 atm.[1] at 25°C. Obviously this solution is not exerting an actual pressure of 27 atm., and this statement merely implies that it has certain properties and potentialities which will become apparent under particular circumstances. Such a statement regarding a solution is analogous to the statement that an idle electric motor has a rating of $\frac{1}{4}$ horsepower; both statements are indices of potential rather than existing capacities.

Used thus as an index, the osmotic pressure characterizes the solution in two ways. In the first place, it tells us that the maximum possible pressure which could be developed in that solution if it were permitted to come to equilibrium with pure water in an osmotic system at 25°C. is 27 atm. The osmotic pressure is thus a rating of the *potential* maximum pressure which can be developed in the solution as a result of osmosis. In the second place, osmotic pressure is an index of the *diffusion-pressure deficit* of the water in a solution *insofar as this results from the presence of solutes*. Commonly used synonyms for osmotic pressure in this index sense are *osmotic concentration, osmotic value, osmotic potential,* and *osmotic power*.

Turgor Pressure.—*Turgor pressure* is the *actual* pressure which develops in a closed osmometer or plant cell as a result of osmosis or imbibition (see later). Use of the term "osmotic pressure" in this sense should be avoided as it only leads to confusion. A given solution has a unique osmotic pressure at a given temperature, but its turgor pressure is variable. Ordinarily the turgor pressure of a solution lies in the range between zero and its osmotic pressure, but under certain conditions it may exceed the osmotic pressure, and under certain other conditions it may be negative in value (Chap. VIII). The turgor pressure prevailing within a solution is also exerted against the confining walls of the system.

---

[1] Osmotic pressures are usually expressed in atmospheres. A better pressure unit is the *bar* which represents a pressure of 1,000,000 dynes per square centimeter—one atmosphere equals 1.013 bars, or 1,013 *millibars*.

Quantitative Aspects of Osmosis.—Let us suppose that a solution with an osmotic pressure of 20 atm. completely fills an essentially inelastic membrane which is permeable only to water and is arranged like that shown in Fig. 19. Let us further suppose this membrane to be immersed in pure water, which has, of course, a zero osmotic pressure. Both the solution within, and the water without, the membrane are initially under atmospheric pressure only, the effect of which (equivalent to a turgor pressure of 1 atm.) is conventionally disregarded when all parts of the system are under atmospheric pressure. From the previous discussion it should be clear that the diffusion-pressure deficit of the water in the enclosed solution is 20 atm.; that of the water outside of the sac, zero. Water, therefore, osmoses across the membrane into the solution. The entering water engenders a gradually increasing turgor pressure throughout the solution in the sac. Subjection of the water in this solution to such a pressure raises its diffusion pressure and hence lowers its diffusion-pressure deficit. An equivalent increase takes place in the diffusion pressure of the solutes present. A dynamic equilibrium will be attained when the turgor pressure of the internal solution reaches 20 atm. At this point the 20 atm. diffusion-pressure deficit which would otherwise result from the presence of solutes is offset by the 20 atm. turgor pressure and the diffusion-pressure deficit of the water in the solution is zero, which is the same as that of the pure water outside the membrane. When the diffusion-pressure deficit of the water on both sides of the membrane becomes equal, osmosis ceases, and the number of water molecules moving through the membrane in the inward direction will be the same as the number moving in the outward direction per unit of time. Since the membrane is assumed to be inelastic or nearly so, osmosis of only a very small amount of water into the solution is necessary to raise its turgor pressure to 20 atm. Since there is virtually no dilution of the solution, its final osmotic pressure, for all practical purposes, is the same as its initial osmotic pressure.

In living organisms water usually osmoses across a membrane from one solution to another, rather than from pure water into a solution. Let us consider, therefore, an analogous situation, exactly like that described above, except that the water on the outside of the membrane is replaced with a solution of 12 atm, osmotic pressure. Initially, before any turgor pressure develops, the diffusion-pressure deficit of the internal solution in this system is 20 atm.; that of the external solution, 12 atm. Water therefore osmoses across the membrane into the solution within the sac. As the turgor pressure of the internal solution increases, the diffusion-pressure deficit of the water in that solution decreases. When a turgor pressure of 8 atm. has been attained, the diffusion-pressure deficit will

have decreased to 12 atm. which is the same as that of the external solution. Dynamic equilibrium is thus attained in this particular system when
the turgor pressure prevailing in the internal solution reaches 8 atm.

In the foregoing discussion an inelastic membrane has been assumed.
Many membranes, however, especially in living organisms, are elastic
within limits. When the membrane is appreciably elastic, the further complication of shifts in the osmotic pressure of the internal solution during
osmosis is introduced. Let us assume an osmotic system identical with
that described in the preceding paragraph, except that the membrane is
elastic enough to permit a 25 per cent increase in the volume of the internal solution before a dynamic equilibrium is attained. As the internal
solution increases in volume it becomes more dilute, *i.e.*, less concentrated. The osmotic pressure of a solution decreases with a diminution
in its concentration (see later). If we assume a proportionate decrease
in osmotic pressure with decrease in concentration, which would be strictly
true only in certain kinds of solutions (see later), the final osmotic pressure in the internal solution would be 16 atm. $(20 : X = 125 : 100)$.
A turgor pressure of only 4 atm. would be required under these conditions to bring the water in the internal solution into dynamic equilibrium
with that in the external solution which has an osmotic pressure of 12
atm. In such a system the turgor pressure of the internal solution is increasing while its osmotic pressure is decreasing. The only difference in
end result when the membrane is elastic is that the turgor pressure and
osmotic pressure at dynamic equilibrium are somewhat less than they
would be otherwise. If the volume of the external solution is large relative to that of the internal solution, variations in the osmotic pressure
of the former are usually negligible.

It should be evident from the foregoing discussion that the diffusion-
pressure deficit of the water in a solution is always equal to the osmotic
pressure of the solution less the turgor pressure which prevails in it. This
relation can be conveniently expressed in the simple equation:

$$D. P. D. = O. P. - T. P.$$

As applied to the initial diffusion-pressure deficits in the second example
given above these equations would work out as follows:

External solution: D. P. D. $= 12 - 0 = 12$ atm.

Internal solution: D. P. D. $= 20 - 0 = 20$ atm.

At dynamic equilibrium the diffusion-pressure deficit of this same external solution is unchanged; that of the same internal solution is then
calculated as follows:

$$D. P. D. = 20 - 8 = 12 \text{ atm.}$$

Factors Influencing the Osmotic Pressure of Solutions.—1. *Concentration.*—Increase in the concentration of a solution invariably results in an increase in its osmotic pressure. If the solute is a non-electrolyte and its molecules do not acquire water of hydration (see later), osmotic pressure is almost strictly proportional to molal concentration, *i.e.*, to the proportion of solute to solvent molecules. The *theoretical* osmotic pressure of a one molal solution of such a solute is 22.4 atm. at 0°C. (van't Hoff, 1887). For various reasons, some of which are discussed later, experimentally determined values of osmotic pressures for many, but not all, substances deviate considerably from such theoretical values. Ethyl and methyl alcohol may be mentioned as examples of solutes for which the experimentally determined values of osmotic pressure agree almost exactly with the theoretical values. For one-molal solutions the osmotic pressures for these two compounds are 22.51 and 22.88 atm., respectively (Jones, 1907).

The figure 22.4 should be recognized as numerically the same as that for the number of liters occupied by one mol of a gas at standard conditions (0°C.; 1 atm. pressure). If this gas be compressed to a volume of one liter, it will exert a pressure of 22.4 atm. (Boyle's Law). In other words, the gas pressure of one mol of a gas confined in a volume of one liter and the osmotic pressure of a solution in which one mol of an unhydrated, nondissociated solute is dissolved in 1000 g. of water at 0°C. are theoretically equal in value. This is one of the several analogies between osmotic pressure and gas pressure first pointed out by van't Hoff in 1887.

In solutions in which the solute is dissociated or hydrated, or both, increase in osmotic pressure is not proportionate with increase in molality.

2. *Ionization of the Solute Molecules.*—Osmotic pressure is a colligative property, *i.e.*, one which depends on the number of solute particles, regardless of kind, in proportion to the number of solvent particles in a solution. The same number of ions, or of solute molecules, or of colloidal micelles in a given weight of water will result in a system with the same osmotic pressure. Actually the concentrations of micelles in colloidal systems are usually so low that their influence on osmotic pressure is negligible or nearly so. If the solute is present as ions, either in part or entirely, the osmotic pressure will be greater than otherwise. If an electrolyte such as NaCl were present at one molal concentration completely in the form of free ions, the theoretical osmotic pressure of the solution would be 44.8 atm. The measured osmotic pressure of a one molal solution of NaCl is 42.7 atm. which indicates that a condition of

maximum ionic mobility is closely approached in such a solution. Solutions of all electrolytes have higher osmotic pressures than equimolal solutions of non-electrolytes. Because of interionic attractions, however, every individual ion in a solution of an electrolyte does not exert its full effect on the osmotic pressure of the solution. Only in electrolytes of the NaCl or KCl type does the osmotic pressure, as a rule, even closely approach the value to be expected if every ion is exerting its full effect on this physical quantity.

3. *Hydration of the Solute Molecules.*—We have previously seen (Chap. III) that the micelles of all hydrophilic sols are highly hydrated. In a somewhat similar fashion water molecules adhere to many kinds of solute molecules and ions. Water thus associated with the particles of a solute is called *water of hydration*. Different species of molecules and ions have different numbers of water molecules associated with them. Water molecules which are bound to solute particles as water of hydration are no longer effective as part of the solvent. In effect a solution containing hydrated solute particles is more concentrated than its molality would indicate, and its osmotic pressure is correspondingly higher. A one molal solution of sucrose, for example, has an osmotic pressure of 24.83 atm. at 0°C. (Table 8) instead of the theoretical value of 22.4 atm. The higher than theoretical value for the osmotic pressure of a sucrose solution is believed to result from hydration of the sucrose molecules. One sucrose molecule binds six molecules of water of hydration. Hence one *mol* of sucrose binds six *mols* of water. One thousand grams of water is equivalent to 55.5 mols of water (1000/18). Since the water of hydration is not free to act as a solvent, in effect the solution consists of 1 mol of sucrose dissolved in 49.5 mols of water. A simple calculation (22.4 × 55.5/49.5) yields the value 25.12 atm. as the theoretical osmotic pressure of a one molal solution of sucrose if hydration

TABLE 8—THE RELATION BETWEEN TEMPERATURE AND THE OSMOTIC PRESSURE OF
A ONE MOLAL SOLUTION OF SUCROSE (DATA OF MORSE, 1914)

Temperature °C.	Osmotic pressure atmospheres
0	24.83
10	25.69
20	26.64
30	27.22
40	27.70
50	28.21
60	28.37
70	28.62
80	28.82

of the molecules is taken into account, a value very close to the one obtained experimentally.

4. *Temperature.*—As shown in Table 8 the osmotic pressure of a solution increases with increase in temperature. For an ideal solution osmotic pressure is proportional to the absolute temperature, another respect in which its behavior parallels that of gas pressure (recall the "Law of Gay-Lussac"). For a sucrose solution this relation does not hold rigidly, but is closely approximated, as can be shown by calculations based on the values in Table 8.

The Measurement of Osmotic Pressures.—The osmotic pressure of a solution, as such, can be measured only by the direct manometric method. Precise results can be obtained by this method only at the cost of an elaborate technique and infinite precautions. Hence the actual number of measurements of osmotic pressures which have been made by this direct method are limited. As is well known there is a direct proportionality between the osmotic pressure, lowering of the vapor pressure, elevation of the boiling point, and depression of the freezing point of solutions. Hence osmotic pressures of solutions can be calculated from measurements of any one of these three physical quantities. Most frequently determinations are made of the depression of the freezing point of a solution, and its osmotic pressure calculated from this. Since the theoretical freezing point depression of a one molal solution of an unionized substance is 1.86°C., and the theoretical osmotic pressure of such a solution is 22.4 atm., an equation relating freezing point depressions and osmotic pressures is easily derived. If we let Δ represent the freezing point depression of a solution, its osmotic pressure (O.P.) may be calculated as follows:

$$O.P. : 22.4 = \Delta : 1.86$$

$$1.86 \; O.P. = 22.4\Delta$$

$$O.P. = \frac{22.4}{1.86} \Delta$$

$$O.P. = 12.04\Delta^2$$

For example, a solution for which the determined freezing point depression is 0.930 would have an osmotic pressure of 11.20 atm. (12.04 × 0.930). This equation appears to be approximately correct over a wide range of concentrations since deviations from the theoretical osmotic pressures of solutions are accompanied by almost strictly proportional

[2] A slightly more accurate form of this equation has been derived by Lewis (1908). The tables of Harris and Gortner (1914, 1915), based on the Lewis equation, are very useful for converting freezing point depressions into osmotic pressures.

deviations from their theoretical freezing-point depression values. This method is often called the <u>cryoscopic method</u> of determining osmotic pressures. The osmotic pressures as determined by this method are as at the freezing point temperature of the solution.

Electro-osmosis.—Under certain conditions pure water will diffuse from one side of a membrane to the other under the influence of a difference of electrical potential, a process which is called *electro-osmosis*. When water is confined in a capillary glass tube, adsorption of OH^- (or HCO_3^-) ions imparts a negative charge to the walls of the tube. Adjoining them is a layer of H^+ ions equal in number to the adsorbed anions. In other words, ions become distributed as an electrical double layer just as they do around a colloidal particle (Fig. 22).

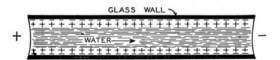

F<small>IG</small>. 22.   Diagram to illustrate electro-osmosis.

If a difference of electrical potential is present between the two ends of the tube, water will travel toward the negative electrode. The anions are firmly adsorbed by the walls of the tube and cannot move. The hydrogen ions, however, are free to move and migrate toward the cathode carrying the water, of which they are a part, along with them. In other words, the moving cations in the water glide past the stationary anions which adhere to the walls of the tube. Since many membranes are essentially porous in structure, conditions similar to those just described may exist in each capillary of the membrane, and electro-osmosis may occur through such membranes in essentially the same way that it occurs through tubes of small bore. Since differences of electrical potential are frequently present in living organisms it seems entirely probable that electro-osmotic flow of water occurs in living tissues.

SUGGESTED FOR COLLATERAL READING

Crafts, A. S., H. B. Currier, and C. R. Stocking. *Water in the Physiology of Plants*. Chronica Botanica Co. Waltham, Mass. 1949.

Findlay, A. *Osmotic Pressure*. 2nd Ed. Longmans, Green & Co. London. 1919.

Parkes, G. B. *Mellor's Modern Inorganic Chemistry*. Longmans, Green & Co. London. 1939.

SELECTED BIBLIOGRAPHY

Berkeley, Earl of, and E. G. J. Hartley. Further determinations of direct osmotic pressure. *Proc. Roy. Soc.* (*London*) **A 92:** 477-492. 1916.

Frazer, J. C. W. The laws of dilute solutions. In *A Treatise on Physical Chemistry*. 2nd Ed. H. S. Taylor, Editor. Vol. I. 353-414. 1931.

Haldane, J. S. The extension of the gas laws to liquids and solids. *Biochem. Jour.* 12: 464-498. 1918.

Harris, J. A. An extension to 5.99° of tables to determine the osmotic pressure of expressed vegetable saps from the depression of the freezing point. *Amer. Jour. Bot.* 2: 418-419. 1915.

Harris, J. A., and R. A. Gortner. Notes on the calculation of the osmotic pressure of expressed vegetable saps from the depression of the freezing point, with a table for the values of P for $\triangle=0.001°$ to $\triangle=2.999°$. *Amer. Jour. Bot.* 1: 75-78. 1914.

Hoff, J. H. van't. Die Rolle des osmotischen Druckes in der Analogie zwischen Lösungen und Gasen. *Zeitschr. Physiol. Chem.* 1: 481-508. 1887.

Jones, H. C. Hydrates in aqueous solution. *Carnegie Inst. Wash. Publ. No. 60*. Washington. 1907.

Lewis, G. N. The osmotic pressures of concentrated solutions and the laws of the perfect solution. *Jour. Amer. Chem. Soc.* 30: 668-683. 1908.

Meyer, B. S. A critical evaluation of the terminology of diffusion phenomena. *Plant Physiol.* 20: 142-164. 1945.

Morse, H. N. The osmotic pressure of aqueous solutions. *Carnegie Inst. Wash. Publ. No. 198*. Washington. 1914.

Pfeffer, W. *Osmotische Untersuchungen*. W. Englemann. Leipzig. 1877.

DISCUSSION QUESTIONS

1. A closed sac-like membrane, completely filled by a solution with an osmotic pressure of 27 atm., is immersed in a solution with an osmotic pressure of 16 atm. Assume the membrane to be permeable to water only and that volume changes in the sac are negligible, *i.e.*, that the membrane is essentially inelastic. What will the diffusion-pressure deficit of the internal solution be at equilibrium? The osmotic pressure? The turgor pressure? Answer the same questions for an external solution with an osmotic pressure of 22 atm. One with an osmotic pressure of 30 atm.

2. The freezing point depression of a plant sap is found to be 3.72°C. What is its osmotic pressure at 25°C.?

3. The two arms of an open U-tube are separated by a membrane permeable only to water. A solution with an osmotic pressure of 15 atm. is placed in arm *A*, one with an osmotic pressure of 20 atm. in arm *B*. Which way will water move? Explain.

4. If the solution in arm *B* (question 3) is subjected to a pressure of 10 atm., in which direction will water move? If a pressure of 5 atm. is used? 3 atm.? If the solution in each arm is subjected to a pressure of 8 atm.?

5. When in a flaccid (turgorless) condition the vacuole of a given plant cell has a volume of $8000\mu^3$ and an osmotic pressure of 18 atm. If in its fully turgid condition its volume is $12000\mu^3$, what is its osmotic pressure? (Assume solution volume of solute is negligible and that there is no appreciable change in dissociation.)

6. Assuming 75 per cent dissociation and no hydration, what is the molal concentration of a KCl solution which exhibits an osmotic pressure of 22.4 atm. at 0°C.?

7. A closed elastic membrane filled with a 0.5 volume molar solution of sucrose is immersed in a beaker of water. After a time its volume is found to have doubled. Assuming that the membrane is permeable to water only, what will then be the osmotic pressure of the solution inside the membrane?

8. A closed, virtually inelastic membrane, permeable to water and glucose but not to sucrose, is completely filled with a sucrose solution of 6 atm. osmotic pressure and is immersed in a glucose solution of 9 atm. osmotic pressure. The volume of the solution inside the membrane is one-half that in the surrounding vessel. Disregarding solution volume effects, what will be the osmotic pressure, turgor pressure, and diffusion-pressure deficit of the solution inside the membrane at equilibrium?

VII

IMBIBITION

If a handful of pea or bean seeds be dropped into water, within a few hours they will have swollen visibly. Seeds of any other species in which the coats are not impermeable to water behave in like fashion when brought into contact with water. Many other materials will swell in a similar way when immersed in water. Among these are starch, cellulose, agar, gelatin, and kelp stipe. Some substances will swell similarly when immersed in other liquids. All of these phenomena are examples of the process called *imbibition*. The amount of water which may enter substances in imbibition is often very great in proportion to the dry weight of the substance which swells. A piece of dried kelp stipe, for example, can absorb as much as fifteen times its own weight of water.

Water may be imbibed as a vapor as well as in the liquid state. The swelling of doors and woodwork during damp weather is a familiar example of this phenomenon. Plant structures, if sufficiently low in water content, also imbibe water-vapor. The water content of "air-dry" seeds, for example, generally fluctuates with the vapor pressure of the atmosphere, rising with an increase in vapor pressure, and *vice versa* (Barton, 1941).

The Dynamics of Imbibition.—Imbibition is usually considered to be basically a diffusion process, but capillary phenomena are probably also involved. Imbibing substances are often permeated with minute submicroscopic capillaries, and it is impossible to determine how much of the liquid enters by diffusion and how much by capillary movement through invisible pores. Fundamentally, however, the cause of imbibition may be regarded as a difference in the diffusion pressure between the liquid in the external medium and the liquid in the "imbibant." As long as the latter is less than the former, movement of water into the imbibing

95

substance will continue. An equilibrium will be reached, as in diffusion or osmotic phenomena, only when the diffusion pressure of the water in the two parts of the system has attained the same value.

A substance which imbibes water does not necessarily imbibe other liquids. Dry kelp stipe, for example, swells enormously when immersed in water, but does not swell when immersed in ether or other organic liquids. Contrariwise, a piece of rubber does not imbibe water, but does imbibe appreciable amounts of ether and other organic compounds when in contact with them in either the liquid or the vapor state. Obviously a difference in diffusion pressures between the liquid in an imbibant and in its surrounding medium is not the only requisite for the occurrence of imbibition. Certain specific attractive forces between the molecules of the imbibant and the imbibed liquid must also be present. In default of such specific attractions imbibition fails to occur, even if all other necessary conditions for the process are fulfilled.

Since in living organisms water is the only liquid imbibed, the further discussion will disregard other types of imbibitional phenomena. The physical relationship between the imbibed water and the imbibant is undoubtedly a complex one. The bulk of the imbibed water in any system is probably adsorbed on the molecules or micelles which constitute the structural units of the imbibing material. The possible relations of adsorbed water to the adsorbing particles in colloidal systems have already been considered (Chap. III). There is good reason for believing that similar physical relations exist between the imbibed water and unit particles in an imbibant. Such water may be pictured as either actually in solution in the adsorbing particles, or as adsorbed as a "shell" of from one to many molecular layers in thickness on their surface. It is possible that either or both of these conditions obtain in many systems containing imbibed water, but the second of these pictures appears to be more likely. It is also probable that a portion of the imbibed water enters and occupies minute submicroscopic capillaries which ramify among the component molecules or micelles of the imbibant. The result of imbibition is often the formation of a system which in its essential properties may be regarded as a gel. The physical status of the water in a system into which it has been imbibed and in an elastic gel is undoubtedly very similar. In fact, the imbibition of a dispersion medium by a dry substance is generally regarded as a method of gel formation.

Volume Changes in Imbibition.—The volume of the *imbibant* always increases during imbibition. The final volume of the entire system (liquid + imbibant) is always less, however, than the sum of the initial volumes of the liquid and the imbibing substance. In other words, a contraction in the volume of the system, liquid + imbibant, occurs during the process of imbibition. This volume shrinkage is not principally a result of the occupancy of minute spaces within the substance of the imbibing material by the liquid, as might be surmised, although in some systems a part of the contraction in volume possibly may be accounted for in this way. The explanation is undoubtedly to be ascribed to the fact that the adsorbed water molecules are definitely oriented in relation to the adsorbing surfaces, and hence occupy less space than when in the free state. This is equivalent to a compression of the adsorbed water so that its density is greater than that of free water.

Energy Relations of Imbibition.—The process of imbibition always results in the release of heat. Liberation of heat during imbibition may be easily detected by allowing dry starch or some other material with a high imbibitional capacity to imbibe water while contained in a calorimeter, and noting the change in temperature (Table 9).

TABLE 9 — HEAT OF IMBIBITION OF DRY STARCH (DATA OF RODEWALD, 1897)

Per cent water imbibed	Heat evolved, g.-cal. per g. starch
0.23	28.11
2.39	22.60
6.27	15.17
11.65	8.43
15.68	5.21
19.52	2.91

The adsorption of water molecules which occurs when they are imbibed results in a loss of a large part of their kinetic energy, which reappears in the system as heat energy. The essential energy change in the process of imbibition is a loss of kinetic energy by the adsorbed molecules, and its transference to the other molecules of the system. Their increased kinetic activity is the cause of the observed rise in temperature. As shown in Table 9, the greatest evolution of heat accompanies the initial stages of imbibition. This is to be expected, as a larger proportion of the first molecules of water imbibed would be firmly adsorbed than of those which enter the imbibant later.

The Effect of Temperature on Imbibition.—As shown in Fig. 23, the rate of imbibition increases with rise in temperature.

Osmotic Effects on Imbibition.—Water moves by imbibition into a substance only when its diffusion pressure exceeds the diffusion pressure of the water in the imbibant. The introduction of a solute into water invariably has the effect, as already discussed, of reducing the diffusion pressure of the water in the resulting solution as compared with pure water. The osmotic pressure of a solution is a measure of its diffusion-pressure deficit, insofar as it results from the presence of solutes. Hence the magnitude of the osmotic pressure influences both the rate of imbibition and the equilibrium water content of an imbibant.

Shull (1916) used the seeds of cocklebur (*Xanthium pennsylvanicum*) as the imbibant in a comprehensive study of osmotic effects on imbibition. Samples of seeds of this species were allowed to come to equilibrium

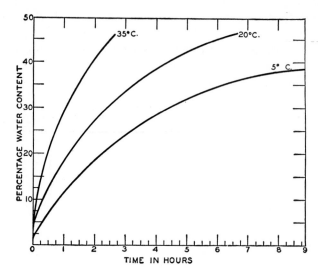

FIG. 23.   Relation between temperature and imbibition of water by *Xanthium* seeds. Data of Shull (1920).

with solutions of sodium chloride and lithium chloride of different osmotic pressures, after which the amount of water which had been imbibed was determined (Table 10). The coats of these seeds are permeable to water, but virtually impermeable to these solutes.

The general principle shown by the results of these experiments is that, with increase in the osmotic pressure of the solution in which the seeds are immersed, the amount of water held by imbibition per unit of dry weight at the equilibrium point decreases. Since at equilibrium the diffusion pressures of the water in the imbibing substance and in the surrounding liquid must be equal, the basis for this osmotic effect upon imbibition is evident. If the diffusion pressure in the solution is relatively low (high osmotic pressure), the diffusion of less water into the imbibing substance is necessary to raise the diffusion pressure of the water in it to a value equal to the diffusion pressure of the water in the circumambient liquid than if the diffusion pressure in the surrounding liquid is high. The relation between the osmotic pressure and the amount of water imbibed is not, however, a strictly proportional one. At the lower end of the range of concentrations employed, an increase of a few atmospheres in osmotic pressure causes a decrease in the amount of water imbibed, in terms of the air dry weight of the seeds, of nearly 15 per cent. Near the upper end of this range of concentrations an increase in osmotic pressure of several hundred atmospheres is required for an equivalent change in the volume of water imbibed. This is further evi-

TABLE 10— IMBIBITION OF WATER BY COCKLEBUR SEEDS IMMERSED IN SOLUTIONS OF DIFFERENT OSMOTIC PRESSURES (DATA OF SHULL, 1916)

Volume molar concentration of solutions	Osmotic pressure of solutions, atmos.	Water imbibed by seeds at equilibrium (48 hours). Per cent of air dry weight
H_2O	0.0	51.58
0.1 M NaCl	3.8	46.33
0.2	7.6	45.52
0.3	11.4	42.05
0.4	15.2	40.27
0.5	19.0	38.98
0.6	22.8	35.18
0.7	26.6	32.85
0.8	30.4	31.12
0.9	34.2	29.79
1.0	38.0	26.73
2.0	72.0	18.55
4.0	130.0	11.76
Sat. NaCl	375.0	6.35
Sat. LiCl	965.0	—0.29

dence that the first increments of water passing into any imbibant are held by tremendously greater forces than those which are imbibed subsequently.

Imbibition Pressure.—Pressures, sometimes of an enormous magnitude, are often exerted by a swelling imbibant if it is confined in some manner. Blocks of rock, for example, have been successfully quarried by drilling holes along the desired cleavage planes, driving tight-fitting wooden stakes into the holes, and pouring water on the stakes. The pressure developed upon imbibition of the water by the wood is sufficient to split the rock.

The term "imbibition pressure" is best employed, however, not as a designation for the actual pressures which develop during imbibition, but with a meaning analogous to that of "osmotic pressure," as an index of certain properties of the imbibant. Used in this sense imbibition pressure is an index of (1) the potential maximum pressure which can develop in an imbibant as a result of imbibition, and (2) the diffusion-pressure deficit of the water in an imbibant as long as its free expansion is not impeded in any way. In a solution, the greater amount of water present in proportion to a given amount of solute, the less the osmotic pressure. Likewise, in an imbibant, the greater the amount of water present in proportion to a given amount of imbibing substance, the less the imbibition pressure. Air-dry pea seeds, for example, have a greater imbibition pressure than half-swollen pea seeds; pea seeds which have reached a condition of maximum swelling have an imbibition pressure of zero.

The *actual* pressures which develop as a result of imbibition, like those which develop as a result of osmosis, can logically be termed *turgor pressures*. No turgor pressure develops in an unconfined imbibant any more than it does in an unconfined solution. Only when complete swelling is prevented, as by enclosure within an inelastic wall, does a turgor pressure develop within an imbibant.

Quantitative Aspects of Imbibition.—The diffusion-pressure deficit of the water in an imbibant is equal to the imbibition pressure less the turgor pressure just as in an osmotic system the diffusion-pressure deficit of the water is equal to the osmotic pressure less the turgor pressure. This relation is expressed in the following equation:

$$D.\ P.\ D. = I.\ P. - T.\ P.$$

Since no turgor pressure develops in an unconfined imbibant, for such systems this equation simplifies to:

$$D.\ P.\ D. = I.\ P.$$

If an imbibant with an imbibition pressure of 100 atm. is immersed in pure water, the initial diffusion-pressure deficit of the water in the imbibant is 100 atm.; when equilibrium has been attained, the imbibition pressure and diffusion-pressure deficit of the water in the imbibant have both become zero. If such an imbibant is immersed in a solution with an osmotic pressure of 20 atm., when equilibrium has been attained both the imbibition pressure and the diffusion-pressure deficit of the water in the imbibant will be 20 atm. In unconfined imbibants equilibrium of the diffusion-pressure deficits of the water in them with the water in outside solutions occurs solely by adjustments in imbibition pressures.

If an imbibant with an initial imbibition pressure of 100 atm. is enclosed in an inelastic, water permeable wall, and immersed in pure water the diffusion-pressure deficit of the water in the imbibant at equilibrium will be zero, not because of a decrease in imbibition pressure but because of the development of a turgor pressure of 100 atm. If a solution of 20 atm. osmotic pressure is substituted for the pure water outside of the imbibing system, then the diffusion-pressure deficit of the water in the imbibant at equilibrium will be 20 atm., again not because of a decrease in imbibition pressure, but because of the development of a turgor pressure of 80 atm.

Measurement of Imbibition Pressures.—The magnitudes of imbibition pressures have been measured in two different ways. One method has been to counterbalance the pressure developed during imbibition by means of a mechanical pressure. Such a method was used by Reinke as long ago as 1879. He stacked disks of dried fronds of *Laminaria* (a sea weed) in a hollow metal cylinder, and inserted above the disks a metal piston bearing a platform at its upper end. Water was then brought into contact with the dry disks. By placing on the platform weights of just sufficient mass to prevent swelling of the kelp, the magnitude of the pressure developed was measured. By this procedure there is measured, in effect, the magnitude of the turgor pressure which is equal to the imbibition pressure, *i.e.*, which keeps the diffusion-pressure deficit of the water in the imbibant at zero and thus prevents any movement of water into the imbibant.

Imbibition pressure can also be measured by an osmotic method. The necessary procedure is to find a solution in which the diffusion-pressure deficit (osmotic pressure) is just great enough to prevent any movement of water into the imbibant. The osmotic pressure of such a solution is equal to the imbibition pressure of the imbibant. This method, in effect, results in the determination of the diffusion-pressure deficit of the water in the imbibant under such conditions that it is equal to the imbibition pressure, *i.e.*, when there is no turgor pressure.

Imbibition pressures of air-dry seeds may be as high as approximately 1000 atm. (Table 10).

SUGGESTED FOR COLLATERAL READING

Crafts, A. S., H. B. Currier, and C. R. Stocking. *Water in the Physiology of Plants*. Chronica Botanica Co. Waltham, Mass. 1949.
Gortner, R. A. *Outlines of Biochemistry*. 3rd Ed. Edited by R. A. Gortner, Jr., and W. A. Gortner. John Wiley & Sons, Inc. New York. 1949.

SELECTED BIBLIOGRAPHY

Barton, Lela V. Relation of certain air temperatures and humidities to viability of seeds. *Contr. Boyce Thompson Inst.* **12:** 85-102. 1941.

Gortner, R. A. Water in its biochemical relationships. *Ann. Rev. Biochem.* **3:** 1-22. 1934.

Meyer, B. S. A critical evaluation of the terminology of diffusion phenomena. *Plant Physiol.* **20:** 142-164. 1945.

Rodewald, H. Thermodynamik der Quellung mit spezieller Anwendung auf die Stärke und deren Molekulargewichtsbestimmung. *Zeitschr. Phys. Chem.* **24:** 193-218. 1897.

Shull, C. A. Measurement of the surface forces in soils. *Bot. Gaz.* **62:** 1-31. 1916.

Shull, C. A. Temperature and rate of moisture intake in seeds. *Bot. Gaz.* **69:** 361-390. 1920.

DISCUSSION QUESTIONS

1. If an imbibant with an imbibition pressure of 100 atm. is immersed in a solution with an osmotic pressure of 35 atm., in which direction will water move? At equilibrium what will be the imbibition pressure of the imbibant? Diffusion-pressure deficit? Turgor pressure?

2. An imbibant with an imbibition pressure of 20 atm. is enclosed within and completely fills an inelastic membrane which is permeable only to water. If this system is immersed in a solution with an osmotic pressure of 12 atm., what will be the imbibition pressure of the imbibant at equilibrium? Diffusion-pressure deficit? Turgor pressure?

3. Cacti and some other desert succulent species retain large quantities of water within their tissues even under conditions of prolonged and severe drought. It has been suggested that such plants possess this capacity because of the imbibitional capacity of hydrophilic colloids within the cells. How would you test this hypothesis?

4. One surface of a block of 2 per cent agar gel is exposed to the atmosphere. How would the rate of evaporation of water from the gel compare with that from a free water surface of equal area under the same conditions during the first hour? After 48 hours? Explain.

5. If a piece of dry kelp stipe is fastened to the base of a hydrometer which is then immersed in a vessel of water, the hydrometer sinks as the kelp swells. Explain.

VIII

THE WATER RELATIONS
OF PLANT CELLS

The Membranes of Plant Cells.—The membranes of plant cells are much more complex in their structure and properties than the nonliving membranes previously discussed in Chap. VI. With very few exceptions the protoplasm of each plant cell is enclosed by a more or less rigid wall which acts as a membrane. Through this wall, which usually consists of several layers, each with a complex organization of its own, must pass all substances moving either into or out of a cell. In addition to the structure of the wall itself, the role of the plasmodesms must be considered in accounting for the movement of substances from one cell to another. Lining the cell wall of all mature plant cells is a layer of cytoplasm. The cytoplasm, or parts thereof, constitutes a second layer through which substances entering or leaving the vacuole of a cell must penetrate. Both theoretical considerations and experimentally observed facts support the view that the two limiting layers of cytoplasm possess different physiochemical properties from the intervening cytoplasm and may be regarded as distinct membranes. The cytoplasmic membrane adjacent to the cell wall is called the _plasmalemma;_ that enclosing the vacuole the _tonoplast_ or _vacuolar membrane._ Since the boundaries between the cytoplasm and the cell wall and the cytoplasm and the vacuole constitute interfaces, certain protoplasmic ingredients probably become adsorbed there in greater concentrations than in the interior of the cytoplasm. For this reason alone the postulation that the cytoplasmic membranes possess different properties from the interior cytoplasm seems justified.

Results from several types of experimental investigations support this hypothesis. The immiscibility of protoplasm with water, already dis-

103

cussed, appears to result at least partly from the fact that protoplasm is coated with a layer of material which is insoluble in water. By means of micropipettes certain nontoxic dyes can be injected into the body of the cytoplasm through which they will spread rapidly. They do not, however, pass through either the plasmalemma or the tonoplast. Neither will they pass into the interior of the cytoplasm from a solution bathing the cell, nor from the vacuole if the latter is injected with the dye (Plowe, 1931). This is direct evidence that the constitution of the plasmalemma and the tonoplast is different from that of the intervening cytoplasm. The presence of cytoplasmic membranes can also be demonstrated by the manipulation of living protoplasm with fine glass needles (Chambers and Höfler, 1931). It has been found possible to withdraw a plasmolyzed protoplast

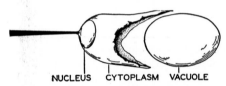

NUCLEUS   CYTOPLASM   VACUOLE

Fig. 24. Removal of the outer cytoplasm from the tonoplast and vacuole of a plasmolyzed cell. Redrawn from Seifriz (1928).

(see later) from its cell wall and to strip off the protoplasm from the vacuole leaving the latter as a free-floating sac full of cell sap enclosed by a delicate membrane —the tonoplast (Fig. 24). Most evidence indicates that the tonoplast and probably also the plasmalemma are thin liquid films which are immiscible with water.

A complete picture of the permeability of a cell to different compounds can be drawn only in terms of the permeability of both the cell wall and the cytoplasmic membranes. In entering a cell a substance must first pass through the various layers of the cell wall, thence in turn through the plasmalemma, the interior cytoplasm, and the tonoplast before reaching the vacuole. Although some investigators prefer to refer all permeability phenomena of plant cells to the cytoplasm as a whole, the evidence that the plasmalemma and the tonoplast exist as distinct membranes with the property of differential permeability must be regarded as very substantial.

Permeability of Cell Membranes.—In general, cell walls composed of cellulose and pectic compounds, such as those in most parenchymatous tissues, are quite permeable to water and solutes. Water and solutes probably penetrate such walls through the hydrophilic intermicellar material. Lignified walls are also quite permeable to water and solutes, but cell walls in which suberin or cutin are present in appreciable quantities, on the other hand, are less permeable both to water and solutes.

In contrast with the walls of most parenchymatous cells, the cytoplasmic membranes exhibit a high degree of differential permeability.

The term "cytoplasmic membranes" is here employed in a loose sense to refer to the entire cytoplasmic system of membranes: plasmalemma plus interior cytoplasm plus tonoplast. Actually many substances entering plant cells are intercepted and utilized in one way or another in the cytoplasm, and do not diffuse in appreciable quantities through the tonoplast. Similarly compounds synthesized in the cytoplasm may pass out of the cell without crossing the tonoplast. Hence the plasmalemma is often regarded as the most important unit in the cytoplasmic system of membranes. It should be realized, however, that substances can move from one cell to another, through the plasmodesms, without crossing the plasmalemma.

Very few general statements can be made regarding the permeability of the cytoplasmic membranes to specific substances which will hold for all or even most plant cells. One such statement which can be made is that the cytoplasm is usually relatively permeable to water. This is also true for certain other small molecules, such as ammonia. Permeability of the cytoplasmic membranes to most solutes of physiological importance such as sugars, electrolytes, and amino acids, on the other hand, appears to be very variable. Studies of many kinds of cells, for example, indicate that their cytoplasmic membranes are relatively impermeable to sucrose and other sugars (Bonte, 1934). The slowness with which many kinds of plant cells recover from plasmolysis (see later) in sugar solutions is also evidence of the relative impermeability of the cytoplasm to such compounds. Nevertheless, there is much indirect evidence that sugars often move into and out of many kinds of cells at relatively rapid rates. Similarly, although many permeability studies indicate the cytoplasmic membranes to be relatively impermeable to electrolytes, they often penetrate relatively rapidly into plant cells, when in an actively metabolizing condition (Chap. XXIV). The probable explanation of these apparent discrepancies is that most studies of permeability have been made upon mature cells which have lost most or all of their capacity for rapid absorption of electrolytes and sugars.

The permeability of the cytoplasmic membranes to specific substances is therefore not a fixed property, but one which differs from one kind of cell to another and varies in the same cell with the age of the cell, the environmental conditions to which it is subjected, and other factors. Furthermore, there are many indications that the cytoplasm is not merely a passive membrane like a sheet of collodion, but that it, at times at least, participates actively in the movement of molecules and ions into or out of cells, or from one part of a cell to another.

Plasmolysis.—If a vacuolate plant cell which is at least partially distended is immersed in a hypertonic[1] solution of some substance to which the membranes are relatively impermeable, a characteristic series of changes takes place in the appearance of that cell. The first detectable occurrence is a gradual shrinkage in the volume of the entire cell as a result of outward osmosis. Consequently there is a reduction in the pressure exerted by the cell sap against the protoplasm and cell wall. This shrinkage in volume can be detected in many cells by measurement under a microscope, although there are some types of plant cells in which little change in volume occurs under such conditions. There is a lower limit to the elasticity of the cell wall, however, and when this is attained no further decrease in the volume of the cell will occur. Since the cell

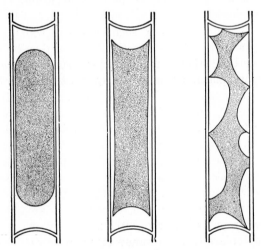

FIG. 25.   Several common types of plasmolysis (diagrammatic).

wall is quite freely permeable to the water and the solutes of the surrounding solution, and hence the hypertonic solution is in contact with the outer surface of the protoplast, the cell sap will continue to lose water by outward osmosis, just as if no cell wall were present. Hence the protoplasm will continue to shrink in volume after the contraction of the cell wall has ceased. At this stage, therefore, the protoplasmic layer will begin to recede from the cell wall. If the hypertonic solution is strong enough, this separation of the protoplasm from the cell wall will become very pronounced. In some types of cells the protoplasm will "ball up" into a more or less spherical mass within the cell. More often the

[1] With reference to a given solution, in this case the cell sap, a hypertonic solution is one with a higher osmotic pressure than the reference solution. Similarly an isotonic solution is one with an osmotic pressure equal to that of the reference solution, while a *hypotonic* solution is one of lesser osmotic pressure.

shrunken protoplasm assumes other configurations as shown in Fig. 25. This phenomenon is called *plasmolysis*. The pattern followed by the shrinkage of the protoplasm in plasmolysis is more or less typical for each kind of cell, although it may be modified somewhat depending upon physiochemical conditions within the protoplasm and the kind of solute used in the plasmolyzing solution. The space between the cell wall and the protoplasm will be filled, after the separation of the latter from the wall, with the external solution.

If a plasmolyzed cell is immersed in water, it will slowly recover and regain a turgid state as a result of osmotic movement of water into the vacuole. Similarly, if immersed in a solution hypotonic to the cell, sap recovery will also ensue, but the degree of turgidity attained will be less than if the cell were immersed in pure water. Rapid "deplasmolysis," however, results in the death of many kinds of plant cells (Iljin, 1934).

Methods of Determining the Osmotic Pressures of Plant Cells and Tissues.—The *plasmolytic* method and the *cryosopic* method are in common use for determining the osmotic pressure of plant cells and tissues. Both methods have many limitations and neither is as accurate as might be desired.

DeVries (1884) was the first to use the plasmolytic method which in principle is very simple. A series of solutions (usually of sucrose), graded according to volume molar concentration, is first prepared. The range of concentrations to be used depends upon the tissue to be studied. Comparable strips or sections of the tissue are then immersed in each solution and left until an osmotic equilibrium is attained. After immersion in the solution the pieces of tissue are observed under a microscope. In the stronger solutions it will be found that all of the cells are severely plasmolyzed, while in the weaker ones little or no sign of plasmolysis can be detected. Somewhere in the series will be found a solution in which about one-half of the cells are not plasmolyzed, and about one-half are more or less plasmolyzed. The average osmotic pressure in the cells of the tissue under investigation is considered to be equal to the osmotic pressure of the solution in which this condition obtains.

The value obtained by the procedure just outlined is called the *osmotic pressure at incipient plasmolysis*. This value is often greater than the usual osmotic pressure of the cells since plasmolysis of many kinds of cells is preceded by a shrinkage in their total volume. A cell which has an osmotic pressure of 15 atm. at incipient plasmolysis might have had an osmotic pressure of (for example) 12 or 13 atm. in its naturally distended state.

Certain more precise methods of determining the osmotic pressure of cells by the plasmolytic method, which take into consideration their volume changes, have also been devised. If incipient plasmolysis is determined to occur for cells of a certain tissue in a sucrose solution with a volume molar concentration of M_i, then the volume molar concentration, M, of sucrose equivalent to that of the cell sap at its original volume (*i.e.*, before the shrinkage due to plasmolysis) is related to M_i by the following equation:

$$M = \frac{M_i V_i}{V}$$

in which V and V_i represent the volume of the cell in its original condition, and at incipient plasmolysis, respectively. Having determined M_i, the corresponding molarity for the cell sap of the "normal" cell can be readily calculated.

The practical difficulty of all such methods is in measuring accurately the volume changes which occur in cells during plasmolysis. The usual practice is to measure the change in the length (sometimes also in the breadth) and to assume that such measurements are proportional to the change in volume of the cell. For some types of cells this assumption is probably valid, but with others it may result in serious errors.

Formerly solutions of a number of different compounds, including certain electrolytes, were used in plasmolytic determinations, but at the present time sucrose solutions are almost universally employed. They are preferred because: (1) sucrose is apparently nontoxic to the protoplasm, (2) it does not penetrate into many plant cells at a very appreciable rate (Höfler, 1926), (3) it apparently has little or no influence on membrane permeability, and (4) the exact osmotic pressures of different molar concentrations of sucrose are known with greater accuracy than for most other solutions.

The principle of the cryoscopic method for determining osmotic pressures has already been described in Chap. VI. Briefly, as usually applied to plants, the method consists in expressing the juice from a sample of plant tissue and determining its freezing-point depression with a suitable thermometer[2] or a thermocouple system (Chap. XI). The osmotic pressure can then be calculated from the freezing-point depression by the usual equation.

It has been found to be impossible to obtain homogeneous samples of sap from plant tissues unless they are first treated in such a way as to kill the cells. Consequently the tissue is usually first subjected to freezing, heating, grinding, or exposure to toxic vapors before the sap is expressed.

Doubtless the expression under high pressure of the sap from tissues

---

[2] A Haidenhain or Beckmann thermometer is generally used.

which have previously been subjected to such treatments has a modifying effect upon the properties of the expressed sap of most tissues as compared with the original cell sap. Furthermore the sap obtained represents a mixture of contributions from all of the cells—living and dead —in the tissues. At the best, determinations of osmotic pressure made on such saps can represent no more than an average of the osmotic pressures of all the cells in the tissue. In spite of the possibility of a considerable modification in the properties of the sap inherent in this method, there is probably a consistent correlation between values obtained in this way and the mean osmotic pressure of the cell sap of the cells in a tissue.

Magnitude of the Osmotic Pressures in Plant Cells.—In many discussions of the osmotic pressure of plant cells no distinction is made between the "osmotic pressure of the cells at incipient plasmolysis" and their osmotic pressure under more or less turgid conditions. When the term osmotic pressure is employed without qualification it can be assumed to refer to the osmotic pressure of cells in their usual distended condition. It is generally considered that the results of determinations by the cryoscopic method represent approximately the osmotic pressure of the cells in this condition.

Different organs or tissues of the same plant may exhibit a wide range of osmotic pressures. Even similar organs on the same plant—leaves, for example—may vary considerably among themselves in the average osmotic pressure of their cells. Furthermore the tissues within the same organ usually show a considerable variation in osmotic pressures. The mesophyll cells of most leaves, for example, show higher values than the epidermal cells.

In general, the osmotic pressures of the plant cells and tissues[3] of the mesic species of North America vary in their extreme range from a fraction of an atmosphere to about 50 atm. Most of the values lie, of course, within a narrower part of this range, probably within the limits of a 4 to 30 atm. span of values. The osmotic pressure of a given plant cell or tissue is by no means a fixed quantity, but often fluctuates considerably. More or less regular daily or seasonal variations occur in the osmotic pressures of many kinds of plant cells or tissues (Chap. XV).

Factors Influencing the Osmotic Pressures of Plant Cells.—Any factor which influences either the water content of a plant cell or the solute content of its cell sap will have an effect on the magnitude of the osmotic pressure of that plant cell. The water content of the plant as a whole, and hence of its constituent cells, is controlled principally by the rela-

[3] It should perhaps be emphasized that the term "osmotic pressure of a tissue" can possess meaning only in the sense of the average osmotic pressure of the cells composing that tissue.

tive rates of transpiration and the absorption of water (Chap. XV). The latter process is influenced very markedly by the water content and other conditions prevailing in the soil. Individuals of the same species invariably have a higher osmotic pressure when growing under drought conditions than when provided with a favorable water supply (Table 11, Fig. 72). This is at least partially a result of the relatively lower water content of the leaves which obtains when the available soil water supply becomes low. Other factors which are also probably involved are a decrease in the growth rate of the plant which often permits an accumulation of mineral salts and soluble foods, and a shift of the starch $\rightleftarrows$ soluble carbohydrates equilibrium toward the side of the soluble carbohydrates (Chap. XX).

TABLE II—THE EFFECTS OF DIFFERENT SOIL WATER CONTENTS UPON THE OSMOTIC PRESSURE OF MAIZE PLANTS (DATA OF HIBBARD AND HARRINGTON, 1916)

Water content of soil. Per cent dry weight	Osmotic pressure of tops	Osmotic pressure of roots
31 per cent	22.06 atmos.	5.91 atmos.
23	23.08	7.23
16	24.36	7.79
14	25.04	9.24
13	25.47	11.34
11	26.48	11.98

The solute content of the cell sap is controlled by the specific metabolic processes of the plant and by the absorption of mineral salts by the plant from its environment. The rate of photosynthesis is an important factor in determining the osmotic pressure of plant cells, particularly those of leaf tissues. The influence of the inherent metabolic processes of any species upon the kinds and concentrations of various types of soluble organic compounds produced, such as simple carbohydrates, organic acids, and amino acids has an important effect on the magnitude of the osmotic pressure in any species. Metabolic conditions and their effects upon osmotic pressures may also be altered by environmental conditions. A well-known example of this is the difference in the osmotic pressures of sun and shade leaves on the same plant. The former almost invariably has the higher osmotic pressure, presumably at least in part as a result of their greater photosynthetic activity.

The mineral salts which contribute to the osmotic pressures of plant cells are all absorbed from the soil or in aquatic species from the water in which part or all of the plant is immersed. Different species of plants vary greatly in their toleration of high concentrations of mineral salts in the soil. All species can become adjusted, within limits, to a change in the mineral-salt content of the substratum. This adjustment takes the form of an increase in the osmotic pressure of the plant with an increase in the osmotic pressure of the medium from which it obtains its mineral salts (Table 12).

Other tissues of plants also show an increase in osmotic pressure with increase in the osmotic pressure of the soil solution, but such increases are generally most pronounced in the roots.

Species indigenous to saline soils usually have relatively high osmotic pressures. Such soils are rich in soluble salts, and the high osmotic pressures found in species native to such soils result from the absorption of relatively large quantities of mineral salts. In fact, the highest recorded osmotic pressure for any species of plant—202.5 atm.—was found in the saltbush (*Atriplex confertifolia*), a saline soil species (Harris, 1934).

TABLE 12— THE EFFECT OF THE OSMOTIC PRESSURE OF THE SOIL SOLUTION UPON THE OSMOTIC PRESSURE OF THE ROOTS OF MAIZE (DATA OF MC COOL AND MILLAR, 1917)

Osmotic pressure of soil solution	Osmotic pressure of sap from root cells
1.21 atm.	4.59 atm.
1.99	5.48
3.38	6.61
4.96	7.51
7.22	8.19

Salt marsh plants also generally have relatively high osmotic pressures. This is also a correlation with the relatively high salt content of the substratum. Except in halophytes, however, a larger proportion of the osmotic pressure of most kinds of plant cells results from the presence of organic solutes than of mineral salts. Root cells are more likely to prove exceptions to this last statement than cells in the aerial organs.

The Osmotic Quantities of Plant Cells.—Let us suppose three similar plant cells, each in a state of incipient plasmolysis (*i.e.*, with a zero turgor pressure), and each with a cell sap osmotic pressure of 10 atm., to be immersed, the first in pure water, the second in a solution with an osmotic pressure of 6 atm., and the third in a solution with an osmotic pressure of 10 atm. (Fig. 26). The volume of the liquid in which each cell is immersed is assumed to be very large in proportion to the volume of the cell.

In order to simplify the discussion, certain assumptions will be made regarding these cells and, unless stated to the contrary, regarding all other cells discussed in the remainder of this chapter. These assumptions are: (1) the cells are at the same temperature, (2) the cytoplasmic membranes are permeable only to water while the cell walls are permeable to both water and solutes, (3) the walls of all the cells are equally elastic, and (4) volume changes in the cells are so small that any resulting effects upon the osmotic pressure of the cell sap are negligible and can be disregarded. A review of the discussion of the quantitative aspects of osmosis in physical systems (Chap. VI) will be helpful in following the ensuing closely analogous discussion with respect to cells.

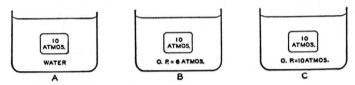

FIG. 26.   Similar cells immersed in solutions of different osmotic pressures.

Osmosis of water into cell A begins immediately upon its immersion, because the diffusion-pressure deficit of the water in the cell sap is 10 atm. and that of the surrounding water is zero. The entrance of water into the cell results in a gradually increasing *turgor pressure* within the cell, just as it does in an osmometer. This pressure not only prevails within the water mass, but is also exerted against the protoplasmic layer and, in turn, against the cell wall. The increase in turgor pressure therefore results in a gradual distension of the cell. Imposition of a pressure of 10 atm. on the water in the cell sap will increase its diffusion pressure by 10 atm. Since the initial diffusion-pressure deficit of the water in the cell sap was 10 atm., imposition of a 10-atm. turgor pressure reduces its diffusion-pressure deficit to zero. This is also the diffusion-pressure deficit of the surrounding water; hence a dynamic equilibrium is attained when the turgor pressure in the cell sap reaches 10 atm.

The diffusion-pressure deficit of the water in the cell sap of cell B is 10 atm., that of the water in the surrounding solution 6 atm. Hence there will be a net inward movement of water into the cell. A turgor pressure thus develops within the cell, but at its maximum under these conditions it will attain a value of only 4 atm. Since the initial diffusion-pressure deficit of the water in the cell sap was 10 atm., imposition of a turgor pressure of 4 atm. reduces this to 6 atm. which is the diffusion-pressure deficit of the water in the surrounding solution. Hence the attainment of a turgor pressure of only 4 atm. results under these conditions in an osmotic equilibrium. Since the magnitude of the turgor pressure developed in cell B will be less than in cell A, the latter cell will be more distended than the former.

Cell C will remain, according to the conditions prescribed for this experiment, in a state of incipient plasmolysis. The diffusion-pressure deficit of the water in the cell sap and in the solution are equal (*i.e.*, their osmotic pressure are equal and neither is under any pressure, except, of course, atmospheric pressures); hence a dynamic equilibrium will be established as soon as the cell is immersed in the solution. Since there is no net movement of water into the cell no turgor pressure will develop, a condition which will obtain in all plant cells in the condition of incipient plasmolysis.

In cells A and B a dynamic equilibrium has been attained by an adjustment of the diffusion-pressure deficit of the water in the cell sap until it is equal to that of the water in the surrounding liquid. This adjustment was attained in each of these cells by a shift in the magnitude of the turgor pressure, which is one of the two components determining the diffusion-pressure deficit of the water in the cell sap, the other being the osmotic pressure. In cell C no shift in the magnitude of the turgor pressure occurred, because the diffusion-pressure deficit was initially the same in the cell sap and in the solution. Unlike a solution exposed to the atmosphere, the diffusion-pressure deficit of a cell is not equal to its osmotic pressure except when the turgor pressure of the cell is zero. The term "diffusion-pressure deficit of a cell" should be considered as an abbreviation for "diffusion-pressure deficit of the water in the cell sap."

The interrelationships among the osmotic pressure, turgor pressure, and diffusion-pressure deficit of a plant cell should be further clarified by a study of Fig. 27. This diagram also takes into account the influence of volume changes in the cell upon these physical quantities. In the interests of simplicity the effects of such volume changes upon the osmotic quantities of the cell have been disregarded in the discussion up to this point. When the cell is completely flaccid (relative volume = 1.0), its diffusion-pressure deficit is equal to its osmotic pressure (20 atm.) while its turgor pressure is zero. As the volume of the cell increases, as a result of influx of water, the osmotic pressure decreases because of the dilution of the cell sap. The pattern of the change in magnitude of the turgor pressure with increase in cell volume is not the same in all kinds of cells, but often follows a trend such as that shown in Fig. 27. The diffusion-pressure deficit, being equal to the difference between the osmotic and turgor pressures, shows a progressive decrease as the turgidity of the cell increases. When the cell attains a condition of maximum turgidity (relative volume = 1.5), its turgor pressure is equal to its osmotic pressure while its diffusion-pressure deficit has fallen to zero.

The dotted extension of the line for turgor pressure to the left indicates that it sometimes has a negative value. Conditions under which this may occur are discussed shortly. The diffusion-pressure deficit of a cell in which the turgor pressure is negative is greater than its osmotic pressure.

In many types of cells volume changes are much less marked than indicated in this figure, and hence they can often be disregarded in gen-

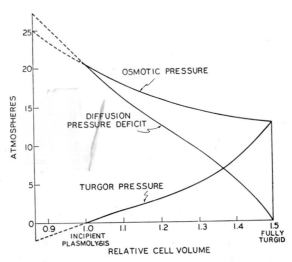

Fig. 27. Interrelationships among the osmotic pressure, turgor pressure, diffusion-pressure deficit, and cell volume of a plant cell. Based on data of Höfler (1920).

eralized considerations of the water relations of plant cells. In some species many of the cells have walls which are virtually inelastic. This is especially true of the tissues of xerophytes and some water plants (Ernest, 1934b).

The fundamental interrelation between the osmotic pressure, turgor pressure, and diffusion-pressure deficit of a plant cell is the same as for an osmometer and is expressed by the same equation:

$$D.\ P.\ D. = O.\ P. - T.\ P.$$

The quantity to which the name "diffusion-pressure deficit" has been given in this discussion has been variously termed by writers in the field of plant physiology (Ursprung, 1935; Meyer, 1945). The more commonly used synonyms for this term are "pressure deficit," "turgor deficit," "net osmotic pressure," "suction force," and "suction tension."

The osmotic pressure, diffusion-pressure deficit, and turgor pressure are collectively called the *osmotic quantities* of plant cells. As previous discussion has shown, a full evaluation of these quantities also requires a consideration of the volume changes of plant cells.

In plant tissues many of the cells are under a pressure imposed upon them by the surrounding cells. In addition to its own turgor pressure the water in such a cell is also subjected to this pressure of external origin. This pressure is just as much a factor in determining the diffusion-pressure deficit of a cell as its own turgor pressure. The true diffusion-pressure deficit of such a cell is therefore less than that of the cell considered as an individual unit by the amount of this added pressure. Hence the equation representing the factors determining the diffusion-pressure deficit of a cell under such conditions becomes:

D. P. D. = O. P. — T. P. — Pressure exerted by surrounding cells

The water in the vessels and cells of plants frequently passes into a state of tension. Imposition of a pressure from an external source raises the diffusion pressure of water. Imposition of a tension, which is in effect a negative pressure, has precisely the opposite effect. In cells and vessels this can happen only if the enclosed water shrinks in volume to such a point that the encompassing protoplasm and cell walls are pulled inward as a result of adhesion between the walls and water. The resulting counter pull exerted by the walls on the water results in throwing it into a state of tension. Under such conditions the turgor pressure is negative in value (Fig. 27), and the tension (negative pressure) developed within the water will be equal to the negative turgor pressure. The equation for the diffusion-pressure deficit of a cell under such conditions becomes:

D. P. D. = O. P. — (−T. P.)

In other words, the diffusion-pressure deficit of the water in a cell or vessel when subjected to a tension is equal to the osmotic pressure plus the tension (negative pressure) imposed on the water.

Dynamics of the Osmotic Movement of Water in Plants.—In order to simplify this part of the discussion, changes in the osmotic pressure of the cell sap resulting from volume changes in the cells, as shown in Fig. 27, will again be disregarded, as usually these are not great enough to modify seriously any generalized picture of the water relations of plant cells.

Let us imagine a certain cell (X) to have an osmotic pressure of 12 atm. and a turgor pressure of 6 atm., and a second cell (Z) to have an osmotic pressure of 10 atm. and a turgor pressure of 2 atm. Let us further suppose that these two cells can be brought into such intimate contact that osmotic movement of water can occur from one to the other (Fig. 28).

The water in the cell sap of X would have a diffusion-pressure deficit of 12 atm. were it under no pressure. The turgor pressure of 6 atm., however, reduces the diffusion-pressure deficit of the water in the cell sap to 6 atm. Similarly the water in the vacuole of cell Z would have a diffusion-pressure deficit of 10 atm. were it not also influenced by the turgor pressure of 2 atm. Hence the diffusion-pressure deficit of cell Z is 8 atm. The diffusion-pressure deficit of cell X is therefore less than that of cell Z. Water will, therefore, osmose from cell X to cell Z. Water will continue to show a net movement from X to Z until the diffusion-pressure deficits of the two cells are equal. In the movement of water from cell to cell in plants, it is the diffusion-pressure deficits and not the osmotic pressures which tend to equilibrate. This is only a special aspect of the fundamental tendency of the diffusion-pressure of water to attain a uniform value throughout any system. It is by no means impossible, therefore, for water to move from a cell of higher to one of lower osmotic pressure.

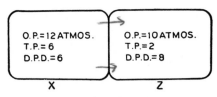

FIG. 28. Diagram of two adjacent cells used in explanation of the mechanism of the cell-to-cell movement of water.

After a dynamic equilibrium has been established between two cells their diffusion-pressure deficits will seldom be an exact average of their initial diffusion-pressure deficits. The only general statement which can be made is that, at equilibrium, the diffusion-pressure deficits of the two cells will be equal, and this value will lie somewhere between the two original values of the cells.

Whenever the diffusion-pressure deficits of two adjacent cells are dissimilar, a *diffusion-pressure-deficit gradient* exists between them. Movement of water from one cell to another can occur only when such a gradient exists. Other conditions being equal, the "steeper" this gradient, *i.e.*, the greater the difference in diffusion-pressure deficits, the more rapidly one cell will gain water from the other. The term "diffusion-pressure deficit gradient" can also be applied to a chain of cells in which the diffusion-pressure deficit increases serially from cell to cell. Several examples of such gradients are discussed in subsequent chapters.

The diffusion-pressure of water is influenced by temperature, although for small temperature differences the magnitude of this effect is not great. If two adjacent plant cells were to be maintained at different temperatures, theoretically this would have an effect on the rate or direction of osmosis. Actually, however, under the thermal conditions ordinarily prevailing in plants, this effect is so slight that it can be disregarded (Curtis, 1937).

Methods of Measuring the Diffusion-Pressure Deficit of Plant Cells.— Most methods of measuring this quantity are based on the principle, previously discussed, that if a cell is immersed in a solution with an osmotic pressure equal to the diffusion-pressure deficit of the cell, a dynamic equilibrium is immediately established, and no change will occur in the volume of the cell because no net movement of water takes place. In solutions with a higher osmotic pressure than the diffusion-pressure deficit of the cell it will decrease in volume; in solutions of lower osmotic pressure than its diffusion-pressure deficit it will increase in volume.

The "simplified method" of measuring diffusion-pressure deficits, introduced by Ursprung (1923), has been one of the most widely used. In this method narrow strips of tissue are cut from such structures as thin leaves or petals. The length of each strip is immediately measured under the microscope, usually while mounted in paraffin oil. Several strips are then immersed in each of a graded series of sucrose solutions in which they are allowed to remain until an equilibrium has been attained in each solution, after which their lengths are measured. The osmotic pressure of the solution in which no change in the length of the strips occurs is considered to equal the average diffusion-pressure deficit of the cells in the strip.

For the measurement of the average diffusion-pressure deficit of the cells in bulky tissues such as potato tubers, masses of tissue such as cylinders of approximately equal dimensions can be employed. The equilibrium point can be determined by measuring changes either in the weight or the volume of the cylinder (Meyer and Wallace, 1941). The solution in which the cylinder neither gains nor loses weight (or volume) is considered to have an osmotic pressure equal to the average diffusion-pressure deficit of the cells in the cylinder.

Determinations of diffusion-pressure deficits by the methods described above should not be confused with plasmolytic determinations of the osmotic pressures of plant cells. In the latter type of determination the critical measurement is the osmotic pressure of the solution with which the cells come to an equilibrium without any turgor pressure, i.e., at incipient plasmolysis. In diffusion-pressure-deficit determinations the critical measurement is the osmotic pressure of the solution with which the cells come to equilibrium without any change in their turgor pressure, i.e., without any change in the volume of the cells. Only when the cell is initially in a completely flaccid condition will determinations of its osmotic pressure and its diffusion-pressure deficit result in the same values.

All of the methods of measuring the diffusion-pressure deficits of plant cells are subject to most of the flaws which are also inherent in plasmolytic determinations of osmotic pressure, as well as some other serious errors (Ernest, 1931, 1934a). Except possibly for a few types of cells which are especially well adapted to such measurements, it is doubtful if the values obtained in determinations of diffusion-pressure deficits are ever more than fair approximations of the true values which obtain in plant cells.

The turgor pressure of a cell cannot be determined directly. However, if the osmotic pressure of a cell or group of cells has been determined, and likewise the diffusion-pressure deficit, the turgor pressure can be calculated from the equations given earlier in the chapter.

The Imbibitional Mechanism of the Movement of Water.—In the preceding discussion, plant cells have been considered purely as osmotic systems. There is no doubt that the osmotic mechanism of the cell-to-cell translocation of water exists and operates in most if not all kinds of plant cells. Certain of the movements of water which occur in plants, however, result from the operation of an imbibitional rather than an osmotic mechanism. As discussed in Chap. VII, whenever the diffusion-pressure deficit of water is greater in an imbibant than in a contiguous solution, water moves from the solution into the imbibant and *vice versa.*

Not only does water pass into dry, mature seeds by imbibition as the first step in germination, but there is evidence that water moves by this process into ovules which are ripening into seeds in the ovulary. During the latter stages of the development of seeds in the cotton boll, for example, their diffusion-pressure deficits exceed their osmotic pressures. This indicates that an osmotic mechanism does not adequately account for the movement of water into the maturing seeds during this period (Kerr and Anderson, 1944). Since no evidence could be found for the existence of a metabolically activated mechanism of water absorption (see later), the most probable explanation of these results is that the diffusion-pressure deficits of maturing cotton seeds are largely imbibitional in origin. It seems likely that imbibition plays a proportionately large role in the movement of water into many other young, actively growing tissues. Other examples of the imbibitional absorption of water can be seen in certain species native to semi-desert regions, such as the resurrection plant (*Selaginella lepidophylla*) or in species such as many kinds of lichens which are indigenous to locally dry habitats such as sun-swept cliffs. Such species may become air-dry during periods of drought, but rapidly imbibe water and resume their physiological activities upon the advent of rain. At least some species of lichens readily imbibe water-vapor as well as liquid water (Scofield and Yarman, 1943).

Within a plant cell the cell sap, the water in the protoplasm, and the water in the cell wall may each be regarded as possessing a diffusion-pressure deficit of its own. The diffusion-pressure deficit of the cell wall is largely of imbibitional origin, and that of the protoplasm partly so. If, for example, the diffusion-pressure deficit of the walls of a mesophyll cell is increased as a result of evaporation during transpirational water loss, water diffuses into the walls from the protoplasm and, in turn, from the cell sap into the protoplasm as long as the diffusion-pressure deficit of the wall exceeds that of the cell sap. In cells in which vacuoles are very small or lacking, or in which the interior of the cell is occupied by hydrophilic colloidal substances, imbibitional phenomena undoubtedly play a greater proportionate role in the movement of water than in cells with prominent vacuoles.

Possible Metabolic Mechanisms of the Movement of Water in Plants.— The osmotic and imbibitional mechanisms may not be the only ones which play a role in the movement of water from cell to cell in plants or from the external environment into plant cells. A number of investigators have suggested that metabolic mechanisms may also be involved, it usually being implied that the energy of respiration is utilized in the transport of water molecules across cell membranes.

Much of the evidence which has been advanced in support of such an hypothesis is highly indirect or otherwise unconvincing. Kelly (1947), however, has shown that a close correlation exists between the rate of respiration and rate of water intake in the oat coleoptile. It has also been shown that certain inhibitors of respiratory enzymes retard water intake by potato tuber tissue (Hackett and Thimann, 1950). The demonstration that auxins accelerate water absorption by potato tuber and other tissues when immersed in pure water (Reinders, 1942; Van Overbeek, 1944; Kelly, 1947) has also been considered to be evidence for the existence of such a mechanism. Auxins are one type of plant hormone (Chap. XXVIII) and are known to influence respiration rates (Commoner and Thimann, 1941). Hence their effect on water absorption might be evidence that respiration plays a role in this process. However, Levitt (1948) failed to find a correlation between the rates of auxin-induced water absorption and respiration in potato tuber tissue, and considers an increased plasticity of the cell walls to be a more likely explanation of this phenomenon.

That correlations do exist between rates of respiration and rates of water movement or absorption in at least some kinds of plant tissues is undeniably true. Whether or not this relationship is a very direct one, however, is not clear. In meristems, for example, passage of water into cells may be a resultant of their increased solute intake, increased fabrication of protoplasm, or expansion in cell-wall area, all processes which appear to be dependent upon respiration as a source of energy. The ✳ influence of respiration on water movement may thus be principally or entirely an indirect one.

While respiration undoubtedly exerts at least indirect effects on the movement of water in plants, there is almost no positive evidence that the energy of this process is utilized directly in the transport of watei molecules. Furthermore, according to calculations of Levitt (1947), it appears improbable that a metabolic mechanism of movement of water of any appreciable magnitude could be maintained in most kinds of plant cells at the expense of respiratory energy. The question of meta-bolically activated mechanisms of the movement of water is discussed further in Chap. XIV.

SUGGESTED FOR COLLATERAL READING

Brooks, S. C., and Matilda M. Brooks. *The Permeability of Living Cells.* Edwards Bros. Ann Arbor. 1944.

Crafts, A. S., H. B. Currier, and C. R. Stocking. *Water in the Physiology of Plants.* Chronica Botanica Co. Waltham, Mass. 1949.

Davson, H., and J. F. Danielli. *The Permeability of Natural Membranes.* The Macmillan Co. New York. 1943.

Harris, J. A. *The Physico-chemical Properties of Plant Saps in Relation to Phytogeography.* University of Minnesota Press. Minneapolis. 1934.

Walter, H. *Die Hydratur der Pflanze.* Gustav Fischer. Jena. 1931.

SELECTED BIBLIOGRAPHY

Bonte, H. Vergleichende Permeabilitätsstudien an Pflanzenzellen. *Protoplasma* **22:** 209-242. 1934.

Broyer, T. C. The movement of materials into plants. Part I. Osmosis and the movement of water into plants. *Bot. Rev.* **13:** 1-58. 1947.

Chambers, R., and K. Höfler. Micrurgical studies on the tonoplast of *Allium cepa. Protoplasma* **12:** 338-355. 1931.

Commoner, B., and K. V. Thimann. On the relation between growth and respiration in the *Avena* coleoptile. *Jour. Gen. Physiol.* **24:** 279-296. 1941.

Curtis, O. F. Vapor pressure gradients, water distribution in fruits, and so-called infra-red injury. *Amer. Jour. Bot.* **24:** 705-710. 1937.

De Vries, H. Eine Methode zur Analyze der Turgorkraft. *Jahrb. Wiss. Bot.* **14:** 427-601. 1884.

Ernest, Elizabeth C. M. Suction-pressure gradients and measurement of suction pressure. *Ann. Bot.* **45:** 717-731. 1931.

Ernest, Elizabeth C. M. The effect of intercellular pressure of the suction pressure of cells. *Ann. Bot.* **48:** 915-918. 1934a.

Ernest, Elizabeth C. M. The water relations of the plant cell. *Jour. Linn. Soc. (London) Bot.* **49:** 495-502. 1934b.

Hackett, D. P., and K. V. Thimann. The action of inhibitors on water uptake by potato tissue. *Plant Physiol.* **25:** 648-652. 1950.

Hibbard, R. P., and O. E. Harrington. The depression of the freezing point in triturated plant tissue and the magnitude of this depression as related to soil moisture. *Physiol. Res.* **1**: 441-454. 1916.

Höfler, K. Ein Schema für die osmotische Leistung der Pflanzenzelle. *Ber. Deutsch. Bot. Ges.* **38**: 288-298. 1920.

Iljin, W. S. Die Veränderung des Turgors der Pflanzenzellen als Ursache ihres Todes. *Protoplasma* **22**: 299-311. 1934.

Kelly, Sally. The relationship between respiration and water uptake in the oat coleoptile. *Amer. Jour. Bot.* **34**: 521-526. 1947.

Kerr, T., and D. B. Anderson. Osmotic quantities in growing cotton bolls. *Plant Physiol.* **19**: 338-349. 1944.

Kramer, P. J., and H. B. Currier. Water relations of plant cells and tissues. *Ann. Rev. Plant Physiol.* **1**: 265-284. 1950.

Levitt, J. The thermodynamics of active (non-osmotic) water absorption. *Plant Physiol.* **22**: 514-525. 1947.

Levitt, J. The role of active water absorption in auxin-induced water uptake by aerated potato discs. *Plant Physiol.* **23**: 505-515. 1948.

McCool, M. M., and C. E. Millar. The water content of the soil and the composition and concentration of the soil solution as indicated by the freezing-point lowerings of the roots and tops of plants. *Soil Sci.* **3**: 113-138. 1917.

Meyer, B. S. The water relations of plant cells. *Bot. Rev.* **4**: 531-547. 1938.

Meyer, B. S. A critical evaluation of the terminology of diffusion phenomena *Plant Physiol.* **20**: 142-164. 1945.

Meyer, B. S., and A. M. Wallace. A comparison of two methods of determining the diffusion pressure deficits of potato tuber tissues. *Amer. Jour. Bot.* **28**: 838-843. 1941.

Plowe, Janet Q. Membranes in the plant cell. *Protoplasma* **12**: 196-240. 1931.

Reinders, Dirkje E. Intake of water by parenchymatic tissue. *Rec. Trav. Bot. Nèerland* **39**: 1-140. 1942.

Scofield, H. T., and L. E. Yarman. Some investigations of the water relations of lichens. *Ohio Jour. Sci.* **43**: 139-146. 1943.

Seifriz, W. New material for microdissection. *Protoplasma* **3**: 191-196. 1928.

Ursprung, A. Zur Kenntnis der Saugkraft. VII. Eine neue vereinfachte Methode zur Messung der Saugkraft. *Ber. Deutsch. Bot. Ges.* **41**: 338-343. 1923.

Ursprung, A. Osmotic quantities of plant cells in given phases. *Plant Physiol.* **10**: 115-133. 1935.

Van Overbeek, J. Auxin, water uptake and osmotic pressure in potato tissue. *Amer. Jour. Bot.* **31**: 265-269. 1944.

DISCUSSION QUESTIONS

Note: In all questions on osmotic quantities of cells, unless stated to the contrary, assume membranes to be permeable to water only and that the cell walls are so nearly inelastic that volume changes in the cells can be disregarded.

1. A decrease in temperature apparently causes a decrease in the permeability of the cytoplasmic membranes to water. What are some possible explanations?

2. An algal filament is immersed in a dilute solution of glycerol from which evaporation of water is allowed to proceed slowly. Even when the concentration of glycerol reaches as much as 50 per cent the cells of the filament show no signs of plasmolysis. Explain. If transferred to pure water the cells of the filament swell and burst almost immediately. Explain.

3. Why does NH_4OH apparently penetrate into many plant cells more rapidly than most other bases?

4. If a NH_4Cl solution is injected directly into the cell sap of a plant cell it becomes more acid, but if the cell is immersed in the NH_4Cl solution the sap becomes more alkaline. Explain.

5. Cell A has an osmotic pressure of 12 atm. and is immersed in a solution with an osmotic pressure of 6 atm. Cell B has an osmotic pressure of 10 atm. and is immersed in a solution with an osmotic pressure of 8 atm. Assume both cells are first allowed to come to equilibrium with the solution in which each is immersed, the volume of which is assumed to be large, and that they are then removed and brought into intimate contact. Which direction will water move? Why?

6. A cell with an osmotic pressure of 12 atm. manifests three-fourths of its maximum turgidity. What is the diffusion-pressure deficit of the cell?

7. A flaccid cell with an osmotic pressure of 15 atm. is immersed in a solution with an osmotic pressure of 5 atm. and increases 25 per cent in volume in coming to equilibrium with this solution. Assuming the osmotic pressure to vary proportionately with the concentration of the cell sap, what will be the osmotic pressure of the cell at equilibrium? Diffusion-pressure deficit? Turgor pressure?

8. Cells A, B, and C, having osmotic pressures of 6, 8, and 3 atm. respectively, constitute a chain of three cells in the order named. A part of the lowest cell, C, dips into a solution with an osmotic pressure of 2 atm. None of the other cells is in contact with the solution, which is large in volume in comparison with the cells. Evaporation from the cells is prevented. What will be the osmotic pressure, diffusion-pressure deficit, and turgor pressure of each cell at equilibrium?

9. Suppose that evaporation is occurring from the surface of cell A (question 8). How would your answer to the question differ?

10. If all three of the cells (question 8) were completely immersed in the solution, what would be the diffusion-pressure deficit, osmotic pressure, and turgor pressure of each cell at equilibrium?

11. If a small block of plant tissue, such as that from a potato tuber, be immersed in a solution with an osmotic pressure of 8 atm., what will be the diffusion-pressure deficit of the cells in the tissue after a dynamic equilibrium has been established? Would there be any exceptions?

12. A chain of cells, each of which has an osmotic pressure of 8 atm., is arranged so that one terminal cell dips in a solution with an osmotic pressure of 3 atm., and the other in a solution with an osmotic pressure of 6 atm. The volume of these solutions is very large in comparison with the size of the cells. Evaporation is prevented. Will any movement of water occur? Explain.

13. What effect will a change of starch to sugar in a cell have upon its diffusion-pressure deficit? An increase in the permeability of the cell membranes to solutes? To water?

14. A cell has an osmotic pressure of 15 atm. and water evaporates from it until the cell walls are pulled inward enough that the enclosed water is subjected to a tension of 12 atm. What is then the diffusion-pressure deficit, osmotic pressure, and turgor pressure of the cell?

15. Pollen grains of cotton and many other species germinate readily upon the stigma, but burst rapidly if floated upon water or a dilute sugar solution. Explain.

IX

THE LOSS OF WATER FROM PLANTS

It is commonplace knowledge that all plants require water for their existence and development and that most plants require it in considerable quantities. It is not so generally recognized, however, that in most species of plants an overwhelmingly large proportion of the water absorbed from the soil is lost by the plant into the atmosphere and takes no permanent part in its development or in its metabolic processes. The lack of this general realization probably results from the fact that, while water is supplied to and absorbed by plants in its familiar liquid form, by far the greater part of that lost escapes in the invisible form of water-vapor.

The loss of water-vapor from living plants is known as *transpiration*. Loss of water-vapor may take place from any part of a plant which is exposed to the air. This applies even to roots in contact with the soil atmosphere. Generally speaking, however, the leaves are the principal organs of transpiration. Most of the transpiration from leaves occurs through the stomates; this is termed *stomatal transpiration*. Smaller amounts of water-vapor are lost from leaves by direct evaporation from the epidermal cells through the cuticle; this is called *cuticular transpiration*. All aerial parts of plants lose some water by transpiration, although, because of the presence on some organs of superficial layers almost impervious to water, the rate of loss from most such organs is very low. Some of the transpiration from herbaceous stems, flower parts, and fruits is of the cuticular type, but is small in amount. Most herbaceous stems, fruits, and flower parts bear stomates which permit the occurrence of stomatal transpiration from such organs. Loss of water-vapor also takes place through the lenticels of fruits and woody stems; this is called *lenticular transpiration*.

The Mechanics of Foliar Transpiration.—The subsequent discussion will deal almost entirely with transpiration from leaves, since, in most plants, the amount of water-vapor lost from other organs is comparatively small. The mechanics of foliar transpiration can be adequately discussed only in reference to the anatomy of the leaves from which it occurs (Figs. 29, 30, 31). It should be recalled that the vacuoles of all of the living cells of a leaf are filled with water, which also saturates the protoplasm

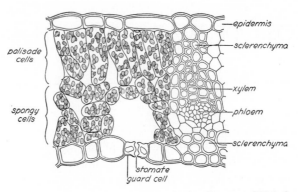

FIG. 29.   Cross section of a portion of a leaf of tulip tree (*Liriodendron tulipifera*).

and the cell walls, this water being supplied to the leaf cells through the water conducting tissues of the vascular bundles. Hence evaporation of water will occur from these wet cell walls into the internal atmosphere of the intercellular spaces just as it will occur from any wet surface into the surrounding air. The intercellular spaces constitute a connected system, ramifying throughout the leaf. Under certain unusual conditions the in-

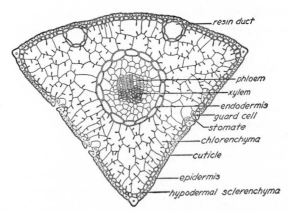

FIG. 30.   Cross section of a leaf of white pine (*Pinus strobus*).

tercellular spaces can become injected with liquid water but under all normal conditions they are occupied by air.

If the stomates are closed the only effect of evaporation from the mesophyll cell walls will be the saturation of the entire volume of the intercellular spaces with water-vapor. When the stomates are open, however, diffusion of water-vapor may occur through them into the outside atmosphere. Such outward diffusion will always take place unless the atmosphere has a vapor pressure equal to, or greater than, that of the intercellular spaces, a condition which does not commonly exist during the daylight hours. The rate of such diffusion will depend principally upon

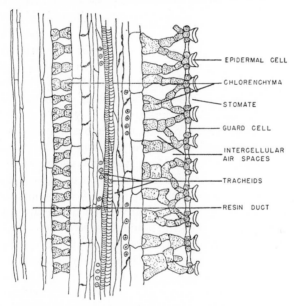

EPIDERMAL CELL

CHLORENCHYMA

STOMATE

GUARD CELL

INTERCELLULAR
AIR SPACES

TRACHEIDS

RESIN DUCT

Fig. 31.   Longitudinal section through a small portion of a leaf of white pine
(*Pinus strobus*).

the excess of the vapor pressure in the leaf over that of the atmosphere, although the "diffusive capacity" of the stomates (Chap. X) is also an important factor. The process of stomatal transpiration therefore involves *evaporation* from the cell wall surfaces bounding the intercellular spaces and the *diffusion* of this water-vapor from the intercellular spaces into the atmosphere through the stomates.

One side of every epidermal cell on a leaf is also exposed to the atmosphere. Evaporation of water occurs into the atmosphere directly from these cell surfaces. The surfaces of practically all aerial leaves are covered with a layer of wax-like substance known as *cutin* (Fig. 32). This is not readily permeable to water and hence reduces transpiration directly through the walls of the epidermal cells to a magnitude much less than it would be, were there no such layer present. The thickness of the cutin layer varies with the species of the plant and the environmental conditions under which the leaves have developed. The layer of cutin is usually thicker on leaves which have developed in bright sunlight, for example, than on leaves of the same species which have developed in shade. Even in leaves which are heavily coated with cutin, some cuticular transpiration occurs, possibly largely through tiny rifts in the cutin layer. In most species of plants of the temperate zone less than 10 per cent of the foliar transpiration occurs through the cuticle, the remainder being stomatal transpiration.

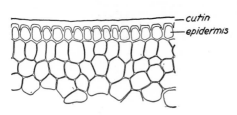

Fig. 32. Cutin layer on the upper epidermis of a leaf of *Clivia nobilis*.

Evaporation.—The fact that transpiration may be regarded as essentially a modified form of the process of evaporation makes desirable a fuller consideration of the dynamics of this process. When an open pan of water is exposed to the atmosphere, the level of the water in the pan slowly drops. Evidently water molecules are being slowly lost into the atmosphere. All of the molecules in a mass of water are not traveling with the same velocity, although for any given temperature the *average* speed of all of the molecules in the liquid mass is a constant. Some of the molecules in the liquid water attain sufficient momentum to overcome entirely the attractive forces holding them in the liquid, and escape into the surrounding atmosphere in the form of vapor. The swiftest molecules present are most likely to be able to overcome the attraction of the other water molecules, therefore they are the most likely to be lost from the liquid. During evaporation any body of water is thus slowly being depleted of its more rapidly moving molecules. The residual water becomes progressively richer in relatively sluggish molecules; in other words, it becomes cooler. This cooling effect is more or less completely offset, however, by physical transfer of heat into the water from its surroundings as soon as its temperature drops below that of the environment. The proportion of "high-speed" molecules in the molecular population of the pan of water is thus maintained at close to its original value, and the rate of evaporation continues with very little diminution.

In the preceding paragraph we have focused our attention only on the water molecules which escape from the liquid. Water-vapor molecules are also returning to the liquid from the atmosphere during the process of evaporation. If a water-vapor molecule in the atmosphere above the evaporating surface, particularly one of the more sluggish ones, strikes the surface of the water at the proper angle and with not too great a velocity, it will be held there by the attractive forces exerted by the liquid water molecules, and again become part of the liquid water. "High-speed" molecules, on the other hand, are much less likely to be captured by the attractive forces exerted by the molecules at the surface of the body of liquid. They impinge upon the bounding film of the liquid with such velocity that, unless they hit that surface at right angles or nearly so, they usually glance off along a new pathway.

This picture of the kinetics of the evaporation process holds for any evaporating surface whether it be the exposed surface of a body of water, a moist piece of cloth, paper, or porous clay, or the mesophyll cell walls of a leaf. Ordinarily the term evaporation is used to refer only to conditions in which the rate of escape of molecules exceeds their rate of return, and its use will be restricted to this sense in this discussion.

If the air above the water surface is confined, as, for example, when a dish of water is covered by a bell jar, the number of water-vapor molecules in the confined space will gradually increase as a result of evaporation from the surface of the water. Since their movement is a random one the water-vapor molecules will be continually colliding with walls of the container, each other, the molecules of other gases present in the air, and surface of the liquid water. Some of those which strike the surface of the liquid will be held there by intermolecular attractive forces. As the concentration of water-vapor molecules in the air increases, the number which plunge back into the water in any unit interval of time increases. Eventually a dynamic equilibrium will be attained at which the number of molecules leaving the surface and the number returning to it in a unit time will be equal. At this point the air will be *saturated* with water-vapor and evaporation will no longer be occurring.

The water-vapor molecules exert a definite pressure against the walls of the container and the surface of the water. This is known as *vapor pressure*. In the illustration given in the preceding paragraph, the vapor pressure of the water increases progressively until the saturation point is reached. The vapor pressure of water under the conditions of such a dynamic equilibrium may conveniently be termed the *saturation vapor pressure*. The vapor pressure of a liquid is usually expressed in terms of millimeters of mercury. The saturation vapor pressure of water at 20°C., for example, is 17.54 mm. Hg. This means that at this temperature the water-vapor exerts a pressure equal to the pressure exerted by a column of mercury 17.54 mm. high. The saturation vapor pressure of any liquid is independent of the area of the evaporating surface, but increases with

increase in temperature (Table 15). In physics and chemistry the saturation vapor pressure is usually referred to simply as "vapor pressure," but
in biological work it is necessary to distinguish between two different
senses in which this latter term is used (Chap. XI).

Botanists are often interested in measuring the rate of evaporation
under a given set of conditions in connection with studies of transpiration and of plant distribution. Many measure-
ments of evaporation rates have been made
with instruments called *atmometers* (Fig. 33).
These consist essentially of surfaces of porous
clay moulded in the form of hollow cylinders
or spheres. Water evaporates from such surfaces in essentially the same way that it evaporates from a free surface of water. Atmometers are attached to a reservoir of water as
shown in the figure, and are usually provided
with mercury valves which prevent absorption
of rain. The loss of water from such instruments can be determined either by measuring
the decrease in volume of water or the loss
of weight of the instrument. Details of atmo-
metric technique are discussed by Livingston
(1935).

Measurement of Transpiration.—Four general methods are in use for measuring transpiration, but only the first two of these as
listed can be used for quantitative determinations of the rate of loss of water-vapor from
plants which are rooted in the soil.

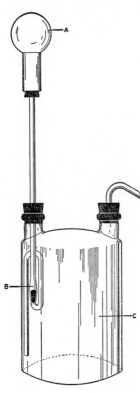

FIG. 33. Arrangement for
the measurement of evapo-
ration rates by means of
an atmometer. (*A*) Porous
clay hollow sphere, (*B*)
mercury valve, (*C*) reservoir.

1. *Method of Weighing Potted Plants.*—
This method can be employed only with plants
which are rooted in pots or other suitable containers. For laboratory experiments potted
plants are often used, the pot generally being
enclosed in a metal shell, and the soil surface
sealed off so that evaporational water loss can
occur only through the plant. For field or
large-scale experiments, metal receptacles
have been found convenient, in which case it is only necessary to seal
off or cover the soil surface in such a way as to prevent evaporation. The
method is limited in practical application to plants which can be grown
in readily portable containers. The transpiration rates of plants as large

as mature maize plants and 5-foot coffee trees have been measured by this method.

The loss of weight of the container and plants for a given time interval may be considered to represent transpiration as the effect of other factors on the weight of the setup is usually negligible. If the experiment is to be continued for more than a relatively short period it is necessary to provide the container with a watering tube through which known volumes of water can be introduced into and distributed throughout the enclosed soil at appropriate intervals.

In employing this method the receptacle in which the plants are growing may be weighed at selected intervals by manual manipulation or may be placed on a balance which is arranged so that each loss of a definite increment of weight (for example, 1 g.) is automatically registered on a recording device (Transeau, 1911, Briggs and Shantz, 1915, Schratz, 1932, Nutman, 1941, and others).

2. *Method of Collecting and Weighing Transpired Water-Vapor.*—This method requires a rather elaborate experimental setup, but is the only way in which the rate of transpiration can be determined quantitatively for plants rooted in out-of-door habitats. A stream of atmospheric air is passed through a glass or cellophane chamber containing the plant or portion of a plant, or through "leaf cups" (Heinicke and Hoffman, 1933) attached to the stomate-bearing side of a leaf. The air stream is then conducted through tubes or vessels containing a water absorbent such as calcium chloride. The gain in weight of these absorption tubes during the experiment represents the water-vapor transpired by the plant plus the water-vapor which was introduced into the system from the outside atmosphere. In order to determine the proportion of the water-vapor which comes from the atmosphere it is necessary to set up a check apparatus, containing no plant, and to pass air through it at the same rate that it is circulated through the setup containing the plant. The gain in weight of the water-absorption tubes in the second apparatus represents water-vapor from the atmosphere. Such a method has been used by Minckler (1936) for measuring transpiration from attached branches of trees and by Heinicke and Childers (1936) for measuring the transpiration rate of attached leaves on apple trees.

3. *Potometer Methods.*—Of a limited usefulness for the measurement of transpirational water loss are instruments known as potometers. The severed base of a leafy shoot is immersed in water in the reservoir of the potometer and the rate of water loss determined by the rate at which the volume of water in the apparatus shrinks. This is usually followed by noting the rate of movement of an air bubble in the water in the capillary sidearm of the instrument. Some potometers are constructed so

that the entire root system of plants which have been specially grown for the purpose in solution cultures can be immersed in the reservoir of the instrument (Fig. 34). A potometer actually measures the rate of absorption of water rather than the rate of transpiration. While under many conditions the rates of these two processes are virtually equal, this is not always true, particularly if an internal water deficit exists in the plant. The rate of transpiration as measured for a cut shoot in a potometer does not necessarily bear any relation to its rate of transpiration while it was still attached to a plant. The reasons for this will become clear in the discussion of the internal water relations of plants (Chap. XV). The prin-

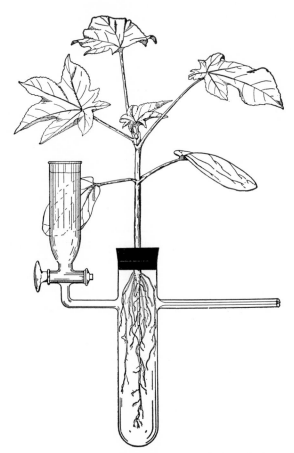

FIG. 34. Potometer as set up for measurement of rate of absorption of water by the root system of a seedling plant. The full length of the capillary tube is not shown.

cipal utility of potometers is in laboratory demonstrations of the effects of various environmental factors upon the rate of transpiration.

4. *Hygrometric Paper Methods.*—When filter paper is impregnated with a dilute (about 3 per cent) solution of cobalt chloride and dried, it becomes a bright blue in color. If exposed to moist air its color gradually changes to pink. The same color change ensues when a piece of such paper is brought into contact with the transpiring surface of a leaf. If small pieces of such paper are mounted so as to be protected from the water-vapor of the atmosphere by glass, mica, or celluloid, and are brought into contact with the surface of a leaf, the rate at which the paper changes in color from blue to pink is an indication of the rate at which water-vapor is being lost by that leaf. A leaf which changes the color of a piece of cobalt chloride from its full blue color to its full pink color in, for example, 30 sec. is losing water to the paper twice as fast as a leaf which requires 60 sec. to accomplish a similar change. This method gives no measure of absolute rates of transpiration, because when a portion of a leaf is covered with a piece of cobalt chloride paper the environmental conditions influencing the leaf under the paper are very different from those which would influence it were it freely exposed to the atmosphere. The leaf under the paper is exposed to a reduced light intensity and an initially lower vapor pressure than freely exposed parts of the same leaf, and furthermore, is completely isolated from any effects of wind. Hence the rate of loss of water-vapor to the paper may be very different from the rate of water-vapor loss of the same area of leaf surface to the atmosphere. Under certain conditions this method can be used for a determination of the *relative* rates of transpiration of different species with a fair degree of accuracy. Even for relative determinations of transpiration rates, however, this method gives valid results only when all of the plants are growing under essentially the same atmospheric conditions. Modifications and limitations of this method are discussed by Livingston and Shreve (1916) and Meyer (1927).

The Magnitude of Transpiration.—Transpiration may be computed per unit of leaf surface or leaf area,[1] per unit of fresh or dry weight, per plant, or per unit area of field or forest. Rates may be calculated for hourly, daily, seasonal, or yearly periods. Transpiration rates show an enormous variation from one kind of a plant to another, and for the same kind of a plant under different environmental conditions.

Transpiration rates in broad-leafed plants of temperate regions range

---

[1] Leaf area is ordinarily used as a basis for expressing rates of transpiration and photosynthesis only for broad-leaved species. In such species leaf surface is always approximately twice the leaf area.

up to about 5 g. per dm.^{2} of leaf area per hour. Usual rates, under conditions favorable for stomatal transpiration, fall within a range of 0.5 to 2.5 g. per dm.^{2} per hour. At night, or during periods when a dry soil, a low temperature, or other conditions unfavorable to stomatal transpiration prevail, the rate may fall to 0.1 g. per dm.^{2} per hour, or even less. Under favorable conditions many herbaceous plants transpire several times their own volume of water in a single day.

The transpiration rates of large plants such as mature trees obviously cannot be measured directly, but can only be estimated from data on the leaf population of the tree and the known rates of transpiration of some of the leaves. To arrive at an accurate estimate of the leaf population of a large tree is in itself a laborious procedure. Among the few such estimates which have been made are those of Turrell (1934), who found a 33-foot open-grown catalpa (*Catalpa speciosa*) to bear 26,000 leaves having an aggregate leaf area of 19,500 dm.^{2}, and of Cummings (1941), who found a 47-foot open-grown silver maple (*Acer saccharinum*) to bear 177,000 leaves having an aggregate leaf area of 68,000 dm.^{2}

Accurate measurements of the transpiration rates of even a small part of a tree can be made only by the air-flow method described previously. Results obtained by the potometer or hygrometric paper methods on small branches or individual leaves may be grossly in error for reasons which have already been discussed. Even if accurate measurements have been made of the transpiration rate of certain branches, a further complication in attempts to estimate the transpiration for the entire tree is introduced by the fact that the rate of the process is known to differ greatly from one leaf or branch to another. All calculations of the transpiration rates of large trees can, therefore, only be approximations, although such estimates are not only of scientific interest but also of practical value.

Likewise, calculations of transpirational water loss per acre of cropped land or of natural vegetation are necessarily only approximations. Results of some such calculations indicate that sufficient water may transpire from maize plants during the course of a growing season to cover the field to a depth of 15 inches (Transeau, 1926) and from apple trees to cover the orchard to a depth of 9 inches. Hoover (1945) estimates the transpiration of a deciduous forest, largely oak, in the southern Appalachian mountains, to be equivalent to 17-22 inches of rainfall per year. This estimate was made on the basis of the effect of removing vegetation from a watershed on the runoff.

Significance of Transpiration.—Opinions regarding the significance of transpiration have ranged all the way from those which would put it practically on a par with such processes as photosynthesis and respiration, to those which would relegate it to the category of a "necessary evil" (Curtis, 1926). The principal roles which have been ascribed to the transpiration of plants can be summarized under the following three headings:

1. *Supposed Role in the Movement of Water.*—It is often claimed or assumed that the movement of water through the plant requires the occurrence of transpiration from the leaves. That this concept is entirely erroneous will be clear from the discussion of the mechanism of the conduction of water through plants in Chap. XII. Under conditions of high transpiration the movement of water through plants is, in general, more rapid than under conditions of low transpiration. The mechanism causing ascent of water through a plant operates in such a way that any increase in the diffusion-pressure deficit of the mesophyll cells favors a more rapid movement of water toward those cells. Hence a rapid transpiration rate, which invariably results in a considerable increase in the diffusion-pressure deficit of the mesophyll cells, usually speeds up the rate at which water ascends through the plant. However, translocation of water to the extent that it is used in restoring the turgor of leaf cells, in photosynthesis or in growth, continues even during periods when the transpiration rate is negligible.

2. *Supposed Role in the Absorption and Translocation of Mineral Salts.* —It has often been assumed that the more rapid the rate of transpiration, the greater the rate of absorption of mineral salts. This view implies that the dissolved mineral salts are swept into the plant along with the absorbed water, a postulation which ignores much evidence that the mechanisms operating in the absorption of water are very different from the mechanisms operating in the absorption of mineral salts (Chap. XIV, Chap. XXIV). The results of certain experiments do indicate that a somewhat larger quantity of mineral salts accumulates in plants under conditions favoring high transpiration rates than in similar plants growing under conditions favoring low transpiration (Freeland 1937, Wright 1939). The work of Broyer and Hoagland (1943), however, indicates that such results are only obtained under certain metabolic conditions, and that there is no consistent correlation of the rate of transpiration with the rate of absorption of mineral salts.

Upward translocation of the mineral salts absorbed by the roots occurs principally in the xylem (Chap. XXVII). The dissolved mineral salts are passively carried upward in the ascending water columns. Since the rates of translocation of water show a fairly close correlation with the rates of transpiration, a similar correlation also exists between rates of upward movement of mineral salts through the plant and rates of transpiration. Although high transpiration rates undoubtedly often result in more rapid upward transport of mineral salts through the plant than low rates, there is no reason to attach any critical significance to this fact. There is no evidence that inadequacies in the distribution of absorbed mineral salts throughout plants ever result from low transpiration rates.

3. *Supposed Role in the Dissipation of Radiant Energy.*—Leaves exposed to direct sunlight absorb large quantities of radiant energy which, unless dissipated in some other way, will be converted into heat energy and raise the temperature of the leaf. The possibilities of such an effect are indicated by the following approximate calculations: In direct noonday summer sunlight, the rate of receipt of solar energy is often as much as 1.3 g.-cal. per square centimeter of leaf area per minute and not uncommonly even greater. The proportion of this actually absorbed varies with the kind of leaf, but will be assumed to be only 50 per cent, which is probably a representative value. The incident radiant energy which is not absorbed by the leaf is all transmitted or reflected. Such a small proportion of the absorbed energy is used in photosynthesis that it can be neglected in a rough calculation. Hence about 0.65 g.-cal. of energy is absorbed per square centimeter of leaf area per minute. If the mass of a square centimeter of a leaf is taken as 0.020 g. and its specific heat as 0.879 g.-cal.,[2] the rise in temperature per minute would be $\dfrac{0.65}{0.020 \times 0.879}$ or about 37°C. Since the thermal death point of most plant protoplasm lies between 50° and 60°C., it should not require more than a few minutes to heat the leaves of most plants to a lethal temperature. Actual measurements of leaf temperatures, however, show that they seldom even approach their thermal death points. Leaf temperatures usually do not exceed atmospheric temperatures by more than a few degrees centigrade. Evidently some efficient energy-dissipating mechanism is at work which prevents the accumulation of heat energy in leaves.

Since transpiration is an energy-consuming process it has often been assumed that it is in the evaporation of water from the leaves that most of the energy absorbed by them is dissipated. We might well inquire, therefore, regarding the possible efficiency of transpiration as an energy-dissipating process. The evaporation of a gram of water at 20°C. requires 584 g.-cal. For the dissipation of 0.65 g.-cal. of heat, therefore, the evaporation of 0.0011 g. (0.65/584) of water per square centimeter of leaf area per minute is required. This is equivalent to 6.6 g. (0.0011 × 100 × 60) of water per square decimeter of leaf area per hour, a rate of transpiration which is seldom attained by plants for any sustained period of time under natural conditions. Evidently transpiration, even when occurring at its

---

[2] These are the actual values as determined for a sunflower leaf by Brown and Escombe (1905). See also Shull (1930).

maximum rate, can seldom account for dissipation of more than part of the radiant energy which is absorbed by leaves in intense sunlight.

The fact that transpiration is often inadequate in direct sunlight to account for the dissipation of all the absorbed radiant energy leads naturally to the question of whether it is at all essential for this process. Observations have shown that leaves in which the transpiration rate is greatly reduced—as, for example, those in which the stomates are plugged with vaseline, leaves in a wilted condition, or the leaves of plants in xeric habitats during dry seasons, in which the occurrence of any appreciable amount of transpiration is precluded by the lack of soil water—seldom have temperatures which are anywhere near the thermal death point, even when exposed to direct sunlight. Although transpiration often accounts for the dissipation of some or even most of the absorbed radiation, in so doing it apparently plays no essential role since absorbed radiation can be dissipated by purely physical means. As soon as the temperature of a leaf exceeds that of the surrounding atmosphere, it will lose heat to the atmosphere in the same way that any other object heated above its environmental temperature does, i.e., by one or more of the purely physical processes of conduction, radiation, and convection. The term *thermal emission* is frequently applied to this physical loss of heat energy by leaves and other objects. As will be shown in Chap. XI, the thermal emission of leaves is adequate to account for the dissipation of all absorbed radiant energy.

Actually, instead of benefiting plants, transpiration may often be detrimental. Under conditions of deficient soil water or of high transpiration rates even when the soil water supply is adequate, this process results in a diminution in the water content of a plant and in the turgidity of its cells. Prolonged drought conditions ultimately result in a severe desiccation with the consequent death of all except the most drought resistant species. When the diminution in water content is less severe, a train of other effects such as a decrease in the turgidity of the cells, stomatal closure, and reduction in rate or cessation of photosynthesis are induced, all of which have the end result of checking the growth of the plant. It is probably true that lack of water is more often the limiting factor in plant growth than any other single factor. Furthermore, deficiency of water is probably responsible for the death of more plants under natural or even cultural conditions than any other single cause.

The fundamental effects of transpiration upon the plant are not to be sought in any hypothetical "advantages" of the process to the plant, but in its very real and readily ascertainable influences upon the water relations of plant cells and tissues, and through these its effects upon other plant processes. In spite of the fact that transpiration may be regarded in a sense as an incidental phenomenon, its indirect influence upon the metabolic processes of plants is a profound one. It is this fact, more than any other, which justifies intensive and critical studies of this process.

The Loss of Water from Plants in Liquid Form.—If a pot of young oat plants is copiously watered and then enclosed in a bell jar, in a relatively short time a slow exudation of water begins at the tip of each leaf. The drops which form at the leaf apexes gradually enlarge and eventually may run down the side of the leaf or fall off. This process of the escape

Fig. 35. Guttation from tomato leaves. Photograph, courtesy of Dr. J. H. Gourley.

of liquid water from uninjured plants is called *guttation* (Fig. 35). It is of very general occurrence, having been recorded in plants of more than 300 genera, although there are many species in which it has not been observed. Guttation occurs most frequently and abundantly under conditions which favor rapid absorption of water by the roots, but which result in a reduced rate of transpiration. In most temperate regions such conditions occur most frequently during the late spring when there is often an alternation between relatively cool nights and relatively warm days. Guttation is frequently observed at that season, usually taking place at night or during the early hours of the morning. The drops of guttation water which form at the tips of grass blades and the tips or edges of the leaves of other plants are often erroneously considered to be dew.

The process of guttation occurs from pore-like structures known as _hydathodes_ (Fig. 36). These structures are also sometimes referred to as _water stomates_ or _water pores_. As the figure indicates, a typical hydathode consists of an enlarged stomate-like opening below which is a rather large chamber, bordered by a mass of thin-walled, loosely arranged cells called the _epithem_. The xylem elements of a vascular bundle terminate just below the epithem.

The exudation of water through hydathodes is considered to result from a pressure which develops in the sap of the xylem elements, and not to any locally developed pressure in the hydathode itself. This pressure is generally believed to be identical with the so-called "root pressure" (Chap. XII). It is supposed that the water is forced from the vessels through the intercellular spaces of the epithem layer and out of the plant through the pore of the hydathode. This water is not pure but contains at least traces of solutes, including sugars, amino acids, and mineral salts. Guttation water sometimes evaporates so rapidly as to leave deposits of salts on the margins or tips of leaves. Reabsorption of drops of guttation water also sometimes occurs, such reabsorbed water often containing a

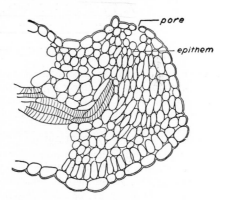

FIG. 36. Hydathode at the margin of a tomato leaf as seen in sectional view (semi-diagrammatic). Note termination of vessels just back of the epithem.

greater concentration of salts than the original exudate because of solution in it of previously deposited encrustations of salts. Either evaporation, or reabsorption of guttated water, or both, may result in injurious effects on plants and are a probable cause of tip burn in leaves of some species (Curtis, 1943). While the volume of water exuded by most plants of temperate regions in guttation is usually small, some tropical species lose large quantities in this process. A young leaf of _Colocasia nymphaefolia_, a native of India, has been observed to lose as much as 100 ml. of liquid water in a single night by guttation.

Glands are found on leaves, flower parts, and other organs of the plant. Certain types of glands secrete water or, more accurately, a dilute solution. The exudation of water or a dilute solution by glands is apparently caused by a physiological mechanism within the gland itself, and not by a pressure developed in the sap of the xylem conduits as appears to be true of hydathodes. Sugars (as in nectar) and certain mineral salts are secreted by some glands. Non-water-soluble substances, such as resins and volatile oils, are secreted by glands on some kinds of plants.

SUGGESTED FOR COLLATERAL READING

Burgerstein, A. *Die Transpiration der Pflanzen.* I, II, and III. Gustav Fischer. Jena. 1904, 1920, 1925.

Eames, A. J., and L. H. MacDaniels. *An Introduction to Plant Anatomy.* 2nd Ed. McGraw-Hill Book Co., Inc. New York. 1947.

Hayward, H. E. *The Structure of Economic Plants.* The Macmillan Co. New York. 1938.

Maximov, N. A. *The Plant in Relation to Water.* R. H. Yapp, Editor. George Allen and Unwin. London. 1929.

SELECTED BIBLIOGRAPHY

Briggs, L. J., and H. L. Shantz. An automatic transpiration scale of large capacity for use with freely exposed plants. *Jour. Agric. Res.* **5**: 117-132. 1915.

Brown, H. T., and F. Escombe. Researches on some of the physiological processes of green leaves, etc. *Proc. Roy. Soc. (London)* **B 76**: 29-137. 1905. (4 papers)

Broyer, T. C., and D. R. Hoagland. Metabolic activities of roots and their bearing on the relation of upward movement of salts and water in plants. *Amer. Jour. Bot.* **30**: 261-273. 1943.

Cummings, W. H. A method for sampling the foliage of a silver maple tree. *Jour. Forestry* **39**: 382-384. 1941.

Curtis, L. C. Deleterious effects of guttated fluids on foliage. *Amer. Jour. Bot.* **30**: 778-781. 1943.

Curtis, O. F. What is the significance of transpiration? *Science* **63**: 267-271. 1926.

Freeland, R. O. Effect of transpiration upon the absorption of mineral salts. *Amer. Jour. Bot.* **24**: 373-374. 1937.

Heinicke, A. J., and N. F. Childers. The influence of water deficiency in photosynthesis and transpiration of apple leaves. *Proc. Amer. Soc. Hort. Sci.* **33**: 155-159. 1936.

Heinicke, A. J., and M. B. Hoffman. The rate of photosynthesis of apple leaves under natural conditions. *Cornell Univ. Agric. Expt. Sta. Bull. 577.* 1933.

Hoover, M. D. Effect of removal of forest vegetation upon water yields. *Amer. Geophysical Union Trans. of 1944.* Part VI. 969-975. 1945.

Livingston, B. E. Plant water relations. *Quart. Rev. Biol.* **2**: 494-515. 1927.

Livingston, B. E. Atmometers of porous porcelain and paper; their use in physiological ecology. *Ecology* **16**: 438-472. 1935.

Livingston, B. E., and Edith B. Shreve. Improvements in the method for determining the transpiring power of plant surfaces by hygrometric paper. *Plant World* **19**: 287-309. 1916.

Meyer, B. S. The measurement of the rate of water-vapor loss from leaves under standard conditions. *Amer. Jour. Bot.* **14**: 582-591. 1927.

Minckler, L. S. A new method of measuring transpiration. *Jour. Forestry* **34**: 36-39. 1936.

Nutman, F. J. Studies of the physiology of *Coffea arabica*. III. Transpiration rates of whole trees in relation to natural environmental conditions. *Ann. Bot.* **5:** 59-81. 1941.

Raber, O. Water utilization by trees, with special reference to the economic forest species of the north temperate zone. *U. S. Dept. Agric. Misc. Publ. No. 257.* 1937.

Schratz, E. Untersuchungen über die Beziehungen zwischen transpiration and Blattstruktur. *Planta* **16:** 17-69. 1932.

Shull, C. A. The mass factor in the energy relations of leaves. *Plant Physiol.* **5:** 279-282. 1930.

Transeau, E. N. Apparatus for the study of comparative transpiration. *Bot. Gaz.* **52:** 54-60. 1911.

Transeau, E. N. The accumulation of energy by plants. *Ohio Jour. Sci.* **26:** 1-10. 1926.

Turrell, F. M. Leaf surface of a twenty-one year old catalpa. *Proc. Iowa Acad. Sci.* **41:** 79-84. 1934.

Wright, K. E. Transpiration and the absorption of mineral salts. *Plant Physiol.* **14:** 171-174. 1939.

DISCUSSION QUESTIONS

1. How would you measure separately the rates of stomatal and cuticular transpiration in a broad-leafed plant?

2. Is it harmful to prune grapevines or other woody plants at a season when they bleed profusely?

3. When a leaf exposed to bright light is surrounded by a bag of cellophane, which checks transpiration, the temperature of the leaf rises. This has been interpreted as evidence of a result of the retardation in the rate of transpiration. What is a more probable interpretation of this effect?

4. How can you tell whether the water present on leaves in the early morning hours after a clear night is dew or water of guttation?

5. If a leaf is absorbing 0.65 g.-cal. of radiant energy per cm.^{2} per minute, what proportion of this will be dissipated by thermal emission if the transpiration rate is 2 g. per dm.^{2} of leaf area per hour?

X

THE STOMATAL MECHANISM

The most important physiological fact about the stomates is that they are sometimes open and sometimes closed. When open, they serve as the principal pathways through which gaseous exchanges take place between the intercellular spaces of the leaf and the surrounding atmosphere. When closed, gaseous exchanges between a leaf and its environment are greatly retarded. The gases of greatest physiological importance which enter or depart from a leaf principally through the stomates are oxygen, carbon dioxide, and water-vapor. The movement of gases through the stomates in either direction is primarily a diffusion phenomenon, although under certain conditions, as discussed later, mass movement of gases may occur through the stomates. Although the stomates are the principal portals through which entry and escape of gases take place, the fact should not be overlooked that at least small quantities of gases pass directly through the epidermis and cuticular layers of all leaves. This appears to be true, in particular, of carbon dioxide (Chap. XIX). In submerged vascular aquatics all gaseous exchanges between the plant and its environment occur through the epidermis.

Structure of the Stomates.—The *stomates* or *stomata* (singular *stomate* or *stoma*) are minute pores which occur in the epidermis of plants. They are surrounded by two distinctive epidermal cells known as the *guard cells*. Stomates may occur on any part of a plant except the roots, but in most species are most abundant upon the leaves. The size of the stomatal pore varies in most plants depending upon the turgidity of the guard cells and often, especially at night, it is entirely closed. In Fig. 37 are depicted surface and cross-sectional views of several of the commoner types of stomates. The structure of stomatal apparatus shows marked variations in detail in different species of plants, but the essential feature of a pore between two guard cells is common to all species of vascular

140

plants. Guard cells which are roughly kidney or bean-shaped as seen in surface view are typical of more species of plants than any other kind (Fig. 37A). In some species the epidermal cells bordering on the guard cells are different in configuration from other cells in the same tissue; these are called *subsidiary cells* or *accessory cells* (Fig. 37B). In many species of the grass and sedge families the guard cells are distinctly

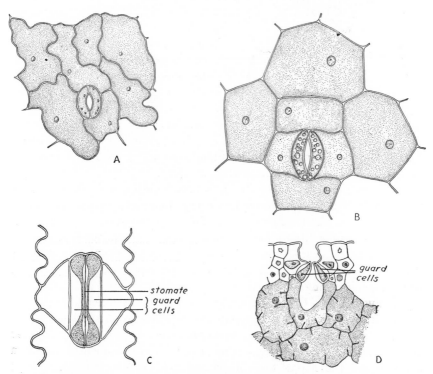

FIG. 37. Structure of stomates. (A) Surface view of sunflower stomate, (B) surface view of *Zebrina* stomate, showing four subsidiary cells around the guard cells, (C) surface view of maize stomate, (D) cross sectional view of Austrian pine stomate.

elongate (Fig. 37C). In most species of conifers and in certain other species, stomates are of the "sunken" type (Fig. 37D). A perspective view of a stomate and the surrounding guard cells is shown in Fig. 38. Unlike other epidermal cells, the guard cells contain chloroplasts. They also appear to contain a larger proportion of cytoplasm than the epidermal cells.

Size and Distribution of Stomates.—The size of the stomatal pore varies greatly according to the species of plant, and somewhat among the individual stomates on any one plant. The pores are always very minute, however, their dimensions being expressed in terms of microns (Table 13).

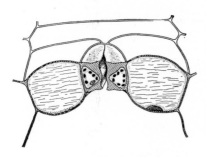

Minute as these openings appear to be from a human scale of values, they are enormous when compared with the size of the gas molecules which diffuse through them. The calculated diameter of a water molecule is 0.000454 μ. More than 2000 water molecules would have to be placed side by side to measure a distance of 1 μ. The molecules of both carbon dioxide and oxygen are larger than water molecules. Since the stomatal diameters usually are considerably in excess of

Fig. 38. Perspective view of a stomate and adjacent cells (semi-diagrammatic).

1 μ, it is evident that the stomates afford relatively enormous portals to the gas molecules which diffuse through them.

In general, the number of stomates present in the epidermis of leaves may range from a few thousand to over a hundred thousand per square centimeter, the exact number depending upon the species and upon the environmental conditions under which the leaf has developed. A single maize plant has been estimated to bear from 140 to 240 million stomates, whereas the number on a large tree could be expressed only by a figure of astronomical dimensions.

The average numbers of stomates which have been found per square centimeter on the leaves of a number of representative species are listed in Table 13. However, marked deviations from such average values are possible for any species, depending upon the environmental conditions under which the leaves have developed. The number of stomates per unit area of leaf surface may be quite different on leaves of two plants of the same species, if one grew in a greenhouse, and the other grew in the open, or upon the leaves of plants of the same species which have developed during different seasons.

As shown in Table 13, stomates occur in both the upper and lower epidermis of many species of plants. In numerous others, especially woody species, they are confined to the lower epidermis. Even in those species in which stomates occur on both surfaces of the leaf they are commonly, but not always, more abundant in the lower epidermis. In floating leaves, such as those of the water lily, stomates occur only in the upper epidermis. Species in which the stomates are relatively small usually have more per unit area than species in which the stomates are relatively large.

TABLE 13—SIZE AND DISTRIBUTION OF STOMATES ON THE LEAVES OF VARIOUS SPECIES OF PLANTS (DATA OF ECKERSON, 1908; SALISBURY, 1927; KISSER, 1929; MILLER, 1931; AND YOCUM, 1935)

Species	Ave. no. of stomates per cm²		Size (length × breadth) of pore when fully open (lower epidermis)	Reference
	Upper epidermis	Lower epidermis		
Alfalfa (*Medicago sativa*).............	16,900	13,800	....	M
Apple (*Pyrus malus* var.).............	0	29,400	....	M
Barberry (*Berberis vulgaris*)..........	0	22,900	....	K
Bean (*Phaseolus vulgaris*)............	4,000	28,100	7 × 3 μ	E
Begonia (*Begonia coccinea*)...........	0	4,000	21 × 8 μ	E
Black Oak (*Quercus velutina*).........	0	58,000	....	Y
Black Poplar (*Populus nigra*)........	2,000	11,500	....	S
Black Walnut (*Juglans nigra*)........	0	46,100	....	K
Cabbage (*Brassica oleracea*)..........	14,100	22,600	....	M
Castor Bean (*Ricinus communis*)......	6,400	17,600	10 × 4 μ	E
Cherry (*Prunus cerasus* var.).........	0	24,900	....	M
Coleus (*Coleus blumei*)..............	0	14,100	10 × 5 μ	E
English Ivy (*Hedera helix*)...........	0	15,800	11 × 4 μ	E
English Oak (*Quercus robur*).........	0	45,000	....	S
Geranium (*Pelargonium domesticum*)...	1,900	5,900	24 × 9 μ	E
Holly (*Ilex opaca*)..................	0	17,000	12.5 × 6.5 μ	K
Jimson Weed (*Datura stramonium*).....	11,400	18,900	....	K
Lilac (*Syringa vulgaris*).............	0	33,000	....	K
Linden (*Tilia vulgaris*)..............	0	13,000	....	S
Maize (*Zea mais*)...................	5,200	6,800	19 × 5 μ	E
Mulberry (*Morus alba*)..............	0	48,000	....	K
Nasturtium (*Tropaeolum majus*).......	0	13,000	12 × 6 μ	E
Nightshade (*Solanum dulcamara*)......	6,000	26,300	....	K
Oat (*Avena sativa*).................	2,500	2,300	38 × 8 μ	E
Pea (*Pisum sativum*)	10,100	21,600	....	K
Peach (*Prunus persica* var.)..........	0	22,500	....	M
Potato (*Solanum tuberosum*).........	5,100	16,100	....	M
Red Oak (*Quercus rubra*)............	0	68,000	....	Y
Scarlet Oak (*Quercus coccinea*).......	0	103,800	....	Y
Scilla (*Scilla nutans*)...............	5,500	5,100	....	S
Sunflower (*Helianthus annuus*)........	8,500	15,600	22 × 8 μ	E
Sycamore (*Platanus occidentalis*)......	0	27,800	....	K
Tomato (*Lycopersicon esculentum*).....	1,200	13,000	13 × 6 μ	E
Tree of Heaven (*Ailanthus glandulosa*)	0	38,600	....	K
Wandering Jew (*Zebrina pendula*).....	0	1,400	31 × 12 μ	E
Wheat (*Triticum sativum*)............	3,300	1,400	38 × 7 μ	E
Willow Oak (*Quercus phellos*).........	0	72,300	....	Y
Wood Sorrel (*Oxalis acetosella*).......	0	4,500	....	S
Yew (*Taxus baccata*)................	0	11,500	....	S

In general, no correlation has been found between transpiration rates and either the size or distribution of the stomates, other factors being much more important in determining the rate of loss of water-vapor from the intercellular spaces.

Principles Governing Diffusion of Gases through the Stomates.—Since gaseous exchanges between the intercellular spaces and the atmosphere take place principally through the stomates, the problem of the *diffusive capacity* of the stomates is an important one. Although the aggregate area of the fully open stomates of a leaf is probably never more than 3 per cent of the stomate-bearing surface and is often less than 1 per cent, the rate of water-vapor loss from leaves per unit of area may be 50 per cent or even more of the evaporation from an exposed water surface of the same area. Stomatal transpiration from a leaf of birch (*Betula pubescens*), for example, under the most favorable conditions, may be as much as 65 per cent of the evaporation from the same area of an evaporating surface (Stalfelt, 1932). Leaves of this species bear stomates only in the lower epidermis. Assuming the aggregate area of the open stomates to be 1 per cent of the leaf area, it is evident that water-vapor often diffuses through the stomates at rates ranging up to at least fifty times greater than it diffuses away from an equal area of exposed evaporating surface.

This unexpectedly high diffusive capacity of the stomates is intelligible in terms of the results of studies upon the principles of diffusion through small apertures. The classical investigation of this problem was made by Brown and Escombe (1900), who studied the rate of diffusion of carbon

TABLE 14—DIFFUSION OF WATER-VAPOR THROUGH SMALL OPENINGS UNDER UNIFORM
CONDITIONS (DATA OF SAYRE, 1926)

Septum	Diameter of pores, mm.	Loss of water-vapor, grams	Relative areas of pores	Relative perimeters (circumferences) of pores	Relative amounts of water-vapor lost
1	2.64	2.655	1.00	1.00	1.00
2	1.60	1.583	0.37	0.61	0.59
3	0.95	0.928	0.13	0.36	0.35
4	0.81	0.762	0.09	0.31	0.29
5	0.72	0.672	0.07	0.27	0.25
6	0.65	0.590	0.06	0.25	0.22
7	0.56	0.492	0.05	0.21	0.18
8	0.48	0.455	0.03	0.18	0.17
9	0.41	0.393	0.02	0.15	0.15
10	0.35	0.364	0.01	0.13	0.14

dioxide through tubes of known dimensions (Chap. XIX). They first made the important discovery that, if a septum which had been pierced with a small circular aperture was interposed across a column of diffusing gas, the rate at which carbon dioxide diffused through this aperture was much greater than the rate at which it passed through an equal area of the unobstructed tube.

Since the problem at present under consideration is the diffusion of water-vapor rather than carbon dioxide through small apertures, the data presented in Table 14 will be used to illustrate more fully the principles

regarding the diffusion of gases through small openings. These data were obtained by sealing thin septa, through the center of which were cut round openings of known dimensions, across the circular mouths of small bottles which had previously been filled to a certain level with water, and then determining the loss in weight of each bottle after all of them had been kept under uniform conditions for the same period of time.

The results of this experiment illustrate two important general principles: (1) The quantities of water-vapor diffusing through small openings in a given period of time are proportional (essentially) to the perimeters (circumferences) and not to the areas of the pores. This is shown by the close corre-

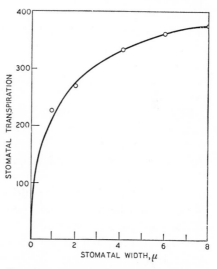

Fig. 39. Relation between width of stomatal pore and rate of stomatal transpiration in leaf of birch in mg. per 25 cm.^{2} leaf area per hr. Data of Stalfelt (1932).

spondence of the figures in the last two columns of Table 14. (2) The smaller the pore, the greater the water loss per unit area. The pore in septum 2, for example, has an exposed area only slightly more than one-third as great as the pore in septum 1, but diffusion through it is nearly two-thirds as great as through septum 1. Similarly, the pore in septum 7, with only 5 per cent of the area of the pore in septum 1, nevertheless permits 18 per cent as much diffusion as the pore in the latter septum.

It has also been found that the diffusion of water-vapor through small pores of elliptical cross section is more nearly proportional to their perimeter than to their area. A stomate attains almost its maximum diffusive capacity considerably before it is fully open (Fig. 39), because the perimeter of a stomatal pore does not increase greatly after the aperture between the guard cells has once widened appreciably.

Diffusion of gases through small apertures is much more nearly proportional to their perimeters than to their areas because of the more rapid diffusion of the molecules through an opening at its periphery than through its center. The concentration of diffusing molecules is much less in outward directions from the rim than it is just above the pore. Hence the number of molecules escaping through the hole near the rim per unit time interval greatly exceeds the number escaping near the center of the opening. Reduction in the area of a circular or elliptical aperture results in increasing its perimeter relative to its area. Hence in small pores such a large proportion of the diffusion is "rim diffusion" and such a small proportion is diffusion through the pore centers that measurements show the rate of diffusion to be essentially proportional to the perimeters of the openings.

Diffusion of gases from or into a leaf through the stomates involves a much more complex system than is represented by a septum pierced by a single aperture. Diffusion is occurring, not through a single opening, but simultaneously through thousands of minute apertures which are relatively close together. Experiments have been performed in analogous physical systems in which multiperforate instead of uniperforate diaphragms have been used. The results of experiments on different spacings of the pores in a septum upon the rate of diffusion of water-vapor per pore and per septum are depicted graphically in Fig. 40 and Fig. 41, respectively.

As shown in Fig. 40, the diffusion *per pore* increases with increase in the distance apart of the apertures, although not proportionately. With pores of this diameter (0.3 mm.) nearly the maximum diffusive capacity per pore is attained when they are spaced at intervals of 20 diameters. In multiperforate septa the molecules diffusing through each aperture invade in part the zones into which the molecules passing through neighboring pores would diffuse were each opening the only one in the septum. Also, the number of molecules diffusing through each pore is not as great as if it were the only pore in the septum because some of those which would diffuse through the pore by chance if it were solitary are now diffusing by chance through neighboring pores. Hence the diffusion pressure gradient is not as steep through each pore as it would be through a single pore, and the rate of diffusion through each pore is correspondingly reduced. The closer together the pores, the less the rate of diffusion through each pore.

The loss of water-vapor by diffusion *per septum* decreases with increase in the distance between the openings, *i.e.*, with decrease in the number of pores per septum (Fig. 41). The decrease in diffusive capacity is not, however, in proportion to the reduction in the aggregate area of the pores in the septum. For example, when the pores are spaced 5 diameters apart, their aggregate area is only 3.38 per cent of the septum area, yet diffusion through them was 62 per cent of that through an open bottle with a mouth of the same area as the septum (compare Table 27). Although with decreasing distance between the pores the diffusion per pore decreases, this effect is more than offset by the increased number of pores per unit of the septum.

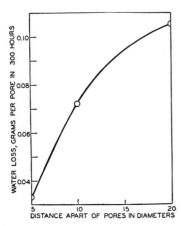

Fig. 40. Relation between water loss per pore and distance in diameters between pores. Data of Weishaupt (1935).

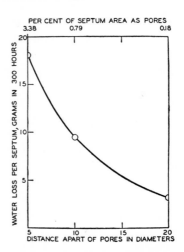

Fig. 41. Relation between water loss per septum and distance in diameters between pores. Data of Weishaupt (1935).

The dimensions of the pores (0.3 mm. diameter, 0.071 mm.² area) used in the experiments just discussed are much greater than those of the average stomate. Pore systems in which the individual pores approach or are within the stomatal range of sizes have still higher diffusive capacities. Huber (1930) found the diffusion through a septum in which the pores were 0.05 mm. (50 μ) in diameter and occupied 3.2 per cent of the septum area to be 72 per cent as great as that from an open evaporating surface of the same area. Similarly Sierp and Seybold (1929) found diffusional water loss through multiperforate diaphragms in which the pores were 10 μ, 20 μ, or 50 μ in diameter and occupied 0.8 per cent of the septum area to be about 70-75 per cent of the water loss from an open evaporating surface of the same area as the septum. Diffusion through a multiperforate septum may thus approach, although it never equals, that from a freely exposed surface.

The relatively high rates of water-vapor loss which occur from leaves in proportion to the aggregate area of the stomatal pores are thus explicable in terms of the principles of diffusion through multiperforate septa. Known rates of transpiration rarely if ever attain the values which calculations based on the principles just discussed indicate to be theoretically possible, even when the stomates are fully open. Evidently some factor other than the diffusive capacity of the stomates is often the limiting factor in stomatal transpiration.

The foregoing discussion of the diffusion of gases through small pores has been based on data obtained when diffusion was allowed to occur into "quiet" air. Even in so-called "quiet" air, it should be realized that considerable convectional movement of air is often taking place. If an air current is blowing across the surface of a multiperforate septum, the usual effect is an increase in the rate of diffusion through the pores. In pore systems within the size and frequency ranges of the stomates of most species, however, the effect of such air movement on the diffusion rate of water-vapor does not appear to be very great (Sierp and Seybold, 1929; Huber, 1930).

In applying the principles of diffusion through small pores to stomates, the further complication that the distance from the rim of one stomate to the next is variable must be considered (Verduin, 1949). The effective diameter of the stomates on tomato leaves, for example, is about 10 mμ., and they are spaced about 10 diameters apart when fully open. At this spacing there is considerable interference with the diffusion of the molecules through one pore by the diffusion through other pores in its vicinity. If these stomates close to half their maximum effective diameter, they will be spaced 20 diameters apart, at which distance there is much less interference with diffusion through one pore by that through another. Decrease in interference during stomatal closure permits the maintenance of a higher diffusive capacity when the stomates are partly closed than would otherwise be possible.

Not all movement of gases through the stomates occurs by diffusion. In a wind, for example, back and forth bending of leaves causes alternate compression and expansion of the intercellular spaces with corresponding outward or inward mass flow of gases. Mass flows of gases also undoubtedly occur when leaf temperatures (Chap. XI) are rapidly fluctuating. This is commonly the situation when wind velocities are variable on a bright day, or when leaves are alternately exposed to direct sunlight and shade, as on a day with scattered clouds in the sky. With each increase in leaf temperature an outflow of gases through the stomates undoubtedly occurs; with each decrease in temperature, an inflow.

Mechanism of the Opening and Closing of the Stomates.—The degree of stomatal opening is influenced both by changes in the turgor of the guard cells and by changes in the turgor of the epidermal cells, although the former usually play a predominant role. In general, an increase in the turgor of the guard cells relative to that of the epidermal cells leads to a widening of the stomatal aperture, and *vice versa*. The greater this turgor difference, the wider the stomatal aperture.

The mechanism of the effect of changes in the turgor of the guard cells upon the size of the stomatal aperture varies with the structure, form, and position of the stomates. In one type of guard cell, found in many different species of plants, the cell wall is thicker on the side bordering the stomatal pore than on the side bordering the epidermal cells (Fig. 38). With an increase in turgor the thinner walls of the guard cells are stretched more than the thicker; this causes the thicker-walled sides to assume a concave shape and results in the appearance of a gap—the stomatal pore—between the two guard cells. Opening of the stomates typical of the grass and sedge families (Fig. 37C), appears to result from swelling of the ends of the guard cells thus separating the abutting walls of the middle portion of the two adjacent guard cells. In the sunken stomates typical of conifers (Fig. 37D), opening of the stomates seems to result largely from a change in the shape of the guard cells as a result of an increased turgor which is unaccompanied by any appreciable stretching of the walls. These various types of stomatal mechanisms are discussed by Copeland (1902).

The three principal factors which influence the opening and closing of the stomates are: (1) light, (2) the internal water relations of the leaf, and (3) temperature.

1. *Influence of the Light Factor in Stomatal Opening and Closing.*—Unless other conditions, to be discussed later, are limiting, the stomates of most species open upon exposure to light and close in its absence. Most commonly, therefore, the stomates are open in the daytime and closed at night, although there are many exceptions to this statement. The reactivity of the guard cells to light undoubtedly varies according to species. It probably differs considerably in shade species, for example, from sun species. Within limits the guard cells appear to react quantitatively to the amount of light they absorb. Stomatal opening apparently will occur in all wave lengths of the visible spectrum, although the influence of radiations in the red region appears to be weaker than the influence of other wave lengths (Sierp, 1933).

Stomatal closure upon the cessation of illumination is generally a gradual process and, according to Stalfelt (1929), the greater the quantity of light which has been absorbed by the guard cells in the course of the day, the longer it takes, at least under some conditions, for the completion of stomatal closure.

Although several theories have been proposed in explanation of the mechanism of stomatal action, as conditioned by light and other factors, the only one for which there is any substantial evidence is the osmotic theory. This does not, of course, eliminate the possibility that other mechanisms may also be operative in this process. The guard cells usually contain starch, but the quantity present is not constant. Sayre (1926) showed that the starch content of the guard cells of dock (*Rumex patientia*) is at its maximum during the night, decreases rapidly during the daylight hours, and increases again toward evening. When the starch content of the guard cells was high the sugar content was low, and *vice versa*. Similarly Alvim (1949) found that opening of stomates of several species as induced by various factors was accompanied by a diminution in the starch content of the guard cells.

The major reaction influencing the proportion of soluble and insoluble carbohydrates present which occurs in the guard cells appears to be the reversible transformation of starch to glucose-1-phosphate in the presence of inorganic phosphates (Chap. XX):

$$\text{Starch} + \text{Phosphate} \xrightarrow[\longleftarrow]{\text{phosphorylase}} \text{glucose-1-phosphate}$$

The enzyme phosphorylase, which catalyzes this reaction, is known to be present in the chloroplasts of the guard cells (Yin and Tung, 1948). The equilibrium position of this reaction is affected by the pH of the medium, being much further to the right at pH values about 7 than at pH values of about 5 (Hanes, 1940). The concentration of soluble glucose-1-phosphate is thus greater at the higher of these two pH values than at the lower.

Illumination of the guard cells of a number of species has been found to result in an increase in their pH; failure of illumination, in a decrease (Scarth, 1932; Small *et al.*, 1942). Scarth, for example, found the pH of the guard cells of zebrina to range from 4.0 or less in the dark to between 6.0 and 7.4 in the light. There is some evidence that the higher pH of the guard cells in the light as compared with the dark may result from a reduction in the carbon dioxide concentration within the leaf as a result of photosynthesis (Scarth and Shaw, 1951). Whether or not photosynthesis occurs in guard cells is not known with certainty, although chlorophyll appears to be present (Freeland, 1951). Reduction of carbon dioxide concentration throughout the leaf could result, however, from occurrence of photosynthesis in the mesophyll cells. In the light, therefore, increase in the pH of the guard cells appears to favor conversion of starch into glucose-1-phosphate under the influence of phosphorylase; in the dark decrease in pH appears to favor the reverse reaction.

Increase in the soluble carbohydrate concentration of the guard cells results in an increase in their osmotic pressure while a decrease in their soluble carbohydrate concentration has the opposite effect. That such changes in the osmotic pressure of the guard cells actually occur has been shown by many investigators. The diurnal changes in the osmotic pressures at incipient plasmolysis of the guard cells and epidermal cells of the English Ivy (*Hedera helix*) are shown in Fig. 42. In general, the osmotic pressure of the guard cells is usually relatively high during the

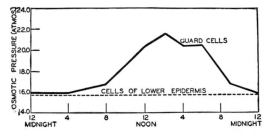

Fig. 42. Daily variations in osmotic pressure of the guard cells and epidermal cells of English ivy (*Hedera helix*). Data of Beck (1931).

daylight hours and relatively low at night. The osmotic pressure of the epidermal cells does not change appreciably during the course of the day and approximates that of the guard cells at night.

Increase in the osmotic pressure of the guard cells in the morning results in an increase in their diffusion pressure deficit relative to that of the contiguous cells. Water therefore moves into the guard cells, increasing their turgor, which in turn leads to a widening of the stomatal aperture. Movement of water into the guard cells from neighboring cells results in a loss of turgor by the latter which probably facilitates opening of the stomate. Decrease in the osmotic pressure of the guard cells leads to the reverse series of processes and results in a narrowing of the stomatal aperture.

2. *Influence of the Water Factor in Stomatal Opening and Closing.*— As discussion in Chap. XV shows, development of an internal water deficit in plants is of frequent occurrence, especially on clear, warm days. A shrinkage in the total volume of water in a plant results in general in a diminution in the volume of water in each individual cell, although all cells will not necessarily be affected equally. Such a decrease in the water

content of the leaf cells, not sufficient to induce visible wilting, is called *incipient wilting*. Under such conditions the guard cells usually decrease in turgor as a result of osmotic movement of water into contiguous cells. Reduction in the turgor pressure of the guard cells as a result of the diminution of the volume of water in them will bring about a partial to complete closure of the stomates. There is also some evidence that diminution in the water content of the guard cells induces a decrease in the pH of their cell sap and a correlated conversion of sugar into starch. The resulting decrease in the osmotic pressure of the guard cells may lead to a further loss of water from them into adjacent epidermal cells. Stomates may thus close even under favorable light and temperature conditions whenever an internal water deficit of sufficient magnitude develops in the leaves.

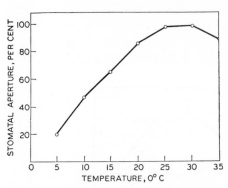

FIG. 43. Relation between temperature and stomatal aperture in cotton. Data of Wilson (1948).

3. *The Temperature Factor in the Opening and Closing of Stomates.*—The effect of temperature upon stomatal opening depends in part upon other prevailing environmental conditions. Under constant and favorable light and other environmental conditions, stomatal opening in cotton (Fig. 43) and tobacco increases with rise in temperature up to 25°–30°C. and decreases at still higher temperatures (Wilson, 1948). In most species stomatal opening fails to occur at temperatures approaching 0°C. or lower. Relatively high temperatures (about 40°C.) induce opening of the stomates of some species in the dark.

Daily Periodicity of Stomatal Opening and Closing.—No kind of living organism is more inescapably at the mercy of its environment than a rooted plant. A number of the factors in the environment of plants (Chap. 30) exhibit more or less regular daily periodicities. The most conspicuous and physiologically important factors of which this is true are solar radiation and temperature, both soil and air. Other usually less significant factors in which daily cyclical variations may occur, at least in some habitats, include wind velocity, atmospheric vapor pressure, and carbon dioxide content of the atmosphere. Since the rates of plant processes are conditioned in part by the environmental factors to which the plant is exposed, they also exhibit more or less regular daily periodicities.

Daily cycles of environmental conditions vary greatly from one plant habitat to another, depending upon latitude, altitude, directional exposure, and local climatic conditions. In a given habitat such cycles vary from season to season and during any one season with day-to-day variations in meteorological conditions. Hence the daily periodicity of any plant process may vary considerably in pattern from one day to another depending upon the prevailing cycle of environmental conditions. In the course of this book we shall have occasion to analyze the hour-to-hour variations of a number of physiological processes occurring in plants. It is desirable, therefore, to choose a definite type of diurnal cycle of environmental factors as a reference standard in terms of which to discuss

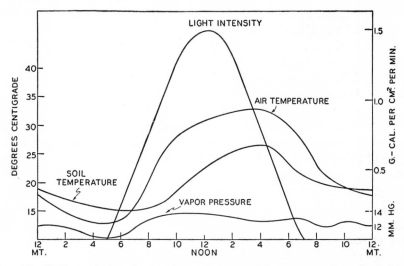

Fig. 44.   Daily variations in certain environmental factors on a "standard day." (Light intensity measured at horizontal incidence.)

daily variations in the rates of various processes. For this purpose we shall select a "representative summer day" as our criterion. We shall consider this hypothetical day to be characterized by a sky which is cloudless or nearly so, a soil with a favorable water supply (*i.e.*, at approximately the field capacity, Chap. XIII), and a maximum temperature in the range of 30°-35°C. (86°-95°F.). Furthermore we will assume that the cyclical daily variations in solar radiation, air and soil temperatures, wind velocity, and atmospheric humidity will be representative of a day upon which the conditions as defined above prevail. In our subsequent discussion we shall refer to these as "standard day conditions" (Fig. 44). Such environmental conditions will actually be approximated on many summer days in moist temperate zone regions.

In all plants which have been studied the stomates exhibit a more or less regular periodicity of opening and closing. Their behavior, however, even on a given plant, may vary greatly from day to day depending upon the daily pattern of environmental factors. Not all of the stomates on a plant are necessarily open at the same time, and different stomates may differ markedly in their degree of opening at a given time. The aggregate diffusive capacity of all of the stomates on a plant must therefore be thought of in terms of the two variables of the average degree of opening of the individual stomates and the number of stomates which are open.

As a rule, under the conditions prevailing on a "standard day," the stomates of most mesic species of plants are open all or most of the daylight period and closed at night, their maximum diffusive capacity being attained during the midday hours. The stomates open in the morning under the influence of the light factor. Maximum opening of the stomates considered in the aggregate usually occurs in less than an hour; some individual stomates may attain a maximum degree of opening very quickly, often within an interval of a very few minutes. Under standard day conditions, however, the water content and turgor of the leaf cells usually decrease progressively during most of the daylight period. Because of this internal water deficit which develops within the leaf, stomatal closure usually begins during the midday hours. Closure of the stomates is often virtually complete before the advent of darkness, because of the predominant effect of the water factor over the light factor during the afternoon hours. Although under some conditions stomates may close very rapidly, in general, under standard day conditions, their closing occurs more gradually than their opening.

Innumerable other types of daily cycles of stomatal behavior are possible, a few of which will be described briefly. The diffusive capacity of the stomates often rises to a mid- or late morning maximum, decreases markedly during the midday hours, rises to a secondary maximum during the early afternoon, and finally falls to a virtually zero value at approximately the termination of the daylight period. The stomates apparently behave in this way when a water deficit develops in the leaves somewhat earlier in the day than under standard day conditions. Partial closure of the stomates results during the morning hours. The resultant reduction in their diffusive capacity permits an increase in the water content of the leaf, and for a time the stomatal apertures again widen. Subsequently the water deficit of the leaf increases again, because of increased transpirational loss, and the stomates enter upon a second cycle of closing which usually continues throughout the remainder of the daylight period.

When the soil water supply is distinctly inadequate the stomates usually open incompletely and seldom remain open for the entire daylight period. Although with the advent of daylight the light factor favors stomatal opening, especially on clear days, the water content of the leaf is so low that opening is seldom complete. Furthermore, the effect of the water factor usually begins to predominate over the light factor relatively early in the day, and stomatal closure may be complete by midday or even sooner. During prolonged droughts the stomates generally close progressively earlier and earlier each day, and ultimately matinal opening may cease almost entirely.

On cloudy or rainy days, especially if the temperature is relatively low, the stomates of most species open less completely than on clear days when the soil is well supplied with water. This results principally from the ineffectiveness of the light factor in inducing stomatal opening under such conditions. Hence opening of the stomates is incomplete and they do not remain open as long under such meteorological conditions as on a "standard day."

During much of the time throughout the winter months in the higher latitudes the stomates of evergreens remain closed. Although low temperatures are undoubtedly the chief causal agent in maintaining the stomates in the closed state under such conditions, the relatively low leaf water contents usually prevailing at low temperatures may be a contributory factor.

Nocturnal opening of the stomates has been reported for a number of species (Loftfield 1921, Desai 1937, and others). In other species, of which maize and other cereals may be mentioned as examples, it has never been possible to demonstrate the occurrence of night opening of the stomates. Apparently this type of stomatal behavior can be brought about by different combinations of environmental conditions, and it seems likely that the conditions leading to nocturnal opening of the stomates may differ according to species. The prevalence of high temperatures, especially at night, appears quite definitely to be one of the environmental conditions which favors this phenomenon. The stomates of many tropical species remain open during the hours of darkness (Faber, 1915). In northern latitudes the near-daylight conditions prevailing during the night hours of summer months favor maintenance of the stomates in the open condition at night (Stalfelt, 1929). A reduced partial pressure of oxygen in the atmosphere has been shown by Scarth *et al.* (1933) to lead to stomatal opening in the dark. This result suggests that a reduced partial pressure of oxygen in the intercellular spaces as a result of night respiration may sometimes induce nocturnal opening of the stomates.

SUGGESTED FOR COLLATERAL READING

Burgerstein, A. *Die Transpiration der Pflanzen.* I, II, and III. Gustav Fischer. Jena. 1904, 1920, 1925.

Loftfield, J. V. G. The behavior of stomata. *Carnegie Inst. Wash. Publ. No. 314.* Washington. 1921.

Maximov, N. A. *The Plant in Relation to Water.* R. H. Yapp, Editor. George Allen and Unwin. London. 1929.

Miller, E. C. *Plant Physiology.* 2nd Ed. McGraw-Hill Book Co., Inc. New York. 1938.

SELECTED BIBLIOGRAPHY

Alvim, P. de T. Studies on the mechanism of stomatal behavior. *Amer. Jour. Bot.* **36:** 781-791. 1949.

Beck, W. A. Variation in the O_g of plant tissues. *Plant Physiol.* **6:** 315-323. 1931.

Brown, H. T., and F. Escombe. Static diffusion of gases and liquids in relation to the assimilation of carbon and translocation in plants. *Phil. Trans. Roy. Soc. (London)* **B 193:** 223-291. 1900.

Copeland, E. B. The mechanism of stomata. *Ann. Bot.* **16:** 327-364. 1902.

Desai, M. C. Effect of certain nutrient deficiencies on stomatal behavior. *Plant Physiol.* **12:** 253-283. 1937.

Eckerson, Sophia F. The number and size of stomata. *Bot. Gaz.* **46:** 221-224. 1908.

Faber, F. C. von Physiologische Fragmente aus einem tropischen Urwald. *Jahrb. Wiss. Bot.* **56:** 197-220. 1915.

Freeland, R. O. The green pigment and physiology of guard cells. *Science* **114:** 94-95. 1951.

Hanes, C. S. The reversible formation of starch from glucose-1-phosphate catalyzed by potato phosphorylase. *Proc. Roy. Soc. (London)* **B 129:** 174-208. 1940.

Huber, B. Untersuchungen über die Gesetze der Porenverdunstung. *Zeitschr. Bot.* **23:** 839-891. 1930.

Kisser, J. Anzahl und Grösse der Spaltöffnungen einiger Pflanzen. In *Tabulae Biologicae* **5:** 242-251. W. Junk. Berlin. 1929.

Salisbury, E. J. On the causes and ecological significance of a stomatal frequency, with special reference to woodland flora. *Phil. Trans. Roy. Soc. (London)* **B 216:** 1-65. 1927.

Sayre, J. D. Physiology of stomata of *Rumex patienta. Ohio Jour Sci.* **26:** 233-266. 1926.

Scarth, G. W. Mechanism of the action of light and other factors on stomatal movement. *Plant Physiol.* **7:** 481-504. 1932.

Scarth, G. W., and M. Shaw. Stomatal movements and photosynthesis in *Pelargonium. Plant Physiol.* **26:** 207-225, 581-597. 1951.

Scarth, G. W., J. Whyte, and A. Brown. On the cause of night opening of stomata. *Trans. Roy. Soc. (Canada)* Sect. 5. **27:** 115-117. 1933.

Sierp, H. Untersuchungen über die Öffnungsbewegungen der Stomata in verschiedenen Spektralbezirken. *Flora* **128:** 269-285. 1933.

Sierp, H., and A. Seybold. Weitere Untersuchungen über die Verdunstung aus multiperforaten Folien mit kleinstem Poren. *Planta* **9:** 246-269. 1929.

Small, J., M. I. Clarke, and J. Crosbie-Baird. pH phenomena in relation to stomatal opening. II-IV. *Proc. Roy. Soc. (Edinburgh)* **B 61**: 233-266. 1942.

Stälfelt, M. G. Die Abhängigkeit der Spaltöffnungsreaktionen von der Wasserbilanz. *Planta* **8**: 287-340. 1929.

Stälfelt, M. G. Der stomatäre Regulator in der pflanzlichen Transpiration. *Planta* **17**: 22-85. 1932.

Verduin, J. Diffusion through multiperforate septa. In *Photosynthesis in Plants*. J. Franck and W. E. Loomis, Editors. Iowa State College Press. Ames. 1949.

Weishaupt, Clara G. Diffusion of water vapor through multiperforate septa. Dissertation Ph.D. Ohio State University. 1935.

Wilson, C. C. The effect of some environmental factors on the movements of guard cells. *Plant Physiol.* **23**: 5-37. 1948.

Yin, H. C. and Y. T. Tung. Phosphorylase in guard cells. *Science* **108**: 87-88. 1948.

Yocum, L. E. The stomata and transpiration of oaks. *Plant Physiol.* **10**: 795-801. 1935.

DISCUSSION QUESTIONS

1. Would you expect the amount of diffusion per unit time through a multiperforate septum to approach more nearly that of an open surface of equal area if the gradient of the diffusing gas is steep or if it is gradual? Explain.

2. Can the size and spacing of the pores in a multiperforate membrane ever be such that the diffusion through the membrane would be equal to that from an open surface of the same area as the membrane?

3. Calculate the percentage of the area of the lower epidermis of a geranium leaf 60 cm.² in area through which diffusion could occur if all the stomates are fully open (see Table 13).

4. Explain why benzene will penetrate rapidly into the intercellular spaces through open stomates when a leaf is brought into contact with it, but water will not similarly penetrate unless applied with considerable force.

5. The intercellular spaces of leaves immersed in recently boiled water often become quickly infiltrated with liquid water, but this does not usually happen to leaves immersed in water drawn from a tap. Explain.

6. What are some of the reasons why there is usually very little correlation between the number of stomates per unit area of a leaf, and its rate of transpiration?

XI

FACTORS AFFECTING TRANSPIRATION

The rate of transpiration of a plant or any leaf on a plant varies from day to day, from hour to hour, and, frequently, from minute to minute. Variations in the rapidity with which water-vapor is lost by plants result from the effects of environmental factors upon physiological conditions within the plant. The important environmental factors influencing the rate of transpiration are: (1) solar radiation, (2) humidity, (3) temperature, (4) wind, (5) soil conditions influencing the availability of water, and (6) atmospheric pressure. This last factor is relatively much less important than the other five listed. While the general effect of variations in the intensity or magnitude of each of these factors upon transpiration is well known and has frequently been demonstrated by experimentation, the precise mechanism of the effect of each is not so easily amenable to experimental treatment. The following interpretation of the mechanism of the effects of these environmental factors upon the rate of transpiration is therefore a somewhat theoretical one, but is in accord with the experimental data available at the present time.

Solar Radiation.—This term refers to the visible light and other forms of radiant energy (infrared and ultraviolet radiations) reaching the earth from the sun (Chap. XVII). The principal effects of solar radiation upon transpiration result from the influence of light upon the opening and closing of the stomates. In most of the species of plants which have been studied the stomates are usually closed in the absence of light, thus causing a virtually complete cessation of stomatal transpiration during the hours of darkness. Since none of the other environmental factors can have any influence upon stomatal transpiration except when the stomates are open, light occupies a position of prime importance among the environmental conditions influencing transpiration.

A second important effect of solar radiation upon transpiration operates

158

through its influence on leaf temperatures. This effect will be analyzed later in this chapter.

Humidity.—Several units are used for designating the humidity conditions of an atmosphere. One of these is the *actual* vapor pressure of the atmosphere. This should not be confused with the *saturation* vapor pressure (Chap. IX). Since the rates of diffusion and evaporation are influenced directly by the vapor pressure of the atmosphere, this is usually the most satisfactory unit in which to express humidity values for physiological purposes.

A more familiar humidity unit is the *relative humidity,* which is the percentage saturation of an atmosphere. Since, at a given temperature, the vapor pressure of an atmosphere is proportional to the concentration of water-vapor molecules present, the relative humidity is equal to the ratio of the actual vapor pressure of the atmosphere to its saturation vapor pressure at the same temperature. For example, a saturated atmosphere at 30°C. has a vapor pressure of 31.82 mm. Hg; its relative humidity is 100 per cent. If only half the amount of vapor is present that would be present at saturation at this temperature, *i.e.*, if the vapor pressure is 15.91 mm. Hg., then the relative humidity of the atmosphere is 50 per cent (Table 15). Change in either the vapor pressure or the temperature of an atmosphere will result in a change in its relative humidity. Change in vapor pressure at constant temperature results in a proportionate change in relative humidity. Increase in temperature, unaccompanied by a change in the amount of water-vapor present, results in a decrease in the relative humidity of an atmosphere, because of the increase in saturation vapor pressure. Contrariwise, decrease in temperature of an atmosphere, without any accompanying change in water-vapor content, results in an increase in relative humidity.

Expression of humidity values in terms of relative humidity, although a common practice, is unsatisfactory for physiological purposes because the same relative humidity, 50 per cent for example, may refer to widely different vapor pressures (Table 15). For a relative humidity of 50 per cent at 10°C., the vapor pressure is only 4.60 mm. Hg. whereas that for a saturated atmosphere at the same temperature is 9.21 mm. Hg. The difference between these two values—4.61 mm. Hg.—is an index of the steepness of the vapor pressure gradient between an evaporating surface and the atmosphere. For a relative humidity of 50 per cent at 50°C., however, the difference between the saturation vapor pressure at an evaporating surface and the vapor pressure of the air above would be 46.25 (92.51-46.26). Hence at a relative humidity of 50 per cent, evaporation from a moist surface would take place many times more rapidly at 50°C. than at 10°C. Only when all relative humidity values are recorded at the same temperature are they an expression of relative differences in vapor pressures.

In general, the greater the vapor pressure of an atmosphere, other factors remaining unchanged, the slower the rate of transpiration. Whenever the stomates are open the rate of diffusion of water-vapor out of a leaf depends upon the difference between the vapor pressure in the intercellular spaces and the vapor pressure of the outside atmosphere, since the vapor pressure is a measure of the diffusion pressure of the water-vapor. Let us suppose that the vapor pressure of the intercellular spaces is 31.82 mm. Hg. which is the value for a saturated atmosphere at 30°C.

TABLE 15—THE RELATION BETWEEN RELATIVE HUMIDITY AND VAPOR PRESSURE AT DIFFERENT TEMPERATURES

Temperature		Actual vapor pressure (mm. Hg) at indicated relative humidity										
°C.	°F.	o	10%	20%	30%	40%	50%	60%	70%	80%	90%	100%
o	32	o	0.46	0.92	1.37	1.83	2.29	2.75	3.21	3.66	4.12	4.58
5	41	o	0.65	1.31	1.96	2.62	3.27	3.92	4.58	5.23	5.89	6.54
10	50	o	0.92	1.84	2.76	3.68	4.60	5.53	6.45	7.37	8.29	9.21
15	59	o	1.28	2.56	3.84	5.12	6.40	7.67	8.95	10.23	11.51	12.79
20	68	o	1.75	3.51	5.26	7.02	8.77	10.52	12.28	14.03	15.79	17.54
25	77	o	2.38	4.75	7.13	9.50	11.88	14.26	16.63	19.01	21.38	23.76
30	86	o	3.18	6.36	9.55	12.73	15.91	19.09	22.27	25.46	28.64	31.82
35	95	o	4.22	8.44	12.65	16.87	21.09	25.31	29.53	33.74	37.96	42.18
40	104	o	5.53	11.06	16.60	22.13	27.66	33.19	38.72	44.25	49.79	55.32
45	113	o	7.19	14.38	21.56	28.75	35.94	43.13	50.32	57.50	64.69	71.88
50	122	o	9.25	18.50	27.75	37.00	46.26	55.51	64.76	74.01	83.26	92.51

Such a vapor pressure is frequently attained in the internal air spaces of leaves. Let us further assume that at the same time the vapor pressure of the atmosphere is only half as great (15.91 mm. Hg.). Such a value would be a representative one for a warm summer's day in the eastern United States. In very quiet air the vapor pressure in the neighborhood of transpiring leaf surfaces may be greater than that in the atmosphere in general but in this discussion it is assumed that there is sufficient air movement to prevent any appreciable accumulation of water-vapor in the vicinity of the leaves.

Under the conditions as stated diffusion of water-vapor would occur through open stomates at a relatively rapid rate. If the vapor pressure of the atmosphere were lowered below this value, the rate of diffusion of water-vapor out of the leaf would be increased; conversely, increase in the vapor pressure of the atmosphere would result in a decrease in the diffusion rate of water-vapor out of the leaf. Similarly, an increase in the vapor pressure of the intercellular spaces would result in an increase in the rate of transpiration, whereas a decrease in the vapor pressure of the intercellular spaces relative to that of the atmosphere would have the opposite effect. On the rare occasions when the vapor pressures of the atmosphere and of the intercellular spaces are equal, no transpiration will occur, even if the stomates are open.

Martin (1943) found the transpiration rate of sunflower (*Helianthus annuus*) and ragweed (*Ambrosia trifida*) in the dark, but with open stomates, to show a linear relation to the relative humidity of the atmosphere at 27° and 38°C. The rate at a relative humidity of 50 per cent, for example, was about twice the rate at a relative humidity of 75 per cent. These results are in agreement with the foregoing theoretical discussion, since, assuming a saturation or near saturation vapor pressure in the intercellular spaces, which the conditions of the experiment favored, the vapor-pressure gradient from the intercellular spaces to the outside atmosphere would be about twice as great at 50 per cent relative humidity as at 75 per cent relative humidity.

Temperature Effects on Transpiration.—1. *Thermal Relations of Leaves.* —While leaf temperatures[1] often do not deviate greatly from surrounding atmospheric temperatures, the discrepancy between the two is often sufficiently great to make it necessary to take it into account in careful experimental work.

Theoretically the temperature of a leaf may be regarded as conditioned by four different influences: (1) thermal absorption, (2) thermal emission, (3) internal endothermic (energy-storing) processes, such as photosynthesis and transpiration, and (4) internal exothermic (energy-releasing) processes such as respiration. The influence of this last factor upon leaf temperatures is practically always negligible and will be disregarded. (*Cf.* Chap. XXI for examples in which internally produced heat of respiration does influence the temperature of plant organs.) Similarly the quantity of energy transformed in photosynthesis is relatively so small that it need not be considered in evaluating the factors determining the temperature of leaves.

Thermal emission refers to the loss of heat from a leaf by the processes of conduction, convection, and radiation (Brown and Escombe, 1905).

---

[1] Leaf temperatures are generally measured by means of thermocouples. A thermocouple is made by twisting together the ends of two fine wires of dissimilar metals— for example, copper and constantan (an alloy of copper and nickel). A difference of electrical potential is set up between two such wires brought into intimate contact, the magnitude of which is very nearly directly proportional to the temperature of the thermocouple. In actual practice two junctions are generally used, one being inserted into the leaf blade, the other being kept at a standard temperature, usually 0°C. The difference in potential between the two thermocouples is usually measured with a potentiometer and is an index of the leaf temperature.

Thermal absorption refers to the gain of energy by a leaf by these same physical processes.

Heat transmission which is brought about by intermolecular contacts is known as (thermal) conduction. The greater the temperature difference between a leaf and its environment the more rapidly conduction of heat will occur from the leaf to the gases of the atmosphere, if its temperature is the higher, or in the opposite direction if the temperature of the atmosphere is the higher.

Whenever loss of heat is occurring by conduction from a leaf to adjacent gas molecules of the atmosphere, convection currents (Chap. V) are set up in the atmosphere in the vicinity of the leaf. Cooler gas will displace the gas in the vicinity of the leaf surfaces which has become warmed as a result of thermal conduction from the leaf. This accelerates the rate at which conduction can occur from the leaf.

Radiation is the transfer of radiant energy across space. The best known types of radiant energy are light, infrared radiations ("heat waves"), and ultraviolet radiations. Radiant energy is commonly pictured as being propagated across space in the form of undulatory waves (see Chap. XVII for discussion of another concept of the nature of radiant energy). Radiation occurs from the molecules of one body to those of another only if the radiating body is at a higher temperature than the receiving body. Thus light, infrared and ultraviolet radiation are transferred from the sun to the earth. In a like manner a warm stove loses heat by radiation of invisible infrared to its environment. Radiation which occurs from leaves is also in the infrared range of wave lengths.

Leaves exposed to strong solar or artificial radiation usually have temperatures from 2° to 10°C. (sometimes even more) in excess of that of the atmosphere. Thermal absorption—in this case direct absorption of radiant energy—proceeds under such conditions at a rapid rate. A portion of the absorbed radiant energy is dissipated (usually) by transpiration, and a portion is lost from the leaf by thermal emission. That part of the absorbed energy which is retained by the leaf goes to raise its temperature. As already shown in Chap. IX, transpiration is usually inadequate to dispose of all absorbed energy if the leaves are exposed to strong insolation. Under such conditions a considerable proportion of the absorbed radiant energy is lost by thermal emission. In general, the lower the rate of transpiration for a given rate of thermal absorption by leaves, the larger the proportion of energy disposal which will be accomplished by thermal emission.

On cloudy days the temperature of leaves seldom deviates very greatly from that of the enveloping atmosphere. Heat exchanges between a leaf and its environment under such conditions probably occur principally by conduction. Similarly, at night the temperature of leaves usually does not deviate greatly from that of the atmosphere.

Leaves sometime have a lower temperature than the surrounding atmosphere. This is generally true, for example, for leaves in the shade or leaves exposed to sunlight of low intensity which are transpiring fairly rapidly. Such leaves are often cooler by several degrees centigrade than the atmosphere. It is also possible for leaves to sometimes lose heat energy by direct radiation to their environment rapidly enough to result in a lowering of their temperature below that of the atmosphere (Curtis, 1936a). This is especially likely to occur on clear nights when the vapor pressure of the atmosphere is low. These conditions favor direct radiation from the leaves to the sky, *i.e.*, to the relatively cold gases of the upper atmosphere.

The temperature of leaves is constantly fluctuating, especially during the daylight hours. Minor fluctuations in leaf temperature result largely from shifts in wind velocity. An increase in wind velocity facilitates heat exchange between the leaf and the atmosphere and hence tends to bring the temperature of the leaf more nearly to that of the atmosphere. Increase in wind velocity therefore results in cooling a leaf which is warmer than the surrounding air. Intermittent sunlight also results in frequent shifts in leaf temperature. Each time the sun is obscured by a cloud there is usually a distinct drop in the temperature of leaves which had been exposed to direct sunlight; each time the sun emerges from behind a cloud there is usually a distinct rise in the temperature of such leaves.

The factors which control the temperatures of other organs of plants are in general similar to those which influence leaf temperatures. The temperature of fleshy leaves, fruits, tree trunks, and succulent stems such as those of cacti may, under direct insolation, often greatly exceed those of the surrounding atmosphere. The side of an apple fruit exposed to direct sunlight, for example, may have a temperature of from 12° to 25°C. higher than the air temperature (Brooks and Fisher, 1926). Similarly, the temperature at the center of cotton bolls exposed to full solar radiation is commonly 6° to 8°C. above that of the air. The temperature of even such an internal tissue shows an immediate and marked shift with changes in the intensity of solar radiation, such as those caused by intermittent cloudiness (Anderson, 1940).

2. *The Influence of Temperature upon Transpiration Rates.*—The effects of temperature upon the rate of stomatal transpiration can be most clearly analyzed in terms of its effect upon the difference in vapor pressures between the intercellular spaces and the outside atmosphere (Renner, 1915). In this part of the discussion it is again assumed that the air movement is sufficient to prevent any appreciable accumulation of

water-vapor in the vicinity of the leaf surfaces. Suppose that the temperature of a leaf with open stomates and the surrounding atmosphere both increase from 20° to 30°C. Unless the leaf is markedly deficient in water this will result in an increase in the vapor pressure of the intercellular spaces from approximately 17.54 mm. Hg to approximately 31.82 mm. Hg, these being the values for saturated atmospheres at 20° and 30°C., respectively. The atmosphere of the leaf intercellular spaces is in direct contact with the relatively extensive evaporating surface of the mesophyll cell walls, hence the vapor pressure in the intercellular spaces tends to remain in equilibrium with the water in the mesophyll cells. In order to simplify this part of the discussion, it will be assumed that the atmosphere of the leaf intercellular spaces maintains essentially a saturation vapor pressure for the prevailing leaf temperature. Under many conditions, as discussed later in this chapter, it seems certain that the intercellular spaces are not maintained in even a near-saturated condition.

In the surrounding atmosphere, however, vapor pressure conditions are very different. On clear days, that is, on the very type of day upon which the highest rates of transpiration occur, there is frequently little change in the vapor pressure of the atmosphere over land surfaces during the course of a single day.[2] Evaporation into the atmosphere is insufficient to permit a rapid building up of the vapor pressure toward the value for a saturated atmosphere as the temperature of the air increases during the day. It might be thought that the process of transpiration itself, occurring on a grand scale from a vegetation-covered area of the earth's surface, would be sufficient to increase the vapor pressure of the lower layers of the atmosphere during the daylight hours. The atmosphere is so vast, however, in relation to the amount of water-vapor lost by plants that, over short periods, transpiration has only a slight effect on its vapor pressure except probably in some local habitats in which free movement of the air is impeded for one reason or another.

Increase in the temperature of the atmosphere does result in an increase in the speed of the water-vapor molecules present. If the volume of the atmosphere remained constant this would result in a small increase in its vapor pressure. But even this effect is never fully realized in the atmosphere because an increase in temperature also results in an expansion of

---

[2] This statement should not be misinterpreted to read that the vapor pressure of the atmosphere is invariable. The magnitude of the vapor pressure of the atmosphere varies greatly from day to day and from season to season, depending upon the prevailing climatic conditions. On cloudy or rainy days, the atmospheric vapor pressure is generally greater than on clear days during the same season; in the summer months it is generally greater than in the winter months, etc. Nevertheless the statement made above that on clear, bright days there is *often* little change in the vapor pressure of the atmosphere is essentially correct (Day, 1917).

the atmosphere, entirely or largely offsetting its influence in increasing vapor pressure.

If we assume, for the purpose of our specific example, that the vapor pressure of the atmosphere at 20°C. was half that of a saturated atmosphere at that temperature—8.77 mm. Hg—then the excess vapor pressure of the leaf over that of the atmosphere at 20°C. was 8.77 mm. Hg (17.54 — 8.77). At 30°C., however, the vapor pressure of the intercellular spaces would have increased to about 31.82 mm. Hg while the increase in the vapor pressure of surrounding atmosphere would in most situations be so small that it can be disregarded in analyzing the effect of temperature upon transpiration. The excess vapor pressure of the intercellular spaces over the atmosphere is now 23.05 mm. Hg (31.82 — 8.77) which will result in diffusion of water-vapor out of the leaf at a rate nearly three times as fast as at 20°C. The effect of a rise in temperature therefore is principally an increase in the steepness of the diffusion pressure gradient (vapor-pressure gradient) of water-vapor through the stomates, and hence an increase in the rate of transpiration.

So far we have considered only examples in which the temperature of a leaf and the surrounding atmospheres are the same. We have already noted, however, that the temperature of leaves exposed to direct sunlight is usually higher than that of the atmosphere. If the temperature of a leaf is increased above that of the surrounding atmosphere by the absorption of solar radiation, the usual effect is an increase in the magnitude of the excess vapor pressure of the intercellular spaces over that of the outside atmosphere. At 30°C. under the conditions stated, the vapor-pressure difference between the intercellular spaces and the atmosphere was about 23.05 mm. Hg. Suppose, however, that, as a result of the absorption of radiant energy, the temperature of the leaf is 35°C. while that of the atmosphere remains at 30°C. Water would evaporate from the walls of the mesophyll cells until the vapor pressure in the intercellular spaces approximates that of a saturated atmosphere at 35°C. (42.18 mm. Hg). The gradient between the intercellular spaces and the atmosphere is therefore increased to about 33.41 mm. Hg (42.18 — 8.77), and the rate of transpiration is correspondingly increased (Curtis, 1936b).

The *rate* of diffusion of water-vapor out of a leaf through the stomates is also influenced by temperature. In general, the higher the temperature for a given gradient, the greater the rate of diffusion. Because of the low temperature coefficient of diffusion (Chap. V), however, this effect is not a very marked one and is decidedly secondary in significance as compared with the effect of temperature on the steepness of the vapor-pressure gradient through the stomates.

Wind.—The effect of wind upon the rate of transpiration is far from simple and depends in part upon the other prevailing environmental con-ditions. Usually, however, increase in wind velocity, within limits, results in an increase in the rate of transpiration (Wrenger, 1935). This is usually explained by assuming that water-vapor often accumulates in the vicinity of transpiring leaves in a quiet atmosphere, especially if they are not exposed to direct sunlight. The result of such an accumulation of water-vapor is a decrease in the steepness of the vapor-pressure gradient through the stomates and hence a decrease in the rate of transpiration. If, how-ever, the leaves are exposed to a wind, any accumulation of water-vapor molecules in the immediate vicinity of the leaf surfaces will be dispersed. The effective result will be an increase in the steepness of the vapor-pres-sure gradient through the stomates, and a consequent increase in the rate of loss of water-vapor.

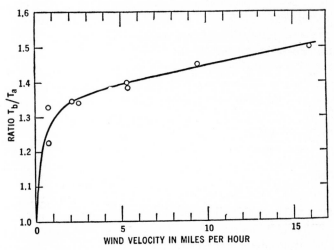

Fig. 45.   Relation between wind velocity and rate of transpiration of sunflower expressed as ratio between plants in wind (T_b) and plants in quiet air (T_a). Data of Martin and Clements (1935).

Whenever a temperature differential exists between a leaf and the sur-rounding atmosphere, convection currents are set up in the gases in the vicinity of a leaf which may largely or entirely prevent any accumula-tion of water-vapor in the immediate vicinity of the leaf. The influence of wind in raising the transpiration rate of leaves is probably more effec-tive, therefore, when they are subjected to such conditions that their temperature does not depart appreciably from that of the surrounding atmosphere. The swaying of branches and shoots, and the bending, twist-ing, and fluttering of leaf blades in the wind also contribute to higher rates of transpiration in moving than in quiet air. It has been shown experimentally that immobile leaves usually transpire less than similar leaves allowed to bend and move freely when both are exposed to wind of equal velocity. Such bending and contortion of leaves may increase the rate of water-vapor loss in part by compressing the intercellular spaces, thus forcing water-vapor and other gases out through the stomates.

A gentle breeze is relatively much more effective in increasing the transpiration rate than winds of greater velocity (Fig. 45). Winds of very high velocity have been observed to have a retarding effect upon transpiration. This probably results from closure of stomates under such conditions. Wind may also exert indirect effects on the rate of transpiration through its influence on the temperature of the leaves, as previously described.

Soil Conditions Influencing the Availability of Water.—Although transpiration can continue for short periods at rates considerably in excess of the rate of absorption of water (Chap. XV), in general, if soil conditions are such that absorption of water is appreciably retarded, the rate of transpiration will soon show a corresponding retardation. The availability of soil water to the plant is therefore an important and, in fact, often the limiting factor in transpiration. The principal soil factors which affect the rate of absorption of water by plants are: (1) available soil water, (2) soil temperature, (3) aeration of the soil, and (4) concentration of solutes in the soil solution (Chap. XIV). All of these factors indirectly influence the rate of transpiration.

Atmospheric Pressure.—It has been demonstrated experimentally that a reduction in atmospheric pressure results in an increase in the rate of transpiration (Sampson and Allen, 1909). This result would be predicted theoretically since reduction in the density of the atmosphere would be expected to permit diffusion of water-vapor to occur into it more rapidly. In any given locality variations in atmospheric pressure are too slight to have any significant effect upon the rate of transpiration. Plants growing at high altitudes are subjected to distinctly lower atmospheric pressures than the plants of lowlands, and in comparative evaluations of the transpiration rates of species growing in these two types of habitats the influence of this factor must be considered.

Effects of Structural Features of Plants on the Rate of Transpiration.—Different kinds of plants, even when growing side by side under virtually identical environmental conditions, may have very different rates of transpiration. In part, such differences in transpiration rate from one kind of a plant to another result from species differences in internal processes and conditions such as osmotic pressures of the leaf cells, imbibitional capacities of the protoplasm and cell walls, and behavior of the stomates. Structural differences, particularly in the leaves, also account in part for unlike rates of water-vapor loss from plants of different species growing in the same environment. It has proved impossible, however, to draw correct inferences regarding the relative rate of transpiration of a plant on the basis of its observed anatomical peculiarities. Many species which, on the basis of their distinctive structural features, have been judged to have a low rate of transpiration, proved upon experimentation to transpire very rapidly when environmental conditions were favorable.

Certain structural features of plants influence the rates of both stomatal and cuticular transpiration. The total leaf surface of the plant is one such factor. The distribution and gross morphology of the root system is another. In a habitat where deep-rooted and shallow-rooted plants grow side by side, the former may transpire more rapidly than the latter during drought periods because their roots penetrate to a soil horizon which still contains available water, while those of the shallow-rooted plants are in a moisture deficient soil. The completeness with which the soil mass is interpenetrated by roots may also influence the rates of water absorption and hence of transpiration. Sorghum, for example, has almost twice as many fibrous roots as maize (Miller, 1916). Rates of water absorption and transpiration can be better maintained, especially in relatively dry soils, by plants with the sorghum type of root system than by those with the maize type. For a given kind of plant, a low shoot-root ratio (Chap. XXXIII) is more favorable to the maintenance of relatively high rates of transpiration than a high shoot-root ratio.

The rates of cuticular transpiration are undoubtedly held to a low value in many species by the cutin layer itself as well as by leaf coatings of waxy or resinous substances which are present on many kinds of plants. The presence of dead epidermal leaf hairs also contributes to maintenance of low rates of cuticular transpiration, but living epidermal hairs have the contrary effect. The presence of dead epidermal hairs on the leaf may also have a retarding effect on the stomatal transpiration of some species, but Sayre (1920) could find little evidence for such an effect in the leaves of mullein (*Verbascum thapsus*).

Rates of stomatal transpiration are influenced by the size, spacing, distribution, and structural peculiarities of the stomates. In some species the stomates are sunken below the general level of the epidermis (Fig. 37D). In general, this should result in a slower rate of diffusion than through stomates of the nonsunken type because of the greater length of the diffusion gradient of water-vapor through sunken stomates. The area of the internal evaporating surface of the mesophyll cell walls in proportion to the surface area of the leaf probably has an influence on the rate of stomatal transpiration, at least under some conditions. Values ranging from 6.8 to 31.3 have been obtained for the ratio of internal exposed surface area to external surface area in leaves of a number of *thicker leaves?* species (Turrell, 1936). The ratio is, in general, higher for xeromorphic than for mesomorphic leaves, and for leaves of a given species which developed under xeric conditions as contrasted with leaves of the same species grown under mesic conditions. Turrell (1944) has shown that xeromorphic leaves of oleander (*Nerium oleander*), with relatively high internal-external surface ratios, transpire more rapidly than the mesomorphic leaves of periwinkle (*Vinca rosea*), with lower internal-external surface ratios. It was also clear from the results, however, that the higher internal-external surface area of the oleander leaves was not the only factor responsible for their higher transpiration rates.

The Daily Periodicity of Transpiration.—All plants exhibit a daily periodicity of transpiration rate which varies somewhat with the species and

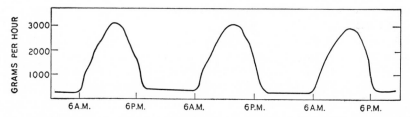

FIG. 46.   Daily periodicity of transpiration of alfalfa on 3 successive days under approximately standard-day conditions. Transpiration expressed as grams per hour per 6-foot square plot of alfalfa (average of two plots). Data of Thomas and Hill (1937).

is greatly influenced by the environmental conditions to which the plant is exposed. We shall first consider the transpiration periodicity upon a standard day as defined in the preceding chapter, since most experiments upon daily variations in transpiration rates have been conducted upon plants growing under approximately such conditions (Briggs and Shantz, 1916; Thomas and Hill, 1937; and others).

During the hours of darkness the transpiration rate (Fig. 46) is generally low, and in most species water loss during this period may be regarded as almost entirely cuticular. It is not justifiable to assume that absolutely no stomatal transpiration occurs at night in any species unless this is definitely known to be true. In some species of plants, as we have already seen, night stomatal opening is a common occurrence, while in others it occurs under certain environmental conditions. Even in those species in which the stomates are normally closed during the hours of darkness, a few may remain open. The transpiration rate shows a steady, and usually consistent, rise during the morning hours which culminates in a maximum rate which is most commonly attained during the early hours of the afternoon.

Following this peak of transpiration, the rate decreases, usually consistently, until the low and virtually steady night rate is attained at approximately the termination of the daylight period.

The daily periodicity in the rate of stomatal transpiration in most species of plants can be interpreted almost entirely in terms of two variable factors: (1) the diffusive capacity of the stomates, and (2) the vapor-pressure gradient between the intercellular spaces of the leaf and the outside atmosphere. In analyzing the daily periodicity of transpiration it is the diffusive capacity of the stomates in the aggregate (*i.e.*, all of the stomates on a plant) which must be considered. The aggregate diffusive capacity of the stomates on a plant on which all of the stomates were half open, for example, would be much greater than that for a similar plant on which half of the stomates were fully open and half fully closed.

With the advent of daylight the stomates open over a period of time which varies in length according to the species and with environmental conditions. Some open earlier or more rapidly than others. The initial rise in the rate of transpiration in the morning is brought about by the opening of the stomates, resulting in a gradual increase in their aggregate diffusive capacity. As each stomate opens a vapor-pressure gradient is established through it between the atmosphere of the intercellular spaces and the outside atmosphere. During the hours of darkness, under standard day conditions, the leaf cells increase in turgidity and the intercellular spaces become saturated with water-vapor. Thus, when the stomates open in the morning the vapor pressure of the intercellular spaces is at the maximum possible for that leaf temperature. This is, on clear days, almost always in excess of the vapor pressure of the atmosphere when the stomates open, and often considerably so. Hence outward diffusion of water-vapor through the stomates usually begins as soon as they are open.

Once a stomate is well open, minor variations in the size of the stomatal aperture have relatively little effect on the rate of water-vapor loss through it. The rate of transpiration continues to increase, however, for some time after the stomates, in the aggregate, have attained their maximum diffusive capacity. This is because of a gradual increase in the steepness of the vapor-pressure gradient through the stomates. As the day progresses the temperatures of both the atmosphere and the leaf increase; if the latter is in direct sunlight its temperature is invariably somewhat in excess of that in the atmosphere. On clear days, as previously described, the vapor pressure of the intercellular spaces usually increases relative to that of the atmosphere with a rise in temperature. The steep-

ness of the vapor-pressure gradient between the internal atmosphere of
the leaf and the external atmosphere therefore usually increases progressively during the earlier part of the day, and this is the important
factor accounting for a rise in the transpiration rate once the stomates
have attained approximately their maximum diffusive capacity.

Almost from the moment when the stomates begin to open in the morning, a train of events is set in operation in the plant which ultimately
causes a reduction in the rate of transpiration. During approximately the
first half of the day, however, these factors are more than offset by the
factors resulting in an increase in the rate of transpiration. In most
plants, while transpiration is occurring rapidly, the rate of absorption of
water does not keep pace with the rate at which water-vapor is lost from
the leaves. This results in a reduction in the water content of the entire
plant, and especially that of the leaves. Under more extreme conditions
wilting results, but under standard day conditions the leaves seldom pass
beyond the stage of *incipient wilting* (Chap. XV), which corresponds
only to a partial loss of turgor by the leaf cells.

In the preceding discussion, in order to simplify analysis of the dynamics of stomatal transpiration, we have always assumed that the intercellular spaces are saturated with water-vapor. There are good reasons
for believing, however, that with a decrease in the water content and
turgidity of the leaf cells, that intercellular vapor pressures are reduced
to considerably less than saturation values. The results of Thut (1939)
offer experimental support for such a view.

The increase in the diffusion-pressure deficit of the leaf cells which
accompanies a decrease in their turgidity would result in a lowering of
the vapor pressure of the intercellular spaces, but this effect is small, the
decrease in vapor pressure being only about 2 per cent, for example, for
a rise in diffusion-pressure deficit of 25 atm.

Of probably greater influence in reducing the vapor pressure of the
intercellular spaces is the reduced permeability of the cell walls to water
resulting from the increase in the osmotic pressure of the leaf cells which
accompanies decrease in their water content (Boon-Long, 1941). Such a
reduction in cell-wall permeability may prevent passage of water across
the walls with sufficient rapidity to permit maintenance of an equilibrium
vapor pressure between the cell sap and the outer surface of the cell walls.
The vapor pressure of the intercellular spaces will be correspondingly
reduced, the steepness of the vapor-pressure gradient between the intercellular spaces and the outside atmosphere decreased, and the rate of
transpiration diminished. The greater the decrease in the water content
of the leaf, in general, the greater this effect should be.

During the course of a day, however, the steepness of the vapor-pressure gradient through the stomates may be decreased in still another and perhaps more important way. When the stomates open in the morning the vapor-pressure gradient between the saturated internal leaf atmosphere and the outside atmosphere is short, being approximately equal in length to the depth of the guard cells. As the day advances the rapid loss of water-vapor molecules out of the intercellular spaces, perhaps coupled with a gradual reduction in the vapor pressure of the cell walls, makes it less and less likely that a condition of saturation or near saturation can be maintained throughout the intercellular spaces. The zone in which a vapor pressure even approaching a saturation value is maintained almost certainly shrinks more and more deeply into the intercellular spaces. Eventually it may be restricted to a thin layer just above the evaporating surfaces of the mesophyll cell walls. This gradual lengthening of the vapor-pressure gradient through the stomates is probably an important factor in bringing about a reduction in the rate of transpiration during the afternoon hours.

By late afternoon the air temperature and the intensity of the solar radiation begin to decrease appreciably, thus inducing a decrease in the temperature of the leaf. This lowering of the leaf temperature may further decrease the vapor pressure of the intercellular spaces, and hence further depress the steepness of the vapor-pressure gradient, since temperature changes have very little influence on the vapor pressure of the outside atmosphere under standard day conditions. Thus the effect of a reduction in the vapor-pressure gradient through the stomates in decreasing the rate of transpiration, which first becomes apparent during the midday period, continues with augmented effect as the hours of darkness approach.

Diminution of leaf water content as a result of an excess of transpiration over absorption of water also results in a decrease in the turgor of the guard cells. This results in a gradual closure of the stomates. Some of the stomates on a plant probably begin to close even before the time at which the peak rate of transpiration is attained. In all likelihood stomates near the margin or tip of a leaf begin to close before those in the middle, since the effects of a deficiency of water usually appear first in the marginal tissues of a leaf. With increasing leaf water deficits gradual closure is induced in more and more of the stomates. As a result there is a gradual reduction in the aggregate diffusive capacity of the stomatal population of the plant during the afternoon hours.

The decreasing effects on stomatal transpiration of the diminishing steepness of the vapor-pressure gradient through the stomates and of gradual stomatal closure probably overlap during most of the afternoon hours. The relative importance of these two effects in reducing the rate of stomatal transpiration varies with environmental conditions and probably also with the kind of plant. At times one of these factors may limit the rate of escape of water-vapor through the stomates, at times the other. In general, whenever the stomates are appreciably open the steepness of the vapor-pressure gradient largely controls the rate of stomatal transpiration, but as the stomates approach complete closure their diffusive capacity becomes the controlling factor. It seems probable that most commonly the former of these two factors usually limits stomatal transpiration during the early afternoon hours under standard day conditions, while the latter is limiting during the later hours of the afternoon. By late afternoon complete closure of virtually all the stomates has occurred and stomatal transpiration is terminated. During the ensuing hours of darkness the rate of water-vapor loss from the plant is controlled by the factors which influence cuticular transpiration.

Under environmental conditions deviating from those which were postulated in the preceding discussion, transpiration periodicity curves may be entirely different from those shown in Fig. 46. Variations in temperature, light intensity, humidity, and soil water supply may all markedly influence both the trend of transpiration periodicity and the magnitude of the daily water-vapor loss.

Low temperatures may result in a complete elimination of stomatal transpiration by inducing stomatal closure.

Low light intensities, such as those existing on cloudy days, are unfavorable to stomatal opening in most species. The stomates seldom open completely under such conditions and the period during which they are open is usually of shorter duration than on clear days. Furthermore, the vapor-pressure gradient through the stomates is seldom as steep on such days as on clear days, since leaf temperatures never appreciably exceed atmospheric temperatures except when exposed to direct sunlight, and atmospheric vapor pressures are usually higher during cloudy days than on clear days at the same season of the year. The magnitude of transpiration under such conditions is usually greatly reduced, and transpiration periodicity curves plotted for plants exposed to such conditions usually present a greatly flattened appearance.

A deficient soil water supply is most commonly the factor which causes marked departures from the type of transpiration periodicity already considered, especially during the summer months. A reduction in soil water content has two pronounced effects upon the daily march of transpiration. The total daily magnitude of water loss is decreased, and the peak of the transpiration curve often occurs somewhat earlier in the day than under conditions of abundant soil water supply. Since, even in temperate regions, periods of decreased soil water supply are of common occurrence during the summer months, and in many habitats are the rule rather than the exception, transpiration periodicity curves of this type (Fig. 47) are, for many species of plants, much of the time more nearly representative than the curves shown in Fig. 46.

Internal factors may also be responsible for transpiration periodicities of a different trend from those which have already been discussed. In some species of plants, as has already been described, the stomates remain open to a greater or lesser extent during the hours of darkness. Such plants have higher transpiration rates at night than those in which the stomates are closed. In some species of cacti there is a complete inversion

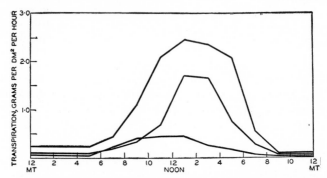

Fig. 47. Daily periodicity of transpiration of bean (*Phaseolus vulgaris*) for 3 successive days during a period when the soil was gradually becoming drier. Data of Chung (1935).

of the usual transpiration periodicity curve, transpiration rates being regularly greater at night than in the daytime. This appears to be a result of a complete or nearly complete stomatal closure during the hours of daylight, while the stomates are, as a rule, open at night (Shreve, 1916).

Seasonal Variations in Transpiration Rates.—In temperate regions transpiration occurs predominantly during the warmer months of the year, and especially during those periods of the warm season when the soil water supply is abundant. Among the deciduous group of woody perennials, the branches are defoliated during most of the autumn, all of the winter, and the earlier part of the spring. Although the twigs and branches which remain exposed to the atmosphere are completely encased in corky layers of bark and the buds are enclosed within cutinized bud scales, some water loss occurs from such species even during the winter months. Young twigs lose water-vapor under such conditions faster than older ones. Winter transpiration rates of deciduous woody plants are always negligible in comparison with summer rates. In most evergreen species of either the needle-leaved or broad-leaved type, the transpiration rates do not differ greatly at most times during the winter from the rates for deciduous trees at that season (Weaver and Mogensen 1919, Kozlowski 1943). Failure of the stomates to open as a result of the prevalence of low temperatures is doubtless one of the causes of low winter transpiration rates in evergreens. The low leaf water contents usually prevailing at that season are probably also a factor in maintaining the stomates in the closed condition during the winter.

Mild periods of any considerable duration often have a detrimental effect upon evergreen species in regions where a cold climate usually prevails during the winter months. The warm air temperatures induce stomatal opening, and a relatively high rate of transpiration ensues. The water in the surface layers of soil may remain frozen, and thus unavailable, during a period of warm air temperatures. Even if none of the soil water is frozen, soil temperatures will be low, and this greatly retards the rate of absorption of water (Chap. XIV). The combined effect of a relatively high transpiration rate and relatively low absorption rate results in a gradual desiccation of the leaves and branches of the plant. This diminution in the water content of the aerial organs during warm periods in winter is more severe in windy weather and is more likely to occur if a sequence of mild days follows immediately after a cold spell. If severe enough, this desiccation results in the death of some of the branches, or in extreme cases of the entire tree or shrub. This is one cause of the phenomenon known as *winter-killing*. Winter-killing resulting from desiccation of the tissues should not be confused with cold injury resulting from low temperatures, which is a different phenomenon (Chap. XXX).

SUGGESTED FOR COLLATERAL READING

Burgerstein, A. *Die Transpiration der Pflanzen.* I, II, and III. Gustav Fischer. Jena. 1904, 1920, 1925.
Maximov, N, A. *The Plant in Relation to Water.* R. H. Yapp, Editor. George Allen and Unwin. London. 1929.
Seybold, A. *Die physikalische Komponente der pflanzlichen Transpiration.* Julius Springer. Berlin. 1929.

SELECTED BIBLIOGRAPHY

Anderson, D. B. The internal temperatures of cotton bolls. *Amer. Jour. Bot.* **27**: 43-51. 1940.
Boon-Long, T. S. Transpiration as influenced by osmotic concentration and cell permeability. *Amer. Jour. Bot.* **28**: 333-343. 1941.
Briggs, L. J., and H. L. Shantz. Hourly transpiration rate on clear days as determined by cyclic environmental factors. *Jour. Agric. Res.* **5**: 583-649. 1916.
Brooks, C., and D. F. Fisher. Some high temperature effects in apples: contrasts in the two sides of an apple. *Jour. Agric. Res.* **32**: 1-16. 1926.

Brown, H., and F. Escombe. Researches on some of the physiological processes of green leaves, etc. *Proc. Roy. Soc. (London)* B **76**: 29-137. 1905.

Chung, C. H. A study of certain aspects of the phenomenon of transpiration periodicity. Dissertation Ph.D. Ohio State University. 1935.

Curtis, O. F. Leaf temperatures and the cooling of leaves by radiation. *Plant Physiol.* **11**: 343-364. 1936a.

Curtis, O. F. Comparative effects of altering leaf temperatures and air humidities on vapor pressure gradients. *Plant Physiol.* **11**: 595-603. 1936b.

Day, P. C. Relative humidities and vapor pressures over the United States. *Mo. Weather Rev. Supplement 6*. 1917.

Kozlowski, T. T. Transpiration rates of some forest tree species during the dormant season. *Plant Physiol.* **18**: 252-260. 1943.

Martin, E. V. Effect of solar radiation on transpiration of *Helianthus annuus*. *Plant Physiol.* **10**: 341-354. 1935.

Martin, E. V. Studies of evaporation and transpiration under controlled conditions. *Carnegie Inst. Wash. Publ. No. 550*. Washington. 1943.

Martin, E. V., and F. E. Clements. Studies of the effect of artificial wind on growth and transpiration in *Helianthus annuus*. *Plant Physiol.* **10**: 613-636. 1935.

Miller, E. C. Comparative study of the root systems and leaf areas of corn and the sorghums. *Jour. Agric. Res.* **6**: 311-332. 1916.

Renner, O. Beiträge zur Physik der Transpiration. *Flora* **100**: 451-547. 1910.

Renner, O. Theoretisches und experimentelles zur Kohäsionstheorie der Wasserbewegung. *Jahrb. Wiss. Bot.* **56**: 617-667. 1915.

Sampson, A. W., and L. M. Allen. Influence of physical factors on transpiration. *Minn. Bot. Studies* **4**: 33-59. 1909.

Sayre, J. D. The relation of hairy leaf coverings to the resistance of leaves to transpiration. *Ohio Jour. Sci.* **20**: 55-86. 1920.

Shreve, Edith. An analysis of the causes of variations in the transpiring power of cacti. *Physiol. Res.* **2**: 73-127. 1916.

Thomas, M. D., and G. R. Hill. The continuous measurement of photosynthesis, respiration, and transpiration of alfalfa and wheat growing under field conditions. *Plant Physiol.* **12**: 285-307. 1937.

Thut, H. F. The relative humidity gradient of stomatal transpiration. *Amer. Jour. Bot.* **26**: 315-319. 1939.

Turrell, F. M. The area of the internal exposed surface of dicotyledon leaves. *Amer. Jour. Bot.* **23**: 255-264. 1936.

Turrell, F. M. Correlation between internal surface and transpiration rate in mesomorphic and xeromorphic leaves grown under artificial light. *Bot. Gaz.* **105**: 413-425. 1944.

Weaver, J. E., and A. Mogensen. Relative transpiration of coniferous and broad-leaved trees in autumn and winter. *Bot. Gaz.* **68**: 393-424. 1919.

Wrenger, Maria. Über den Einfluss des Windes auf die Transpiration der Pflanzen. *Zeitschr. Bot.* **29**: 257-320. 1935.

DISCUSSION QUESTIONS

1. Plot curves which would be representative of the daily variations in the vapor pressure of the atmosphere: (1) out-of-doors on a perfectly clear summer day, (2) out-of-doors on a perfectly clear winter day, (3) in a closed greenhouse

well populated with plants on a clear winter day, (4) out-of-doors on a clear late spring day with a heavy dew in the morning, (5) out-of-doors during a summer day on which a heavy thunderstorm occurs in the late afternoon.

2. Why is the air of the California and Arizona semi-deserts considered "dry" when it contains approximately the same quantity of water-vapor per unit of volume as the "moist" air of the Minnesota lake country?

3. Cell A has an osmotic pressure of 30 atm. and a turgor pressure of 15 atm. Cell B has an osmotic pressure of 30 atm. and a zero turgor pressure. Cell C has an osmotic pressure of 30 atm. and the water within it is under a tension of 15 atm. From which of these cells will water evaporate most rapidly? Least rapidly? Explain.

4. If half the leaves were removed from a plant what effect would this have on the rate of transpiration per unit area from the remaining leaves?

5. Assuming a saturated atmosphere in the intercellular spaces, open stomates, and sufficient air movement to prevent accumulation of water-vapor around the leaves, which plant will lose water-vapor more rapidly—one in an environment of 80 per cent relative humidity and 40°C. temperature or one in an environment of 80 per cent relative humidity and 20°C. temperature? Explain.

6. Making the same assumptions as in the preceding question which would have the greater effect on the rate of transpiration—an increase in leaf temperature from 30° to 35°C., or a decrease in atmospheric relative humidity from 80 to 60 per cent, air temperature remaining at 30°C.? Explain.

7. The following statement is sometimes encountered: "The rate of transpiration usually increases during the forepart of a summer day because of the decrease in relative humidity which occurs during that period." Evaluate.

8. A well-watered potted plant is growing under conditions of constant light, temperature, and humidity in a current of air from a fan. The fan is turned off and the rate of transpiration decreases. After a few minutes the fan is turned on again and the rate of transpiration is found, temporarily at least, to be higher than just before the fan was turned off. Explain.

9. When exposed to direct sunlight and otherwise identical environmental conditions, which will become warmer, a thick leaf or a thin one? Explain.

10. Will the rate of transpiration at night from a plant on which stomates are open necessarily be greater than that from a similar plant under the same conditions in which the stomates are closed? Explain.

11. Can transpiration ever occur in a saturated atmosphere? Explain.

XII

THE TRANSLOCATION OF WATER

Most terrestrial plants obtain the water which is necessary for their existence from the soil. An overwhelmingly large proportion of the water which is absorbed by the roots of land plants is lost in the process of transpiration. Smaller quantities are utilized in growth and in photosynthesis, and in some species limited amounts of water may be lost by guttation. Water must therefore move through the intervening tissues and organs from the absorbing regions of the root to the tissues in which it is utilized, or from which it passes out of the plant. The process whereby water moves through the plant is termed the *conduction, transport,* or *translocation* of water.

In herbaceous species and many shrubby plants the distance through which water moves in passing from the root tips to the leaves is usually not more than a few feet. Even in such plants appearances are sometimes deceptive, as some herbaceous and shrubby species such as alfalfa may have such deep root systems that some of the absorbed water often ascends for distances as great as 20 feet or more before it reaches the level of the soil surface. It is in trees, however, that the most striking illustrations of the upward movement of water occur. The tallest tree of which we have an authentic record is a specimen of the Coast Redwood (*Sequoia sempervirens*) which has attained a height of 364 feet (Tiemann, 1935). Many other individuals of this species and of several others, including the Big Trees (*Sequoia gigantea*) of California, the Douglas Fir (*Pseudotsuga douglasi*) of the Pacific Northwest, and the Blue Gums (*Eucalyptus*) of Australia exceed 300 feet in height. Trees ranging from 100 to 200 feet in height were of common occurrence in the virgin forests of eastern North America. Since the root systems of trees always penetrate at least a few feet into the ground, the actual vertical distance through which at least a part of the water absorbed is elevated is always more than the height of the tree. In trees, therefore, water must ascend to heights ranging up to nearly 400 feet above the level of water absorption.

The mechanism by which this feat is accomplished in tall trees has been the subject of much experimentation and even more speculation. The ensuing discussion of the "ascent of sap" through plants will be principally in terms of its movement through trees, because much of the experimental work on this problem has been performed on woody species. Any explanation of this phenomenon which can be shown to be adequate for tall trees should also prove satisfactory for vascular species of lesser stature.

The water which moves through plants is not pure, but almost invariably contains dissolved in it small quantities of inorganic solutes, and often organic solutes as well (Chap. XXVII). This dilute solution is often called the *xylem sap*.

The Path of Water Through the Plant.—Water enters the plant mainly through the epidermal cells and root hairs at or near the tips of the roots and crosses the cortex, endodermis, and a part of the pericycle before it finally enters the lumina of the vessels or tracheids of the root xylem

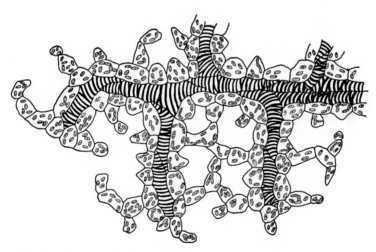

Fig. 48. Termination of vessels in the mesophyll of an apple leaf.

(Fig. 67). Once in the xylem ducts its general direction of movement is upward. The xylem tissue is continuous from just back of the tips of the roots, through the roots, into and through the stems, the petioles of leaves, and ultimately, usually only after much branching, terminates in the mesophyll of the leaf (Fig. 48). Thousands of vascular bundles may terminate within 1 cm.² of leaf area. The xylem tissue through which the water moves is thus a continuous unit system within the body of the plant. Along most of its course the water moves *en masse* through the vessels or tracheids. From the xylem ducts in the leaves the water passes into the mesophyll cells. In the mesophyll it moves from cell to cell, eventually most of it being lost from the cells by evaporation into the intercellular spaces. The movement of water through the cells of the root and leaf mesophyll must be regarded as integral parts of the process of translocation of water.

Although the great bulk of the water which passes through the plant follows the route just described and is lost in the transpirational process, small quantities escape this fate. All along the path of its movement small amounts of water pass into adjacent living cells and are utilized in cell enlargement, especially in the cambium layer. Actively growing stem tips, root tips, and fruits also utilize considerable quantities of water, principally in the enlargement phase of growth, while chlorophyllous cells utilize water in the photosynthetic process. In most species, however, not more than 1 or 2 per cent of the water which enters a plant is utilized in growth and metabolic processes, the remainder being lost from the plant in transpiration.

That the xylem is the principal water-conducting tissue of plants has been recognized at least since the time of the girdling experiments of Malpighi in 1671. Girdling (or "ringing") a stem, so that all of the tissues external to the xylem are removed, does not prevent movement of water to organs attached to that stem above the ring. On the contrary, cutting through the xylem tissue of a stem results in almost immediate wilting of leaves attached to the stem above the ring.

Anatomy of Stems.—Since the mechanism of the movement of water can scarcely be understood intelligently without some knowledge of the anatomy of the tissues through which it moves, a brief review of stem structure is desirable before proceeding further with a discussion of this process. Stems vary greatly in their structure, every species possessing some anatomical features which are peculiar to itself. Nevertheless certain general patterns of tissue arrangement have been found to prevail, and the stem structure of most species approximates one or another of these general arrangements.

The stem anatomy of two representative species is shown in Fig. 49 and Fig. 50, which are self-explanatory. The corn stem represents an herbaceous monocot type of structure while that of the tulip poplar is typical of woody dicot stems.

The structure of woody stems cannot properly be appreciated merely from a consideration of one-year-old stems. The *primary tissues* of such stems develop from tissues formed at the apical growing tip during

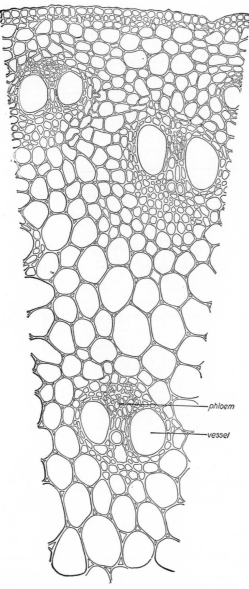

FIG. 49. Segment of young corn (maize) stem as seen in cross section. Three vascular bundles and parts of two others are shown. The large-celled tissue between the bundles is sometimes classed as pith; sometimes as parenchyma.

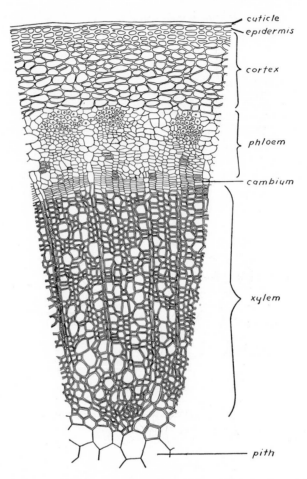

cuticle
epidermis

cortex

phloem

cambium

xylem

pith

FIG. 50. Segment of young stem of tulip poplar (*Liriodendron tulipifera*) as seen in cross section.

growth of the stem in length. Nearly all perennial stems also grow in diameter as a result of the development of *secondary tissues* from the cambium. By successive stages of division, enlargement, and differentiation of cambial cells additional layers of xylem (*secondary xylem*) are laid down on the inner face of the cambium, and new layers of phloem tissue (*secondary phloem*) on its outer face (Fig. 51). Secondary growth of woody stems is initiated during the first season of their development and continues during each growing season thereafter. Hence after a few years the great bulk of any woody stem is composed of secondary tissues. The apical and lateral growth of woody stems and the relation of these processes to the formation of the primary and secondary tissues of the stem are considered in more detail in Chap. XXIX.

Secondary xylem and secondary phloem also develop from the cambium in most herbaceous dicot stems, but in such species the cambium in any one stem is never active for more than one growing season.

The spring-formed xylem tissue, as viewed in cross section, is usually distinctly different in aspect from that formed later in the season. In many angiosperms the "spring" wood contains more and larger vessels, and the cell walls are generally thinner than in the subsequently formed "summer" wood. In the conifers the spring-formed tracheids are thinner-walled and of larger cross-sectional diameter than those formed later in the growing season. The transition from spring to summer wood is often a very gradual one. On the other hand, the more open xylem tissues formed each spring abut directly upon the denser tissues which were produced during the preceding summer, thus giving rise to an abrupt line of demarcation between the zones of xylem formed in any two successive seasons. The result of this growth behavior is that a cross section of the trunk or a branch of any tree appears as a system of concentric layers, the so-called *annual*

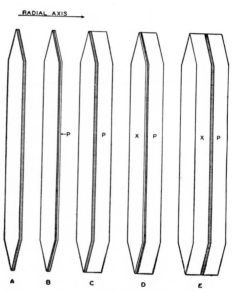

RADIAL AXIS

FIG. 51. Diagram illustrating formation of phloem and xylem elements from the cambium. (*A*) A cambium initial, (*B*) division of cambium cell, (*C*) outer cell resulting from division becomes a phloem element, (*D*) another division of the cambium cell, (*E*) inner cell resulting from second division becomes a xylem element. Actually several xylem or several phloem elements are often formed successively. Upon maturation most of the xylem and phloem elements acquire sizes and shapes which are very different from those of the cambium initials from which they originate.

rings, each representing an annual increment of growth. In rare cases no annual rings or more than one annual ring may be produced in a season, but usually each ring represents the xylem resulting from the activity of the cambium during one season (Glock, 1941).

In many woody species, as the xylem tissues increase in age, important changes occur in the color, composition, and structure of the various elements, resulting in the conversion of *sapwood* into *heartwood*. As sapwood ripens into heartwood the walls of any remaining living cells of the xylem become increasingly lignified, death of these cells soon follow-

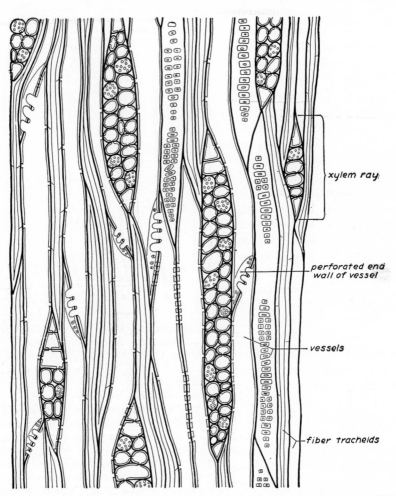

Fɪɢ. 52.   Tangential section of a small portion of the wood of a tulip tree (*Liriodendron tulipifera*). This is a plane section except that the end walls of the vessels have been shown in perspective in order to indicate their structure clearly. Most of the vessels and fiber tracheids show in sectional view, but a few show as the surface view of the tangential wall. Surface and sectional views of bordered pits show in the vessel walls. Simple pits show in the end walls of the ray cells and between ray cells. Half-bordered pits show between vessels and ray cells. Adapted from a drawing by L. G. Livingston.

ing. The water content of the tissues is generally reduced, and such compounds as oils, resins, gums, and tannins accumulate in the cells or cell
walls. The darker coloration of the heartwood of most species as compared
to the sapwood is caused by such accumulations.

In mature trees the heartwood becomes merely a central supporting
column surrounded by a cylinder of sapwood which varies in thickness
from a few to many annual layers, depending upon the species and the

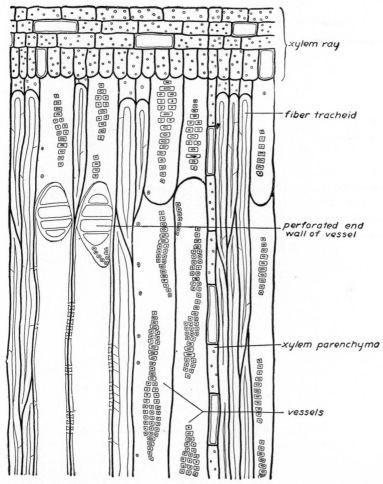

Fig. 53. Radial section of a small portion of the wood of a tulip tree (*Liriodendron tulipifera*). Most of the vessels show as a surface view of the walls; two are in sectional view. Surface and sectional views of bordered pits show in vessel walls. Simple pits show in surface view in the walls of the xylem ray and xylem parenchyma cells. Adapted from a drawing by L. G. Livingston.

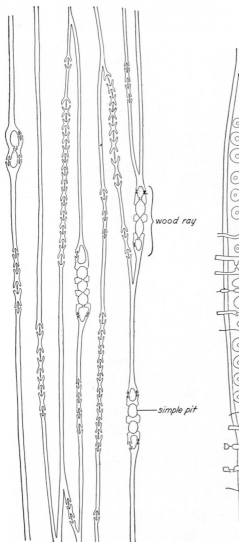

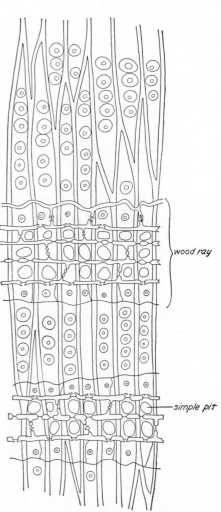

FIG. 54. Tangential section of a small portion of the wood of white pine (*Pinus strobus*). The vertically oriented elongated elements are tracheids. Bordered pits show in sectional view in the tracheid and marginal ray cells. Simple pits show in sectional view in the other ray cells. Half-bordered pits show between marginal ray cells and other ray cells.

FIG. 55. Radial section of a small portion of the wood of white pine (*Pinus strobus*). The vertically oriented elongated elements are tracheids. Bordered pits show in face view in the tracheids; in sectional view in the marginal ray cells. Simple pits show in surface and sectional views in the ray cells. Half-bordered pits show between marginal ray cells and other ray cells. Three rows of marginal ray cells show in outline only.

environmental conditions under which the tree was growing. In some species (apple, elm) the heartwood remains virtually saturated with water, while in others (ash) it becomes relatively dry. The water in the heartwood of such species as apple and elm appears to be largely static and is not directly involved in translocation.

Coincident with the development of secondary xylem, secondary phloem tissues also develop from the cambium (Chap. XXVII). Cork cambiums

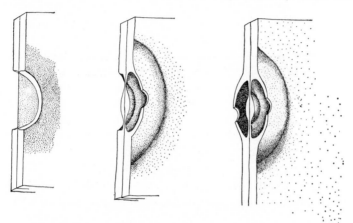

FIG. 56. Perspective diagram illustrating types of pits in white pine (*Pinus strobus*): right, full-bordered pit; middle, half-bordered pit; left, simple pit.

are also initiated in the bark which produce cork layers. Profound modifications therefore occur in the outer tissues as well as in the xylem of woody stems as they grow older.

A somewhat more detailed concept of the structure of the cells and elements of the stems of angiosperms through which the movement of water occurs is presented in Fig. 52 and Fig. 53, which represent longitudinal tangential and radial sections from the xylem of a tulip tree which may be taken as representative for this group of plants. Fig. 54 and Fig. 55 illustrate in a similar way the structure of the xylem tissues of the white pine—a representative gymnosperm. The following discussion merely amplifies somewhat the facts depicted graphically in these two figures.

The xylem tissues of the wood of angiosperms are composed of vessels, tracheids, fibers of several types, wood parenchyma. and xylem ray cells. There is a tremendous variability in the proportional distribution and arrangement of these tissues according to species.

The most characteristic elements in the xylem tissue of angiosperms are the vessels. These are, in general, more or less tubular structures which may extend through many feet of the xylem. In some species cross walls, usually perforated, are of frequent occurrence in vessels, in others such cross walls are infrequent or lacking. In diameter vessels may range in trees from about 20 μ to about 400 μ. In vines they may be as much as 700 μ in diameter. The vessels branch extensively in certain regions of the plant, especially at nodes, within the leaf lamina, and in those parts of root systems where root branching occurs.

The vessels of the *protoxylem* (the first cells of the xylem to mature during the ontogeny of a growing stem or root tip) have cellulose walls, reinforced by distinctive lignified thickenings, which appear as rings, spirals, or other characteristic patterns. The vessels that develop later in the ontogeny of any growing tip have lignified, usually pitted walls which lack any of the thickenings that distinguish the walls of the vessels of the protoxylem.

Pits occur, not only in all parts of vessel walls which are contiguous with other vessels or cells, but also in the walls of the majority of plant cells. Three main types of pits, *simple pits, bordered pits,* and *half bordered pits,* are found in plant cell walls (Fig. 56; *cf.* also Figs. 52, 53, 54, 55). Strictly speaking the term pit refers only to the opening in the secondary wall of one cell, the term *pit pair* often being used to designate the two complementary pits of adjacent cells.

The stages in the development of a vessel, which is a more complex phenomenon than the formation of the other elements of the wood, are

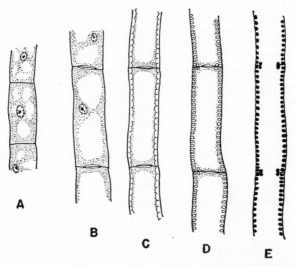

A   B   C   D   E

Fig. 57. Stages in the development of a vessel in the petiole of celery. (*A*) enlarged cambial cell, (*B*) young vessel segment showing lenticular thickenings on the end walls, (*C*) end walls still present in vessel segments with spiral thickenings forming on lateral walls, (*D*) protoplasm disintegrating in vessel segments, spiral thickening on thin portions of end walls, (*E*) mature vessel in which the end walls have disappeared. Redrawn in part from Esau (1936).

indicated in Fig. 57. The original cell resulting from the division of a cambium cell increases rapidly in diameter, simultaneously developing a rather prominent vacuole. Secondary lignified layers develop on the longitudinal walls of the *vessel segment* following which disintegration of the protoplasm and dissolution of the end walls occur. The result of this series of processes is the formation of a typical tubular, nonliving *vessel* by the coalescence of a number of vessel segments each of which has been differentiated from a single cell originating from a division of a cambium cell. In many species, especially of woody plants, vessel formation does not occur in as regular a manner as just described. In many such species the ends of the vessel segments overlap and openings develop in the side walls near the ends (Fig. 52).

Tracheids are found in the wood of many, but not all, species of angiosperms. They are typically more or less spindle-shaped cells with thick walls which are almost always lignified. As viewed in cross section they are usually angular. Mature tracheids contain no protoplasm and hence are nonliving like the xylem vessels. The largest tracheids are about 5 mm. in length, and about 30 μ in diameter. The walls of tracheids are pitted like those of vessels. Tracheids are water-conducting cells, but in most angiosperms they are relatively of much less importance as channels through which water moves than the vessels.

Tracheids are developed from the cambium by a process essentially similar to that by which vessel segments are formed, except that the size and shape of the resulting cells are different, and that there is no coalescence of the individual elements such as occurs in the formation of vessels.

The xylem of the angiosperms also contains fibers of various types, which in general are similar to the tracheids in structure except that usually they have thicker walls, smaller lumina, and fewer and smaller pits. Fiber cells are nonliving and their walls are lignified. Because of their thick walls and small lumina the fibers do not play an important part in the movement of water through stems.

The xylem tissue of practically all angiosperms also contains wood parenchyma cells which, unlike the elements already described, remain alive for some time after their differentiation. Usually death of the wood parenchyma cells does not occur until the wood of which they are a part is converted into heartwood. Wood parenchyma cells are generally somewhat elongate, and roughly four-angled in cross section. They occur in the xylem as vertical series of cells placed end to end. The strands of wood parenchyma thus formed often extend for long distances in a vertical direction through the wood. The distribution of the wood parenchyma strands throughout the annual ring of xylem tissue varies with the species.

In some they are more or less scattered through the xylem, in others they occur in the last layer or two of cells which are produced in the summer wood—in other words, at the termination of the season's growth—and in others only in contact with the vessels, or in contact with other wood parenchyma cells which are themselves in contact with the vessels.

All of the xylem elements previously described are oriented with their long axes in a vertical direction. In addition to this vertical system there is also present in the xylem a transverse, radiating system in which the long axis of the cells is at right angles to the long axis of the stem. These transversely oriented tissue units are known as *vascular rays*. In the stems of most species they are continuous from the outer extremity of the phloem through the cambium into the xylem, which they penetrate to a greater or lesser distance. The portion of the vascular ray found in the xylem is termed the *xylem ray* or *wood ray;* that found in the phloem the *phloem ray*. Xylem rays may vary from one to many cells in thickness and likewise in height, certain types usually being characteristic of any one species (Figs. 52-55). The cells of the xylem rays, like those of the wood parenchyma, usually remain alive until the woody tissue is converted into heartwood. The cells of the xylem ray are typically elongate and more or less angular in cross section. The xylem rays probably serve as routes along which lateral movement of water occurs from the xylem to the cambium and phloem, and along which translocation of soluble foods takes place from the phloem to the living cells of the xylem.

The living cells are in contact at various points with the strands of living wood parenchyma cells. The vertically oriented wood parenchyma strands and transversely oriented xylem ray strands thus form a unit system of living cells within the woody cylinder. Hence there is present a continuous intermeshing network of living cells throughout the greater mass of nonliving vessels, tracheids, and fibers in the younger portions of any woody angiosperm stem. There are probably few if any of the conducting elements—vessels and tracheids—which are not in contact at one or more points with this continuous system of living cells.

The wood of the gymnosperms is simpler in its structure than that of the angiosperms, this group of woody species also showing, in general, a greater uniformity in stem structure than the latter group. The only cell types universally present in the wood of coniferous trees are the tracheids and wood ray cells. Wood parenchyma cells are also present in the wood of most species of conifers, while in many species tracheid-like fiber cells are also present. The most important distinction between the wood of conifers and that of angiosperms is the total absence of vessels in the former.

The tracheids are the distinctive element in conifer wood, constituting as they do the great bulk of all the woody tissues present in such species. In conifers the tracheids form a densely packed type of woody tissue, composed of interlocking cells. Vertically contiguous tracheids always overlap along their tapering portions (Fig. 60). Movement of water and solutes from one tracheid to another is facilitated by means of the pit pairs in the adjacent walls. Because of the numerous cross walls in a xylem tissue composed almost entirely of tracheids, water encounters a greater resistance in moving through such tissues than in traversing woody tissues which contain vessels. Nevertheless it is interesting to note that the tallest trees in the world are conifers in which upward translocation of water occurs through tracheids.

Developmental aspects of the xylem tissues are given further consideration in Chap. XXIX.

Theories of the Mechanism of the Translocation of Water Through Plants. —A number of theories of the mechanism by which the ascent of xylem sap is brought about in plants have been suggested, and it is probable that more than one mechanism is involved in the process. The present state of our knowledge justifies a discussion of three possible mechanisms of the upward transport of water through plants.

"Vital Theories."—Although the vessels and tracheids through which longitudinal transit of water occurs are nonliving, they are always in more or less intimate contact with living cells. Suggestions have therefore been made from time to time that the upward translocation of water is brought about in some manner by the living cells of the stem, although there is almost no direct evidence in favor of such a view. Bose (1923) has been one of the most ardent advocates of a "vital" theory of the upward movement of water in plants.

The experiments of Strasburger (1893) demonstrated quite clearly that the primary mechanism of the rise of sap in trees operates independently of the living cells of the stem. He performed many experiments on the movement of water through woody stems in which the living cells had been killed by one method or another. In one experiment, for example, he used a 75-year-old oak tree about 22 meters high. This was sawed off close to the ground and the cut end of the trunk immersed in a solution of picric acid, which is toxic to living cells. The picric acid solution slowly moved up the stem. Fuchsin, added to the liquid in which the basal end of the tree was immersed 3 days after the picric acid, also ascended to the top of the tree through tissues in which the living cells had been killed by the picric acid. Water also continued to ascend through similar stems after they had been completely killed by exposure to a temperature of 90°C.

Similar experiments have been performed by later investigators, especially Roshardt (1910), Overton (1911), and MacDougal, *et al.* (1929). All of these investigators have confirmed Strasburger's results that water would continue to ascend for some time through stems, segments of which had been exposed to one treatment or another which would kill all living cells present.

In all experiments of the type just described, it has been observed that the leaves at the top of a stem, part or all of which has been killed, sooner or later wilt and wither, although this effect is by no means an immediate one, often appearing only after several days. Proponents of the vital theories have accepted this as evidence that the living cells of a stem are essential for the passage of water through it. Dixon (1914), however, considers that this delayed lethal effect on the leaves results from either or both of two causes. Killing of the stem tissues often causes the formation of substances which plug the vessels or tracheids, thus impeding the upward movement of water. Furthermore, death of the cells in the treated regions causes the release into the conducting channels of toxic compounds which, when transported to the leaves, cause death of the leaf cells. There is still some doubt, however, whether all of the retardation in rate of translocation as a result of such experiments can be explained in these two ways. The possibility remains that the living cells of the xylem may in some way be necessary to the maintenance of the water-conducting capacity of the xylem, or even that they may contribute in some way to the upward movement of water through stems (Ursprung, 1912).

Root Pressure.—An exudation of xylem sap often occurs from the stub of a freshly cut stem, from the stump of a newly cut tree, or from incisions or borings made into plants. Such exudations result from the development of a pressure in the dilute sap of the xylem ducts resulting from the operation of an as yet not fully understood mechanism in the roots (Chap. XIV)—hence, the term "root pressure." Guttation in intact plants (Chap. IX) also results from root pressure.

The magnitude of the root pressure in any plant is usually measured by means of a manometer (Fig. 58). With few exceptions the xylem sap exudation pressures which have been recorded for plants do not exceed 2 atm., and most of them are less than this. In general, there is no correlation between the pressure with which xylem sap is exuded from cut stems and the volume of the flow. In some species, relatively large volumes of sap are exuded under a relatively low pressure; in others, exactly the opposite relation may exist.

Some of the woody plants in which xylem sap exudation occurs are the maples, boxelder, walnut, dogwood, hornbeam (*Ostrya*), sycamore, birches, currant, and grape. Sap flow in the sugar maple and closely related species appears to be a special case, however, which is discussed below. Exudations of xylem sap under pressure from woody plants usually occur only during the seasons of the year when the plants bear no foliage, and most commonly in the early spring months. The popular concept of a "rise of sap" in woody plants in the spring is largely based on the observation of such phenomena. Exudation of xylem sap can also be demonstrated in many species of herbaceous plants, if the soil is relatively moist.

The volume of xylem sap exuded under the influence of root pressures, although usually small, are sometimes very considerable. As many as 28 liters of xylem sap have been exuded per day from a large paper birch tree. Over 100 ml, of xylem sap have been exuded per day from the cut stumps of such herbaceous species as corn, sugar cane, and squash.

Although it is undoubtedly true that root pressure does, in some species of plants, under certain conditions, account for the movement of some water in an upward direction through plants, there are several reasons why this process cannot be considered to be the principal mechanism by which water is moved through plants. In the first place, there are many species in which this phenomenon has never been observed. In the second place, the magnitude of the pressure developed is seldom sufficient to force water to the tops of any except relatively low-growing species of plants. Neither is the rate of flow, as it occurs in most species, adequate to compensate for the known rates of transpira-

Fig. 58. Experimental arrangement for the demonstration of root pressure in a potted plant.

tion. In the third place, root pressures are usually negligible, in temperate regions at least, during the summer period when transpiration is most rapid. During periods of rapid transpiration, the cut surfaces of most plants not only fail to exude sap, but usually absorb water if it is supplied at the cut surface.

The trunks of many species of deciduous trees exhibit a marked seasonal variation in water content (Fig. 59). A minimum water content is attained during middle or late summer, and the trunks gradually fill up

during the fall and spring. Often there is a temporary shrinkage in their
water content during the winter months, but the main period of diminishing trunk water content occurs in the spring and summer. Some authorities consider that intercellular spaces as well as cells become occupied
with water during this increase in the water content of tree trunks
(Priestley, 1930). Root pressure undoubtedly accounts at least in part
for such seasonal replenishments of the store of water in tree trunks. The
living cells of the xylem probably play an active part in this process. It
is possible that there may be slowly ascending streams of water in the
living cells of the xylem which operate independently of the water col-

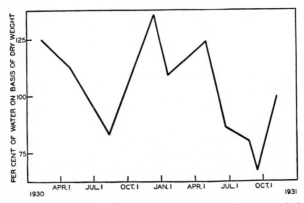

Fig. 59. Seasonal variation in the water content of the trunks of the trembling
aspen (*Populus tremuloides*). Data of Gibbs (1935).

umns in the vessels or tracheids. The trunks of many conifers show no
marked seasonal variations in water content; this is possibly correlated
with the lack of appreciable root pressures in such species.

The Cohesion of Water Theory.—The leading advocate of this theory
has been Dixon (1914, 1924), who has performed much of the experimental work upon which it is based. A number of other workers, notably
Askenasy (1897) and Renner (1911, 1915), have also contributed important theoretical and experimental evidence in support of this theory.

Molecules of water, although ceaselessly in motion, are also strongly
attracted to each other. In masses of liquid water the existence of such
intermolecular attractions is not obvious, but when water is confined in
long tubes of small diameter their existence can often be demonstrated.
If the water at the top of such a tube be subjected to a "pull," the resulting stress will be transmitted all along the column of water, because of
the mutual attraction ("cohesion") between the water molecules. Furthermore, because of an attraction between water molecules and the molecules

of the wall of the tube ("adhesion"), putting the water column under stress does not result in pulling the water away from the encompassing wall. The water-conducting system of plants constitutes just such a system, enclosing continuous, often intermeshing, thread-like columns of water which extend from the top to the bottom of the plant. Because of the cohesion between water molecules and their adhesion to the walls of the xylem ducts, a stress applied at any point in this system will be propagated to all its parts. The application of negative stress tautens the water columns and creates within them a state of tension, which is the equivalent of a "negative pressure."

Whenever evaporation is occurring from the walls of the mesophyll cells into the intercellular spaces, the diffusion-pressure deficit of the water in the mesophyll cell walls increases. Such cell-wall diffusion-pressure deficits are primarily imbibitional in origin (Chap. VIII). Water therefore moves into the walls from the adjacent protoplasm, resulting in turn in a movement of water from the vacuole into the protoplasmic layer. The resulting increase in the diffusion-pressure deficit is in turn propagated to all parts of the cell. Within the lamina of the leaf, gradients of diffusion-pressure deficits, gradually increasing in magnitude from cell to cell in the direction in which water is moving, are established between the xylem ducts and the cells from which evaporation is occurring. Water therefore moves from a given vessel or tracheid into adjacent cells, which results in the development of a tension in the water column occupying that element of the xylem. Concurrently tensions are similarly developing in other xylem ducts within the leaf. The diffusion-pressure deficit of the water in the xylem elements will be increased by the amount of this tension. Water under a tension ("negative pressure") of 13 atm., for example, has a diffusion pressure just 13 atm. less than that of pure water at the same temperature which is not under tension (Chap. VIII). The osmotic pressure of the xylem sap is seldom more than one, or at most 2, atm.; hence this is not an important factor in determining its diffusion-pressure deficit.

While the diffusion-pressure deficits of mesophyll cells probably do not commonly exceed their osmotic pressures, it seems likely that there are certain conditions under which they do. Whenever conditions are such that entry of water into the lower ends of the xylem ducts from adjacent root cells is greatly retarded, tensions of considerable magnitude develop in the water columns, and movement of water from the xylem conduits into the mesophyll cells will be slow or negligible. If, under such conditions, evaporation continues from the mesophyll cells the volume of water within them may continue to diminish even after their turgor pressure had decreased to a zero value. Under such conditions the walls of the cells may be pulled inward as a result of the adhesion between them and the shrinking volume of water, and the counter pull exerted by the walls on the water will throw it into a state of tension (Chap. XV).

The tension developed in the conducting elements is transmitted along their entire length to their lower termination just back of the root tips and probably, very often at least, across the root tissues as well. The magnitude of the tension which develops in the xylem conduits is increased by conditions which favor a rate of water loss from the leaves considerably in excess of the rate at which water enters the roots from the soil.

The movement of water across the cells of the root from the soil into the lower ends of the water-conducting elements must be considered as an integral part of the translocation process. At their lower terminations the xylem vessels or tracheids are in contact with the pericycle, or more rarely, directly with the endodermal cells of the root (Fig. 67). Water moves from the adjacent root cells into the conducting elements because the tension (diffusion-pressure deficit) developed in these elements exceeds the diffusion-pressure deficit of the cells of the root. When the tension in the water columns is relatively low, a gradient of diffusion-pressure deficits will be established across the root cells similar to those which are established in the leaf mesophyll cells when water is moving through them. The diffusion-pressure deficits will increase from cell to cell along this gradient in the direction in which water is moving, i.e., from the periphery of the root toward the xylem.

Since, however, the osmotic pressures of root cells are usually lower than those of the mesophyll cells (Hannig, 1912), it is probable that the tension developed in the water columns often exceeds the highest osmotic pressures of any of the root cells through which water passes on its way from the soil to the xylem. Under such conditions a tension may develop in the root cells in a manner similar to that already described for mesophyll cells (Livingston, 1927).

Regardless of the exact mechanism involved, the essential fact is that the development of tensions in the water columns induces the establishment of a gradient of diffusion-pressure deficits, increasing consistently from cell to cell across the root from its peripheral cell layer to the conducting elements, and water will move along this gradient from the epidermal layer to the xylem tissue. Water enters the peripheral cells of a root whenever the diffusion-pressure deficit of water in the soil is less than that of the water in the epidermal cells and root hairs in the absorbing zone of the root (Chap. XIV).

In most trees practically all upward movement of water occurs in the vessels or tracheids of a few of the outermost annual rings of the sapwood and in some species, especially those with ring-porous wood (Huber, 1935), is almost entirely confined to the outermost ring. As is well known, in some species of trees (beech, sycamore, redwood, etc.) the heartwood of the trunk may disappear completely by decay. The fact that such hollow trees continue to live and thrive is conclusive evidence that the heartwood plays no essential role in the upward movement of water in such species.

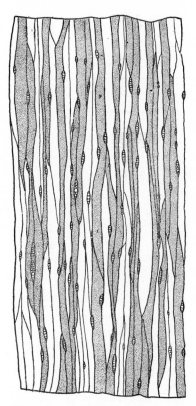

The water-conductive system of plants should be regarded as a unit system; the individual threads or columns of water not operating separately, but each as a part of a more or less complicated meshwork. Fig. 60 illustrates the continuity of the water columns through a woody tissue, in which part of the elements have become blocked with air. The air-plugged tracheids or vessel sections become merely "islands" in the meshwork of intact water columns; and the capacity of the tissues as a whole to conduct water, although somewhat impaired by the presence of air in some of the conducting elements, is by no means destroyed.

Magnitude of the Cohesion of Water. —If water is to move through the xylem ducts as postulated by this theory, its cohesion must be of sufficient magnitude to resist the stresses which are imposed upon it. The maximum height to which water ever moves in plants does not exceed 400 feet. This height is equivalent to about 12 atm. which represents the maximum stress which the

Fig. 60. Continuity of water columns through the wood of a conifer. Redrawn from Dixon (1914).

water columns could develop as a result of their own weight. Water, however, encounters a certain amount of resistance in moving through the conducting tissues. The greater the velocity of the current of water, the greater the resistance which it will encounter. Dixon has showed that, at the velocity corresponding to the usual rates of transpiration, the resistance is approximately equal to the pressure required to support water to the height of the plant. He used the wood of the yew (*Taxus baccata*) for his determinations, in which higher values for resistance would be expected than in nonconifers in which most water traverses vessels rather than tracheids. For high rates of conduction, Huber (1924) estimates the resistance to be several times as great as this. Accepting Dixon's estimates as an average value, the minimum adequate value for the cohesion of water becomes 24 atm. To this must be added the resistance encountered by water crossing the tissues of the root and the mesophyll cells of the leaf which is equivalent to only a few atmospheres. The estimated minimum cohesion required to lift water to the top of the tallest tree is therefore about 30 atm. Even if we assume a resistance three times as great as that found by Dixon, the required value for the cohesion of water becomes only about 50 atm.

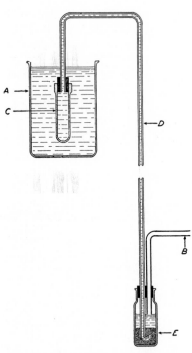

Fig. 61. Apparatus for demonstrating the development of tension in a water column as a result of evaporation. (A) Beaker of boiled water, (B), glass tube, (C) porous clay cup filled with water, (D) capillary glass tube filled with water, (E) mercury layer in bottle. For successful operation it is essential that the water in (C) and (D) be free of air bubbles. This is accomplished by boiling the water in (A) and allowing the hot water to siphon through the apparatus and out at (B). To perform the demonstration the beaker (A) is removed from around the porous cup (C).

Experimentally determined values for the cohesion of water range up to 350 atm. Dixon obtained values as high as 207 atm. for sap centrifuged from branches of holly (*Ilex aquifolium*). The cohesion of water is therefore much in excess of the minimum required for the lifting of water to the tops of even the tallest trees.

The existence of cohesion in water can be demonstrated by means of an apparatus such as that shown in Fig. 61. The first experiment of this type was performed by Askenasy (1897). As evaporation proceeds from the porous clay cup, water moves up the vertical glass tube, followed by mercury from the reservoir. If the demonstration is successful the mercury will continue to rise above the level to which it will stand in a barometer. The water is now being pulled up the tube, a phenomenon which is possible only because of the cohesion between water molecules. The water in the tube is thus thrown into a state of tension which is transmitted to the mercury column below it because of the strong adhesion between water and mercury. The pull exerted on the water column originates at the evaporating surface of the cup, and results from the attractions between molecules operative in maintaining numerous microscopic water menisci in the pores of the clay cup. Thut (1928) succeeded in demonstrating a rise of mercury to a height of 226.6 cm. in such an apparatus. This is approximately three times as high as a column of mercury will be supported by atmospheric pressure acting alone. While the maximum tension developed in the water column in these experiments does not exceed 2 atm., this demonstration illustrates a physical system which is analogous to that which is believed to operate in the plant.

Experiments similar to that just described have also been performed using small branches or twigs of plants as an evaporating surface instead of a porous clay cup. These are attached at the upper end of a glass tube in place of the clay cup; otherwise the setup for such an experiment is similar to that just described. While it has not been possible to obtain as great a rise of mercury in such experiments as when a porous clay evaporating surface is used, upward traction of mercury for distances well in excess of atmospheric pressure can be demonstrated if a suitable technique is followed (Thut, 1932).

Development of Tension in the Water Columns.—Convincing evidence that the water in the xylem vessels is often in a state of tension has been obtained by direct observations of vessels under a microscope. The stems of some species of herbaceous plants, especially the cucurbits, are especially suitable for such observations. Such a stem of an intact, rapidly transpiring plant can be fastened in position across the stage of a microscope and, by careful dissection, vessels examined individually. If one of the vessels under observation be jabbed with the point of a fine needle, an immediate jerking apart of the water column at the point of the rupture will be seen to occur, indicating that the water in the intact vessel was in a state of tension.

Interesting evidence that the water in the xylem ducts of woody stems is, at times at least, under tension has been obtained by means of an instrument known as the *dendrograph*. This is a self-recording instrument which measures variations in the diameters of tree trunks. It is constructed so that its sensitivity is very great and its recordings are not influenced by temperature effects upon the instrument. Dendrographs are used principally to measure periodic variations in the diameter growth of trees. However, even in trees in which diameter growth has ceased,

slight diurnal periodic variations in the diameter of trees have been found
to be of regular occurrence.

A record of the periodic variations in the diameter of a tree trunk for
a period of several days at a season when little diameter growth was
occurring is pictured in Fig. 62. The trunk attained its minimum diameter
during the afternoon hours, at a period when the water columns are
undoubtedly under their maximum tension. While under tension the
water columns become taut and decrease in diameter. Because of the

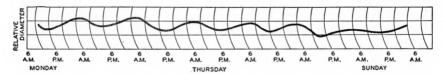

Fig. 62. Daily variations in the diameter of the trunk of a Monterey pine
(*Pinus radiata*) as measured with a dendrograph. Data of MacDougal (1936).

enormous adhesion between water and the walls of the ducts, a slight
contraction occurs in their diameter. Such diurnal changes in the diameter of a tree trunk result from alternate contraction of the vessels or
tracheids when the water in them is under tension followed by their dila-
tion when the tension is slackened.

Although there is ample evidence for the existence of tensions in the
water columns of plants, it is not easy to get good estimates of their exact
magnitudes. They probably do not ordinarily exceed a few atmospheres
in herbs and a few tens of atmospheres in woody plants. Under conditions
of severe internal water deficit, such as may be induced under drought
conditions (Chap. XV), however, it seems probable that tensions ranging
up to at least 100 atm. may develop in the water columns of at least
some species.

Whenever a root pressure is present the water in the xylem ducts is
under a positive pressure; at most other times it is under a tension. In
some plants, especially herbaceous species, daily alternations between
a positive pressure in the water columns at night and a tension in the
daytime are a common occurrence whenever the soil water supply is
abundant. Stocking (1945) has calculated that the physical status of the
water in the xylem of squash ranges from a positive pressure of about
1 atm. during the night, to tensions of about 4 atm. on a warm summer
day and about 9 atm. during wilting.

Vessels and tracheids normally contain water at the time of their
differentiation and remain filled with water for varying periods of time
thereafter. Ultimately most of the water columns in a plant break, but
this does not happen to all of them at any one time except under such

extreme conditions as prolonged drought. Breaking of water columns occurs principally at times when they are subjected to high tensions.

The Relation of Transpiration to the Movement of Water Through the Plant.—In most discussions of the cohesion of water theory of the rise of water in plants, the relation of transpiration to this process is so greatly emphasized that it has come to be almost indelibly associated with this concept. Transpiration is not, however, the fundamental cause of the upward movement of water in plants. Water ascends in the xylem ducts only when an adequate diffusion-pressure deficit has been created in the water of the vacuoles or the walls of cells in organs in the upper parts of the plant. Since evaporation of water from the walls of the mesophyll cells is the most frequent cause of such diffusion-pressure deficits, the process of transpiration has been generally linked in discussions with the mechanism of the ascent of sap. It is only because of its effect in increasing the diffusion-pressure deficit of the water in the mesophyll cells that transpiration sets in motion the entire train of water through the plant. Any other process which results in an increase in the diffusion-pressure deficit in the cells at the terminus of any plant axis may also induce the translocation of water. Upward movement of water often continues during the night hours after transpiration has virtually ceased. This lag results from the residual high diffusion-pressure deficit of the leaf cells at the end of the daylight period. Water will continue to enter these cells until they reattain the maximum turgidity of which they are capable under the conditions prevailing. Similarly movement of water will occur into any rapidly growing stem tip or fruit because the binding up of water in certain phases of the growth process creates a diffusion-pressure deficit in the cells of such organs, thus inducing the migration of water toward such centers of growth activity.

At the present time most plant physiologists are agreed that the cohesion theory is a correct representation of the principal mechanism by which water is transported through plants, be they the tallest of trees or herbs only a few feet in height. It is also generally agreed that root pressure plays a minor role in this process at least under certain conditions and in some species. There is no doubt that living cells are involved in the phenomena generally described under the term root pressure, and there is at least a possibility that living cells of the xylem are in some way essential to the maintenance or operation of the cohesion mechanism.

Rates of Movements of Water Through Plants.—The rate at which water ascends through the xylem ducts may vary from a movement so slow as to be almost imperceptible to speeds of at least 75 cm. per minute (Huber, 1932) and probably higher. In general, daily variations in the rate of ascent of water approximately parallel daily variations in transpiration rate (Baumgartner, 1934); the maximum velocity of the transpiration stream is often not attained, however, until several hours after the peak of transpiration.

Lateral Movement of Water.—A cell-to-cell lateral movement of water in a radial direction undoubtedly occurs along the vascular rays in the stems of most species of plants. In woody stems there is probably also a lateral movement of water around the stem in a tangential direction. Except in trees in which the "grain" of the wood is twisted, the conducting vessels on one side of the tree generally connect with branches on that side of the tree at their upper extremity, and with roots on the same side of the tree at their lower extremity. If no lateral movement of water occurs in woody stems, it would be expected that removal of the roots from one side of a tree would result in a dearth of water, or perhaps even death of the leaves or branches on that side of the tree.

Experiments have been performed on apple, peach, oak, and other woody species in which the roots on one side of the plant were removed in an attempt to ascertain whether or not lateral movement of the water occurs (Auchter, 1923). Although the water content and growth of the plants treated in this manner diminished, there was no difference in the moisture content of the leaves on the two sides of the tree. Neither did the leaves on the side from which the roots had been removed show any greater tendency to wilt on clear, warm days than those on the other side. These results indicate very strongly that lateral movement of water occurs in woody stems, and that the water conductive system of plants acts as a unit system.

Downward Movement of Water.—There are a number of experiments on record which indicate that downward movement of water can occur in stems. For example, Dixon (1924) found that, if the tip of the leaf of a potato plant be cut off under an eosin solution, the liquid will descend through the xylem tissue of the leaf, petiole, and stem, and eventually reach the underground organs. In general, however, such an effect is to be expected only when an internal water deficit exists in a plant.

The cohesion theory of the movement of water will account equally well for the conduction of water in either an upward or a downward direction through the plant. Whenever conditions are such that the diffusion-pressure deficit of the cells of an organ, which is basally situated relative to another, is greater than that of the cells of a more nearly apical organ, a reversal in the direction of the movement of the water will occur (Chap. XV).

Sap Flow in the Maple.—Sap flow from cuts or bore holes in maple trees occurs only during the late winter and early spring months when cold nights alternate with days upon which the temperature rises above freezing (Jones, *et al.*, 1903). The flow is largely or entirely confined to the daylight hours. A single sugar maple tree will generally yield from 25 to 75 liters of sap per season, the sucrose content of which is usually between 2 and 3 per cent. In other woody species that exhibit a pre-foliation sap flow, such as birch and grape, exudation usually will not occur until later in the spring at a period when freezing temperatures have become uncommon. Xylem sap flow in such species is a root pressure phenomenon and continues during both day and night hours.

Sap flow in the red maple is not a result of root pressure because sap exuded as freely from borings into the xylem of cut trees with their bases immersed in water as from similar borings into rooted trees during the late winter and early spring whenever the necessary alternation of cold nights and warm days occurred (Stevens and Eggert, 1945). These investigators suggest that the crystallization of water within the trunk and branches, especially in the outer layers of the xylem, indirectly causes upward movement of water through the tree. As a result of the conversion of some of the water present into ice, the osmotic pressure of the cells increases, which in turn induces upward movement of water through the xylem. It must also be assumed that at least some of the roots are in soil layers warm enough to permit the absorption of water. When, under the influence of daytime rising air temperatures or direct insolation, the temperature of the trunk and branch tissues reaches or exceeds the freezing point, the ice melts and the tissues become flooded with sap. This sap exudes through any sort of an incision made into the outer xylem of the tree.

[handwritten: Mech. in Sugar maple]

SUGGESTED FOR COLLATERAL READING

Crafts, A. S., H. B. Currier, and C. R. Stocking. *Water in the Physiology of Plants.* Chronica Botanica Co. Waltham, Mass. 1949.

Dixon, H. H. *Transpiration and the Ascent of Sap in Plants.* The Macmillan Co. London. 1914.

Dixon, H. H. *The Transpiration Stream.* Univ. London Press. London. 1924.

Eames, A. J. and L. H. MacDaniels. *An Introduction to Plant Anatomy.* 2nd Ed. McGraw-Hill Book Co., Inc. New York. 1947.

Hayward, H. E. *The Structure of Economic Plants.* The Macmillan Co. New York. 1938.

SELECTED BIBLIOGRAPHY

Askenasy, E. Beiträge zur Erklärung des Saftsteigens. *Verhandl. Naturhist.-Med. Ver. Heidelberg* **5**: 429-448. 1897.

Auchter, E. C. Is there normally a cross transfer of foods, water, and mineral nutrients in woody plants? *Maryland Agric. Expt. Sta. Bull. No. 257*: 33-62. 1923.

Baumgartner, A. Thermoelektrische Untersuchungen über die Geschwindigkeit des Transpirationsstromes. *Zeitschr. Bot.* **28:** 81-136. 1934.

Bose, J. C. *Physiology of the Ascent of Sap.* Longmans, Green and Co. London. 1923.

Esau, Katherine. Vessel development in celery. *Hilgardia* **10:** 479-488. 1936.

Gibbs, R. D. Studies of wood. II. On the water content of certain Canadian trees, and on changes in the water-gas system during seasoning and flotation. *Canad. Jour. Res.* **12:** 727-760. 1935.

Glock, W. Growth rings and climate. *Bot. Rev.* **7:** 649-713. 1941.

Hannig, E. Untersuchungen über die Verteilung des osmotischen Druckes in der Pflanze in Hinsicht auf die Wasserleitung. *Ber. Deutsch. Bot. Ges.* **30:** 194-204. 1912.

Huber, B. Die Stromungsgeschwindigkeit und die Grösse der Widerstände in den Leitbahnen. *Ber. Deutsch. Bot. Ges.* **42:** 27-32. 1924.

Huber, B. Beobachtung und Messung pflanzlicher Saftströme. *Ber. Deutsch. Bot. Ges.* **50:** 89-109. 1932.

Huber, B. Die physiologische Bedeutung der Ring- und Zerstreutporigkeit. *Ber. Deutsch. Bot. Ges.* **53:** 711-719. 1935.

Jones, C. H., A. W. Edson, and W. J. Morse. The maple sap flow. *Vt. Agric. Expt. Sta. Bull. No. 103.* 1903.

Livingston, B. E. Plant water relations. *Quart. Rev. Biol.* **2:** 494-515. 1927.

MacDougal, D. T. Studies in tree growth by the dendrographic method. *Carnegie Inst. Wash. Publ. No. 462.* Washington. 1936.

MacDougal, D. T., J. B. Overton, and G. M. Smith. The hydrostatic-pneumatic system of certain trees; movements of liquids and gases. *Carnegie Inst. Wash. Publ. No. 397.* Washington. 1929.

Overton, J. B. Studies on the relation of the living cells to transpiration and sap flow in *Cyperus. Bot. Gaz.* **51:** 28-63, 102-120. 1911.

Priestley, J. H. Studies in the physiology of cambial activity. III. The seasonal activity of the cambium. *New Phytol.* **29:** 316-354. 1930.

Renner, O. Experimentelle Beiträge zur Kenntnis der Wasserbewegung. *Flora* **103:** 171-247. 1911.

Renner, O. Theoretisches und Experimentelles zur Kohäsionstheorie der Wasserbewegung. *Jahrb. Wiss. Bot.* **56:** 617-667. 1915.

Roshardt, P. A. Über die Beteiligung lebender Zellen am Saftsteigen bei Pflanzen von niedrigem Wuchs. *Beih. Bot. Centralbl.* **25:** I: 243-357. 1910.

Stevens, C. L., and R. L. Eggert. Observations on the causes of the flow of sap in red maples. *Plant Physiol.* **20:** 636-648. 1945.

Stocking, C. R. The calculation of tensions in *Cucurbita pepo. Amer. Jour. Bot.* **32:** 126-134. 1945.

Strasburger, E. *Über das Saftsteigen.* S. Fischer. Jena. 1893.

Thut, H. F. Demonstration of the lifting power of evaporation. *Ohio Jour. Sci.* **28:** 292-298. 1928.

Thut, H. F. Demonstrating the lifting power of transpiration. *Amer. Jour. Bot.* **19:** 358-364. 1932.

Tiemann, H. D. What are the largest trees in the world? *Jour. Forestry* **33:** 903-915. 1935.

Ursprung, A. Zur Frage nach der Beteiligung lebender Zellen am Saftsteigen. *Beih. Bot. Centralbl.* **28:** I: 311-322. 1912.

White, P. R. "Root-pressure"—an unappreciated force in sap movement. *Amer. Jour. Bot.* **25:** 223-227. 1938.

DISCUSSION QUESTIONS

1. What would be reasonable estimates of the tensions existing in the water columns under the following conditions: In a tomato plant in the mid-afternoon of "standard day"? In a tomato plant just after sunrise on a cool late spring morning? In a 100-foot oak tree in the mid-afternoon of a "standard day"? In a birch tree in the spring just before development of leaves starts? In a permanently wilted tomato plant? In a desert shrubby plant after a period of prolonged drought?

2. When colored dyes are applied to the cut ends of the upper branches on a tree they often move downward for considerable distances and out into lateral branches. Is this phenomenon consistent with the idea that tensions exist in the water columns? Explain.

3. Is it logical to assume that, since the coast redwoods are the tallest of trees, they must have the most effective water-conducting system?

4. If a branch is sawed off from near the top of a 100-foot oak tree about noon on a clear warm summer day, what change if any would occur in the water content of the topmost or outermost twig on that branch?

5. Suppose the primary xylem of a young root of a 20-year-old tree to be injected with a dye. Assuming no lateral movement of the dye to adjacent tissues. trace the exact course of the dye as it rises through the tissues of the root, stem and leaf.

6. If you wished to inject a solution into a tree, how would you proceed in order to insure its most widespread and rapid distribution throughout the tree?

7. Why is not atmospheric pressure considered to be a factor in the upward movement of water through plants?

8. When flowers are cut for vases many of the vessels in the stems become plugged with air bubbles. Observation has shown, however, that these air bubbles gradually disappear. Explain.

XIII

SOILS AND SOIL-WATER RELATIONS

Most vascular plants are rooted in the soil from which they obtain both water and mineral salts. The entrance of water from the environment into any of the organs of a plant is called the *absorption, intake,* or *uptake* of water. In most terrestrial vascular species only a negligible quantity of water is absorbed through organs other than the roots. Any thorough consideration of the entrance of water into roots requires a consideration of the properties of soils, particularly as they affect the movement of water from the soil into the root.

Constitution of the Soil.—The soil matrix, which is the habitat of most roots, is an extremely complex system. In general, five different components of this system are distinguished:

1. *The Mineral Matter of the Soil.*—The parent substance of practically all soils is rock, of which there are numerous varieties. By various weathering processes rock strata are reduced to fragments of diverse sizes, and these compose the bulk of most soils. The rock particles in soils may vary in size from stones and gravel down to sub-microscopic particles of colloidal clay. The mineral portion of the soil is customarily classified into several fractions depending upon the size of the particles. Such classifications usually disregard the very large particles of the soil (rock fragments, pebbles, etc.). The classification now generally used is as follows:

Fraction	Diameter limits of particles
Coarse sand	2.0 –0.2 mm.
Fine sand	0.2 –0.02
Silt	0.02–0.002
Clay	Less than 0.002

206

The proportions of the different fractions present are very different in different kinds of soils.

The clay fraction of the mineral portion of soils requires special consideration. Unlike the coarser fractions which are composed of small fragments of unmodified rock minerals such as quartz, feldspar, and mica, the clay portion of soils is made up almost entirely of the products of chemical weathering of the rock minerals and hence differs, not only in its physical state, but in its chemical composition, from the particles in the coarser fractions. The particles in the clay fraction are flat and plate-like. Most of them are of colloidal dimensions and exhibit the characteristic properties of colloidal systems. The particles of the clay complex, like those of many other colloidal systems, retain water within the structure of the particle. On the contrary, the sand and silt particles of the soil retain water only on their surfaces. The presence of a considerable proportion of clay in a soil therefore endows it with a high water retaining capacity. Changes in the water content of colloidal clay result in marked changes in its volume. One result of such changes in volume is the commonly observed cracking of a soil rich in clay upon drying. The plasticity and cohesiveness of soils are also due very largely to the colloidal clay present.

Like other colloidal systems colloidal clay is markedly sensitive to the influence of electrolytes. The micelles of colloidal clay usually bear a negative charge when in contact with water. In the presence of calcium ions the individual clay particles are more or less completely flocculated into compound particles. Much of the colloidal clay in most soils exists as enveloping films around the larger soil particles and is also closely associated with organic material in the soil. Flocculation of the clay particles therefore usually results in the formation of compound granules including sand and silt particles and organic matter in addition to the clay. These are called soil crumbs. For agricultural purposes a well-developed granular structure of the soil is highly desirable because such a structure favors both a high moisture-retaining capacity and a good aeration of the soil. "Calcium soils," that is, those with a high calcium content, are in general the most suitable and most valuable for agricultural purposes partly because calcium favors the development of a crumb structure. In the presence of an excess of univalent cations (Na^+, etc.). on the other hand, a greater proportion of the clay fraction of the soil disperses into its ultimate particles, and the soil has a single-grain structure. In this condition the soil is in the least desirable structural condition for agricultural purposes. Many soils contain hydrogen ions in excess. Such soils often develop a good crumb structure, but the crumbs are less stable than those developed in a calcium soil. The addition of lime improves the physical structure of such soils. The crumb structure of a soil, especially in its surface layers, can also be destroyed by purely mechanical effects, such as trampling, or beating by heavy rains.

2. *The Organic Matter of the Soil.*—Most soils contain organic matter which has been derived principally from the partial decomposition of plant residues. Small quantities may also originate from animal residues and excretions. The proportion of organic matter present may vary from almost none as in some sand deposits to 95 per cent or better in some peat soils. In ordinary agricultural soils the amount present seldom exceeds 15 per cent. In forests organic matter comes from falling leaves, dead branches and trunks of woody plants, roots which die and decay underground, and from dead herbaceous vegetation. In grasslands, the underground roots and rhizomes as well as the aerial parts of the plants all contribute their quota to the organic matter of the soil. In well-managed agricultural soils attempts are made to maintain the organic matter content by supplying them with organic fertilizers.

The organic matter is the seat of most of the microbiological processes occurring in the soil. One of the most important of these is the oxidation of the organic matter, a process resulting largely from the metabolic activities of bacteria and fungi, although a limited amount of purely chemical decomposition probably also occurs. Under conditions that are exceptionally favorable for the activities of microorganisms, the organic matter of the soil is oxidized completely and disappears. For this reason the organic matter of soils in tropical regions, particularly when under cultivation, is very low. Even in more temperate regions cultivation of the soils generally results in a rapid reduction in organic matter content, principally as a result of the better aeration induced by tillage.

As a result of the decay process there is present in most soils organic matter in various stages of decomposition. A large proportion of the organic material which is added to some soils survives in the form of a dark-colored amorphous substance called *humus*. Humus is composed principally of the degradation products of the cellulose and lignin derived from plant remains. The accumulation of humus in soils is furthered by conditions unfavorable to the oxidative decomposition of organic matter. The decomposition of organic matter in bogs, ponds, swamps, and water-logged soils under conditions which are largely, if not entirely, anaerobic results in the production of relatively large quantities of humus. Where the organic matter supplied is distinctly acid, as under coniferous forests, or heath plants, humus usually accumulates as a definite layer at the surface. Decomposition of the organic remains under these conditions is largely effected by fungi. In prairie and steppe regions, where a grassland vegetation is predominant, humus usually accumulates in considerable quantities as a result of the decay of both underground and aerial organs of plants. The amount of humus which accumulates in any soil depends upon the relative rates of the addition of organic residues and of its disappearance as a result of oxidation. Soils with a low humus content may result from a sparse contribution of organic matter, as in desert or semi-desert regions, or from a rapid oxidation of organic material which prevents accumulation of humus even when the supply of organic residues to the soil is large. This latter condition obtains in many tropical and subtropical soils.

Humus is essentially colloidal in its properties and possesses an even greater imbibitional capacity than the colloidal clay particles of the soil. The plasticity and cohesiveness of the colloidal organic matter, while considerably less than of the colloidal clay, are much greater than in the noncolloidal fractions of the soil. Humus is rather inert chemically, its influence on the soil being largely a physical one. Its presence in soils favors, in general, a looser structure and hence a better aeration. In sandy soils, especially, humus increases the water-holding capacity of the soil and in clay soils, especially, it decreases the cohesiveness of the soil.

Since the clay fraction and the humus are the two essentially colloidal fractions of the soil and are associated in an intimate physical relationship, many soil scientists refer to these two soil fractions, considered jointly, as the *colloidal complex* of the soil. A large part of this colloidal complex occurs, in many soils, as films enveloping the larger soil particles. The relation of these films to the maintenance of the crumb structure of the soil has already been mentioned. Many other important soil properties are greatly influenced by the colloidal complex.

3. *Soil Water and the Soil Solution.*—Water is universally a component of soils, although the amount present may vary from the merest trace to a quantity sufficient to saturate the soil, *i.e.*, completely fill all of the spaces between the soil particles. Dissolved in the soil water are varying quantities of numerous chemical compounds. These originate principally from the dissolution or chemical weathering of the rock particles, from the decomposition of organic matter, from the activities of microorganisms, and from reactions between the roots of plants and the soil constituents. It is thus more accurate to speak of the *soil solution* than of the soil water, although in discussions of the water relations of soils it is often a common practice to disregard the presence of solutes in the soil water. The concentration of the soil solution in any given soil varies with the proportion of water present. While in most soils the soil solution is very dilute, in saline and alkali soils it may be so concen-

trated that only a few species of plants can survive with their roots in contact with it. The principal cations found in the soil solution are Ca^{++}, Mg^{++}, K^+, Na^+, Al^{+++}, and Fe^{+++} (or Fe^{++}); the principal anions are HCO_3^-, $H_2PO_4^-$, Cl^-, NO_3^-, SO_4^{--}, and SiO_3^{--}. Other solutes too numerous to mention may also occur in the soil solution but are usually present only in very low concentrations. Soil-water relations receive a more detailed discussion later in this chapter, and the soil solution is discussed more fully in Chap. XXV.

4. *The Soil Atmosphere.*—The irregularity of the soil particles in size, shape, and arrangement insures the existence of a certain amount of space among them, even in the most tightly packed soils. This is termed the *pore space* of a soil. The pore space of soils varies from approximately 30 per cent of the volume of the soil in sandy soils to about 50 per cent of the volume in clay soils, or even higher in soils which are very rich in organic matter. More important from the standpoint of plants than the total pore space is the relative proportion of large and small pores. A soil in which the pore space is about equally divided between large and small pores is a more favorable environment for the roots of most kinds of plants than one in which most of the pores are large or in which most of the pores are small. In such a soil the large pores permit adequate drainage and aeration, while the small pores permit considerable capillary retention of water. The pore space of any given soil depends upon the physical and chemical conditions to which the soil is subjected. Conditions favoring a crumb structure of a soil, for example, usually result in an increase in its pore space. The interstitial spaces of a soil may be occupied entirely by gases, as in desiccated soils, entirely by water, as in saturated soils, or, as in most usually true, partly by water and partly by gases. The relative proportions of water and gases present in any given soil vary, depending upon the water content of the soil.

In well-aerated soils the *soil atmosphere* often does not deviate greatly in the proportion of gases present from the atmosphere proper. Oxygen concentrations in the soil atmosphere may range from approximately the usual atmospheric concentration down to near-zero values. Very low oxygen concentrations, however, are seldom found except in excessively wet soils. Concentrations of carbon dioxide as high as 10 per cent are not uncommon in some soils, and even higher values have occasionally been found. The highest concentrations of carbon dioxide in the soil atmosphere usually occur during the late spring and summer months. Except in very dry soils the soil atmosphere is usually saturated with water vapor or nearly so.

5. *Soil Organisms.*—The soil flora includes bacteria, fungi, and algae.

The bacteria are generally the most abundant of all the living organisms present in any soil. Among them are the nitrifying, sulfofying, nitrogen-fixing, ammonifying, and cellulose-decomposing bacteria. The bacteria accomplishing the oxidative decomposition of cellulose and similar compounds are the most important agents in the formation of humus. The numbers of bacteria present vary greatly from soil to soil, and in any one soil vary with seasonal and other fluctuations in soil conditions. Most soils contain between two million and two hundred million individual bacteria per gram of soil. The number of bacteria decreases rapidly with increasing depth, subsoils being sterile or practically so. In general an abundant representation of most species of bacteria is favored in soils by warm temperatures (35°-40°C.), good aeration, and a good but not superabundant water supply. Some species of bacteria, on the other hand, are anaerobic and thrive when aeration of the soil is deficient. The denitrifying bacteria and certain of the nitrogen-fixing bacteria (*Clostridium* spp.) are examples of anaerobes.

Fungi are, in general, most abundant in soils of acid reaction. In such soils they largely replace bacteria as agents of decomposition of organic matter. The fungal components of mycorrhizas (Chap. XXIV) are also important soil organisms.

The soil fauna includes protozoa, nematodes, earthworms, insects, insect larvae, and burrowing species of the higher animals. The earthworms are generally credited with having the most important effects on soil structure, at least in many soils. Their activities result principally in a general loosening of the soil, which facilitates both aeration and distribution of water. Many of the other soil animals have similar effects on the structural organization of the soil.

Soil-Water Relations under Field Conditions.—In a region of moist climate, if a hole is dug or bored into the ground at almost any place where the soil is deep enough, a level at which the soil is completely saturated with water will be encountered at some depth or other. Water will stand in this hole up to this level of complete saturation which is called the *water table.* In river valleys or in close proximity to large bodies of water the water table will usually be reached at a depth of only a few feet under the soil surface. Even in regions of arid climate there are some local situations in which a water table is present. The depth of the water table in any locality usually fluctuates, sometimes very markedly, with seasonal and periodic changes in the relative rates of rainfall, evaporation, transpiration, and other factors. Relatively impermeable soil layers sometimes impede downward percolation of water sufficiently to cause the development of temporary water tables which may be far above the level of the true water table. Such temporary water tables have essentially the same effects on soil-water relations as true water tables, except that their influence is often only a transient one.

For many years an important role was ascribed to the capillary rise of the water from the water table into the soil above in maintaining the moisture conditions within that soil. Recent investigations have shown, however, that the importance of this source of water in soils has been overemphasized. Experiments upon the rise of water through columns of soil indicate that water seldom rises through the soil by capillarity from the water table at an appreciable rate for heights of more than a few feet (Keen, 1928). In a typical loam soil the absolute maximum capillary rise of water is about 8 feet (Shaw and Smith, 1927). Not only is the height to which water moves in a soil by capillarity much less than it was once thought to be, but the actual rate of movement in most soils is very slow.

In many soils the water table lies so far below the soil surface that it has little or no effect on the soil moisture conditions in the soil layers which are penetrated by the roots of most plants. Generally speaking, even in loam or clay loam soils, a capillary rise of water from a zone of complete saturation is probably ineffective in providing the roots of most species of plants with any considerable part of the water which they absorb unless the water table is within about 15 feet of the surface. Some of the more deeply rooted species may obtain some water from a water table located at depths as great as about 30 feet, but the presence of a water table at greater depths than this is a negligible factor in supplying the roots of any species of plants with water. A capillary rise of water from a water table is usually an important source of water for plants in such locations as river bottomlands, or in fields or forests in close proximity to ponds or lakes. In many and perhaps most agricultural soils in moist climate regions plants obtain some water from the water table at least during the earlier part of the growing season. However the widespread practice of drainage of agricultural regions has often resulted in such a marked lowering of the water table as to reduce greatly the possibility that capillary rise of water from below will supply crop plants with any significant part of the water which they absorb.

The other important source of soil water is that part of the precipitation—usually rain, although often melting snow or ice—which percolates downward into the soil. In dry regions this is the only source of water naturally available to plants. Even in more humid regions this is the principal or only source of available soil water in most soils during the dry season of the year. In many dry regions irrigation is an important way in which water is supplied to crop plants. The percolation behavior of irrigation water is essentially similar to that of the water from natural precipitation.

Let us now consider how percolating water becomes distributed in a soil. We will assume that the soil under consideration is relatively dry, *i.e.*, that its water content is substantially below the field capacity (see later), and that it is essentially homogeneous in structure to a depth of a number of feet. Furthermore, we will assume that the water table is so far below the soil surface that it has no effect on soil-water conditions in the upper layers of the soil.

Let us now assume that 2 inches of rain falls on this soil. After an approximate capillary equilibrium has been attained the soil will be moistened to a certain depth which will vary greatly depending upon its porosity and other properties. In general, the depth of this moist blanket of soil will lie within a range of a few inches in heavy clay soils to perhaps 2 feet in very sandy soils. In this hypothetical example let us assume that the soil has been moistened to a depth of one foot. The rain that enters

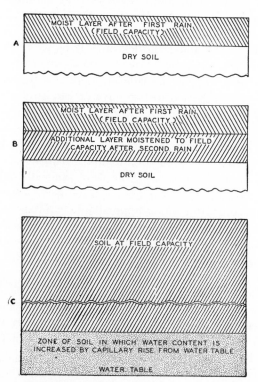

Fig. 63. Diagram illustrating manner in which water becomes distributed through a soil under certain field conditions.

the soil through its surface layer increases its water content sufficiently so that capillary distribution of water within the soil begins, capillary movement under such conditions being in the downward direction. The force of gravity also has an influence, but under the conditions as postulated it is so small in comparison with the capillary forces at work that it may be disregarded. As the water becomes distributed through a soil the water films gradually become attenuated until eventually capillary movement of water becomes negligible. When this attenuation of the soil water has reached its limit, water is believed to occupy only the smaller interstices in the soil.

The depth of this moist blanket of surface soil will depend, therefore, upon the limit to which water can be transferred in the downward direction by capillary movement. Furthermore, the water content of this moist layer of soil will be approximately uniform, and the boundary between it and the zone of drier soil below will be fairly sharp (Fig. 63A). The attainment of this condition has required the movement of water until it comes to an approximate equilibrium with the capillary and gravitational forces influencing its translocation through the soil (Veihmeyer and Hendrickson, 1927).

Following Viehmeyer and Hendrickson (1931) we shall use the term *field capacity* for the water content of the moist layer of soil after capillary movement of water has become negligible. Most soils reach their field capacity within a period of two days or less after a rain or irrigation, unless a water table is present within a few feet of the surface. It is important to realize that a soil at its field capacity is far from being saturated. Field capacities range from about 5 per cent in very sandy soils to about 45 per cent of the dry weight in clays.

Let us now assume that another 2 inches of rain falls on this same soil before any appreciable amount is lost from its upper layers by evaporation or transpiration. After a new approximate capillary equilibrium has been attained the upper foot of soil will not have increased in water content, but a layer of the soil approximately 2 feet in depth will now be moistened up to its field capacity (Fig. 63B). In other words, addition of a second increment of water equal in volume to the first does not increase the water content of the already moist layer of the soil above its field capacity, but results, because of further capillary movement, in raising to its field capacity a second layer of soil, lying directly under the zone which had been moistened by the addition of the first increment of rain, and approximately equal to it in thickness. Although the exact mechanics of the distribution of water under these conditions is probably more complicated, the effect produced is as if the second increment of water simply flows through the moist blanket of soil under the pull of gravity, after which it is distributed to the dry soil layer underneath by capillarity (Shantz, 1927).

Successive rainfalls would thus continue to deepen the layer of soil which has been moistened up to its field capacity. If the water table is not too deep and if sufficient rainfall penetrates the soil, not too much of which is utilized by plants growing thereon, eventually the entire soil from its surface down to the water table will be moistened to its field capacity. A zone several feet in height just above the water table may be enriched somewhat above field capacity by upward capillary movement from the water table (Fig. 63C). If additional water is applied to the soil, after the entire soil mass down to the water table has attained its field capacity, this water percolates down through the soil under the influence of gravity and becomes a part of the ground water. Such conditions obtain in many of the soils of more humid regions at least during the wetter seasons of the year, provided that the water table is not located at too great a depth. This downward percolation of water to the water table is an important factor in influencing its depth below the soil surface, which usually fluctuates considerably from season to season.

In the preceding discussion only the simplest possible situation, that of a homogeneous soil, has been considered. However, most soils consist of a vertical succession of several distinct horizons, each with more or less distinctive physical and chemical properties. Even after long continued disturbance of a soil by plowing or other cultural activities, at least some semblance of the original soil stratification usually persists. In the horizons below those reached by the plow the original structural organization of the soil is usually maintained practically intact. Although the individual horizons of a soil are often fairly homogeneous within themselves, each such horizon in a given soil may have a distinct field capacity of its own. The water contents of the different horizons, even after an equilibrium in the capillary distribution of water has been attained, may therefore be very different.

A somewhat erratic distribution of rainfall to an underlying soil often results from cracks or channels which are opened into the soil by one agency or another. Many soils crack upon drying, sometimes to depths of several feet. Such cracks often facilitate a mass flow of water to a considerable depth in the soil. Similarly in forest soils the decomposition of roots may leave channels through which water flows down into the deeper layers of the soil. The burrows of animals may also facilitate the entry of water into a soil. The presence of rock strata, or of relatively impervious layers of soil close to the surface, will also modify very markedly the simple picture which has been presented of soil-water conditions.

Laboratory Measurements of Soil-Water Relations.—The problem of the water relations of soils has also been approached from the standpoint of laboratory measurements. All such measurements of soil-water relations are open to the criticism that the soil as used in the laboratory does not retain the same structural relationships which it possessed in the field. Nevertheless, laboratory measurements on soil-water relations, made according to usual procedures, yield, with most soils, results close enough to those obtained with undisturbed soil samples to be very useful. Only several of the more significant of such measurements will be described.

1. *Water Content.*—The water content of a soil is commonly expressed as the percentage of water present on the basis of the dry weight of the soil. Samples of soil are brought from the field in closed containers, weighed, and dried to constant weight at (usually) 105°C. The loss in weight represents the water which was present in the soil. Measurements of the water content of soils without regard to the physical status of the water present are of little significance. Laboratory determinations of the water content of soils under certain specified conditions, as in measurements of field capacity, moisture equivalent, and permanent wilting percentage (see below), on the other hand, yield data of considerable value in interpreting the water relations of soils.

2. *Field Capacity.*—Reasonably accurate estimates of the field capacity of many soils can be made by a relatively simple laboratory procedure. The soil is first air-dried and then tapped into place so as to nearly fill a tall glass cylinder. A small quantity of water is then poured on top of the soil and the cylinder capped to prevent evaporation. The water will move slowly downward through the soil but, after two or three days, further downward movement will have virtually ceased. The water content of the upper, moist part of the soil column is then determined by the usual method of oven-drying; this, expressed on the basis of the dry weight, is the *field capacity*. If so much water is added that the entire soil column is moistened from top to bottom, the determination is invalidated (why?) and must be repeated using a smaller quantity of water.

3. *Moisture Equivalent.*—The moisture equivalent is defined as the percentage water content that a soil can retain in opposition to a pull one thousand times that of gravity (Briggs and McLane, 1907). It is determined by placing samples of the soil in especially designed cups with a perforated bottom and whirling them in a centrifuge for (usually) one-half hour (Veihmeyer *et al.*, 1924). This displaces all of the more loosely held water; that retained by the soil is determined by the usual method of oven-drying, and expressed as a percentage of dry weight; this is the *moisture equivalent*.

Although the moisture equivalent of a soil is an arbitrary value, in many kinds of soils it has been found to approximate the field capacity very closely. The principal utility of this measurement, therefore, has been that of a quick laboratory method of indicating the approximate field capacity of a soil. However, the correspondence between these two values is close only in soils of intermediate properties; in sandy or heavy clay soils the divergence between the field capacity and moisture equivalent is often considerable (Veihmeyer and Hendrickson, 1931; Work and Lewis, 1934; Browning, 1941). Hence considerable caution must be exercised in accepting moisture equivalents as valid indices of field capacities.

4. _Permanent Wilting Percentage._—The previously described measurements of the water relations of soils are all purely physical determinations. In contrast the *permanent wilting percentage* (also called *wilting percentage, wilting point*, or *wilting coefficient*) is a physiological measurement. This quantity is defined as the percentage water content to which a soil is reduced when the plant or plants growing in it have just reached a condition of permanent wilting (Briggs and Shantz, 1912a). A permanently wilted plant is one that will not recover its turgidity unless water is supplied to the soil (Chap. XV).

In order to determine the permanent wilting percentage of a soil, a sample is first enclosed in a waterproof vessel. The test plant—sunflower is most commonly used (Hendrickson and Veihmeyer, 1945; Veihmeyer and Hendrickson, 1949)—is generally allowed to develop from seed in the soil sample until it has attained a suitable size. The soil surface is then sealed over in some manner so that all loss of water from the system occurs through the plant. The plants eventually pass into a state of permanent wilting as a result of loss of water by transpiration. When the sunflower is used, permanent wilting of the lowest pair of leaves, judged to have occurred when they fail to recover if placed in a saturated atmosphere overnight, is generally taken as the critical point in the determination. As soon as this occurs a sample of the soil is removed and its water content is determined.

Prior to extensive determinations of permanent wilting percentages it was supposed that plants differed very markedly in their capacity to reduce the water content of a soil. It was assumed, for example, that species which could endure drought conditions could deplete the moisture content of a soil to a lower percentage before showing permanent wilting than could those species which were soon injured or killed when subjected to drought. Extensive investigations have shown, however, that hydrophytes, mesophytes, and xerophytes all reduce the water content of a given type of soil to about the same value before the condition of permanent wilting is induced (Table 16).

Although the permanent wilting percentage for a given soil shows no appreciable variation when measured by means of different plants growing in it, the value varies greatly with the type of soil. The percentage of water remaining in a soil when permanent wilting of the plants growing in it occurs ranges from approximately 1 per cent in some sands to approximately 25 per cent in heavy clays.

According to Caldwell (1913) and Shive and Livingston (1914), a greater percentage of water is left in the soil at permanent wilting if the plants are transpiring rapidly than if they are transpiring slowly. Later investigations by Veihmeyer and Hendrickson (1934) and Furr and Reeve (1945), however, indicate that the permanent wilting percentage is not materially affected by the rate of transpiration of the test plants. In gen-

TABLE 16—RELATIVE WILTING PERCENTAGES FOR DIFFERENT SPECIES OF PLANTS   (DATA OF BRIGGS AND SHANTZ, 1912b)

Species	Relative wilting percentage	Species	Relative wilting percentage
Corn......................	1.03	Coleus.....................	0.99
Wheat.....................	0.994	Potato.....................	1.06
Oats......................	0.995	Buckwheat.................	1.05
White sweet clover........	1.03	Red beet...................	1.06
Red clover................	1.04	Flax.......................	0.99
Tomato....................	1.06	Hydrophytes (several species)..	1.10
Cotton....................	1.05	Xerophytes (several species)...	1.06

The value of the wilting percentage for each species was determined by calculating the ratio of the individual determination to the mean of all determinations made with that soil.   The values given in this table are the average mean ratios for a number of determinations on each species.

eral, this quantity appears to be controlled largely by soil conditions and is only slightly affected by the species used or by the climatic conditions to which the plants are exposed.

The significance of the permanent wilting percentage lies in the fact that it is the percentage of soil moisture below which no growth of a plant occurs. Wilted plants continue to reduce the water content of a soil, but at such a slow rate that restoration of turgidity is impossible because the rate of transpiration even from a wilted plant exceeds the rate of absorption of water from a soil at its permanent wilting percentage or lower. From a physiological viewpoint the permanent wilting percentage is probably the most significant index of soil-water conditions since it appears to be a relatively stable value for a given soil, and because it marks the lower limit of the range of soil-water contents at which growth of plants occurs.

5. *Wilting Range.*—As the previous discussion has indicated, plants can survive and even absorb limited amounts of water at soil-water contents below the permanent wilting percentage. The range of soil-moisture contents between the first permanent wilting of the basal leaves of sunflower plants and the permanent wilting of all of the leaves on a plant ("ultimate wilting point") has been called the *wilting range* (Taylor *et al.*, 1934). The wilting range is usually narrower in coarse-textured soils than in fine-textured ones (Furr and Reeve, 1945). As little as 11 per cent to as much as 30 per cent of the soil-water content between the moisture equivalent and the ultimate wilting point may lie within the

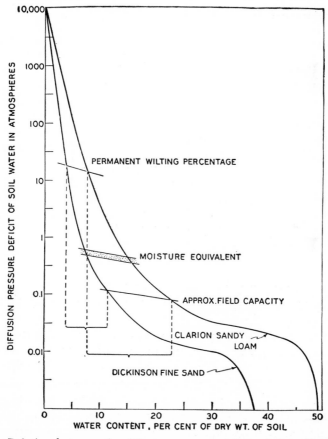

FIG. 64. Relation between the diffusion-pressure deficit of the soil water and soil-water content in two soils over the entire soil-water range. The horizontal brackets indicate the range over which water is readily available to plants. It should be noted that the vertical scale in this figure is a logarithmic one. Data of Russell (1939).

wilting range. In general, growth of plants cannot occur while the soil in which they are rooted is within the wilting range. Many, although not all, kinds of plants can survive, however, often for long periods, under such conditions.

Interrelationships between soil-water content and the various indices of soil-water relations are shown graphically in Fig. 64.

The Diffusion-Pressure Deficit of the Water in Soils.—In preceding discussions of the water relations of plant cells and tissues, it has been shown that the most significant unit for the expression of the dynamics of water relations of plant cells is the diffusion-pressure deficit. Since all problems of the absorption of water by plants involve a consideration of the relation of the water in the soil and the water in the plant, it is desirable that

TABLE 17—DIFFUSION PRESSURE DEFICIT VALUES OF AN "OSWEGO SILT LOAM SOIL" AT DIFFERENT WATER CONTENTS, AS INDICATED BY THE ABSORPTION OF WATER BY COCKLEBUR SEEDS (DATA OF SHULL, 1916)

Soil moisture, per cent of dry weight	Water imbibed by seeds, per cent of air-dry weight	Diffusion pressure deficit of the soil water, atm.
5.83 ("air-dry")	0.00	965
9.36	6.47	375
11.79	11.94	130
13.16	21.36	72
14.88	28.61	38
17.10	37.70	19
17.93	43.25	11.4
18.07	45.15	7.6
18.87 (approx. wilting percentage)	47.26	3.8

this concept of the diffusion-pressure deficit of water be extended to the soil water if the absorption of water is to be interpreted in terms of dynamic units.

One of the first successful attempts to measure the retentive capacity of the soil for water was made by Shull (1916). Air-dry seeds of the cocklebur (*Xanthium pennsylvanicum*) were used as the "instrument" for measuring the diffusion-pressure deficit of the soil. Seeds of this species were first placed in salt solutions of various osmotic pressures and the percentage of water which had been imbibed when an equilibrium was attained in each solution was first determined (Chap. VII).

Once the percentages of water held by these seeds when in equilibrium with solutions of different osmotic pressures had been determined, the diffusion-pressure deficit of any medium in which they might be immersed could be measured. For example, if some of these seeds were immersed in a medium of unknown osmotic pressure (diffusion-pressure deficit) until a dynamic equilibrium was established, after which it was determined that their moisture content was 32.8 per cent, a diffusion-pressure deficit of 26.6 atm. was indicated for the medium (Table 10). This principle was applied to the measurement of the diffusion-pressure deficit of soils at different water contents. A sample of soil at a known water content was shaken with some of the seeds until an equilibrium was attained, after which the water content of the seeds was determined.

As the data in Table 17 indicate, the diffusion-pressure deficit of the water in an air-dry soil is of the order of magnitude of 1000 atm. With an increase in the soil-water content, its diffusion-pressure deficit decreases. In the range of low water contents, a small increase in water content corresponds to a very large decrease in the diffusion-pressure deficit of the soil. As the water content of the soil is increased further, the diffusion-pressure deficit continues to decrease but at a progressively slower rate.

Diffusion-pressure deficit values for soil water can be calculated from the results of a number of other types of measurements. Among these

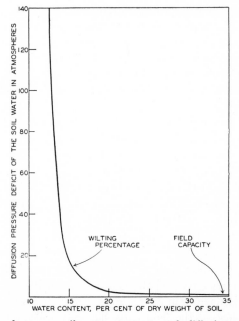

Fig. 65. Relation between soil-water content and diffusion-pressure deficit of the soil water in a silty clay loam soil. In contrast with Fig. 64 this figure shows only a small portion of the soil-water scale. Data of Magistad and Brezeale (1929).

are vapor-pressure measurements (Thomas, 1924), determinations of the freezing-point depression of the soil (Bodman and Day, 1943), measurements of the amount of water retained by a soil in equilibrium with tensions of a known magnitude (Gradmann, 1928), and measurements of the quantity of water retained by a soil in equilibrium with pressures of a known magnitude (Richards, 1941, 1949). Each of these methods is suitable only for a certain range of soil-water contents.

From data obtained by one or more of these methods it is possible to construct for any soil a water-content diffusion-pressure deficit curve (Fig. 65). Most of the important soil-water relations can be interpreted in terms of such curves.

Such a curve is characterized by a marked rise in diffusion-pressure deficit in the region of low soil-water contents. As already shown by the results presented in Table 17, in this zone of soil-moisture contents a very small decrease in soil-water content corresponds to a very considerable increase in diffusion-pressure deficit.

Experimentally determined values for the diffusion-pressure deficit of the water in a soil at the permanent wilting percentage vary somewhat depending upon the kind of soil and the method of determination, but appear to be commonly in the neighborhood of 15 atm. (Richards and Weaver, 1943). The position of the permanent wilting percentage is just above the region of the sharp upward inflection of the diffusion-pressure-deficit soil-water content curve. The position of this value on the curve makes understandable the fact that further absorption of water by plants from soils at water contents below the permanent wilting percentage occurs very slowly.

The diffusion-pressure deficit of the soil water when the soil is at field capacity is not more than a few tenths of an atmosphere (Richards and Weaver, 1944). Absorption of water by plants occurs readily at such a low soil-water diffusion-pressure deficit. At the field capacity the diffusion-pressure deficit of the soil water results principally from the osmotic effects of the dissolved salts (Bodman and Day, 1943). At lower soil-water contents, on the contrary, the diffusion-pressure deficit of the soil water results principally from attractions between the soil particles and the water molecules.

In most soils the water readily available to plants is that in the range between the field capacity and the permanent wilting percentage. In general, this range is narrow in sandy soils, wider in loam soils, and widest in clay soils. Hence, at the field capacity, clay soils contain the greatest quantities of both available and unavailable water, loam soils the next, and sandy soils the least. The total quantity of available water in a soil often becomes a limiting factor in plant growth. In the absence of rainfall or irrigation it is obvious that a plant can develop longer if rooted in a loam soil, for example, than in a sandy soil, if both were initially at their field capacity.

The foregoing discussion of this topic refers primarily to soils in which the concentration of solutes in the soil solution is negligible or nearly so. This is the prevailing situation in the vast majority of agricultural, grassland, and forest soils. In some soils, however, the concentration of the soil solution may become appreciable. The most extreme examples of this situation are found in alkali and saline soils in which the osmotic pressures of the soil solution may reach, in extreme cases, 100 atm. or more. Although certain species of halophytes can survive in extremely saline soils, most plants are markedly retarded in growth if the osmotic pressure of the soil solution exceeds a few atmospheres. Because of the higher osmotic pressure of the soil solution, the diffusion-pressure deficit of a saline soil at the field capacity is greater than that of a nonsaline soil. With decreasing water content of a saline soil its osmotic pressure increases. Furthermore, the shape of the diffusion-pressure deficit soil-water content curve will be different for a saline soil from that for an otherwise similar but nonsaline soil (Wadleigh, 1946). In general, the upward trend to the left will be more gradual in the curve for a saline than for a nonsaline soil.

SUGGESTED FOR COLLATERAL READING

Baver, L. D. *Soil Physics.* 2nd Ed. John Wiley and Sons, Inc. New York. 1948.

Kramer, P. J. *Plant and Soil Water Relationships.* McGraw-Hill Book Co., Inc. 1949.

Robinson, G. W. *Soils, Their Origin, Constitution, and Classification.* 3rd Ed. John Wiley and Sons, Inc. New York. 1950.

Russell, E. J. *Soil Conditions and Plant Growth.* 8th Ed. Longmans, Green and Co. London. 1950.

U. S. Department of Agriculture. *Soils and Men.* Yearbook, 1938.

SELECTED BIBLIOGRAPHY

Briggs, L. J., and J. W. McLane. The moisture equivalent of soils. *U. S. Bureau Soils Bull. No. 45.* 1907.

Briggs, L. J., and H. L. Shantz. The wilting coefficient for different plants and its indirect determination. *U. S. Dept. Agric. Bur. Plant Ind. Bull. No. 230.* 1912a.

Briggs, L. J., and H. L. Shantz. The relative wilting coefficients for different plants. *Bot. Gaz.* **53:** 229-235. 1912b.

Bodman, G. B., and P. R. Day. Freezing points of a group of California soils and their extracted clays. *Soil Sci.* **55:** 225-246. 1943.

Browning, G. M. Relation of field capacity to moisture equivalent in soils of West Virginia. *Soil Sci.* **52:** 445-450. 1941.

Caldwell, J. S. The relation of environmental conditions to the phenomenon of permanent wilting in plants. *Physiol. Res.* **1:** 1-56. 1913.

Edlefsen, N. E., and A. B. C. Anderson. Thermodynamics of soil moisture. *Hilgardia* **15**: 31-298. 1943.

Furr, J. R., and J. O. Reeve. Range of soil-moisture percentages through which plants undergo permanent wilting in some soils from semiarid irrigated areas. *Jour. Agric. Res.* **71**: 149-170. 1945.

Gradmann, H. Untersuchungen über die Wasserhaltnisse des Bodens als Grundlage des Pflanzenwachstums. *Jahrb. Wiss. Bot.* **69**: 1-100. 1928.

Hendrickson, A. H., and F. J. Veihmeyer. Permanent wilting percentages obtained from field and laboratory trials. *Plant Physiol.* **20**: 517-539. 1945.

Keen, B. A. The limited role of capillarity in supplying water to plant roots. *Proc. First Int. Cong. Soil Sci.* **1**: 501-511. 1928.

Magistad, O. C., and J. F. Breazeale. Plant and soil relations at and below the wilting percentage. *Univ. Ariz. Tech. Bull. No. 25.* 1929.

Richards, L. A. A pressure membrane extraction apparatus for soil solution. *Soil Sci.* **51**: 377-386. 1941.

Richards, L. A. Methods of measuring soil moisture tension. *Soil Sci.* **68**: 95-112. 1949.

Richards, L. A., and L. R. Weaver. Fifteen-atmosphere percentage as related to the permanent wilting percentage. *Soil Sci.* **56**: 331-339. 1943.

Richards, L. A., and L. R. Weaver. Moisture retention by some irrigated soils as related to soil-moisture tension. *Jour. Agric. Res.* **69**: 215-235. 1944.

Russell, M. B. Soil moisture sorption curves for four Iowa soils. *Proc. Soil Sci. Soc. Amer.* **4**: 51-54. 1939.

Shantz, H. L. Drought resistance and soil moisture. *Ecology* **8**: 145-157. 1927.

Shaw, C. F., and A. Smith. Maximum heights of capillary rise starting with soil at capillary saturation. *Hilgardia* **2**: 399-409. 1927.

Shive, J. W., and B. E. Livingston. The relation of atmospheric evaporating power to soil moisture content at permanent wilting in plants. *Plant World* **17**: 81-121. 1914.

Shull, C. A. Measurement of the surface forces in soils. *Bot. Gaz.* **62**: 1-31. 1916.

Taylor, C. A., H. F. Blaney, and W. W. McLaughlin. The wilting range in certain soils and the ultimate wilting point. *Trans. Amer. Geophys. Union* **15**: 436-444. 1934.

Thomas, M. D. Aqueous vapor pressure of soils. II. Studies in dry soils. *Soil Sci.* **17**: 1-18. 1924.

Veihmeyer, F. J., and A. H. Hendrickson. Soil-moisture conditions in relation to plant growth. *Plant Physiol.* **2**: 71-82. 1927.

Veihmeyer, F. J., and A. H. Hendrickson. The moisture equivalent as a measure of the field capacity of soils. *Soil Sci.* **32**: 181-193. 1931.

Veihmeyer, F. J., and A. H. Hendrickson. Some plant and soil-moisture relations. *Amer. Soil Survey Assoc. Bull.* **15**: 76-80. 1934.

Veihmeyer, F J., and A. H. Hendrickson. Methods of measuring field capacity and permanent wilting percentage of soils. *Soil Sci.* **68**: 75-94. 1949.

Veihmeyer, F. J., and A. H. Hendrickson. Soil moisture in relation to plant growth. *Ann. Rev. Plant Physiol.* **1**: 285-304. 1950.

Veihmeyer, F. J. *et al.* The moisture equivalent as influenced by the amount of soil used in its determination. *Univ. Calif. Coll. Agric. Tech. Paper 16:* 1-64. 1924.

Wadleigh, C. H. The integrated soil moisture stress upon a root system in a large container of saline soil. *Soil Sci.* **61**: 225-238. 1946.

Work, R. A. and M. R. Lewis. Moisture equivalent, field capacity, and permanent wilting percentage and their ratios in heavy soils. *Agric. Eng.* **15**: 1-20. 1934.

DISCUSSION QUESTIONS

1. Why is the water content of a clay soil much greater than that of a sandy soil when both are at the permanent wilting percentage?

2. A waterproof pot is filled with a known weight of dry soil which has a field capacity of 20 per cent. Water equal in weight to 10 per cent of the entire soil mass is poured on the surface of the soil. How would this water be distributed in the soil at equilibrium?

3. For experimental purposes how would you keep the water content in a pot in which a plant was growing at approximately its field capacity? At approximately three-fourths its field capacity?

4. A greenhouse bench filled with a loam soil is drenched with water. After all drainage of water from the bench has ceased, would the water content of the bench be at approximately the field capacity? More than the field capacity? Less than the field capacity? Explain.

5. What are some of the effects of tiling a field on the water relations of soil?

6. Dust mulches are often recommended as a means of conserving water in a soil. Evaluate this practice.

7. A corn plant, a young pine tree, and a fern were planted in equal-sized pots containing a silt loam, a sandy loam, and a clay loam, respectively, and the pots sealed against water loss. The soil water was initially at the field capacity in each pot. How will the water content of the soils compare when the permanent wilting percentage is reached? The diffusion-pressure deficits of the soil water? The amounts of water lost from each soil before the permanent wilting percentage is reached? The times required for the plants to reach permanent wilting?

XIV

ABSORPTION OF WATER

Roots and Root Systems.—The root system of a plant is often as distinctive in form and structure as its aerial portions. Each species has, when growing in its usual type of habitat, a characteristic set of roots, just as it has a recognizably distinctive top when growing within its usual range of climatic conditions. Root systems are subject to modifications as a result of the influence of various soil factors, just as the form, height, spread or other features of the tops may be modified in accordance with the climatic conditions to which they are subjected. A coniferous tree may produce a stately, cone-shaped crown if growing in a favorable habitat, while another individual of the same species will be only a straggling, scrawny shrub if located near the timber line on a mountain. Similarly, a plant may develop a deep, profusely branched root system in a well-drained soil, while another individual of the same species will produce a shallow root system of entirely different configuration in a soil which is water-logged to within a foot or two of its surface.

Superficially roots resemble stems, inasmuch as both are usually elongate, more or less cylindrical structures. There are, however, a number of important distinctions between the two types of organs. Roots are generally much more irregular in shape than stems. They are not differentiated into distinct nodes and internodes, and hence the branching of roots follows a much less regular pattern than the branching or bearing of lateral organs by stems. With few exceptions the growing tip of every root is capped with a distinctive zone of cells known as the *root cap;* such a tissue is absent from the stem tips. The origin of lateral roots is very different from that of lateral stems; the former develop from deep-seated meristems; the latter from peripheral meristems. The arrangement of the primary tissues in roots is usually different from the arrangement of the primary tissues of stems. Roots bear no appendages which are

226

comparable to leaves or flowers, and lack stomates which are present in many stems.

When a seed germinates the first root which appears is called the *primary root*. This develops from an apical growing region which is already differentiated in the embryo. The primary root, which may be considered as a downward extension of the main axis of the plant, gradually elongates, grows in diameter, and produces lateral branches. Branches and sub-branches of the primary root are called *secondary roots*.

The primary root and its branches considered collectively are called the *primary root system*. In the seed plants primary root systems develop only from embryos. In many species the primary root system remains the only, or at least the conspicuous, root system throughout the life of the plant. In perennial plants, especially certain tree species, such primary root systems may attain an enormous size.

All other roots, regardless of the organ of the plant on which they develop, are termed *adventitious roots*. The roots which develop from bulbs, tubers, corms, rhizomes, and cuttings are classed in this category. Adventitious roots may even arise from the leaves of some species such as begonia, bryophyllum, and walking fern. Such roots also develop from the lower nodes of the vertical stems of many species, especially monocots. In some species, maize for example, they may arise from nodes above the soil surface, becoming the so-called prop roots. When they develop from the stems adventitious roots most commonly arise at the nodes.

Two very generalized types of root systems which are often distinguished are *tap root systems* and *fibrous root systems*. Practically all adventitious root systems belong in the latter category. In the former, the primary root system is predominant, the primary root itself often being conspicuous.

The root system of a plant is often more extensive than its top. The relative development of the top and roots of a plant is greatly influenced, however, by a number of soil and climatic conditions (see discussion of shoot-root ratio in Chap. XXXIII).

The depth to which roots penetrate into soils is in part a species characteristic, some species being typically more deep-rooted than others. However, prevailing soil conditions usually exert a pronounced effect upon the depth of penetration of roots. Rock strata are frequently so close to the soil surface that the penetration of roots to any great depth is prevented. Similarly the presence of hardpan or otherwise extremely tight layers of soil not far below the surface checks or at least greatly hinders the invasion of the lower soil layers by roots. If a water table is close to the soil surface downward growth of roots of most species is retarded because of the deficient aeration of saturated soils. Only the roots of hydrophytes, as a rule, can penetrate very far into saturated soils. In dry climates, as for example the western plains area of North America, the lower limit of root growth is determined by the depth of infiltration into the soil of the scanty rainfall, as, generally speaking, roots cannot grow into dry soils. In deep, moist, well-drained soils, on the other hand, the depth of penetration of roots is limited not by soil conditions but by factors inherent within the plant.

Extensive investigations have been conducted by Weaver (1926) and Weaver and Bruner (1927) on the depth of penetration and general distribution in the soil of the roots of many crop plants as well as of some species in their natural habitats. Formerly the concept was prevalent that the roots of crop plants do not penetrate greatly below the depth to which the soil is plowed. These investigators showed, however, that in well-drained soils the bulk of roots of most crop plants is located in a zone between the surface and a depth of 3 to 5 feet. Some individual roots penetrate to greater distances; with most crop plants a few roots were found to reach depths of 6 to 8 feet depending upon the species.

Contrary to popular opinion the roots of trees do not usually penetrate for very great distances into the soil. As a rule most of the root system of the vast majority of trees will be found in the upper few feet of the soil. If soil conditions permit, a few roots penetrate to greater depths, but growth of tree roots to a depth of more than 10 feet beneath the soil surface is uncommon. Trees growing in deep, well-drained soils, especially if sandy or gravelly, may sometimes be exceptions to this statement. Under such conditions the roots of some species, such as cottonwood, may penetrate into the soil for 20 feet or more.

The lateral extent as well as the depth of penetration is an important gross feature of any root system. In general, the lateral roots lying close to the soil surface attain the greatest horizontal spread. This varies greatly according to the environmental conditions to which the root system of a plant is subjected. In the more arid climates of the world it is a common observation that the scantier the rainfall the more extensive the lateral development of the root system of many species. Corresponding with this increased lateral development there is usually, under such conditions, a decrease in the depth of penetration.

The density of the vegetation is also a factor of importance in determining the lateral spread of roots. The influence of this factor has been observed largely with crop plants. Generally a plant which is closely surrounded by other plants will have a more restricted lateral spread to its root system than one growing at some distance from its neighbors. The lateral spread of the roots of a crop plant such as wheat, growing in a dense stand, is always less than that of an isolated plant of the same species. Isolated trees or those growing in open stands often have root systems which extend far beyond the spread of the crown. In artificial tree plantations the density of the stand affects the lateral spread of the roots just as it does in crop plants. The same principle also operates in natural forests but is there complicated by the greater diversity of species and of age groups than is usually present in an artificial planting of trees.

The Absorbing Region of Roots.—Most of the absorption of water and mineral salts occurs in the terminal portions of roots. Because of the extensive branching of roots there are often millions of root tips on the root system of a mature plant. From a physiological point of view the number of root tips borne by a root system is probably the most important index of its effectiveness in obtaining water and mineral salts from the soil.

The external morphology of a root tip can be observed most easily in roots which have developed in moist air. Upon close examination of a root tip, four distinct, but intergrading, regions can usually be discerned with no greater magnification than that afforded by a hand lens or, in many species, even with the naked eye. At the apex of the root is an extremely short region, white in color, which is known as the *root cap*. Just above the root cap, and partly covered by it, is the *meristematic region*, the zone of maximum cell division, which is seldom more than a millimeter in length and which is usually distinguishable by a yellowish color. Next above the meristematic region is the *region of cell enlargement*, usually not more than a few millimeters in length, in which most increase in length of the root occurs. Above this region is usually present the *root-hair zone* which bears the slender hair-like outgrowths of the epidermal cells known as the root hairs. The root-hair zone varies in length depending on the species and the conditions to which the root is subjected during its development.

Most evidence indicates that the region of the root tip in which maximum absorption of water occurs corresponds to the root-hair zone or the zone in which the root hairs would be present if they had developed. The rate of absorption of water in the zone of cell enlargement is also high, but relatively little movement of water into the root occurs through the root cap and meristematic region. In contrast with the absorption of water, maximum absorption of mineral salts appears to occur in the meristematic region of a root tip (Chap. XXIV).

Measured from the apex, the length of the absorbing region of a root varies greatly with species, age of the root, and conditions under which it has developed. Above the root-hair zone one or more of the outer cell layers of the root become suberized or lignified, or both, and in older roots cork cambiums develop (see later). In general, relatively little absorption occurs through such regions of a root, although appreciable amounts can be absorbed through the older suberized roots of at least some species (Kramer, 1946).

Anatomy of Roots.—If a longitudinal median section be cut through a root tip such as has just been described, and examined under a microscope, the anatomy of the several regions of the root can be observed (Fig. 66). The root cap is a more or less thimble-shaped assemblage of cells covering the distal end of the meristematic region. It apparently minimizes mechanical abrasion of the root tip as it grows through the soil. Such abrasion gradually tears off the outer terminal cells of the root cap, but these are replaced by new root-cap cells which are formed by cell divisions occurring in the lowermost layers of the cells of the meristematic regions.

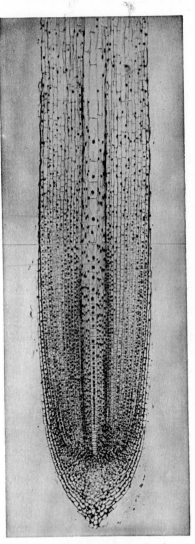

FIG. 66. Median longitudinal section (approximately 3 mm. in length) of onion root tip. Photomicrograph by Tillman Johnson.

The meristematic tissue of a root tip is composed of small, thin-walled cells with prominent nuclei. As new cells are formed by cell division they begin to enlarge, principally in the direction of the long axis of the root. The division of meristematic cells and their subsequent elongation result in projecting the growing region and root cap forward through the soil and account for the growth in length of the roots. The region of cell elongation is seldom more than a few millimeters in length. This contrasts markedly with the corresponding region of a stem tip which may be as much as 10 cm. in length or even longer in some species. Only a small part of the root tip—a few millimeters in length at most—is pushed through the soil. Since, in a growing root tip, the elongation of cells ensues as soon as they are formed by cell division, a cell which is one day in the region of cell division is the next day in the region of cell elongation, subsequent divisions in the meristematic tissue having produced additional layers of cells beyond it (Chap. XXIX).

The anatomy of a representative root, as shown in cross section through the root-hair zone, is illustrated in Fig. 67. The structure of a young root shows a number of distinctive features. The cortex is relatively thicker than that of stems. This characteristic is especially noticeable in fleshy roots in which the thickness of the cortex is often many times the radius of the stele. The intercellular spaces of the root cortex are also more prominent than those in the stem cortex in which the cells are rather densely packed. An endodermis is almost invariably present in roots; this is generally considered to represent the innermost layer of the cortex. While an endodermis is found in the stems of many species, it is by no means of universal occurrence. Just within the endodermis is present a narrow zone of parenchymatous pericyclic tissue. Usually this is continuous, but in some species, as described below, it may be discontinuous. Lateral roots most commonly originate in the pericycle.

In roots the primary xylem and the primary phloem are present in a radial pattern. The primary xylem as seen in cross section appears as a number (usually 2 to 5, although sometimes as many as 20) of radially situated strands. In many roots the center of the stele is composed of xylem; in some, especially monocots, it is composed of pith. Usually the xylem strands terminate radially in contact with the pericycle, but in

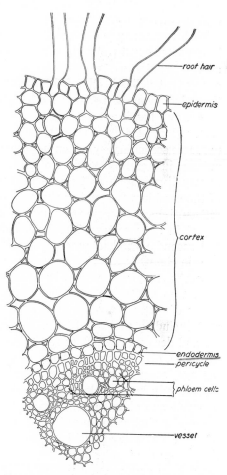

FIG. 67.   Cross section of a segment of a young maize root through the root-hair zone. Only a portion of each root hair is shown.

some species they abut directly on the endodermis, breaking up the pericycle, as seen in cross section, into a discontinuous series of arcs. The primary phloem of roots occurs as patches of tissue (as seen in cross section) which alternate with the strands of xylem (Fig. 68).

The structure of the individual types of cells occurring in the root tissues is essentially similar to the structure of corresponding types of cells occurring in the stem.

With few exceptions the roots of all perennials and many annuals grow in diameter as they increase in age by means of a cambium layer much as do most stems. The cambium layer is initiated in young roots in such a way that it lies inside of the strands of phloem tissues, and outside of the xylem strands. In cross section the original cambium layer appears as a wavy band, passing inside of each phloem strand, and outside of each xylem strand (Fig. 68). Once differentiated this cambium layer produces secondary xylem on its inside face, and secondary phloem on its outside, just as the cambium of stems does. The initial formation of secondary tissues by a root cambium is usually more rapid in the segments of the cambium internal to the primary phloem strands. Because of this differential growth rate the cambium of a root rapidly attains a circular aspect in cross section. The further differentiation of secondary phloem and secondary xylem proceeds in essentially the same manner that it does in stems.

Most perennial roots sooner or later become encased in layers of cork cells. The initial cork cambium often originates in the pericycle. As layers of cork cells are produced by the cork cambium the cortex of the root, including the endodermis, is ruptured and the cells of these tissues die and decay away. Older roots therefore have a characteristic smooth, brownish, corky covering that is pierced only by lenticels. With increasing age, secondary cork cambiums may arise progressively more and more deeply in the phloem tissues. This results in the gradual loss of the pericycle and older phloem tissues. The bark of older roots, therefore, is essentially similar to that of the trunks or larger branches of trees (Chap. XXIX). Thick layers of bark do not as a rule accumulate on roots as they do on the trunks of some species of trees because of the rapid decay of all dead underground tissues.

In the roots of species in which no secondary thickening occurs, as in many monocots, the epidermal layer of cells may persist intact, usually becoming suberized. In other such species the epidermis may die and decay, but when this occurs an underlying layer of the cortex cells in turn becomes suberized.

Lateral branches of the primary root system usually originate in the

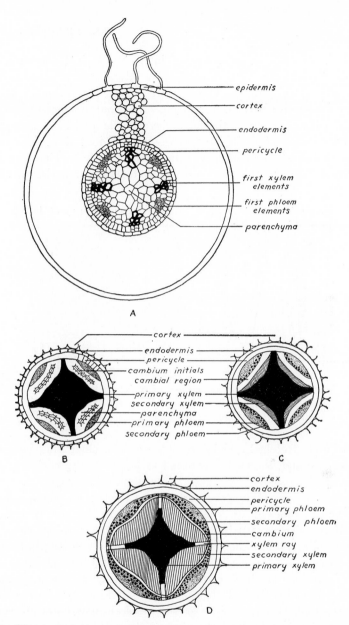

FIG. 68. Diagrammatic representation of the development of secondary phloem and xylem in a dicotyledonous root. (A) Cross section showing first xylem and phloem elements, (B) central region of root showing development of primary xylem (black), primary phloem (stippled), and first cambial elements. Note that the entire center of the root has become primary xylem, (C) later stage showing development of secondary xylem and phloem, (D) still later stage showing more extensive secondary phloem and xylem with cambium now entirely encircling the xylem.

pericycle, most of them being formed in the region just above the root-hair zone. Usually the locus of origin of a lateral root is opposite one of the primary xylem strands. The first step in the formation of a lateral root in most species is the development of a group of meristematic cells by the division of several adjacent pericycle cells in the layer just inside of the endodermis (Fig. 69). By successive divisions these cells rapidly form an apical root meristem with its characteristic root cap, region of cell division, etc. As this develops the endodermis and tissues exterior

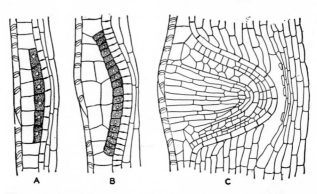

FIG. 69. Three stages in the formation of a lateral root. Meristematic cells (stippled) arise in the pericycle and the cells of the lateral root develop from these. Redrawn from Holman and Robbins (1938) after van Tieghem.

to it are first stretched and later ruptured. The elongating lateral root penetrates through the tissues external to it, partly by mechanical pressure, and perhaps partly by digesting the tissues through which it passes. Eventually the lateral rootlet emerges from the root of which it forms a branch and becomes an externally visible part of the root system.

Root Hairs.—These structures are confined to the root-hair zone, which may be from a few millimeters to many centimeters in length, depending on the species and the conditions under which the root develops. Since the root-hair zone lies back of the region of cell enlargement, there is no forward progression through the soil of the individual root hairs along the axis of the root. In any rapidly growing root tip new hairs are continually developing just back of the zone of elongation. New root hairs are thus constantly developing in contact with different portions of the soil, a fact which is of fundamental significance in the absorption of water and perhaps of mineral salts. Many root hairs are short-lived structures and often die within a few weeks or even less after they develop. In certain species, at least, some of the root hairs may remain alive for an entire growing season, and in a few species they may become suberized or lignified and persist for a year or longer.

Very little information is available regarding the abundance and distribution of root hairs on the root systems of mature plants. Dittmer (1937) found root hairs to be present on all of the roots of a four-months-old rye plant. This plant bore a total of about 14 billion root hairs. On the other hand, some tree species, especially certain conifers, bear few or no root hairs. The roots of some species, such as maize, produce an abundance of root hairs when they develop in the soil or moist air, but few or none when they develop under water as in a so-
lution culture. The roots of
other species, on the contrary,
produce root hairs in abundance whether they develop in
the soil or in water. Under
field conditions maximum development of root hairs on
most terrestrial plants appears
to occur in soils with a moisture content between the field
capacity and permanent wilting percentage.

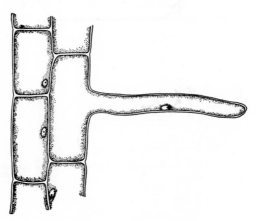

A root hair is essentially a
tubular outgrowth of the pe-
Fig. 70.   A young root hair.

ripheral wall of an epidermal cell, closed at its distal extremity, projecting more or less at right angles from the long axis of the epidermal cell of which it is an integral part (Fig. 70). Root hairs develop only from certain of the epidermal cells. They range in length from less than a millimeter to about a centimeter and are usually about 10 μ in diameter. On some roots as many as several hundred root hairs may be borne on a square millimeter of root surface, although the number per unit area is usually less. The presence of root hairs on a given area of a root often increases the exposed surface of that area from three- to tenfold.

The cell wall of a root hair is composed principally of cellulose and pectic compounds. The outer lamella of the wall seems to be composed entirely of pectic compounds, largely calcium pectate. The tenacity with which root hairs and soil particles adhere is accounted for by this pectic coating. Because of this intimate contact between the root hairs and soil particles it is difficult to separate the two by washing or in any other way without injuring or destroying most of the root hairs. The inner wall

of a root hair is lined with a thin layer of cytoplasm which is continuous
with the cytoplasm of the epidermal cell of which the root hair is a part.
In water or in moist air the root hairs are usually straight, but in soil
they are more or less contorted, and sometimes even branched, conform-
ing to the shape and distribution of the soil particles among which they
penetrate. Detailed investigations of the development of root hairs have
been made by Sinnott and Bloch (1939) and Cormack (1949).

The Pathway of Water Through the Root.—Water enters the roots principally through the walls of the root hairs and epidermal cells of the
root tips. Absorption of water by individual root hairs has been demonstrated experimentally with micropotometers (Rosene, 1943; Rosene and
Walthall, 1949). From the epidermal cells the water passes through suc-

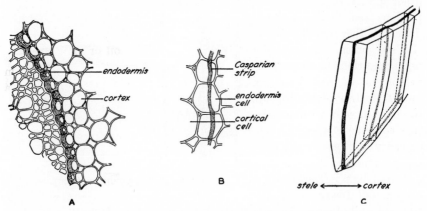

Fig. 71. (A) Thickened tangential walls of endodermis of a maize root, as seen
in cross section. (B) Casparian strip in stem endodermis of *Piper macrophylla*,
as seen in cross section. (C) Perspective diagram showing position of Casparian
strip in an endodermal cell.

cessive rows of thin-walled cortical cells, and then through the cells of
the endodermis (Fig. 67).

The structure of the walls of the endodermal cells is peculiar. Two
main types of such cells have been recognized. In one type (Fig. 71A)
the inner tangential and radial walls, or sometimes the entire wall, is
thickened. These thickened walls are suberized and sometimes partly
lignified. In a second type (Fig. 71B and C) a thickened strip is present
on the inner surface of the radial and transverse walls, this thickening
often being suberized. The width and general configuration of these
Casparian strips, as they are called, vary with the species. Regardless of
type, most thickened endodermal walls are pitted. In some species having
the thick-walled type of endodermis, there are present, opposite the

outer end of each area of xylem tissue (as seen in cross section) isolated thin-walled endodermal cells called *passage cells*. These are supposed to facilitate the movement of water and dissolved salts through the endodermis. Passage of water and mineral salts through the endodermis is probably also facilitated by the presence of lateral root initials which usually have developed by the time the endodermis is mature.

After passing through the endodermis water moves into the xylem ducts, in most species after traversing a few intervening layers of pericyclic cells. The route followed by water through the rest of the plant has already been described in Chap. XII.

The Relation between Roots and Soil Water.—From the standpoint of the absorption of water by plants, a clear distinction should be made between conditions under which capillary movement of water occurs readily in a soil and those under which such movement of water is slow or nonexistent. If capillary movement occurs readily, translocation of water may take place toward the young roots whenever they are absorbing water. There are two principal conditions under which capillary translocation of water can occur in soils at appreciable rates: (1) in any zone of soil which is not more than a few feet above a water table, and (2) in the upper layers of any soil after a heavy rain or irrigation, but before the water content of the soil has decreased to its field capacity. As the water in the films surrounding the soil particles with which the root tips are in contact becomes depleted, more water moves toward those particles by capillarity. The actual rate of such capillary movement of water through the soil may become a factor influencing the rate of absorption. Root systems, however, are not static, but are more or less continually growing through the soil. The rate of root growth of most species decreases, as a general rule, with increasing wetness of the soil above the field capacity, because of the corresponding reduction in soil aeration. Hence in soils in which capillary movement of water occurs—which are necessarily relatively wet—the rate of elongation of roots is generally less than in otherwise similar but somewhat dryer soils. This continued growth of root tips through the soil brings them into contact with other portions of the soil water, so that, even if capillary movement to certain parts of the soil ceases, capillary movement of water to the roots may be re-established by the extension of the root tips themselves into zones of the soil that have not yet been depleted of water which can move by capillarity.

Many plants, much of the time, grow in soils at water contents between the permanent wilting percentage and the field capacity. In this range of soil-water contents capillary movement of water is very slow. Once most of the film water present on the soil particles with which the root tips are in contact has been absorbed it cannot be replaced in any significant quantity by capillary movement from adjacent regions of soil if the soil water content is below the field capacity. Neither does water move in vapor form through soils toward the absorbing regions of roots at appreciable rates. Under such conditions the absorbing region of every rootlet often becomes surrounded with a narrow cylindrical zone of soil which has been depleted to a water content much below that of the surrounding soil.

Since, in soils at a water content below the field capacity, movement of water toward the roots is very slow, the principal method by which the roots come in contact with additional increments of water is by continually growing through the soil (Burr, 1914). Mature root systems of many species of plants bear millions of root tips. Each of these numerous root tips may be pictured as progressing through the soil and absorbing most of the water present in the smaller interstices between the soil particles with which they come in contact (Livingston, 1927). Relatively large quantities of water can be absorbed in this way, at least by some species of plants. For example, the total length of all the roots on a four-months-old rye plant was found by Dittmer (1937) to be 387 miles. On the average, therefore, the aggregate daily increase in the length of the roots on this plant was more than 3 miles. In addition, nearly 55 miles of new root hairs were formed, on the average, per day. Kramer and Coile (1940) calculated that such a rate of root extension would permit the absorption by such a plant of about 1.6 liters of water daily from a sandy loam, or about 2.9 liters from a heavy clay loam, when both soils were at the field capacity.

This picture of the role of root elongation in the absorption of water (and mineral salts) from the soil under certain conditions is probably an accurate one for many and perhaps most species of plants. The root systems of some species of plants, however, are of a sparse, sparingly branched type which would suggest that the quantities of water which they can absorb in the manner just described would be relatively small. Mycorrhizae (Chap. XXIV) may aid in the absorption of water by some species. Elongation of roots would also be less effective in contributing to the absorption of water by terrestrial species in which the roots bear few or no root hairs than in species on which root hairs develop in abundance.

The root-tip population of any plant is usually so large that often not all of the root tips are subjected to the same soil-water conditions. Some may be located in lower soil horizons which, under certain conditions, contain more water than the upper layers of the soil. Under other conditions the reverse situation may prevail. After light rainfalls on a comparatively dry soil, for example, the root tips closer to the surface may be in contact with soil at a higher water content than those at greater depths. Hence the quantity of water absorbed in a given interval of time may differ greatly from one root tip to another as they advance through the soil. In general, however, roots do not grow appreciably in soils which have a water content less than that of the permanent wilting percentage (Hendrickson and Veihmeyer, 1931).

Mechanism of the Absorption of Water.—In Chap. XII it was shown that the development of a diffusion-pressure deficit in the mesophyll cells of leaves causes the water in the xylem vessels or tracheids to pass into a state of tension which results in an increase in the diffusion-pressure deficit of the water in the xylem ducts by the amount of the imposed tension. As soon as the diffusion-pressure deficit of the water in the xylem ducts in the absorbing region of the root exceeds that in contiguous cells, a gradient of diffusion-pressure deficits is established across the root, increasing consistently from cell to cell from its epidermal layer to the xylem conduits. Many authorities believe that the water in the cells in absorbing regions of roots often passes into a state of tension under conditions such as those just described. If this occurs greater diffusion-pressure deficits could develop in the peripheral cell walls of young roots than otherwise would be possible. However, the mechanism as just described will operate even if the water in the root cells never passes into a state of tension. The osmotic pressure of the root epidermal and root-hair cells of most species for which measurements are available is about 3-5 atm., although higher values undoubtedly occur in some species. Hence diffusion-pressure deficits of this magnitude can develop in the peripheral cells of roots even if the water in them is never under tension.

Whenever the diffusion-pressure deficit of the water in the peripheral walls of the young root cells exceeds that of the water in the soil, water will move from the soil into the root. Since the osmotic pressure of the soil solution in most soils is only a fraction of an atmosphere, the diffusion-pressure deficit of the absorbing cells of a root does not have to be very great before water will enter them from any soil with a water content equal to or greater than the field capacity.

The absorption process which has just been described is often called "passive absorption" because the entry of water into the roots is brought about by conditions which originate in the top of the plant and the root cells seemingly play only a subsidiary role. Although the general picture of this mechanism of absorption which has just been presented is probably correct in its essentials, it is almost certainly oversimplified. The influence of certain environmental factors upon absorption, particularly temperature and oxygen (see later), suggests that the metabolic activities of living cells in the absorption zone of roots also play at least an indirect part in this process.

The mechanism of absorption just described undoubtedly accounts for the intake of most of the water which enters the roots of plants, but it is not the only mechanism of absorption which is known to operate in plants. In many species an internal pressure known as root pressure often develops in the xylem (Chap. XII). The occurrence of sap exudation resulting from root pressure can be strikingly demonstrated with some species by immersing the root system of a decapitated plant in a potometer (Fig. 34). After a time a dilute sap will begin to ooze from the cut stem, and the absorption of water will be indicated by the movement of the meniscus on the capillary arm of the potometer. If the volume of water exuded is measured it will be found to be not sensibly different from the volume absorbed. In other words, water is being absorbed and is moving in an upward direction through the plant as a result of processes which take place in the root cells. This type of absorption, in which the mechanism involved is localized within the root system, is often called "active absorption." Root pressure, or guttation, and active absorption are usually considered to be different aspects of the same phenomenon.

There is good evidence for the existence of a relatively simple osmotic mechanism of active absorption, but it is by no means certain that this is the only mechanism responsible for root pressure, xylem sap exudation, and guttation. The essentials of an osmotic theory of active absorption were first clearly suggested by Atkins (1916). Priestley (1920, 1922) has also advocated a similar hypothesis. In a number of species it has been shown that, although the osmotic pressure of the sap in the xylem ducts is relatively low, seldom exceeding 2 atm., it is higher than the diffusion-pressure deficit of most soils at the field capacity or a higher water content. Osmotic movement of water from the soil to the xylem ducts could therefore occur through the "multicellular membrane" of the intervening root cells in spite of the fact that such cells have a higher osmotic pressure than either the soil solution or the xylem sap. The mechanism of such a movement of water can be interpreted in terms of the establishment of a consistently increasing gradient of diffusion-pressure deficits from cell to cell across the root from the epidermis to the xylem ducts. Kramer (1932) has shown that in an analogous situation water will move across the cells of the petiole of the tropical papaw (Carica papaya).

Eaton (1943) found an almost proportional relation between the difference in osmotic pressures of the xylem sap and the external solution and the rate of exudation from decapitated young cotton plants. His results also indicated that exudation would cease when the value of this osmotic differential fell to zero suggesting that, under the conditions of these experiments at least, the osmotic mechanism was the only one in operation. The sensitivity of the osmotic mechanism is very great; reversals occur in less than a minute from exudation to cessation of exudation and back to exudation upon transfer of the root systems of young plants from water to a dilute sucrose solution and back to water (Kramer, 1941).

Although there is little doubt of the existence of an osmotic mechanism of active absorption, the results of certain experiments are difficult to reconcile with the view that this process can be accounted for entirely by such a mechanism. The findings of Grossenbacher (1938, 1939) and Skoog et al. (1938) that an autonomous, more or less regular diurnal fluctuation occurs in the rate of exudation of xylem sap from detopped seedlings, with the maximum about noon and the minimum about midnight, suggests a more complex mechanism than the one described above. A retarding effect of deprivation of oxygen on absorption of water by isolated onion roots, and by root hairs of radish, has been demonstrated by refined experiments with potometers (Rosene, 1950; Rosene and Bartlett, 1950), suggesting that respiration plays at least an indirect part in the active absorption mechanism. The enhancing effect of auxin (Chap. XXVIII) on xylem sap exudation rates (Skoog et al., 1938) also suggests that respiration plays a part in active absorption, since auxins are known to influence respiration rates. It has therefore been postulated that a second mechanism of active absorption exists which is dependent for its operation upon the metabolic activity of the root cells.

The influence of metabolic processes on active absorption of water may, however, be largely or entirely an indirect one. The absorption of mineral salts by cells is markedly influenced by the metabolic conditions prevailing within them, especially their rate of aerobic respiration (Chap. XXIV). Furthermore, there are good reasons for believing that the passage of salts into the xylem ducts is largely controlled by the metabolic conditions in adjacent living cells (Crafts and Broyer, 1938). Metabolic conditions, therefore, may influence the steepness of the osmotic gradient between the xylem sap and the soil because of their effect on the absorption and cell-to-cell movement of mineral salts; and their influence on the active absorption of water may be exerted largely or entirely in this or in other indirect ways.

Although some plants, under certain conditions, exude relatively large quantities of water as a result of active absorption (Chap. XII), in general, the volumes of water moving into plants as a result of this process are relatively small compared with the volumes entering plants as a result of passive absorption (Kramer, 1939). The effectiveness of active absorption in reducing the water content of a soil also appears to be considerably less than that of passive absorption. Detopped herbaceous plants cease exuding water when the soil-water content has been reduced to about halfway between the permanent wilting percentage and the field capacity (Kramer, 1941). The active absorption mechanism apparently does not absorb water against a diffusion-pressure deficit of more than 1 or 2 atm.; whereas the passive absorption mechanism results in absorption of water at relatively rapid rates until the diffusion-pressure deficit of the substrate approaches the permanent wilting percentage value (approximately 15 atm.).

Environmental Factors Influencing the Rate of Absorption of Water.— Any factor which influences the diffusion-pressure deficit of the water in the peripheral walls of the young roots or the diffusion-pressure deficit of the water in the soil will influence the rate of absorption of water. Furthermore the roots of a plant are more or less continually growing through the soil, and, when the water content of a soil is less than the field capacity, absorption of water at any appreciable rate can occur only if growth of roots through the soil continues. Factors which in-

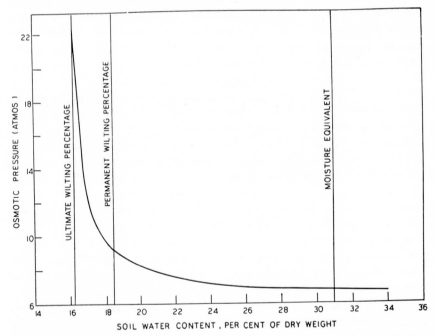

FIG. 72.   Relation between soil-water content and osmotic pressure of leaves of sunflower plants. Data of Furr and Reeve (1945).

fluence the rate of root growth may therefore also have important effects on the amount of water which can be absorbed.

For reasons which should be clear from the preceding discussion, the rate of absorption of water is greatly influenced by the rate of transpiration. Hence any factor which influences the rate of transpiration will indirectly influence the rate of absorption of water. Contrariwise, as already shown in the discussion of transpiration, any factor which influences the rate of absorption will also influence the rate of transpiration. The more important soil factors which influence the rate of absorption of water will now be discussed.

1. *Available Soil Water.*—In general, the term available soil water is used to refer to that fraction of the soil moisture in excess of that present at the permanent wilting percentage. Absorption of water appears to take place almost equally well over the range of soil-water contents between the field capacity and the permanent wilting capacity, especially in light- and medium-textured soils (Veihmeyer, et al., 1943; and others). In heavier textured soils there is considerable evidence that the rate of absorption of water is somewhat retarded in the lower part of this range (Martin, 1940; and others). A significant fact in this connection is that the osmotic pressure of the leaves increases as the soil-water content decreases (Fig. 72). Hence as the diffusion-pressure deficit of the soil water becomes greater, the potential diffusion-pressure deficit of the water in the plant likewise becomes greater. The effectiveness of the passive absorption mechanism undoubtedly increases accordingly. This upward adjustment in the osmotic pressures of the cells of the plant with decrease in soil-water content is one of the main factors resulting in a nearly uniform rate of absorption from many soils in the range of soil-water contents between the field capacity and the permanent wilting percentage.

At soil-water contents below the permanent wilting percentage, water intake is so slow that the turgidity of the leaf cells ordinarily cannot be maintained. Relatively high soil-water contents, in the range above the field capacity, result in a diminution in the rate of absorption by many species, because of the accompanying decrease in soil aeration (see later).

2. *Soil Temperature.*—Reduction in the absorption rate of water occurs in many kinds of plants at soil temperatures well above freezing, but the exact magnitude of this effect differs according to species (Döring, 1935; Arndt, 1937; Brown, 1939; Kramer, 1942; Kozlowski, 1943; and others). In general, plants native to warm climates undergo a greater reduction in rate of water intake when the soil is chilled than those which are habitants of cooler climates. For example, Kramer (1942) found that watermelon and cotton, warm season crops, absorbed only 20 per cent as much water at 10°C. as at 25°C., while collards, a cool season crop, absorbed 75 per

cent as much water at the lower of these two temperatures as at the higher. The relation between soil temperature and the rate of absorption of water (for which the rate of transpiration is taken as the index) by sunflower is shown in Fig. 73. In this species, the rate of transpiration diminishes rapidly with a decrease in soil temperature below about 55°F. (13°C.). A similar relation doubtless holds for other species, except that the soil temperature at which an appreciable diminution in the rate of water influx is initiated differs from one kind of a plant to another. For obvious reasons, virtually no water is absorbed by roots from frozen soils.

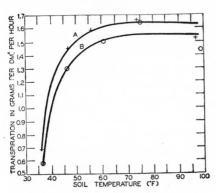

Fig. 73. Relation between rate of transpiration of sunflower plants and soil temperature. Each curve represents the results of a different experiment. Data of Clements and Martin (1934).

The mechanism whereby low soil temperatures cause a retardation in the rate of absorption of water is doubtless a complex one. The principal factors involved are: (1) retardation in the rate of root elongation, (2) decreased rate of movement of water from soil into roots, (3) decreased permeability of cell membranes, (4) increased viscosity of the protoplasm and cell walls, (5) increased viscosity of water, (6) decreased vapor pressure of water, and (7) decreased metabolic activity of root cells (Kramer, 1949).

Soil temperatures may sometimes become high enough to exert a retarding effect on the rate of absorption of water. For example, Haas (1936) found that absorption of water by lemons, oranges, and grapefruits decreased when soil temperatures exceeded 30° or 35°C.

3. *Aeration of the Soil.*—In general, absorption of water by the roots of most species of plants proceeds more rapidly in soils which are well aerated than in those which are not. In such soils oxygen concentrations may approach a zero value, and carbon-dioxide concentrations ranging up to 10 per cent are not uncommon. The comparative effects of a maintained near zero oxygen content and a maintained relatively high (20 per cent) carbon-dioxide content in the soil atmosphere on the intake of water by tomato, tobacco, sunflower, coleus, cotton, and corn plants were investigated by Whitney (1942). Severe oxygen deficiency, obtained by passing nitrogen through the sand medium, resulted in a marked reduction in water absorption by all of these species as compared with plants whose roots were aerated with atmospheric air, although the effect was

more pronounced on some than on others. When the roots of these species were exposed to excess carbon dioxide in the presence of oxygen, a condition which was obtained by passing a mixture of 20 per cent carbon dioxide, 20 per cent oxygen, and 60 per cent nitrogen through the sand, there was no significant decrease in the rate of water intake by corn or sunflower plants, and only a relatively small decrease in the rate for tobacco, tomato, coleus, and cotton plants as compared with similar plants aerated with atmospheric air. When the roots were exposed to the combined effects of oxygen deficiency and carbon-dioxide excess (gaseous phase in the sand consisting of 80 per cent nitrogen and 20 per cent carbon dioxide), the retarding effects on water absorption by all species investigated except coleus and tomato were little if any greater than the effect of severe oxygen deficiency alone. In general, these results indicate that a near absence of oxygen has a greater influence in retarding the rate of water intake by many kinds of plants than the presence of carbon dioxide in concentrations considerably in excess of those usually found in soils. Exposure of roots to pure carbon dioxide, or to high concentrations (50 per cent or more) of this gas, at least for short periods, however, has a marked retarding effect on absorption of water by a number of species (Kramer 1940, Chang and Loomis 1945). Hoagland and Broyer (1942) interpret this result as being caused by an initial decreasing effect of carbon dioxide on the permeability of root cells to water.

Saturation or near-saturation of a soil with water is the most common cause of deficient soil aeration. Under such conditions it appears probable that the reduced rates of water absorption which are evidenced by most plants result more from a severe oxygen deficiency than from an accumulation of carbon dioxide. A drastic reduction in the supply of available oxygen in the soil reduces the rate of respiration of the root cells and this, in turn, influences other metabolic processes as well as the rate of root growth. One of the results of this sequence of disturbed physiological conditions is a lower rate of absorption of water. While the roots of most kinds of plants can survive for at least short periods in soils practically devoid of oxygen, as a result of the occurrence of anaerobic respiration (Chap. XXII), maintenance of this process for any considerable interval of time leads to death of roots of many species.

In contrast with other species, the roots of hydrophytes naturally grow in water-saturated soils and absorb water readily from such soils. Some species of hydrophytes have well-developed intercellular air spaces which are continuous from the leaves through the stems into the roots. It has been shown in some such species that oxygen moves to the roots through such channels (Conway 1937, Laing 1940) and such movement of oxygen doubtless occurs in many other kinds of hydrophytes. In other species which grow with their roots submerged, however, no such prominent system of air passages is present. Even in such species some movement may occur to the roots from aerial organs through intercellular spaces of usual dimensions. The roots of these species in which little or no oxygen becomes available through downward movement from the tops apparently are able to carry on their metabolic processes at relatively low oxygen concentrations.

4. *Concentration of the Soil Solution.*—The concentration of the soil solution in most soils in humid regions is so small that it has only a slight effect on the diffusion-pressure deficit of the soil water. In alkali or saline soils, on the other hand, the concentration of the dissolved salts in the soil water is often sufficient to raise the osmotic pressure to a very considerable value—in extreme situations to 100 atm. or even higher. Copious applications of fertilizers to greenhouse or agricultural soils, especially if sandy, or irrigation with water containing dissolved salts in considerable concentration, often result in raising the osmotic pressure of the soil solution to a value of several atmospheres or more.

The diffusion-pressure deficit of the soil water, except when soils are relatively dry, *i.e.*, below the field capacity, is essentially equal to the osmotic pressure of the soil solution. In general, the rate of absorption of water decreases, often almost proportionately, with increase in the osmotic pressure of the substrate (Rosene 1941, Hayward and Spurr 1943, Long 1943, and others). The effect of solutes on the movement of water into roots appears to be principally an osmotic one, specific effects of ions playing only a secondary role. Plants may, within limits, become adjusted to an increase in the concentration of the substrate solution, inasmuch as the osmotic pressure of the cells of a plant may increase under such conditions (Table 12). Hence a plant in which the absorption rate is markedly reduced when its roots are first brought into contact with a substrate solution of higher osmotic pressure than the one in which it had been growing may, after an interval of time, largely or entirely regain its original rate of water absorption. Most plants can develop normally only when the osmotic pressure of the substrate solution does not exceed a few atmospheres. Halophytes, *i.e.*, plants indigenous to saline or alkali soils or substrates, are the only important exception to this statement.

Absorption of Water and Water Vapor by Leaves.—Leaves and other aerial parts of plants frequently become wet as a result of rain, dew, or fog. Floods also sometimes result in a temporary immersion of aerial plant organs. Wetzel (1924) found that, of a large number of species investigated, practically all absorbed some water directly through the leaves. The turgidity of the leaves was restored from the wilted condition in most species after immersion in water for 24 hr. or less. Absorption of water occurred directly through the epidermal cells rather than through the stomates. In nature, however, absorption of water through the leaves is only rarely a factor of importance in the water economy of the plant.

Prolonged immersion of the leaves of many species in water leads to opening of the stomates and, under certain conditions, also to an injection of the intercellular spaces with liquid water. Tiny droplets of water are sometimes projected through the stomates as a result of splashing during heavy rains or during the artificial spraying of leaves. Partial or complete injection of the intercellular spaces with liquid water is sometimes brought about in this way, especially in species with large stomates.

Under certain conditions leaves and other aerial organs can absorb water vapor directly from the atmosphere. Stone, *et al.* (1950) have shown that seedlings of Coulter pine (*Pinus coulteri*), in a state of permanent wilting, absorb water-vapor from saturated or near-saturated atmospheres.

SUGGESTED FOR COLLATERAL READING

Cannon, W. A. Physiological features of roots, with especial reference to the relation of roots to the aeration of the soil. *Carnegie Inst. Wash. Publ. No. 368.* Washington. 1925.

Clements, F. E. Aeration and air content. The role of oxygen in root activity. *Carnegie Inst. Wash. Publ. No. 315.* Washington. 1922.

Crafts, A. S., H. B. Currier, and C. R. Stocking. *Water in the Physiology of Plants.* Chronica Botanica Co. Waltham, Mass. 1949.

Eames, A. J., and L. H. McDaniels. *An Introduction to Plant Anatomy.* 2nd Ed. McGraw-Hill Book Co., Inc. New York. 1947.

Hayward, H. E. *The Structure of Economic Plants.* The Macmillan Co. New York. 1938.

Kramer, P. J. *Plant and Soil Water Relationships.* McGraw-Hill Book Co., Inc., New York. 1949.

SELECTED BIBLIOGRAPHY

Arndt, C. H. Water absorption in the cotton plant as affected by soil and water temperatures. *Plant Physiol.* **12:** 703-720. 1937.

Atkins, W. G. R. *Some Recent Researches in Plant Physiology.* Whittaker and Co. London. 1916.

Brown, E. M. Some effects of temperature on the growth and chemical composition of certain pasture grasses. *Mo. Agric. Expt. Sta. Res. Bull. 299.* 1939.

Broyer, T. C. The movement of materials into plants. Part I. Osmosis and the movement of water in plants. *Bot. Rev.* **13:** 1-58. 1947.

Burr, W. W. The storage and use of soil water. *Neb. Agric. Expt. Sta. Res. Bull. No. 5.* 1914.

Chang, H. T., and W. E. Loomis. Effect of carbon dioxide on absorption of water and nutrients by roots. *Plant Physiol.* **20:** 221-232. 1945.

Clements, F. E., and E. V. Martin. Effect of soil temperature on transpiration in *Helianthus annuus. Plant Physiol.* **9:** 619-630. 1934.

Conway, Verona M. Studies in the autecology of *Cladium mariscus*. III. The aeration of the subterranean parts of the plant. *New Phytol.* **36:** 64-96. 1937.

Cormack, R. G. H. The development of root hairs in angiosperms. *Bot. Rev.* **15:** 583-612. 1949.

Crafts, A. S., and T. C. Broyer. Migration of salts and water into xylem of the roots of higher plants. *Amer. Jour. Bot.* **25:** 529-535. 1938.

Dittmer, H. J. A quantitative study of the roots and root hairs of a winter rye plant (*Secale cereale*). *Amer. Jour. Bot.* **24:** 417-420. 1937.

Döring, B. Die Temperaturabhängigkeit der Wasseraufnahme und ihre ökologische Bedeutung. *Zeitschr. Bot.* **28:** 305-383. 1935.

Eaton, F. M. The osmotic and vitalistic interpretations of exudation. *Amer. Jour. Bot.* **30:** 663-674. 1943.

Esau, Katherine. Developmental anatomy of the fleshy storage organ of *Daucus carota*. *Hilgardia* **13:** 175-226. 1940.

Furr, J. R., and J. O. Reeve. Range of soil-moisture percentages through which plants undergo permanent wilting in some soils from semiarid irrigated areas. *Jour. Agric. Res.* **71:** 149-170. 1945.

Grossenbacher, K. A. Diurnal fluctuation in root pressure. *Plant Physiol.* **13:** 669-676. 1938.

Grossenbacher, K. A. Autonomic cycle of rate of exudation of plants. *Amer. Jour. Bot.* **26:** 107-109. 1939.

Haas, A. R. C. Growth and water losses in citrus as affected by soil temperature. *Calif. Citrograph* **21:** 467, 469. 1936.

Hayward, H. E., and Winifred B. Spurr. Effects of osmotic concentration of the substrate on the entry of water into corn roots. *Bot. Gaz.* **105:** 152-164. 1943.

Hendrickson, A. H., and F. J. Veihmeyer. Influences of dry soil on root extension. *Plant Physiol.* **6:** 567-576. 1931.

Hoagland, D. R., and T. C. Broyer. Accumulation of salt and permeability in plant cells. *Jour. Gen. Physiol.* **25:** 865-880. 1942.

Kozlowski, T. T. Transpiration rates of some forest tree species during the dormant season. *Plant Physiol.* **18:** 252-260. 1943.

Kramer, P. J. The absorption of water by root systems of plants. *Amer. Jour. Bot.* **19:** 148-164. 1932.

Kramer, P. J. The forces concerned in the intake of water by transpiring plants. *Amer. Jour. Bot.* **26:** 784-791. 1939.

Kramer, P. J. Causes of decreased absorption of water by plants in poorly aerated media. *Amer. Jour. Bot.* **27:** 216-220. 1940.

Kramer, P. J. Soil moisture as a limiting factor for active absorption and root pressure. *Amer. Jour. Bot.* **28:** 446-451. 1941.

Kramer, P. J. Species differences with respect to water absorption at low soil temperatures. *Amer. Jour. Bot.* **29:** 828-832. 1942.

Kramer, P. J. Absorption of water through suberized roots of trees. *Plant Physiol.* **21:** 37-41. 1946.

Kramer, P. J., and T. S. Coile. An estimation of the volume of water made available by root exudation. *Plant Physiol.* **15:** 743-747. 1940.

Laing, H. E. The composition of the internal atmosphere of *Nuphar advenum* and other water plants. *Amer. Jour. Bot.* **27:** 861-868. 1940.

Livingston, B. E. Plant water relations. *Quart. Rev. Biol.* **2:** 494-515. 1927.

Long, E. M. The effect of salt additions to the substrate on intake of water and nutrients by roots of approach-grafted tomato plants. *Amer. Jour. Bot.* **30:** 594-601. 1943.

Martin, E. V. Effect of soil moisture on growth and transpiration in *Helianthus annuus*. *Plant Physiol.* **15**: 449-466. 1940.

Priestley, J. H. The mechanism of root pressure. *New Phytol.* **19**: 189-200. 1920.

Priestley, J. H. Further observations on the mechanism of root pressure. *New Phytol.* **21**: 41-47. 1922.

Rosene, Hilda F. Control of water transport in local root regions of attached and isolated roots by means of the osmotic pressure of the external solution. *Amer. Jour. Bot.* **28**: 402-410. 1941.

Rosene, Hilda F. Quantitative measurement of the velocity of water absorption in individual root hairs by a microtechnique. *Plant Physiol.* **18**: 588-607. 1943.

Rosene, Hilda F. The effect of anoxia on water exchange and oxygen consumption of onion root tissues. *Jour. Cell. and Comp. Physiol.* **35**: 179-193. 1950.

Rosene, Hilda F., and L. E. Bartlett. Effect of anoxia on water influx of individual radish root hair cells. *Jour. Cell. and Comp. Physiol.* **36**: 83-96. 1950.

Rosene, Hilda F., and A. M. J. Walthall. Velocities of water absorption by individual root hairs of different species. *Bot. Gaz.* **111**: 11-21. 1949.

Sinnott, E. W., and R. Bloch. Cell polarity and the differentiation of root hairs. *Proc. Nat. Acad. Sci. (U.S.A.)* **25**: 248-252. 1939.

Skoog, F., T. C. Broyer, and K. A. Grossenbacher. Effects of auxin on rates, periodicity, and osmotic relations in exudation. *Amer. Jour. Bot.* **25**: 749-759. 1938.

Stone, E. C., F. W. Went, and C. L. Young. Water absorption from the atmosphere by plants growing in dry soil. *Science* **111**: 546-548. 1950.

Veihmeyer, F. J., N. E. Edlefsen, and A. H. Hendrickson. Use of tensiometers in measuring availability of water to plants. *Plant Physiol.* **18**: 66-78. 1943.

Weaver, J. E. *Root Development of Field Crops*. McGraw-Hill Book Co., Inc. New York. 1926.

Weaver, J. E., and W. E. Bruner. *Root Development of Vegetable Crops*. McGraw-Hill Book Co., Inc. New York. 1927.

Wetzel, K. Die Wasseraufnahme der höheren Pflanzen gemässigter Klimate durch oberirdische Organe. *Flora* **117**: 221-269. 1924.

Whitney, J. B., Jr. Effects of composition of the soil atmosphere on the absorption of water by plants. *Abst. Doctoral Dissertations, Ohio State University* **38**: 97-103. 1942.

DISCUSSION QUESTIONS

1. Under what conditions would the transpiration rate be a fairly accurate index of the rate of absorption of water? Under what conditions not?

2. How would you ascertain, for a given plant, exactly how much the absorption of water by the plant during its lifetime had exceeded loss of water by transpiration and guttation?

3. Why do tobacco plants often exhibit wilting immediately after a heavy rain?

4. In a given soil under which of the following conditions would you expect the most extensive root development of most kinds of plants: (1) at the field capacity, (2) at a water content considerably above the field capacity, (3) at a water content close to the permanent wilting percentage? Explain.

5. Why do not many kinds of seeds germinate in a soil at the permanent wilting percentage when they will absorb water from solutions with a diffusion deficit

corresponding to a value less than that of the permanent wilting percentage (Table 10)?

6. Two similar, small potted tomato plants are selected and the root systems of one killed by heating the soil to 70°C. The soil in both pots is then saturated with water and the plants set in a greenhouse and allowed to remain there until death results from water deficiency. Plot curves showing how you would expect the rate of water absorption to vary in each pot as the soil dries out.

7. Some kinds of plants have a much larger "water requirement" (amount of water absorbed per unit dry weight accumulated) than others. How can such differences be accounted for?

8. Why is the watering of some kinds of house or greenhouse plants with water from a tap often harmful during the winter months?

9. Assuming the soil moisture to be at the field capacity and "standard day" conditions, show by means of two curves how the rates of active and passive absorption would vary in a vigorous tomato plant over a 24-hour period.

10. Assuming a clear, warm summer day, and soil moisture at the field capacity, what will be the effect on the rate of water absorption of severing the stem of a vigorous herbaceous plant at the soil level at noon? Illustrate by means of a curve.

XV

THE INTERNAL WATER RELATIONS OF PLANTS

In preceding chapters the loss of water from plants, the movement of water through plants, and the absorption of water by the roots of plants have been considered more or less as independent processes, although it should have become increasingly evident as the discussion progressed that the internal hydrostatic system of plants is essentially a unit in its behavior. This point cannot be too strongly stressed as no adequate picture of the water relations of plants can be drawn in terms of these processes considered separately. Many of the more succulent species of plants may, in fact, be regarded as physically little more than a mass of water held in position and shape by an amount of cellular structure which is remarkably small in relation to the volume of water thus retained. Even in woody species of plants, in which the proportion of cellular material to water is greater, the water in the plant is maintained as a continuous unit system. Within this unit system diffusion and mass flow of water are continually in progress. A shift in the diffusion-pressure deficit of the water in any part of this unit system will show its influence, sooner or later, but usually within a relatively short time, in other parts of the system. Such effects of changes in the diffusion-pressure deficit of the water in one part of this system upon the diffusion-pressure deficit of water in other parts of the same system are more pronounced when the rate of absorption of water is slow, or has ceased entirely, than when water is moving into the roots of a plant at a relatively rapid rate.

Wilting.—One of the commonest of observations among agriculturists and gardeners is that the leaves of many species of plants often wilt on hot summer afternoons, only to regain their turgidity during the night even if the plants are not provided with additional water by rainfall or irrigation. In dry, hot regions, or during hot weather in more temperate regions, such a phenomenon may be a regular daily occurrence, even during periods when the soil is well supplied with water. This familiar reaction of plants is called *temporary* or *transient wilting* and clearly results from a temporary excess of the rate of transpiration over that of absorption. As a result the total volume of water in the plant shrinks, although not equally in all the tissues. In general, diminution of water content is greatest in the leaf cells. The condition commonly called wilting is induced whenever the shrinkage in the volume of water in the leaf cells is sufficient to cause them to lose all or most of their turgor.

Wilting as a visible phenomenon is confined chiefly to species in which the leaf tissues are composed largely of thin-walled, parenchymatous mesophyll cells, and in which the leaves are maintained in their usual firm, expanded condition principally by the turgidity of such cells. External manifestations of wilting can also be observed frequently in young succulent stem tips, floral parts, and even fruits. Root hairs also wilt very commonly, although such wilting usually cannot be observed except under experimental conditions.

In many species of plants the leaves are supported largely by lignified tissues. Examples of species bearing such leaves include many of the evergreens such as pines, holly, mountain laurel, etc., and numerous sclerophyllous species common in the semi-arid regions of many parts of the world. Such leaves wilt just as do parenchymatous ones in the sense that a marked loss of turgor may occur in the leaf cells. The wilting of such leaves is not usually characterized, however, by the drooping, folding, or rolling which are the visible symptoms of wilting leaves composed principally of parenchymatous tissues.

Even on days upon which visible wilting does not take place, *incipient wilting* is of frequent occurrence. Incipient wilting is the term applied when loss of turgor by the leaf cells is only partial; it does not result in visible drooping, rolling, or folding of the leaves. Incipient wilting is of almost universal occurrence in the leaves of terrestrial plants on bright, warm days whenever environmental conditions are not severe enough to induce the more extreme and visibly discernible temporary wilting. Leaves passing into a state of transient wilting always first pass through the stage of incipient wilting. Both incipient and transient wilting are to be distinguished from permanent wilting (see later) which results, not from a temporary excess of transpiration over absorption, but from a deficiency of water in the soil. Plants do not recover from permanent wilting unless the water content of the soil in which they are rooted increases.

As a general rule the leaves wilt first, because they are the organs from which the great bulk of all water loss occurs, but the decrease in turgor gradually spreads throughout the plant as the internal deficiency of water becomes more severe. Loss of turgor is thus general, although not usually equal throughout all of the tissues of a plant whenever wilting of any duration occurs. Any living cell in a plant may wilt, if this term is used to designate an approximately complete loss of turgor, which will be the general sense in which it will be employed in this discussion. The longer the condition of wilting persists, the more pronounced such a systemic loss of turgor will be. We may speak, therefore, not only of wilted leaves, or other plant parts, but also of "wilted plants."

As a general rule the stomates close during wilting, although in at least some species their closure is preceded by a transient widening of the stomatal aperture (Müller, 1937). This passing enlargement in the size of the stomatal pore may result from a more rapid loss of turgor by the contiguous epidermal cells than by the guard cells, thus permitting a slight further expansion of the latter. Prolonged wilting has been observed to lead to a reopening of the stomates of a number of species. According to Iljin (1932), although a moderate decrease in the water content of a leaf causes conversion of sugar to starch in the guard cells (Chap. X), a more pronounced water loss induces the reverse action. Hence the diffusion-pressure deficit of the guard cells on wilted leaves often attains such a value that movement of water occurs into them even from adjacent cells which are in a flaccid condition. The resulting increase in turgor of the guard cells causes them to open.

Because of its effects on the dynamics of the internal hydrostatic system and upon the stomates, wilting initiates a train of far-reaching effects upon physiological conditions and processes. Some of these effects have received attention earlier in the discussion of factors influencing the periodicity of transpiration; other such effects, particularly those upon photosynthesis and growth, will receive consideration in later chapters.

Daily Variations in the Water Content of Leaves.—Although a daily variation in the total volume of water present in the body of a plant is a common and almost regular occurrence whenever transpiration is occurring at appreciable rates, because of the experimental difficulties involved no studies have been made of this phenomenon in terms of entire plants. A number of investigations have been made, however, of the diurnal variations in the water content of leaves and other plant organs.

Stanescu (1936) has studied the daily variations in the water content of the leaf blades of Boston Ivy (*Ampelopsis tricuspidata*). The determinations were made on a clear day in early November, but there is no rea-son for believing that results would be greatly different under standard day conditions (Chap. X). As shown by his data (Fig. 74), the leaf-water content decreased during the morning and early afternoon hours, reaching a minimum at about 5:00 P.M. Thereafter the leaf-water content increased, culminating in a maximum which was attained at about 1:00 A.M. During the early morning hours the leaf-water content again decreased. Similar observations have been made by Kramer (1937) on leaves of several species. In the sunflower, for example, the minimum leaf-water content was attained at about 4:00 P.M., and the maximum at about midnight. The most probable explanation of the occurrence of the maximum leaf-water content during the middle hours of the night is that during the early morning hours the leaves lose water by translocation to other organs of the plant. The mechanism of such internal redistributions of water in the body of a plant is discussed later in this chapter. Under such con-

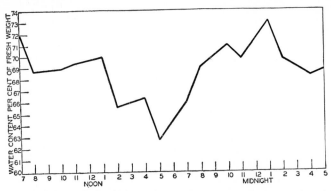

Fig. 74.   Daily variation in the water content of leaves of Boston ivy (*Ampelopsis tricuspidata*). Data of Stanescu (1936).

ditions the water content of the plant as a whole might be increasing as a result of continued absorption of water, while that of certain organs, such as the leaves, might be diminishing.

The magnitude of the frequently recurrent diurnal reduction in the water content of the leaves and other organs of a plant varies not only with the species, but also with the environmental conditions and their influence on the relative rates of transpiration and absorption of water. On cool, cloudy or rainy days when the soil is well provided with water often little or no water deficit develops within the plant during the daylight hours. On bright, sunny, but not extremely hot days, while the soil water supply is abundant, an internal water deficit will develop, but it seldom is severe enough to induce more than incipient wilting. On clear, hot days, especially when the soil water supply is not entirely adequate, a more marked shrinkage in the volume of water within the plant usually occurs which is often of sufficient magnitude to induce temporary wilting. Only if the available water supply in the soil becomes so low that absorption of water virtually ceases will the plant pass into a state of permanent wilting.

The magnitude of the reduction in the water content of the leaves required to induce wilting varies greatly depending upon the species of plant. According to Maximov (1929) leaves of many "sun" species may lose from 20 to 30 per cent of the total water present before wilting ensues, while typical "shade" species wilt upon a reduction in the amount of water present of 3 to 5 per cent. Only in the leaves of the "sun" type can incipient wilting be distinguished as a distinct phase; in "shade" species incipient wilting is extremely transitory. The discussion of wilting and related phenomena in this chapter refers primarily to wilting of the type that is characteristic of plants indigenous to sunny, exposed habitats.

Diminution in the water content of leaves with its concomitant reduction in leaf turgor also influences the total volume of the leaf. The area of leaves may decrease as much as 5 per cent during the midday hours of a bright warm day, the exact magnitude of this shrinkage in area depending upon the species and the prevailing environmental conditions (Thoday, 1909). Not only the area, but even the thickness of the leaves may decrease with a reduction in the turgor of the leaf cells. Bachmann (1922) has shown that a reduction of as much as 5-6 per cent occurs in the thickness of the leaves of many species as they pass from a turgid into a flaccid condition.

Comparative Daily Periodicities of Transpiration and the Absorption of Water.—The observed phenomenon of wilting, and the experimental results showing that a daily diminution in the water content of leaves and other plant organs is of frequent occurrence, are both indirect evidence that the transpiration rate frequently exceeds the rate of absorption of water during the daylight hours. Only a few investigations have been undertaken, however, in which simultaneous measurements have been made of transpiration and absorption rates of the same plant over periods of 24 hr. or longer.

Kramer (1937) grew plants in metal containers which were provided with auto-irrigators of porous clay buried in the soil. Each of these irrigators was connected by tubing with a reservoir of water which was set at a lower level than the container. As water is absorbed by the plant from the soil, more moves into the soil from the porous clay irrigator which is kept filled by the pressure of the atmosphere on the water in the reservoir. Prior to an experiment the containers were sealed so that all loss of water occurred as transpiration from the plant. By weighing the container plus the reservoir at appropriate intervals and simultaneously making an observation upon the volume of water which had been absorbed from the reservoir it was possible to make parallel determinations of the rates of transpiration and absorption. Except for the fact that the soil was irrigated the plants were grown under approximately standard day conditions.

The results of one of the experiments in which loblolly pine (*Pinus taeda*) was used are shown in Fig. 75. As shown in this figure there was a distinct lag in the rate of absorption as compared with the rate of transpiration during the daylight hours—*i.e.*, during the period of relatively high transpiration rates. There was also a fairly well marked tendency, shown clearly on the second day of the experiment, for the peak absorp-

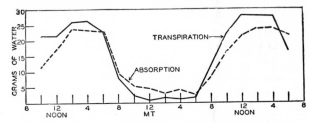

Fig. 75. Comparative daily periodicities of transpiration and absorption of water in the loblolly pine (*Pinus taeda*). Data of Kramer (1937).

tion rate to occur somewhat later in the day than the peak transpiration rate. This effect was more pronounced in experiments performed on other species by the same investigator. During the night hours the rate of absorption was continuously higher than the rate of transpiration. In other words, the tissues of the plant were being progressively depleted of water during the daylight hours, while their water supply was being replenished at night.

In this type of experimental setup it is possible that part of the water deficit observed to develop during the daylight hours may have occurred in the soil rather than in the plant. That this source of error is not serious enough to invalidate the conclusions just drawn can be shown by similar experiments in which plants are grown with their roots in potometers adapted to weighing. Even when the roots of plants are immersed in water an internal water deficit develops during periods of high transpiration because of a lag in the rate of absorption of water as compared with the rate of transpiration.

In all probability in soils in which the water content is at the field capacity or lower, the rate of absorption often shows a more pronounced lag as compared with transpiration than in soils in which capillary movement of water can occur more readily, as is the case when water is supplied by auto-irrigators. The lag in the rate of water absorption behind the rate of transpiration results largely from the relatively high resistance of the living root cells to the passage of water across them (Kramer, 1938).

Diurnal Variations in the Osmotic Quantities of Plant Cells.—Determinations of daily variations in the water content of leaves and other plant organs have been valuable in elucidating the principle that development of an internal water deficit is a phenomenon of almost daily occurrence in most plants during their growing season. However, such determinations alone are inadequate to give a complete picture of the dynamic aspects of the internal water relations of plants. The same change in water content, for example, which induces a certain shift in the turgor pressures or diffusion-pressure deficits of the leaf cells of one species may have a very

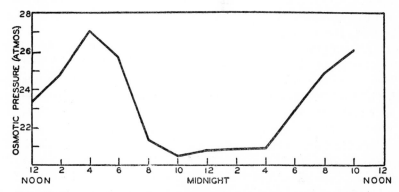

Fig. 76.   Daily variation in the osmotic pressure of the leaves of *Andropogon scoparius*. Data of Stoddart (1935).

different effect upon the turgor pressures or diffusion-pressure deficits in the leaf cells of another species. The influence of fluctuations in water content upon internal movements of water and upon physiological processes can only be fully interpreted if the status of the water present is expressed in terms of diffusion-pressure deficits or analogous dynamic units.

Daily variations in the osmotic pressures of leaves and other plant organs are of common occurrence. Such variations are more pronounced in aerial than in underground organs of plants. Their magnitude and direction are strongly influenced by the environmental conditions to which the plant is subjected. Daily variations in osmotic pressures have been studied more extensively in leaves than in other organs of the plant. The data for the leaves (Fig. 76) of the prairie grass, *Andropogon scoparius*, were obtained under drought conditions, but similar, although less marked diurnal variations in the osmotic pressures of leaves are undoubtedly of regular occurrence in most species, at least on clear, warm days.

The rather consistent increase in the osmotic pressures of leaves which usually occurs during the daylight hours is undoubtedly conditioned principally by two factors: the accumulation of soluble carbohydrates or other organic compounds resulting directly or indirectly from photosynthesis, and the decrease in the water content of the cells resulting from an excess in the rate of transpiration over the rate of absorption of water. The minimum leaf osmotic pressure, which is usually attained between midnight and dawn, probably corresponds to a period when the leaf cells are at a relatively high water content, and at a minimum organic solute content as a result of continuance of translocation of organic solutes out of the leaves during the night.

Under standard day conditions (Chap. X) the diffusion-pressure deficit of the leaf cells is usually low in the early morning hours, rises until late afternoon, and then decreases during the night hours. During the early morning hours the cells often approach their maximum turgidity. In the late afternoon their turgidity is often low (incipient wilting) and their diffusion-pressure deficit approaches the osmotic pressure of the cells (Herrick, 1933). When the diffusion-pressure deficits of the leaf cells become equal to their osmotic pressures, the turgor pressure of those cells is zero, and the leaves are in a distinctly wilted condition. As already mentioned in Chap. XII, and as discussed more fully later in this chapter, in at least some kinds of plants it is possible for the diffusion-pressure deficits of leaf cells to exceed their osmotic pressures because of the development of tensions within the cells.

The increase in the diffusion-pressure deficits of leaf cells which usually occurs during the forepart of the daylight period results from the simultaneous operation of the factors of increasing osmotic pressures and decreasing turgor pressures, the latter in turn resulting from the gradual diminution in the volume of water in the cells. Similarly the decrease in diffusion-pressure deficits of leaf cells which usually begins sometime during the afternoon, and continues during the night hours, results from the concurrent effects of decreasing osmotic pressures, and a gradual replenishment of the cells with water, the latter in turn resulting in a progressive increase in the turgor pressures of the cells.

Similar, although probably less marked, diurnal variations undoubtedly also occur in the osmotic quantities of the cells in the other organs of plants.

Permanent Wilting.—This term refers only to wilting from which a plant will not recover unless the water content of the soil is increased. It is engendered by the development in the soil water of a diffusion-pressure deficit so great that the rate of movement of water into the plant is inadequate for the maintenance of turgor. As with transient wilting, visible symptoms of permanent wilting are apparent only in thin-leaved species of plants, but physiologically equivalent conditions may develop in practically all terrestrial species.

In a soil that is slowly drying out, temporary wilting slowly grades over into permanent wilting. Under such conditions, each night recovery of the plant from temporary wilting occurs more slowly and is less complete until finally even the slightest nocturnal recovery fails to take place and the plant passes into a continuous state of permanent wilting which grows progressively more drastic the longer that it persists.

Since plants enter the state of permanent wilting by a gradual transition from a condition of temporary wilting, the early stages of this phenomenon are not greatly different from those of transient wilting except that there is no nocturnal recovery of turgor. As the available water in the soil becomes depleted, continuity of the soil water with the water in the plant is interrupted, and the water mass in the plant becomes essentially an isolated unit hydrostatic system. When this condition prevails the stress in the hydrostatic system gradually becomes intensified, since, even if the stomates are closed as they usually are in permanently wilted plants, cuticular transpiration continues, thus gradually reducing the total volume of water within the plant. The water content of the leaves of permanently wilted plants is less than that of plants in a state of transient wilting, and gradually decreases during the continuance of permanent wilting. This is also true of the other organs of plants. Maintenance of plants in a state of permanent wilting for more than a few days often results in death of the root hairs as a result of a deficiency of water. This is one reason why recovery of many plants from permanent wilting takes place very slowly even after water again becomes available in the soil.

Continued gradual reduction in the volume of water in the plant ultimately may throw some or all of the residual mass of water into a state of tension, just as a reduction in the volume of water in a single cell may have the same effect. A tension generated in the water columns, if of sufficient magnitude, will, in some species at least, be propagated into the leaf cells and other tissues of the plant. Although it is customary to think of the tensions developed in the internal hydrostatic systems of plants largely in terms of the water columns, the existence of water under tension in plants is not necessarily confined to the conductive system. Continued withdrawal of water from a cell after its turgor pressure has fallen to a zero value can have one of two results—either the water in the cell ruptures or else it is thrown into a state of tension. Tensions of a very considerable magnitude undoubtedly develop in at least some of the cells of many species when subjected to permanent wilting. According to Chu (1936), under conditions of a severe internal water deficiency, the water in the leaf cells of many species of trees, both coniferous and deciduous, passes into a state of tension.

Shrinkage in the volume of water in a cell to the point at which it passes into a state of tension results in the protoplasm and cell walls being subjected to an inward pull because of the strong adhesion between the water and the cell walls. Under such a condition the turgor pressure of a cell has a negative value. The greater the tension to which the water in the cell is subjected the greater the pull exerted by the contracted mass of water upon the cell walls. The cell walls of plants are often distorted by the centripetally directed pull which they sustain when the water within them is under tension. It has been observed that the shrinkage in the volume of the cells of a number of species during wilting results in an inward folding or crinkling of the cell walls because of the centripetal pull to which they are subjected (Thoday, 1931; Engmann, 1934). On the other hand, the walls of some plant cells are so rigid that they can sustain the development of a considerable tension in the enclosed water without any apparent distortion.

It is generally believed that tensions of a very considerable magnitude can develop in the water columns of permanently wilted plants, probably ranging up to 100 atm. and perhaps even higher. In some drought resistant species the water columns apparently can be maintained in a state of high tension for weeks or even months without breaking. In many species, however, gradual intensification of the tension in the water columns sooner or later leads to the entrance of air and consequent breaking of the columns.

Internal Redistributions of Water in Plants.—Although the possibility that metabolically activated mechanisms of water movement operate in plants (Chap. VIII, XIV) cannot be overlooked, the preponderance of available evidence indicates that the primary mechanism of water movement in plants is purely a physical one. Whenever a plant is replete with water, differences in diffusion-pressure deficits from one organ or tissue to another sink to a minimal value. But whenever absorption of water by a plant is occurring at a rate which does not compensate for the rate of transpiration, an internal water deficit develops and marked differences in diffusion-pressure deficit may be engendered in some parts of the plant as compared with others. Under such conditions redistribution of the water present in the plant may occur from one organ to another. The greater the internal water deficit, the greater the likelihood that such internal movements of water will occur.

Internal movements of water from fruits to leaves or *vice versa* seem to be of especially common occurrence. The results of Bartholomew (1926) on the diurnal expansion and contraction of lemon fruits illustrate this phenomenon (Fig. 77). Such measurements are made with an auxograph, an instrument which automatically records variations in the diameter of plant organs. As shown in this figure the lemon fruit began to contract in volume each day at about 6:00 A.M. and continued to shrink until about 4:00 P.M. Evidently during this part of the day, which corresponds to the period of high transpiration rates, water was moving out of the fruits into the other organs of the tree. Transpirational water loss from the fruit itself was negligible. Between the hours of 4:00 P.M. and 6:00 A.M. the next morning the volume of the fruit gradually increased, indicating that water was moving back into the fruit during this period. These results illustrate strikingly the fact that water can move in either

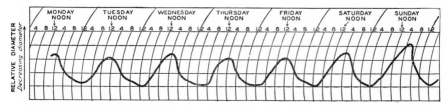

FIG. 77. Daily variations in the diameter of lemon fruits. Data of Bartholomew (1926).

direction through the xylem, depending upon the relative magnitudes of the diffusion-pressure deficits in different parts of the plant. Marked daily fluctuations in the diameter of lemon fruits were apparent even under environmental conditions which resulted in no observable wilting of the leaves. Greater diurnal fluctuations in the diameter of the fruits were found to occur after the trees had gone without irrigation for several weeks than when irrigation water had recently been applied.

The behavior of cotton bolls, however, during their enlargement period of about 16 days is quite different from that just described for lemon fruits (Anderson and Kerr, 1943). Auxographic measurements of bolls during this period show that their diameters increase consistently, although at a somewhat greater rate during the daylight than during the night hours (Fig. 78). The bolls continue to enlarge even during periods when the leaves are severely wilted, indicating that, even under such conditions, water continues to move into the growing fruits. After enlargement of the cotton bolls has ceased, however, reversible changes in diameter occur similar to those which take place in well-developed lemon fruits. Such daily variations in volume doubtless are of frequent occurrence in many other kinds of succulent fruits in which enlargement growth has ceased.

Growing stem tips may continue to obtain water even when the older parts of the stem are losing it (Wilson, 1948). By attaching auxometers in pairs to stems of tomato plants, one to the growing tip, and another at the first node below the growing tip (above which elongation occurs) this investigator was able to determine changes in length of the stem both above and below the first node. Growth in length of the stem above the first node was at approximately the same rate both day and night. The stem below the first node, however, showed a measurable shrinkage in length during the daytime, and an equal elongation at night, undoubtedly

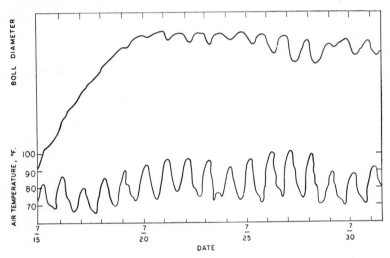

FIG. 78. Daily variations in the diameter of a cotton boll. During the first five days the boll was still growing. After attaining full size a marked shrinkage occurs in the boll during the warm part of each day. Data of Anderson and Kerr (1943).

corresponding to reversible changes in the turgidity of the stem cells. Obviously the meristematic stem tip cells continued to obtain water during the daylight hours while the rest of the stem was losing water, and some of the water utilized in their growth probably came from the older stem cells.

It seems probable that, as a general rule, actively meristematic regions such as growing stem and root tips, and enlarging fruits, under conditions of internal water deficiency, develop higher diffusion-pressure deficits than other tissues. There are experimental indications that the diffusion-pressure deficits of such tissues are largely of imbibitional rather than of osmotic origin (Chap. VIII). Hence even under conditions which induce temporary wilting of the leaves, water often continues to move into meristematic regions in quantities sufficient to permit a continuation of growth. Under conditions of severe internal water deficiency, approaching or corresponding to a state of permanent wilting, however, growth of all meristems is greatly retarded or inhibited (Chap. XXIX).

Drought Resistance.—Some species of plants are better able than others to survive and develop in habitats in which a dearth of water is frequent or usual. This capacity of surviving periods of drought with little or no injury is termed *drought resistance*. All perennial species of plants native to semi-arid regions are more or less drought resistant. This same statement is true for those species indigenous to local habitats which, for one reason or another, are unduly dry, even in humid climates. Drought resistant species or varieties of plants are important in the agricultural economy of certain regions, such as the "dry-farming" areas of western United States. Certain varieties of crop plants are much more productive in dry regions than other varieties of the same species. Examples are the durum and emmer varieties of wheats.

The term "drought" is not in itself subject to any rigid definition. In general, however, this term refers to periods during which the soil contains little or no water which is available to plants. In the more humid climates of the world such periods are relatively infrequent and seldom last very long except in certain local habitats. The more arid a climate, in general, the more frequent the occurrence of periods of drought, and the longer their duration. Most species of plants can survive short dry periods without serious injury, but only those possessing a well-developed capacity for drought resistance can avoid death or serious injury during prolonged periods of soil-water deficiency.

Soil drought conditions are often accompanied by atmospheric conditions—high temperature, low humidity, and often relatively high wind velocities—which favor high transpiration rates. Such "atmospheric drought" is not only a frequent accompaniment of soil drought, but sometimes occurs in the absence of soil-water deficiency. Atmospheric drought often induces transient wilting of plants during the daylight hours. Sometimes atmospheric drought alone may have devastating effects upon plants. Hot, dry winds sometimes sweep across grain fields of the western United States, killing or seriously injuring plants, even during periods when the soil-water content is still relatively high.

Most species which grow in semi-arid regions, such as the "deserts" of the southwestern United States, or in locally dry habitats, can be conveniently classified into three groups: (1) ephemerals, (2) succulents, and (3) drought-enduring species.

The ephemerals are a prominent feature of the vegetation of all semi-arid regions which are characterized by definite rainy seasons. With the aavent of rains the seeds of such species germinate, and the entire life cycle of the plant is completed within a few weeks. The new crop of seeds survives the intervening dry period until the next rainy season. Such plants have been termed "drought-escaping" (Shantz, 1927). They are no more drought resistant than many mesic annual plants.

Succulents constitute a considerable proportion of the vegetation of most semi-arid regions (Fig. 79) and are frequently found in locally dry

Fig. 79. Succulents of the semi-deserts of southern Arizona. Left, sahuaro (*Cereus giganteus*); right, century plant (*Agave parryi*) in fruit. Photographs by B. S. Meyer.

habitats such as sand dunes and beaches in regions of humid climate. The most conspicuous succulents of the American semi-desert regions mostly belong to the cactus family (Cactaceae). The other more important families of plants which include a number of succulent species are the Euphorbiaceae, Liliaceae, Crassulaceae, Aizoaceae, and Amaryllidaceae. The succulents are a distinctive group of plants not only in structure, but in metabolism (Spoehr, 1919) and water economy as well. Species of the succulent habit of growth are able to survive dry periods because of the relatively large reserves of water which accumulate in the inner tissues of the fleshy stems or (in some species) in the fleshy leaves. A relatively thick cuticle and the fact that in many succulents the stomates are generally open only at night are important factors in permitting the conservation of water by such species. Many cacti can live for months on this stored water even if entirely uprooted from the soil.

Neither the ephemerals nor the succulents can be regarded as truly drought resistant in the sense that their cells can endure a severe reduction in water content for extended periods of time without injury. This is true only of species which have been classed in the "drought enduring" group. One of the most extreme examples of such a species among higher plants is the creosote bush (*Larrea tridentata*), which is the dominant plant through large areas of the semi-arid regions of the southwestern United States and northern Mexico. This species carries the same set of leaves through both the wet and dry seasons. During drought periods the water content of the leaves of the creosote bush is sometimes less than 50 per cent of their dry weight (Runyon, 1936). The water contents of the leaves of most woody mesic species, on the other hand, generally range between 100 and 300 per cent of their dry weight.

Some species of plants, including especially many mosses, lichens, and algae, can be reduced to a virtually air-dry condition during drought periods, yet remain viable, and resume their life processes very quickly when they are again provided with a supply of moisture. The seeds of many species are drought resistant in the sense that they may be reduced to a nearly air-dry condition without losing their viability.

All attempts to explain drought resistance of "drought-enduring" plants upon a purely morphological basis have proved inadequate, although certain structural features of plants undoubtedly aid in their survival in dry habitats. Many xerophytes, for example, have extensive root systems in proportion to their tops. Such root systems may efficiently tap a very considerable volume of soil; hence the aerial portions of the plant may receive a fairly adequate supply of water, even when the rainfall is scanty.

Similarly, many drought resistant species are characterized by relatively small leaves, hence the total area of foliage exposed may be small in proportion to the absorbing capacity of the root system. The leaves of others abscise with the advent of the dry season, and their transpiring surface is thus relatively small during the period of greatest stress upon the hydrostatic system.

The structural peculiarities of xeromorphic leaves such as thick cuticle and hypodermal sclerenchyma are such as to greatly retard cuticular transpiration. Since during drought periods the stomates of xerophytes are closed most or all of the time, the low rate of cuticular transpiration aids in the conservation of the water remaining in the plant.

Formerly it was believed that drought-resistant species were characterized by low transpiration rates and that they are able to withstand drought conditions largely because of their economical expenditure of water. Investigations by Maximov (1929) and others have shown clearly that the transpiration rates of most such species are as great as those of typical mesophytes, whenever the soil water supply is adequate. The frequently observed low transpiration rates of xerophytes result, not from any inherent peculiarities of structure or physiological behavior, but from the fact that the water content of the soil in which they are rooted is so low that little or no absorption can occur.

Another misconception, long current, was that xerophytes are more efficient in reducing the soil-water content than mesophytes. The previous discussion of the effect of the type of plant upon the permanent wilting percentage of a soil indicates that there is no valid evidence for such a belief (Chap. XIII).

As the prior discussion has indicated, during a prolonged period of soil-water deficiency the store of water in a plant is gradually depleted, largely as a result of cuticular transpiration. This is true even of xerophytes. One result of this gradual water loss is a progressive increase in the severity of the stress in the internal hydrostatic system. The ensuing gradual dehydration of the tissues sooner or later results in the death of species possessing relatively little drought resistance. Many "drought-enduring" species, on the other hand, can endure this condition, which is physiologically equivalent to permanent wilting, for months at a time without suffering irrecoverable injury.

It seems clear, therefore, that one of the basic factors in the drought resistance of plants is a capacity of the cells to endure desiccation without suffering any irreparable injury. According to Iljin (1930), death of plant cells as a result of drying is not due primarily to the desiccation of the protoplasm, but to the destructive effects upon the protoplasm of various mechanical disturbances resulting from dehydration of the cell. Purely mechanical effects such as pressure, stretching and tearing often are destructive to protoplasm. During drying of cells the protoplasm is often subjected to just such effects. The vacuole usually contracts more than the cell wall thus leading to distortion and tearing of the protoplasm. Such drastic disturbances in the protoplasmic system usually result in its death.

As shown by the same investigator cells with a small surface in proportion to their volume and cells in which the size of the vacuole is small relative to the protoplasmic mass are usually less subject to injury during desiccation than cells of structurally opposite types. In cells which fall into one or both of these classes, dehydration results in relatively little mechanical deformation of the protoplasm.

Iljin (1933), Etz (1939), and others have shown that many kinds of plant cells, including some from highly parenchymatous tissues, can be slowly dried until all water disappears from their vacuoles and subsequently restored to their turgid condition without killing them. This appears to indicate that desiccation of the protoplasm *per se* does not necessarily cause its death. The turgidity of desiccated cells can be restored without injury only if they are allowed to imbibe water very slowly from concentrated solutions. If immersed directly in water the ensuing rapid absorption results in mechanical deformations of the protoplasm which are lethal. Death of cells which would otherwise endure desiccation apparently can be brought about by either a too rapid drying, or by a too rapid absorption of water after severe desiccation.

SUGGESTED FOR COLLATERAL READING

Kramer, P. J. *Plant and Soil Water Relationships.* McGraw-Hill Book Co., Inc. New York. 1949.
Maximov, N. A. *The Plant in Relation to Water.* R. H. Yapp, Editor. George Allen and Unwin. London. 1929.
Walter, H. *Die Hydratur der Pflanze.* Gustav Fischer. Jena. 1931.

SELECTED BIBLIOGRAPHY

Anderson, D. B., and T. Kerr. A note on the growth behavior of cotton bolls. *Plant Physiol.* **18:** 261-269. 1943.
Bachmann, F. Studien über Dickenänderungen von Laubblättern. *Jahrb. Wiss. Bot.* **61:** 372-429. 1922.
Bartholomew, E. T. Internal decline of lemons. III. Water deficit in lemon fruits caused by excessive leaf evaporation. *Amer. Jour. Bot.* **13:** 102-117. 1926.
Chu, Chien-Ren. Der Einfluss des Wassergehaltes der Blätter der Waldbäume auf ihre Lebensfähigkeit, etc. *Flora* **130:** 384-437. 1936.
Engmann, K. F. Studien über die Leistungsfähigkeit der Wassergewebe sukkulenter Pflanzen. *Beih. Bot. Centralbl.* **A 52:** 381-414. 1934.
Etz, K. Über die Wirkung des Austrocknens auf den Inhalt lebender Pflanzenzellen. *Protoplasma* **33:** 481-511. 1939.
Herrick, E. M. Seasonal and diurnal variations in the osmotic values and suction tension values in the aerial portions of *Ambrosia trifida. Amer. Jour. Bot.* **20:** 18-34. 1933.
Iljin, W. S. Die Ursachen der Resistenz von Pflanzenzellen gegen Austrocknen. *Protoplasma* **10:** 379-414. 1930.
Iljin, W. S. Über Öffnen der Stomata bei starkem Welken der Pflanzen. *Jahrb. Wiss. Bot.* **77:** 220-251. 1932.
Iljin, W. S. Über Absterben der Pflanzengewebe durch Austrocknung und über ihre Bewahrung vor dem Trockentode. *Protoplasma* **19:** 414-442. 1933.
Kramer, P. J. The relation between rate of transpiration and rate of absorption of water in plants. *Amer. Jour. Bot.* **24:** 10-15. 1937.
Kramer, P. J. Root resistance as a cause of the absorption lag. *Amer. Jour. Bot.* **25:** 110-113. 1938.

Maximov, N. A. Internal factors of frost and drought resistance in plants. *Protoplasma* **7**: 259-291. 1929.

Müller, H. Untersuchungen über der Transpirationansteig bei welkenden Blättern von *Coleus. Angew. Bot.* **19**: 369-427. 1937.

Runyon, E. H. Ratio of water content to dry weight in leaves of the creosote bush. *Bot. Gaz.* **97**: 518-553. 1936.

Shantz, H. L. Drought resistance and soil moisture. *Ecology* **8**: 145-157. 1927.

Spoehr, H. A. The carbohydrate economy of cacti. *Carnegie Inst. Wash. Publ. No. 287.* Washington. 1919.

Stanescu, P. P. Daily variations in products of photosynthesis, water content, and acidity of leaves towards end of vegetative period. *Amer. Jour. Bot.* **23**: 374-379. 1936.

Stoddart, L. A. Osmotic pressure and water content of prairie plants. *Plant Physiol.* **10**: 661-680. 1935.

Thoday, D. Experimental studies on vegetable assimilation and respiration. V. A critical examination of Sachs' method for using increase of dry weight as a measure of carbon dioxide assimilation in leaves. *Proc. Roy. Soc. (London)* **B 82**: 1-55. 1909.

Thoday, D. On the behavior during drought of leaves of two cape species of *Passerina*, with some notes on their anatomy. *Ann. Bot.* **35**: 585-601. 1921.

Wilson, C. C. Diurnal fluctuations of growth in length of tomato stems. *Plant Physiol.* **23**: 156-157. 1948.

Yapp, R. H., and Una C. Mason. The distribution of water in the shoots of certain herbaceous plants. *Ann. Bot.* **46**: 159-181. 1932.

DISCUSSION QUESTIONS

1. Which of the osmotic quantities of the mesophyll cells of the leaves on a maple tree will show the greatest variation during a 24-hour period in midsummer under "standard day" conditions? Why?

2. Leaves of "shade" plants usually wilt upon a reduction in their water content of 5 per cent or less, while most "sun" species do not wilt unless the reduction in leaf water content is 20 per cent or more. Explain.

3. At 6 A.M. the water content of the leaves on a certain species of plant is found to be 90 per cent; at 4 P.M. on the same day 88 per cent. In terms of water per gram of dry weight, what per cent of the water originally present has been lost?

4. In lumbering practice it has been found that logs of yellow pine and some other species float more readily if the side branches are not trimmed off until several weeks after the tree is felled than if they are removed immediately. Explain.

5. Tomato plants which develop during wet seasons are more apt to wilt on hot, sunny days than tomato plants which develop under drier conditions. Explain.

6. Plot curves which might reasonably be expected to represent the daily variations in transpiration, absorption of water, and tension in the water columns of a sunflower plant (1) on a "standard day," (2) on an otherwise "standard day" with the soil water content approaching the permanent wilting percentage, (3) on a cool, cloudy day with the soil water content at about the field capacity.

7. Plot curves which might reasonably be expected to represent the daily variations in the osmotic pressure, turgor pressure, and diffusion-pressure deficit of the mesophyll cells of a sunflower plant under the several conditions listed in question 6.

8. Why should the tearing of the protoplasm away from the cell wall during drying usually be more harmful to a plant cell than separation of the protoplasm from the wall during plasmolysis?

9. Why do the lower leaves of a plant usually wilt before the upper leaves? The inner, more shaded leaves before the outer, more exposed leaves?

10. Why do light showers which do not result in penetration of water to the roots often result in restoring the turgidity of wilted plants? Why do such showers not always have this effect?

11. Hollow beech trees usually suffer more severely as a result of a prolonged drought than those with solid trunks. Suggest possible explanations.

XVI

ENZYMES

Every actively metabolizing cell is a seat of hundreds of chemical reactions, the speed and direction of which are controlled and regulated according to complex and integrated patterns. Each of these many diverse chemical reactions constitutes a link in some reaction chain leading ultimately to some stable or relatively stable product of cellular metabolism. Reaction follows reaction in regular order, each setting the stage for the next. The inherent control and regulation of the metabolic system is so delicate that physiological processes of great complexity move smoothly and rapidly to completion.

This precise and orderly regulation of the chemical reactions occurring in living cells suggests the presence of some mechanism of control. For many years this control was believed to be inseparable from the protoplasm itself. During the nineteenth century, however, evidence began to accumulate which indicated that the mechanism of control might reside in certain specific compounds rather than in the protoplasm as a whole. This theory received important support when Buchner in 1897 discovered that extracts from crushed, lifeless cells of yeast plants could bring about the fermentation of sugar solutions. Here for the first time was tangible evidence that protoplasm was unnecessary for the oxidation of sugar to alcohol and carbon dioxide. Apparently such fermentation occurred only in the presence of certain specific compounds formed in yeast cells and the presence of these active molecules in small quantities was sufficient to bring about the oxidation of sugars. The term *enzyme* (literally *in yeast*) was coined to designate these active substances. Since Buchner's original discovery, many other enzymes have been discovered and isolated from living cells.

It is now recognized that the orderly progress of each of the many chemical reactions in living cells is achieved through the agency of enzymes. In digestions, for example, complex molecules are split into simpler ones through the action of enzymes. The enzyme β *amylase* (Chap. XX) converts one fraction of starch into the much simpler molecules of the sugar maltose which in turn are hydrolyzed to glucose molecules by the enzyme *maltase:*

$$2n\ (C_6H_{10}O_5) + n\ H_2O \xrightarrow{\text{Amylase}} n\ C_{12}H_{22}O_{11}$$
$$\text{Starch} \qquad\qquad\qquad\qquad \text{Maltose}$$

$$C_{12}H_{22}O_{11} + H_2O \xrightarrow{\text{Maltase}} 2\ C_6H_{12}O_6$$
$$\text{Maltose} \qquad\qquad\qquad \text{Glucose}$$

In similar reactions other carbohydrates (Chap. XX) as well as fats (Chap. XXIII) and proteins (Chap. XXVI) are hydrolyzed into simpler molecules through the action of specific enzymes. All of the many oxidation and reduction reactions which are steps in respiration (Chap. XXII) also depend upon the presence of enzymes. It follows, therefore, that living cells must contain large numbers of enzymes. Experimental work supports this assumption since hundreds of enzymes have been isolated from the cells of a small yeast colony (Green, 1946).

Enzymes are indispensable compounds which play a key role in metabolism by bringing direction and control to the physiological processes of living cells. It is the enzyme systems of cells which determine the kinds of chemical reactions that can occur. The particular kinds of food substances made or used by plants, for example, depend upon the enzymes which are present. A cell lacking enzymes which can hydrolyze starch or cellulose cannot use these compounds as food materials. Any change in the enzyme complement of living cells is immediately reflected in a change in the physiological processes of the cell (Beadle, 1948).

Enzymes and Catalysts.—Catalysts are compounds which influence the velocity of chemical reactions without themselves being destroyed or permanently altered in the process. Characteristically, catalysts accelerate chemical reactions and this is the usual sense in which the term is employed, although negative catalysts are known. Catalysts are effective in very small quantities; their influence upon reaction velocities is proportional to the quantity of catalyst present; they are often specific in that they influence the rate of only one kind of reaction; and, finally, the catalyst is present in the same amount and in the same form at the end of the reaction as at the beginning.

Enzymes appear to have most, but not all, of the characteristics of

TABLE 18—A CLASSIFIED LIST OF SOME OF THE MORE IMPORTANT ENZYMES

HYDROLYZING ENZYMES

Enzyme	Substrate	End Products
I. Carbohydrases		
1. Sucrase (invertase)	Sucrose	Glucose + fructose
2. α-Glycosidases		
A. Maltase	Maltose	Glucose
3. β-Glycosidases		
A. Emulsin	Glycosides	Glucose + nonsugar
B. Cellobiase	Cellobiose	Glucose
4. α-Galactosidases		
A. Melibiase	Raffinose	Sucrose + galactose
5. β-Galactosidases		
A. Lactase	Lactose	Glucose + galactose
6. Polysaccharidases		
A. Amylases		
α-Amylase	Starch	Dextrins
β-Amylase	Dextrins	Maltose, dextrins
B. Cellulase	Cellulose	Cellobiose
C. Hemicellulases	Hemicelluloses	Hexoses and pentoses
D. Lichenase	Lichenin	Cellobiose
E. Inulase	Inulin	Fructose
F. Protopectinase	Protopectin	Pectin
G. Pectinase	Pectic acid	Galactose + uronic acid
II. Esterases		
1. Lipase	Fats	Glycerol + fatty acids
2. Chlorophyllase	Chlorophyll *a*	Phytol + chlorophyllide *a*
3. Pectase	Pectin	Pectic acid + methyl alcohol
4. Tannase	Tannin	Glucose + digallic acid
5. Phosphatases	Phosphates or compounds containing phosphate groups	Phosphate + non-phosphate
6. Phosphorylases		
A. α-Glucosan phosphorylase	Glycogen or starch + H_3PO_4	Glucose-1-phosphate
B. Sucrose phosphorylase	Sucrose + H_3PO_4	Fructose + glucose-1-phosphate
III. Enzymes hydrolyzing nitrogen compounds		
1. Proteases		
A. Pepsin	Proteins	Peptones
B. Trypsin	Proteins	Polypeptides + amino acids
C. Papain	Proteins	Polypeptides + amino acids
D. Bromelin	Proteins	Polypeptides + amino acids
2. Peptidases	Polypeptides	Amino acids
3. Amidases		
A. Urease	Urea	Ammonia + carbon dioxide
B. Asparaginase	Asparagine	Aspartic acid + ammonia
C. Arginase	Arginine	Urea + ornithine

TABLE 18—CONTINUED

DESMOLYZING ENZYMES

Enzyme	Substrate	End Products
I. Catalase	Hydrogen peroxide	Water + Oxygen
II. Peroxidases	Hydrogen peroxide + reduced compounds	Oxidized compounds + water
III. Carbonic anhydrase	Carbonic acid	Carbon dioxide + water
IV. Oxidases		
1. Cytochrome oxidase	Reduced cytochrome c	Oxidized cytochrome c
2. Tyrosinase	Phenols	Quinones
3. Ascorbic acid oxidase	Ascorbic acid	Dehydroascorbic acid
V. Dehydrogenases		
1. Succinic dehydrogenase	Succinic acid	Fumaric acid
2. Alcohol dehydrogenase	Ethyl alcohol	Acetaldehyde
3. Malic dehydrogenase	Malic acid	Oxalacetic acid
4. Lactic dehydrogenase	Lactic acid	Pyruvic acid
5. α-Glycerophosphate dehydrogenase	Dihydroxyacetone-phosphate	α-Glycerophosphate
6. Diphosphoglyceraldehyde dehydrogenase	1,3 Diphosphoglyceraldehyde	1,3-Diphosphoglyceric acid
7. Glutamic dehydrogenase	Glutamic acid	α-Ketoglutaric acid + NH$_3$
VI. Transphosphorylases		
1. Hexokinase	Glucose or fructose + adenosine triphosphate	Adenosine diphosphate + glucose- or fructose-6-phosphate
2. Phosphoglucomutase	Glucose-1-phosphate	Glucose-6-phosphate
3. Phosphohexosisomerase	Glucose-6-phosphate	Fructose-6-phosphate
4. Phosphohexokinase	Fructose-6-phosphate + adenosine triphosphate	Fructose 1,6-diphosphate + adenosine diphosphate
5. Phosphoglyceric transphosphorylase	1,3-Diphosphoglyceric acid + adenosine diphosphate	3-Phosphoglyceric acid + adenosine triphosphate
6. Phosphoglyceromutase	3-Phosphoglyceric acid	2-Phosphoglyceric acid
7. Phosphopyruvate transphosphorylase	2-Phosphopyruvic acid + adenosine diphosphate	Pyruvic acid + adenosine triphosphate
8. Phosphotriose isomerase	3-Phosphoglyceraldehyde	Dihydroxyacetone phosphate
VII. Desmolases		
1. Aldolase	Fructose-1,6-diphosphate	Dihydroxyacetone phosphate + 3-phosphoglyceraldehyde
VIII. Hydrases		
1. Enolase	2-Phosphoglyceric acid	2 phosphopyruvic acid + H$_2$O
2. Aconitase	Aconitic acid + H$_2$O	Isocitric acid
3. Fumarase	Fumaric acid + H$_2$O	L Malic acid
IX. Carboxylases		
1. Pyruvic acid carboxylase	Pyruvic acid	Acetaldehyde + carbon dioxide
2. Oxalacetic carboxylase	Oxalacetic acid	Pyruvic acid + carbon dioxide
3. Amino acid carboxylases	Amino acids	Amines + carbon dioxide
X. Transaminases	Amino acids + organic acid	Deaminated amino acid + aminated organic acid

catalysts, and are often defined as organic catalysts made by living cells. They enormously accelerate the rate of chemical reactions; they are effective in very minute amounts; they are specific, since each enzyme is associated with only one chemical reaction or with only one kind of chemical reaction. The apparent differences between enzymes and catalysts are, first, that some of the molecules of enzymes are inactivated or destroyed during the course of the reaction which they catalyze and, secondly, the velocity of enzymatically controlled reactions is not always strictly proportional to the concentration of the enzyme. These differences between enzymes and catalysts may be more apparent than real. The destruction of enzymes during the course of the reactions they catalyze seems, almost certainly, to be the result of incidental side reactions and not a consequence of the participation of the enzyme molecules in the primary reaction. It is also probable that, because of the complexity of enzyme systems, all of the enzyme molecules are not equally free to act as catalysts. For this reason, an exact proportionality between concentration and reaction velocity may not always exist.

The Kinds of Enzymes.—The compound upon which an enzyme acts is known as the *substrate*. Enzymes are usually named by adding the suffix *ase* to the name of the substrate. Thus, the enzyme which brings about the hydrolysis of cellulose is called *cellulase* and the enzymes which hydrolyze fats (lipoids) are known as *lipases*. Sometimes the name given an enzyme describes the kind of reaction in which it participates rather than the particular substrate molecule utilized. Enzymes which catalyze the transfer of hydrogen atoms from one compound to another, for example, are known as *dehydrogenases*. Both the substrate molecules and the kind of reaction are sometimes indicated in the name of the enzyme as in *succinic acid dehydrogenase* or *cytochrome oxidase*. The compounds that are formed as a result of the action of an enzyme on a substrate are known as the *end products* of the reaction. Thus, when the enzyme sucrase acts upon cane sugar (sucrose), equal numbers of glucose and fructose molecules are formed:

$$C_{12}H_{22}O_{11} + H_2O \xrightarrow{\text{Sucrase}} C_6H_{12}O_6 + C_6H_{12}O_6$$
$$\text{Sucrose} \qquad\qquad\qquad \text{Glucose} \qquad \text{Fructose}$$

Glucose and fructose are, therefore, the end products of this reaction.

Enzymes are generally classified on the basis of the kinds of reactions which they catalyze. Most of them can be classified under one or the other of two great groups: (1) the hydrolyzing enzymes, and (2) the desmolyzing enzymes. Enzymes in the former group cause cleavages in substrate molecules by the addition of water. Digestive enzymes, in general, are of this type. The reactions catalyzed by desmolyzing enzymes are more diverse than those catalyzed by hydrolyzing enzymes. In general they catalyze other than hydrolyzing reactions such as the breaking of linkages *Decarboxylase* between carbon atoms, the addition or removal of atoms or atomic groups *transferases* from molecules, and the shifting of atoms or groups from one part of a *transphosidases* molecule to another. Enzymes involved in respiration and fermentation (Chap. XXII) are of the desmolyzing type. In Table 18 are listed most of the enzymes known to be of importance in the higher plants. Many of the enzymes tabulated catalyze the reverse reaction as well as the one indicated. All details of all of the reactions cannot be shown in a summary table of this kind. The roles of many of these enzymes are considered more fully in later chapters.

The Chemical Structure of Enzymes.—Many of the early studies of enzymes showed that they exhibited properties such as heat sensitivity, colloidal dimensions and pH sensitivity which suggested that they possessed many of the properties of proteins. All efforts of earlier investigators to isolate enzymes as pure substances failed, however, and not until 1926 did Sumner succeed in isolating the enzyme urease in pure crystalline form and showing it to be a protein. Since then a number of enzymes have been isolated from plant and animal tissue, each one proving, upon critical study, to be a protein. A number of the enzymes have been obtained in the form of beautifully shaped crystals (Fig. 80). It is now generally recognized that all enzymes are basically proteins, although many of them also have non-protein groups attached to the protein molecules. The fact that many enzymes have been crystallized and shown to be

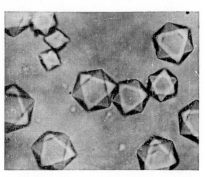

FIG. 80. Crystals of the enzyme urease from jack bean (*Canavalia ensiformis*). Photograph courtesy of Dr. J. B. Sumner.

protein molecules of varying complexity has not greatly increased our understanding of their behavior, however. The intricate and enormously complicated architecture of protein molecules (Chap. XVI), which still baffles the most skillful chemists, stands in the way of any very satisfactory comprehension of the way in which enzymes accomplish their catalytic action.

The molecular structure of enzyme molecules appears to be of two general types: (1) Simple protein molecules (simple only in a relative sense!) and (2) protein molecules to which some non-protein (prosthetic) group is attached. The prosthetic group may itself be highly complex in its molecular architecture.

Enzyme molecules of the first group include a number of the hydrolyzing enzymes such as urease, amylase, and papain. These enzymes appear to consist only of protein and to possess no non-protein groups. In enzyme molecules of this kind the molecular orientation of each of the many amino acid groups which together make up the protein molecule probably plays a role in determining its catalytic activity.

The oxidizing-reducing enzymes (Chap. XXII) all belong in the second group. In some of these enzymes the prosthetic (active) group is a metal or an organic group which includes a metal. Iron, copper, and zinc are all known to form a part of the molecules of some of these enzymes. Other oxidizing enzymes contain organic groups, often of great complexity, in addition to the protein moiety.

Many of the desmolyzing enzymes can be separated into a protein fraction and a *coenzyme* which represents the prosthetic group. Because of differences in dissociability it appears that the active groups of some such enzymes are usually attached to the protein as prosthetic groups, while the active groups of others exist in the protoplasm apart from the protein and are called coenzymes. Although the coenzymes are often referred to as the active groups of the system they must be linked to or closely associated with the protein component for the enzyme to be fully effective as a catalyst. Coenzymes include a wide variety of compounds, some of which are built up in part from vitamins (Chap. XXVIII).

Enzyme precursors, often called *zymogens,* are sometimes present in cells. Such precursors are inactive until converted into enzymes. The compounds which bring about the transformation of precursors to enzymes are called *kinases.* A number of kinases have been identified, but relatively little is known about the mechanism of their action.

For more detailed discussion of the structure of enzymes such references as Northrup *et al.* (1948), Stern (1944), Sumner and Somers (1947) and Lardy (1949) should be consulted.

General Properties of Enzymes.—1. *Catalytic properties.*—Catalysts are substances which, although present in only small amounts and unaffected by the reactions they accelerate, bring about chemical changes in relatively large quantities of reacting materials. Similarly, a very small quantity of an enzyme can catalyze the transformation of vastly larger quantities of the substrate. It has been estimated, for example, that the enzyme sucrase ("invertase") can effect the hydrolysis of at least 1,000,000 times its own weight of sucrose without exhibiting any appreciable diminution in its activity. The enzyme catalase brings about the reduction of hydrogen peroxide to water and molecular oxygen:

$$2 H_2O_2 \xrightarrow{\text{Catalase}} 2 H_2O + O_2$$

turnover no.

Catalase is one of the more efficient enzymes, one molecule of this enzyme being able to catalyze the conversion of 5,000,000 molecules of H_2O_2 per minute when conditions are favorable (Sumner and Somers, 1947).

Chemical reactions proceed in the direction of stable equilibria, *i.e.*, in the direction which will reduce the energy of the system to the lowest possible level under the existing conditions. Neither enzymes nor catalysts can alter this situation, although they may enormously increase the rate at which equilibria are reached. No enzyme can cause a reaction to occur in a direction that is inconsistent with the laws which govern energy changes between reacting molecules.

2. *Colloidal Condition.*—All enzymes that have been isolated and purified are molecules of very large dimensions, so large in fact as to fall within the size limits which characterize the particles of colloidal systems. They are, therefore, compounds of high molecular weights. The enzyme catalase, for example, has a molecular weight of 248,000 (Sumner and Gralen, 1938), and the enzyme urease has a molecular weight of 483,000 (Sumner *et al.*, 1938). Some enzyme molecules undoubtedly exceed these dimensions, probably by very large margins. Because of their great size the molecules of enzymes diffuse very slowly, a fact that makes it possible to separate them from readily diffusible substances by dialysis.

The enormous surface area exposed by particles of colloidal dimensions has been emphasized earlier (Chap. III). Since enzymes dispersed in water are colloidal systems, they present an extensive surface area at which catalyzed reactions can occur. The association between enzyme and substrate is considered by some to be a loose chemical combination, by others, a true adsorption phenomenon.

3. *Specificity.*—Each enzyme is specific in the sense that it can operate only upon a certain substrate or group of substrates. This does not mean that there must be a separate enzyme for every substrate but that each enzyme acts only upon substances having a certain molecular pattern. Apparently each individual enzyme can affect only one particular type of chemical bond. When a number of different compounds possess this bond in common, they can be acted upon by the same enzyme. For example, the enzyme emulsin can hydrolyze any β-glycoside (Chap. XX) since the chemical linkage between the sugar and non-sugar groups in all such glycosides is the same.

Enzyme specificity is also illustrated by the fact that different end products are formed from the same substrate under the influence of different enzymes. In the presence of sucrase, for example, the trisaccharide raffinose (Chap. XX) is hydrolyzed into melibiose and fructose while, in the presence of emulsin, the end products of the reaction are sucrose and galactose. Pyruvic acid (Chap. XXII) is notable for the large number of compounds into which it may be converted by the action of different enzymes.

Many enzymes apparently act on only a single kind of substrate. The enzyme urease, for example, can act only upon urea and no other molecule. Cytochrome oxidase (Chap. XXII) appears to be another example of absolute specificity since it can catalyze only the oxidation of cytochrome c by oxygen. Often enzymes are not so restricted in their activity and can act upon a specific kind of chemical linkage or even upon related bondings. When this is true, however, one kind of bond is acted on preferentially and related bonds are usually affected at a slower rate.

4. *Reversibility of Action.*—A true catalyst is able to cause the acceleration of a given reaction in either direction provided suitable sources of energy are available. Although the capacity of enzymes to catalyze reactions in both directions has been demonstrated experimentally for relatively few of them, there is little reason to doubt the reversibility of enzyme action. The synthesis of fats from glycerol and fatty acids under the influence of the enzyme lipase has been accomplished. Similarly, it has been shown that under proper conditions other enzymes such as some of the proteases and urease can synthesize the compounds which, under other conditions, serve as their substrates. Glycosides have also been synthesized from the end products of their hydrolysis under the influence of the enzyme emulsin. Hence, it is often inferred that most hydrolytic enzymes possess the capacity of catalyzing not only the hydrolysis of a certain substrate, but also, under proper conditions, the synthesis of that same substrate from the end products of its hydrolysis.

It does not necessarily follow, however, that the same enzyme invariably catalyzes both the synthesis and degradation of a given kind of molecule. It is known that some molecules are synthesized by the operation of reaction chains which involve other compounds and other enzymes than those which bring about their hydrolysis. Urea, for example, is synthesized in animal cells by the action of the enzyme arginase upon arginine, but urea is hydrolyzed by the enzyme urease. Another example of this principle is illustrated by the two different enzymes which catalyze the hydrolysis and synthesis of sucrose. Sucrose is hydrolyzed to glucose and fructose by the enzyme sucrase (invertase), but its synthesis apparently requires the action of the enzyme sucrose phosphorylase (Chap. XX).

5. *Heat Sensitivity.*—Unlike most inorganic catalysts, enzymes are inactivated or destroyed at temperatures considerably below the boiling

point of water. At temperatures above 50°C. most enzymes in a liquid medium are rapidly inactivated. Inactivation, although at a slower rate, may also occur at somewhat lower temperatures. Most enzymes in a liquid medium are completely destroyed at temperatures between 60° and 70°C. A few, however, will endure temperatures as high as 100°C., at least for short periods of time. The destruction of enzymes in this range of temperatures is in all probability a heat coagulation phenomenon.

The enzymes of dry tissues such as seeds and spores can endure temperatures of 100° to 120°C., or even higher, for considerable periods without suffering deleterious effects. The same is also true of dried enzyme extracts.

The exact temperature at which a given enzyme will be destroyed varies greatly, depending upon the conditions prevailing in the medium in which it is dispersed. The pH of the medium has a marked effect upon the heat sensitivity of the enzyme. The presence of either the substrate or the end products of an enzyme in the medium in which it is dispersed greatly retards or may even entirely prevent its destruction at a temperature which would otherwise result in its demolition. The substrate or end products of an enzyme exerts a similar protective effect against other destructive agents (Table 19).

TABLE 19—THE ACTION OF FRUCTOSE IN PROTECTING A SUCRASE EXTRACT FROM DESTRUCTION BY ACIDS, ALKALIES, ALCOHOL, AND HEAT (DATA OF HUDSON AND PAINE, 1910)

Concentration of fructose, %	Destructive agent			
	0.04 N HCl, 30° C.	0.03 N NaOH, 30° C.	50 per cent alcohol, 30° C.	Distilled water 61° C.
	Relative rates of destruction			
0	100	100	100	100
2.7	26	3	1	32
5.4	12	3	1	16
10.9	2	4	1	24

Temperatures near or below the freezing point usually result in the inactivation of enzymes, but not commonly in their destruction. When the temperature is raised to within a suitable range, enzymes which have been exposed to relatively low temperatures are generally found to be little if any impaired in their properties.

Occurrence and Distribution of Plant Enzymes.—Every living cell contains enzymes, usually hundreds of them, but they are not uniformly distributed throughout the cells of a plant. Certain enzymes, notably those associated with respiration, are present in all living cells, but others may be restricted in their distribution to certain organs or tissues. The leaves of the garden beet, for example, are reported to contain sucrase, maltase, and amylase; the stems, sucrase, amylase, inulase, and emulsin, while the roots contain amylase, inulase, and emulsin (Robertson *et al.*, 1909). Germinating seeds are the richest of all organs of higher plants in enzymes and are frequently used as the source of enzymes in experimental work.

In some tissues the enzyme and corresponding substrate are both present but are separated from each other by cellular membranes. This is true, for example, in the seeds of the bitter almond where the enzyme emulsin and its substrate amygdalin both occur but not in the same cells. When bitter almond seeds are crushed, the enzyme and its substrate are brought into contact and hydrolysis of the glycoside proceeds (Chap. XX). More frequently the substrate and the enzyme which catalyzes its hydrolysis both occur in the same cell. Whether or not hydrolysis of the substrate will occur is dependent upon conditions within the cell. It is almost invariably true that plant tissues which are rich in a certain substrate will be relatively rich in the corresponding enzyme and *vice versa*.

Some plant enzymes, at least, maintain their potency for long periods of time. Miehe (1923) has demonstrated that rye seeds which were at least 112 years old still contained amylase which would hydrolyze starch. The death of plant cells does not cause the simultaneous destruction of all of the enzymes present in the cells.

The cells of bacteria and fungi are rich in enzymes, some of which bring about the hydrolysis of the substrate upon which these plants live. Although these hydrolyzing enzymes are synthesized inside the cells, they pass outward through the cellular membranes and cause the hydrolysis of the substrate material outside of the cells of the organism. Many kinds of bacteria and fungi can live and grow on a wide variety of substrate materials. The cells of these organisms apparently can synthesize a number of different hydrolyzing enzymes, and there is good reason to believe that the particular hydrolyzing enzymes actually made by the cells of these plants are determined at least in part by the chemical composition of the substrate.

Factors Affecting Enzymatic Reactions.—The influence of various factors upon the reactions of the enzymes of the higher plants has been studied almost entirely *in vitro*. The usual procedure has been to prepare a more or less purified extract of the enzyme to be studied, then to bring this extract into contact with the substrate under controlled conditions, and finally to determine the rate of the ensuing reaction. Enzymatic reactions as they occur in living cells are influenced by conditions within the protoplasmic matrix, and in this respect differ greatly from such reactions occurring *in vitro*. Since the conditions which affect the action of an enzyme in an artificial medium are usually very different from those obtaining in a living cell, it is certain that the effects of various factors on extracted enzymes are quantitatively unlike those which they would have on that same enzyme *in vitro*, although qualitatively the effects are probably very similar.

1. *Temperature.*—The rate at which an enzymatic reaction proceeds is influenced not only by the temperature, but also by the length of time which the reaction mixture has already been at that temperature. In other words, a "time factor" (Chap. XIX) must be recognized in considering the effects of temperature upon the rate of an enzymatic reaction. In general, the initial velocity of enzymatic reactions is accelerated with increase in temperature until a certain "optimum" is attained. The initial velocity of the reaction may be maintained almost indefinitely at lower temperatures, but, the higher the temperature, the more markedly it decreases with time.

There are, therefore, two distinctly separate and often opposing factors to be considered in all studies of the effect of temperature upon enzymatic reactions: (1) The direct effect of temperature change upon the reaction rate and (2) the effect of the temperature upon the enzyme itself. The former increases as the temperature rises, but the destructive effect of temperature upon most plant enzymes increases rapidly as the temperature rises above 40°C. The optimum temperature is that at which the accelerating effect of temperature increase is just balanced by the destructive action of the temperature upon the enzyme system.

In general, the Q_{10} of enzymatic reactions is somewhat lower than that

TABLE 20—THE TEMPERATURE COEFFICIENTS OF THREE ENZYMATIC REACTIONS
(DATA OF HALDANE AND STERN, 1932)

Enzyme	Substrate	Temperature interval, °C.	Temperature coefficient (Q_{10})
Yeast maltase	Maltose	10–20	1.90
		20–30	1.44
		30–40	1.28
Malt amylase	Starch	20–30	1.96
		30–40	1.65
		40–50	1.43
Root peroxidase	H_2O_2	5–15	2.0
		15–25	2.0

of uncatalyzed reactions. Uncatalyzed chemical reactions have a Q_{10} of 2 or 3 while in most enzymatic reactions the Q_{10} falls between 1.4 and 2.0 (Table 20).

The optimum temperature for most enzymatic reactions, if measured in terms of hours, lies between 40° and 50°C., although for a few it is as high as 60°C. If only a very short interval of time is allowed to elapse before a determination of the amount of substrate hydrolyzed is made, a higher optimum will usually be found than if longer time intervals are used as a basis of measurement. The optimum is influenced, however, not only by the time factor, but also by other conditions prevailing in the medium such as the pH, relative concentration of enzyme, substrate, end products, and so forth.

At temperatures above the optimum point for any enzymatic reaction, inactivation of the enzyme occurs so fast that the rate of the reaction is rapidly decreased. It is also possible that the retarding influence of relatively high temperatures may sometimes result from a greater acceleration of the reverse reaction (whereby the substrate is resynthesized from the end products) than the hydrolytic reaction.

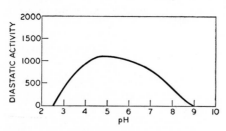

FIG. 81. Relation between pH and activity of diastase from malt. Data of Sherman *et al.* (1919).

2. *Hydrogen-ion Concentration.*—The activity of enzymes is greatly influenced by the hydrogen-ion concentration of the medium in which the reaction occurs. This is one of the most important known effects of hydrogen-ion concentration in the realm of biological phenomena. In general, the activity of an enzyme appears to be at its maximum at a certain optimum hydrogen-ion concentration, and to decrease, usually rapidly, on each side of this value (Fig. 81). At still higher or lower pH values the enzyme is inactivated, at first reversibly, and later irreversibly. The optimum and limiting pH values for activity differ from one enzyme to another. Optimum values may range from as low as pH 1.5 for some enzymes to as high as pH 10 for others. The optimum pH value for a given enzyme may vary, however, depending upon the source of the enzyme, the substrate, nature of other substances in the medium, temperature, etc.

Curves such as those shown in Fig. 81 are the resultant of a number of different pH effects. Among these are the effects of pH upon the enzyme itself, effects on the substrate, and effects on coenzymes, activators, or inhibitors. The direct effects of hydrogen-ion concentration upon enzymes appear to result largely from their influence upon the dissociation of the enzyme molecules.

3. *Hydration.*—The effect of increased hydration upon the enzyme activity of plant tissues is most easily demonstrated during the germination of seeds. The enzyme activity, measured in terms of any specific enzyme known to be present, is usually low in dry but viable seeds. As imbibition of water proceeds during germination the activity of the enzyme increases more or less progressively, an effect which can be ascribed, at least indirectly, to the increase in the hydration of the tissues of the seed (Pickler, 1919). Sometimes, however, this apparent increase in the activity of an enzyme with

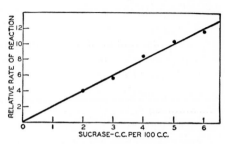

FIG. 82. Relation between concentration of sucrase and its hydrolytic activity. Data of Nelson and Hitchcock (1921).

increase in the hydration of the tissues during seed germination can be ascribed to the conversion of zymogens into enzymes. Similar effects upon enzyme activity are undoubtedly shown in other plant tissues in which considerable changes in hydration occur.

4. *Concentration of the Enzyme.*—With very few exceptions, the rates of enzymatic reactions increase linearly with the enzyme concentration. Doubling the quantity of the enzyme doubles the reaction rate provided that pH, temperature, and other conditions are not limiting. A few apparent exceptions to this general rule are known, but it is often possible to account for these divergent results. For example, the products of some enzymatic reactions possess an affinity for the enzyme and thus render a portion of the enzyme inactive; in other enzymatic reactions the failure of rates to vary directly as enzyme concentrations may be ascribed to changes in the pH of the medium during the reaction. In spite of a few exceptions for

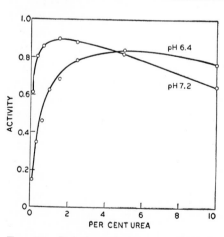

FIG. 83. Relation between substrate concentration and activity of the enzyme urease. Data of Howell and Sumner (1934).

which no entirely satisfactory explanation has been suggested, the rule holds for so many enzymatic reactions that it may be considered generally applicable (Fig. 82).

5. *Concentration of the Substrate*.—The velocity of an enzymatic reaction usually increases with increase in the concentration of the substrate up to a certain maximum, after which the relative amount acted upon per unit of time decreases with increase in the substrate concentration (Fig. 83). The retarding effect of relatively high concentrations of the substrate upon enzyme activity may be caused in part by the more rapid accumulation of the end products of the reaction (see next section). Furthermore as the concentration of the dissolved or dispersed substrate in a reaction mixture increases, the concentration of water decreases. The smaller proportion of water present at higher substrate concentrations prevents the action of the enzyme at its maximum efficiency.

6. *Concentration of the End Products*.—Enzymatic reactions, like all other chemical reactions, are subject to the laws of chemical equilibrium and mass action. Hence as the end products of the reaction accumulate the apparent rate of the reaction decreases. Similarly, if the concentration of the end products in the reaction mixture is initially high, the rate of the reaction will be slower than if the end products are lacking. In some enzymatic reactions the enzyme itself combines with one of the end products. This results in a reduction in the active concentration of the enzyme, and the velocity of the reaction is slowed down.

7. *Activators*.—Activators are specific chemical compounds which accelerate the rate of enzymatic reactions. The exact mechanism of their action is not understood. Some activators seem to be general; *i.e.*, increase the activity of all or most enzymes, while others are specific for certain enzymes. Among the former are low concentrations (2-5 per cent) of the salts of the alkali and alkaline earth metals. Cobalt, manganese, nickel, magnesium, and chlorine ions are more or less specific activators for some enzymes.

Activators may exert their influence either by some direct effect upon the enzyme or by eliminating the effect of some substance or factor which inhibits the operation of the enzyme.

8. *Inhibitors*.—Just as some compounds increase the rate of enzymatic reactions so others are known which check or inhibit the action of enzymes. These latter compounds are known as *inhibitors*. Inhibitors are often grouped into two classes: (1) competitive inhibitors and (2) noncompetitive inhibitors.

One theory of the mechanism of enzyme action is that the enzyme enters into a loose chemical or physical union with substrate molecules. The possibilities of such unions depend, of course, upon the geometry of the enzyme and substrate molecules. The structure of the enzyme molecule must bear such a relationship to the structure of the substrate molecule that combinations between the two can take place.

Competitive inhibitors are compounds sufficiently similar, in their molecular architecture, to the usual substrate molecules as to combine with the active groups of the enzyme. When such a combination between enzyme and inhibitor occurs, further progress of the reaction is blocked and the enzyme is rendered inactive. In a sense the inhibitor competes with the substrate for the enzyme. The union of substrate molecules and enzymes is very transitory and the enzyme is quickly restored to its original condition, but the union between an inhibitor and an enzyme may endure and effectively eliminate the enzyme molecule from further participation in the reaction. The molecules of the end products of an enzymatic reaction sometimes act as inhibitors in this way.

Competitive inhibitors also may work in other ways. For example, the sulfa drugs so effective against certain kinds of bacteria are very similar in their molecular architecture to para-aminobenzoic acid, a vitamin of the B complex (Chap. XXVIII) that is essential for the growth of many bacteria. This vitamin appears to owe its importance to the fact that it is an essential component of enzymes participating in certain of the reactions of respiration. The close similarity in the chemical structure of para-aminobenzoic acid and the sulfa molecule makes it possible for the sulfa drug to combine with the protein component of the enzyme forming a unit which has no catalytic action. The sulfa molecules, therefore, may be considered as competing with the vitamin molecules for the same positions in the enzyme molecules. When the sulfa molecule combines with the protein portion of the enzyme molecule, the resulting molecule is no longer capable of acting as an enzyme. Cyanides also inhibit some enzyme reactions by combining with certain atoms in the prosthetic groups of enzymes and thus preventing the enzyme from functioning in the reaction chains in which they normally operate.

Noncompetitive inhibitors may act in different ways. One mode of action appears to be a union of the inhibitor with the enzyme at some other location on the enzyme molecule than that utilized by the substrate molecule. When this occurs, the molecular architecture of the enzyme is altered so as to destroy its effectiveness. Noncompetitive inhibitors also block enzyme reactions by breaking the sequence of step-wise reactions so characteristic of biological processes. This may be accomplished by a combination of the inhibitor with one of the compounds essential to the sequence of reactions thus preventing the use of this compound in the reaction series. Some of the better known enzyme inhibitors and their effective concentrations are listed in Table 21.

TABLE 21—EFFECTIVE CONCENTRATIONS OF SOME ENZYME INHIBITORS
(DATA OF STERN, 1944, AND SUMNER AND SOMERS, 1947)

Inhibitor	Effective concentration	Enzyme inhibited
Cyanide	10^{-3} M	Cytochrome oxidase
Carbon monoxide	70% by volume	Cytochrome oxidase
Heavy metals	—	Many
Fluorides	10^{-3} M	Phosphatases
Malonic acid	10^{-2} M	Succinic dehydrogenase
Iodoacetates	10^{-3} M	Papain, alcohol dehydrogenase and others
Sodium azide	—	Catalase, peroxidase, cytochrome oxidase and others

9. *Radiant Energy.*—Radiations of various wave lengths often have inhibitory or inactivating effects upon enzymes *in vitro.* This is especially true of wave lengths in the ultraviolet. The shorter wave lengths of the visible spectrum usually have more marked effects upon enzymatic activity than the longer wave lengths of visible light. Very little is known, however, regarding the effects of radiant energy upon enzymes as they exist in living cells.

The Synthesis of Enzymes.—Until recent years little more was known about the origin of enzymes than the fact that they were products of the metabolic processes of living cells. Experimental studies by Beadle (1945, 1946), Horowitz (1947), and others, have demonstrated beyond reasonable doubt that the synthesis of enzymes is controlled by genes in the chromosome complement of the cell. A species of bread mold (*Neurospora crassa*) was used as the experimental organism by these investigators. This fungus can be grown in a culture medium containing only sucrose, certain mineral salts including nitrates, and biotin (a vitamin, Chap. XXVIII). By various treatments of the spores such as exposure to X-rays or ultraviolet irradiation, mutant strains of this organism can be obtained. Some of these mutants will not grow on the basic medium described above but require the presence of one or more additional compounds. Apparently such a mutant is incapable of making some necessary compound which could be synthesized by the original strain of the organism.

One such mutant, for example, was found not to grow unless the amino acid tryptophane (Chap. XXVI) was present in the medium. The tryptophane-synthesizing capacity of this strain of the mold had been lost. Loss of this capacity was found to result from a failure to take place within the organism of one specific step in the chain of reactions whereby tryptophane is synthesized. Furthermore, the enzyme which catalyzes this particular reaction was also found to be absent from the mutant. Genetic studies showed that the absence of this particular enzyme was correlated with a difference in the properties of a certain gene as compared with its properties in the original strain of mold. The inference seems clear that synthesis of this particular enzyme is controlled by a certain gene.

In similar fashion synthesis of other enzymes in *Neurospora* appears to be controlled by other genes. Genes are composed of proteins of the type known as nucleoproteins (Chap. XXVI). Evidence from other organisms also points to the now widely entertained view that enzyme synthesis is controlled by genes and that the synthesis of a given enzyme is controlled by a given gene or genes.

A widely held hypothesis is that there are present in the cytoplasm self-duplicating units called *plasmagenes* which are responsible for the formation of enzymes (Spiegelman, 1946; and others). This view is not necessarily in conflict with the concept that enzyme synthesis is controlled by genes since it might be supposed that the plasmagenes are formed under the influence of the genes and that they may even be replicas of them. The plasmagenes may either be centers of enzyme synthesis or may themselves operate as enzymes. This theory further holds that the rate of multiplication of a given plasmagene may be different in different kinds of cells, thus accounting for variations in the quantities of enzymes present from one cell to another.

The Relation of Enzymes to Vitamins and Hormones.—Enzymes, vitamins, and hormones are all similar in at least one important respect. Each of these substances is capable of inducing important physiological reactions in living cells when present in only minute amounts. In recent years the relationships between these three classes of substances has been clarified greatly by the discovery that several of the vitamins form a part of the prosthetic groups of important enzymes. Among these are such vitamins of the B complex as thiamime, nicotinic acid, riboflavin, and pyridoxine (Chap. XXVIII).

The relationship between hormones and enzymes is less clear. There is evidence, however, that the important plant hormones known as auxins (Chap. XXVIII) play some role in an enzyme system involved in carbo- ✷ hydrate metabolism. In view of the close similarity in the physiological roles of hormones and vitamins, it seems probable that hormones also will be found to act either as actual components of enzyme systems or as agents which powerfully affect enzyme activity.

The Mechanism of Enzyme Action.—Chemical reactions occur when molecules or ions collide with each other. Only a small portion of these molecular collisions result in chemical reactions, however, because, to combine with another, a molecule must be at a higher energy level than most of its associates—it must be "activated." The frequency with which chemical combinations occur depends upon the proportion of activated molecules in the medium. Energy is necessary to bring molecules into this activated state. The so-called "activation energy" of a reaction represents the energy required to bring molecules up to the energy levels at which chemical combinations can occur. The role of an enzyme seems to be that of bringing about chemical reactions at lower energy levels, or, in other words, of decreasing the energy of activation. When the activation energy is reduced, a larger proportion of molecules in the medium are in an active state and as a result more chemical combinations between molecules occur. The difference in the energy of activation brought about by the presence of an enzyme is shown for three specific chemical reactions in Table 22.

TABLE 22—THE INFLUENCE OF ENZYMES UPON ACTIVATION ENERGY
(DATA OF LINEWEAVER, 1939)

Reaction	Activation energy in cal./mol.		Enzyme
	Without enzyme	With enzyme	
Decomposition of H_2O_2	18,000	5,500	Catalase
Hydrolysis of sucrose	26,000	11,500	Yeast Invertase
Hydrolysis of sucrose		13,000	Malt Invertase
Hydrolysis of casein	20,600	12,000	Trypsin

The chemical reaction catalyzed by an enzyme often appears to occur between the coenzyme and the substrate, yet no reaction will occur if coenzyme and substrate molecules alone are present. When the protein component of the enzyme is added to the mixture, the reaction proceeds at once and often at a very rapid rate. These facts suggest that the protein fraction of the enzyme in some way increases the reactivity of the substrate molecules, probably as a result of a very temporary union between protein and substrate. This union must be fleeting indeed, for one enzyme molecule may bring about the chemical combination of thousands of substrate molecules in a single minute.

Indirect evidence of such combinations between enzyme and substrate is furnished by the effect of inhibitors. The specificity of the enzyme probably depends upon the architecture of the protein component. Studies of inhibitors have shown that compounds similar to substrate molecules in their chemical architecture may block the action of an enzyme. This is interpreted as evidence that the properties of the protein and the inhibitor molecules permits at least a partial union between them to occur but that the resulting linkage is not complete nor perfect enough for the reaction to continue.

The protein fraction of the enzyme is believed to be analogous in a sense to a complicated lock. Only when a substrate molecule has the complementary pattern—that of a key to the lock—can the two work together. If the key does not fit precisely, the lock may be jammed—*i.e.*, the reaction inhibited.

The temporary combination of protein and substrate activates the latter so that reactions may occur. These reactions often involve the transfer of atoms or molecules between coenzymes and substrate. This, in general terms, is one widely accepted theory of the way in which enzymes operate.

The ingenious experiments of Rothen (1947) indicate that direct union between substrate and enzyme may not always be necessary for catalysis to occur. In these experiments enzyme and substrate molecules were separated by extremely thin barriers of plastic that prevented any direct contact between them. In spite of this barrier, the enzyme catalyzed chemical changes in the substrate molecules. Although these experiments have not been carried out upon a sufficient scale to permit any generalization, they suggest the interesting possibility that enzymes may be capable of activating substrate molecules by forces that are effective over a distance of at least 20 mμ.

The Production of Enzymes by Plants.—A distinction is often made between intracellular or endoenzymes and extracellular or exoenzymes. The former operate within the cells in which they are synthesized; the latter are secreted by cells and operate externally to the cells in which they originate. The enzymes of the digestive tract of higher animals are of the extracellular type, being secreted from certain cells into the various organs of the alimentary system. Extracellular digestion as a result of the release of exoenzymes is a regular feature of the metabolism of many bacteria and fungi.

In higher plants, however, exoenzymes are the exception rather than the rule. There are only two well-known examples of the extracellular operation of enzymes in the higher plants. One of these is in the so-called insectivorous plants such as the pitcher plants and sundews. The leaves of these species have been shown to secrete proteases into the liquid in the "pitcher" or, in the sundews, on the surface of the leaf.

Certain tissues of the embryo in the grains of various members of the grass family also synthesize exoenzymes (Brown and Escombe, 1898, and others). This phenomenon cannot be appreciated without a knowledge of the various parts of the grain type of fruit. These are illustrated in Fig. 84 which represents a longitudinal section cut through a corn grain across the shorter of the two transverse axes. The structure of the other grains (wheat, barley, rye, etc.) is, in general, very similar to that of the corn grain.

Shortly after a grain of corn, barley, or one of the other closely related species begins to imbibe water striking changes take place in the appearance of the epithelial cells of the scutellum (Fig. 85). The protoplasmic contents of these cells, originally finely granulated and nearly transparent, become much coarser in texture and clouded in appearance. The

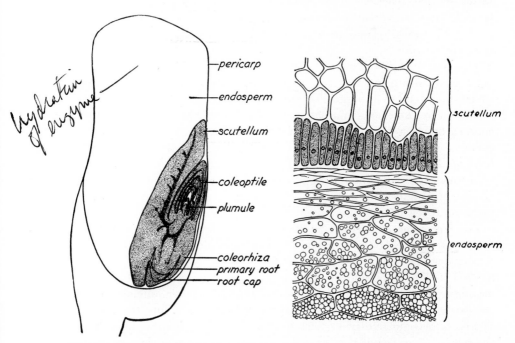

FIG. 84. Longitudinal section through a corn (maize) grain to show the principal parts of the grain and embryo.

FIG. 85. Section through a small portion of a corn (maize) grain. Starch has been digested in several layers of endosperm cells adjacent to the scutellum.

nucleus, originally clearly visible, is obscured by this change in the physical properties of the cytoplasm. The epithelial cells also swell to several times their original volume during the first few days of germination.

Not long after these changes occur in the appearance of the cells of the epithelium the cell walls of the endosperm cells adjacent to the epithelial layer begin to disappear, and the starch grains in the cells of the endosperm begin to show corrosion. Shortly afterward transitory starch grains appear in the parenchymatous cells of the scutellum. Enzymes produced in the layer of epithelial cells apparently have moved into the endosperm and there set in operation digestive processes, the products of which subsequently pass into the scutellum. This seems to be the mechanism whereby the embryo obtains food from the endosperm during the process of germination. The principal enzymes secreted by the embryo are hemi-cellulase which results in the dissolution of the endosperm cell walls, and diastase (amylase plus maltase) which results in the digestion of starch. Similar phenomena undoubtedly occur during the germination of other kinds of seeds.

SUGGESTED FOR COLLATERAL READING

Lardy, H. A., Editor. *Respiratory Enzymes*. Burgess Publishing Co. Minneapolis 1949.

Northrup, J. H., M. Kunitz, and R. M. Herriott. *Crystalline Enzymes*. 2nd Ed. Columbia University Press. New York. 1948.

Sumner, J. B., and K. Myrbäck, Editors. *The Enzymes*. Vol. I (Parts 1, 2); Vol. II (Parts 1, 2). Academic Press, Inc. New York. 1950, 1951, 1951, 1952.

Sumner, J. B., and G. F. Somers. *Chemistry and Methods of Enzymes*. Academic Press, Inc. New York. 1947.

Tauber, H. The chemistry and technology of enzymes. John Wiley & Sons, Inc. New York. 1949.

SELECTED BIBLIOGRAPHY

Beadle, G. W. Genetics and metabolism in *Neurospora*. *Physiol. Rev.* **25**: 643-663. 1945.

Beadle, G. W. Genes and the chemistry of the organism. *Amer. Scientist* **34**: 31-53. 1946.

Beadle, G. W. The gene and biochemistry. In *Currents in Biochemical Research*. D. E. Green, Editor. 1-12. Interscience Publishers, Inc. New York. 1946.

Beadle, G. W. Genes and biological enigmas. *Amer. Scientist* **36**: 69-74. 1948.

Beadle, G. W. Physiological aspects of genetics. *Ann. Rev. Biochem.* **17**: 727-752. 1948.

Brown, H. T., and F. Escombe. On the depletion of the endosperm of *Hordeum vulgare* during germination. *Proc. Roy. Soc.* (*London*) **B 63**: 3-25. 1898.

Cohen, P. P., and R. W. McGilvery. Nonoxidative, nonproteolytic enzymes. *Ann. Rev. Biochem.* **19**: 43-66. 1950.

Green, D. E. Enzymes and trace substances. *Advances in Enzymol.* **1**: 177-198. 1941.

Green, D. E. Biochemistry from the standpoint of enzymes. In *Currents in Biochemical Research*. D. E. Green, Editor. 149-164. Interscience Publishers, Inc. New York. 1946.

Greenberg, D. M., and T. Winnick. Enzymes that hydrolyze the carbon-nitrogen bond: Proteinases, peptidases, and amidases. *Ann. Rev. Biochem.* **14**: 31-68. 1945.

Haldane, J. B. S., and K. G. Stern. *Allgemeine Chemie der Enzyme*. Stankopff. Dresden. 1932.

Hopkins, R. H. The actions of the amylases. *Advances in Enzymol.* **6**: 389-414. 1946.

Horowitz, N. H. Methionine synthesis in *Neurospora*. The isolation of cystathionine. *Jour. Biol. Chem.* **171**: 255-264. 1947.

Howell, S. F., and J. B. Sumner. The specific effects of buffers upon urease activity. *Jour. Biol. Chem.* **104**: 619-626. 1934.

Hudson, C. S., and H. S. Paine. The inversion of cane sugar by invertase. V. The destruction of invertase by acids, alkalies, and hot water. *Jour. Amer. Chem. Soc.* **32**: 985-989. 1910.

Laskowski, M. Proteolytic enzymes. *Ann. Rev. Biochem.* **19**: 21-42. 1950.

Lineweaver, H. The energy of activation of enzyme reactions and their velocity below 0°C. *Jour. Amer. Chem. Soc.* **61**: 403-408. 1939.

Lu Valle, J. E., and D. R. Goddard. The mechanism of enzymatic oxidations and reductions. *Quart. Rev. Biol.* **23**: 197-228. 1948.

Miehe, H. Über die Lebensdauer der Diastase. *Ber. Deutsch. Bot. Ges.* **41**: 263-268. 1923.

Nelson, J. M., and D. I. Hitchcock. Uniformity in invertase action. *Jour. Amer. Chem. Soc.* **43**: 2632-2655. 1921.

Pickler, W. E. Water content and temperature as factors influencing diastase formation in the barley grain. *Plant World* **22**: 221-238. 1919.

Robertson, R. A., J. C. Irvine, and Mildred E. Dobson. A polarimetric study of the sucroclastic enzymes in *Beta vulgaris*. *Biochem. Jour.* **4**: 258-273. 1909.

Rothen, A. On the mechanism of enzymatic activity. *Jour. Biol. Chem.* **163**: 345-346. 1946. **167**: 299-300. 1947.

Sherman, H. C., A. W. Thomas, and M. E. Baldwin. Influence of hydrogen-ion concentration upon enzyme activity of three typical amylases. *Jour. Amer. Chem. Soc.* **41**: 231-235. 1919.

Spiegelman, S. Nuclear and cytoplasmic factors controlling enzymatic constitution. *Cold Spring Harbor Symposia Quant. Biol.* **11**: 256-277. 1946.

Stern, K. G. Enzymes. In *The Chemistry and Technology of Food and Food Products*. Vol. I. M. B. Jacobs, Editor. 185-228. Interscience Publishers, Inc. New York. 1944.

Sumner, J. B. The isolation and crystallization of the enzyme urease. *Jour. Biol. Chem.* **69**: 435-441. 1926.

Sumner, J. B. Nonoxidative enzymes. *Ann. Rev. Biochem.* **17**: 35-66. 1948.

Sumner, J. B., and N. Gralén. The molecular weight of crystalline catalase. *Jour. Biol. Chem.* **125**: 33-36. 1938.

Sumner, J. B., N. Gralén, and I. Eriksson-Quensel. The molecular weight of urease. *Jour. Biol. Chem.* **125**: 37-44. 1938.

XVII

THE CHLOROPHYLLS AND
THE CAROTENOIDS

Radiant Energy.—An elementary knowledge of the physical properties of light and other kinds of radiant energy is essential for a proper understanding of photosynthesis, the synthesis and properties of chlorophyll, and many other plant processes to be discussed in the subsequent chapters of this book. Radiant energy, as judged from some of its properties, appears to be propagated across space as undulatory waves. Ordinary sunlight or "white light" from any artificial source seems homogeneous to the human eye but after it has passed through a prism appears as a spectrum of colors. This dispersion of light by a prism was first demonstrated by Newton in 1667, but man had already long been familiar with the similar phenomenon which occurs in rainbows. The order of the more prominent colors in a spectrum of sunlight is red, orange, yellow, green, blue-green, blue, and violet. Each of these colors corresponds to a different range of *wave lengths* of light (Fig. 86). The wave length is the dis-

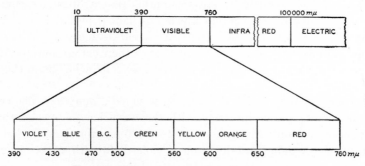

Fig. 86.   The spectrum of radiant energy.

293

tance between two successive crests of a wave. The wave lengths which induce the sensation of light, range from about 390 mμ to about 760 mμ.[1]

Visible light, however, constitutes only a very small part of the spectrum of radiant energy (Fig. 86). Beyond the visible red lies the long zone of infrared or "heat waves" which range up to a wave length of about 100,000 mμ. Electric waves are still longer and range in length up to a kilometer or more. The waves used for radio transmission are in this portion of the spectrum of radiant energy.

Just below the region of visible light in the radiant energy scale lies the ultraviolet zone which ranges down to wave lengths as short as 10 mμ. Even shorter are the X-rays (0.01-10 mμ) much used for their therapeutic effects in medicine. Below them on the scale lie the gamma rays (0.0001-0.01 mμ) which are emitted by radium, also used in medical therapy. Shortest of all are the cosmic rays, which are less than 0.0001 mμ in wave length.

The wave lengths which reach the earth's surface from the sun range from about 300 mμ in the ultraviolet to about 2600 mμ in the infrared. In their natural habitats plants are also subjected to bombardment by the extremely long electric waves, and the extremely short cosmic waves, but there is no experimental evidence that either of these kinds of radiant energy has any effect upon plants.

In the preceding discussion we have referred to radiant energy as a wave phenomenon with an air of finality which is not justified by observed facts. Many radiant energy phenomena, such as the behavior of light in optical systems, can only be satisfactorily explained at the present time in terms of the postulate that light travels as waves. Other effects, however, appear completely unintelligible in terms of this hypothesis. The most important of these are photochemical reactions such as the effect of light upon sensitized photographic paper and its role in the process of photosynthesis. At the present time such phenomena can only be explained satisfactorily by the assumption that light is particulate in nature. According to this concept a beam of light is pictured as a stream of tiny particles. Each of these particles is called a _photon._ When such photons impinge against a suitable substance their energy may be transferred to the electrons which they strike, thus inducing photochemical reactions.

The energy manifestation of a photon is called a _quantum._ The energy value of quanta varies inversely with the wave length. A quantum of ultraviolet radiation with a wave length of 100 mμ, for example, has four times the energy value of a quantum of violet light with a wave length of

[1] A millimicron (mμ) is one-thousandth of a micron.

400 mμ., and eight times that of a quantum of infrared radiation with a wave length of 800 mμ.

Radiant energy, therefore, apparently possesses a dual nature, and at present it is impossible to reconcile its corpuscular with its undulatory manifestations. All we can say with certainty is that, in some of its effects, radiant energy behaves *as if* it traveled in waves, in others *as if* it is propagated across space as a stream of photons.

Light and all other kinds of radiant energy vary in several different ways, the most important of which are: (1) irradiance ("intensity"), (2) quality, and (3) duration.

Irradiance is the radiant energy receipt per unit area per unit of time. It is commonly expressed as ergs per cm.² per sec., microwatts per cm.², or as g.-cal. per cm.² per min. (Withrow, 1943). On a clear summer's day

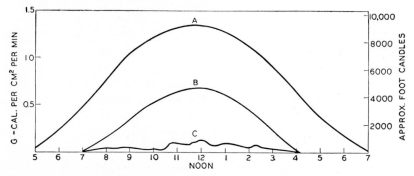

Fig. 87. Daily variations in light intensity (horizontal incidence): (*A*) on a clear day in early July, (*B*) on a clear day in early January, (*C*) on an early January day with heavy clouds. Curves based on measurements made at Columbus, Ohio. (40° N. latitude).

in the midtemperate zones the impinging solar radiant energy has an irradiance of between 1.2 and 1.5 g.-cal. per cm.² per min. at noon. The irradiance of light and its "brightness" are not the same, the latter being an index of the illuminating capacity of light as perceived by the human eye. Neither are they expressed in the same units. Nevertheless there is usually a fairly close correlation between these two quantities. Illumination values corresponding to the irradiance mentioned above range from about 8,000 to 10,000 foot-candles. On a cloudy winter's day in the same latitudes, irradiance and illumination values are commonly only 10 per cent or even less of those at corresponding hours on a clear summer's day (Fig. 87).

"Quality" refers to the wave-length composition of light. The quality of light from a tungsten filament bulb, for example, is very different from that of sunlight. The latter is relatively richer in blue light and relatively poorer in infrared than the former. Similarly, the quality of light from one artificial source, such as a fluorescent tube, is different from that from another artificial light source such as a tungsten bulb.

"Duration," as applied to the light-relations of plants, refers to the number of hours a day during which a plant is exposed to illumination.

The Chloroplast Pigments.—Green is the predominant color of the plant kingdom. With only a few exceptions all leaves are green in color as are also many other plant organs such as herbaceous and young woody stems, young fruits, and sepals of flowers. The green coloring of plants is often termed chlorophyll, although actually a number of kinds of chlorophyll occur in plants.

Less evident is the fact that the leaves and many other organs of plants also contain yellow pigments. These are seldom apparent except in leaves in which the chlorophyll fails to develop, or in which it is destroyed as a result of senescence or other physiological changes. Corn plants that have grown from seed in the dark, for example, do not synthesize chlorophyll, but are usually yellow in color because of the presence of yellow pigments. In the autumn disintegration of the chlorophyll in the leaves of many woody species results in unmasking the yellow pigments which are also present in the leaves. The yellow chloroplast pigments of leaves belong to the group of compounds called _carotenoids_ (see later).

Except in blue-green algae and the photosynthetic bacteria, chlorophylls occur only in the chloroplasts. The carotenoids of leaves are also restricted to the chloroplasts, and this also appears to be true of the carotenoids in the cells of most algae. All of these pigments appear to be present only in the grana of the chloroplasts (Chap. IV). In certain other plant organs, such as flower petals, the yellow pigments occur in chromoplasts. The chlorophylls and associated carotenoids are often called the _chloroplast pigments_. In some kinds of algae pigments of another group, called the _phycobilins_, also occur in the chloroplasts. The best known of these are the _phycoerythrin_ of most red and some blue-green algae, and the _phycocyanin_ of most blue-green and some red algae. These two pigments are closely related chemically. Both are colloidal proteinaceous pigments and can be extracted from the cells with hot water.

The Chlorophylls.—A number of different kinds of chlorophyll occur in the plant kingdom (Strain, 1944). Of these, chlorophyll _a_ is most nearly of universal occurrence being present, as far as is known, in all photosynthetic organisms except the green and purple bacteria. Chlorophyll _b_ is found in all higher plants and in the green algae, but is not present in algae of most other phyla. Chlorophyll _c_ is found in the brown algae and diatoms, which do not contain chlorophyll _b_. Similarly red algae contain chlorophyll *d* but no chlorophyll *b*. In the purple bacteria still another kind of chlorophyll called *bacteriochlorophyll* is present, whereas the green bacteria contain another apparently similar pigment called *bacterioviridin*. All of these chlorophylls are very similar in chemical composition, and all of them are compounds which contain magnesium.

Chlorophylls *a* and *b* are the characteristic chlorophylls of the higher plants. Neither is water soluble, but both are soluble in a number of organic reagents. Chlorophyll *a* is readily soluble in absolute ethyl alcohol, ethyl ether, acetone, chloroform, and carbon bisulfide. Chlorophyll *b* is soluble in the same reagents, although generally less so. Chlorophyll *a* is blue-green in solution, and blue-black in the solid state; chlorophyll *b* is almost pure green in solution, and greenish-black in the solid state.

All of the chlorophylls possess the property of *fluorescence.* This term refers to the peculiar property possessed by certain substances when illuminated of re-radiating light of wave lengths other than those absorbed by the substance. Usually the radiated light (fluorescent light) is longer in wave length than the incident light. Chlorophyll *a* in ethyl alcoholic solution exhibits a deep blood red fluorescence, best seen by viewing the solution in reflected light. Similar solutions of chlorophyll *b* exhibit a brownish-red fluorescence. Chlorophyll in living cells also exhibits fluorescence (Stern, 1920; Lloyd, 1924).

The Chemistry of the Chlorophylls.—Willstätter and his associates have isolated chlorophylls *a* and *b* in pure form from over two hundred different species of higher plants and found them to be identical in chemical composition. They also succeeded in determining the molecular formulas of these two chlorophylls. For chlorophyll *a* this is $C_{55}H_{72}O_5N_4Mg$; for chlorophyll *b* it is $C_{55}H_{70}O_6N_4Mg$.

Each chlorophyll yields a separate series of degradation products, but one of the products derived from both after mild hydrolysis is an unsaturated primary alcohol which is called *phytol* ($C_{20}H_{39}OH$). Splitting of the phytol group from the chlorophyll molecule can also be accomplished by the enzyme *chlorophyllase*, which occurs in leaves. Phytol makes up about one-third of the chlorophyll molecule. It has a strong affinity for oxygen and may be responsible for the reducing action of chlorophyll.

When ashed pure chlorophyll leaves a residue composed solely of magnesium oxide. Although iron and other minerals seem essential for the formation of chlorophyll in living cells, magnesium is the only metallic constituent of the chlorophyll molecule.

From the results of the intensive study of the chemistry of the degradation products of chlorophyll the probable structural formulas of both chlorophyll a and chlorophyll b (Fig. 88) have been determined (Fischer and Wenderoth, 1939).

As shown in Fig. 88 the nucleus of a molecule of chlorophyll a consists of a complex ring structure composed principally of four pyrrol nuclei linked together by intermediate atomic groupings. Each such ring bears side chains, the most prominent of which is the phytyl ($C_{20}H_{39}O$—) grouping which upon hydrolysis gives rise to phytol.

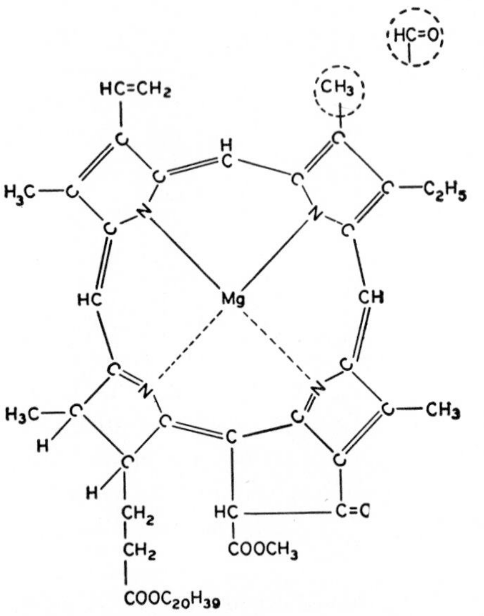

FIG. 88. Structural formula of chlorophyll a (Fischer and Wenderoth, 1939). Another arrangement of the double bonds in this formula is possible. The formula for chlorophyll b is the same, except that a HC=O group occurs in place of the CH_3 group enclosed in the dotted circle.

Absorption Spectra of the Chlorophylls.—When a colored solution such as an ether solution of a chlorophyll is interposed between a source of "white light" and a spectroscope, it can readily be shown that certain wave lengths of light are much more completely absorbed than others. The regions of the spectrum in which complete or nearly complete absorption takes place appear as dark bands. Chlorophylls a and b both show a definite and characteristic absorption spectrum when in solution. The exact appearance of such absorption spectra will vary, however, depending upon the kind of solvent and the concentration and thickness of the layer of solution which is examined. Absorption curves for chlorophyll a and b in ether solution as determined by photoelectric measurements are shown in Fig. 89. Both chlorophylls exhibit maximum absorption in the blue-violet region and a secondary maximum in the short red.

As a rule the absorption spectrum of a leaf does not correspond very closely with the spectrum of a solution of the pigments from that same leaf. In general there is relatively more absorption of light by leaves in those spectral regions where absorption by solutions is low, and a relatively less absorption of light by leaves in those spectral regions where absorption by solutions is high (Fig. 97). Some of the principal reasons for this are: (1) the pigment in the leaf is not continuous, but located only in the plastids; hence some light may pass through the leaf without traversing any pigment; (2) actual or apparent absorption, the latter a result of scattering of light within the leaf, by the nonpigmented parts of cells affects the overall absorption of light by the leaf; and (3) the concentration of the pigment in the leaf is usually different from its concentration in extracts; as a result specific absorption values of pigments in the leaf are different from those in a solution.

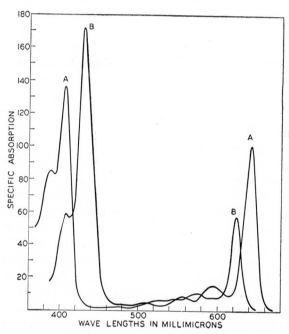

FIG. 89. Absorption spectra of chlorophylls *a* and *b* in ether solution. Data of Zscheile and Comar (1941).

Physicochemical State of the Chlorophylls in the Chloroplasts.—Although the extensive investigations of extracts of chlorophylls in organic solvents have advanced our knowledge of their physical and chemical properties, it should be remembered that these are only *extracts* and the physicochemical state of the chlorophylls in them bears little or no relation to its condition in the chloroplasts. One necessary step in learning how the chlorophylls of living cells operate will be to discover how they are related physically and chemically to the other constituents of the chloroplasts. Any acceptable picture of the physicochemical relationships of the chlorophylls within the chloroplasts must also be reconcilable with the known structural arrangement of the chlorophylls in the grana of the chloroplasts (Chap. IV).

A number of investigators (Lubimenko, 1926, 1927, 1928; Price and Wycoff, 1941; Smith, 1941; Anson, 1941; and others) have shown that green, opalescent, aqueous extracts can be prepared from the leaves of many species by grinding them with sand in water or solutions and clarifying by filtration, precipitation, or centrifugation. These extracts possess many of the properties of protein sols or suspensions and the chlorophyll molecules seem to be definitely associated with the protein micelles or particles. These results have led to the postulation of the existence of a chlorophyll-protein compound of constant composition in plants, analogous to the hemoglobin (hemin plus globin, a protein) of the blood. Although results of these experiments indicate that some sort of an association of chlorophylls with proteins in the chloroplasts is highly probable, there are strong reasons for doubting that this association takes the form of a protein-chlorophyll compound in the strictly chemical sense.

Actual chemical analyses of the chloroplast substance have been made by Chibnall (1939), Menke (1940), Granick (1938), Comar (1942), and others. The protein content of the chloroplast material from several species has been found to lie within a range of 35 to 55 per cent, and the lipid content within a range of 18 to 32 per cent on the dry weight basis (chloroplasts are probably about 50 per cent water). In the leaf cells of spinach most of the lipids present are constituents of the chloroplasts. In such chemical analyses the chlorophylls and carotenoids (see later) constitute a part of the lipid fraction, about 5-10 per cent of which is chlorophylls and 2-4 per cent carotenoids. The relatively large quantity of lipids in the chloroplasts suggests that the pigments commonly present in some manner may be associated with lipids as well as with proteins. The physicochemical properties of the lipids are such that it seems more probable that any association between them and the chlorophylls or carotenoids is of a physical rather than a chemical nature.

Chlorophyll Synthesis.—Chlorophylls, in common with practically all the other organic substances which occur in plants, are products of the synthetic activities of the plant. A number of conditions are known to be necessary for, or at least to influence greatly, the synthesis of chlorophylls in plants. Absence of any one of these factors will inhibit chlorophyll synthesis resulting in the condition often called <u>chlorosis</u>. This term is most frequently applied when the failure of chlorophylls to develop is the result of a deficiency of one of the essential mineral elements. Different types of chlorosis may develop in the leaves of any species depending upon the factor limiting chlorophyll formation. The following discussion of the factors influencing chlorophyll synthesis refers primarily to the formation of chlorophylls a and b in the higher plants.

1. *Genetic Factors*.—That certain genetic factors are necessary for the development of chlorophylls is shown by the behavior of some varieties of maize in which a certain proportion of the seedlings produced cannot synthesize chlorophylls, even if all environmental conditions are favorable for their formation. As soon as the food stored in the grain is exhausted such "albino" seedlings die. This trait is inherited in such strains of maize as a Mendelian recessive and hence is apparent only in plants homozygous for this factor. More or less similar genetic effects on chlorophyll synthesis have been demonstrated in a number of other species.

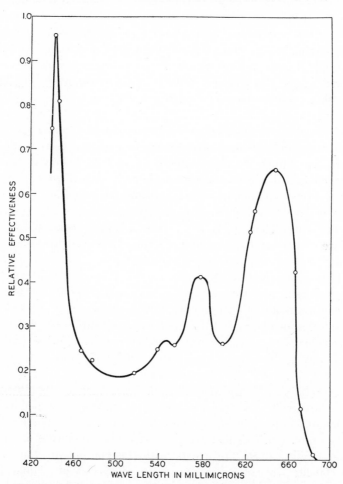

Fig. 90.   Relative effectiveness of different wave lengths in the formation of chlorophyll. Data of Frank (1946).

2. *Light.*—Light is usually necessary for the development of chlorophyll in the angiosperms. In the algae, mosses, ferns, and conifers, however, chlorophyll synthesis can occur in the dark as well as in the light, although the quantity produced is often less in the absence of light than in its presence. In a few angiosperms such as seedlings of the water lotus (*Nelumbo*), and in the cotyledons of citrus embryos chlorophylls can also develop in the absence of light.

Relatively low intensities of light are generally effective in inducing chlorophyll synthesis in those species in which light is required for this process. All wave lengths of the visible spectrum will, if their energy value is adequate, cause chlorophyll development in etiolated seedlings (chlorophyll-free seedlings which have been grown in the dark) except those longer than 680 mμ. (Sayre, 1928). For equal irradiances, a narrow band of wave lengths in the blue at about 445 mμ. is most effective in inducing chlorophyll formation in oat seedlings, a broader wave band in the orange red (about 620-660 mμ.) being next most effective (Fig. 90).

Like other complex compounds synthesized in plants, chlorophyll undoubtedly represents the terminal product of a long chain of reactions. Most of the steps in this sequence of reactions are unknown, but the evidence regarding the final step in chlorophyll synthesis seems clear. Dark-grown seedlings of higher plants are usually yellow in color, but actually contain traces of a green pigment, called *protochlorophyll*. Chemically this compound is closely related to the other chlorophylls, differing from chlorophyll *a* only in having two less hydrogen atoms in the molecule. There is good evidence that protochlorophyll is the immediate precursor of chlorophyll *a* (Smith, 1948). Reduction of protochlorophyll to chlorophyll *a* appears to be the last step in the synthesis of this latter compound. In the higher plants, at least, this reaction occurs only in the light, and the protochlorophyll is the light-absorbing agent for its own transformation to chlorophyll *a* (Koski, *et al.*, 1951).

If a solution of chlorophyll in an organic solvent is exposed to bright light its color soon fades because of a destructive effect of light upon the chlorophyll. This is in all probability a photo-oxidation process, since it is accomplished by the absorption of oxygen. Strong light also brings about the disintegration of the chlorophylls in leaves, although at a less rapid rate than in chlorophyll solutions (*cf.* discussion of photo-oxidation in Chap. XIX). In leaves exposed to intense light, therefore, synthesis and decomposition of chlorophylls are probably going on simultaneously. In accord with this concept are the results of Shirley (1929) who found in a number of species of plants that the chlorophyll content per unit leaf weight or per unit leaf area increased with decreasing light intensity until a relatively low intensity was reached.

Further decrease in light intensity below this value caused a decrease in chlorophyll content.

3. *Oxygen.*—In the absence of oxygen etiolated seedlings fail to develop chlorophylls even when illuminated under conditions otherwise favorable for chlorophyll formation. Oxygen must therefore be required in some of the steps in the sequence of reactions whereby chlorophyll is synthesized.

4. *Carbohydrates.*—Etiolated leaves which have been depleted of soluble carbohydrates fail to turn green even when all of the other conditions to which they are exposed favor chlorophyll synthesis. When such leaves are floated on a sugar solution, sugar is absorbed and chlorophyll formation occurs rapidly. A supply of carbohydrate foods is therefore essential for the formation of chlorophyll.

5. *Nitrogen.*—Since nitrogen is a part of chlorophyll molecules it is not surprising to find that a deficiency of this element in the plant retards chlorophyll formation. Failure of chlorophylls to develop is one of the commonly recognized symptoms of nitrogen deficiency in plants.

6. *Magnesium.*—Like nitrogen this element is also a part of chlorophyll molecules. Deficiency of magnesium in plants results in the development of a characteristic mottled chlorosis of the older leaves (Chap. XXV).

7. *Iron.*—In the absence of iron in an available form green plants are unable to synthesize chlorophylls and the leaves soon become blanched or yellow in color (Chap. XXV). While not a constituent of chlorophyll molecules, iron is essential for its synthesis.

8. *Other Mineral Elements.*—In the absence of manganese, copper, or zinc, more or less characteristic chloroses develop in plants (Chap. XXV). These substances apparently play at least indirect roles in the synthesis of chlorophyll.

9. *Temperature.*—In general, chlorophyll synthesis can occur over a wide range of temperatures. In etiolated wheat plants synthesis of chlorophylls occurs at any temperature within the range 3°-48°C., but is most rapid between 26° and 30°C. (Lubimenko and Hubbenet, 1932). Somewhat similar results have been obtained by Larsen (1950) on chlorophyll synthesis in potato tubers except that synthesis appears to be most rapid in the approximate range 11°-19°C. The range of temperatures over which chlorophyll synthesis occurs as well as the temperature of most rapid synthesis undoubtedly varies considerably from one species to another.

10. *Water.*—Desiccation of leaf tissues not only inhibits synthesis of chlorophylls but seems to accelerate disintegration of the chlorophylls already present. A familiar example of this effect is the browning of grass during droughts.

The mechanism of chlorophyll synthesis is very sensitive to any type of physiological disturbance within the plant. Many other conditions besides those already discussed, such as lack of certain other mineral elements, deficient aeration of the roots, infestations of insects, or infection with bacterial, fungous or viral diseases, may induce, directly or indirectly, partial or complete chlorosis of the leaves. The failure of chlorophyll synthesis to take place normally is often one of the first observable symptoms of almost any derangement in the metabolic conditions within a plant.

The Carotenoids.—This group of orange, red, yellow, and brownish pigments includes a number of chloroplast pigments. At least sixty different carotenoids are known to be present in plants. Best known of the pigments in this group is the orange-yellow *carotene*. This is a hydrocarbon with the formula $C_{40}H_{56}$ and exists in three isomeric forms. β-carotene is the most abundant of these in plants, and appears to be invariably present in the chloroplasts. This compound is the precursor of vitamin A (Chap. XXVIII), which is formed in the animal body by a simple hydrolytic splitting of the molecules of β-carotene, as follows:

$$C_{40}H_{56} + 2\,H_2O \rightarrow 2\,C_{20}H_{29}OH$$

Lycopene, a red pigment found in the fruits of tomato, red peppers, roses, and other species, is also isomeric with carotene.

The *xanthophylls* or *carotenols* are mostly yellow or brownish pigments, many, but not all, of which have molecular formula $C_{40}H_{56}O_2$. Chemically the carotenols are closely related to carotene, and undoubtedly transformations from one kind of carotenoid to another occur readily in plants.

Luteol is by far the most abundant carotenol in leaves (Strain, 1938); other leaf xanthophylls include zeaxanthol, violaxanthol, cryptoxanthol, flavoxanthol, and neoxanthin.

Numerous other xanthophylls occur in the various phyla of algae. Among the most abundant of these pigments are the fucoxanthins which impart to brown algae their distinctive color. Several brownish carotenols are also present in the diatoms, including fucoxanthins, diatoxanthin, and diadinoxanthin.

The carotenoids are not water soluble, but they can be extracted from plant tissues by use of suitable organic solvents. Carotene, for example, is soluble in ethyl ether, chloroform, and carbon bisulfide. Leaf xanthophylls are soluble in chloroform and ethyl alcohol, but only slightly soluble in carbon bisulfide.

All of the carotenoids are highly unsaturated compounds, and hence readily oxidizable. Loss of a considerable proportion of the carotenoids present in a plant tissue may be occasioned by oxidation during extraction procedures.

As shown by its absorption spectrum (Fig. 91), β-carotene absorbs only wave lengths in the blue-violet portion of the visible spectrum. The absorption spectra of other carotenoids are similar to that of carotene.

✗Most, if not all, of the carotenoid pigments can be synthesized by plants in the absence of light.

blue-violet

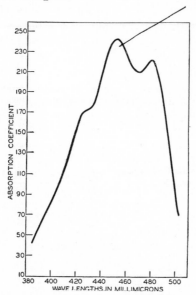

Fɪɢ. 91.   Absorption spectrum of β-carotene in ether-alcohol solution. Data of Miller *et al.* (1935).

Relative Quantities of the Chloroplast Pigments Present in Green Leaves.
—Data regarding the molecular proportions of the chloroplast pigments in the leaves of several species are presented in Table 23. The leaves listed in this table contain about three molecules of the chlorophylls to one molecule of the carotenoids, about three molecules of chlorophyll *a* to each molecule of chlorophyll *b,* and about two molecules of xantho- phylls to each molecule of carotene. Although these values can be taken as representative, considerable variation in the proportions of the chloroplast pigments occurs as a result of differences in genetic factors, environmental conditions, and the age of the leaf. As shown in Table 23, with senescence of leaves in the autumn there is a marked increase in the proportion of carotenoids to chlorophylls as a result of the disintegration

a = 3 X
b = X
c = X
Xa = 2X

of the chlorophylls. The proportion of chlorphyll a to b in leaves may vary considerably depending upon the light intensity to which the leaves have been exposed. Willstätter and Stoll (1928) and others, for example, have shown that the proportion of chlorophyll b to a is higher in shade leaves of many species than in sun leaves of the same species. As an example of genetic differences in the pigment content of leaves, results obtained with dark and burley varieties of tobacco may be taken as illustrative (Griffith et al., 1944). Although the ratio of chlorophyll a to b was virtually the same in all varieties studied the total chlorophyll content per gram of dry weight was, on the average, more than 50 per cent greater in the dark varieties than in the burley varieties. Carotene content of the dark varieties was also appreciably higher than in the burley varieties.

TABLE 23—MOLECULAR PROPORTIONS OF THE CHLOROPLAST PIGMENTS PRESENT IN LEAVES AT DIFFERENT SEASONS (DATA OF WILLSTÄTTER AND STOLL, 1918).

Species	Date	Appearance of leaves	Molecular proportions		
			Chlorophyll a / Chlorophyll b	Carotene / Xanthophylls	Chlorophyll a and b / Carotene and Xanthophylls
European Elder (*Sambucus nigra*)	July	Green	2.74	0.59	3.33
	Oct. 21	Green	2.61	0.60	3.15
Sunflower (*Helianthus annuus*)	Oct. 7	Green	2.86	0.54	3.66
	Nov. 5	Yellow green	4.01	0.26	1.27
	Nov. 5	Yellow	4.95	0.17	0.32
Horse Chestnut (*Aesculus hippocastanum*)	Oct. 24	Green	4.23	0.47	3.06
	Oct. 24	Yellow green	4.23	0.20	0.81

SUGGESTED FOR COLLATERAL READING

Bragg, W. *The Universe of Light*. The Macmillan Co. New York. 1941.

Duggar, B. M., Editor. *Biological Effects of Radiation*. McGraw-Hill Book Co., Inc. New York. 1936.

Franck, J., and W. E. Loomis, Editors. *Photosynthesis in Plants*. Iowa State College Press. Ames. 1949.

Karrer, P. and E. Jucker. *Carotenoids*. Translated and revised by E. A. Braude. Elsevier Publishing Co. New York. 1950.

Rabinowitch, E. *Photosynthesis and Related Processes*. Vol. I, II. Interscience Publishers, Inc. New York. 1945, 1951.

Willstätter, R., and A. Stoll. *Untersuchungen über die Assimilation der Kohlen säure.* Julius Springer. Berlin. 1918.

Willstätter, R., and A. Stoll. *Investigations on Chlorophyll.* Translated by F. M Schertz and A. R. Merz. Science Press. Lancaster, Pa. 1928.

SELECTED BIBLIOGRAPHY

Anson, M. L. On Lubimenko extracts of chlorophyll-protein. *Science* **93**: 186-187. 1941.

Aronoff, S. Chlorophyll. *Bot. Rev.* **16**: 525-588. 1950.

Chibnall, A. C. *Protein Metabolism in the Plant.* Yale University Press. New Haven. 1939.

Comar, C. L. Chloroplast substance of spinach leaves. *Bot. Gaz.* **104**: 122-127. 1942.

Fischer, H., and H. Wenderoth. Zur Kenntnis von Chlorophyll. *Ann.* **537**: 170-177. 1939.

Frank, Sylvia R. The effectiveness of the spectrum in chlorophyll formation. *Jour. Gen. Physiol.* **29**: 157-179. 1946.

Granick, S. Chloroplast nitrogen of some higher plants. *Amer. Jour. Bot.* **25**: 561-567. 1938.

Granick, S. Biosynthesis of chlorophyll and related pigments. *Ann. Rev. Plant Physiol.* **2**: 115-144. 1951.

Griffith, R. B., W. D. Valleau, and R. N. Jeffrey. Chlorophyll and carotene content of eighteen tobacco varieties. *Plant Physiol.* **19**: 689-693. 1944.

Koski, Violet M., C. S. French, and J. H. C. Smith. The action spectrum for the transformation of protochlorophyll to chlorophyll a in normal and albino corn seedlings. *Arch. Biochem.* **31**: 1-17. 1951.

Larsen, E. C. Chlorophyll formation in potato tubers as influenced by temperature and time. *Science* **111**: 206-207. 1950.

Lloyd, F. E. The fluorescent colors of plants. *Science* **59**: 241-248. 1924.

Lubimenko, V. N. Recherches sur les pigments des plastes et sur la photosynthèse. *Rev. Gen. Bot.* **38**: 307-328, 381-400. 1926. **39**: 547-559, 619-637, 698-710, 758-766. 1927. **40**: 23-29, 88-94, 146-155, 226-243, 303-318, 372-381, 415-447, 486-504. 1928.

Lubimenko, V. N., and E. R. Hubbenet. The influence of temperature on the rate of accumulation of chorophyll in etiolated seedlings. *New Phytol.* **31**: 26-57. 1932.

Menke, W. Untersuchungen über das Protoplasma grüner Pflanzenzellen. II. Der Chlorophyll gehalt der Chloroplasten aus Spinatblättern, *Zeitschr. Physiol. Chem.* **263**: 100-103. 1940.

Miller, E. S., G. MacKinney, and F. P. Zscheile. Absorption spectra of alpha and beta carotenes and lycopene. *Plant Physiol.* **10**: 375-381. 1935.

Price, W. C., and R. W. G. Wyckoff. The ultracentrifugation of the proteins of cucumber viruses 3 and 4. *Nature* **141**: 685-686. 1941.

Sayre, J. D. The development of chlorophyll in seedlings in different ranges of wave lengths of light. *Plant Physiol.* **3**: 71-77. 1928.

Shirley, H. L. The influence of light intensity and light quality upon the growth of plants. *Amer. Jour. Bot.* **16**: 354-390. 1929.

Smith, E. L. The chlorophyll-protein compound of the green leaf. *Jour. Gen. Physiol.* **24**: 565-582. 1941.

Smith, J. H. C. Protochlorophyll, precursor of chlorophyll. *Arch. Biochem.* **19:** 449-454. 1948.

Stern, K. Untersuchungen über Fluorescenz und Zustand des Chlorophylls in lebenden Zellen. *Ber. Deutsch. Bot. Ges.* **38:** 28-35. 1920.

Strain, H. H. Leaf xanthophylls. *Carnegie Inst. Wash. Publ. No. 490.* Washington. 1938.

Strain, H. H. Chloroplast pigments. *Ann. Rev. Biochem.* **13:** 591-610. 1944.

Withrow, R. B. Radiant energy nomenclature. *Plant Physiol.* **18:** 476-487. 1943.

Zscheile, F. P. Plastid pigments. *Bot. Rev.* **7:** 587-648. 1941.

Zscheile, F. P., and C. L. Comar. Influence of preparative procedure on the purity of chlorophyll components as shown by absorption spectra. *Bot. Gaz.* **102:** 463-481. 1941.

XVIII

PHOTOSYNTHESIS

The biological world, with only negligible exceptions, runs at the expense of the material and energy capital accumulated as a result of photosynthesis, a process which occurs only in chlorophyllous (green) plants. From the products of photosynthesis and from a few simple inorganic compounds obtained from the environment are built up in living organisms all of the multifarious and often complex kinds of molecules which constitute the cellular structure of plants and animals, or which are otherwise essential to their existence. Some of the sequences of reactions resulting in the synthesis of such compounds from photosynthetic products occur in the bodies of green plants. Others occur in the bodies of animals or non-green plants after they have ingested or utilized as food compounds which had their ultimate origin in the photosynthetic process.

Not only do most of the materials which enter into the cellular structure of plant and animal bodies derive from the photosynthetic capital, but the energy expended in the operation of living organisms also derives from this source. Plants and animals are constituted so that only energy released as a result of the oxidation of foods can be used in metabolic processes, growth, locomotion, or in other ways. The chemical energy of foods, releasable upon oxidation, all represents converted energy of sunlight which was originally entrapped within the molecules of organic compounds during photosynthesis.

A goodly share of what economists term wealth originates directly or indirectly as a consequence of photosynthesis. This is true not only of all plant and animal products, but also of our heritage of coal, oil, and gas from past geological ages. These latter products all derive from the remains of living organisms and also represent photosynthetic capital. The energy released from them upon combustion represents sunlight

309

of past geological ages which was captured and converted into chemical energy by the photosynthesis of plants which flourished during geological epochs long antedating the advent of man.

Man's stake in photosynthesis is thus even greater than that of any other living organism. Not only is he, like plants and all other animals, dependent for his very existence upon this process, but he is also indebted to it for many of the goods and most of the energy which contribute to maintenance of his standard of living above a mere subsistence level.

The average human being in the United States consumes foods with an energy value of about 3000 kg.-cal. per day. Many of the human inhabitants of this globe are not this fortunate, and substantial numbers exist more or less constantly on the verge of starvation. Intensifying the problem of maintaining adequate food supplies for mankind is the never-ending increase in the total human population of the earth. The demand of men for more food is not likely to diminish in the foreseeable future. There is no substitute for photosynthesis as the ultimate source of all human food.

Advanced industrial civilizations, such as those of North America and Europe, are dependent for their maintenance upon the continuous and lavish expenditure of energy. The indirect per capita consumption of energy per day for each inhabitant of the United States—about 147,000 kg.-cal.—is vastly greater than that used directly as foods. This is the energy which is used for heat and power in industry, for turning the wheels of trains and automobiles, and for the generation of electricity. The great bulk of this energy comes from the combustion of coal, oil, and gas. The only important nonphotosynthetic source of energy is water power.

Man's need to augment power resources is not as pressing as his need to increase food supplies. The reservoir of fossil fuels, on which the wheels of our civilization turn, will not be depleted in the next year, nor even in the next century. But the veins of coal and the pools of oil beneath the earth's surface are not inexhaustible. Sooner or later the problem of replacement sources for these fuels will confront the human race. Some foresight in meeting this ultimate problem would be a wise insurance against the inevitable.

Spectacular hopes have been expressed that the future will see the harnessing of atomic energy for peaceful purposes, and undoubtedly this imagination-challenging possibility exists. But atomic energy sources of heat and power will be developed slowly, and there is as yet no certainty that they can supplant fuels as a major source of energy. To bank solely on atomic energy as our future source of heat and power would be premature in the present state of knowledge.

On this sun-drenched planet solar radiation would seem to be the most promising source to which to turn for additional energy. Particularly does this seem to be true when it is realized that the efficiency of photosynthesis is very low. The proportion of the total solar energy falling on the earth's surface which is converted into chemical energy by green plants is of the order of a few tenths of one per cent (see further *light energy utilized* discussion later in this chapter). For well-recognized thermodynamic reasons it is improbable that man will ever be able to harness any major fraction of the solar radiation intercepted by the earth, but there is no doubt that some increase could be made in the proportion of this solar energy which can be diverted to human use.

One major possibility is that of an increase in the total annual photosynthetic production. In this connection a digression should be made to point out that the currently available photosynthetic product is by no means fully exploited by man as a source of energy. A larger supply of available foods and fuels can be achieved by a more efficient utilization of the present annual photosynthetic output, but measures designed to accomplish this objective should not be confused with procedures which might be undertaken to increase the total annual production of photosynthate.

There are a number of possible ways of utilizing the present organic material output of photosynthesis more efficiently. One would be the conversion of inedible products such as wood and straw into foods. Technological methods of obtaining large yields of sugars from such plant materials, which are composed largely of cellulose, have been developed. Carbohydrate foods obtained in this way could be used, either directly or indirectly, as supplementary sources of human food. An alternative procedure would be to convert such plant materials into alcohol—also a technologically feasible procedure—which could then be used as fuel. Another way of increasing available foods would be by making a greater use of aquatic plants which constitute the least tapped of all photosynthetic resources. Still another method of achieving a more complete utilization of present photosynthetic resources lies in the breeding of better varieties of grazing animals which are more efficient than existing ones in the conversion of the photosynthetic product of grasslands into foods which can be eaten by humans.

The primary goal, however, should be an increase in the total annual production of photosynthate. Some enhancement in the overall efficiency of the process on an acre-year basis undoubtedly can be achieved in many parts of the world by the use of improved varieties of plants, better agricultural and silvicultural methods, and other practices. A gain of only 0.01 per cent in the total radiant energy incident on land areas converted into chemical energy in photosynthesis would increase enormously the food resources of the world. Proposals have also been made that commercial-scale artificial culture of *Chlorella* or other unicellular algae in solution be undertaken as an additional source of basic foods. Preliminary experiments indicate at least a possibility that this somewhat revolutionary approach to the problem of food production may be feasible.

A second major possibility of channeling more solar energy to human use is that of its direct conversion to usable energy without the intermediation of the green plant. This dream has long been entertained, and many schemes for its realization have been elaborated. Of various proposals which have been made the most promising appears to be the development of some sort of an artificial photosynthetic mechanism. A thorough understanding of photosynthesis as it occurs in the green plant —the only known mechanism of this kind—should yield clues as to how analogous mechanisms might be devised and operated to convert now wasted radiant energy of sunlight into chemical energy which can be used by man.

The key to further progress in adding to the food or energy resources of man clearly lies in a thorough understanding of the mechanism of the one known effective radiant energy converter—the chlorophyllous plant cell. This is true whether progress is to be made by a more efficient utilization of the green plant itself as an energy converter, or by the development of artificial photosynthetic systems which circumvent the plant.

Photosynthesis as a Process.—The process in which certain carbohydrates are synthesized from carbon dioxide and water by chlorophyllous cells in the presence of light, oxygen being a by-product, is generally called *photosynthesis*. On the continent of Europe and to a lesser extent in Great Britain, the terms *carbon assimilation* and *assimilation* are often used to designate this process. The common use of the word "assimilation" to denote the process in which foods are incorporated into the structures of the plant body (Chap. XXIX) makes the employment of this term or carbon assimilation as a synonym for photosynthesis undesirable.

The *summary* equation representing the process of photosynthesis is conventionally written as follows:

$$6\ CO_2 + 6\ H_2O \xrightarrow[\text{chlorophyllous cells}]{\substack{\text{673 kg.-cal. of} \\ \text{radiant energy}}} C_6H_{12}O_6 + 6\ O_2$$

It should be clearly understood that this equation does not purport to indicate the mechanism of the process, but is merely a statement of the net exchanges which occur in the shorthand of chemical symbols. As usually written, a hexose sugar is designated as the carbohydrate formed in photosynthesis, but this is by no means certain. The question of the actual first products of photosynthesis will be discussed later. The value 673 kg.-cal. is, strictly speaking, correct only for glucose; the energy requirement of the reaction is approximately the same, per CH_2O group, however, for the synthesis of any of the hexoses, or for any disaccharide or polysaccharide derived from hexoses.

Leaf Anatomy in Relation to Photosynthesis.—In the vascular plants photosynthesis occurs chiefly in the leaves, which in the majority of species are thin, expanded organs possessing a large external surface in proportion to their volume. This type of structure permits the display of a large number of chloroplast-containing cells to light in proportion to the volume of the leaf. The labyrinth of intercellular air passages in the interior of the leaf is so extensive that practically every green cell is in contact with the internal atmosphere of the leaf. As a result of this loose cellular structure the internal leaf surface (surface of the leaf cells in contact with the intercellular spaces) is much greater than the surface of the epidermal cells exposed to the outside atmosphere. In a lilac leaf, for example, the internal surface is about thirteen times as great as its external surface (Turrell, 1936). Most of the carbon dioxide absorbed by mesophyll cells passes into them from the intercellular spaces after first having diffused into the leaf through the stomates, although substantial quantities of carbon dioxide are absorbed directly by the epidermal cells of some species (Freeland, 1948). The presence of intercellular spaces in a leaf therefore provides a much more extensive carbon dioxide absorbing surface than if all of this gas were absorbed directly through the external leaf surfaces. Since the walls of all of the cells within a leaf are normally more or less saturated with water, the vapor pressure of the internal air spaces is usually higher than that of the outside atmosphere. This makes it possible for the leaf cells to absorb atmospheric carbon dioxide without being exposed to the usually relatively dry external atmosphere. Whenever the stomates are open the internal atmosphere of the intercellular spaces is continuous with that of the outside atmosphere, and carbon dioxide can diffuse with little impediment from the outside air into the intercellular spaces. After passing into solution in the water saturating the mesophyll cell walls part of the carbon dioxide reacts with water forming carbonic acid (H_2CO_3). Some of the carbon dioxide diffuses to the chloroplasts in this form and some simply as dissolved carbon dioxide.

The Products of Photosynthesis.—The products of photosynthesis are generally considered to be carbohydrates and oxygen. Most of the latter diffuses out of the cells in which it is set free and plays no further part in the metabolism of the plant. Some of the oxygen, however, may be chemically intercepted and utilized in respiration within the cells. The products of importance in plant nutrition are the energy-rich carbohydrates which are built up in the chloroplasts.

Only four carbohydrates commonly appear in leaf cells during or immediately after photosynthesis. These are the hexoses, D-glucose and D-fructose, the disaccharide sucrose, and the polysaccharide starch (Chap. XX). Numerous attempts have been made to determine how many of these carbohydrates are direct products of photosynthesis and also which is the "first" product in this process, but to date there is no entirely satisfactory answer to this question. It appears quite probable, in fact, that the products of photosynthesis may differ somewhat from one photosynthetic tissue to another.

The work of some investigators seems to indicate that the principal leaf carbohydrates are formed sequentially in the order of their complexity. Weevers (1924), for example, showed that if geranium plants, the leaves of which had been depleted of sugars by keeping them in the dark, were allowed to photosynthesize for a very short period, only hexoses accumulated. A longer exposure was required for the appearance of sucrose, and a still longer one for the appearance of starch.

On the other hand, a number of investigators have claimed that sucrose ($C_{12}H_{22}O_{11}$) is the first sugar to be formed in photosynthesis. The fact that the sucrose content of the leaves of a number of species increases during periods of active photosynthesis and decreases rapidly upon the cessation of photosynthesis, while the hexose content of those same leaves remains much more nearly constant throughout the day (Parkin, 1912, and others), has been taken as evidence for this postulation. Further evidence that sucrose is probably the first free carbohydrate to be formed in photosynthesis, at least in some species, is given later under the discussion of the carbon pathway in photosynthesis.

Still different results were obtained by Smith (1944). He found that sucrose and starch are formed simultaneously during photosynthesis in sunflower leaves, presumably from a common precursor, and also obtained evidence that most of the hexoses present in the leaf cells arise from the digestion of sucrose (Chap. XX), rather than as direct products of photosynthesis.

Both starch and sucrose serve principally as temporary storage carbohydrates in mesophyll cells. Sucrose is readily translocated from the leaves as such. Starch, however, being insoluble, is immobile until digested to simpler, soluble carbohydrates which can move out of the mesophyll cells.

There is some evidence that other types of stable organic compounds may arise more or less directly in the photosynthetic process, at least under some conditions or in some species. Burström's (1943) results with young, excised wheat leaves indicate that a direct reduction of nitrates resulting in the formation of amino acids (Chap. XXVI) or related compounds may occur as an integral part of photosynthesis. Indications of a similar close relationship between nitrogen metabolism and photosynthesis has also been found in *Chlorella* (Myers, 1949). Evidence of an intermeshing of the processes of photosynthesis and amino acid synthesis also comes from studies of the carbon pathway in photosynthesis as revealed by the use of radioactive isotopes, discussed later.

Results indicating that amino acid synthesis occurs in young leaves of at least some species as an apparently integral part of photosynthesis contrasts with the results of Smith (1943), who found an exact equivalence between the quantity of carbon dioxide photosynthesized and the quantity of carbohydrates made in sunflower leaves. It seems highly probable that the course of photosynthesis is not exactly the same in all photosynthetic tissues. The process may follow a different course in young, growing leaves, for example, than it does in older and more mature leaves, even in the same species.

Starch Synthesis.—One of the most familiar facts about photosynthesis is that starch accumulates in the chloroplasts of many species shortly, if not immediately, after the onset of the process at any appreciable rate. Although the possibility of the direct formation of starch in photosynthesis in some species cannot be excluded, in general starch synthesis and photosynthesis are independent processes. Since starch is insoluble in water the presence of starch grains in a cell must signify that the grains have been built up in that cell. Starch grains often occur abundantly in the cells of non-green tissues or in the tissues of roots or other plant organs which are never exposed to light. Obviously photosynthesis cannot take place in such cells and the starch present must have been synthesized from sugars translocated to them from the green organs of the plant.

Since starch synthesis in the non-green cells of plants is obviously a distinct process from photosynthesis, it seems probable that this is also true of the starch synthesis which occurs in green cells. The fact that starch synthesis will take place in the chloroplasts of green leaves floated on a sugar solution in the dark also supports this view. Photosynthesis occurs only in the presence of light and, in the higher plants, only in the chloroplasts. Starch synthesis may occur in the chloroplasts, most probably as the product of a secondary reaction, but also may take place in many non-green cells and in either the light or dark. In non-green cells starch is synthesized in the leucoplasts.

The critical concentration of simple sugars required for starch formation in the leaves of many species is very low and has been reported to be less than 0.5 g. per 100 g. of fresh leaves in some species. In the mesophyll cells of most species, therefore, starch formation in the leaves quickly follows photosynthesis, much of the sugar made in the latter process being converted into starch. Under conditions favorable to photosynthesis the starch content of the leaves of most species usually increases during much of the daylight period. During the night hours the starch content of leaves usually decreases because of digestion of part or all of the starch back to glucose and translocation out of the cells in the form of this sugar or other soluble carbohydrates produced therefrom.

That starch synthesis is an entirely independent process from photosynthesis is also indicated by the fact that this process does not occur in the mesophyll cells of a number of species of plants, yet photosynthesis takes place in these cells in the same manner as in all other green plants. Failure of the leaves to synthesize starch is a characteristic feature of the metabolism of many species of the Liliaceae, Amaryllidaceae, Gentianaceae, Compositae, and Umbelliferae.

Similarly the non-green portions of at least some kinds of variegated leaves do not normally synthesize starch. However, if the sugar concentration within the chlorophyll-free cells is artificially increased by floating such leaves on glucose solutions, starch synthesis can be induced. For the leaves of the variegated geranium a glucose solution of about 0.5 M concentration has been found to be optimum for the induction of starch synthesis in the non-green portions (Chapman and Camp, 1932).

The chemical mechanism of starch synthesis is discussed in Chap. XX.

The Measurement of Photosynthesis.—Measurements of photosynthesis are complicated by the fact that certain other processes involving the same materials are proceeding in the cells at the same time. The process of respiration is continually in progress in all cells, resulting in an oxidation of part of the carbohydrates synthesized in photosynthesis. This introduces an error which is inherent in all methods of measuring photosynthesis. Determinations of the quantity of photosynthate formed in a given time are always less than the true value by the amount of carbohydrate which has been consumed in respiration. In many measurements of photosynthesis the simultaneous occurrence of respiration is disregarded, and the results obtained are designated as the _apparent,_ or _net_ photosynthetic rate, or, in other words, as the rate of photosynthesis minus the rate of respiration. Since in rapidly photosynthesizing tissues the rate of photosynthesis is often ten to twenty times as great as the rate of respiration, the apparent photosynthetic rate is often not greatly less than the true rate. For many purposes measurements of the rate of apparent photosynthesis have as great or greater significance as determinations of the "true" rate. Values for the actual rate of photosynthesis are obtained by correcting apparent rates for the quantity of carbohydrates consumed in respiration during the period of the measurement. The values used for such corrections are obtained by measuring the respiration rate of the same plant or organ when treated so that photosynthesis cannot occur—as, for example, by subjection to complete darkness.

Quantitative measurements of photosynthesis in terrestrial plants are usually based on determinations of the rate of oxygen evolution or rate of carbon dioxide consumption. The plants or parts of plants are enclosed in transparent chambers, or leaf cups (Chap. IX) are attached to the leaves. Outside air is passed through the chambers or leaf cups at a relatively rapid rate. The air is collected upon emergence from the chamber and analyzed for oxygen, or carbon dioxide, or both. Another procedure is to analyze small samples of the air for these gases at frequent intervals. By a comparison of the results of these analyses with similar analyses of the outside atmosphere, the rate of carbon dioxide consumption or oxygen evolution can be computed, either of which will serve as an index of the rate of apparent photosynthesis (Heinicke and Hoffman, 1933; Thomas and Hill, 1937). The rate of carbon dioxide

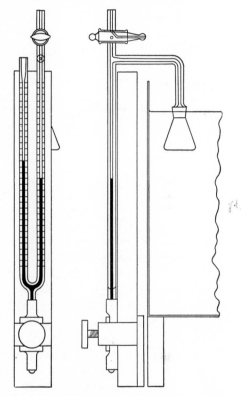

Fig. 92. Warburg manometer. Left, front view. Right, side view, showing attached flask which is immersed in, and oscillates in, a constant temperature bath. In the simplest application of this method to the measurement of photosynthesis, algae or other small units of photosynthetic tissue are suspended in a bicarbonate buffer (which serves as the CO_2 source) in the flask, and the rate of O_2 evolution, measured manometrically, taken as the index of the rate of apparent photosynthesis. The same type of apparatus is also widely used for the measurement of the rates of respiration as indicated by the rate of O_2 consumption. Redrawn from Dixon (1943).

consumption, under field conditions favorable for photosynthesis, is usually between 10 and 20 mg. CO_2 per dm.^{2} of leaf area per hr.

Many of the most fundamental investigations of photosynthetic rates have been made by very sensitive manometric techniques which are intrinsically limited in their application to determinations of photosynthesis in small units of plant tissue. Manometric methods of measuring photosynthesis have been used most widely with suspensions of algae such as *Chlorella*. In these techniques the rate of oxygen evolution, or carbon dioxide consumption, or both, are measured by pressure changes in a closed system in which the photosynthesizing tissue is enclosed (Fig. 92). Detailed descriptions of the various manometric techniques are given by Dixon (1943) and Umbreit *et al.* (1949).

The simplest method of making rough quantitative measurements of the rate of photosynthesis in terrestrial plants is to determine the increase in the dry weight of leaves during a given interval of time. One method of procedure is as follows: a representative sample of disks, usually 100 or more, is cut from the leaves by means of a cork borer at the beginning of the period for which the determination is to be made. These disks are transferred to an oven and dried to constant weight. At the end of a chosen period of time, the plant having been meanwhile exposed to the desired environmental conditions, a second sample consisting of the same number of disks as the first is cut from the leaves. Various precautions must be taken to insure the two samples being as nearly comparable as possible. The dry weight of the second sample of disks is also determined. Any gain in dry weight is considered to represent carbohydrates which have accumulated in the leaves as a result of photosynthesis. This method is subject to several serious errors (Thoday, 1909) and yields only approximate results. The gain in dry weight of leaves under conditions favorable for photosynthesis is usually between 0.5 and 2.0 g. per square meter per hour. The "twin leaf" method described by Denny (1930) is a variation of this method.

The Use of Isotopes as Tracers in Physiological Investigations.—The atoms of most chemical elements exist in more than one variety. Each kind of a given element has a different atomic weight, but all of them carry the same nuclear charge. For example, there are three different kinds of magnesium atoms with atomic weights of 24, 25, and 26, respectively. Such different varieties of atoms of a given element are called *isotopes*. Differences in the chemical behavior of two isotopes of the same element are so slight as to be barely detectable, and ordinarily they cannot be separated by chemical methods. The chemical properties of all isotopes of a given element are virtually identical, because all have the same electron configuration; one isotope differs from another only in the constitution of the atomic nucleus which is composed of protons and neutrons.

In addition to the stable isotopes described above there are many radioactive isotopes of various elements. Radioactive isotopes of certain heavy elements such as uranium and radium occur in nature. The atoms of many elements not normally radioactive may be made so by bombardment with various types of elementary particles such as neutrons, protons, deuterons, and alpha particles. Such bombardments are usually accomplished with the aid of a cyclotron or an uranium pile reactor.

Atoms of all radioactive elements gradually disintegrate, emitting charged particles and radiations in the process. For the artificially radioactive elements which are of greatest significance in biological sciences, the charged particles emitted are electrons and positrons. As a result cf the loss of particles and radiations by radioactive isotopes one element is transmuted into another. Radioactive Na^{24}, for example, with the loss of an electron, is converted into the stable naturally occurring Mg^{24} isotope. The *half-life* of a radioactive isotope is the length of time required for half of any given weight of the isotope to be converted into the kind of atom into which it is degraded. The half-lives of radioactive isotopes range from less than a second to many hundreds of years.

The situation with regard to isotopes is well illustrated by the biologically important element carbon. Naturally occurring carbon consists almost entirely of the stable C^{12} isotope. The C^{13} isotope is also stable and occurs in traces in nature. The atomic weight of naturally occurring carbon is a little more than 12, because of the presence of a slight admixture of the C^{13} isotope. In addition, three radioactive isotopes can be made: C^{10}, with a half-life of 9 sec., C^{11}, with a half-life of 21 min.; and C^{14}, with a half-life of about 5000 years.

A radioactive isotope betrays its presence wherever it may be by the continual emission of charged particles which can be detected with an electroscope or Geiger counter. Similarly, the presence of any of the rarer stable isotopes in a system can be detected, because of their unusual mass, by means of the instrument known as the mass spectograph. Hence, if molecules of any compound are tagged, by incorporating into them atoms that are radioactive or atoms of the rarer kinds of stable isotopes, it is possible to trace such molecules through a system. After the absorption or ingestion of such molecules by an organism it is possible to follow their subsequent distribution through the organism and often to determine the reactions in which they participate. This is not possible by ordinary methods of chemical analysis because by such methods it is impossible to distinguish between introduced molecules and others of the same species which were already present in the organism.

If a compound containing tagged atoms is introduced through the roots of a plant, for example, subsequent distribution of the labeled atoms in the plant can be followed (Chap. XXVII). Furthermore, if tissues in which the labeled substance is found to be present—leaves, for example —are analyzed, the kinds of compounds in which the tagged atoms are present at the end of the experiment can often be ascertained. It is in this latter manner that the steps in metabolic reactions can often be followed.

The availability of the rarer kinds of stable isotopes of some elements and of artificially made radioactive isotopes of others has placed a new tool in the hands of investigators of the physiology of plants and animals. Some of the more widely used isotopes in plant research are the stable isotopes H^2, O^{18}, C^{13}, and N^{15}, and the radioactive isotopes Na^{24}, P^{32}, K^{42}, C^{11}, C^{14}, S^{35}, and Ca^{45}. Many of these isotopes will be referred to in the following pages in connection with investigations in which they have been employed as tracers. For further information on this topic, such reference books as Kamen (1947) and Hevesey (1948) should be consulted.

The Mechanism of Photosynthesis.—From the standpoint of fundamental chemistry the overall process of photosynthesis is an oxidation-reduction reaction between carbon dioxide and water. The carbon dioxide is reduced, and the water is oxidized largely as a result of a transfer of hydrogen atoms from water to carbon dioxide. Because this reaction occurs against the existing energy gradient, *i.e.*, the energy content of the products is greater than that of the initial reactants, energy must be supplied from an outside source. Since, in actuality, the external source of energy is light, the overall process is, in essence, a photochemical reduction of carbon dioxide.

The summary chemical equation for photosynthesis actually represents a complex of reactions. Although some progress has been made in the direction of unraveling the various steps in this process, our knowledge of its mechanism is still very fragmentary.

Certain topics contributing to an understanding of the mechanism of photosynthesis have already been considered: (1) the structure of the chloroplasts (Chap. IV), (2) the physical and chemical properties of the chloroplast pigments, and (3) the products of photosynthesis. Other aspects of this problem will now be discussed briefly under appropriate subheadings. For comprehensive reviews of this topic, see Rabinowitch (1945, 1951) and Franck and Loomis (1949).

Role of the Chloroplast Pigments.—All of the chlorophylls appear to participate in photosynthesis in fundamentally the same ways. Their role appears to be twofold: (1) they absorb certain wave lengths of radiant energy and either convert this energy into other wave lengths which are used in photosynthesis, or else transfer the absorbed energy directly to compounds involved in the reaction; (2) they act in the capacity of a catalyst at some stage or stages of the photosynthetic process. The first of these roles is the more obvious of the two, since neither carbon dioxide nor water absorbs radiant energy in the visible range. It is essential, therefore, that the reaction be "sensitized" by a pigment. The further role of the chlorophylls is a catalytic one. The chlorophyll content of leaves shows no change during a period of photosynthesis, and the proportion of chlorophyll a to chlorophyll b is just the same after a period of active photosynthesis as before. These facts indicate that no permanent destruction or transformation of chlorophyll occurs during the process and indirectly, at least, support the concept that one of the roles of chlorophyll in photosynthesis is a catalytic one.

The universal presence of the carotenoid pigments in the chloroplasts suggests very strongly that they also participate in photosynthesis, but no evidence has yet been found that they actually play any role in the process in the higher plants. There is good evidence, on the other hand, that at least some of the light absorbed by certain carotenoid pigments in diatoms (Dutton and Manning, 1941; Tanada, 1951); and green and brown algae (Haxo and Blinks, 1950) is used in photosynthesis. Similarly light absorbed by phycocyanin in some blue-green algae (Emerson and Lewis, 1942) and by phycobilins (phycocyanin and phycoerythrin) in some red algae (Haxo and Blinks, 1950) is used in the process. In some red algae the phycobilins appear to be the primary light absorbers rather than chlorophyll. While other pigments may thus supplement chlorophylls as light-absorbers in the photosynthetic mechanism of at least some species, they cannot substitute for chlorophyll in its catalytic role. No example has ever been found of photosynthesis occurring in a cell which did not contain at least one of the chlorophylls.

Other Protoplasmic Factors.—It has never been found possible to accomplish the complete process of photosynthesis *in vitro* by the use of chlorophyll solutions or dispersions, or by means of chloroplasts which have been isolated from cells. The complete process occurs only in intact chlorophyll-containing cells, indicating that other constituents of the living cell system besides the chlorophylls, or even the chloroplasts, are essential for the occurrence of photosynthesis.

At least several enzymes undoubtedly play a part in photosynthesis, although no enzyme which is known to be a specific participant in the process has ever been isolated from plant cells. The evidence for the intermediation of enzymes comes chiefly from the temperature behavior of photosynthesis and from the effects of certain specific chemical compounds on the process (Chap. XIX).

Carbon Dioxide Absorbing Mechanism of Leaves.—Independently of photosynthesis, and preliminary to its actual participation in the over-all mechanism of the process, carbon dioxide may be absorbed and accumulated in the cells of leaves and other plant organs in considerable quantities. Green leaves can absorb much more carbon dioxide than can be accounted for by simple solution in the cell sap (Shafer, 1938; Smith, 1940). This process is reversible and is not related to the presence of chlorophyll or the occurrence of photosynthesis because it occurs almost equally well in non-green organs and in the dark. At least three mechanisms of accumulation of carbon dioxide have been shown to operate in sunflower leaves: (1) solution in the cell sap, (2) reaction with soluble buffers, largely phosphates, and (3) reaction with insoluble carbonates, probably largely calcium carbonate (Smith and Cowie, 1941). Still another mechanism whereby cells accumulate carbon dioxide is described later in this chapter.

The "Light" and "Dark" Reactions of Photosynthesis.—Over a temperature range of about 10°-25°C., if light intensity and carbon dioxide concentration are relatively high, the Q_{10} (Chap. V) of photosynthesis is approximately two. Strictly chemical reactions characteristically have a Q_{10} of from two to three. This fact indicates that at least one of the reactions involved in photosynthesis is of a purely chemical type. Since this fact was first pointed out by Blackman, this reaction is often called the *Blackman reaction*. It is also frequently referred to as the *dark reaction*, since it does not require light, and therefore may take place in either the light or the dark. It now seems certain that there is not just one, but several, "dark" reactions involved in photosynthesis.

A chemical reaction which proceeds only at the expense of absorbed light is called a *photochemical reaction*. That photosynthesis involves such a reaction or reactions can be inferred from the fact that it occurs only in the light. The Q_{10} of a photochemical reaction is approximately one. Under low light intensities, even with a relatively high carbon dioxide concentration and other conditions favorable for photosynthesis, the temperature coefficient of the process is about one, indicating that under such conditions the rate of photosynthesis is limited by a photochemical phase.

That photosynthesis involves both photochemical and chemical reactions is also shown by the results of investigations in which plants are exposed to intermittent light. As shown by Emerson and Arnold (1932), when cultures of the green alga *Chlorella* were exposed to the intermittent illumination at the rate of 50 flashes per second, the periods of illumination being much shorter (0.0034 sec.) than the intervening dark periods

(0.0166 sec.), the photosynthetic yield *per unit of light* was increased about 400 per cent as compared with the rate in continuous light.

Assuming that a photochemical reaction comes first, the results just described can be explained as follows. When illumination is continuous the products of a light reaction are formed faster than they can be utilized in a relatively slower dark reaction. When the light is intermittent, however, all or most of the products of a photochemical reaction are removed by a dark reaction during the intervening dark period, and the photosynthetic output per unit of light is considerably greater.

By experimenting to find out how long a dark period was required for the best yield per unit of light, *i.e.*, for the complete removal of the product resulting during each light flash, the same investigators were able to estimate the duration of each reaction. The dark reaction was found to proceed in less than 0.04 sec. at 25°C., and to be greatly influenced by temperature. The light reaction, on the other hand, takes place with great speed, requiring only about 0.00001 sec. for its completion, and is unaffected by temperature.

These results indicate that the rate of photosynthesis is limited by the stage of the process which occurs at the slowest rate. With low light intensities and adequate carbon dioxide supply, a photochemical reaction is limiting and temperature will have little effect on the rate of the process. With high light intensities and adequate carbon dioxide supply but low temperatures, the rate of photosynthesis is limited by a dark reaction, and will increase considerably with a rise in temperature.

Source of the Oxygen Released in Photosynthesis.—A knowledge of the source of the oxygen released in photosynthesis is one of the keys to an understanding of the mechanism of the process. Many investigators of photosynthesis have assumed in the past that the oxygen released came from the carbon dioxide, an assumption which the equivalence between the oxygen released and the oxygen in the carbon dioxide made plausible. By using water and carbon dioxide made with the heavy isotope of oxygen (O^{18}) as the raw materials of photosynthesis, Ruben *et al.* (1941) have shown that the oxygen set free in the process comes from water molecules and not from carbon dioxide molecules. This extremely fundamental discovery has been confirmed by Dole and Jenks (1944). A necessary corollary of this finding is that more water molecules (at least twelve per molecule of hexose formed) must participate in the overall photosynthetic reaction than are shown in the conventional *summary* equation, because more oxygen is released than can be provided by only six water molecules. The following equation is therefore a more accurate representation of the overall reaction:

$$6 \ CO_2 + 12 \ H_2O \xrightarrow[\text{chlorophyllous cells}]{\substack{\text{673 kg. -cal. of} \\ \text{radiant energy}}} C_6H_{12}O_6 + 6 \ H_2O + 6 \ O_2$$

The Hill Reaction.—Hill (1937, 1939) and subsequently others have shown that illumination of suspensions of chloroplasts in water in the presence of a suitable hydrogen acceptor (oxidant) results in the release of oxygen. This reaction also occurs in suspensions of grana from disintegrated chloroplasts (Warburg and Lüttgens, 1944; Aronoff, 1946). This phenomenon, now generally called the *Hill reaction,* can be represented by the following summary equation, A standing for a hydrogen acceptor:

$$2 \ H_2O + 2 \ A \xrightarrow[\text{chloroplasts}]{\text{light}} 2 \ AH_2 + O_2$$

Some of the compounds which act as hydrogen acceptors in this reaction are ferricyanides, chromates, certain quinones, and certain indophenols. Holt and French (1948), by use of the O^{18} isotope of oxygen, showed that the oxygen released in the Hill reaction, as in the overall process of photosynthesis, comes from the water molecules.

It is now quite generally considered that the Hill reaction, which is essentially a photocatalyzed splitting of water, represents one of the constituent reactions of photosynthesis. A probable role of this reaction in the overall process is the formation of a reducing agent which, in turn, directly or indirectly, results in the transfer of hydrogen to carbon dioxide.

Oxygen liberation without simultaneous reduction of carbon dioxide can also occur in intact plants. When, for example, suspensions of *Chlorella* cells were illuminated in the absence of carbon dioxide, but in the presence of certain hydrogen acceptors, such as benzaldehyde, oxygen, presumably coming from water molecules, was released (Fan, *et al.,* 1943).

If the assumption that the Hill reaction is a constituent reaction of photosynthesis is correct, then the *summary* equation for the other phase of the process (*i.e.,* the reduction of carbon dioxide) would be:

$$CO_2 + 2 \ AH_2 \rightarrow (CH_2O) + 2 \ A + H_2O$$

in which (CH_2O) represents a carbohydrate-type molecule.

The Carbon Pathway in Photosynthesis.—Considerable progress has been made in tracing the pathway of carbon through the photosynthetic mechanism by the use of radioactive isotopes. When a suspension of the alga *Chlorella* or of the alga *Scenedesmus* was allowed to photosynthesize for the very short period of 5 sec. in the presence of carbon dioxide made with radioactive C^{14} isotope, a very large proportion (about 70 per cent) of the labeled carbon was found by subsequent analysis of the cells to be present in the compound phosphoglyceric acid (Calvin and Benson, 1949; Benson and Calvin, 1950). This was also found to be true for barley and geranium leaves after very short periods of photosynthesis. Similarly Aronoff and Vernon (1950) found glyceric acid and phosphoglyceric acid to be the principal compounds containing radioactive carbon after very short periods of photosynthesis in soybean leaves. Glyceric (or phosphoglyceric) acid thus appears to be a key intermediate in photosynthesis. It is also a known intermediate compound in the process of respiration (Chap. XXII). After slightly longer, but still very short periods of photosynthesis, radioactive carbon is also present in other compounds, some of which are also intermediates in respiration. It is a plausible hypothesis, therefore, that the carbon dioxide reduction phase of photosynthesis may proceed at least in part by a reversal of the sequence of reactions occurring in one phase of respiration.

Radioactive carbon also appears in sucrose molecules after relatively short periods of photosynthesis. The actual order in which sugars appear is not clearly indicated by the results obtained to date in experiments with radioactive carbon dioxide. It is entirely possible that the sequence in which sugars are formed in photosynthesis may be different in different species of plants or even in the same plant under different conditions.

Radioactive carbon is also found after very short periods of photosynthesis to be present in alanine, serine, and other amino acids (Chap. XXVI). This is evidence in favor of the previously expressed view that the synthesis of amino acids in photosynthetic tissues is closely intermeshed with the intermediate steps in photosynthesis.

Although the discoveries which have been made regarding the carbon path in photosynthesis are very significant, they do not clarify the problem of how energy is actually incorporated into the products of photosynthesis. If the photochemical splitting of water is a fundamental constituent reaction of photosynthesis, some mechanism, as yet undiscovered, must exist whereby the reductants formed in this reaction transfer their energy to the products formed in the carbon dioxide reducing phase of the process.

Ruben et al. (1940), Calvin and Benson (1948), Brown et al. (1949), and others have studied the fixation of radioactive carbon dioxide in several species of plants in the dark. It has been presumed that a clue to the first step in the utilization of carbon dioxide in photosynthesis might be found in this way. The results of such experiments have shown that in the dark most of the radioactive carbon is quickly incorporated into the carboxyl groups of various organic acids including certain amino acids such as alanine and aspartic acid. This is a fundamentally different process from the one previously described under the topic of the carbon dioxide-absorbing mechanism of leaves.

However, interpretation of experimental results on dark fixation of carbon dioxide is complicated by the fact that this process is not necessarily related to photosynthesis. Wood and Werkman (1936) were the first to show that bacteria can incorporate carbon dioxide into metabolic products by a reversal of the decarboxylation process (Chap. XXII). It is now known that similar processes occur very widely in plant tissues, both green and non-green (Chap. XXII). Just how close a relation exists between such carbon dioxide fixation processes and the fixation which represents a first step in photosynthesis is not certain at the present time.

Variant Mechanisms of Photosynthesis.—Although, as far as is known, the process of photosynthesis follows the same general course in all of the higher plants, somewhat different mechanisms occur in some species of the lower plant phyla. Investigations of van Niel (1941) and others have shown that in the photosynthesis of the anaerobic green and purple bacteria the reaction is similar to that occurring in the higher plants, except that substances other than water act as the hydrogen "donors." For example, green sulfur bacteria, which contain the pigment *bacterioviridin,* can use hydrogen sulfide as a source of hydrogen in photosynthesis, the overall reaction being:

$$6 CO_2 + 12 H_2S \rightarrow C_6H_{12}O_6 + 6 H_2O + 12 S$$

The purple sulfur bacteria, containing the pigment *bacteriochlorophyll,* are metabolically more versatile. Not only can they photosynthetically accomplish a chemical transformation similar to the above, in which, however, oxidation is carried all the way to a sulfate, but they also can use many other compounds besides hydrogen sulfide as hydrogen donors. Still another group, the purple "non-sulfur" bacteria, use principally various organic compounds as reductants in photosynthesis, although a few species in this group can also oxidize sulfur compounds. No oxygen is released in these bacterial photosyntheses, further evidence that the oxygen released in ordinary photosynthesis comes from water. In this kind of photosynthesis light energy appears to be used mainly in activation of the reactions rather than as a major source of the energy. Furthermore, the purple sulfur bacteria, at least, as a consequence of the absorption spectrum of bacteriochlorophyll, can accomplish photosynthesis in the infrared up to a wave length of about 900 mμ, as well as in visible light.

A discussion of photosynthesis is not complete without a brief consideration of the *chemosynthetic* bacteria. A number of species of colorless, aerobic bacteria are known which synthesize carbohydrates using energy derived from oxidation reactions, rather than radiant energy. Among these are the nitrifying bacteria, *Nitrosamonas* and *Nitrobacter* (Chap. XXVI) which oxidize ammonia to nitrite, and nitrite to nitrate respectively; the nonpigmented sulfur bacteria such as *Beggiatoa*, which oxidize hydrogen sulfide to sulfates; the iron bacteria which oxidize ferrous hydroxide to ferric hydroxide, and others (Stephenson, 1939).

Chemosynthetic and photosynthetic bacteria play an insignificant part in the world's production of carbohydrates as compared with green photosynthetic plants. Distribution of chemosynthetic bacteria is strictly limited to habitats in which the appropriate oxidation substrates are present. Likewise, distribution of the photosynthetic bacteria is confined to habitats in which the particular compounds which serve as hydrogen donors occur. Many different hydrogen donors have apparently been experimented with in evolution's laboratory in the development of the mechanism of photosynthesis. Eventually, however, that version of the mechanism in which hydrogen is taken from its most abundant source—water—largely prevailed, and green photosynthetic plants are now the most prominent type of living organism on the face of the earth.

Investigations of the chemosynthetic and photosynthetic bacteria have been important, not only in elucidating the metabolism of these organisms, but study of these variant, and presumably more primitive, mechanisms of carbohydrate synthesis in these simple plants has broadened insight into the chemical machinery of the much more significant process of photosynthesis in the green plants.

Quantum Requirement.—The quantum requirement of photosynthesis, *i.e.*, the number of quanta required for the reduction of each molecule of carbon dioxide, is an important consideration in attempting to visualize the mechanism of the process. If the radiant energy required in the synthesis of one mol of glucose (673 kg. cal.) be divided by the number of carbon atoms in a mol ($6 \times 6 \times 10^{23}$), the amount of energy per carbon atom is found to be approximately three times that of one quantum at 600 mμ. (3.27×10^{-12} erg). The absolute minimum light requirement of photosynthesis would therefore be about 3 quanta per molecule of carbon dioxide reduced. However, since 4 hydrogen atoms must receive sufficient energy to move them from water to carbon dioxide in this process, and since a quantum is an indivisible unit, it appears that the theoretical minimum requirement would actually be about 4 quanta per molecule of carbon dioxide reduced.

As early as 1923 experiments by Warburg seemed to indicate that only 4 quanta were required per molecule of carbon dioxide reduced and later investigations by him and co-workers have led to similar conclusions

(Burk *et al.*, 1949). Such a quantum requirement would indicate an amazing efficiency of about 70 per cent for photosynthesis in converting absorbed radiant energy into chemical energy. Investigations of Manning *et al.* (1938), Emerson and Lewis (1941), Tanada (1951) and others indicate, on the other hand, that about 10 quanta are required per molecule of carbon dioxide reduced. Even this quantum requirement represents an efficiency of about 25 per cent for the process. A similar quantum requirement has been found by French and Rabideau (1945) for the Hill reaction. It is obvious that the question of the quantum requirement of photosynthesis has not yet been settled with finality.

A clear implication of the quantum requirement of photosynthesis is that the process must proceed as a series of steps with an energy utilization of one quantum per step. A unique feature of the process is that a high energy product is constructed by the successive introduction into the reaction sequence of smaller units of energy (quanta). Franck's (1949) theory, in accord with this line of reasoning, proposes that there are eight intermediate steps in photosynthesis, each requiring one quantum for its activation.

Induction Period.—As shown by McAlister (1937), Smith (1937), and others, when illumination of a plant starts, the rate of photosynthesis is at first low and gradually increases until it reaches the maximum value for the prevailing conditions. The length of this "induction period" is typically 1-3 min., but it may be shorter or longer, depending upon the species, its previous treatment, and the prevailing environmental conditions. The causes of such an initially low rate of photosynthesis are complex and are not the same under all conditions (Franck, 1951), but the existence of such induction periods must be reconciled with any postulated mechanisms of photosynthesis.

Magnitude and Efficiency of Photosynthesis.—Because of its primary role in the biological economy of the earth, considerable interest attaches to the world magnitude of photosynthesis (Table 24) and the efficiency of the process.

The figures in Table 24 are for net carbon accumulation, *i.e.*, for photosynthesis minus respiration. These data are in terms of organic carbon; the figures as given must be multiplied by a factor of 2.5 to give the equivalent values in terms of a hexose. It should perhaps be emphasized that estimates of the photosynthetic productivity of marine plants are necessarily much more approximate than those of land plants. Even on the basis of the lowest limit of the estimate given in Table 24 it is clear, however, that aquatic organisms (largely diatoms) account for a larger proportion of the annual photosynthate than do terrestrial plants.

Approximately 3×10^{18} kg-cal. of radiant energy are converted into

TABLE 24—ESTIMATED WORLD PRODUCTION OF ORGANIC CARBON
(DATA OF SCHROEDER (1919) FOR LAND PLANTS; OF RILEY (1944) FOR MARINE PLANTS)

	Area, km.^{2}	Metric tons[1] organic C per km.^{2} per year	Metric tons organic C, total annual production
Forest.................	44×10^6	250	11.0×10^9
Cultivated land.........	27×10^6	160	4.3×10^9
Grassland..............	31×10^6	36	1.1×10^9
Desert.................	24×10^6	7	0.2×10^9
Total land.............	126×10^6		16.6×10^9
Ocean.................	371×10^6	340 ± 220	$126 \pm 87 \times 10^9$

[1] A metric ton equals 1000 kg.

chemical energy per year by the photosynthesis of the earth's population of green plants. This is only a small fraction, however, of the total quantity of radiant energy impinging on the earth's surface—estimated at about 5×10^{20} kg-cal. annually—indicating that more than 99 per cent of the incident radiant energy escapes capture by photosynthesis. Even so, the energy converted by photosynthesis annually is about one hundred times greater than the heat of combustion of all the coal mined on the earth in one year, and it is about ten thousand times greater than all the energy derived by man from water power during one year (Rabinowitch, 1945).

Some conception of the magnitude and efficiency of photosynthesis in terms of a familiar crop plant is afforded by calculations based on a

TABLE 25—QUANTITY OF PHOTOSYNTHATE PRODUCED BY ONE ACRE OF CORN (MAIZE) IN A GROWING SEASON (DATA OF TRANSEAU, 1926)

Dry weight of average corn plant.........	Grain......................	216 g.
	Stalk......................	200
	Leaves.....................	140
	Roots.....................	44
		600 g.

Total dry weight of an acre of corn (10,000 plants) at end of season........ 6000 kg.
Total ash (5.37 per cent of dry weight)............................. 322 kg.
Total organic matter in the plants................................... 5678 kg.
Total carbon accumulated (44.58 per cent of the organic matter).......... 2675 kg.
Glucose equivalent of accumulated carbon ($C_6H_{12}O_6 : C_6 = 180 : 72$)...... 6687 kg.
Glucose equivalent of respired carbon (calculated from estimated rate of
  CO_2 release $= 1$ per cent of dry weight per day)..................... 2045 kg.
Total sugar manufactured in terms of glucose........................... 8732 kg.

hypothetical acre of corn (10,000 plants) growing in north central Illinois and yielding 100 bu. per acre (average yield in the United States in 1946 was 33 bu. per acre). The growing season is assumed to be 100 days. The magnitude of photosynthesis for such a field of corn is shown in Table 25.

The quantity of radiant energy falling on an acre of land surface in north central Illinois during the growing period of 100 days is known from measurements made at Madison, Wisconsin, not far from the region of north central Illinois. Using these data together with his own estimates of the total sugar synthesized by the corn plants, Transeau was able to calculate the photosynthetic efficiency of corn (Table 26).

TABLE 26—EFFICIENCY OF PHOTOSYNTHESIS IN CORN (MAIZE). (DATA OF TRANSEAU, 1926)

Energy required for synthesis of 1 kg. glucose.................	3760 kg.-cal.
Total energy utilized in photosynthesis by an acre of corn plants in manufacture of 8732 kg. glucose.........................	33 million kg.-cal.
Total solar energy available on the acre during growing season...	2043 million kg.-cal.
Per cent of available energy used by corn plant in photosynthesis— *i.e.* its photosynthetic efficiency...........................	1.6 per cent

Since, of the total carbohydrate synthesized, about one-fourth is consumed in respiration, the efficiency in terms of net photosynthesis is not 1.6 per cent (Table 26) but 1.2 per cent. Of the net photosynthetic product only about one-third is present in the grain. The 100 bu. of corn harvested at the end of the growing season, therefore, represents only about 0.4 per cent of the radiant energy which fell on the acre during that period.

However, a corn crop occupies the land for less than one-third of the year. The same is true for many other temperate zone crop plants. Very little of the incident radiant energy during the rest of the year is utilized in photosynthesis, even under suitable crop rotation systems, since environmental conditions are not very favorable to photosynthesis during most of the months that corn does not occupy the land. On an annual basis, therefore, the photosynthetic efficiency of this acre of corn land was about 0.4-0.5 per cent. Such a value can only be attained on an acre of land on which a superior crop is raised. The annual photosynthetic efficiency of *average* temperate zone crop land is only about 0.1-0.2 per cent; computations indicate a similar efficiency in temperate zone forest lands (Daniels, 1950). In some warmer regions, where agriculture can be practiced on a year-round basis, and in some tropical forest regions an average annual photosynthetic efficiency of several times this value is probably attained.

SUGGESTED FOR COLLATERAL READING

Duggar, B. M., Editor. *Biological Effects of Radiation.* McGraw-Hill Book Co., Inc. New York. 1936.

Franck, J., and W. E. Loomis, Editors. *Photosynthesis in Plants.* Iowa State College Press. Ames. 1949.

Rabinowitch, E. I. *Photosynthesis and Related Processes.* Vol. I, II. Interscience Publishers, Inc. New York. 1945, 1951.

Stephenson, Marjory. *Bacterial Metabolism.* 3rd Ed. Longmans, Green, and Co. London. 1949.

SELECTED BIBLIOGRAPHY

Aronoff, S. Photochemical reduction of chloroplast grana. *Plant Physiol.* **21:** 393-409. 1946.

Aronoff, S., and L. Vernon. C^{14} O_2 assimilation by soybean leaves. *Arch. Biochem.* **27:** 239-240. 1950.

Aronoff, S., and L. Vernon. Metabolism of soybean leaves. I. The sequence of formation of soluble carbohydrates during photosynthesis. *Arch. Biochem.* **28:** 424-439. 1950.

Benson, A. A., and M. Calvin. Carbon dioxide fixation by green plants. *Ann. Rev. Plant Physiol.* **1:** 25-42. 1950.

Brown, A. H., E. W. Fager, and H. Gaffron. Kinetics of a photochemical intermediate in photosynthesis. In *Photosynthesis in Plants.* J. Franck and W. E. Loomis, Editors. 403-422. Iowa State College Press. Ames. 1949.

Burk, D., S. Hendricks, M. Korzenovsky, V. Schocken, and O. Warburg. The maximum efficiency of photosynthesis: a rediscovery. *Science* **110:** 225-229. 1949.

Burström, H. Photosynthesis and assimilation of nitrate by wheat leaves. *Ann. Roy. Agric. Coll. Sweden* **11:** 1-50. 1943.

Calvin, M., and A. A. Benson. The path of carbon in photosynthesis. *Science* **107:** 476-480. 1948.

Calvin, M., and A. A. Benson. The path of carbon in photosynthesis IV. *Science* **109:** 140-142. 1949.

Chapman, A. G., and W. H. Camp. Starch synthesis in the variegated leaves of *Pelargonium. Ohio Jour. Sci.* **32:** 197-217. 1932.

Daniels, F. Atomic and solar energy. *Amer. Scientist* **38:** 521-548. 1950.

Denny, F. E. The twin-leaf method of studying changes in leaves. *Amer. Jour. Bot.* **17:** 818-841. 1930.

Dixon, M. Manometric methods. 2nd Ed. The Macmillan Co. New York. 1943.

Dole, M., and G. Jenks. Isotopic composition of photosynthetic oxygen. *Science* **100:** 409. 1944.

Dutton, H. J., and W. M. Manning. Evidence for carotenoid-sensitized photosynthesis in the diatom *Nitzschia closterium. Amer. Jour. Bot.* **28:** 516-526. 1941.

Emerson, R., and W. Arnold. A separation of the reactions in photosynthesis by means of intermittent light. *Jour. Gen. Physiol.* **15:** 391-420. 1932.

Emerson, R., and C. M. Lewis. Carbon dioxide exchange and the measurement of the quantum yield of photosynthesis. *Amer. Jour. Bot.* **28:** 789-804. 1941.

Emerson, R., and C. M. Lewis. The photosynthetic efficiency of phycocyanin in

Chroococcus and the problem of carotenoid participation in photosynthesis. *Jour. Gen. Physiol.* **25**: 579-595. 1942.

Fan, C. S., J. F. Stauffer, and W. W. Umbreit. An experimental separation of oxygen liberation from carbon dioxide fixation in photosynthesis by *Chlorella*. *Jour. Gen. Physiol.* **27**: 15-28. 1943.

Franck, J. A critical survey of the physical background of photosynthesis. *Ann. Rev. Plant Physiol.* **2**: 53-86. 1951.

Freeland, R. O. Photosynthesis in relation to stomatal frequency and distribution. *Plant Physiol.* **23**: 595-600. 1948.

French, C. S. Photosynthesis. *Ann. Rev. Biochem.* **15**: 397-416. 1946.

French, C. S., and G. S. Rabideau. The quantum yield of oxygen production by chloroplasts suspended in solutions containing ferric oxalate. *Jour. Gen. Physiol.* **28**: 329-342. 1945.

Gaffron, H. Photosynthesis and the production of organic matter on earth. In *Currents in Biochemical Research.* D. E. Green, Editor. 25-48. Interscience Publishers, Inc. New York. 1946.

Gaffron, H., and E. W. Fager. The kinetics and chemistry of photosynthesis. *Ann. Rev. Plant Physiol.* **2**: 87-114. 1951.

Haxo, F. T., and L. R. Blinks. Photosynthetic action spectra of marine algae. *Jour. Gen. Physiol.* **33**: 389-422. 1950.

Heinicke, A. J., and M. B. Hoffman. The rate of photosynthesis of apple leaves under natural conditions. *Cornell Univ. Agric. Expt. Sta. Bull. 577.* 1933.

Hevesy, G. von. *Radioactive Indicators.* Interscience Publishers, Inc. New York. 1948.

Hill, R. Oxygen evolved by isolated chloroplasts. *Nature* **139**: 881-882. 1937.

Hill, R. Oxygen evolved by isolated chloroplasts. *Proc. Roy. Soc. (London)* **B 127**: 192-210. 1939.

Holt, A. S., and C. S. French. Isotopic analysis of the oxygen evolved by illuminated chloroplasts in normal water and in water enriched with O^{18}. *Arch. Biochem.* **19**: 429-435. 1948.

Kamen, M. D. *Radioactive Tracers in Biology.* 2nd Ed. Academic Press, Inc. New York. 1951.

Manning, W. M., J. F. Stauffer, B. M. Duggar, and F. Daniels. Quantum efficiency of photosynthesis in *Chlorella. Jour. Amer. Chem. Soc.* **60**: 266-274. 1938.

McAlister, E. D. Time course of photosynthesis for a higher plant. *Smithsonian Misc. Coll.* 95. No. 24. 1937.

Myers, J. The pattern of photosynthesis in *Chlorella.* In *Photosynthesis in Plants.* J. Franck and W. E. Loomis, Editors. 349-364. Iowa State College Press. Ames. 1949.

Ochoa, S. Enzymatic mechanisms of carbon dioxide assimilation. In *Currents in Biochemical Research.* D. E. Green, Editor. 165-185. Interscience Publishers, Inc. New York. 1946.

Parkin, J. The carbohydrates of the foliage leaf of the snowdrop (*Galanthus nivalis*) and their bearing on the first sugar of photosynthesis. *Biochem. Jour.* **6**: 1-47. 1912.

Riley, G. A. The carbon metabolism and photosynthetic efficiency of the earth as a whole. *Amer. Scientist* **32**: 129-134. 1944.

Ruben, S., M. D. Kamen, W. Z. Hassid, and L. H. Perry. Photosynthesis with radioactive carbon. II, III, IV. *Jour. Amer. Chem. Soc.* **62**: 3443-3455. 1940.

Ruben, S., M. Randall, M. Kamen, and J. L. Hyde. Heavy oxygen (O^{18}) as a tracer in the study of photosynthesis. *Jour. Amer. Chem. Soc.* **63**: 877-879. 1941.

Schroeder, H. Die jährliche Gesamtproduktion der grünen Pflanzendecke der Erde. *Naturwiss.* **7**: 8-12, 23-29. 1919.

Shafer, J., Jr. Effect of light on CO_2 in leaves. *Plant Physiol.* **13**: 141-156. 1938.

Smith, E. L. The induction period in photosynthesis. *Jour. Gen. Physiol.* **21**: 151-163. 1937.

Smith, J. H. C. The absorption of carbon dioxide by unilluminated leaves. *Plant Physiol.* **15**: 183-224. 1940.

Smith, J. H. C. Molecular equivalence of carbohydrates to carbon dioxide in photosynthesis. *Plant Physiol.* **18**: 207-223. 1943.

Smith, J. H. C. Concurrency of carbohydrate formation and carbon dioxide absorption during photosynthesis in sunflower leaves. *Plant Physiol.* **19**: 394-403. 1944.

Smith, J. H. C., and D. B. Cowie. Absorption and utilization of radioactive carbon dioxide by sunflower leaves. *Plant Physiol.* **16**: 257-271. 1941.

Tanada, T. The photosynthetic efficiency of carotenoid pigments in *Navicula minima. Amer. Jour. Bot.* **38**: 276-283. 1951.

Thoday, D. Experimental studies on vegetable assimilation and respiration. V. A. critical examination of Sachs' method for using increase of dry weight as a measure of carbon dioxide assimilation in leaves. *Proc. Roy. Soc. (London)* **B 82**: 1-55. 1909.

Thomas, M. D., and G. R. Hill. The continuous measurement of photosynthesis, respiration, and transpiration of alfalfa and wheat growing under field conditions. *Plant Physiol.* **12**: 285-307. 1937.

Transeau, E. N. The accumulation of energy by plants. *Ohio Jour. Sci.* **26**: 1-10. 1926.

Turrell, F. M. The area of the internal exposed surface of dicotyledon leaves. *Amer. Jour. Bot.* **23**: 255-264. 1936.

Umbreit, W. W., R. H. Burris, and J. F. Stauffer. *Manometric Techniques and Tissue Metabolism.* Burgess Publishing Co. Minneapolis. 1949.

Van Niel, C. B. The bacterial photosyntheses and their importance for the general problem of photosynthesis. *Advances in Enzymol.* **1**: 263-328. 1941.

Warburg, O., and W. Lüttgens. Weitere Experimente zur Kohlensäureassimilation. *Naturwiss.* **32**: 301. 1944.

Weevers, T. The first carbohydrates that originate during the assimilatory process. A physiological study with variegated leaves. *Proc. Kon. Acad. Wetensch. (Amsterdam)* **27**: 1-11. 1924.

Wood, H. G., and C. H. Werkman. The utilization of CO_2 in the dissimilation of glycerol by the proprionic acid bacteria. *Biochem. Jour.* **30**: 48-53. 1936.

DISCUSSION QUESTIONS

1. What would be the effect upon plants of the disappearance of all animals from the earth? The effect upon animals of the disappearance of all plants?

2. Is it true that no life could exist on the earth in the absence of photosynthesis?

3. When leaves of some species are submerged in water a slow infiltration of the intercellular spaces occurs if they are kept in the dark, but this does not take place if they are kept in the light. Explain.

4. Masses of filamentous algae are often found floating near the surface of a pond after several days of clear weather, but the same algal masses are often submerged after a period of several cloudy days. Explain.

5. What method would you recommend for measuring the rate of apparent photosynthesis of a bean plant growing in the field. Point out the possible sources of error in the method.

6. Since only a small percentage of the light incident on a leaf is utilized in photosynthesis, why cannot the light intensity be reduced to this value without retarding the rate of photosynthesis?

7. A large culture tube, A, is filled with a dilute bicarbonate solution and stoppered so that no air bubbles are entrapped within the tube. Tubes B and C are similarly prepared, except that a shoot of waterweed is also suspended in the solution in each tube. The volume of solution is the same in each tube. Tubes A and B are kept in the dark while tube C is exposed to strong illumination, all tubes being kept at the same temperature. At the end of one hour analysis shows the oxygen contents of the tubes to be: A, 0.250 ml.^{2}; B, 0.210 ml.^{2}; C, 0.625 ml.^{2}. Assuming the two shoots to be physiologically similar, calculate approximate rates of respiration, apparent photosynthesis, and "true" photosynthesis per shoot.

8. Assuming a light intensity of 1 g.-cal. per cm.^{2} per min., calculate the photosynthetic efficiency of a leaf in which hexose is synthesized at the rate of 10 mg. per dm.^{2} per hr.

XIX

FACTORS AFFECTING PHOTOSYNTHESIS

The Principle of Limiting Factors.—Earlier investigators of the effects of various conditions upon the rate of photosynthesis attempted to distinguish among *minimum, optimum,* and *maximum* values for each factor in relation to photosynthesis. In evaluating the effect of temperature upon photosynthesis, for example, it was generally considered that there was a minimum temperature below which no photosynthesis occurred, an optimum at which the process takes place most rapidly, and a maximum above which photosynthesis ceases. Advocates of this point of view, however, soon found themselves confronted with the anomalous situation of a fluctuating "optimum." The "optimum" carbon dioxide concentration was found to be greater at high light intensities than at low ones, the "optimum" temperature was found to vary with the light intensity, and the "optimum" light intensity was different for plants well supplied with water than for those which were inadequately supplied.

The first important step in the clarification of this problem of the influence of various factors upon photosynthesis was taken when Blackman (1905) enunciated the "principle of limiting factors." This principle is essentially an elaboration of Liebig's "law of the minimum" (Chap. XXX) and was stated by its author as follows: "When a process is conditioned as to its rapidity by a number of separate factors, the rate of the process is limited by the pace of the 'slowest' factor."

The explanation of this principle can best be presented in terms of the illustration given by Blackman (Fig. 93). Assume the intensity of light to be just great enough to permit a leaf to utilize 5 mg. of carbon dioxide per hour in photosynthesis. If only 1 mg. of carbon dioxide can enter the leaf in an hour, the rate of photosynthesis is limited by the carbon dioxide factor. As the carbon dioxide supply is increased the rate of photosynthesis is also increased until 5 mg. of carbon dioxide enter the leaf per hour. Any further increase in the supply of carbon dioxide will have no influence upon the rate of photosynthesis, unless a sufficient concentration is present to bring about retarding effects, because insufficient light energy is available to permit its utilization. Light has now become the limiting factor and further increase in the rate of photosynthesis can be brought about only by an increase in the intensity of light. These results are indicated graphically as *A B C* in Fig. 93. This theory assumes a progressive increase in the rate of the process with a quantitative increase in the limiting factor (in this example, carbon dioxide) until the point is reached at which some other factor becomes limiting (in this example, light intensity). At this point the increase stops abruptly (point *B* in Fig. 93), and the rate of photosynthesis becomes constant (*B C* of Fig. 93). According to this concept, when the magnitude of photosynthesis

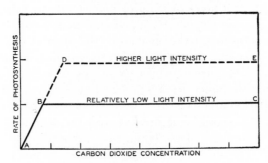

Fɪɢ. 93.   Diagram to illustrate Blackman's interpretation of the principle of limiting factors.

is limited by one of a set of factors, only a shift in that factor toward a condition more favorable for the process will result in an increase in the rate of photosynthesis.

If the light intensity is sufficient to permit the leaf to utilize 10 mg. of carbon dioxide per hour, then the rate of photosynthesis will rise with increase in the carbon dioxide concentration to a value about twice as great as that at which the maximum rate of photosynthesis was attained at the lower light intensity. The results under these conditions can be indicated graphically by *A D E* (Fig. 93).

Light and carbon dioxide are not the only factors which can be limiting in the photosynthetic process. Theoretically, as examples given later in the chapter will show, any of the factors which influence this process can, under certain conditions, become limiting.

Most subsequent workers (Harder, 1921, James, 1928, and others) have been unable to accept the principle of limiting factors in quite the simple form in which it was first proposed by Blackman. Most investigators have found that, when the rate of increase of photosynthesis is plotted along the ordinate with the quantitative variations in some one factor as the abscissa, the resulting curve is not found to show an abrupt transition to the horizontal (points B and D, Fig. 93) as postulated by Blackman's formulation of this principle, but shows instead a gradual transition to a position approximately parallel to the abscissa (Fig. 96). Within this transition region it is evident that increase in either of the two factors involved will result in an increase in the rate of photosynthesis.

The explanation for the occurrence of this gradual transition in the direction of the curve, rather than the abrupt change postulated by the original Blackman theory, results at least in part from the fact that the seat of the photosynthesis is in the chloroplasts of which there are millions in even a small leaf. Patently it is impossible that each and every chloroplast will be subjected to exactly the same conditions at exactly the same time. All of the chloroplasts are not equally exposed to light; neither are all of them equally well supplied with carbon dioxide. As a factor approaches a limiting value it may check the rate of photosynthesis in some chloroplasts sooner than in others. It is quite possible therefore for light to be the limiting factor for some chloroplasts, while carbon dioxide is simultaneously the limiting factor for other chloroplasts. Similar comments apply to most of the other factors influencing photosynthesis. Hence the rate of photosynthesis, as measured in terms of entire organs, will exhibit only a gradual change when factors affecting the process are modified, and there exist well-defined regions in curves such as those shown in Fig. 96, in which two or even more factors may be considered to act simultaneously as limiting factors.

It should be clearly understood that, in speaking of "limiting factors" as applied to physiological processes, it is not their absolute magnitude which is significant, but their relative magnitude in proportion to the amounts actually required in the process. The quantitatively smallest factor does not necessarily condition the rate of the process, since it may be necessary only in traces, while larger amounts of some other material, or a greater intensity of some other factor may be necessary. To illustrate, suppose that we assume ten units of a, two units of b, and one unit of c are necessary for the formation of one unit of d. If we suppose that only five units of a are available, none of d can be formed regardless of the quantities of b and c available. Although c may be in absolute minimum, a is in relative minimum and thus acts as the limiting factor.

For this reason many authorities consider it to be more satisfactory to speak of the "relatively limiting factor," "factor in relative minimum," or "most significant factor," rather than of the "limiting factor."

One other qualification of the theory of limiting factors not envisaged in the original Blackman formulation should also be mentioned. When present in a high enough intensity or concentration, as discussed later in this chapter, most of the factors influencing the rate of photosynthesis exert a depressing or inhibitory effect on the process.

The modifications which have been imposed upon the original concept of limiting factors do not invalidate this principle as a good approximation to the facts, nor do they destroy its value as a point of view from which to interpret the influence of various factors upon the rate of photosynthesis. The significant fact is that the rate of the process, except in relatively narrow transition regions, is usually determined in the main by the least favorable factor, which may for convenience be spoken of either as the limiting factor or as the factor in relative minimum.

The principle of limiting factors is applicable to all physiological processes and will receive further evaluation in relation to growth phenomena in Chap. XXX.

The Role of Carbon Dioxide.—All of the carbon dioxide used by green plants reaches the chloroplasts as dissolved carbon dioxide, carbonic acid, or one of the salts of the latter. In land plants the atmosphere is the only important source of carbon dioxide. Carbon dioxide released in respiration may be utilized in photosynthesis without leaving the plant, but under conditions favorable for photosynthesis this does not constitute a very large fraction of the total used. Submersed water plants use carbonates and bicarbonates as well as dissolved carbon dioxide and carbonic acid as substrates of photosynthesis.

The atmosphere is composed chiefly of two gases, nitrogen (about 78 per cent) and oxygen (about 21 per cent), but also contains, in addition to a variable but never large amount of water-vapor, small quantities of other gases. One of its minor constituents, carbon dioxide, which constitutes on the average only about 0.03 per cent by volume of the atmosphere, plays a role of the greatest significance in the biological world. As a result of the photosynthetic activity of green plants, the carbon dioxide from the air becomes chemically bound for periods of indefinite length in the organic molecules which are the basis of all life. In view of its important biological role, the proportion of carbon dioxide in the atmosphere seems precariously small. The absolute amount present, however, is enormous. Estimates, necessarily very approximate, place the total quantity of carbon dioxide in the atmosphere at about 2×10^{15} kg. According to Schroeder (1919), the quantity of carbon dioxide used annually in photosynthesis by land plants is about 6×10^{13} kg. This is only about one-thirtieth the amount actually present in the atmosphere.

1. *Sources of the Atmospheric Carbon Dioxide.*—While green plants are continually removing carbon dioxide from the atmosphere, other processes are continually replenishing the atmospheric reservoir with this gas. Carbon dioxide is continually being returned to the atmosphere as a product of the respiration of plants and animals. Plants are more important producers of carbon dioxide than animals. Carbon dioxide is released into the atmosphere as a result of the respiration of both green and non-green plants. The relatively great importance of the latter group of organisms as generators of this gas is not always appreciated. The organic residues of plants and animals are decomposed as a result of the activities of bacteria and fungi. During such decay processes the carbon of these residues is mostly released in the form of carbon dioxide as a result of the metabolic activities of these organisms and escapes into the air. The evolution of carbon dioxide gas from soils is often very considerable and is frequently referred to as "soil respiration"; this represents largely the respiration of microorganisms (see later). The respiration of the soil bacteria alone probably results in a greater return of carbon dioxide to the atmosphere than the respiration of all animals.

Carbon dioxide is also released into the atmosphere from volcanos, mineral springs, and in the combustion of coal, oil, gasoline, wood, and other fuel materials, but the total annual increment from these sources is very small relative to the amount present in the atmosphere. On the other hand, the weathering of certain igneous rocks (feldspars) combines carbon dioxide and thus reduces the quantity of this gas in the atmosphere.

Oceans are much more important reservoirs of carbon dioxide than the atmosphere. The oceans occupy nearly three-fourths of the earth's surface and are estimated to contain about eighty times as much carbon in forms available to plants as the atmosphere. The carbon dioxide in ocean waters is involved in a complex series of chemical and biological cycles which have never been fully evaluated. Marine plants consume carbon dioxide in photosynthesis and release it in respiration. Marine animals feed either upon marine plants or other animals, but ultimately, as with land animals, all of their food comes from the process of photosynthesis. A part of the carbon in the food consumed by such organisms is released into the water as carbon dioxide in the process of respiration. Aquatic microorganisms accomplish the decay of dead plants and animals, releasing most of the carbon in these organic remains in the form of carbon dioxide. Complex equilibria between the dissolved carbon dioxide, carbonates, and bicarbonates also exist. Large quantities of carbonates are tied up by certain marine animals in the formation of shells. Other marine animals precipitate large quantities of carbon dioxide in chemically combined form as the calcium carbonate of calcareous rocks. The conversion of bicarbonates into carbonates results in the release of carbonic acid and thus increases the available carbon dioxide content of the water. Eventually such rocks (limestones, etc.) may be raised above sea level, and the carbon dioxide tied up in the form of carbonates again is released to the atmosphere or dissolved in running water during dissolution of the rock.

Similar although not quite such complex cycles of carbon dioxide exist in the bodies of fresh water.

There is also a constant exchange of carbon dioxide between the oceans and the atmosphere. In fact, on theoretical grounds, there is good reason to suppose that the carbon dioxide concentration of the atmosphere is more or less effectively maintained in dynamic equilibrium with that of the oceans. Carbon dioxide probably escapes from the oceans whenever

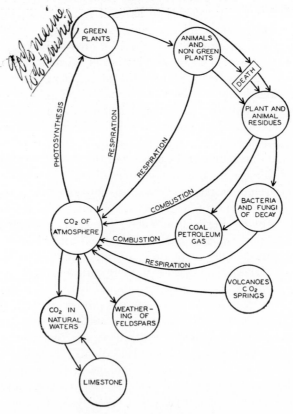

Fig. 94.   The carbon cycle.

its atmospheric concentration falls below the usual value, and dissolves in the oceans whenever a contrary shift in atmospheric carbon dioxide concentration occurs. The maintenance of such a large-scale dynamic equilibrium between the oceans and the atmosphere is probably the principal factor accounting for the constancy of the carbon dioxide concentration of the atmosphere.

The cycle of carbon in nature is shown diagrammatically in Fig. 94.

2. *The Entrance of Carbon Dioxide.*—Although the bulk of the carbon dioxide entering the leaves of land plants undoubtedly passes in through the stomates, substantial amounts may diffuse directly into the epidermal cells in some species. For example, a considerable proportion of the carbon dioxide used in photosynthesis in certain species which have stomates only in the lower epidermis, such as coleus, begonia, and avocado, passes into the leaves through the upper epidermis (Freeland, 1948). By the use of carbon dioxide made with the radioactive C^{14} isotope, Dugger (1950) has also shown that this gas can pass into the leaves of coleus and hydrangea through their upper, unstomated surfaces (Fig. 95).

All entrance of carbon dioxide, bicarbonates, or carbonates into the leaves of submersed hydrophytes, occurs directly through the epidermis.

The rate of entrance of carbon dioxide through stomates is very considerable in proportion to the aggregate area of the stomatal pores. Under conditions favorable for photosynthe-

FIG. 95. Radioautograph of a coleus leaf a part of the upper (unstomated) surface of which has been exposed to 1 per cent radioactive carbon dioxide. The white area, in which radioactive carbon is present, lies mostly below the area of upper leaf surface to which the leaf cup was attached through which the air stream containing radioactive carbon dioxide was passed.

sis Brown and Escombe (1900) found that carbon dioxide would diffuse into a catalpa leaf from the atmosphere at the rate of 0.07 cc. per cm.^{2} of leaf surface per hour. Since the stomates in this leaf occupy only 0.9 per cent of the surface, diffusion of carbon dioxide gas through them took place at a rate of 7.77 cc. per cm.^{2} of stomatal aperture per hour. (The assumption was made that all carbon dioxide entered through the stomates.) Under the same conditions a normal solution of sodium hydroxide absorbs from the atmosphere, even in rapidly moving air, only 0.177 cc. of carbon dioxide per cm.² per hour. In other words, carbon dioxide gas diffuses through the stomates at a rate approximately fifty times as fast as it diffuses into an efficient absorbing surface.

The extremely rapid rate of diffusion of carbon dioxide gas through the stomates can be interpreted in the light of principles of diffusion of gases through small openings. Table **27**, condensed from the work of Brown and Escombe, indicates that these same principles hold, in general, for carbon dioxide as well as water-vapor (Chap. X).

TABLE 27—DIFFUSION OF CARBON DIOXIDE THROUGH MULTIPERFORATE SEPTA. PORES 0.380 MM. IN DIAMETER; SEPTA I CM. FROM SODIUM HYDROXIDE SOLUTION (DATA OF BROWN AND ESCOMBE, 1900)

Septum	Area of tube, cm.²	Distance apart of pores in diameters	Diffusion CO_2 through septum, cc. per hour	Diffusion CO_2 through open tube, cc. per hour	Per cent of septum area occupied by pores	Diffusion through pores as per cent of diffusion through open tube
1	9.347	2.63	0.433	0.771	11.34	56.1
2	9.186	5.26	0.401	0.775	2.82	51.7
3	9.456	7.80	0.312	0.768	1.25	40.6
4	9.511	10.52	0.241	0.767	0.70	31.4
5	9.186	13.10	0.156	0.744	0.45	20.9
6	9.347	15.70	0.106	0.740	0.31	14.0

The most important principle illustrated, that the rate of diffusion does not decrease proportionately with reduction in the aggregate area of pores, is shown in the last two columns. For septum 4 (pores 10.52 diameters apart), for example, the diffusion is 31.4 per cent of that from the open tube, although only 0.70 per cent of the septum surface is occupied by the apertures.

3. *Effects of Variations in the Atmospheric Concentration of Carbon Dioxide upon the Rate of Photosynthesis.*—Although the average carbon dioxide content of the atmosphere is 0.03 per cent, the actual range in plant habitats is from about half to several times this value. Lower than average values are not infrequent in relatively quiet air in zones in which high rates of photosynthesis prevail. In a field of corn, for example, the carbon dioxide content of the air surrounding the plants may become measurably less than the average atmospheric value during daylight hours whenever high rates of photosynthesis occur. Similarly, in the atmosphere on the level with the crowns of trees in a dense forest the carbon dioxide content is sometimes considerably less than the average atmos-

pheric value during hours when rapid photosynthesis is in progress. In a tightly closed greenhouse the carbon dioxide content of the air may decrease materially during the course of a bright day.

Investigations of Lundegardh (1931) and others indicate that a considerable part of the carbon dioxide utilized by plants in many habitats is released locally as a result of "soil respiration," *i.e.*, in the respiration of soil microorganisms. Such a release of carbon dioxide is especially pronounced in well-fertilized soils, soils rich in organic matter, and in many forest soils. "Soil respiration," when marked, may result in a local enrichment of the carbon dioxide concentration in the air stratum close to the surface of the ground. Such a rise in carbon dioxide content is greatest during the night hours when the offsetting effect of photosynthesis in low-growing plants is absent. On a well-fertilized field the formation of carbon dioxide as a result of "soil respiration" during a 24-hr. period may equal or exceed the consumption in photosynthesis during the daylight hours.

The carbon dioxide content of the air is also influenced by fogs and mists. The quantity present per unit volume of air is measurably higher on foggy mornings than on clear mornings, and rates of apparent photosynthesis are correspondingly increased in a foggy as contrasted with a clear atmosphere if no other conditions are limiting (Wilson, 1948).

Although it is customary to express atmospheric concentrations of carbon dioxide as percentage by volume, such units are valid only when all of the concentrations to be compared are at approximately the same atmospheric pressure. The rate of diffusion of carbon dioxide into a leaf is a function of its partial pressure which varies directly as the total atmospheric pressure. Hence, although the percentage of carbon dioxide in the atmosphere is about 0.03 per cent both at sea level and, for example, at an altitude of 15,000 feet, its partial pressure is very different. At sea level the partial pressure of this gas is about 0.23 mm. Hg; at 15,000 feet altitude, about 0.13 mm. Hg. In terms of fundamental units, therefore, the effective concentration of carbon dioxide varies considerably with altitude, and this may be a factor to be taken into consideration when photosynthetic rates or development of plants at different altitudes is being compared (Decker, 1947).

In general, at least over relatively short periods, with increase in the concentration of atmospheric carbon dioxide, there is an increase in the rate of photosynthesis until some other factor, most commonly light, becomes limiting. The results of an experiment on the relation of carbon dioxide concentration to the rate of photosynthesis are shown in Fig. 96 in which, it should be noted, the highest light intensity used was only about 10 per cent of noonday summer sunlight.

If no other factor is limiting, the rate of photosynthesis rises in most species, at least for a while, with increase in the carbon dioxide concentration up to, at a minimum, 15-20 times the usual atmospheric concentration. Relatively high concentrations of carbon dioxide, in general, retard photosynthesis. The concentration at which such depressant effects are initiated varies with the kind of plant, stage of development of the photosynthetic tissue, length of exposure to carbon dioxide, and other prevailing environmental conditions. In the leaves of *Hydrangea otaksa*, for example, the rate of photosynthesis, although considerably retarded,

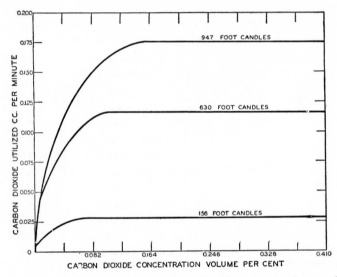

Fig. 96.   Relation between different carbon dioxide concentrations and rate of photosynthesis in wheat at three different light intensities. Data of Hoover *et al.* (1933).

is not entirely inhibited in short time experiments at concentrations as great as 20 per cent carbon dioxide (Livingston and Franck, 1946).

Under natural conditions during summer months in moist, temperate regions the carbon dioxide concentration of the atmosphere is most frequently the limiting factor in photosynthesis for all photosynthetic tissues which are well exposed to light. There seems to be little doubt that increase in the atmospheric concentration of this gas to at least several times its average value of 0.03 per cent has a continuously favorable effect on photosynthesis, as long as no other factors are limiting. There is evidence, however, that only slightly higher concentrations of carbon dioxide which favor enhanced photosynthesis over periods of a few hours or days may have a detrimental effect on the process over longer periods. Thomas and Hill (1949), for example, found that tomato plants exposed to ten times the atmospheric concentration of carbon dioxide during daylight hours showed detrimental effects within less than 2 weeks.

The Role of Light.—The energy stored by green plants in the molecules of carbohydrates during photosynthesis can be supplied only by light. Any source of radiant energy which includes wave lengths within the range of the visible spectrum will induce photosynthesis, provided its intensity is sufficiently great. Although a few of the longer wave lengths of ultraviolet apparently are effective in photosynthesis, and some of the shorter wave lengths of infrared can be used by sulfur bacteria, in general this process can occur only in the visible part of the spectrum. Under natural conditions sunlight, either direct or reflected from the sky or other objects, is the only source of radiant energy including wave lengths which can be used in photosynthesis. Photosynthesis will occur under electric lights or other artificial sources of illumination if of sufficient intensity. Such light sources are often used in experimental work on photosynthesis and to some extent in greenhouses as supplementary sources of illumination.

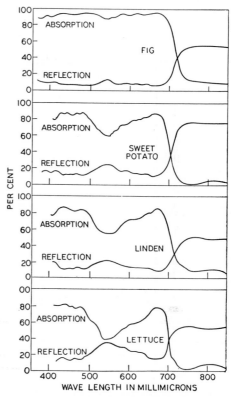

Fig. 97. Absorption and reflection spectra of leaves of four species. Data of Rabideau *et al* (1946).

Light, like all forms of radiant energy, varies in intensity (irradiance), quality, and duration (Chap. XVII), and the influence of this factor upon photosynthesis will be discussed under these three headings. Before the various effects of light upon photosynthesis are considered, however, it will be desirable to analyze the physical relations between leaves and incident light.

1. *The Optical Properties of Leaves.*—Of the visible light which falls

on leaves, as with radiant energy generally, a part is reflected, a part is transmitted through the leaf, and a part is absorbed by the leaf.

The proportion of the *visible light* incident upon a leaf which is absorbed varies considerably according to the kind of leaf and the intensity of light, but it is frequently in the neighborhood of 80 per cent (Seybold, 1932) and probably often higher. A clear distinction should be drawn between the proportion of visible light absorbed by a leaf and the proportion of the total incident radiant energy absorbed, the latter being in the neighborhood of 50 per cent for many kinds of leaves (Chap. IX).

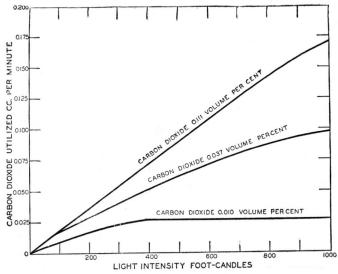

Fig. 98. Relation between different light intensities and rate of photosynthesis of wheat plants at three different carbon dioxide concentrations. Data of Hoover *et al.* (1933)

For any given kind of leaf the proportions of incident light reflected, transmitted, and absorbed vary considerably according to wave length (Fig. 97). In general a larger proportion of the incident light is absorbed by thick than by thin leaves. For normally green leaves maximum reflection in the range of visible light occurs in the extreme long red with a secondary, but less pronounced, maximum in the green. Conversely, maximum absorption is in the blue-violet and orange-short red regions, corresponding approximately with the prominent absorption bands of the chlorophylls. Reflection of infrared by leaves is about 50-60 per cent in the wave length range of 760-1100 mμ. (Billings and Morris, 1951).

2. *Effects of Variations in the Intensity of Light upon the Rate of*

Photosynthesis.—In general, with increase in light intensity there is an increase in the rate of photosynthesis until some other factor, in this example, the carbon dioxide concentration, becomes limiting (Fig. 98). At relatively low light intensities, as long as carbon dioxide is not the limiting factor, the rate of photosynthesis is approximately proportional to the light intensity. For the maximum concentration of carbon dioxide indicated in Fig. 98 (0.11 per cent), the maximum light intensity used was not great enough for the carbon dioxide factor to have become limiting. It should also be noted that the maximum light intensity employed— 1000 foot-candles—is much inferior in intensity to usual summer sunlight, which at noon on a clear day usually is equivalent to 8,000-10,000 foot-candles.

At usual atmospheric carbon dioxide concentrations, maximum photosynthetic rates are attained when leaves are exposed to light intensities considerably less than the maximum sunlight intensity. In apple leaves, for example, peak photosynthetic rates are reached at light intensities one-fourth to one-third full sunlight (Heinicke and Childers, 1937). Similarly in maize leaves maximum rates are attained at about one-fourth the peak intensity of summer sunlight (Verduin and Loomis, 1944) and in loblolly pine (*Pinus taeda*) needles at about one-third full sunlight (Kramer and Clark, 1947). On the other hand, in pronounced shade species, the highest rates of photosynthesis under otherwise favorable natural conditions are reached at light intensities no higher than 1000 foot-candles (Lundegardh, 1931).

Results such as those discussed above will be obtained only when a single leaf or a small plant, in which there is little or no shading of one part by another, is used as the experimental material. When the effect of light on photosynthesis is considered in terms of an entire tree, however, a different relation holds. Thus Heinicke and Childers (1937) showed that the rate of photosynthesis for an entire apple tree increased progressively with increase in light intensity up to or nearly that of full sunlight. This is undoubtedly because many of the interior leaves on a large tree are heavily shaded. Although, in general, maximum rates of photosynthesis are attained in the leaves of most (probably all) species at light intensities considerably below that of full sunlight, these investigators showed that many of the interior leaves of an apple tree receive as little as 1 per cent or less of the sunlight received by peripheral leaves. Even in full sunlight, therefore, many of the leaves on an apple tree do not photosynthesize at their maximum capacity. The lower the light intensity the greater the proportion of the leaves of which this will be true. Hence the greater the intensity of the incident light, the greater the average rate of photosynthesis per unit of leaf area. The total photosynthesis per tree, therefore, increases progressively with increased illumination up to or at least close to the maximum possible sunlight intensity.

Internal shading effects on the rate of photosynthesis have been demonstrated experimentally for such diverse plants as the loblolly pine (*Pinus taeda*) by Kramer and Clark (1947) and the hornwort (*Ceratophyllum demersum*)—a submersed aquatic—by Meyer (1939) and doubtless occur in many other kinds of plants with densely arranged foliage. Similar effects exist in compact stands of plants such as fields of some crop species. Mutual shading of the plants in plots of alfalfa is sufficiently marked so that the photosynthetic rate of such plots considered as a unit is highest at peak light intensities, or at intensities close thereto, as in an apple tree (Thomas and Hill, 1937). In fields of maize, on the other hand, the plants apparently do not shade each other sufficiently to have any appreciable effect on the aggregate rate of photosynthesis on bright days (Verduin and Loomis, 1944).

The intensity of the sunlight incident on the earth's surface varies from hour to hour and from season to season, as well as with meteorological conditions. Clouds, fogs, dust, and atmospheric humidity, all influence the intensity of the radiation which reaches the surface of the earth. The exposure and pitch of a slope are also factors influencing the intensity of the light impinging upon a given location, and are particularly of importance in hilly or mountainous country. Other conditions being equal the intensity of sunlight also increases with increase in altitude. In aquatic habitats light intensity decreases with depth below the surface of the water. Most variations in the intensity of natural light are accompanied by variations in light quality of greater or lesser magnitude. Usually, however, under out-of-doors conditions, variations in the intensity component of light are of greater physiological influence than the accompanying variations in the quality component.

Ecologically one of the most important factors causing different species of plants to be exposed to differences in light intensity is the effect of taller plants in shading those of lesser stature. Some species thrive and photosynthesize efficiently only in fully exposed locations; others can complete their normal life cycle in intensely shaded habitats.

Even under a tree with a rather open crown the light intensity is only one-tenth to one-twentieth that of full sunlight. Hence light is usually the limiting factor for photosynthesis in most species of plants when growing in the shade of trees. Species which normally grow in deep shade are often exceptions to this statement. On cloudy days light is also usually the limiting factor in photosynthesis. Because of the prevalence of cloudy weather in many regions during the winter, plants under glass often photosynthesize at very low rates during those months. The short length of the daylight period also contributes to low daily rates of photosynthesis during the winter season.

A number of studies have been made of the minimum light intensities at which various species of plants are just barely able to survive. Unless foods have previously accumulated, the minimum light intensity at which a plant will remain alive for indefinite periods during its normally active seasons must permit sufficient photosynthesis to compensate for both day and night respiration, and in all probability must also allow for some assimilation (Chap. XXIX).

Bates and Roeser (1928) studied the effects of low light intensities upon the growth of a number of species of evergreens native to the western United States. The seedlings were exposed to a 200 watt, blue tungsten lamp for 10 hours a day. Differences in light intensity were obtained by growing the seedlings at different distances from the source of illumination. Their results (Fig. 99) show that redwood seedlings were able to maintain their initial dry weight in a light intensity less than 1 per cent of full sunlight, while pinon pine required about 6 per cent, and the other three species were intermediate in their requirements.

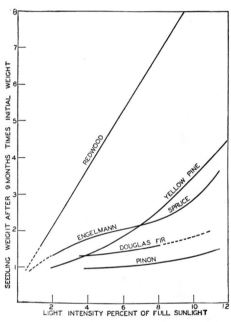

Fig. 99. Relation between light intensity and weights of conifer seedlings after 9 months. Data of Bates and Roeser (1928).

Extremely high light intensities exert an inhibitory effect on photosynthesis, a phenomenon called *solarization*. Holman (1930) showed that bean leaves exposed to an illumination of 6800 foot-candles accumulated starch readily, but that little starch was synthesized at twice this illumination value. This effect is exerted upon the photosynthetic mechanism itself and not on the process of starch synthesis.

Solarization effects appear to result principally, and probably entirely, from the phenomenon of *photo-oxidation*, in which leaves consume oxygen in the light, and use it in the oxidation of certain cell constituents, carbon dioxide being released in the process. The data shown graphically in Fig.

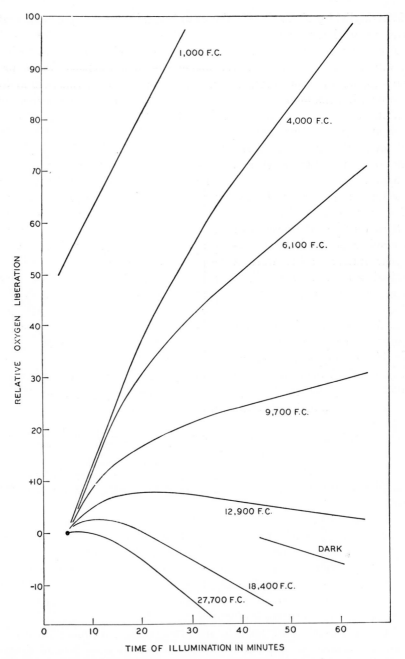

Fig. 100. Relation between light intensity in foot-candles and oxygen liberation by *Chlorella*. Oxygen consumption (photoxidation) occurs under the higher intensities. Data of Myers and Burr (1940).

100 illustrate the occurrence of photo-oxidation in *Chlorella,* but the existence of this phenomenon has also been demonstrated in other species. At lower light intensities a steady or nearly steady rate of photosynthesis is maintained by *Chlorella* but the higher the light intensity above 4000 foot-candles the more markedly the rate falls off with time. At 27,700 foot-candles, the highest intensity used, oxygen consumption (photo-oxidation) sets in almost immediately.

Photo-oxidation should not be confused with ordinary respiration as it is an entirely different process. It operates through at least a part of the photosynthetic mechanism and may occur at a rate three or four times greater than respiration. In a sense photo-oxidation may be regarded as a variant of photosynthesis in which oxygen is used as the substrate instead of carbon dioxide. Oxygen consumption at high light intensities results not merely from a superimposing of photo-oxidation upon photosynthesis but at least partly from an inactivation of the latter process by the former.

Short periods of photo-oxidation are usually not harmful to leaves or other photosynthetic organs, but continuation of this process for more than a few hours commonly results in decolorization of chlorophylls and ultimately in death of the cells in which it is occurring.

Light may exert indirect as well as direct effects upon photosynthesis. Low light intensities favor stomatal closure and hence may sometimes check photosynthesis by restricting the entrance of carbon dioxide as well as by acting as a direct limiting factor. Similarly high light intensities often cause increased rates of transpiration. Indirectly this causes a reduced water content of the leaf cells, which may in turn cause a dimin-

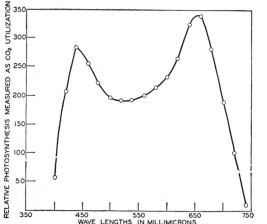

FIG. 101. Relative rates of photosynthesis of wheat in different wave lengths of light of equal intensity. Data of Hoover (1937).

ished rate of photosynthesis. A high light intensity also has the usual effect of raising leaf temperatures somewhat above the prevailing temperatures of the surrounding atmosphere and may thus influence photosynthesis indirectly by its effect on thermal conditions within leaves. Very high light intensities also have a destructive effect upon chlorophyll and other cell constituents as mentioned in the preceding paragraph.

3. *Effects of Different Light Qualities upon Photosynthesis.*—Hoover (1937) investigated the effect of different wave lengths of radiation upon the rate of photosynthesis of wheat plants (Fig. 101). By the use of suitable filters he was able to irradiate the plants with narrow spectral bands. All measurements were made with equal but low intensities of radiation incident upon the plants and under such conditions that no other factor was limiting for photosynthesis. The results of his investigation indicate the occurrence of maximum photosynthesis at a wave length of (655)mμ. in the red, and a secondary maximum of 440 mμ. in the blue. It is worthy of note that this curve does not show a very close agreement with the absorption spectrum of chlorophyll (Fig. 89).

The results of all investigators on the relation between light quality and photosynthesis do not agree with those just described. Gabrielsen (1948), for example, found in several species, including wheat, that the highest rates of photosynthesis occurred in orange-red light, the next highest in green-yellow light, and the lowest in violet-blue light. With *Ulva lactuca* (a marine alga), however, results were obtained similar to those of Hoover for wheat.

It is not certain whether the differences in the effect of light quality on photosynthesis from one species to another which appear to exist are real or not. It is possible that the relation between light quality and photosynthesis is not the same in all kinds of plants, and may even be different in two plants of the same species which have developed under different conditions. On the other hand, the technical difficulties in this type of experimentation are considerable, and it is not clear just how much of the available data has been obtained under sufficiently critical conditions. It is also possible, therefore, that the diverse results which have been recorded are more apparent than real, and are largely the outcome of the different experimental techniques which have been used.

There are a number of conditions under which plants growing in their natural habitats are exposed more or less continuously to light of a different quality from that of full sunlight at the earth's surface. On cloudy days, for example, the intensity of light is not only less than on clear days, but it is proportionately richer in blue and green wave lengths.

Light which has been filtered through the crown of a tree is usually proportionately richer in green rays than direct sunlight because of the greater proportionate absorption by leaves in the red and blue portions of the spectrum. This effect upon light quality is most marked in hardwood forests in which the tree crowns form an almost continuous canopy. The herbs, shrubs, and smaller trees growing in such forests are subjected to light which is not only of much lower intensity than full sunlight, but is also different in quality from the light impinging upon the forest canopy.

In habitats of submerged aquatics both the intensity and quality of the light are usually very different from the intensity and quality of the sunlight at the earth's surface. Pure water absorbs radiations in the red-orange portion of the spectrum much more effectively than in the blue-green region. While the absorption coefficients of natural waters for various wave lengths of light vary somewhat, depending upon the substances dissolved or dispersed in the water, in general shorter wave lengths penetrate to greater depths than longer wave lengths. Hence with increasing depth in either fresh or ocean water not only is the intensity of the light reduced, but its quality is greatly modified. Aquatic plants growing at a depth of 20 meters, for example, will be exposed to light proportionately much richer in blue-green rays, although of lower intensity, than those at a depth of 1 meter.

Alpine plants are also exposed to light of different composition than species at lower altitudes. The atmosphere absorbs the shorter wave lengths of the sun's radiation more effectively than the longer ones. Because of the shorter column of atmosphere through which it passes, sunlight at high altitudes is therefore not only more intense than at lower elevations, but is also relatively richer in the shorter wave lengths of visible radiation and the ultraviolet.

4. *Effects of Duration of the Light Period upon Photosynthesis.*—In general a plant will accomplish more photosynthesis in the course of a day if exposed to illumination of favorable intensity for ten or twelve hours than if suitable light conditions prevail for only four or five hours. In arctic regions photosynthesis may occur continuously throughout the 24-hr. day of the summer months (Müller, 1928), although the rate may vary cyclically throughout the day. A considerable capacity for sustained photosynthesis under continuous light is indicated by the results of Böhning (1949). Leaves on young apple trees, exposed to a continuous illumination of about 3200 foot-candles at 25°C. and the usual atmospheric concentration of carbon dioxide, were shown to photosynthesize at an undiminished rate for periods of at least 18 days.

Temperature Effects on Photosynthesis.—The measurement of the effect of temperature upon photosynthesis in terrestrial plants is complicated by the fact that the leaf temperatures of such plants are seldom the same as atmospheric temperatures. Whenever leaves are exposed to direct illumination, which is almost invariably the situation when photosynthesis is occurring at a rapid rate, their temperatures exceed those of the surrounding atmosphere. It is difficult, therefore, if not impossible, to maintain the temperature of the leaves of land plants at a desired value while they are exposed to light of any considerable intensity. Evaluation of the effect of the temperature of leaves upon photosynthesis is possible only if the actual leaf temperature is measured. For this reason many of the more critical studies of the effect of temperature upon photosynthesis have been made with submerged water plants, in which a close thermal equilibrium is maintained between the plant body and the surrounding water.

1. *Temperature Limits of Photosynthesis.*—Photosynthesis can take place over a wide range of temperatures. It has been reported to occur in some species of conifers at temperatures as low as −35°C. and in some kinds of lichens at −20°C. Freeland (1944) has shown that the photosynthetic rate may exceed the rate of respiration in several species of conifers at temperatures as low as −6°C. Tropical plants cannot carry on photosynthesis at temperatures as low as those at which many temperate zone plants do. In most tropical species photosynthesis apparently will not occur at temperatures below about 5°C. At the other end of the temperature range for photosynthesis stand the species of algae indigenous to hot springs which can survive 75°C. and probably carry on photosynthesis at temperatures close to this value. Many semi-desert and tropical species can withstand air temperatures of 55°C. and probably photosynthesize at temperatures not far below this. In most plants of temperate regions the range of temperatures within which photosynthesis occurs at a relatively rapid rate is about 10°-35°C.

2. *The Effect of Temperature on the Rate of Photosynthesis.*—*If neither carbon dioxide, nor light, nor any other factor is limiting,* the rate of photosynthesis increases with rise in temperature up to a point which varies somewhat from one kind of a plant to another. Further increase in temperature results in a rapid decline in the rate of photosynthesis, resulting primarily from injurious effects of higher temperatures on the protoplasm. Furthermore, as first clearly shown by Matthaei (1905) for cherry laurel (*Prunus laurocerasus*) but since confirmed by other investigators for other species (Fig. 102), the rate of photosynthesis at all higher temperatures decreases with time. The higher the temperature the sooner this decline in rate sets in, and the more rapidly that it occurs. In the cherry laurel, for example, the rate of photosynthesis is essentially constant for a number of hours at temperatures of 23.7°C. and lower. At 30.5°C., however, the rate is measurably less after several hours than at the beginning of the photosynthetic period. At 37.5°C., at which the highest initial photosynthetic rate is attained, the rate falls off still more

rapidly, and within a few hours is markedly less than initially.   Under such conditions, within a favorable temperature range (about 10°-35°C.), the temperature coefficient of photosynthesis is about two.

The diminution in the rate of photosynthesis with time, particularly marked at higher temperatures, is evidence of the increasingly limiting effect of some internal factor, generally called the "time factor." The exact nature of this time factor is unknown, and it is possible that it may represent the composite influence of several internal conditions. One of the more probable mechanisms of this effect is that of an inactivation of

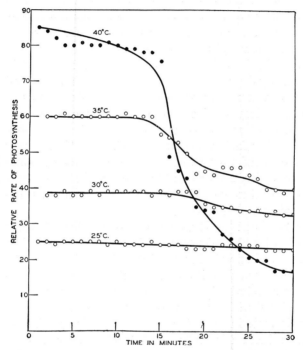

Fig. 102.   Relative rates of apparent photosynthesis in waterweed (*Anacharis canadensis*) at different temperatures over a period of 30 minutes.

enzymes at higher temperatures. The temperature relations of enzymatic reactions (Chap. XVI) are similar to those of the photosynthetic reaction, a fact which supports this view. Other possible components of the time factor are the destructive effects of relatively high temperatures upon other constituents of the protoplasm than enzymes, the accumulation of the end products of the reaction which may exert a retarding effect on the rate of photosynthesis (see later), or failure of the diffusion of carbon dioxide toward the chloroplasts to keep pace with its use in photosynthesis, even though the external supply is not limiting. As discussed in later chapters, similar time factor effects are present in the temperature relations of other plant processes, such as respiration and growth.

It should be emphasized again that the relation between photosynthesis and temperature described above holds only when no other environmental factor is limiting. Such experiments on the overall temperature character- istics of the process must therefore be conducted with the plants exposed to an atmosphere in which the carbon dioxide concentration is consider- ably higher than the usual atmospheric concentration of 0.03 per cent.

In nature the maximum rate of photosynthesis which might be achieved under the prevailing temperature is often not realized because of the limit- ing effect of some other factor. Temperature, within the ordinary physio- logical range for plants, has little effect on the rate of photosynthesis of plants growing in deep shade or of plants exposed to the low light in- tensities of cloudy days. Under such conditions light is the limiting factor.

Similarly, on warm days, well-watered plants exposed to bright light often do not photosynthesize at the maximum rate possible under the prevailing temperature because carbon dioxide at atmospheric concentra- tion is the limiting factor. Thomas and Hill (1949), for example, found that temperature had very little influence on the rate of photosynthesis of alfalfa under field conditions within a range of 16.4° to 29°C. In other words the temperature coefficient of the process under such conditions is approximately one.

The Role of Water in Photosynthesis.—Less than 1 per cent of the water absorbed by a plant is used in photosynthesis. It therefore seems probable that the indirect effects of the water factor upon photosynthesis are more pronounced than its direct effect. In other words, deficiency of water as a raw material is rarely if ever a limiting factor in photosyn- thesis. Nevertheless a reduction in the water content of leaves usually results in a decrease in the rate of photosynthesis as is illustrated by the results of Schneider and Childers (1941). These investigators studied the effects of withholding water upon the rate of apparent photosynthesis in apple trees. When the soil was allowed to dry out gradually, starting from the field capacity, reduction in the rate of apparent photosynthesis (and transpiration) became evident within a few days at an air temperature of 26.7°C. and was pronounced before visible wilting took place. When the soil water content had fallen to the permanent wilting percentage, and the leaves were distinctly wilted, apparent photosynthesis was 87 per cent less than the initial rate. Upon watering the soil the leaves regained turgidity within a few hours, but the original rates of apparent photo- synthesis were not reattained until 2-7 days had passed. An important implication of this last observation is that the retarding effects of drought on photosynthesis linger for some time after water has again become available in the soil.

Submersion of roots also has a pronounced retarding effect on apparent photosynthesis (and transpiration) in apple (Childers and White, 1942), usually becoming evident within 2-7 days after flooding the soil with water. With continued water-logging of the soil around the roots, rates of apparent photosynthesis often become immeasurable. This effect is doubtless largely the result of a retardation in water absorption (Chap. XIV).

The influence of a reduction in the water content of leaves upon the rate of photosynthesis probably results from either or both of two principal causes: (1) a reduction in the diffusive capacity of the stomates, and (2) a decrease in the hydration of the chloroplasts and other parts of the protoplasm which in some manner diminishes the effectiveness of the photosynthetic mechanism.

Decrease in the water content of leaves unquestionably causes a reduction in the diffusive capacity of the stomates. Mitchell (1936) and others have observed, however, that in some plants relatively high rates of photosynthesis may prevail at times when the stomates appear to be closed. There are several possible explanations for this apparently anomalous observation. One is that stomates which appear closed to microscopic observations are not entirely closed to the passage of gases. A second is that reservoired carbon dioxide (Chap. XVIII) within the leaf cells may be used in photosynthesis while the stomates are closed or nearly so. A third is that considerable amounts of carbon dioxide may enter the leaves of some species directly through the epidermis as described earlier.

The evidence in favor of the view that the decreased hydration of the protoplasm which accompanies a reduction in cell turgidity causes a decreased rate of photosynthesis comes chiefly from experiments with water plants. Walter (1929), for example, has studied the effect upon their rate of photosynthesis of immersing plants of waterweed (*Anacharis canadensis*) in sucrose solutions of various concentrations. The greater the concentration of the sucrose solution the less the turgidity of the cells, the less the hydration of protoplasm and the slower the rate of photosynthesis. In one experiment the rate of photosynthesis was appreciably retarded by immersion of the plants in an 0.3 molal solution and almost entirely stopped in an 0.7 molal solution of sucrose with an osmotic pressure of about 18 atm. Plasmolysis of the cells occurred at a solution concentration of between 0.3 and 0.4 molal. The rate of respiration, on the other hand, was practically unaffected by sucrose solutions at any concentration up to and including 1.0 molal. Since the waterweed is a submerged aquatic with thin leaves which bear no stomates, any reduction in the rate of photosynthesis resulting from a diminution in cell turgor most likely results from direct effects upon the hydration of the protoplasm of the photosynthesizing cells.

In general, it appears that the rate of photosynthesis is less affected by reduction in leaf water content than the rate of transpiration. This is indicated by the results of Heinicke and Childers (1936) who determined the average rates of photosynthesis and transpiration over a one-week period in two apple trees, one of which was well watered while the other was growing in soil which was gradually drying out. The rate of photosynthesis of the plant in the dry soil was about half as great as in the plant which was watered. The rate of transpiration, however, was only about one-fourth as great in the former plant as in the latter.

Effect of Oxygen Concentration on Photosynthesis.—The photosynthetic organs of terrestrial plants are seldom exposed to oxygen concentrations which deviate appreciably from the usual atmospheric concentration of about 21 per cent. Hence studies of the effect of oxygen concentration on

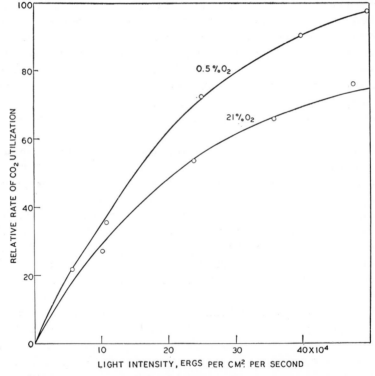

Fig. 103. Comparative rates of photosynthesis in wheat at low and high oxygen concentrations under different light intensities. (10×10^4 ergs per sec. = 0.143 g.-cal. per cm.^{2} per min.) Data of McAlister and Myers (1940).

the rate of photosynthesis are principally of theoretical interest. In at least some, and probably all, plants, increase in the oxygen concentration results in a decrease in the rate of photosynthesis, and the normal atmospheric concentration is sufficiently high to induce a slower photosynthetic rate than obtains at lower oxygen concentrations. For example, McAlister and Myers (1940) showed that the rate of photosynthesis in young wheat plants was about 30-50 per cent higher in 0.5 per cent oxygen than in 20 per cent oxygen at a high light intensity and atmospheric carbon dioxide concentration (Fig. 103). This effect of oxygen is not merely a decrease in apparent photosynthesis resulting from an enhanced respiration rate at the higher oxygen concentration but is on the process of photosynthesis *per se.* Neither is this effect one of photo-oxidation offsetting photosynthesis, because the magnitude of the retardation in photosynthesis under relatively high concentrations of oxygen is too great to be accounted for in this way. The only satisfactory explanation appears to be that oxygen actually exerts a direct inhibitory effect on photosynthesis, and the greater the concentration of oxygen the greater this effect.

Effects of Certain Chemical Compounds on Photosynthesis.—Many different kinds of chemical compounds, upon absorption by plant cells, have effects—direct or indirect—upon the rate of photosynthesis. Especially noteworthy are the effects of certain substances which markedly influence the rate of photosynthesis when present only in minute quantities. Among these are hydrocyanic acid, hydroxylamine, hydrogen sulfide, and certain *Enzyme* compounds containing the iodoacetyl radical. Hydrocyanic acid, for example, has a pronounced retarding effect on the photosynthesis of *Chlorella* at a concentration of only 4×10^{-5} molar. All of these substances appear to act as enzyme inhibitors (Chap. XVI, XXII) and each of them appears to affect one specific enzyme system of the several which operate in the mechanism of photosynthesis. This fact has been used to advantage by investigators of the chemical dynamics of photosynthesis, who have thereby been enabled to inhibit the process at different stages, and thus to differentiate more clearly among the several partial reactions of photosynthesis. For example, the enzyme system which is sensitive to hydroxylamine participates only in the oxygen-releasing stage of photosynthesis.

Narcotics, of which chloroform, ether, and the urethans are examples, also exert retarding or inhibitory effects on photosynthesis when present in very low concentrations. Unless the concentration is too high, in which *general-surface* case death of the cells may result, the effect of such substances is reversible. Narcotic inhibition of photosynthesis does not appear to result from effects on specific enzymes, but from some more general influence, which is believed to be related to their surface activity.

The Effects of Internal Factors on the Rate of Photosynthesis.—In addition to the environmental factors which influence photosynthesis, the rate of the process is also influenced by certain factors within the plant. In general, because of the experimental difficulties encountered in their investigation, the effects of such internal factors on photosynthesis are less well understood than those of external factors. Some discussion of several of these factors is warranted, however, by the present state of our knowledge.

1. *Chlorophyll Content.*—In their extensive study of the relationship between chlorophyll content and photosynthesis Willstätter and Stoll (1918) devised the *photosynthetic number* ("Assimilationszahl") as an index to this relation. The photosynthetic number is the number of grams of carbon dioxide absorbed per hour per gram of chlorophyll. These two investigators studied the relation between chlorophyll content and photosynthesis in green-leaved and yellow-leaved varieties of the same species (Table 28). In this experiment the leaves were exposed to strong light in an atmosphere of 5 per cent carbon dioxide at 25°C.

TABLE 28—THE RELATION BETWEEN PHOTOSYNTHESIS AND CHLOROPHYLL CONTENT IN GREEN AND YELLOW-LEAVED VARIETIES OF ELM AND ELDER (DATA OF WILLSTÄTTER AND STOLL, 1918)

| Species | Variety | Chlorophyll content of 10 g. fresh leaves in mg. | CO_2 absorbed per hr. in mg. | | Photo-synthetic number |
			Per 10 g. leaf tissue	Per dm.^{2} leaf surface	
Elm...............	Green	16.2	111	21	6.9
Elm...............	Yellow	1.2	98	24	82.
European Elder.......	Green	22.2	146	34	6.6
European Elder.......	Yellow	0.81	97	21	120.

As shown in this table the rate of photosynthesis in green-leaved varieties is not much in excess of that in yellow-leaved varieties of the same species, and, when expressed in terms of the photosynthetic number, the yellow-leaved varieties are much more efficient per unit of chlorophyll present. Other investigations by the same workers also seem to point to the conclusion that there is no proportional relationship between chlorophyll content and photosynthesis in the leaves of vascular plants. In other words, it appears that the chlorophyll content of the leaves is seldom the limiting factor in photosynthesis in such species even when all external conditions are favorable for the process.

2. *Hydration of the Protoplasm.*—That the hydration of the protoplasm

is an important internal factor influencing photosynthesis has already been shown in the discussion of the water factor in photosynthesis.

3. *Leaf Anatomy.*—The rate of photosynthesis in any leaf is partly conditioned by the anatomy of that leaf. The size and distribution of the intercellular spaces, the relative proportions and distribution of palisade and spongy layers, the size, position, and structure of the stomates, the thickness of the cuticular and epidermal layers, the amount and position of sclerenchyma, proportion and distribution of non-green mesophyll tissues, and the size, distribution and efficiency of the vascular system, all influence the rate of photosynthesis. The effects of the structure of leaves upon the rate of photosynthesis result principally from influences upon the rate of entrance of carbon dioxide, upon the intensity of light penetrating to chlorenchyma cells, upon the maintenance of the turgidity of the leaf cells, and upon the rate of translocation of soluble carbohydrates out of the photosynthesizing cells.

4. *Protoplasmic Factors.*—Evidence from various types of experiments, some of which has been presented on the foregoing pages, indicates conclusively that certain other conditions resident in the protoplasm of plant cells, other than chlorophyll content and hydration, influence the rate of photosynthesis. The most important of such factors is undoubtedly the enzyme complement of the protoplasmic system. That a number of enzymes play a part in photosynthesis is beyond question. There is also little doubt that the proportions and quantities of these enzymes may vary in different kinds of photosynthetic cells, or in the same cell under different conditions, but until more is known of the physicochemical nature of the photosynthetic catalysts no discussion of them beyond these generalized statements is warranted.

5. *Accumulation of the End Products of Photosynthesis.*—During photosynthesis the carbohydrates synthesized in the process, or in immediately following secondary reactions, accumulate in the photosynthesizing cells more rapidly than they are translocated toward other tissues. Under at least some conditions accumulation of carbohydrates appears to exert a retarding effect upon photosynthesis (Kurssanow, 1933; Mönch, 1937; and others). The results of Boysen-Jensen and Müller (1929), Kjär (1937), and others, however, appear to indicate that there is no consistent relationship between the concentration of carbohydrates in the leaf cells of intact plants and the rate of photosynthesis.

Daily Variations in the Rate of Photosynthesis.—Thomas and Hill (1937) measured the daily variation in rates of apparent photosynthesis for small plots of alfalfa (Fig. 104) under conditions approximating a "standard day." Well-watered plots of alfalfa 6 feet square were enclosed in transparent celluloid cabinets and air circulated through each cabinet at rates ranging up to several hundred cubic feet per minute. The net consumption of carbon dioxide by the plants was ascertained by measuring the difference in the concentration of this gas in the inflowing and outflowing streams of air. In general, as with the apple tree previously described, the rate of photosynthesis under these conditions showed a close correlation with the light intensity.

Innumerable other types of daily periodicities of photosynthesis are possible. The pattern of any such periodicity depends in part on the kind

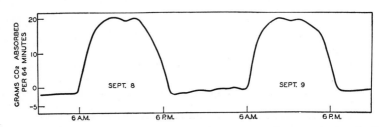

FIG. 104. Daily variations in the rate of apparent photosynthesis of alfalfa. Data of Thomas and Hill (1937).

of plant and on the unit of plant material for which photosynthesis is measured—whether a single leaf, a small plant, a large plant, such as a tree, or a plot of vegetation. It will also obviously vary with the daily cycle of environmental conditions which not only differs in a general way from one climatic center to another, but also shows seasonal and daily variations within any climatic region.

SUGGESTED FOR COLLATERAL READING

Duggar, B. M., Editor. *Biological Effects of Radiation.* McGraw-Hill Book Co., Inc. New York. 1936.

Franck, J., and W. E. Loomis, Editors. *Photosynthesis in Plants.* Iowa State College Press. Ames. 1949.

Lundegardh, H. *Environment and Plant Development.* Translated and edited by E. Ashby. Edward Arnold and Co. London. 1931.

Rabinowitch, E. I. *Photosynthesis and Related Processes.* Vol. I, II. Interscience Publishers, Inc. New York. 1945, 1951.

SELECTED BIBLIOGRAPHY

Bates, C. G., and J. Roeser, Jr. Light intensities required for growth of coniferous seedlings. *Amer. Jour. Bot.* **15:** 185-194. 1928.

Billings, W. D., and R. J. Morris. Reflection of visible and infrared radiation from leaves of different ecological groups. *Amer. Jour. Bot.* **38:** 327-331. 1951.

Blackman, F. F. Optima and limiting factors. *Ann. Bot.* **19:** 281-295. 1905.

Blackman, F. F., and G. L. Matthaei. Experimental studies on vegetable assimilation and respiration. IV. A quantitative study of carbon dioxide assimilation and leaf temperature in natural illumination. *Proc. Roy. Soc. (London)* **B 76**: 402-460. 1905.

Böhning, R. H. Time course of photosynthesis in apple leaves exposed to continuous illumination. *Plant Physiol.* **24**: 222-240. 1949.

Boysen-Jensen, P., and D. Müller. Die maximale Ausbeute und der tägliche Verlauf der Kohlensäureassimilation. *Jahrb. Wiss. Bot.* **70**: 493-502. 1929.

Brown, H. T., and F. Escombe. Static diffusion of gases and liquids in relation to the assimilation of carbon and translocation in plants. *Phil. Trans. Roy. Soc. (London)* **B 193**: 223-291. 1900.

Childers, N. F., and D. G. White. Influence of submersion of the roots on transpiration, apparent photosynthesis, and respiration of young apple trees. *Plant Physiol.* **17**: 603-618. 1942.

Decker, J. P. The effect of air supply on apparent photosynthesis. *Plant Physiol.* **22**: 561-571. 1947.

Dugger, W. M. The permeability of certain epidermal membranes to gaseous carbon dioxide. Dissertation Ph.D. North Carolina State College. 1950.

Freeland, R. O. Apparent photosynthesis in some conifers during winter. *Plant Physiol.* **19**: 179-185. 1944.

Freeland, R. O. Photosynthesis in relation to stomatal frequency and distribution. *Plant Physiol.* **23**: 595-600. 1948.

Gabrielsen, E. K. Influence of light of different wave-lengths on photosynthesis in foliage leaves. *Physiol. Plantarum* **1**: 113-123. 1948.

Harder, R. Kritische Versuche zu Blackmans Theorie der "begrenzenden Faktoren" bei der Kohlensäureassimilation. *Jahrb. Wiss. Bot.* **60**: 531-571. 1921.

Heinicke, A. J., and N. F. Childers. The influence of water deficiency in photosynthesis and transpiration of apple leaves. *Proc. Amer. Soc. Hort. Sci.* **33**: 155-159. 1936.

Heinicke, A. J., and N. F. Childers. The daily rate of photosynthesis . . . of a young apple tree of bearing age. *Cornell Univ. Agric. Expt. Sta. Mem. 201.* 1937.

Holman, R. On solarization of leaves. *Univ. Calif. Publ. in Botany* **16**: 139-151. 1930.

Hoover, W. H. The dependence of carbon dioxide assimilation in a higher plant on wave length of radiation. *Smithsonian Misc. Coll.* **95**: No. 21. 1937.

Hoover, W. H., E. S. Johnston, and F. S. Brackett. Carbon dioxide assimilation in a higher plant. *Smithsonian Misc. Coll.* **87**: No. 16. 1933.

James, W. O. Experimental researches on vegetable assimilation and respiration. XIX. The effect of variations of carbon dioxide supply upon the rate of assimilation of submerged water plants. *Proc. Roy. Soc. (London)* **B 103**: 1-42. 1928.

Kjär, A. Der Schwankungen der Assimilationsintensität der Blätter von *Sinapsis alba* in Laufe des Tages in Abhängigkeit von inneren Faktoren. *Planta* **26**: 595-607. 1937.

Kramer, P. J., and W. S. Clark. A comparison of photosynthesis in individual pine needles and entire seedlings at various light intensities. *Plant Physiol.* **22**: 51-57. 1947.

Kurssanow, A. L. Über den Einfluss der Kohlenhydrate auf den Tagesverlauf der Photosynthèse. *Planta* **20**: 535-548. 1933.

Livingston, R., and J. Franck. Assimilation and respiration of excised leaves at high concentrations of carbon dioxide. *Amer. Jour. Bot.* **27**: 449-458. 1940.

Matthaei, Gabrielle L. C. Experimental researches on vegetable assimilation and respiration. III. On the effect of temperature on carbon dioxide assimilation. *Phil. Trans. Roy. Soc. (London)* **B 197**: 47-105. 1905.

McAlister, E. D., and J. Myers. The time course of photosynthesis and fluorescence observed simultaneously. *Smithsonian Misc. Coll.* **99**, No. 6. 1940.

Meyer, B. S. The daily cycle of apparent photosynthesis in a submerged aquatic. *Amer. Jour. Bot.* **26**: 755-760. 1939.

Mitchell, J. W. Effect of atmospheric humidity on rate of carbon fixation of plants. *Bot. Gaz.* **98**: 87-104. 1936.

Mönch, Ingeborg. Untersuchungen über die Kohlensäurebilanz von Alpenpflanzen am natürlichen Standort. *Jahrb. Wiss. Bot.* **85**: 506-553. 1937.

Müller, D. Die Kohlensäureassimilation bei arktischen Pflanzen und die Abhängigkeit der Assimilation von der Temperatur. *Planta* **6**: 22-39. 1928.

Myers, J., and G. O. Burr. Studies on photosynthesis. Some effects of high light intensity on *Chlorella. Jour. Gen. Physiol.* **24**: 45-67. 1940.

Rabideau, G. S., C. S. French, and A. S. Holt. The absorption and reflection spectra of leaves, chloroplast suspensions, and chloroplast fragments as measured in an Ulbricht sphere. *Amer. Jour. Bot.* **33**: 769-777. 1946.

Schneider, G. W., and N. F. Childers. Influence of soil moisture on photosynthesis, respiration, and transpiration of apple leaves. *Plant Physiol.* **16**: 565-583. 1941.

Schroeder, H. Die jährliche Gesamtproduktion der grünen Pflanzendecke der Erde. *Naturwiss.* **7**: 8-12, 23-29. 1919.

Seybold, A. Über die optischen Eigenschaften der Laubblätter. I, II. *Planta* **16**: 195-226. 1932; **18**: 479-508. 1932.

Shirley, H. L. Light as an ecological factor and its measurement. I, II. *Bot. Rev.* **1**: 355-381. 1935; **11**: 497-532. 1945.

Thomas, M. D., and G. R. Hill. The continuous measurement of photosynthesis, respiration, and transpiration of alfalfa and wheat growing under field conditions. *Plant Physiol.* **12**: 285-307. 1937.

Thomas, M. D., and G. R. Hill. Photosynthesis under field conditions. In *Photosynthesis in Plants*. J. Franck and W. E. Loomis, Editors. 19-52. Iowa State College Press. Ames. 1949.

Verduin, J., and W. E. Loomis. Absorption of carbon dioxide by maize. *Plant Physiol.* **19**: 278-293. 1944.

Walter, H. Plasmaquellung und Assimilation. *Protoplasma* **6**: 113-156. 1929.

Willstätter, R., and A. Stoll. *Untersuchungen über die Assimilation der Kohlensäure*. Julius Springer. Berlin. 1918.

Wilson, C. C. Fog and atmospheric carbon dioxide as related to apparent photosynthetic rate of some broadleaf evergreens. *Ecology* **29**: 507-508. 1948.

DISCUSSION QUESTIONS

1. What environmental factor would be most likely to be the limiting factor in photosynthesis in the east central United States in July? In January? In a greenhouse in the same region in July? In January? In a semidesert region during the rainy season? During the dry season? In a lake at a depth of 10 meters?

2. If, under the conditions prevailing on a "standard day," half of the leaves are removed from a tree, how will the daily rate of photosynthesis per unit of leaf area compare with the rate before the leaves were removed? Explain. Answer the same question for a day with heavy clouds. Would the distribution of the removed leaves make any difference? Explain.

3. If the carbon dioxide concentration is usually the limiting factor during the summer months for plants well exposed to light, why is it possible to increase the production of many crop plants by adding fertilizers to the soil?

4. Explain exactly why a leaf appears green to the human eye.

5. Under what conditions would the addition of water to the soil around a plant be expected to result in an appreciable increase in the rate of photosynthesis? No very great change? A measurable decrease?

6. Why does adding carbon dioxide to the atmosphere of greenhouses in the northeastern United States during the winter months often have little or no beneficial effect on plants?

7. Assuming otherwise "standard day" conditions, would you expect the rate of photosynthesis of an entire apple tree to be greater on a perfectly clear day or on one with scattered cumulus clouds in the sky?

8. Waterweed plants immersed in a dilute solution of $KHCO_3$ and exposed to sunlight show an immediate increase in the rate of photosynthesis if the temperature is raised from 25° to 30°C. The rate of photosynthesis in leaves of land plants exposed to full sunlight, however, usually increases only slightly or not at all with the same rise in temperature. Explain.

9. Cite some examples of situations in which solarization might be expected to occur under natural conditions.

10. If you wished to obtain maximum production of photosynthate in a potted herbaceous plant over a 2-hr. period, what procedure would you suggest? Maximum production of photosynthate over a period of a week?

XX

CARBOHYDRATE METABOLISM

The physiological processes of green plants revolve around molecules which belong to the great chemical group known as carbohydrates. Included in this group of compounds are the molecules put together in photosynthesis, the molecules which make up the structural framework of plants, some of the most important food reserves, and a large number of less prominent compounds that participate in a wide variety of processes which occur within plant cells. The carbohydrate molecule serves as the principal vehicle in which the energy of sunlight is captured, stored, transported, and from which it is finally released and utilized by living cells.

The name carbohydrate was given to the group many years ago when the first chemical analyses revealed that the molecules of these compounds contained only carbon, hydrogen, and oxygen, the latter two being present in the same ratio in which they are found in the water molecule. It has been known for a long time, however, that carbohydrates are not, as the name suggests, hydrates of carbon. Most of the compounds in the group do have the empirical formula $C_m (H_2O)_n$, but this is not true for all carbohydrate molecules. Furthermore, there are a number of compounds which have this same empirical formula but which are chemically unrelated to the carbohydrates. Carbohydrates are now defined as aldehydic or ketonic derivatives of polyhydric alcohols of the aliphatic series and their condensation products. The significance of this statement will become clearer in the light of the following discussion.

A large number of different kinds of carbohydrates have been isolated from plants, and doubtless many more remain to be discovered. They compose the bulk of the dry matter of plants. Although some of the carbohydrates are of universal occurrence in plants, or practically so, others seem to be restricted to a very few species. Certain carbohydrates are the important structural components of the cell walls of plants, others are integral parts of the protoplasm, some are in solution in the cell sap, while large quantities of others accumulate in plant cells as insoluble storage products.

Classification of the Carbohydrates.—A classification of the principal carbohydrates is presented in Table 29. This table is not complete, but it does list all of the more important carbohydrates, and includes all of those known to be of especial significance in the metabolism of plants.

TABLE 29—A CLASSIFICATION OF THE PRINCIPAL CARBOHYDRATES

I. Monosaccharides or Simple Sugars	1. Bioses 2. Trioses 3. Tetroses 4. Pentoses...	Aldoses........	1. Xylose 2. Arabinose 3. Ribose	
		Ketoses		
	5. Hexoses...	Aldoses........	1. Glucose 2. Mannose 3. Galactose	D-and L-forms
		Ketoses........	1. Fructose 2. Sorbose	
	6. Heptoses 7. Octoses 8. Nonoses 9. Decoses			
II. Oligosaccharides or Compound Sugars 2-4	1. Disaccharides..............		1. Sucrose 2. Maltose 3. Gentiobiose 4. Trehalose 5. Melibiose 6. Cellobiose 7. Lactose	
	2. Trisaccharides.............		1. Raffinose 2. Gentianose 3. Melezitose	
	3. Tetrasaccharides...........		1. Stachyose	
III. Polysaccharides...	5-? 1. Pentosans.................		1. Araban 2. Xylan	
	2. Hexosans..	1. Glucosans...	1. Starch 2. Glycogen 3. Cellulose 4. Lichenin	
		2. Fructosans....Inulin 3. Mannans 4. Galactans		
	3. Pectic compounds............		Pectic Acid Pectin Protopectin	
	4. Gums 5. Mucilages 6. Amino-hexosans.............. Chitin			

The *monosaccharides* are the group of carbohydrates from which no simpler carbohydrates can be produced by hydrolysis. They are classified according to the number of carbon atoms which they contain. Although monosaccharides of all of the groups included in Table 29 have been identified, only the 5-carbon atom (pentose) and 6-carbon atom (hexose) monosaccharides are important in plants. Most of the sub-groups of monosaccharides can be further divided into aldoses and ketoses. Aldoses are monosaccharides containing an aldehydic group $\begin{matrix} H \\ | \\ (-C=O) \end{matrix}$ while ketoses contain a ketonic group $(=C=O)$.

The *oligosaccharides* or compound sugars can all be hydrolyzed into simple sugars. They may therefore be regarded as condensation products of the simple sugars. Disaccharides yield two molecules of monosaccharides upon hydrolysis; trisaccharides, three; and tetrasaccharides, four. All of the important compound sugars known to occur in plants are condensation products of hexose sugars. The hexose molecules formed upon hydrolysis of compound sugars may be all of one kind, or of more than one kind, depending upon the specific oligosaccharide.

The polysaccharides are condensation products of large numbers of monosaccharide molecules, or of molecules which are close derivatives of monosaccharide molecules. In most of the polysaccharides all of the condensing molecules are of the same kind, although there are some important exceptions to this statement.

General Properties of the Sugars.—The mono, di, tri, and tetrasaccharides are collectively called the sugars. All of these compounds possess the property of sweetness and all of them are white, more or less crystalline compounds which are soluble in water.

1. *Reducing and Nonreducing Sugars.*—All of the monosaccharides and some of the more complex sugars act as reducing agents. This action is made possible by the presence of an aldehydic or ketonic group in the sugar molecule. Those compound sugars in which the linking of the monosaccharides has occurred in such a manner that the aldehydic or ketonic groups have lost their usual reactivity are nonreducing. Sugars are commonly classified on this basis as *reducing sugars* or *nonreducing sugars*. The reducing action of sugars is most commonly determined by means of Fehling's or Benedict's solution, in which, upon heating, a reducing sugar converts cupric hydroxide into cuprous oxide. The latter compound separates from the solution in the form of a reddish precipitate. These solutions are used not only for the qualitative demonstration of reducing sugars but for their quantitative estimation, since the quantity of precipi-

tate formed, although not directly proportional, bears a definite relation to the amount of sugar taking part in the reaction.

2. *Optical Activity.*—Most of the soluble carbohydrates are, like many other organic compounds, optically active when in solution. The *optical activity* of a solution of carbohydrate refers to its property of rotating the plane of polarized light. The *specific rotary power* of a sugar is expressed in terms of the number of degrees of angular rotation of the plane of polarized sodium light caused by a solution made in the proportion of 1 g. of the sugar to 1 ml. of solution, observed through a depth of 10 cm. at a temperature of 20°C. Measurements of the rotary power of substances are made with an instrument known as a *polarimeter.* Compounds which rotate the plane of polarized light to the right (in a clockwise direction) are called *dextrorotatory;* those which rotate it to the left (in a counterclockwise direction) are called *levorotatory.*

3. *Isomerism.*—An important fact regarding the sugars is that many isomers may exist with the same molecular formula. There are two important types of these, ordinary chemical isomers and *stereoisomers.* The former result from differences in atomic groupings within the molecule. The difference between the isomers of this type may be seen by comparing the structural formulas for D-glucose and D-fructose, both of which have the same empirical formula ($C_6H_{12}O_6$) :

$$
\begin{array}{cc}
\text{CHO} & \text{CH}_2\text{OH} \\
| & | \\
\text{H—C—OH} & \text{C=O} \\
| & | \\
\text{HO—C—H} & \text{HO—C—H} \\
| & | \\
\text{H—C—OH} & \text{H—C—OH} \\
| & | \\
\text{H—C—OH} & \text{H—C—OH} \\
| & | \\
\text{CH}_2\text{OH} & \text{CH}_2\text{OH} \\
\text{D-Glucose} & \text{D-Fructose}
\end{array}
$$

Stereoisomers are molecules that have exactly the same atomic groupings but these groupings are arranged in different patterns around the asymmetric carbon atoms. An asymmetric carbon atom is one in which each of the four valences is satisfied with a different kind of atom or group. Such carbon atoms are indicated in bold face in the structural formulas for monosaccharides given in this chapter. D-Glucose and D-mannose, for example, are stereoisomers:

$$
\begin{array}{cc}
\text{H} & \text{H} \\
| & | \\
\text{C}=\text{O} & \text{C}=\text{O} \\
| & | \\
\text{H}-\text{C}-\text{OH} & \text{HO}-\text{C}-\text{H} \\
| & | \\
\text{HO}-\text{C}-\text{H} & \text{HO}-\text{C}-\text{H} \\
| & | \\
\text{H}-\text{C}-\text{OH} & \text{H}-\text{C}-\text{OH} \\
| & | \\
\text{H}-\text{C}-\text{OH} & \text{H}-\text{C}-\text{OH} \\
| & | \\
\text{H}-\text{C}-\text{OH} & \text{H}-\text{C}-\text{OH} \\
| & | \\
\text{H} & \text{H} \\
\text{D-Glucose} & \text{D-Mannose}
\end{array}
$$

Two exactly opposite stereoisomeric forms exist for each of the simple sugars, the arrangement for L-glucose and L-mannose being the mirror images of the above patterns. One of the stereoisomeric forms rotates the plane of polarized light to the right; the other rotates the plane to the left. It is impossible to know which form actually is associated with either rotation, and, therefore, the designation of the two molecular types as D and L forms does not represent their action on polarized light. A D molecule is one in which the asymmetric carbon atom farthest from the reducing group and adjacent to the terminal CH_2OH group has its OH group shown on the right. In the L form the OH group of the same carbon atom is shown on the left. When it is desired to show the direction of rotation, this is indicated by the use of a plus sign for rotation to the right and a minus sign for rotation to the left, thus:

D-glucose	or if desired	D (+) glucose
D-fructose	or if desired	D (−) fructose

4. *Ring Structure.*—Although it has long been customary to write the formulas of monosaccharides as straight carbon chains, some of the properties of such sugars cannot be explained satisfactorily by such a molecular structure. It has been necessary to assume that the monosaccharides actually possess a ring structure. In fact, molecules of glucose and other hexose sugars may exist in two different ring forms which are unlike in their stability and reactivity. In the more stable ring form (the pyranose ring) carbon atoms 1 and 5 are linked by an oxygen atom, while in the less stable ring form (the furanose ring) the oxygen atom is shared by carbon atoms 1 and 4. The ring formulas are now commonly written as closed hexagons or pentagons (Haworth, 1929), but they may also be expressed as straight carbon chains with an oxygen atom shared between appropriate carbon atoms:

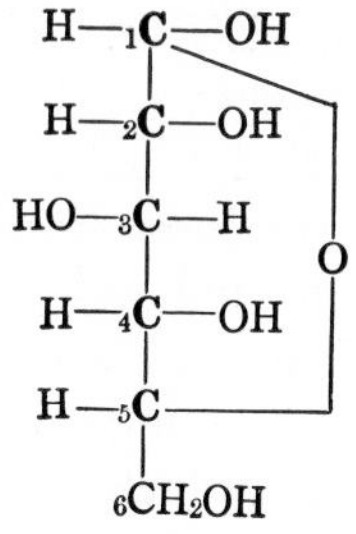

$$H-{}_1C-OH$$
$$H-{}_2C-OH$$
$$HO-{}_3C-H$$
$$H-{}_4C-OH$$
$$H-{}_5C$$
$$O$$
$${}_6CH_2OH$$

D glucose
(pyranose ring)

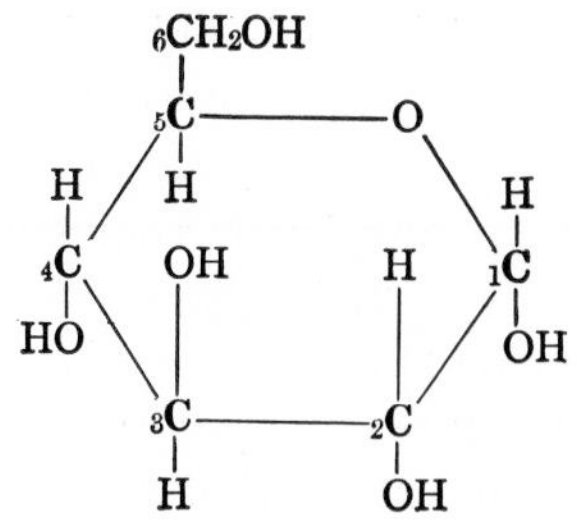

$${}_6CH_2OH$$
$${}_5C \quad O$$
$${}_4C \quad OH \quad H \quad {}_1C$$
$$HO \quad OH$$
$${}_3C \quad {}_2C$$
$$H \quad OH$$

D glucose
(pyranose ring)

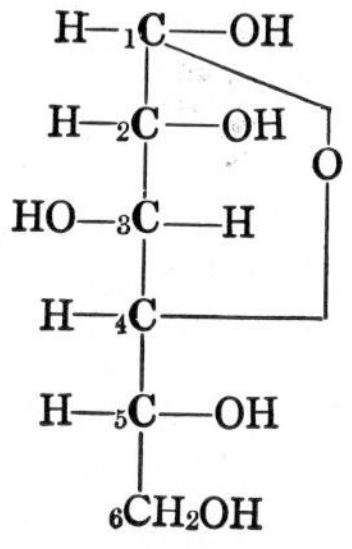

$$H-{}_1C-OH$$
$$H-{}_2C-OH$$
$$HO-{}_3C-H$$
$$H-{}_4C$$
$$H-{}_5C-OH$$
$$O$$
$${}_6CH_2OH$$

D glucose
(furanose ring)

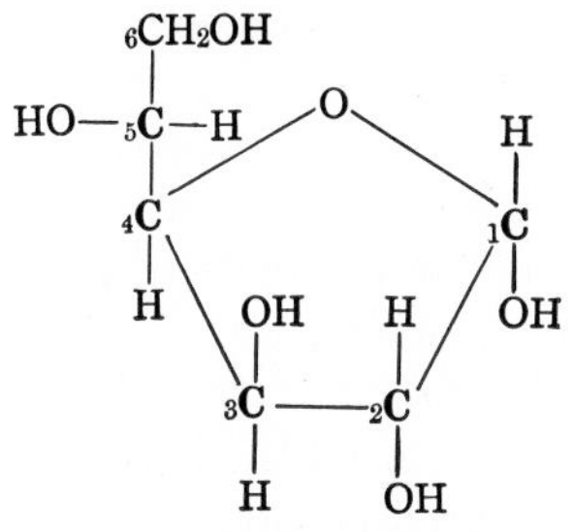

$${}_6CH_2OH$$
$$HO-{}_5C-H \quad O$$
$${}_4C \quad H$$
$$H \quad OH \quad H \quad {}_1C$$
$${}_3C \quad {}_2C \quad OH$$
$$H \quad OH$$

D glucose
(furanose ring)

Pentose sugars also have ring structures of both forms. Because of their greater reactivity the furanose forms commonly have a transitory existence, but because of their lability probably play an important role in metabolic processes.

Each of the hexoses exists in α and β forms, depending upon the position of attachment of the H and OH groups to the number 1 carbon atom, which is also asymmetric in the pyranose and furanose rings:

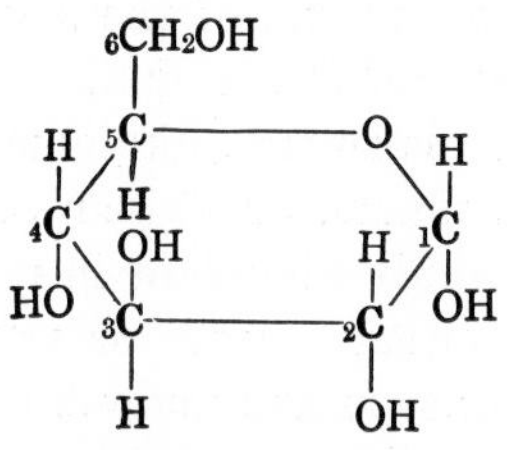

$${}_6CH_2OH$$
$$H \quad {}_5C \quad O \quad H$$
$${}_4C \quad H$$
$$OH \quad H \quad {}_1C$$
$$HO \quad {}_3C \quad {}_2C \quad OH$$
$$H \quad OH$$

α D-Glucose

$${}_6CH_2OH$$
$$H \quad {}_5C \quad O \quad OH$$
$${}_4C \quad H$$
$$OH \quad H \quad {}_1C$$
$$HO \quad {}_3C \quad {}_2C \quad H$$
$$H \quad OH$$

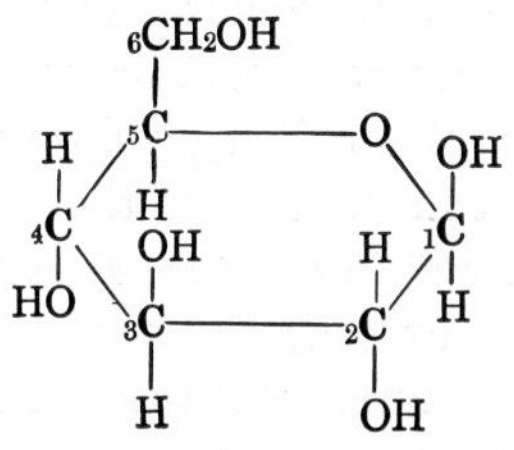

β D-Glucose

The Monosaccharides.—The *pentoses* are sugars with five carbon atoms ($C_5H_{10}O_5$). Pentoses occur in plants principally as their condensation products—the pentosans, as constituents of certain glycosides, and as a part of nucleic acid molecules (Chap. XXVI). L-Arabinose and D-xylose are the common pentose sugars obtained by the hydrolysis of the pentosans. The former is also one of the products formed in the hydrolysis of vegetable gums and pectic compounds. D-Arabinose has been obtained by hydrolysis of certain glycosides. D-Ribose and desoxy-D-ribose are constituents of the nucleic acids of the cytoplasm and nuclei respectively.

The pentose sugars are, therefore, important building blocks in the synthesis of certain more complex molecules, some of which are essential components of all living cells. The origin of the pentoses in plants is unknown, but it is highly probable that they are formed from the hexose sugars.

The *hexoses* are six carbon atom sugars represented by the molecular formula $C_6H_{12}O_6$. Sixteen stereoisomeric aldoses and eight stereoisomeric ketoses having this formula are known to be possible. Of all these, only two, D-glucose (an aldose) and D-fructose (a ketose), are commonly found in plants in the free state. D-Mannose and D-galactose, both aldoses, are hydrolytic products of a number of the more complex carbohydrates found in plants.

D-Glucose (also called dextrose, blood sugar, corn sugar, or grape sugar) is the most familiar of all the hexoses, and is of widespread occurrence in plants. It is apparently present in practically every living plant cell. D-Glucose rotates the plane of polarized light to the right. Transformation of glucose to fructose, as well as the reverse reaction, occurs readily in plant cells. Glucose is a substrate of respiration and is probably also a common translocation form of carbohydrate. Its condensation products include starch, cellulose, and glycogen. It is also a hydrolytic product of certain di-, tri-, and tetrasaccharides.

D-Mannose and D-galactose are both found in plants of the free state only in traces, and are evidently only transitory products in the metabolism of plants. Their condensation products are mannans and galactans respectively, both discussed later. Galactans are commonly associated with the pectic compounds and galactose is one of the sugars produced upon the hydrolysis of lactose, raffinose, stachyose, gums and mucilages.

D-Fructose (also called levulose, or fruit sugar), like glucose, is nearly always present in the cells of the higher plants. Fructose rotates the plane of polarized light to the left. It is especially abundant in many fruits in which it often exceeds the amount of either glucose or sucrose present. Fructose is a common substrate of respiration and undoubtedly is readily translocated from cell to cell in plants. Condensation of fructose molecules produces *inulin*, an important storage carbohydrate in some species of plants. Fructose is also one of the hydrolytic products of sucrose and of several of the tri- and tetrasaccharides.

The Disaccharides.—Sucrose, a nonreducing sugar, is the most abundant of all the disaccharides in the higher green plants. It is widely distributed throughout plant tissues and often accumulates to high concentrations in storage organs. The roots of sugar beets and the stalks of sugar cane, for example, may contain sucrose ("cane sugar") in sufficient quantities to make up 20 per cent of their fresh weight.

Upon hydrolysis sucrose yields equimolar quantities of α D-glucose and β D-fructose. Following is the structural formula of sucrose:

The left-hand portion of the molecule is derived from the pyranose ring form of glucose and the right-hand portion from the furanose ring of fructose.

Maltose is a reducing disaccharide which is widely distributed in plants but is seldom present in more than small amounts. It yields two molecules of D-glucose upon hydrolysis. Maltose is produced by the action of the amylase enzymes on starch (see later). It is, therefore, commonly found in germinating seeds of cereals and in other tissues in which starch is being digested by amylases.

Cellobiose is a reducing disaccharide which is produced from cellulose by the action of the enzyme cellulase. Upon hydrolysis it yields two mole-cules of glucose. Cellobiose differs from maltose in that it is formed by the condensation of two molecules of β D-glucose, while a molecule of maltose results from the condensation of two molecules of α D-glucose.

Trehalose is a nonreducing disaccharide found in fungi in which it con-stitutes an important food reserve.

Other disaccharides found in plants are listed in Table 29.

Tri- and Tetrasaccharides.—Trisaccharides are sugars with the molec-ular formula $C_{18}H_{32}O_{16}$. *Raffinose* is a nonreducing trisaccharide present in small quantities in many of the higher plants and in fungi. It is found in appreciable quantities in cotton seeds and sugar beets. Upon complete hydrolysis it yields one molecule each of D-galactose, D-glucose, and D-fructose. Partial hydrolysis may yield either fructose and melibiose, or galactose and sucrose, depending upon the enzyme used.

The trisaccharide *gentianose* has been found in the roots of the yellow gentian (*Gentiana lutea*). Upon partial hydrolysis it yields one molecule each of fructose and gentiobiose; upon complete hydrolysis one molecule of fructose and two of glucose. *Melezitose* is a very sweet trisaccharide which has been found in the exudates of certain trees, especially some conifers such as the European larch and Douglas fir. Upon complete hydrolysis this sugar yields two molecules of glucose and one of fructose.

The only known tetrasaccharide is stachyose ($C_{24}H_{42}O_{21}$) which has been isolated from the roots of the hedge nettle (*Stachys tubifera*). Upon complete hydrolysis this carbohydrate yields one molecule of glucose, one of fructose, and two of galactose.

The Polysaccharides.—The polysaccharides are complex carbohydrates of high molecular weight. They are condensation products of monosaccharides, or of close derivatives of monosaccharides. Large numbers of these simpler molecules are combined in the formation of one molecule of a polysaccharide. Some polysaccharides are built up solely out of the molecules of one kind of sugar. Starch and cellulose, for example, are both condensation products of D-glucose. Other polysaccharides are built up from two or even more different kinds of molecules of sugars or related compounds. This more complex type of structure is characteristic, for example, of the gums and mucilages. The polysaccharides are not sweet like the sugars and they are not soluble in water. Some, such as the pectic compounds, are extremely hydrophilic, readily forming colloidal sols and gels.

1. *The Pentosans.*—These compounds are the condensation products of pentose sugars. The best known pentosans are the *arabans* and *xylans*. The molecules of these compounds apparently consist of long chains of arabinose or xylose residues, similar in structure to cellulose molecules described later. Arabans and xylans apparently occur principally in the cell walls of plants. Arabans are often closely associated with pectic compounds in cell walls. In some species, such as the cacti, they are also important constituents of the mucilaginous materials present in the cells, and contribute largely to the hydrophilic properties of such substances. Arabans are one of the constituents of cherry, peach, and plum gum, while xylans are found very commonly in wood, straw, corncobs, and seed coats. Xylans may constitute as much as 25 per cent of the woody tissues of some trees.

2. *The Hexosans.*—The important polysaccharides which are synthesized in plants from D-glucose are cellulose, starch, and glycogen.

Cellulose is the principal constituent of the cell walls of all of the higher plants (Chap. IV). In terms of absolute amounts it is probably the most abundant organic compound present on the earth. Much of the cellulose as it occurs in the plant is in intimate mixture with, or encrusted by, other materials. Some fibers, however, such as those of the cotton plant, are practically pure cellulose.

Cellulose "molecules" are long, ribbon-like structures. These chain-like molecules are built up by the linear condensation of β D-glucose molecules Each cellulose molecule consists of a chain of at least 1000 and probably many more glucose residues linked together by oxygen bridges:

Chemically cellulose is relatively inert, being insoluble in water and all organic solvents. One of the few liquids which will dissolve it is an ammoniacal solution of copper hydroxide (Schweitzer's reagent). Concentrated sulfuric acid will gradually hydrolyze cellulose into glucose, while dilute sulfuric acid causes it to swell and converts it into "hydrocellulose." In sodium hydroxide solutions of about 15 per cent, cellulose swells, also producing a "hydrocellulose"; this effect is the basis of the process of mercerization. Stepwise hydrolysis of cellulose results first in the production of *cellobiose*, a disaccharide, each molecule of which is in turn hydrolyzed into two molecules of glucose.

Cellulose-digesting enzymes are present in many bacteria and molds and in some invertebrates, but not in the higher plants or animals. A number of species of bacteria and molds contain the enzyme *cellulase* which hydrolyzes cellulose to the disaccharide cellobiose. Virtually nothing is known of the chemical mechanism of cellulose synthesis in plants.

Starch is the most abundant hexosan, next to cellulose, occurring in plants. It is found throughout the vegetative tissues of most species of green plants and often accumulates in large quantities in storage organs. A temporary accumulation of starch occurs in the leaves of many species during photosynthesis.

In plants starch is always synthesized in chloroplasts or leucoplasts, usually in the form of small grains or granules. The grains synthesized in the chloroplasts are usually small and seem to be formed within the interior of the plastid. Most of the larger and more prominent starch grains built up in plant cells are synthesized by the leucoplasts. Each leucoplast apparently produces only a single starch grain. The starch grains vary greatly in size (from 1-150 μ in diameter) and number in different cells, but their shape is so nearly constant for a given species that the plant source of the starch in flour can often be determined by examining a small sample under the microscope (Fig. 105).

Commonly starch grains appear to be built up of a number of layers of lamellae which have been deposited about a central locus. The lamellae probably represent different degrees of compactness (Frey-Wyssling, 1948) of the starch molecules making up the grain. The innermost parts of each lamella apparently are denser than the outer portion, and it is

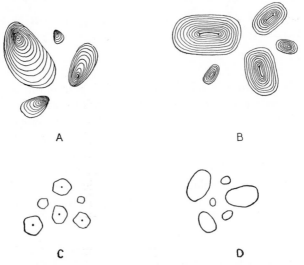

A   B

C   D

FIG. 105.   Starch grains: (A) from potato tuber, (B) from bean seed, (C) from corn (maize) grain, (D) from wheat grain.

this regular variation in density which causes the laminated appearance of the grain. Starch grains formed under continuous illumination lose all appearance of lamination (Badenhuizen, 1937).

Starch consists of two components, *amylose* and *amylopectin*, which differ in their physical properties. The former is more water soluble and less viscous in solution than the latter. Amylose gives an intense blue reaction with I_2KI solution; amylopectin a light blue-violet color.

The percentages of amylose and amylopectin differ widely in starch from different kinds of plants. Waxy starch, found in certain varieties of maize and other cereals, is composed wholly of amylopectin, while starch from some varieties of peas may be 60-70 per cent amylose. About 20-30 per cent of the starch of most species of plants is amylose.

Both components of starch are condensation products of α D-glucose.

Amylose consists solely of straight chains in which glucose molecules in the pyranose form are linked together between carbon atom 1 of one molecule and carbon atom 4 of the adjacent molecule, a molecule of water being split out. Each straight chain molecule of amylose is built up of 300-1000 glucose residues.

Amylopectin molecules are larger than those of amylose and have a multiple-branched rather than a straight chain structure. Straight chains are constructed as in amylose, but there also exist many side chains in which carbon atom 6 of certain glucose residues is linked with carbon atom 1 of other glucose residues, thus giving rise to a branched structure:

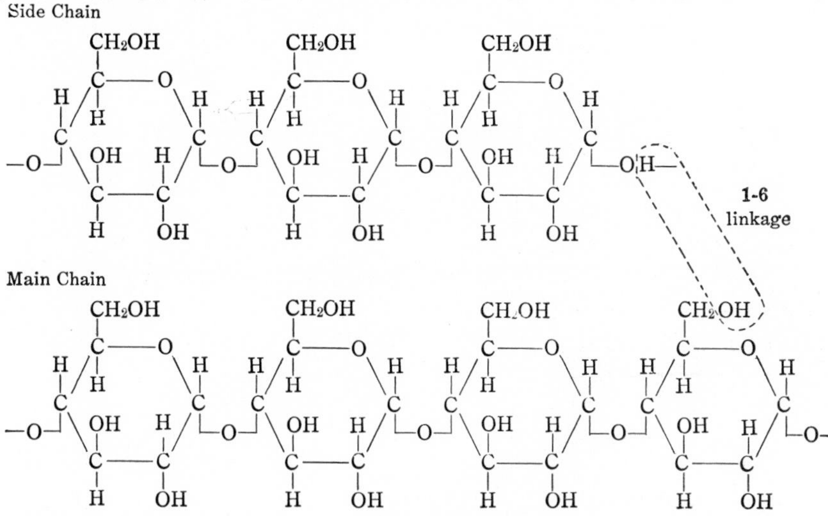

Side Chain

$$
\begin{array}{ccc}
CH_2OH & CH_2OH & CH_2OH \\
\end{array}
$$

1-6 linkage

Main Chain

$$
\begin{array}{cccc}
CH_2OH & CH_2OH & CH.OH & CH_2OH \\
\end{array}
$$

Each branch chain of an amylopectin molecule may in turn bear other side chains. A diagrammatic representation of the structure of an amylopectin molecule is shown in Fig. 106.

Glycogen (sometimes called animal starch) serves as a storage carbohydrate in animal tissue, being especially abundant in the muscles and liver. It is found in some species of fungi and bacteria, but rarely occurs in the higher plants. A compound very similar to glycogen has been isolated from Golden Bantam sweet corn. Glycogen consists entirely of branched molecules in which glucose residues are linked through 1-4 and 1-6 carbon atom bonds, much as in amylopectin. Glycogen, like starch (see later) is hydrolyzed to maltose by the combined action of α and β amylases.

The only well-known fructosan is *inulin* which is accumulated as a storage product in a number of plants, especially members of the composite family. Some species in which inulin is found are the dahlia, chickory, salsify, dandelion, Jerusalem artichoke, and goldenrod. Inulin is seldom if ever found in the aerial organs of plants, but may constitute as much as 15 per cent of the dry weight of some underground parts. Some species (Jerusalem artichoke) accumulate starch in the aerial parts, but inulin in the underground portions. Inulin is a white powder-like compound which forms colloidal sols in water. It is dispersed in the cell sap of those cells in which it accumulates and can be precipitated as crystals in the cells by immersing them in alcohol. Inulin is hydrolyzed

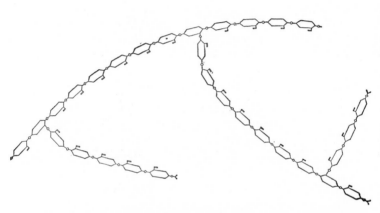

Fig. 106.   Diagrams showing arrangement of α D-glucose residues in an amylose molecule (above) and in an amylopectin molecule (below).

in plants to D-fructose by the enzyme *inulase*. Other plant fructosans are discussed by Archbold (1940).

Mannans are found commonly in the wood of coniferous trees and as cell-wall constituents of the endosperms of some kinds of seeds.

Galactans are commonly associated with the pectin compounds in cell walls.

Hemicellulose is a widely used, but ill-defined term employed to refer to certain polysaccharides found in the cell walls of plants. This blanket designation includes xylan, mannans, and galactans, already mentioned, together with a number of similar, but less common, polysaccharides. Hydrolytic products of hemicelluloses include D-glucose, D-glucuronic acid, D-xylose, D-galactose, D-galacturonic acid, L-arabinose, and D-mannose. The hemicelluloses present in many seeds are used as food by the young seedlings during germination. Compounds of this type, although cell-wall constituents, may therefore serve as reserve foods. The hemicellu-loses found in the cell walls of the woody tissues of some trees, as for example the apple tree, also serve as reserve food which is digested and utilized when growth of the stems is resumed in the spring.

3. *Pectic Compounds.*—Three principal types of pectic compounds are recognized as occurring in plants: pectic acid, pectin, and protopectin. All of these compounds are important constituents of the cell walls of plants Pectic acid is the simplest of these three compounds and most of our knowledge of the chemical composition of the pectic compounds has been derived from studies of pectic acid. This compound appears to be a long straight chain molecule built up by the condensation of a large number (about one hundred) of α galacturonic acid molecules. The structure of a galacturonic acid molecule is the same as that of a galactose molecule except that carbon 6 is in a carboxyl (—COOH) group instead of in a —CH₂OH group as in the latter compound. The arrangement of the galac-turonic acid residues in a molecule of pectic acid is indicated in the fol-lowing diagram:

Pectin differs from pectic acid in that many of the carboxyl groups of the pectic acid have been esterified with methyl groups and that the number of galacturonic residues per chain is greater. Pectin forms viscous colloidal sols in water which "set" into firm gels under proper conditions. Among these are the presence of a dehydrating agent such as a high concentration (65-70 per cent) of sugar. Household jellies owe their "gelling" property to the pectin derived from the fruits. Neither proto-pectin nor pectic acid forms gels, and for this reason over-ripe fruits (in which much of the pectin has been converted into pectic acid) are less satisfactory for making jellies than green or immature fruits. Because of its usefulness in making fruit jellies, pectin is extracted from fruits on a commercial scale. As much as 35 per cent of the dry weight of lemon rind and 10-15 per cent of the dry weight of crushed apple fruits may be pectin. Protopectin differs from pectin in having a still greater length of the molecular chain. Protopectin occurs in the middle lamella where it serves to bind the cell walls of the tissue firmly together. It also makes up a portion of the primary cell wall where it seems intimately associated with cellulose and often with lignin. Protopectin is insoluble in water. During the ripening of fruits, protopectin is converted into "soluble" pectin and the cells of the tissue are no longer held firmly together. It is this conversion of protopectin into pectin that is responsible for the softening of many fruits during ripening.

The pectic compounds, because of the presence of carboxyl groups, form salts and the calcium salt is an important constituent of the middle lamella of plant cell walls.

Several enzymes are known which catalyze reactions in which pectic compounds are broken down into simpler ones. Protopectinase converts protopectin into pectin. Pectase de-esterifies pectin, resulting in the formation of pectic acid and methyl alcohol. Pectinase hydrolyzes pectic acid into galacturonic acid. This enzyme may also act on some pectins and on pectates. All of these enzymes are found in the higher plants and in many bacteria and fungi.

Practically nothing is known of the synthetic processes whereby the pectic compounds are built up in plants.

4. *Gums and Mucilages.*—These are complex kinds of carbohydrates which resemble in some respects the pectic compounds and so-called hemicelluloses. The gums and mucilages cannot be sharply differentiated from each other.

The gums appear to have a branched chain molecular structure which has been built up by condensation of various pentoses, hexoses, and acids derived from such sugars. Hydrolytic products of the gums include L-rhamnose (a methyl pentosan-hexosan), L-fuctose (a methyl pentose), L-arabinose, D-mannose, D-galactose, D-galacturonic acid, and D-glucuronic acid.

Gum arabic (gum acacia), an exudate from an African species of acacia, is a well-known example of a gum. This compound is actually a salt in which calcium, magnesium, and potassium have replaced some of the hydrogens on the carboxyl groups. Other gums include gum tragacanth from Asiatic species of *Astragalus,* and the familiar gums which exude from the stems of cherry, plum, and peach trees.

The molecular structure of the mucilages appears, in general, to be similar to that of the gums. Examples of this kind of polysaccharide include the mucilage from the bark of the slippery elm (*Ulmus fulva*), the mucilage which coats the surface of flax seeds, and certain polysaccharides which accumulate in the seeds of some legumes such as the carob, locust, and honey locust.

5. *Amino-hexosans.*—The only well-known carbohydrate of this group

is *chitin* which occurs in some fungi and in many invertebrates, especially insects. The structure of chitin is analogous to that of cellulose except that the structural unit is not glucose, but a molecule in which the —OH group of carbon 2 has been replaced by an acetylamino (—NH—CO—CH₃) group.

Carbohydrate Transformations in Plants.—There are many lines of evidence which show that transformations of one kind of carbohydrate molecule to other kinds are continually and rapidly in progress in physiologically active cells. Utilization of carbohydrates in the synthesis of fats, proteins, and other compounds is also constantly going on in such cells, but consideration of such transformations will be deferred to later chapters. Experiments in which detached leaves have been artificially supplied with various kinds of sugars show that one kind of sugar can be converted into another in plant cells. Sucrose, for example, is synthesized in barley leaves (McCready and Hassid, 1941) and sorghum and cotton leaves (Leonard, 1939) which are supplied artificially with glucose, fructose, or certain other monosaccharides.

Experiments with albino plants also furnish evidence of the ready conversion of one kind of carbohydrate to others. Such chlorophyll-lacking plants usually starve to death within a few weeks after germination as soon as the foods in the seed have been used up. Albino maize plants, however, have developed to maturity if the leaves are artificially supplied with sucrose (Spoehr, 1942). The cells of the albino maize plant are able to use sucrose as the starting point in the synthesis of all of the many organic compounds in the plant. Cellulose, starch, and hexose sugars were among the carbohydrates formed from the sucrose artificially supplied to the leaves.

Some of the more important reactions in which carbohydrates are known to participate in living cells will now be considered. Many of these reactions involve the conversion of one kind of carbohydrate into another.

Formation of Phosphate Esters.—One of the commonest and metabolically most fundamental of the reactions of the sugars is the formation of phosphate esters. Such esters serve as the substrate of respiration (Chap. XXII), and are involved in various reactions in which one kind of carbohydrate is converted into another.

A primary hexose ester is glucose-6-phosphate, a compound in which a phosphate group is attached to carbon atom 6 of glucose. This compound is synthesized by the transfer of phosphate groups from adenosine triphosphate (ATP) to glucose, resulting in the formation of glucose-6-phosphate and adenosine diphosphate (ADP). The role of the adenosine phosphates is discussed in greater detail in Chap. XXII. This reaction is essentially irreversible and is catalyzed in animal tissues and in yeasts by the enzyme *hexokinase*. This enzyme has not yet been isolated from the cells of higher plants but there is little doubt that it, or some similar enzyme, is present. Glucose-6-phosphate can be broken down into glucose and inorganic phosphate by a *phosphatase* enzyme. This reaction is irreversible.

Migration of the phosphate group so that it is attached to carbon atom 1 instead of carbon atom 6 of glucose results in the formation of glucose-1-phosphate. This reaction, which is reversible, is catalyzed by the enzyme *phosphoglucomutase*, which occurs in both plants and animals.

Under the influence of the enzyme *phosphohexose isomerase* glucose-6-phosphate is converted into its isomer fructose-6-phosphate. This reaction is reversible, and the enzyme involved has been found in the higher plants. This is the only reaction known to occur in plants whereby glucose and fructose are interconverted. Fructose-6-phosphate can also be formed from fructose and ATP in a manner analogous to that by which glucose-6-phosphate is formed. Irreversible breakdown of fructose-6-phosphate into fructose and phosphate can be accomplished by a phosphatase enzyme.

Still another common transformation in living cells is the conversion of fructose-6-phosphate into fructose-1, 6-diphosphate. Fructose-6-phosphate reacts with ATP in such a way that phosphate groups are transferred from the latter compound to the former. The end products of the reaction are fructose-1, 6-diphosphate and ADP. This reaction is catalyzed by the enzyme *phosphohexokinase* and does not appear to be reversible. Action of a phosphatase on this compound converts it back to fructose-6-phosphate with the release of inorganic phosphate.

Synthesis and Hydrolysis of Sucrose.—As previously discussed, sucrose synthesis occurs during or immediately following photosynthesis in many chlorophyllous cells. Synthesis of sucrose can, however, occur entirely independently of photosynthesis. This sugar is readily synthesized, for example, in detached leaf blades infiltrated with glucose or fructose and kept in the dark. Sucrose synthesis does not occur in the absence of oxygen (McCready and Hassid, 1941). In the bacterium *Pseudomonas saccharophila* it has been shown by Hassid *et al.* (1944) that sucrose synthesis is accomplished according to the following reaction:

$$\text{Glucose-1-phosphate} + \text{Fructose} \rightleftharpoons \text{Sucrose} + \text{Phosphate}$$

This reversible reaction is catalyzed by *sucrose phosphorylase*. The exact mechanism of sucrose synthesis in the cells of higher plants is not known, but it is probable that it occurs by this reaction or one similar to it.

Hydrolysis of sucrose into glucose and fructose is accomplished by the enzyme *sucrase,* but this reaction is apparently not reversible.

Synthesis, Phosphorolysis, and Hydrolysis of Starch.—Certain general aspects of the process of starch synthesis discussed in Chap. XVIII will now be supplemented by a more detailed consideration of its mechanism. As first clearly shown by Hanes (1940a, 1940b), starch is synthesized in plant cells from glucose-1-phosphate under the influence of the enzyme *α-glucosan phosphorylase.* The nature of the reaction between two of the reacting molecules is indicated in the following diagram:

Phosphoric acid is formed by the reaction between an OH group of one molecule and the H_2PO_3 group of another, as indicated. The two glucose residues, one of them still phosphorylated, are then linked together by an oxygen bridge. The glucose-1-phosphate molecules which participate in this reaction are very probably derived from molecules of glucose-6-phosphate. Hundreds of glucose-1-phosphate molecules must be combined in this manner in the synthesis of a single starch (amylose) molecule. The plastids in which starch grains are formed have been shown to be centers of phosphorylase activity (Yin and Sun, 1949). In actively respiring cells the phosphate released in this reaction is quickly utilized in the resynthesis of adenosine triphosphate.

The same phosphorylase which catalyzes the synthesis of starch also catalyzes the reverse reaction whereby starch is converted into glucose-1-phosphate. The cleavage of the starch molecule is accomplished by linking inorganic phosphate groups to the bonds between the glucose residues of the molecular chain. No water enters into this reaction, the process being a *phosphorolysis* rather than a hydrolysis. The energy change involved in this reversible reaction is very small.

Starch is *hydrolyzed* into dextrins and maltose by amylases. The two principal enzymes of this type are α-amylase and β-amylase. The former hydrolyzes starch to dextrins; the latter hydrolyzes the amylose fraction of starch to maltose and the amylopectin fraction partly to maltose and partly to dextrins. These reactions are not reversible. Other enzymes

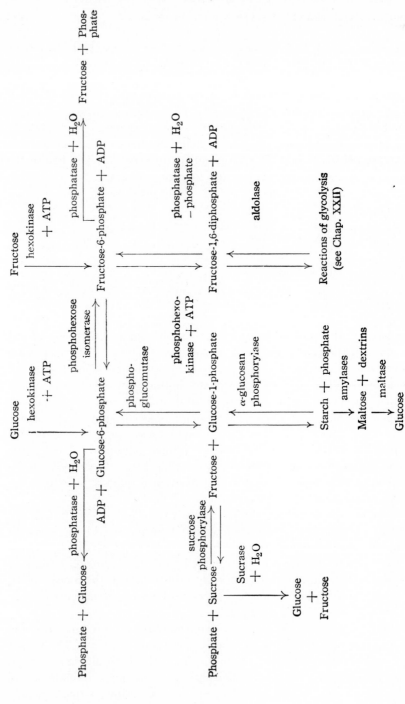

Fig. 107. Some important carbohydrate transformations occurring in plants.

apparently convert dextrins into maltose, and this sugar is hydrolyzed to glucose by the enzyme maltase.

The carbohydrate transformations discussed in this section are indicated schematically in Fig. 107.

Some Factors Influencing Carbohydrate Transformations in Plants.— The rate and direction of various carbohydrate transformations occurring in plants are known to be influenced by a number of factors. Some of the better known of these effects will now be considered.

1. *Temperature.*—Low temperatures in general favor the starch-to-sugar transformation in plant cells. This fact is illustrated by the seasonal behavior of the carbohydrates in the leaves of evergreen species and in woody stems (Winkler and Williams, 1945; and others) in regions where low winter temperatures prevail. During the colder months of the year

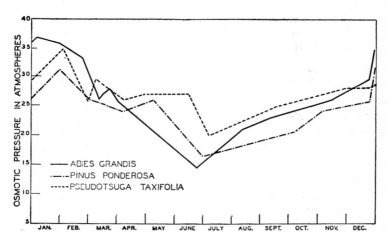

Fig. 108.   Seasonal variations in the osmotic pressure of the leaves of evergreens. Data of Gail (1926).

soluble carbohydrates accumulate in the cells of such tissues at the expense of starch, while during the warmer months the reverse situation prevails. Correlated with these seasonal shifts in the starch $\rightleftarrows$ soluble carbohydrate equilibrium are seasonal variations in the osmotic pressure of the cell sap. Midwinter osmotic pressure of the cell sap of such tissues is often as much as twice as high as midsummer values (Fig. 108).

Another interesting example of a shift in the starch-sugar equilibrium with temperature occurs in potato tubers (Hopkins, 1924). If stored at too low a temperature a gradual accumulation of sugars (principally sucrose) will occur in the tubers at the expense of the starch present. This accounts for the sweet taste which is sometimes found in potatoes purchased on the market. Contrary to popular opinion this sweetening is not necessarily a result of freezing of the tubers, since it has been found that temperature of the inception of sugar accumulation is about 5° or 6°C. (41°-43°F.). Storage of potatoes at temperatures in this range just above the freezing point will therefore induce sugar formation in the tubers.

Starch-to-sugar transformations in the potato tuber are activated principally by a phosphorylase (Arreguin-Lozano and Bonner, 1949). At low temperature glucose-1-phosphate accumulates in the tubers in detectable quantities, but it is absent at higher temperatures. Glucose-6-phosphate and fructose-6-phosphate are both present in the tubers over a wide range of temperatures, but the proportion of the latter to the former is much greater at temperatures approaching zero than at higher temperatures.

Apparently it is only in a zone of intermediate temperatures that starch formation at the expense of sugars is favored in potato tubers, as relatively high temperatures (35°-45°C.) also appear to favor hydrolysis of starch to sugar. It is possible, however, that this shift in equilibrium toward sugars at the higher temperatures is a result of the reduction in water content which may be induced by such temperatures (Wolff, 1926).

Similar effects of temperature on carbohydrate equilibria are shown by other species. In sweet potato roots sucrose accumulates rapidly at the expense of starch at temperatures below a critical range of 13°-16°C., but above this range most of the stored carbohydrates remain in the form of starch (Hopkins and Phillips, 1937). In ripening banana fruits hydrolysis of starch occurs rapidly at temperatures between 21° and 26°C. but there is practically no starch hydrolysis at 10°C. It is evident that the critical temperature ranges for hydrolysis and synthesis of starch vary greatly according to species.

2. _Water Content._—In wilting leaves much of the starch present is converted into sugars (Molisch, 1921; Ahrns, 1924; Spoehr and Milner, 1939). A relatively high water content apparently favors "starchiness" in the leaf tissues of many species, while a severe reduction in water content induces a conversion of starch into sugar. Sucrose, as well as simple sugars, accumulates during wilting. That many species of plants do accumulate sugars rather than starch under drought conditions has already been pointed out in Chap. XV. In certain succulent plants, such as cacti, desiccation favors the accumulation of polysaccharides, rather than soluble sugars (Spoehr, 1919), so evidently no single general principle regarding the influence of the water content of the cells upon carbohydrate equilibria within them can be formulated.

3. _H-ion Concentration._—The action of enzymes is very sensitive to the H-ion concentration of the medium wherein they operate (Chap.

XVI). Since most of the carbohydrate transformations occurring in plants are catalyzed by enzymes, the pH of the medium in which these reactions occur may have an important effect upon the rate of these transformations. Apparently the pH of the medium may influence not only the rate of an enzymatic reaction but may also influence its direction. The reversible carbohydrate transformations occurring in the guard cells of the stomates are a well-known example of this effect.

4. _Concentration of Sugars._—Theoretically, a high concentration of sugars in a cell would favor starch synthesis, and _vice versa._ The daytime accumulation of starch in green leaves which are photosynthesizing rapidly apparently results from the maintenance of a relatively high concentration of sugars in the cell sap, since under conditions unfavorable for rapid photosynthesis the accumulation of starch is greatly reduced. During the hours of darkness, when a high sugar concentration of the cells is no longer maintained by photosynthesis, the accumulated starch is rapidly reduced in amount by transformation to sugars, in which form it is translocated out of the leaf.

The Glycosides.—These are compounds formed by a reaction between a sugar (most commonly glucose) and one or more compounds which are non-sugars. All glycosides may exist in two forms, α or β, but all of those known to occur in plants are of the β type. Although of widespread occurrence in plants the glycosides are never present in large quantities. They may be found in almost any part of the plant. In a pure state they are mostly levorotatory, crystalline, colorless, bitter, and soluble in either water or alcohol. All β-glycosides can be hydrolyzed by the enzyme _emulsin_ or by dilute mineral acids. A large number of different glycosides have been isolated from plant tissues. Their role in the metabolism of plants, if any, is obscure although it is possible that they may serve in a minor way as storage foods.

Several representative glycosides will be discussed briefly in order to indicate more clearly the general nature of these compounds.

Salicin is found in the bark and leaves of the willow tree. Upon hydrolysis with emulsin it yields glucose and the alcohol _saligenol_ according to the following equation:

$$\underset{\text{Salicin}}{C_{13}H_{18}O_7} + H_2O \xrightarrow{\text{Emulsin}} C_6H_4 \underset{\text{Saligenol}}{\overset{\displaystyle CH_2OH}{\underset{\displaystyle OH}{<}}} + \underset{\text{Glucose}}{C_6H_{12}O_6}$$

Amygdalin occurs in the seeds of almonds, apples, peaches, and plums. Upon hydrolysis with emulsin it produces glucose, hydrocyanic acid, and benzaldehyde:

$$C_{20}H_{27}NO_{11} \quad + \quad 2\,H_2O \xrightarrow{\text{Emulsin}} 2\,C_6H_{12}O_6 \quad + \quad HCN \quad + \quad C_6H_5CHO$$

Amygdalin   Glucose   Hydrocyanic   Benzaldehyde
                                                 acid

Similar cyanogenetic glycosides occur in other plant materials such as the leaves of cherries and peaches and in Sudan grass and other sorghums. Under certain conditions domestic animals may be poisoned from eating plant materials containing such glycosides. Such poisoning results from release of hydrocyanic acid upon hydrolysis of the glycoside.

Sinigrin is called the mustard oil glycoside. It is found in the black mustard (*Brassica nigra*) and is hydrolyzed as follows:

$$C_{10}H_{16}O_9NS_2K \quad + \quad H_2O \xrightarrow{\text{Emulsin}} C_3H_5CNS \quad + \quad C_6H_{12}O_6 \quad + \quad KHSO_4$$

Sinigrin   Allyl isothio-   Glucose   Potassium
                               cyanate ("Mustard   hydrogen
                                    oil")   sulfate

The Anthocyanins.—Most of the red, blue, and purple pigments of plants belong to the group known as the *anthocyanins*. These compounds are glycosides which have been formed by a reaction between a sugar and one of a group of complex, cyclic compounds known as the *anthocyanidins*. Known sugar components of the anthocyanins are glucose, galactose, rhamnose, and gentiobiose.

A number of chemically different anthocyanins have been isolated from seed plants in which they are of widespread occurrence. They are also present in some species of ferns and mosses, but no anthocyanins are known to occur in the algae or fungi. The anthocyanins are water-soluble and are usually dissolved in the cell sap, the cytoplasmic membranes being impermeable to them. Less commonly these pigments are found in plant cells in the form of crystals or amorphous solid bodies. Red pigmentation caused by anthocyanins is of frequent occurrence in flowers, fruits, bud scales, developing leaves, and less commonly, in stems, mature leaves (red cabbage, copper beech, red coleus, etc.) and other plant parts. The reds and purplish reds of autumn foliage also result from the presence of anthocyanins. Blue and purple pigmentation caused by anthocyanins is largely restricted to flowers and fruits.

Anthocyanin pigmentation, especially of flowers, is a very complex phenomenon. Factors affecting the color of plant tissues resulting from anthocyanins include the concentration of the pigment present, the proportions of the different pigments when two or more are present in the cells, the modifying effects on color of the presence of other substances such as tannins and anthoxanthins (see later), the physical state of the anthocyanins (whether in solution or adsorbed), and the pH of the cell sap (Blank, 1947). Practically all anthocyanins are red in acid solution, and many of them change in color through violet to blue as the pH of the medium increases. Because of the modifying effect of other factors listed above, however, this relation often does not show up in a clear-cut fashion.

Although anthocyanin pigments have been studied extensively in the laboratory from the chemical standpoint, very little is known of the mode of their formation in plants. The genetic capacity for anthocyanin synthesis differs considerably from one kind of plant to another. Extensive investigations have been made of the inheritance of anthocyanin pigmentation, particularly in relation to the coloration of flowers (Scott-Moncrieff, 1939; Lawrence and Price, 1940). Synthesis of anthocyanins will not occur in a plant, however, even if the necessary genes are present, unless environmental conditions are also favorable. The formation of anthocyanins seems to be commonly associated with accumulation of sugars in plant tissues. Any environmental factor such as high light intensity, low temperature, drought, or low nitrogen supply, which favors an increase in the sugar content of a given plant tissue, often favors synthesis of anthocyanin in that tissue. On the other hand, environmental factors which check the formation or accumulation of sugars often have a similar effect on anthocyanin synthesis.

Light influences anthocyanin synthesis directly in some plant tissues. Autumnal red coloration, for example, usually develops its full intensity only in leaves which are directly exposed to light. Arthur (1932, 1936) showed that all visible wave lengths up to about 600 mμ. are effective in inducing anthocyanin synthesis in apple fruits picked green in the late summer, although the shorter wave lengths in this range are more effective than the longer ones. The 290-313 mμ. range in the ultraviolet is more effective than any of the visible wave lengths. In some species anthocyanins are synthesized in the absence of light. This is true, for example, in etiolated seedlings or red cabbage and in the roots of a number of species, of which the beet is the most familiar.

The Anthoxanthins.—Exposure of the petals of almost any white flower to ammonia vapor will cause them to turn yellow. This is because of the presence in such tissues of what may be regarded as a colorless form of one of the *anthoxanthins*. These compounds are chemically quite similar to the anthocyanins and usually occur in plants in the form of glycosides. Most of the anthoxanthins are colorless or nearly so as they occur in the plant but upon extraction and treatment in various ways their typical yellow or orange color develops. Like the anthocyanins they are water-soluble, and are usually found in the cell sap. In some plant tissues, the anthoxanthins present are yellow in color. The yellow pigment in the inner bark of the black oak (*Quercus velutina*) is an anthoxanthin called *quercitrin.* Similar pigments occur in the wood of various other species (osage orange, sumac, etc.), and in certain fruits (oranges). Some flowers, as for example yellow snapdragons, owe their yellow color to anthoxanthins. The color of most yellow flowers results, however, from the plastid pigments carotene and the xanthophylls.

Autumnal Leaf Coloration.—The most spectacular display of pigmentation in the plants of temperate regions is the annual autumnal coloration of leaves, especially of woody species. The "turning" of leaves in the autumn is not a result, as is commonly believed, of the effects of frost. In fact, early frosts will greatly reduce the abundance and brilliance of the autumn leaf colors by killing or severely injuring the leaves before the pigments reach their maximum development. The sequence of events leading to the coloration of leaves in the autumn seems to be about as follows: In late summer or early autumn chlorophyll synthesis in the leaves ceases, while the destruction of the chlorophyll already present apparently proceeds at an accelerated rate. As the chlorophyll disappears the residual yellow plastid pigments—carotene and xanthophylls—become apparent. The yellow color of the leaves of many species at this season, as for example, the tulip polar, sycamore, and birch, is a result of the disappearance of the chlorophyll which has masked the presence of the yellow pigments during the summer season. The golden yellow effect produced in some leaves, such as those of beeches, results from the presence in the cells of a brownish pigment, probably a tannin, in addition to the yellow pigment.

The more prominent colors in most autumn landscapes, however, are the various shades of red and purplish red which develop in the leaves of such species as the red maple, many oaks, sumac, dogwood and black gum. These result from the synthesis of anthocyanins in the leaf cells of such species. Autumnal development of anthocyanins is favored by periods of bright, clear, dry weather, during which cool, but not freezing temperatures, prevail.

Tannins.—These are a rather heterogeneous group of complex compounds of widespread occurrence in plants. Very little is known of their physiological role in plant tissues, but they are of importance commercially because of their property of forming an insoluble colloidal compound (leather) with the hides of animals. Some tannins cannot be hydrolyzed by acids or by any known enzyme, others may be hydrolyzed and yield complex acids, a sugar, commonly D-glucose, and sometimes other substances. The proportion of sugar found in the hydrolytic products of the tannins is relatively small. While the tannins may be regarded as remotely related to the glycosides, their properties are distinctive as compared with the glycoside type of compound, and they must be considered as a separate class of substances.

Tannins vary greatly in amount from one species to another. They are sometimes present in the cell sap but are of more frequent occurrence in the cell walls, often accumulating in very considerable amounts in dead tissues. Tannins are found in the leaves of many species such as tea (15 per cent of the dry weight) oaks, and many conifers. The woody tissues of many species contain tannins. The bark of oaks, chestnut, hemlock, sumac, and other species is very rich in tannins. In some species of oak they may compose as much as 40 per cent of the dry weight of the bark. Unripe fruits of some species (persimmon, plum, etc.) contain relatively large quantities of tannins.

SUGGESTED FOR COLLATERAL READING

Bonner, J. *Plant Biochemistry*. Academic Press, Inc. New York. 1950.

Gortner, R. A. *Outlines of Biochemistry*. 3rd Ed. Edited by R. A. Gortner, Jr., and W. A. Gortner. John Wiley and Sons, Inc. New York. 1949.

Howes, F. W. *Vegetable Gums and Resins*. Chronica Botanica Co. Waltham, Mass. 1949.

SELECTED BIBLIOGRAPHY

Ahrns, W. Weitere Untersuchungen über die Abhängigkeit des gegenseitigen Mengenverhältnisses der Kohlenhydrate in Laubblatt vom Wassergehalt. *Bot. Archiv.* **5**: 234-259. 1924.

Archbold, H. K. Fructosans in the monocotyledons. A review. *New Phytol.* **39**: 185-219. 1940.

Arreguin-Lozano, R., and J. Bonner. Experiments on sucrose formation by potato tubers as influenced by temperature. *Plant Physiol.* **24**: 720-738. 1949.

Arthur, J. M. Red pigment production in apples by means of artificial light sources. *Contr. Boyce Thompson Inst.* **4**: 1-18. 1932.

Arthur, J. M. Radiation and anthocyanin pigments. In *Biological Effects of Radiation*. II. B. M. Duggar, Editor. 841-852. McGraw-Hill Book Co., Inc. 1936.

Badenhuizen, N. P. Die Struktur des Stärkekorns. *Protoplasma* **28**: 293-326. 1937.

Barr, C. G. Polysaccharides of the vegetative tissues of maize. *Plant Physiol.* **14**: 737-753. 1939.

Bernstein, L. Amylases and carbohydrates in developing maize endosperm. *Amer. Jour. Bot.* **30**: 517-526. 1943.

Blank, F. The anthocyanin pigments of plants. *Bot. Rev.* **13**: 241-317. 1947.

Bonner, J. The chemistry and physiology of the pectins. *Bot. Rev.* **2**: 475-497. 1936. **12**: 535-537. 1946.

Frey-Wyssling, A. *Submicroscopic Morphology of Protoplasm and Its Derivatives*. Translated by J. J. Hermans and M. Hollander. Elsevier Publishing Co. 1948.

Gail, F. W. Osmotic pressure of cell sap and its possible relation to winter killing and leaf fall. *Bot. Gaz.* **81:** 434-445. 1926.

Hanes, C. S. The breakdown and synthesis of starch by an enzyme system from pea seeds. *Proc. Roy. Soc. (London)* **B 128:** 421-450. 1940a.

Hanes, C. S. The reversible formation of starch from glucose-1-phosphate catalyzed by potato phosphorylase. *Proc. Roy. Soc. (London)* **B 129:** 174-208. 1940b.

Hassid, W. Z., and E. W. Putnam. Transformation of sugars in plants. *Ann. Rev. Plant Physiol.* **1:** 109-124. 1950.

Hassid, W. Z., M. Doudoroff, and H. A. Barker. Enzymatically synthesized crystalline sucrose. *Jour. Amer. Chem. Soc.* **66:** 1416-1419. 1944.

Haworth, W. N. *The Constitution of Sugars.* Longmans, Green and Co. London. 1929.

Hehre, E. J. Enzymic synthesis of polysaccharides. A biological type of polymerization. *Advances in Enzymol.* **11:** 297-337. 1951.

Hopkins, E. F. Relation of low temperatures to respiration and carbohydrate changes in potato tubers. *Bot. Gaz.* **78:** 311-325. 1924.

Hopkins, E. F., and J. K. Phillips. Temperatures and starch-sugar change in sweet potatoes. *Science* **86:** 523-525. 1937.

Lawrence, W. J. C., and J. R. Price. The genetics and chemistry of flower colour variation. *Biol. Rev. Cambridge Phil. Soc.* **15:** 35-58. 1940.

Leonard, O. A. Carbohydrate transformations in leaf blades with special reference to sucrose synthesis. *Amer. Jour. Bot.* **26:** 475-484. 1939.

McCready, R. M., and W. Z. Hassid. Transformation of sugars in excised barley shoots. *Plant Physiol.* **16:** 599-610. 1941.

Molisch, H. Über den Einfluss der Transpiration auf das Verschwinden der Stärke in den Blättern. *Ber. Deutsch. Bot. Ges.* **39:** 339-344. 1921.

Scott-Moncrieff, Rose. The genetics and chemistry of flower colour variation. *Ergeb. Enzymforsuch.* **8:** 277-306. 1939.

Spoehr, H. A. The carbohydrate economy of cacti. *Carnegie Inst. Wash. Publ. No. 287.* 1919.

Spoehr, H. A. The culture of albino maize. *Plant Physiol.* **17:** 397-410. 1942.

Spoehr, H. A., and H. W. Milner. Starch dissolution and amylotic activity of leaves. *Proc. Amer. Phil. Soc.* **81:** 37-78. 1939.

Winkler, A. J., and W. O. Williams. Starch and sugars of *Vitis vinifera. Plant Physiol.* **20:** 412-432. 1945.

Wolff, C. J. de Die Saccharosebildung in Kartoffeln während des Trocknens. *Biochem. Zeitschr.* **176:** 225-245. 1926.

Yin, H. C., and C. N. Sun. Localization of phosphorylase and of starch formation in seeds. *Plant Physiol.* **24:** 103-110. 1949.

DISCUSSION QUESTIONS

1. Why does sweet corn lose its sweetness soon after being picked?

2. Why should bananas not be kept in a refrigerator?

3. Wild cherry leaves are much more poisonous to cattle after they have wilted than when they are fresh. Explain.

4. What, in general, will be the effect of girdling a stem through the phloem on the time of appearance and the intensity of red color in leaves of species in which anthocyanins are synthesized?

5. Heavy fertilization of red coleus plants with nitrogenous fertilizer greatly decreases the red color of the leaves. What is a probable explanation?

6. Why are the leaves of some species, such as the black cherry, usually yellow at the time of falling if they drop from the tree during a midsummer drought, but generally red at the usual time of abscission in the autumn?

XXI

RESPIRATION

When seeds germinate in a dark room, the total weight of the developing seedlings increases for a number of days, but their dry weight consistently decreases. This can be shown by calculating the dry weight of the seeds at the time of planting from a water content determination of other seeds from the same batch and determining the dry weight of the resulting seedlings after they have been allowed to develop for several weeks. For example, Boussingault found many years ago that the dry weight of ten pea seedlings allowed to develop in the dark was 1.076 g. while the dry weight of the original seeds was 2.237 g. In other words, 1.161 g. or 52 per cent of the dry substance initially present in the seeds disappeared during the course of the experiment. By chemical analysis it can be shown that the loss of dry weight of seedlings growing in the absence of light results entirely from the disappearance of a portion of the stored foods in the seed. The gain in total weight of such seedlings is a consequence of the absorption of water which occurs during the early stages of germination in quantities far surpassing any loss of dry weight resulting from the disappearance of foods. The quantity of mineral salts absorbed by young seedlings in the course of a week or two is usually too small to have any appreciable effect upon either their dry or total weight.

If seedlings developing in the dark are enclosed in a chamber which is constructed so that a slow, continuous stream of air can be passed through it, and frequent analyses made of the air, it can be demonstrated that the air emerging from the chamber contains a lower percentage of oxygen and a higher percentage of carbon dioxide than the air which entered.

Furthermore, if such seedlings are enclosed in a calorimeter, and other suitable precautions taken which will be described later, it can also be shown that heat—which is one kind of energy—is continuously escaping from them.

All of these phenomena—disappearance of food resulting in a decrease in dry weight, absorption of oxygen, evolution of carbon dioxide, and liberation of energy—are different external manifestations of the process of *respiration* which occurs, not only in germinating seeds and seedlings, but in living cells generally.

The gaseous exchanges accompanying respiration were discovered and extensively studied before any especial significance was attached to them. This was true for plants as well as animals, in both of which oxygen is usually consumed and carbon dioxide is usually released during respiration. The term respiration has therefore long been used to refer to these externally apparent gaseous exchanges and is still commonly employed in this sense by many animal physiologists. As thus employed with reference to higher animals the term is essentially synonymous with "breathing."

However, as shown in the latter discussion, gaseous exchanges of the usual type are not invariable accompaniments of respiration. Carbon dioxide is not always released nor is oxygen always used in respiration. Furthermore, plants never "breathe" in any fundamentally acceptable sense of the word, frequently popular and semi-popular statements to the contrary notwithstanding. For these reasons plant physiologists use the term "respiration" primarily to refer to the oxidation of foods in living cells with the resulting release of energy. A part of the energy released is transferred to compounds other than those which are oxidized and some is used in the activation of certain cell processes. The formation of certain kinds of highly reactive molecules which occurs during the course of the process is also an important role of respiration. These fundamental aspects of the process are discussed in greater detail later.

Aerobic Respiration.—Respiration of the type described in the preceding paragraphs is, strictly speaking, called *aerobic respiration* since it proceeds at the expense of atmospheric oxygen. A type of respiration known as *anaerobic respiration* is also of common occurrence in plant cells. Anaerobic respiration, as the name indicates, does not require atmospheric oxygen but may occur in its presence. The basic difference between the two kinds of respiration is that atmospheric oxygen participates as a reactant in some of the stages of aerobic respiration but not at any stage of the process when the respiration is strictly anaerobic. When the term "respiration" is used without qualification it usually refers to aerobic respiration.

On the assumption that a hexose is the substrate, the summary chemical equation for aerobic respiration is:

$$C_6H_{12}O_6 + 6\ O_2 \rightarrow 6\ CO_2 + 6\ H_2O + 673 \text{ kg.-cal.}$$

The value 673 kg.-cal.[1] is based on the assumption that glucose is the hexose oxidized. However the quantity of energy released by the oxidation of other hexose sugars deviates only slightly from this value. This equation is exactly the reverse of the photosynthetic equation and the same quantity of energy is required in the synthesis of one mol of a hexose sugar as is released when one mol of it is oxidized in respiration.

The oxidation of a hexose in plant cells does not take place in a single step as indicated in this convenient summary equation. The possible intermediate steps in the respiratory process are considered in the next chapter. This equation merely tells us that for the oxidation of one mol of a hexose, six mols of oxygen are required; that six mols each of carbon dioxide and water result from this oxidation; and that 673 kg.-cal. of energy are released. Since equimolar weights of gases occupy the same volume (Avogadro's hypothesis) the volume of oxygen consumed when a hexose is oxidized is equal to the volume of carbon dioxide released.

The water formed as a result of respiration becomes a part of the general mass of water present in the respiring cells. Since it is seldom possible to measure experimentally the quantities of water released in respiration, the conclusion that it is an end product of this process is based largely on theoretical considerations. The water produced in respiration is often termed *metabolic water*.

Hexose sugars are most commonly the substrates which are oxidized in the cells of higher green plants. When plant cells contain both carbohydrates and fats, the former apparently are consumed first in respiration, before any inroads are made upon the fats. When fatty seeds are allowed to germinate in contact with a sugar solution it has been found that the sugar is oxidized first. When fats serve as the respiratory substrate in plants they must first be hydrolyzed to fatty acids and glycerol before oxidation can proceed. Utilization of proteins in the respiration of plant cells does not appear to occur commonly except in tissues which have been depleted of carbohydrates and fats. In starved leaves, for example, proteins are hydrolyzed to amino acids, which are then oxidized, a process which is commonly accompanied by the synthesis of asparagine and other amides. Subsequently oxidation of the amides may occur resulting in the release of ammonia in plant tissues (Chap. XXVI). Under such conditions it is believed that the protoplasmic proteins may themselves be hydrolyzed and oxidized.

In most plant organs the rate of respiration is relatively so slow that

---

[1] This value represents the heat of combustion of the reaction. The actual decrease in free energy (calculated from chemical affinities) in this reaction under "biological conditions" is 710 kg.-cal. (Wohl and James, 1942).

any heat released is rapidly dissipated into the environment and thus escapes detection. The evolution of heat during the respiration of certain plant organs can, however, be demonstrated under natural conditions. Temperatures as high as 15°C. in excess of the surrounding atmosphere have been found in the spadices of the skunk cabbage (*Symplocarpus foetidus*) while the temperatures within the spadices of *Arum italicum* have been shown to sometimes exceed atmospheric temperatures by as much as 36°C. This latter, however, must be regarded as an extreme example. Such a self-induced increase in the temperature of a plant organ in itself results in an increase in the rate of respiration and other metabolic processes occurring within that organ.

Heat release during respiration can be demonstrated most easily by enclosing plant material with a relatively high rate of respiration in a calorimeter. Among such materials are rapidly growing stem tips, opening buds, floral parts (especially during the earlier stages in their development), and germinating seeds. The latter are most frequently used. To conduct the demonstration two Dewar flasks or thermos bottles are partially filled, the one with germinating seeds, the other with an equal mass of germinating seeds which have been killed just before starting the experiment. The calorimeters are then plugged with cotton through which is inserted a thermometer, and the temperature changes are noted over a period of time. If the results obtained are to be considered at all critical, the seeds and all parts of each apparatus must be sterilized at the beginning of the determination; otherwise most of the temperature rise observed will result from the respiration of micro-organisms. Such a rise indicates the evolution of heat during the respiration of such organisms, but invalidates the experiment as a demonstration of heat release by the seeds. In general, in a properly set up experiment of this type, the temperature within the mass of living seeds will rise to a value considerably in excess of that recorded for the dead ones. The sterilized dead seeds will show little or no change in temperature. In such experiments 100 g. of germinating seeds may release heat with sufficient rapidity as to acquire temporarily a temperature as much as 20°C. higher than that of the dead seeds in the check experiment. In the more critical experiments upon heat release by plant tissues the heat evolved is expressed in terms of calories per unit of time.

Although the energy released in respiration is generally expressed in terms of heat units (*i.e.*, calories or kilogram-calories), not all of the energy is evolved as heat. That portion of the energy which is released as heat is all lost to the cells in which respiration occurs. It is pure waste from the standpoint of supplying the plant with energy and is roughly analogous to the frictional loss of energy in a machine. In warm-blooded animals, in contradistinction to plants, the heat released in the respiratory process is important in maintaining the body temperature.

Energy becomes manifest in living cells as well as in inorganic systems as chemical energy, heat energy, radiant energy, surface energy, mechanical energy, potential energy, etc. All of the energy released from molecules during respiration represents radiant energy which was previously entrapped in the process of photosynthesis. Upon release this energy may be transformed into any of the kinds listed above.

In young, growing tissues a significant proportion of the energy of respiration is not released as heat, but takes other manifestations. The most important way in which such energy is used, especially in younger cells, is in certain synthetic processes. Among these are the syntheses of fatty and amino acids, glycerol, and acetaldehyde. In all of these reactions the releasable energy of some of the products of the reaction is greater than that of a molecularly equivalent quantity of hexose. In other words, in such syntheses, chemical energy is transferred by the oxidation of certain molecules (usually hexoses or derivatives therefrom) to other molecules which thereby become enriched in chemical energy. Most such molecules are highly reactive, and the reactions in which they participate lead to the synthesis of a number of important compounds in plants.

Among the other energy-requiring processes occurring in plants, especially in younger organs or tissues, are the migration of the chromosomes and other cell constituents during cell division, streaming of the protoplasm, accumulation of solutes by cells (Chap. XXIV), translocation of solutes (Chap. XXVII), growth of stems in opposition to gravity, growth of root tips against the frictional resistance of the soil, and maintenance of differences of electrical potential in plants. Although most, if not all, of the energy used in these processes comes from respiration, the amounts used in such processes are very small relative to the total energy output of respiration.

In mature plant tissues practically all of the energy released in respiration escapes as heat (Wohl and James, 1942). Although there is some difficulty in visualizing the role which respiration plays in such tissues, continuation of the process is essential, death of the cells in most mature plant tissues soon ensuing if they are deprived of oxygen. Maintenance of the controlled chains of reactions (Chap. XXII) which constitute the respiration process can only be accomplished by the stepwise transfer of energy from molecule to molecule. Even though most of the energy involved is ultimately released as heat it appears that maintenance of these reaction chains is necessary if the protoplasm is to remain in a living condition.

However, not all plant processes rely upon the energy derived from respiration for their motive power. Transpiration, for example, is essentially a modified evaporation process, and the energy used in the vaporization of water mostly comes either directly from the radiant energy of sunlight, or from the heat energy of the surrounding atmosphere.

Methods of Measuring Respiration.—Respiration rates are usually measured in terms of the rate of oxygen consumption, or the rate of carbon dioxide evolution, or both. Rates of carbon dioxide release are more commonly determined than rates of oxygen consumption, since the chemical and physicochemical methods of detecting changes in the rates of carbon dioxide evolution are easier to work with. Respiration rates are often determined by enclosing the plant in a suitable chamber through which air is allowed to flow at an appropriate rate. The carbon dioxide in the effluent gas stream can be precipitated as $BaCO_3$ by bubbling the gas through a solution of $Ba(OH)_2$. The quantity of this compound formed can be measured either volumetrically (i.e., by titration), gravimetrically (by determining the weight of $BaCO_3$ precipitate formed), or by measuring the rate of change of electrical conductivity of the $Ba(OH)_2$ solution. A commonly used variation of this method is to pass the effluent gas stream through a NaOH solution (usually about 0.2 N). At the end of the experimental period the Na_2CO_3 formed is precipitated as $BaCO_3$ with a saturated $BaCl_2$ solution and its quantity determined by titration. From the quantity of carbonate formed under any of these procedures the amount of carbon dioxide which has been evolved from the plant tissue can be calculated. In all such methods it is also necessary either to remove the carbon dioxide from the gas stream before it passes through the plant chamber or else to make a check analysis of its carbon dioxide content.

If it is desired to determine carbon dioxide liberation and oxygen consumption simultaneously, the simplest procedure is to collect the gas stream in a reservoir after it has passed through the plant chamber and analyze it for the proportions of these two gases present. If the volume of each of these gases which has passed into the plant chamber is also known, the gaseous exchanges of the plant can be computed.

Rates of respiration are expressed in terms of either carbon dioxide evolution or oxygen consumption per unit of time and are usually calculated on the basis of a unit dry weight of tissue. Obviously accurate determinations of respiration rates of chlorophyllous plant organs can be obtained only if they are enclosed in a respiration chamber which is impervious to light.

Some caution must be exercised, however, in accepting the rate of carbon dioxide release or of oxygen consumption as an index of respiration. The most fundamental measures of respiration would be the rates of energy release or transfer, or of the formation of highly reactive compounds. Neither the rate of carbon dioxide release nor the rate of oxygen consumption is invariably a consistent index of the rate at which the fundamental transformations of respiration occur. This is especially true when comparisons are being made between aerobic and anaerobic respiration, between tissues in which different substrates are being oxidized, or between a given tissue under one set of conditions as compared with that same tissue under a markedly different set of conditions. A certain rate of carbon dioxide release, for example, from a tissue which is respiring largely anaerobically is not an index of the same amount of respiration as the same rate of evolution of carbon dioxide from an equivalent amount of tissue which is respiring aerobically. For a given plant tissue, however, over a range of not too widely differing environmental conditions, either rate of carbon dioxide liberation or oxygen consumption is a convenient and usually a fairly accurate index of respiration.

Comparative Rates of Respiration.—Rates of respiration as expressed either in terms of oxygen consumption or carbon dioxide liberation vary greatly, depending upon the plant organ or tissue and the environmental conditions. Since the seat of respiration lies in the protoplasm a correlation often exists between the proportion of protoplasm present in a tissue and the intensity of the respiration process in that tissue. As a general rule, respiration rates are found to be greatest in meristematic tissues, such as growing root or stem tips or the embryos of germinating seeds. It is precisely in such tissues that the proportion of protoplasm is greatest in relation to the total dry weight of the tissue. In mature tissues, such as photosynthetically active leaves, a larger proportion of the dry weight of the tissue mass is composed of inert cell-wall materials, hence the respiration rates of such tissues, expressed in the usual terms, are almost invariably less than those of meristems under comparable conditions. Senescent tissues, such as yellowing leaves or ripe fruits in which the proportion of protoplasm to dry weight is still smaller, generally have lower rates of respiration than the same tissues had when in a metabolically active condition. The lowest rates of respiration are found in dormant seeds and spores, a marked increase in the rate of respiration being one of the striking physiological aspects of germination. The relatively slow rate of respiration in such structures is not, however, primarily the result of a low proportionate amount of protoplasm, but of other factors, among which deficient hydration of the tissues is one of the most important.

Representative rates of respiration for a number of plant organs are listed in Table 30. Even for the plant parts tabulated these rates are to be regarded as only approximations, since the rate for any one plant organ or tissue is subject to marked fluctuations due to the influence of various internal and external factors.

TABLE 30—RESPIRATION RATES OF VARIOUS PLANT TISSUES IN TERMS OF VOLUME OF OXYGEN ABSORBED OR VOLUME OF CARBON DIOXIDE RELEASED IN 24 HOURS PER GRAM OF DRY WEIGHT (FROM DATA COMPILED BY KOSTYCHEV, 1927)

Plant	Organ	Temperature	Respiration Rate
Wheat (*Triticum satirum*)	Young roots	15–18° C.	67.9 cc. O_2 absorbed
Red Clover (*Trifolium pratense*) .	Leaves	20–21°	27.2 " " "
Rice (*Oryza sativa*)	Young roots	14–17°	44.4 " " "
Mint (*Mentha aquatica*)	Roots	18–19°	37.2 " " "
Lilac (*Syringa vulgaris*)	Leaf buds	15°	35.0 cc. CO_2 liberated
Linden (*Tilia europea*)	Leaf buds	. . . .	66.0 " " "
Lettuce (*Lactuca sativa*)	Germ. seeds	16°	82.5 " " "
Poppy (*Papaver somniferum*)	Germ. seeds	16°	122.0 " " "
Mold (*Aspergillus niger*)	Mycelium	. . . .	1800 " " "

The Compensation Point.—In the leaves or other chlorophyllous tissues the rate of photosynthesis usually exceeds the rate of respiration during the daylight hours. In maize, for example (Table 25), the rate of photosynthesis during the daylight hours is, on the average, about eight times the rate of respiration. (See also Fig. 104 for similar data on alfalfa.) The carbon dioxide released in respiration is re-utilized by the cells in photosynthesis, but since the latter process is occurring more rapidly than the former, additional carbon dioxide is continuously diffusing into the plant from the outside environment. Similarly photosynthesis produces more oxygen than is used in respiration, the surplus diffusing out of the plant. Hence during the daylight hours, as long as conditions favorable for photosynthesis prevail, there is a net movement of carbon dioxide into the green parts of plants, and a net loss of oxygen from them. Under such conditions the occurrence of the gaseous exchanges accompanying respiration in green leaves is completely masked.

At night or in the dark the reverse condition obtains, oxygen moving into the green parts of a plant and carbon dioxide passing out of them. Similar gaseous exchanges are characteristic of the non-green organs of a plant, whether in the light or in the dark. The magnitude of the gaseous exchanges occurring between a green plant organ and its environment in the absence of light are usually less than those which generally take place—but in the opposite direction—in its presence.

Since at low intensities light is usually the limiting factor in photosynthesis it is evident there should be a certain light intensity at which the rate of photosynthesis and the rate of respiration in a leaf or other chlorophyllous organ are exactly equal. At this light intensity, often called the *compensation point,* the volume of carbon dioxide being released in respiration is exactly equal to the volume being consumed in photosynthesis, while the opposite is true for oxygen. In other words, at the compensation point apparent photosynthesis is zero. The light intensity corresponding to the compensation point varies considerably with different species of plants. The compensation point for any one species is also influenced by various environmental factors, especially temperature, and is markedly affected by the conditions to which the leaves or other photosynthetic organs have been exposed during their development. Compensation points have been measured more extensively in submersed aquatics than in land plants. Meyer *et al.* (1943) found the compensation point for a number of such species to be of the order of 1-2 per cent of the intensity of full midday summer sunlight. The leaves of some shade species of land plants also have compensation points of approximately this magnitude, but in sun species the compensation point is usually higher.

No plant can survive indefinitely in nature at the light intensity of the compensation point. Under such conditions there is no photosynthesis which compensates for night respiration. Also, the compensation point is usually measured only for the leaves or aerial organs of the plant, no allowance being made for the respiration of the roots or other underground organs. Hence the actual minimum light intensity at which any species could survive in nature would necessarily be somewhat greater than the compensation point. As shown in Fig. 99, the minimum light intensities for the survival of several species of conifers lie within a range of 1-6 per cent. Compensation points for these species would presumably show a slightly lower range of values.

The Respiratory Ratio.—The ratio of the volume of CO_2 released to the volume of O_2 absorbed in the respiratory process is termed the *respiratory ratio* or *quotient.* When complete oxidation of a hexose sugar occurs, as already pointed out:

$$\frac{CO_2}{O_2} = 1$$

The respiratory ratio for any plant or plant part can be determined by making parallel measurements of the rates of carbon dioxide release and oxygen consumption.

The respiratory ratio of germinating seeds in which the accumulated foods are principally in the form of carbohydrates is invariably found to be approximately one as long as oxygen has free access to such seeds. This is true, for example, of the germinating grains of practically all of the cereals (wheat, maize, oats, etc.). Similarly the respiratory ratios for the leaves of many species of plants have been found to be in the neighborhood of one (Table 31), and flowers usually have a respiratory ratio of approximately one (Pringsheim, 1935). The proportion of the volume of carbon dioxide evolved to the volume of oxygen absorbed may vary greatly from a unit value, however, depending upon the respiratory substrate, the completeness of the oxidation, and other conditions. Many studies have been made of the respiratory quotient of various plant organs. Most such investigations have dealt with germinating seeds. The principal internal conditions under which it has been found that the respiratory ratio of the higher green plants deviates from one are as follows:

TABLE 31—RESPIRATORY RATIOS OF THE LEAVES OF VARIOUS SPECIES
(DATA OF MAQUENNE AND DEMOUSSY, 1913)

Begonia	1.11	Pea	1.07
Castor Bean	1.03	Pear	1.10
Chrysanthemum	1.02	Privet	1.03
Corn (maize)	1.07	Rose	1.02
Grape	1.01	Tobacco	1.03
Lilac	1.07	Wheat	1.03

1. *Respiration of Compounds in Which the Proportion of Oxygen to Carbon Is Relatively Low as Compared with Hexoses.*—The proportion of oxygen to carbon is invariably less in fats than in carbohydrates. Many studies of the respiratory ratio of seeds in which the stored foods are mostly in the form of oils have shown that the respiratory ratio of such seeds is always less than one. The following summary equation represents the complete oxidation of tri-palmitin, a representative fat:

$$C_{51}H_{98}O_6 + 72.5\ O_2 \rightarrow 51\ CO_2 + 49\ H_2O + 7590\ \text{kg.-cal. (approx.)}$$

Actually fats, being insoluble compounds, are not oxidized directly as indicated in the above equation, but only after hydrolysis to fatty acids and glycerol (Chap. XXIII) and probably only after further conversions to simple carbohydrates or related compounds. Regardless of the exact course of the respiratory process, however, the sequence of reactions followed will require the absorption of oxygen in excess of the quantity of carbon dioxide released. The summation effect, therefore, of the various reactions involved in the respiration of fats will be a respiratory ratio of less than one.

Similarly oxidation of the hydrolytic products of the proteins results in a respiratory ratio of less than one (usually 0.8-0.9) since the proportion of oxygen to carbon in such compounds is less than in carbohydrates.

2. *Respiration of Compounds in Which the Proportion of Oxygen to Carbon Is Relatively High as Compared with Hexoses.*—In some species of plants, particularly those of the succulent habit of growth, organic acids are often oxidized. Such compounds are relatively rich in oxygen as compared with carbohydrates. The equations for the complete oxidation of oxalic and malic, two of the common plant organic acids, are as follows:

$$2 \begin{array}{c} COOH \\ | \\ COOH \end{array} + O_2 \rightarrow 4\,CO_2 + 2\,H_2O + 60.2 \text{ kg.-cal.}$$

Oxalic acid

$$\begin{array}{c} COOH \\ | \\ CHOH \\ | \\ CH_2 \\ | \\ COOH \end{array} + 3\,O_2 \rightarrow 4\,CO_2 + 3\,H_2O + 320.1 \text{ kg.-cal.}$$

Malic acid

The theoretical respiratory ratio for oxalic acid is therefore 4; for malic acid $\frac{4}{3}$ or 1.33. For tartaric acid, another organic acid which occurs in plants, the respiratory ratio is 1.6. Oxidation of any compound of this type results in a respiratory ratio in excess of one.

3. *Occurrence of Oxygen Liberation or Utilization without Corresponding Carbon Dioxide Consumption or Release.*—As seeds which store fats mature, simple carbohydrates are converted into fats. Oxygen is eliminated in this process without any corresponding utilization of carbon dioxide, since the molecules of fats contain much less oxygen in proportion to the carbon and hydrogen present than do the molecules of sugars. The freed oxygen serves as an internal supply which can be transferred to other molecules in respiration. The volume of oxygen absorbed by seeds from the exterior atmosphere during this period will hence be less than it otherwise would be, and the respiratory ratio is theoretically greater than one. This expectation has been confirmed for the seeds of a number of species in which fats accumulate; for example the respiratory ratio of maturing flax seeds is about 1.22.

Essentially the opposite situation prevails during the germination of fatty seeds in which very low respiratory quotients sometimes prevail after several days. Murlin (1934), for example, found values for the respiratory ratio of germinating castor bean seeds as low as about 0.3 and explained this finding on the assumption that transformation of fat to sugar—an oxygen-consuming process in which no carbon dioxide is released—is proceeding much more rapidly than oxidation of sugar.

A situation similar to the last obtains in many succulent species in which incomplete oxidation of sugars to organic acids occurs. In species of the Crassulaceae, for example, some of the sugar present is often incompletely oxidized to malic acid:

$$2 \ C_6H_{12}O_6 + 3 \ O_2 \rightarrow 3 \ C_4H_6O_5 + 3 \ H_2O + 386 \ \text{kg.-cal.}$$

Other organic acids are formed in succulent species as a result of similar respiratory processes. The synthesis of such compounds requires absorption of oxygen for which there is no corresponding evolution of carbon dioxide. Such metabolic conditions will obviously result in an apparent respiratory ratio of less than one.

4. *Occurrence of Carbon Dioxide Utilization or Liberation without Corresponding Oxygen Release or Consumption.*—The leaves of *Bryophyllum* and some other species make direct use of carbon dioxide absorbed in the dark in the synthesis of organic acids (Chap. XXII). The effect of the occurrence of this process would be to give such leaves an apparent respiratory ratio of less than one.

Release of carbon dioxide without any corresponding utilization of atmospheric oxygen is characteristic of *anaerobic respiration,* which occurs in higher green plants under certain conditions. Sometimes, especially when the oxygen supply is deficient, both aerobic and anaerobic respiration occur simultaneously in a plant tissue. Some cells may be respiring anaerobically, while others are carrying on aerobic respiration. In the early stages of respiration of seeds in which the seed coats are relatively impermeable to oxygen, such as those of peas, a limited amount of aerobic respiration may be carried on, accompanied by a larger proportion of anaerobic respiration. Under such conditions the volume of carbon dioxide evolved may be very large in proportion to the volume of oxygen absorbed, and the respiratory ratio is much greater than one. As soon as the seed coat is ruptured, thus permitting free access of oxygen to the developing embryo, anaerobic respiration largely or entirely ceases.

In addition to the various internal conditions which influence the value of the respiratory quotient, its magnitude may also vary with certain factors of external origin. Increase in temperature within the physiological range, for example, causes an increase in the respiratory quotient of many plant tissues. A probable reason for this effect, especially in bulky tissues, is that at higher temperatures oxygen does not gain access to the cells fast enough to keep up with the accelerated rate of respiration, and there is a partial substitution of anaerobic for aerobic respiration. Another environmental factor which affects the magnitude of the respiratory ratio is the carbon dioxide concentration of the atmosphere (Table 32).

The principal justification for study of the respiratory quotients of plants is that the results of such investigations afford important clues regarding the nature of the respiratory process itself. Certain inferences regarding the type of substrate being oxidized, transformations in the foods present in cells, and even the chemical mechanism of respiration can often be drawn from the results of determinations of respiratory ratios. Some caution is always necessary, however, in interpreting the results of such experiments. A number of different processes are often occurring simultaneously in plant cells, each of which will influence the magnitude of the respiratory ratio. Several types of substrates may be undergoing oxidation concurrently, or other reactions may be occurring which affect the oxygen or carbon dioxide intake or output of cells. If one of these several reactions is strongly predominant, it will in the main determine the value of the respiratory ratio, and the quotient will be a valid indicator of the nature of the respiratory process. If, on the contrary, several different processes are proceeding at approximately equal rates, their net influence on the gaseous exchanges of the tissue may be such that the apparent respiratory ratio will bear no relation whatever to any one of the processes and may even lead to entirely erroneous inferences.

Factors Affecting the Rate of Aerobic Respiration.—A number of factors, some internal, others external, are definitely known to influence the rate of respiration of plant cells. Under some conditions the pathway of the respiration process, as well as its rate, may be influenced by prevailing factors. Whenever the magnitude of the respiratory quotient changes with a shift in one or more of the factors influencing respiration, this is evidence that a change in the pathway of the respiration process has occurred. Such an effect of temperature has already been discussed in the preceding section, and a similar effect of carbon dioxide concentration is illustrated in Table 32. Other examples of this effect are the action of certain chemicals, such as cyanides, which inhibit aerobic respiration, but in at least some plant tissues do not inhibit anaerobic respiration (Chap. XXII).

1. *Protoplasmic Conditions.*—Young, meristematic tissues, which are relatively rich in protoplasm, usually have higher rates of respiration than older tissues in which the proportion of cell walls is greater. Not

nature of the tissue

only is the gross amount of protoplasm present a factor, but various internal conditions in that protoplasm also influence the respiration rate. In view of our incomplete knowledge of the physicochemical structure and dynamics of the protoplasm, the influence of only a few of these protoplasmic factors can be recognized at the present time. One of these is the degree of hydration of the protoplasm. The effect of this factor will be discussed later under a separate heading. The quantities and kinds of respiratory enzymes (Chap. XXII) present in the protoplasm undoubtedly are also factors which affect the rate of respiration.

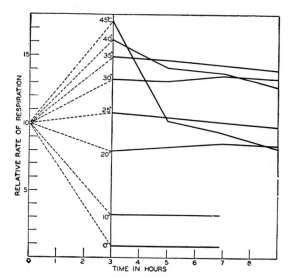

Fig. 109. Relation between time, temperature, and rate of respiration of pea seedlings. Dotted lines represent period during which temperature of seedlings was changed from 25°C. to indicated temperatures. Data of Fernandes (1923).

2. *Temperature.*—As is true of most other biological processes temperature effects upon the rate of respiration are rather complex. In general, within certain limits, increase in temperature results in an increase in the respiration rate. As in photosynthesis and in enzymatic reactions a definite time factor effect is often evident (Fig. 109). In the temperature range between 0° and 45°C., increase in temperature resulted in an increase in the initial rate of respiration of the pea seedlings. At temperatures above approximately 30°C. the rate of respiration showed a decrease with time, which became more marked the higher the temperature.

For the pea seedlings used in this experiment the optimum temperature would appear to be about 30°C., as this is approximately the maximum temperature at which there is a maintained rate of respiration. The optimum temperature for respiration, considered in this sense, is not the same for all plant tissues. For some it is clearly higher than the value obtained in this experiment with pea seedlings and for others it is lower.

The exact nature of the "time factor" which becomes increasingly effective in causing reduction in the rate of respiration with rise in temperature is unknown. One of the seemingly more probable explanations is that this effect results from a progressively more pronounced inactivation of enzymes with increase in temperature. Other possibilities are: (1) oxygen may not gain access to the cells fast enough at higher temperatures to permit maintenance of the respiration rate, (2) carbon dioxide may accumulate in the cells in such concentrations at higher temperatures as to check the rate of respiration, and (3) the supply of oxidizable foods may be inadequate to maintain high rates of respiration.

As the temperature is decreased below 0°C., the rate of respiration gradually diminishes until it becomes imperceptible. Measurable rates of respiration have been recorded, however, in some plant tissues at temperatures as low as −20°C.

The Q_{10} of respiration for plant tissues within the temperature range 10°-30°C. is usually between 2.0 and 2.5. At temperatures below 10°C., higher Q_{10} values have been found for a number of tissues (Platenius, 1942). Above 30°C., determination of the Q_{10} values for plant respiration with any degree of certainty is difficult because of the time factor effect.

The temperature to which a plant organ is exposed sometimes has important *indirect* effects on the rate of respiration. When the temperature of a potato tuber is lowered from a few degrees above to about 0°C., the respiration rate *increases*. According to Hopkins (1924) this is a result of the effect of low temperatures in causing a shift in the starch-sugar equilibrium toward the sugar side (Chap. XX). Increase in the quantity of respiratory substrate in plant cells results in an increase in the rate of respiration whenever it is the limiting factor, a condition which apparently obtains in potato tubers under these conditions. Similar indirect effects of temperature upon the rate of respiration are probably of frequent occurrence in other plant tissues.

3. *Food.*—As a general rule increase in the soluble food content of plant cells results in an increase in the respiration rate up to a certain point at which some other factor becomes limiting. One example of the effect of the concentration of foods in cells upon the rate of respiration has just been described in the previous section. The effect of this factor on respiration rates can also be demonstrated in etiolated leaves. For example, Palladin (1893) found that 100 g. of carbohydrate deficient etiolated bean leaves released an average of 89.6 mg. of carbon dioxide per hour at room temperature. After floating the same leaves upon a

sucrose solution for two days, during which considerable absorption of sugar occurred, the average rate of carbon dioxide release increased to 148.8 mg. per hr.

4. *Oxygen Concentration of the Atmosphere.*—The effect of the oxygen concentration of the atmosphere on the rate of respiration varies with the kind of tissue, concentration of oxygen, period of exposure, and other prevailing environmental conditions. The apparent magnitude of the effect, and sometimes also its direction, may also differ, depending upon whether carbon dioxide output or oxygen intake is used as the index of respiration. Variations in the oxygen content of the aerial atmosphere are too slight to have any appreciable effect on respiration rates, but this is not true of the soil atmosphere (Chap. XIV). In general, unless the oxygen concentration deviates by at least 5 per cent from the usual atmospheric concentration, effects on rates of respiration are small or negligible.

Choudhury (1939) found that the rate of carbon dioxide output of potato tubers was essentially the same over a range of oxygen concentrations from 6.2 to 98.6 per cent. With artichoke (*Helianthus tuberosus*) tubers the rate of carbon dioxide release was essentially the same in oxygen concentrations above atmospheric as in air; but, in oxygen concentrations below atmospheric, the rate showed a progressive lowering with decrease in concentration. With carrot roots irregular results were obtained at oxygen concentrations below atmospheric; but, at oxygen concentrations above atmospheric, the higher the concentration, the greater the rate of carbon dioxide output. In a somewhat similar investigation Platenius (1943) showed that the rate of respiration, measured either as carbon dioxide output or as oxygen intake, was progressively reduced as oxygen concentrations were lowered below atmospheric in the following plant materials: asparagus stalks, bean fruits, spinach tops, shelled peas, and carrot roots.

One of the factors accounting for such differences in the relation between oxygen concentration and the rate of respiration is the usual atmospheric rate of respiration. The respiration rate of tissues in which the usual atmospheric rate is relatively low—as, for example, in potato tubers —appears to be less affected by a lowering of oxygen concentration than that of tissues in which the atmospheric rate is higher.

Another factor accounting for differences in the effect of oxygen concentration on respiration is the greater capacity of some tissues than others for anaerobic respiration. An example of this effect is the contrasting behavior of wheat and rice seedlings (Taylor, 1942). At low oxygen concentrations carbon dioxide output by rice seedlings was much greater than that by wheat seedlings. In the total absence of oxygen, carbon

dioxide output of wheat seedlings was only about half that in air, while
that of rice seedlings was about 50 per cent greater than in air (Fig. 110).
The difference in the behavior of these two kinds of seedlings is ascribed
to the possession by rice seedlings of a much more effective anaerobic
respiration system than is possessed by wheat seedlings. On the other
hand, if oxygen consumption was used as the index of respiration,
this was greater at low oxygen concentrations in the wheat seedlings than in the rice seedlings.
An effect similar to that in rice seedlings has been shown in
slices of carrot root tissue by Marsh and Goddard (1939).
With decrease in oxygen concentration below 5 per cent, carbon
dioxide output of this tissue increased, but its oxygen consumption decreased.

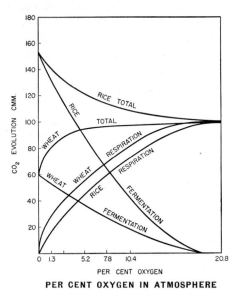

FIG. 110. Relation between oxygen concentration and respiration and fermentation of wheat and rice seedlings. Data of Taylor (1942).

5. *Carbon Dioxide Concentration of the Atmosphere.*—The
effect of carbon dioxide concentration on respiration, like that
of oxygen, differs with its concentration, the kind of tissue, the
period of exposure, and other prevailing environmental conditions. As with oxygen, usual atmospheric fluctuations in carbon dioxide concentration of the aerial atmosphere are not sufficient to have appreciable effects on respiration rates,
but the contrary is true of the soil atmosphere.

In a study of white mustard seedlings it was shown that the rate of
respiration decreased with increase in carbon dioxide concentration (Table
32). This effect was shown whether respiration was measured in terms of
carbon dioxide release or oxygen absorption. The decreasing effect on the
rate of carbon dioxide release was more marked than on the rate of absorption of oxygen. Hence the higher the carbon dioxide concentration of
the atmosphere, the lower the respiratory ratio.

The rate of respiration of other plant tissues, on the contrary, is increased when they are exposed to relatively high concentrations of carbon
dioxide. For example, Thornton (1933) studied the rate of respiration of
potato tubers at 25°C. in various concentrations of carbon dioxide. The

initial concentration of oxygen in the atmosphere was 20 per cent in all experiments. Exposure of the tubers to concentrations of carbon dioxide in excess of about 20 per cent for periods of greater than 20-24 hr. resulted in a marked increase in respiration rate as measured in terms of oxygen consumption. In 60 per cent carbon dioxide the rate of respiration sometimes exceeded that of the controls by more than 200 per cent. This increased rate of respiration is undoubtedly to be explained, at least in part, by the increase in the concentration of sugar which occurs in the cells under such conditions. Shorter periods of exposure of the potato tuber to high concentrations of carbon dioxide resulted in a decreasing rather than an increasing effect upon respiration. Similar effects of high

TABLE 32—EFFECT OF CARBON DIOXIDE CONCENTRATION UPON THE RATE OF RESPIRATION OF GERMINATING WHITE MUSTARD SEEDS. INITIAL CONCENTRATION OF O_2 IN EACH EXPERIMENT 20 PER CENT. DURATION OF EXPERIMENTS, 14 HOURS. (DATA OF KIDD, 1915)

	Percentage of CO_2 initially present					
	0	10	20	30	40	80
CO_2 evolved (cc.).............	58	48	38	33	26	17
O_2 absorbed (cc.).............	71	57	49	45	38	32
Respiratory ratio.............	0.82	0.84	0.77	0.73	0.69	0.53

concentrations of carbon dioxide were found for onion and tulip bulbs and for beet roots. With asparagus shoots and shelled lima beans, on the other hand, high concentrations of carbon dioxide resulted in a reduction in respiration rate as in germinating mustard seeds.

The most marked effects of variations in the oxygen and carbon dioxide concentrations of the atmosphere upon respiration are doubtless those upon roots, underground stems, and seeds. The carbon dioxide concentration of the soil atmosphere may sometimes be as much as 10 per cent and occasionally even higher, while the oxygen content may, in some soils, at some times, approach a zero value (Chap. XIII). The usual effect of either or both of these conditions is a retardation in the rate of respiration. As a result of such diminished respiration rates such fundamental processes as absorption of water (Chap. XIV) and of mineral salts (Chap. XXIV) by roots, growth of roots (Chap. XXIX), and germination of seeds (Chap. XXXIV) may be retarded or even entirely inhibited.

6. *Hydration of the Tissues.*—As is true of a number of other processes, the effect of the hydration of the tissues upon the rate of respiration can best be observed in germinating seeds (Fig. 111). The marked rise in

the rate of respiration as the water content of wheat seeds increases from 16 to 17 per cent, as contrasted with the small effect of increase in water content in the range below 16 per cent, is probably a result of practically all of the water in the seeds being in the bound condition at water contents below 16 per cent. The data in Fig. 111 show why it is highly desirable that the water content of grains be below a certain value before they are placed in storage.

Similar results have been obtained with tissues of some of the more extreme xerophytes, such as many species of lichens, which can be desiccated to an air-dry condition without losing their viability. As the water content of such tissues is increased, often no great effect upon the rate of respiration is observed until a certain water content (which varies according to the tissue) is attained, after which the respiration rate increases rapidly.

Minor variations in the water content of well-hydrated plant tissues do not have any great influence upon the rate of respiration. When the tissues of leaves or other plant organs approach a wilting condition, accumulated starch is often converted into sugars. This increase in sugar content of the cells presumably accounts for the rise in respiration rate which is often observed in wilting tissues.

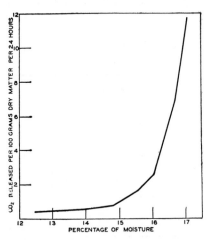

FIG. 111. Relation between water content of wheat grains and rate of respiration. Data of Bailey and Gurjar (1918).

7. *Light*.—Numerous investigators have reported increasing or decreasing effects of light on respiration in plants (Weintraub, 1944) but, with rare exceptions, these can be interpreted as indirect influences. Although direct effects of light on respiration appear to be exceptional, a few undeniable examples are known. Emerson and Lewis (1943) have found that light absorbed by carotenoid pigments in *Chlorella* has an enhancing effect on respiration. Weintraub and Johnston (1944) likewise appear to have demonstrated a direct effect of light on the respiration of etiolated barley seedlings. On the other hand, light clearly has a number of indirect effects on the rate of oxidation of foods in plants. In chlorophyllous organs light may affect the rate of respiration because of its influence upon the supply of respiratory substrate resulting from photosynthesis. Plant organs exposed to direct il-

lumination almost always have a temperature in excess of that of similar organs not so exposed. The heating effect of light is one of its most important indirect effects on respiration.

8. *Injury.*—Wounding of plant tissues almost invariably results in a temporarily increased rate of respiration. If a potato tuber is cut in half, for example, the loss of carbon dioxide from the two halves will be considerably greater than from the intact tuber. Similar results have been observed for many other plant tissues. The increased respiratory activity of wounded or otherwise injured plant tissues gradually rises to a maximum which is generally attained within a day or two, after which a diminution in rate sets in until approximately the rate which prevailed in the uninjured tissues is re-established.

Hopkins (1927) and others have shown that this increased respiration of potato tubers following wounding is correlated with an increase in the sugar content of the tuber. This increase, which amounted in Hopkins' experiments to from 53 to 68 per cent of the sugar originally present, occurs gradually, the maximum not being attained until several hours after the injury. The increase in sugar content is greater in the cells close to the cut surface than in those which are more remote from it. This increase in the quantity of the respiratory substrate is apparently an important factor in accounting for the increased loss of carbon dioxide by potato tubers following wounding, and probably of many other tissues as well.

9. *Mechanical Effects.*—A purely mechanical "stimulation" of respiration has been demonstrated in the leaves of a number of species by Audus (1939, 1940, 1946). A gentle rubbing or bending of the leaf blade was sufficient to induce a marked rise in the respiration rate (often over 100 per cent) which persisted for some hours. No such effect was found for leaves in an atmosphere of nitrogen, indicating that the influence is on the aerobic phases of respiration. The mechanism of this effect is unknown, but it is obvious that it should be taken into account in any experiments on respiration which require handling of the plant material.

10. *Effects of Certain Chemical Compounds on Respiration.*—Although the rate of respiration, like that of other metabolic processes, may be influenced by many different kinds of compounds, particular interest attaches to certain substances which act more or less as enzymatic inhibitors when present in very low concentrations at one stage or another of the respiratory mechanism. Among these are cyanides, azides, carbon monoxide, fluorides, malonates, and iodoacetate (Chap. XVI, XXII).

Narcotics, such as chloroform and ether, also have pronounced effects on respiration in low concentrations. Although in very low concentrations the effect of such compounds is sometimes an enhancement of the respiration rate, most commonly their effect is an inhibitory one. If the concentration of the narcotic is not too high and the exposure not too prolonged, this inhibitory effect is reversible; otherwise irreparable injury of the protoplasm itself may soon result.

SUGGESTED FOR COLLATERAL READING

Kostychev, S. *Plant Respiration.* Translated and edited by C. J. Lyon. P. Blakiston's Son and Co. Philadelphia. 1927.
Stiles, W., and W. Leach. *Respiration in Plants.* Dial Press. New York. 1932.

SELECTED BIBLIOGRAPHY

Audus, L. J. Mechanical stimulation and respiration in the green leaf. II, III, VI. *New Phytol.* **38:** 284-288. 1939. **39:** 65-74, 1940. **45:** 243-253. 1946.
Bailey, C. H., and A. M. Gurjar. Respiration of stored wheat. *Jour. Agric. Res.* **12:** 685-713. 1918.
Choudhury, J. K. Researches on plant respiration. V. On the respiration of some storage organs in different oxygen concentrations. *Proc. Roy. Soc. (London)* **B 127:** 238-257. 1939.
Emerson, R., and C. M. Lewis. The dependence of the quantum yield of *Chlorella* photosynthesis on wave length of light. *Amer. Jour. Bot.* **30:** 165-178. 1943.
Fernandes, D. S. Aerobe und anaerobe Atmung bei Keimlingen von *Pisum sativum. Rec. Trav. Bot. Nèerland* **20:** 107-256. 1923.
Hopkins, E. F. Relation of low temperatures to respiration and carbohydrate changes in potato tubers. *Bot. Gaz.* **78:** 311-325. 1924.
Hopkins, E. F. Variation in sugar content in potato tubers caused by wounding and its possible relation to respiration. *Bot. Gaz.* **84:** 75-88. 1927.
Kidd, F. The controlling influence of carbon dioxide. III. The retarding effect of carbon dioxide on respiration. *Proc. Roy. Soc. (London)* **B 89:** 136-156. 1915.
Maquenne, L., and E. Demoussy. Sur la valeur des coefficients chlorophylliens et leur rapports avec les quotients respiratoires réels. *Compt. Rend. Acad. Sci. (Paris)* **156:** 506-512. 1913.
Marsh, P. B., and D. R. Goddard. Respiration and fermentation in the carrot, *Daucus carota. Amer. Jour. Bot.* **26:** 724-728; 767-772. 1939.
Meyer, B. S., F. H. Bell, L. C. Thompson, and Edythe I. Clay. Effect of depth of immersion on apparent photosynthesis in submersed vascular aquatics. *Ecology* **24:** 393-399. 1943.
Murlin, J. R. The conversion of fat to carbohydrate in the germinating castor bean. I. The respiratory metabolism. *Jour. Gen. Physiol.* **17:** 283-302. 1933.
Palladin, W. Recherches sur la respiration des feuilles vertes et des feuilles étiolées. *Rev. Gen. Bot.* **5:** 449-473. 1893.
Platenius, H. Effect of temperature on the respiration rate and respiratory quotient of some vegetables. *Plant Physiol.* **17:** 179-197. 1942.
Platenius, H. Effect of oxygen concentration on the respiration of some vegetables. *Plant Physiol.* **18:** 671-684. 1943.
Pringsheim, E. G. Untersuchungen über den Respirationsquotienten verscheidener Pflanzenteile. *Jahrb. Wiss. Bot.* **81:** 579-608. 1935.
Stiles, W. Respiration. I. II. *Bot. Rev.* **1:** 249-268. 1935; **12:** 165-204. 1946.

Taylor, D. L. Influence of oxygen tension on respiration, fermentation, and growth in wheat and rice. *Amer. Jour. Bot.* **29**: 721-738. 1942.

Thornton, N. C. Carbon dioxide storage. III. The influence of carbon dioxide on the oxygen uptake by fruits and vegetables. *Contr. Boyce Thompson Inst.* **5**: 371-402. 1933.

Vlamis, J., and A. R. Davis. Germination, growth, and respiration of rice and barley seedlings at low oxygen pressures. *Plant Physiol.* **18**: 685-692. 1943.

Weintraub, R. L. Radiation and plant respiration. *Bot. Rev.* **10**: 383-459. 1944.

Weintraub, R. L., and E. S. Johnston. The influence of light and of carbon dioxide on the respiration of etiolated barley seedlings. *Smithsonian Misc. Coll.* Vol. 104, No. 4. 1944.

Wohl, K., and W. O. James. The energy changes associated with plant respiration. *New Phytol.* **41**: 230-256. 1942.

DISCUSSION QUESTIONS

1. How can respiration occur at night in leaves in which the stomates are closed?

2. How would you proceed to measure the rate of respiration of a potted plant? Evaluate the method chosen for sources of error.

3. How valid is the belief that it is harmful to keep flowers in a sick room at night?

4. In a certain experiment etiolated corn seedlings were measured for daily variation in rate of respiration in the dark. It was found that the rate per hour remained virtually constant in spite of the fact that marked variations in temperature occurred during the day. Explain.

5. What are some of the ways in which the respiration of plant tissue might alter immediately surrounding environmental conditions?

6. Why do starchy seeds decrease proportionately more in dry weight during germination than oily seeds?

7. Would the complete elimination of all animal life from the earth alter the relative proportions of oxygen and carbon dioxide in the air?

8. List specific ways in which the rate of respiration of a given plant tissue might be increased. Decreased.

XXII

THE MECHANISM OF RESPIRATION

The summary chemical equation commonly used to represent the process of respiration:

$$C_6H_{12}O_6 + 6 \; O_2 \rightarrow 6 \; CO_2 + 6 \; H_2O + 673 \text{ kg.-cal.}$$

represents equally well the combustion of sugar. It might be taken to imply that the release of energy in respiration is achieved in a manner analogous to that by which heat energy is liberated in combustion. Actually the two processes are not remotely similar in mechanism. Sugar and atmospheric oxygen are much too stable to unite directly within any temperature range in which living organisms could survive.

Unlike the combustion type of oxidation which would result from a direct combination of oxygen with sugar, the respiration of a hexose to carbon dioxide and water involves long sequences and cycles of reactions in which many kinds of organic molecules participate. Some of these chains of reactions are known, at least for some tissues; others seem very probable, but are less well supported by experimental evidence. These reaction chains are not the same for all tissues, and for a given tissue may differ depending upon various conditions and especially on whether or not atmospheric oxygen is available. Regardless of the exact pathway which the reaction sequence follows, however, oxidation occurs very gradually, step by step, with only small units of energy being released or transferred at a time.

As shown in the later discussion, the component reactions of respiration are of a number of different kinds. The most significant from the standpoint of energy release or transfer are the oxidation-reduction reactions. Many of the oxidation-reduction reactions occurring in the protoplasm are achieved by transfers of hydrogen from molecule to molecule.

416

The molecules which lose hydrogen are oxidized and those which gain hydrogen are reduced. The terminal reaction in many of the sequences in which hydrogen is shuttled from molecule to molecule is the transfer of hydrogen to oxygen; it is principally in such of the component reactions of respiration that oxygen is used and water is formed.

Many enzymes, co-enzymes, and carriers play a role in the stepwise oxidation of carbohydrates or of other molecules which serve as respiratory substrates. Each reaction in the chain is controlled by a specific enzyme and often also requires the presence of a co-enzyme or carrier or both. Many of these enzymes have been isolated, and their part in the respiratory mechanism has been ascertained. Most of our understanding of the respiratory process has resulted from the study of these enzymatic reactions. The action of a specific enzyme may be checked or blocked by certain compounds known as inhibitors (Chap. XVI). By the use of a suitable inhibitor it is possible to block the action of one enzyme without checking the activity of others. The respiratory sequence of reactions can, therefore, be stopped at a given point and the products which accumulate studied. By systematically interrupting the chain of reactions at various points in this way considerable information can be obtained regarding the nature of different steps in the overall process.

Anaerobic Respiration.—The external aspects of aerobic respiration have been considered in some detail in the preceding chapter; a similar consideration will now be given to anaerobic respiration before the mechanism of the overall process is discussed.

Alcoholic Fermentation.—The term "fermentation" is applied rather loosely to a variety of oxidation processes which are features of the metabolism of various species of bacteria and fungi. Some of the better known fermentations are alcoholic fermentation, acetic acid fermentation, lactic acid fermentation, butyric acid fermentation, oxalic acid fermentation, and citric acid fermentation. Some fermentation reactions are widely used in industry for the commercial production of certain chemical compounds. The chemical aspects of many of the fermentation processes occurring in bacteria and fungi have been investigated much more thoroughly than the similar processes which take place in the tissues of higher plants.

Most fermentation reactions are anaerobic, but some are aerobic. In all of them incompletely oxidized compounds accumulate as end products, and this is the most characteristic feature of fermentation processes. Some authorities also use the term fermentation to apply to the closely analogous processes which occur in the tissues of higher plants under certain conditions (see later).

Of the many known kinds of fermentations the most thoroughly investigated is the process of alcoholic fermentation. Although this process has been familiar to the human race for time out of mind, it was not until the classical researches of Pasteur, begun in 1857, that it was recognized that alcoholic fermentation resulted from the metabolic activities of yeast plants, and that it was an anaerobic process. Yeasts, it should be recalled, are single-celled fungi belonging to the Ascomycetes. Yeasts can multiply by budding and under certain conditions produce ascospores (Fig. 112).

A further step in the understanding of alcoholic fermentation was furnished by Buchner's demonstration in 1897 that an active agent or enzyme ("zymase") could be extracted from yeast cells, and that this enzyme could catalyze the process in the total absence of yeast cells.

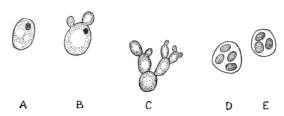

A   B   C   D   E

FIG. 112.   Yeast plants. (A) Vegetative cell, (B) "budding" of a yeast cell, (C) "colony" of cells resulting from budding, (D) and (E) asci containing ascospores.

Zymase is now recognized to be a complex of enzymes rather than a single enzyme.

Alcoholic fermentation may occur in almost any moist sugar-containing medium or sugar solution, such as a fruit juice, which is inoculated with yeast or which is left exposed to the air. Since various species of wild yeasts are blown about through the atmosphere, inoculation of such media will occur without human intervention.

The following summary equation represents the net chemical changes occurring in alcoholic fermentation:

$$C_6H_{12}O_6 \xrightarrow{\text{"Zymase"}} 2\ C_2H_5OH + 2\ CO_2 + \underline{\underline{21\ \text{kg.-cal}}}.$$

As this equation shows, fermentation of one mol of a hexose sugar results in the production of two mols of ethyl alcohol and two mols of carbon dioxide, energy to the amount of approximately 21 kg.-cal.[1] being released in the process. The carbon dioxide evolved escapes as a gas, accounting for the effervescence of a fermenting liquid. Certain by-products such as glycerol, succinic acid, amyl alcohol, and other compounds

[1] This value represents the energy evolved as calculated from the heat of reaction. The actual decrease in free energy (calculated from chemical affinities) under "biological conditions" is 72 kg.-cal. (Wohl and James, 1942).

are also usually produced in small quantities as a result of subsidiary reactions. The chemical mechanism of this process is considered later in the discussion.

Yeasts can ferment glucose, fructose, galactose, and mannose directly. Since yeast cells also contain the enzymes sucrase and maltase, the disaccharides sucrose and maltose can also be fermented after being hydrolyzed to hexose sugars. On the other hand, most kinds of yeasts cannot ferment starch because they do not synthesize amylases. This is the reason that germinated barley (malt) is used rather than the ungerminated grains in the brewing industry, since the sugar content of the grains increases greatly during germination.

Alcoholic fermentation is an anaerobic process, occurring without any utilization of atmospheric oxygen. Oxidation is accomplished by intermolecular atomic shifts which take place in such a manner that the sum total of the energy remaining in the resulting compounds is less than that present in the original substrate. Alcoholic fermentation results in only an incomplete oxidation of hexose molecules, hence the quantity of energy released is much less than in aerobic respiration. In spite of its relative inefficiency the process of fermentation is the method by which yeast plants obtain all necessary energy under anaerobic conditions.

It might be supposed that efficient aeration of a sugar solution containing yeast plants would result in complete oxidation of the sugars by a process of aerobic respiration. On the contrary, ethyl alcohol and carbon dioxide are the principal end products whether the reaction occurs in the presence or absence of oxygen. Some aerobic respiration (as much as one-third of the total, according to some investigators) does occur when oxygen has access to the yeast cells. The predominance of fermentation even in the presence of oxygen is generally ascribed to the possession by yeast cells of a relatively ineffective respiratory enzyme mechanism, as compared to a highly active fermentative system. In the presence of oxygen, however, multiplication of yeast cells occurs at a much more rapid rate than in its absence. This is undoubtedly a consequence of the markedly greater energy release resulting from the occurrence of some aerobic respiration.

When sugar in solution is fermented by yeast one of the end products—ethyl alcohol—accumulates in the solution, while the other—carbon dioxide—escapes as a gas. However, there is a definite limit to the accumulation of the alcohol. When the proportion of alcohol in the liquid reaches a certain value, which may range from 9-18 per cent depending upon the species or strain of yeast, the cells are poisoned and the fermentation process stops.

Anaerobic Respiration in the Tissues of Higher Plants.—Under anaerobic conditions, and sometimes in the presence of oxygen, processes identical with, or similar to alcoholic fermentation occur in many of the tissues of the higher plants. The several terms *fermentation, intramolecular respiration,* and *anaerobic respiration* are in common use to designate such processes. The occurrence of such a process in any higher plant tissue results in the evolution of carbon dioxide and often, although by no means invariably, in the accumulation of ethyl alcohol within the cells. In some higher plant tissues alcohol is not a product of anaerobic respiration, and in others the quantity of alcohol formed does not correspond quantitatively to the amount of hexose broken down. Various organic acids, such as oxalic acid, tartaric acid, malic acid, citric acid, and lactic acid are also common end products of anaerobic respiration in the tissues of higher plants.

At least a few tissues of higher plants possess such a powerful anaerobic respiration mechanism that the process predominates over aerobic respiration even in the presence of oxygen in considerable concentrations. In germinating rice grains, for example, in oxygen concentrations as high as about 8 per cent, the rate of anaerobic is equal to the rate of aerobic respiration and even in germinating wheat grains, a more markedly aerobic tissue, a considerable amount of anaerobic respiration occurs at this oxygen concentration (Taylor, 1942). Anaerobic respiration also takes place in the presence of oxygen in at least some kinds of tissues in which the usual course of aerobic respiration has been interrupted by cyanide or some other specific enzyme inhibitor.

In the majority of the tissues of the higher plants, however, anaerobic respiration is induced only when the access of atmospheric oxygen to the tissues is largely or entirely cut off. This process can be initiated in almost any tissue of a higher plant by subjecting it to an atmosphere which is devoid of oxygen or to an atmosphere in which the oxygen concentration is below a certain relatively low critical value. Different tissues of higher plants differ greatly in their toleration of lack of oxygen and the resultant anaerobic respiration which takes place in the cells. Some plants or plant organs can survive under such conditions for long periods, others succumb within a day or two. Maize seedlings, for example, do not remain alive much more than a day in an atmosphere devoid of oxygen. Apple and pear fruits, on the other hand, can survive storage in an atmosphere of pure hydrogen or pure nitrogen for months without injury. These fruits continue to evolve carbon dioxide under such conditions, thus indicating the occurrence of a type of respiration for which atmospheric oxygen is not necessary.

Many of the known examples of anaerobic respiration in higher plants result from structural features of plant organs which prevent ready access of oxygen to interior tissues. For example, the seed coats of a number of species are only slightly permeable to oxygen. During the earlier stages of the germination of such seeds, before the coats are ruptured, anaerobic preponderates over aerobic respiration. The best known example of this is in pea seeds, which in the early stages of germination evolve a volume of carbon dioxide three or four times as great as the volume of oxygen absorbed. Similarly, anaerobic respiration also occurs in corn grains, oat grains (especially if the glumes are left intact), and sunflower fruits during the early stages of germination (Frietinger, 1927). A similar condition probably obtains in many other seeds and dry fruits.

Anaerobic respiration also occurs naturally in some fleshy fruits. The "skin" of some fruits, of which the grape is the most familiar example, is relatively impermeable to oxygen, hence this process undoubtedly occurs in such organs.

It has been rather generally supposed that the interior tissues of most bulky fruits such as bananas, citrus fruits, melons, etc., often suffer from a deficiency of oxygen and that anaerobic respiration is of frequent occurrence in such tissues. Gustafson (1930) has shown that tomato fruits respire anaerobically when enclosed in an atmosphere of nitrogen or hydrogen and considers it possible that some anaerobic respiration may occur in them even when they are exposed to usual atmospheric conditions. On the other hand, analysis of the internal atmosphere of some of the cucurbitaceous fruits has shown the oxygen concentration to be almost as high as in the atmosphere. While it is impossible to draw a definite conclusion regarding the prevalence of anaerobic respiration in fleshy fruits, it seems probable that this process occurs in at least some fruits of this type.

Cacti will respire anaerobically when enclosed in an atmosphere of pure nitrogen (Gustafson, 1932), and it seems likely that the deep-seated tissues of succulent species may carry on anaerobic respiration under natural conditions.

When freshly harvested grains, hay, shelled beans or other such rapidly respiring plant materials are stacked compactly or packed tightly in containers, free access of oxygen to all parts of the mass may be impeded. Under such conditions anaerobic may replace aerobic respiration in many of the cells. Spoilage of the material for consumer use may result as an outcome of the accumulation of products of anaerobic respiration; this is especially likely if the plant material is kept at a relatively high temperature.

The adverse effect of a flooding of the soil upon many species of plants appears to result from the substitution of anaerobic for aerobic respiration, such a flooded soil being practically devoid of oxygen. Submergence of a field of almost any crop plant—a common occurrence in some localities—

soon results in serious injury to the plants, even if only the roots are immersed. If the flooded condition of the soil continues very long, death of the plants commonly results. The plants often exhibit many of the symptoms of desiccation, suggesting a likelihood that the physiological processes of the roots have been altered in such a fashion that absorption of water is no longer occurring at an adequate rate.

At least two probable reasons can be advanced for the injurious effects of substitution of anaerobic for aerobic respiration in normally aerobic tissues. One of these is the much lower energy output of the former process as compared with the latter. Anaerobic respiration releases only a small fraction as much energy per molecule of hexose oxidized as aerobic respiration. In metabolically active tissues, especially, the curtailed rate of energy release is probably inadequate for the normal maintenance of cell processes and deleterious effects are soon engendered within the cells. Another probable cause of impairment of cells as a result of fermentation is the accumulation of substances which exert toxic effects on the protoplasm. During anaerobic respiration ethyl alcohol and other more or less toxic compounds accumulate in cells in which this process is occurring and may be translocated to other parts of the plant which are still under aerobic conditions. In tissues in which anaerobiosis commonly occurs, considerable concentrations of such compounds can be tolerated without harm. In normally aerobic tissues, however, the tolerance for such substances is much less and their accumulation within the cells soon leads to injurious effects.

In contrast with most terrestrial plants are the many aquatic species in which the rhizomes and roots, and in some species other organs as well, are continuously submerged. In some such species considerable quantities of oxygen diffuse into the submerged organs through aerenchyma tissue from the aerial organs (Chap. XIV). At times such an internal movement of oxygen gas is adequate to maintain a completely aerobic respiration in the submerged organs, but at many times, at least in some species, it is inadequate, and at least some anaerobic respiration occurs. This latter process has been shown to be of regular or frequent occurrence in the roots and rhizomes of the spatterdock (*Nymphaea advena*) and several other aquatic species (Laing, 1940). In such organs respiration is at times preponderantly aerobic and at times preponderantly fermentative, although there is seldom a time at which some anaerobic respiration is not occurring at least in those tissues which are most remote from the supply of oxygen.

When many tissues are transferred from anaerobic to aerobic conditions fermentation is largely or entirely suppressed and the rate of consumption of respiratory substrate is reduced. This phenomenon is called the *Pasteur effect*. Although the rate of utilization of the substrate is diminished by the shift to aerobic conditions, the energy made available in the cells is usually increased because of the greater efficiency of aerobic as compared with anaerobic respiration as an energy-releasing process. The existence of the Pasteur effect has long been known in yeasts and in animal tissues. Such a mechanism has also been reported to operate in various tissues of higher plants as, for example, the roots of carrots (Marsh and Goddard, 1939), barley leaves (James and Hora, 1940), rice (Taylor, 1942), apple fruits (Thomas and Fidler, 1941), carrot and parsnip roots and potato (McCormick variety) tubers (Appleman and Brown, 1946) and doubtless occurs in many others. The exact mechanism of this effect is not known, although several more or less theoretical explanations have been offered for it (Turner, 1951).   *E/N Schume*

Glycolysis.—For purposes of discussion it is convenient to distinguish two major phases of respiration; (1) the oxidation of carbohydrate to pyruvic acid, a process called _glycolysis,_[2] and (2) the subsequent oxidation of pyruvic acid. The first of these phases appears to take place in the same general way in many kinds of tissues in either the presence or absence of atmospheric oxygen. The second phase may follow a number of diverse patterns, however, depending upon the kind of tissue and especially upon whether it occurs under aerobic or anaerobic conditions. The reactions of glycolysis have been investigated most thoroughly in yeasts and in the muscle tissue of animals, but there is good evidence for the occurrence of a similar, if not identical, chain of reactions in the cells of the higher plants (James, 1946; Bonner and Wildman, 1946; Stumpf, 1950).

The first important reactions in glycolysis are those which result in the phosphorylation of hexose molecules. The roles of adenosine diphosphate (ADP) and adenosine triphosphate (ATP) in transfers of phosphate from one molecule of carbohydrate to another have already been mentioned in Chap. XX. These same compounds play similar roles in some of the subsequent reactions of glycolysis. They act as phosphate carriers in a manner analogous to that in which other compounds act as hydrogen carriers (see later). Especial significance attaches to the energy-rich phosphate bonds. As discussed more in detail later, energy obtained in the stepwise degradation of hexose molecules is stored in phosphorylated compounds and passed from molecule to molecule by transfers of phosphate. Throughout all of the reactions of glycolysis the molecules of carbohydrates or derivatives therefrom remain in the phosphorylated state, and certain of the glycolytic reactions are catalyzed by enzymes of the transphosphorylase type.

Starting with fructose-1,6-diphosphate (Fig. 107) the probable sequence of the further reactions of glycolysis is shown in Fig. 113.

[2] As mentioned later, some authors use this term in a slightly different sense.

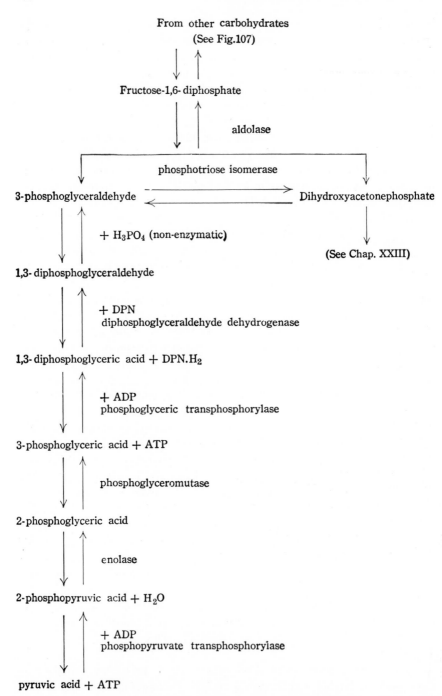

FIG. 113. Reactions of glycolysis from fructose-1,6-diphosphate to pyruvic acid.

A major step in this series of reactions is the cleavage of fructose-1, 6-diphosphate into the trioses: 3-phosphoglyceraldehyde and dihydroxyacetonephosphate, a reaction which is catalyzed by the enzyme *aldolase*.

The 3-phosphoglyceraldehyde is then converted into 1,3-diphosphoglyceric acid in two steps, as follows:

$$
\begin{array}{l}
\text{H—C=O} \\
| \\
\text{H—C—OH} \quad + \; H_3PO_4 \rightleftarrows \\
| \\
\text{H—C—O—}H_2PO_3 \\
| \\
\text{H}
\end{array}
\qquad
\begin{array}{l}
\text{OH} \\
| \\
\text{H—C—O—}H_2PO_3 \\
| \\
\text{H—C—OH} \\
| \\
\text{H—C—O—}H_2PO_3 \\
| \\
\text{H}
\end{array}
$$

3-phosphoglyceraldehyde   1,3-diphosphoglyceraldehyde

$$
\begin{array}{l}
\text{OH} \\
| \\
\text{H—C—O—}H_2PO_3 \\
| \\
\text{H—C—OH} \\
| \\
\text{H—C—O—}H_2PO_3 \\
| \\
\text{H}
\end{array}
\; + \; DPN
\xrightleftharpoons{\substack{\text{diphosphoglyceraldehyde} \\ \text{dehydrogenase}}}
\begin{array}{l}
\text{O} \\
\| \\
\text{C—O—}H_2PO_3 \\
| \\
\text{H—C—OH} \\
| \\
\text{H—C—O—}H_2PO_3 \\
| \\
\text{H}
\end{array}
\; + \; DPN \cdot H_2
$$

1,3-diphosphoglyceraldehyde   1,3-diphosphoglyceric acid

The compound which acts as a hydrogen acceptor in this reaction is diphosphopyridine nucleotide (DPN) and the catalyst is a dehydrogenase enzyme (see later). Subsequent regeneration of the reduced hydrogen acceptor $DPN \cdot H_2$ to DPN under aerobic conditions will require $\tfrac{1}{2} O_2$ so this reaction indirectly results in the ultimate utilization of this quantity of oxygen. Under anaerobic conditions reoxidation of the $DPN \cdot H_2$ takes place at the expense of the reduction of other compounds.

The 1,3-diphosphoglyceric acid is then transformed to 3-phosphoglyceric acid and then to 2-phosphoglyceric acid as indicated in Fig. 113. Under the influence of the enzyme *enolase* this latter compound is then converted to 2-phosphopyruvic acid as follows:

$$
\begin{array}{l}
\text{O} \\
\| \\
\text{C—OH} \\
| \\
\text{H—C—O—}H_2PO_3 \\
| \\
\text{H—C—OH} \\
| \\
\text{H}
\end{array}
\xrightleftharpoons{\text{enolase}}
\begin{array}{l}
\text{O} \\
\| \\
\text{C—OH} \\
| \\
\text{C—O—}H_2PO_3 \; + \; H_2O \\
\| \\
\text{C—H} \\
| \\
\text{H}
\end{array}
$$

2-phosphoglyceric acid   2-phosphopyruvic acid

The final reaction in this series is the transfer of phosphate from 2-phosphopyruvic acid to ADP resulting in the formation of pyruvic acid and ATP.

It is worthy of emphasis that the reactions of glycolysis do not involve atmospheric oxygen. It is not difficult to understand, therefore, how the series of reactions comprising this first phase of respiration can be the same, or at least closely similar, both in cells which have ready access to oxygen and those which do not. It is also noteworthy that very little energy is made available to cells by the reactions of glycolysis.

Although pyruvic acid is probably formed in living cells as a result of other sequences of reactions, glycolysis appears to be of widespread occurrence in living organisms. Pyruvic acid occupies a pivotal position in the sequence of respiratory reactions, because from it further reaction chains may diverge in a number of directions. The chemical pathway along which this compound undergoes further modifications depends in part upon whether prevailing conditions are aerobic or anaerobic. Some of the better known compounds into which pyruvic acid can be converted, in one kind of organism or another, as a result of relatively simple, enzymatically catalyzed reactions, are acetaldehyde, lactic acid, acetic acid, oxalacetic acid, and the amino acid alanine (Chap. XXVI).

Anaerobic Oxidation of Pyruvic Acid.—In the absence of oxygen, and under certain other conditions, anaerobic oxidation of pyruvic acid usually occurs, but the course of the reaction differs in different tissues and organisms. In general the products of the anaerobic respiration of pyruvic acid are incompletely oxidized compounds such as alcohols and organic acids.

In the yeasts and many other fungi, and in at least some higher plants under some conditions, anaerobic respiration results in the formation of ethyl alcohol.

The first step in this reaction is the decarboxylation of pyruvic acid, as follows:

$$CH_3 \cdot CO \cdot COOH \underset{\text{pyruvic}}{\overset{\text{pyruvic carboxylase}}{\rightleftarrows}} CH_3 \cdot CHO + CO_2$$

pyruvic acid   acetaldehyde

A second step is the reduction of acetaldehyde to ethyl alcohol, which in yeast occurs as follows:

$$CH_3 \cdot CHO + DPN \cdot H_2 \overset{\text{alcohol dehydrogenase}}{\rightleftarrows} CH_3CH_2OH + DPN$$

The $DPN \cdot H_2$ used in this reaction may be that formed in the previous glycolytic reaction in which diphosphoglyceraldehyde is converted to diphosphoglyceric acid.

In the muscle tissue of animals and in some bacteria, anaerobic respiration results in the conversion of pyruvic acid to lactic acid:

$$CH_3 \cdot CO \cdot COOH + DPN \cdot H_2 \underset{\longleftarrow}{\overset{\text{lactic acid}}{\underset{\text{dehydrogenase}}{\longrightarrow}}} CH_3 \cdot CHOH \cdot COOH + DPN$$

Both of the last two reactions are further examples of reactions in which diphosphophyridine nucleotide (DPN) participates as a hydrogen acceptor or donator (see later). Among animal physiologists the conversion of pyruvic acid to lactic acid is generally included as one of the reactions of glycolysis.

Relatively little energy becomes available to cells as a result of the further conversion of pyruvic acid to other compounds under anaerobic conditions.

Aerobic Oxidation of Pyruvic Acid.—Under aerobic conditions the oxidation of pyruvic acid usually occurs along entirely different pathways than under anaerobic conditions and the end products of its oxidation are usually carbon dioxide and water.

The most fruitful suggestion regarding the mechanism of the aerobic oxidation of pyruvic acid is that it is accomplished through a "tricarboxylic acid cycle." Several variations of this scheme have been proposed, one of which, based largely on the suggestions of Wood et al. (1942) and Krebs (1943) is represented in Fig. 114. No attempt is made to indicate in this diagram the numerous enzymes, coenzymes, and carriers which participate in these reactions nor the fact that many of the compounds which participate in this reaction are phosphorylated. The roles of some of these are discussed later in the chapter.

As shown in this figure, according to this hypothesis, a tricarboxylic acid (cis-aconitic acid) is first formed in a reaction between pyruvic and oxalacetic acids. This larger molecule then undergoes stepwise degradation until oxalacetic acid is regenerated as the final step in the cycle, the equivalent of one molecule of pyruvic acid having meanwhile been completely oxidized.

It is important to realize that this diagram presents a greatly telescoped picture of the manner in which many of these reactions proceed. This is particularly true of those four reactions in which $\frac{1}{2} O_2$ is indicated as a reactant and H_2O as a product. Actually in such reactions 2 H are usually lost from the organic acid molecule by transfer to another molecule, whence they may be transferred, stepwise, to other molecules under the catalytic influence of dehydrogenases (see later). The terminal step in each such reaction chain, however, is the transfer of the 2 H to O and the

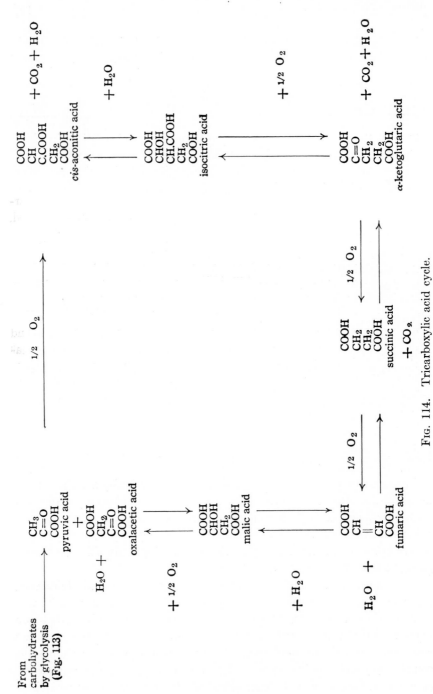

From
carbohydrates
by glycolysis
(Fig. 113)

CH₃
C=O
COOH
pyruvic acid

$H_2O +$

+

COOH
CH₂
C=O
COOH
oxalacetic acid

$+ \frac{1}{2}\ O_2$

COOH
CHOH
CH₂
COOH
malic acid

$+ H_2O$

$H_2O +$

COOH
CH
‖
CH
COOH
fumaric acid

$\frac{1}{2}\ O_2$

COOH
CH₂
CH₂
COOH
succinic acid
$+ CO_2$

$\frac{1}{2}\ O_2$

$\frac{1}{2}\ \ O_2$

COOH
CH
C.COOH
CH₂
COOH
cis-aconitic acid
$+ CO_2 + H_2O$

$+ H_2O$

COOH
CHOH
CH.COOH
CH₂
COOH
isocitric acid

$+ \frac{1}{2}\ O_2$

COOH
C=O
CH₂
CH₂
COOH
α-ketoglutaric acid
$+ CO_2 + H_2O$

Fig. 114. Tricarboxylic acid cycle.

formation of H_2O, under the catalytic influence of an oxidase enzyme (see later).

Carbon dioxide is eliminated in this cycle in the formation of aconitic, α-ketoglutaric and succinic acids, respectively. Water is eliminated in four of the reactions in this cycle, but is a reactant in two of the others, hence the net liberation of water is two molecules per molecule of pyruvic acid oxidized. The total consumption of oxygen is one-half molecule in each of five different reactions, a total of two and one-half molecules for each molecule of pyruvic acid oxidized. The summary equation for this phase of respiration is therefore:

$$CH_3 \cdot CO \cdot COOH + 2\tfrac{1}{2} O_2 \rightarrow 3 CO_2 + 2 H_2O + \text{energy}$$

If the $\tfrac{1}{2} O_2$ required to oxidize the hydrogen acceptor (DPN) which is reduced in one of the reactions of glycolysis and the H_2O eliminated in the formation of pyruvic acid (Fig. 113) be added to the equation above, the resulting equation will be that for the complete oxidation of a triose sugar such as glyceraldehyde.

Evidence for the existence of a cycle of reactions of the general nature of that depicted in Fig. 114 is much stronger for animal tissues than for the tissues of the higher plants. However, it is well known that most of the organic acids and enzymes involved in such a cycle are common plant constituents, and evidence that such a cycle operates in plants has been steadily accumulating (Henderson and Stauffer, 1944; Bonner and Wildman, 1946; Bonner, 1948; Laties, 1949).

In aerobic respiration most of the energy release occurs during the later aerobic phase of the process, rather than during the earlier reactions of glycolysis. Energy is liberated or transferred to other molecules principally during the dehydrogenation reactions of the cycle. In these reactions hydrogen is transferred to oxygen, not directly, but through intermediate enzymes and carriers not shown in Fig. 114.

Although some energy release occurs during anaerobic respiration, this energy is either inadequate in amount or unavailable for maintenance of physiological processes in most tissues of higher plants. Many fundamental physiological processes are completely arrested in plant tissues in the absence of oxygen. Among these are cell division, absorption of electrolytes, streaming of protoplasm, translocation of solutes, tropisms, and various synthetic processes. In other words all of these processes, and doubtless many others, can proceed only under the driving force of aerobic respiration. In some tissues disintegration of protoplasm ensues within 48 hr. if aerobic respiration is stopped. Although oxygen apparently participates in only a few of reactions of respiration, nevertheless its presence induces the establishment of chains of reactions of such a nature that at least some of the energy released is diverted to the accomplishment of essential energy-consuming reactions.

Other mechanisms of aerobic respiration besides the one described above probably also operate in plant cells. There is limited evidence, for example, that other substances in the glycolytic chain of reactions besides pyruvic acid may serve as the starting points for divergent pathways of aerobic respiration. The available information is too meager, however, to warrant discussion of other possible mechanisms.

Energy Transfer During Respiration.—So far the discussion has centered on the kinds of compounds formed at different stages of respiration. Even more at the heart of the process are the transfers of energy which occur from molecule to molecule. Such energy transfers are the mainspring of life.

Any detailed treatment of the intricate and far from fully understood mechanisms of energy transfer in biological oxidations is beyond the scope of this book. Only a few of the most fundamental aspects of this topic can be discussed briefly. Many, probably most, of the energy transfers occurring during respiration hinge on the formation of labile high-energy phosphate bonds. The term "high energy" does not mean that the phosphate is strongly bonded—the contrary is usually true—but that when such a bond is disrupted in a chemical reaction, that a relatively large amount of energy is released. Not all phosphate bonds are of the high-energy type. The ester type phosphate bonds in the phosphorylated sugars, for example, are all relatively low-energy bonds.

Several kinds of compounds in which high-energy phosphate bonds are present are known to exist in living organisms. The best known, and probably most important, of these are adenosine triphosphate (ATP) and adenosine diphosphate (ADP). These two compounds are derivatives of adenosine-5-monophosphate (AMP) which is a complex compound constructed from one molecule each of adenine (a purine base), ribose, and phosphoric acid. ADP differs from AMP in having a second phosphate group linked to the one present in AMP, and ATP has a third phosphate group linked to the second one of ADP. Thus an ATP molecule contains a chain of three phosphate groups linked together. The chemical bonds of the second and third phosphate groups of ATP and of the second phosphate group of ADP, but not the first group in any of the adenosine phosphates, are high-energy bonds. The energy liberated on hydrolysis of either of the high-energy phosphate groups of ATP is about 12,000 calories per mol. In contrast that released upon hydrolysis of the ester type phosphate bond such as occurs in phosphorylated sugars is only 2000-3000 calories per mol.

In general, energy is stored in high-energy phosphate bonds as a result of reactions in which phosphorylated compounds are oxidized. The conversion of 1,3-diphosphoglyceraldehyde to 3-phosphoglyceric acid is one example of a reaction in which ATP is synthesized (Fig. 113). The glyceraldehyde is first oxidized (by loss of 2 H to DPN) to 1,3 phosphoglyceric acid. As a result of this reaction one of the phosphate groups in this molecule becomes a carboxyl phosphate group $\overset{O}{\overset{\|}{C}}\cdot O\cdot H_2PO_3$ which contains another type of high-energy phosphate bond. Because of the high energy of this bond it can be transferred in an immediately following reaction to ADP, becoming a high energy phosphate bond of ATP.

From the standpoint of cellular energetics the number of ATP molecules generated per molecule of hexose oxidized is very significant. In certain animal tissues from 12 to 24 mols of energy rich phosphate are formed for each mol of hexose completely oxidized. It appears that roughly about half of the total energy released in respiration is stored in this way. It is a reasonable presumption that an approximately similar situation prevails in plant tissues. Some ATP molecules are synthesized during glycolysis (Fig. 113); still more are generated in certain reactions of the tricarboxylic cycle. Many of the compounds which participate in this cycle are undoubtedly in a phosphorylated state, although in the present incomplete status of our knowledge it is not practicable to represent them in this way in Fig. 114.

By release of energy stored in energy-rich phosphate bonds, energy-requiring metabolic reactions which would otherwise not take place are made to occur. Such phosphate bonds are thus a connecting link between the energy-releasing reactions of respiration and the numerous energy-consuming reactions which are integral steps in metabolism. The reaction in which the ATP was synthesized is said to "drive" the reaction in which the phosphate bond energy is used, the two reactions thus being connected through ATP as a common reactant.

Organic Acid Metabolism.—It is clear from the previous discussion that respiration, particularly in its aerobic phases, represents largely the metabolism of organic acids. Apart from the fatty and amino acids, which are considered in later chapters, the more important organic acids occurring in plants are oxalic, tartaric, succinic, fumaric, malic, oxalacetic, pyruvic, aconitic, citric and isocitric, and α-ketoglutaric. Some of these, such as oxalic, malic, tartaric, and citric, are present in considerable quantities in some tissues; others, such as pyruvic, oxalacetic, succinic, fumaric, and aconitic, are seldom if ever present in appreciable amounts, but are important metabolites as discussed previously. Although present in all parts of the plant these organic acids are, in general, found in the greatest quantities in leaves and fruits.

The organic acids integrally involved in the respiratory process are also metabolically related to the synthesis of fatty acids (Chap. XXIII) and amino acids (Chap. XXVI). The former are one of the kinds of compounds from which fats and oils are made; the latter are the compounds out of which proteins are synthesized. Since the organic acids that serve as respiratory intermediates are derived from carbohydrates they occupy a metabolic crossroads between carbohydrates on the one hand and fats and proteins on the other.

Any compound containing a carboxyl ($-\overset{\displaystyle O}{\overset{\displaystyle \|}{C}}-OH$) group or groups falls into the category of an organic acid. Some of the important plant acids, such as α-ketoglutaric, oxalacetic, succinic, fumaric, and malic are dicarboxylic; others such as aconitic, citric, and isocitric, are tricarboxylic. Several of them, such as pyruvic, oxalacetic, and α-ketoglutric, are keto-acids, *i.e.*, contain a ketone ($-C=O$) group. Certain of the plant acids, such as isocitric, malic, and tartaric are hydroxy acids, *i.e.*, contain hydroxyl groups other than those in the carboxyl groups.

The fact that many plant tissues can metabolically fix carbon dioxide from the atmosphere in nonphotosynthetic processes has already been referred to in Chap. XVIII. This phenomenon is especially prominent among many plants of the succulent habit of growth (Bennet-Clark, 1949), and appears to be closely related to the organic acid metabolism of plants.

In some succulent species the organic acid content shows a regular daily cycle of increase during the night hours and decrease during the daylight hours. The synthesis of organic acids in the leaves of some succulents is directly related to the carbon dioxide concentration of the atmosphere. In *Bryophyllum crenatum*, for example, virtually no organic acids are synthesized in the dark in the absence of carbon dioxide, but the greater the carbon dioxide concentration in the air up to 10 per cent the greater the quantity of organic acids synthesized (Bonner and Bonner, 1948). The principal acids formed are citric, malic, and isocitric. The diurnal variation in the organic acid content of the leaves of certain succulents is therefore probably to be explained on the basis that, during the daytime, carbon dioxide concentration in the photosynthetic tissues is maintained at a low value and little or no synthesis of organic acids occurs. At night the carbon dioxide content of the tissues builds up as a result of respiration and synthesis of organic acids is favored.

Carbon dioxide fixation in the leaves of nonsucculents also involves organic acids. For example, when leaves of tomato, tobacco, or barley were exposed to carbon dioxide containing radioactive carbon for 15 min. in the dark and then analyzed, most of the radioactive carbon was found in malic or succinic acid (Stutz and Burris, 1951).

Carbon dioxide fixation in a species of bacterium has been shown to take place by the following reaction:

$$\text{CH}_3 \cdot \text{CO} \cdot \text{COOH} + \text{CO}_2 \underset{}{\overset{\text{oxalacetic carboxylase}}{\rightleftarrows}} \text{HOOC} \cdot \text{CH}_2 \cdot \text{CO} \cdot \text{COOH}$$

pyruvic acid   oxalacetic acid

This reaction is called the Wood and Werkman (1936) reaction after its discoverers. It is probable that carbon dioxide fixation in the tissues of higher plants occurs either by this or other similar reactions. Support for this view is afforded by the fact that oxalacetic carboxylase, which catalyzes the Wood and Werkman reaction, has been found in a number of species of plants (Vennesland, 1949). The enzyme oxalsuccinic carboxylase, which catalyzes a similar reaction in which carbon dioxide is fixed by reacting with α-ketoglutaric acid, forming oxalsuccinic acid, has also been found in higher plants (Ceithaml and Vennesland, 1949). This latter acid is readily converted into iso-citric acid.

The organic acids synthesized by direct fixation of carbon dioxide undoubtedly enter into the stream of metabolic reactions, particularly the chains and cycles of reactions which constitute the respiratory process. That dark fixation of carbon dioxide in organic acids is a possible first step in photosynthesis has already been mentioned in Chap. XVIII.

Respiratory Enzymes.—As the previous discussion has indicated, many different kinds of enzymes participate in the reactions of respiration. Respiratory enzymes possess, in general, the properties of enzymes already discussed in Chap. XVI. Most, if not all, of the respiratory enzymes either have a prosthetic group or else have a coenzyme associated with them. Among the oxidizing-reducing enzymes it is the prosthetic group or coenzyme which readily undergoes oxidation and reduction. The same prosthetic group or coenzyme can be associated with any of a number of different proteins, and enzyme specificity appears to depend upon the protein fraction of the enzyme.

The principal categories of enzymes involved in respiratory reactions are transphosphorylases, desmolases, carboxylases, hydrases, dehydrogenases, and oxidases.

Transphosphorylases.—The principal enzymes of this type are listed in Table 18, and examples of reactions which they catalyze are shown in

Fig. 107 and Fig. 113. In general, these enzymes catalyze transfers of phosphate groups, either from one kind of molecule to another, or from one position to another position in the same kind of molecule. Very little is known of the chemical constitution of the transphosphorylases. The presence of magnesium ions is necessary for at least some of the transphosphorylases to exert their catalytic activity.

Desmolases.—These are enzymes which catalyze reactions in which carbon chains are broken or lengthened. The best known example is *aldolase* (Fig. 113). This enzyme is known to be present in the tissues of the higher plants (Tewfik and Stumpf, 1949).

Carboxylases.—Enzymes of this type catalyze the reversible carboxylation of certain organic acids and related compounds. These enzymes are sometimes classified under the desmolases. Equations for reactions catalyzed by pyruvic carboxylase and oxalacetic carboxylase are given earlier in the chapter. A close relationship between thiamine (Chap. XXVIII) and pyruvic carboxylase has been recognized since the work of Lohmann and Schuster (1937). The compound diphosphothiamine is now recognized to be the coenzyme of pyruvic carboxylase and of several other similar enzymes.

Hydrases.—These are enzymes which catalyze the addition or subtraction of water from molecules without causing their splitting. One example is *enolase* which catalyzes one of the reversible reactions of glycolysis (Fig. 113). This enzyme is a metalloprotein, most probably a magnesium compound. *Fumarase*, which catalyzes the reversible conversion of L-malic acid to fumaric acid, and *aconitase*, which catalyzes the reversible transformation of aconotic to isocitric acid (*cf.* tricarboxylic acid cycle, Fig. 114), are other examples of hydrases.

Dehydrogenases.—Enzymes which accomplish intercellular oxidations and reductions by the transfer of hydrogen from one kind of molecule to another kind are called dehydrogenases. The essential effect of such enzymes is that of activating the hydrogen of metabolites. Dehydrogenases are widely and probably universally distributed throughout the plant and animal kingdoms.

Some dehydrogenases can transfer hydrogen directly to oxygen, thus resembling oxidases (see later) in their action. Such "aerobic dehydrogenases" appear to be more common in animals than in plants. "Anaerobic dehydrogenases" transfer hydrogen to other compounds than oxygen and hence can operate under either aerobic or anaerobic conditions. The majority of plant dehydrogenases are of this latter type.

Dehydrogenases operate simultaneously on two substrates, one of which is oxidized (dehydrogenated) while the other is reduced (hydrogenated). The former is called the *hydrogen donator;* the latter the *hydrogen accep-*

tor. Some, and perhaps all, dehydrogenases can catalyze the same reaction in both directions. Alcohol dehydrogenase, mentioned earlier in the discussion, can, for example, catalyze both the dehydrogenation (oxidation) of alcohol to acetaldehyde, and the hydrogenation (reduction) of acetaldehyde to alcohol. Dehydrogenases are commonly named for the substrate which serves as the hydrogen donor. Some of the principal dehydrogenases known to occur in plants are listed in Table 18.

Other examples of dehydrogenase-catalyzed reactions are shown in the scheme for glycolysis (Fig. 113) and for aerobic respiration by the tricarboxylic acid cycle (Fig. 114). Among the latter is the oxidation of succinic to fumaric acid under the influence of succinic acid dehydrogenase. Under anaerobic test tube conditions the dye methylene blue serves as a hydrogen acceptor in this reaction:

$$
\begin{array}{ccccc}
\underset{\substack{\text{Succinic}\\ \text{acid}}}{\overset{\displaystyle \text{CH}_2\text{COOH}}{\underset{\displaystyle \text{CH}_2\text{COOH}}{|}}}
& + \underset{\substack{\text{Methylene}\\ \text{blue}}}{\text{Mb}}
& \xrightarrow{\text{Succinic acid dehydrogenase}}
& \underset{\substack{\text{Fumaric}\\ \text{acid}}}{\overset{\displaystyle \text{CHCOOH}}{\underset{\displaystyle \text{CHCOOH}}{\parallel}}}
& + \underset{\substack{\text{Reduced}\\ \text{Methylene}\\ \text{blue (color-}\\ \text{less)}}}{\text{MbH}_2}
\end{array}
$$

In this reaction hydrogen atoms are shuttled from succinic acid molecules to dehydrogenase molecules to methylene blue molecules, the dehydrogenase being transitorily reduced in the process.

Indicators such as methylene blue are not natural constituents of living cells, but cells do contain numerous substances which act in a manner analogous to such indicators, *i.e.*, as hydrogen acceptors. One of the most important of these is the complex compound *cytochrome* which is of widespread occurrence in both plant and animal tissues (Keilin 1925).

Actually three cytochromes, *a, b,* and *c,* have been identified in living tissues, but for the purpose of this discussion it will not be necessary to differentiate among them. Cytochrome is a complex pigmented compound containing iron and is closely related chemically to chlorophyll and the hematin of hemoglobin.

Cytochrome performs in a biological oxidation-reduction system as a hydrogen *carrier.* Under the influence of certain dehydrogenases, hydrogen atoms are transferred from the substrate to the cytochrome. The substrate is thus oxidized; the cytochrome reduced. The reduced cytochrome is then oxidized back to its original condition under the influence of cytochrome oxidase (see later). This cycle can be repeated an indefinite number of times. Although usually classed as a hydrogen carrier, the behavior of cytochrome is substantially that of an enzyme. In fact, it is difficult to draw any hard and fast distinction between an enzyme and a carrier. The

cycle of reduction and subsequent oxidation of cytochrome, assuming succinic acid as the hydrogen donator, can be indicated as follows:

$$\begin{array}{c} CH_2COOH \\ | \\ CH_2COOH \\ \text{succinic acid} \end{array} + Cyt \xrightarrow{\text{succinic acid dehydrogenase}} \begin{array}{c} CHCOOH \\ || \\ CHCOOH \\ \text{fumaric acid} \end{array} + Cyt \cdot H_2$$

$$Cyt \cdot H_2 + \tfrac{1}{2} O_2 \xrightarrow{\text{cytochrome oxidase}} Cyt + H_2O$$

Certain other dehydrogenases in addition to succinic acid dehydrogenase are linked to cytochrome in their operation. Many dehydrogenases
are linked in their action, however, not to cytochrome, but to certain
compounds of the class called nucleotides. The best known of these are
diphosphorypridine nucleotide (DPN), also called coenzyme I or cozy-
mase, and *triophosphopyridine nucleotide* (TPN), also called coenzyme
II. Diphosphopyridine nucleotide is the coenzyme of, for example, alcohol
dehydrogenase; triphosphopyridine nucleotide of, for example, glucose-6-
phosphate dehydrogenase. Either of these nucleotides can apparently
serve as the coenzyme for malic dehydrogenase or for lactic dehydrogenase from animal tissues. Both of these compounds are in part derivatives of nicotinic acid, one of the B-complex vitamins (Chap. XXVIII).
The pyridine nucleotides are widely distributed in the tissues of plants
and animals.

The pyridine ring of the nicotinic acid amide is the active group in both
of these compounds, being reversibly oxidized or reduced by the loss or
gain, respectively, of pairs of hydrogen atoms. Under the influence of a
nucleotide-linked dehydrogenase, hydrogen is transferred from the substrate to the nucleotide, whence it is usually transferred, under the influence of other enzymes, to other molecules. The nucleotide coenzymes thus
act, in effect, as hydrogen carriers. Under aerobic conditions, the chain
of molecule-to-molecule transfers of hydrogen usually terminates with the
transfer of hydrogen to oxygen, forming water, under the catalytic influence of an oxidase enzyme.

Examples of reactions in which a nucleotide coenzyme plays a role have
already been given under the discussion of glycolysis and the anaerobic
respiration of pyruvic acid.

For some of the aerobic dehydrogenases the prosthetic group or coenzyme is the compound isoalloxanthine-adenine-dinucleotide, which is in
part a derivative of riboflavin (Chap. XXVIII), another of the B-complex
vitamins. This compound acts as a hydrogen carrier in certain oxidation-
reduction reactions in a manner analogous to that of other carriers previ-

ously described. The riboflavin group is the active one in this compound, each of two of the nitrogen atoms of the riboflavin reversibly losing or gaining a hydrogen in oxidation or reduction reactions, respectively.

The activity of dehydrogenases may be greatly retarded or completely blocked by various organic inhibitors. Some dehydrogenase inhibitors are more or less specific in their action. For example, malonic acid and pyrophosphate are strong inhibitors of succinic acid dehydrogenase, but scarcely affect other enzymes of this type. Similarly iodoacetate is a much stronger inhibitor of alcohol dehydrogenase than of most other dehydrogenases. Other inhibitors, such as urethane, have a generally retarding or checking effect on the activity of all dehydrogenases.

Oxidases.—These are enzymes which activate molecular oxygen to which hydrogen is then transferred from oxidizable substrates. The usual products of an oxidase-catalyzed reaction are an oxidized (dehydrogenated) substrate and reduced oxygen, *i.e.*, water. It is obvious that oxidases can operate only under aerobic conditions. The three principal oxidases known to occur in plants are *cytochrome oxidase, tyrosinase,* and *ascorbic acid oxidase.* Enzymes of this type catalyze, for example, the final step in those reactions of the tricarboxylic acid cycle (Fig. 114) in which oxygen is a reactant and water is an end product.

Cytochrome oxidase is probably the most widely distributed of the oxidases and is known to be present in the tissues of a number of plants and of many animals. The enzyme catalyzes the oxidation (dehydrogenation) of cytochrome which has previously been reduced (hydrogenated) by the action of a dehydrogenase as described above.

Tyrosinase (polyphenol oxidase, catechol oxidase) is widely distributed in both green and non-green plants but is uncommon in animals. This enzyme catalyzes the oxidation (dehydrogenation) of a large number of phenolic compounds such as guaiacol, catechol, pyrogallol, and tyrosine (Nelson and Dawson, 1944). Oxidation probably takes place to the corresponding hydroxyquinone, as the following representative reaction for the oxidation of catechol shows:

catechol   o-hydroxyquinone

Rapid polymerization of the hydroxyquinone results in formation of some of the dark-colored pigments which are characteristic end products of this reaction.

The frequently observed reddish, brownish, or blackish discolorations in cut or crushed plant tissues, or in expressed juices, result largely from the oxidative activities of tyrosinase or from the activities of its oxidation products, such as the hydroquinones.

Ascorbic acid oxidase is found in many, although by no means all, plant tissues but is not known to occur in animals. This enzyme catalyzes the oxidation (dehydrogenation) of ascorbic acid, also called vitamin C (Chap. XXVIII), to dehydro-ascorbic acid as follows:

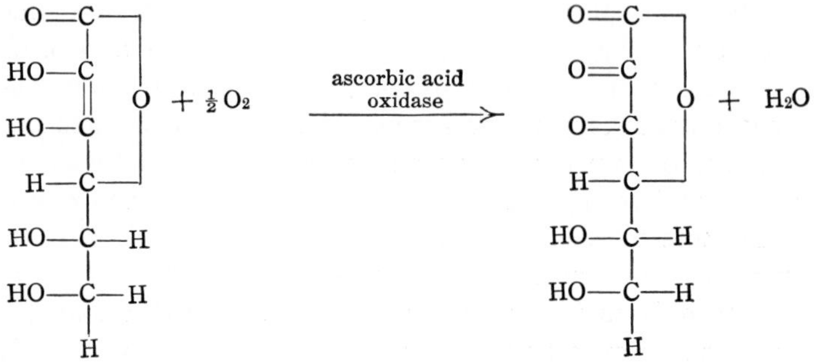

L ascorbic acid   dehydro-L-ascorbic acid

The reverse of the above reaction also occurs readily in plant tissues, under the influence of reducing agents, suggesting that ascorbic acid may operate in plants as a hydrogen carrier. Ascorbic acid can also be oxidized indirectly in plant tissues by a reaction with a quinone resulting from the action of polyphenol oxidase.

More than one of the principal plant oxidases may occur in the cells of some tissues. In some kinds of cells, however, one such enzyme system appears to be the only, or at least the predominant, one present. Cytochrome oxidase has been found in the embryos of wheat (Goddard, 1944) and other plants, and in various other plant tissues. Among the wide variety of plant tissues in which tyrosinase is found are potato tubers (Baker and Nelson, 1943). Cytochrome oxidase is also present in this tissue (Goddard and Holden, 1950). Ascorbic acid oxidase appears to play a role in the respiration of barley shoots (James *et al.*, 1944) and has been shown to be present in a number of other kinds of plants.

All of the oxidases appear to be metalloprotein compounds. Cytochrome oxidase is an iron or copper compound. The tyrosinase of potatoes is a copper proteinate (Kubowitz, 1937), and this also appears to be true of ascorbic acid oxidase (Powers *et al.*, 1944). In all of these enzymes the metallic group appears to be both the prosthetic and catalytically active group.

All of the oxidases are strongly inhibited by certain substances such as cyanides, sulfides, and azides, which react readily with the metallic groups. Many oxidases are also inhibited by carbon monoxide. For cytochrome oxidase, and perhaps some other oxidases, such carbon monoxide-inhibited systems can be reactivated by exposure to light.

Peroxidases.—Enzymes of this group are widely distributed in plants and animals. One of the best sources of a plant peroxidase is horseradish root. Peroxidases catalyze the oxidation of phenolic compounds and certain other closely related substances, using oxygen derived from hydrogen peroxide. This latter compound is formed in at least small quantities in cells, as a result of the activity of certain aerobic dehydrogenases and perhaps also of other enzymes. Peroxidases are supposed to operate by transferring hydrogen from a substrate (*i.e.*, oxidizing the substrate) to hydrogen peroxide, thus converting the latter into water. The reaction is analogous to that of oxidases, except that hydrogen peroxide serves as the hydrogen acceptor instead of oxygen.

The exact physiological role of peroxidases is not clear although it is considered probable that these enzymes participate in metabolically important reactions. Peroxidase from horseradish root is an iron protein compound with the iron in a hematin group, this latter acting as the prosthetic group (Theorell, 1947). Like oxidases, peroxidases are strongly inhibited by cyanides, sulfides, and azides.

Catalase.—This enzyme is widely distributed in living organisms. Catalase, like peroxidases, acts on hydrogen peroxide, catalyzing its decomposition into water and molecular oxygen:

$$2 \text{ H}_2\text{O}_2 \xrightarrow{\text{Catalase}} 2 \text{ H}_2\text{O} + \text{O}_2$$

In spite of the fact that it is one of the most ubiquitous of enzymes, the role of catalase is obscure. It is commonly considered that the presence of catalase prevents any accumulation of hydrogen peroxide in cells. This compound, which in any appreciable concentration is toxic, is known to be a product of certain types of enzymatic activity.

Catalase is an iron-protein compound with the iron in a hematin group. It has a molecular weight of about 250,000 and has been prepared in pure crystalline form by Sumner and Dounce (1937). Catalase activity is strongly inhibited by sulfides, cyanides, and azides. It is not active under anaerobic conditions.

Metabolically active plant tissues usually exhibit a high rate of respiration and a correlated high enzymatic activity. Hence a correlation usually exists between the catalase activity of a tissue and its metabolic status. Measurements of the catalase activity of a tissue are therefore often accepted as an index of the intensity of metabolic activity in that tissue.

SUGGESTED FOR COLLATERAL READING

Bonner, J. *Plant Biochemistry*. Academic Press, Inc. New York. 1950.

Goddard, D. R. The respiration of cells and tissues. In *Physical Chemistry of Cells and Tissues*. R. Höber, *et al.* 371-391. The Blakiston Co. Philadelphia. 1945.

Lardy, H. A., Editor. *Respiratory Enzymes*. Burgess Publishing Co. Minneapolis. 1949.

Sumner, J. B., and K. Myrbäck, Editors. *The Enzymes*. Vol. I (Parts 1, 2); Vol. II (Parts 1, 2). Academic Press, Inc. New York. 1950, 1951, 1951, 1952.

Sumner, J. B., and G. F. Somers. *Chemistry and Methods of Enzymes*. 2nd Ed. Academic Press, Inc. New York. 1947.

SELECTED BIBLIOGRAPHY

Appleman, C. O., and R. G. Brown. Relation of anaerobic to aerobic respiration in some storage organs with special reference to the Pasteur effect in higher plants. *Amer. Jour. Bot.* **33:** 170-181. 1946.

Baker, D., and J. M. Nelson. Tyrosinase and plant respiration. *Jour. Gen. Physiol.* **26:** 269-276. 1943.

Barron, E. S. G. Mechanisms of carbohydrate metabolism. An essay on comparative biochemistry. *Advances in Enzymol.* **3:** 149-189. 1943.

Bennet-Clark, T. A. Organic acids of plants. *Ann. Rev. Biochem.* **18:** 639-654. 1949.

Berger, J., and G. S. Avery, Jr. Dehydrogenases of the *Avena* coleoptile. *Amer. Jour. Bot.* **30:** 290-297. 1943.

Bonner, J. Biochemical mechanisms in the respiration of the *Avena* coleoptile. *Arch. Biochem.* **17:** 311-326. 1948.

Bonner, J., and S. G. Wildman. Enzymatic mechanisms in the respiration of spinach leaves. *Arch. Biochem.* **10:** 497-518. 1946.

Bonner, W., and J. Bonner. The role of carbon dioxide in acid formation by succulent plants. *Amer. Jour. Bot.* **35:** 113-117. 1948.

Ceithaml, J., and Birgit Vennesland. The synthesis of tricarboxylic acids by carbon dioxide fixation in parsley root preparations. *Jour. Biol. Chem.* **178:** 133-143. 1949.

Frietinger, G. Untersuchungen über die Konlensäureabgabe und Sauerstoffaufnanme bei keimenden Samen. *Flora* **122:** 167-201. 1927.

Goddard, D. R. Cytochrome *c* and cytochrome oxidase from wheat germ. *Amer. Jour. Bot.* **31:** 270-276. 1944.

Goddard, D. R., and Constance Holden. Cytochrome oxidase in the potato tuber. *Arch. Biochem.* **27:** 41-47. 1950.

Goddard, D. R., and J. D. Meeuse. Respiration of higher plants. *Ann. Rev. Plant Physiol.* **1:** 207-232. 1950.

Gustafson, F. G. Intramolecular respiration of tomato fruits. *Amer. Jour. Bot.* **17:** 1011-1027. 1930.

Gustafson, F. G. Anaerobic respiration of cacti. *Amer. Jour. Bot.* **19:** 823-834. 1932.

Henderson, J. H. M., and J. F. Stauffer. The influence of some respiratory inhibitors and intermediates on growth and respiration of excised tomato roots. *Amer. Jour. Bot.* **31:** 528-535. 1944.

James, W. O. The respiration of plants. *Ann. Rev. Biochem.* **15:** 417-434. 1946.

James, W. O., C. R. C. Heard, and Gladys M. James. On the oxidative decomposition of hexosediphosphate by barley. The role of ascorbic acid. *New Phytol.* **43:** 62-74. 1944.

James, W. O., and F. B. Hora. The effect of cyanide on the respiration of barley. *Ann. Bot.* **4:** 107-118. 1940.

Keilin, D. On cytochrome, a respiratory pigment common to animals, yeasts, and higher plants. *Proc. Roy. Soc. (London)* **B 98:** 312-339. 1925.

Keilin, D., and E. F. Hartree. Cytochrome *a* and cytochrome oxidase. *Nature* **141:** 870-871. 1938.

Keilin, D., and T. Mann. On the haematin compound of peroxidase. *Proc. Roy. Soc. (London)* **B 122:** 119-133. 1937.

Krebs, H. A. The intermediary stages in the biological oxidation of carbohydrates. *Advances in Enzymol.* **3:** 191-252. 1943.

Kubowitz, F. Über die chemische Zusammensetzung der Kartoffeloxydase. *Biochem. Zeitschr.* **292:** 221-229. 1937.

Laing, H. E. The composition of the internal atmosphere of *Nuphar advenum* and other water plants. *Amer. Jour. Bot.* **27:** 861-868. 1940.

Laties, G. G. The role of pyruvate in the aerobic respiration of barley roots. *Arch. Biochem.* **20:** 284-299. 1949.

Lohmann, K., and P. Schuster. Untersuchungen über die Cocarboxylase. *Biochem. Zeitschr.* **294:** 188-214. 1937.

Marsh, P. B., and D. R. Goddard. Respiration and fermentation in the carrot, *Daucus carota. Amer. Jour. Bot.* **26:** 724-728. 767-772. 1939.

Nelson, J. M., and C. R. Dawson. Tyrosinase. *Advances in Enzymol.* **4:** 99-152. 1944.

Powers, W. H., S. Lewis, and C. R. Dawson. The preparation and properties of highly purified ascorbic acid oxidase. *Jour. Gen. Physiol.* **27:** 167-180. 1944.

Stotz, E. Pyruvate metabolism. *Advances in Enzymol.* **5:** 129-164. 1945.

Stumpf, P. K. Carbohydrate metabolism in higher plants. III. Breakdown of fructose diphosphate by pea extracts. *Jour. Biol. Chem.* **182:** 261-272. 1950.

Stutz, R. E., and R. H. Burris. Photosynthesis and metabolism of organic acids in higher plants. *Plant Physiol.* **26:** 226-243. 1951.

Sumner, J. B., and A. L. Dounce. Crystalline catalase. *Jour. Biol. Chem.* **121:** 417-424. 1937.

Taylor, D. L. Influence of oxygen tension on respiration, fermentation, and growth in wheat and rice. *Amer. Jour. Bot.* **29:** 721-738. 1942.

Tewfik, S., and P. K. Stumpf. Carbohydrate metabolism in higher plants. II. The distribution of aldolase in plants. *Amer. Jour. Bot.* **36:** 567-571. 1949.

Theorell, H. Heme-linked groups and mode of action of some hemoproteins. *Advances in Enzymol.* **7:** 265-303. 1947.

Thimann, K. V., and W. D. Bonner, Jr. Organic acid metabolism. *Ann. Rev. Plant Physiol.* **1:** 75-108. 1950.

Thomas, M., and J. C. Fidler. Studies in zymasis. VIII, IX. *New Phytol.* **40:** 217-261. 1941.

Thunberg, T. The hydrogen-activating enzymes of the cells. *Quart. Rev. Biol.* **5:** 318-347. 1930.

Turner, J. S. Respiration (The Pasteur effect in plants). *Ann. Rev. Plant Physiol.* **2:** 145-168. 1951.

Vennesland, Birgit. The β-carboxylases of plants. II. *Jour. Biol. Chem.* **178:** 591-597. 1949.

Wohl, K., and W. O. James. The energy changes associated with plant respiration. *New Phytol.* **41:** 230-256. 1942.

Wood, H. G., and C. H. Werkman. The utilization of CO_2 in the dissimilation of glycerol by propionic acid bacteria. *Biochem. Jour.* **30:** 48-53. 1936.

Wood, H. G., C. H. Werkman, A. Hemingway, and A. O. Nier. Fixation of carbon dioxide by pigeon liver in the dissimilation of pyruvic acid. *Jour. Biol. Chem.* **142:** 31-45. 1942.

XXIII

FAT METABOLISM

Fats and fat-like substances are present in every living cell. They are essential constituents of the protoplasmic system and one of the principal kinds of food substances. In storage organs fats and oils may accumulate until they make up nearly half of the dry weight of the tissues. Fats are composed of the same three elements—hydrogen, carbon, and oxygen—that make up carbohydrates. As food substances, however, they are distinguished by their high energy content. This results from the very low percentage of oxygen in the fat molecule. A single molecule of the fat palmitin, for example, contains fifty-one carbon atoms, and only six oxygen atoms. Chemically, fats and oils are similar; the distinction between them rests on differences in their physical properties. Fats are solids at room temperature while oils are liquids. In addition to their great importance as foods, fats and their chemical relatives serve in a number of other indispensable roles in plants as the succeeding discussion will show.

Esters.—Fats and most other lipids are compounds of the type termed *esters*. Esters are compounds formed by the reaction between an alcohol and an acid. The reaction between ethyl alcohol and acetic acid, for example, results in the formation of ethyl acetate, a typical ester:

$$\underset{\substack{\text{Ethyl} \\ \text{alcohol}}}{C_2H_5OH} + \underset{\substack{\text{Acetic} \\ \text{acid}}}{CH_3COOH} \rightleftarrows \underset{\substack{\text{Ethyl} \\ \text{acetate}}}{CH_3COOC_2H_5} + H_2O$$

Fats and most other lipids are esters of fatty acids of relatively high molecular weight with complex alcohols.

The Lipids.—In general, lipids may be considered to be compounds which are insoluble in water but soluble in fat solvents (ether, chloroform, benzene, etc.) and which chemically are either esters of fatty acids or hydrolytic products of such esters. The following classification is based on a somewhat more elaborate one given by Bloor (1943):

I. Simple Lipids—esters of fatty acids with various alcohols.
   1. Fats—esters ("glycerides") of fatty acids with glycerol that are solid at room temperature.
   2. Oils—esters ("glycerides") of fatty acids with glycerol that are liquid at room temperature.
   3. Waxes—esters of fatty acids with alcohols other than glycerol.
II. Compound Lipids—esters of fatty acids containing groups in addition to alcohol and fatty acid radicals.
   1. Phospholipids (often called phosphatides)—substituted fats containing phosphoric acid and nitrogen. *Lecithin* and *cephalin* are the best known examples.
   2. Glycolipids—compounds of fatty acids with a carbohydrate, also containing nitrogen. Compounds of this group are not definitely known to occur in plants.
III. Derived Lipids—certain substances derived from compounds in the above groups by hydrolysis.
   1. Fatty acids of various series.
   2. Sterols—mostly alcohols of large molecular weight, soluble in fat solvents. Examples: *cholesterol* ($C_{27}H_{45}OH$), and ergosterol ($C_{28}H_{43}OH$).

Fatty Acids.—There are two principal groups of fatty acids, the saturated and the unsaturated. With very few exceptions the fatty acids found in living organisms contain an even number of carbon atoms. The general formula of fatty acids of the saturated series is $C_nH_{2n+1}COOH$. The following are the principal acids in this series:

Formic	HCOOH	or	CH_2O_2
Acetic	CH_3COOH	or	$C_2H_4O_2$
Propionic	$CH_3(CH_2)COOH$	or	$C_3H_6O_2$
Butyric	$CH_3(CH_2)_2COOH$	or	$C_4H_8O_2$
Caproic	$CH_3(CH_2)_4COOH$	or	$C_6H_{12}O_2$
Caprylic	$CH_3(CH_2)_6COOH$	or	$C_8H_{16}O_2$
Capric	$CH_3(CH_2)_8COOH$	or	$C_{10}H_{20}O_2$
Lauric	$CH_3(CH_2)_{10}COOH$	or	$C_{12}H_{24}O_2$
Myristic	$CH_3(CH_2)_{12}COOH$	or	$C_{14}H_{28}O_2$
Palmitic	$CH_3(CH_2)_{14}COOH$	or	$C_{16}H_{32}O_2$
Stearic	$CH_3(CH_2)_{16}COOH$	or	$C_{18}H_{36}O_2$
Arachidic	$CH_3(CH_2)_{18}COOH$	or	$C_{20}H_{40}O_2$

The first four homologues in the above series do not commonly occur in fats. Caproic, caprylic, and capric acids occur as glycerides in palm and coconut oils. Lauric acid has been found as a glyceride in laurel, coconut, and palm oils. Palmitic acid is found as glycerides in bayberry wax, palm oil, and many other plant and animal fats. Stearic acid is similarly a constituent of many plant and animal fats. Arachidic acid is found abundantly as a glyceride in peanut oil.

The great bulk of the plant fatty acids are of the unsaturated type. The molecules of such compounds contain one or more pairs of carbon atoms united by a double bond. Molecules of such acids are not entirely "saturated" with hydrogen as they possess the capacity of combining with two additional atoms of hydrogen for each double bond present. The best known of the unsaturated fatty acids is oleic acid which contains one double bond located at the midpoint of the carbon chain. Its formula can therefore be indicated as follows: $CH_3(CH_2)_7CH=CH(CH_2)_7COOH$. Linoleic acid ($C_{18}H_{32}O_2$) is an example of a fatty acid which contains two double bonds. Oleic and linoleic are the most abundant in the form of glycerides (fats and oils) of all plant fatty acids. Linolenic acid ($C_{18}H_{30}O_2$), found in linseed oil, contains three double bonds. A number of other less common unsaturated fatty acids have been isolated from the tissues of plants and animals.

All of the unsaturated fatty acids combine with hydrogen, oxygen, or the halogens. The "drying" properties of linseed, sunflower, and certain other oils are a consequence of the capacity of the highly unsaturated fatty acid radicals of the oil for reacting with oxygen of the air, resulting in the formation of solid, waxy compounds.

None of the fat-forming fatty acids—saturated or unsaturated—is appreciably soluble in water. The lower members of the saturated series are liquids at ordinary temperatures, while those containing ten or more carbon atoms are solids. Most of the unsaturated fatty acids found in plants are liquids at ordinary temperatures. In general, the fatty acids resemble the fats proper in most of their properties.

Fat Synthesis.—It is generally considered that fats, being insoluble in water, cannot readily diffuse from cell to cell. It seems probable, therefore, that fats are usually synthesized in the cells in which they occur. Fat synthesis is linked with the complicated series of chemical reactions that occur in respiration. Certain intermediate compounds which are formed as a result of the oxidation of carbohydrates are utilized in the synthesis of fats. Many of the reactions involved are reversible, so rapid interconversions of carbohydrates and fats readily take place in living cells.

Fat molecules are synthesized in living organisms by the condensation of one molecule of the trihydric alcohol glycerol with three molecules of the same or different fatty acids. Both the glycerol and the fatty acid molecules are derived from carbohydrates during respiration. The general scheme of fat synthesis may be therefore represented as follows:

$$\text{Carbohydrates} \nearrow \text{Glycerol} \searrow \atop \searrow \text{Fatty Acids} \nearrow \text{Fats} + \text{Water}$$

During the maturation of many oily seeds an increase in oil content occurs concurrently with a decrease in the quantity of carbohydrate present (Table 33). This indicates that the carbohydrates in the seed are being converted into fats, and is in accord with the generally accepted theory of fat synthesis.

TABLE 33—CHANGES IN THE PROPORTIONS OF FATS AND CARBOHYDRATES IN THE KERNEL OF ALMOND SEEDS DURING MATURATION (DATA OF LE CLERC DU SABLON, 1896)

Date of collection	Per cent fat	Per cent glucose	Per cent sucrose	Per cent starch and dextrins
June 9...................	2	6	6.7	21.6
July 4....................	10	4.2	4.9	14.1
August 1.................	37	0	2.8	6.2
September 1..............	44	0	2.6	5.4
October 4................	46	0	2.5	5.3

From the preceding discussion it is evident that there are three principal steps in the synthesis of fats in plants: (1) synthesis of glycerol, (2) synthesis of fatty acids, and (3) condensation of fatty acids and glycerol resulting in the formation of fats.

1. *Synthesis of Glycerol.*—It is probable that more than one mechanism exists whereby glycerol is synthesized in living cells. One known method of synthesis is from the dihydroxyacetonephosphate which is one of the products into which fructose diphosphate is split under the influence of the enzyme aldolase in the glycolytic chain of reactions (Fig. 113). Re-

$$
\begin{array}{l}
\text{H} \\
| \\
\text{H—C—O—H}_2\text{PO}_3 \\
| \\
\text{C=O} \\
| \\
\text{H—C—OH} \\
| \\
\text{H} \\
\text{dihydroxyacetonephosphate}
\end{array}
\; + \text{DPN.H}_2 \xrightarrow[\text{dehydrogenase}]{\alpha\text{-glycerophosphate}}
\begin{array}{l}
\text{H} \\
| \\
\text{H—C—O—H}_2\text{PO}_3 \\
| \\
\text{H—C—OH} \\
| \\
\text{H—C—OH} \\
| \\
\text{H} \\
\alpha\text{-glycerophosphate}
\end{array}
\; + \text{DPN}
$$

duction of dihydroxyacetonephosphate converts it into α-glycerophosphate.

Subsequent dephosphorylation of the α-glycerophosphate results in its conversion into glycerol:

$$
\begin{array}{c}
\text{H} \\
|\\
\text{H—C—O—H}_2\text{PO}_3 \\
|\\
\text{H—C—OH} \\
|\\
\text{H—C—OH} \\
|\\
\text{H}
\end{array}
\quad + \text{H}_2\text{O} \xrightarrow{\text{phosphatase}}
\begin{array}{c}
\text{H} \\
|\\
\text{H—C—OH} \\
|\\
\text{H—C—OH} \\
|\\
\text{H—C—OH} \\
|\\
\text{H}
\end{array}
\quad + \text{H}_3\text{PO}_4
$$

α-glycerophosphate   glycerol

From the standpoint of energy relations it is important to note that the energy content of glycerol is higher than that of the triose sugar from which it is derived.

2. *Fatty Acid Synthesis.*—With few exceptions fatty acid molecules occur only in traces in healthy plant tissues. Apparently fatty acids are utilized in fat synthesis about as rapidly as they are synthesized. The common and important fats of plant cells are formed from fatty acid molecules that have an even number of carbon atoms, the eighteen carbon atom and sixteen carbon atom fatty acid molecules being most abundant.

Although there is little doubt that fatty acids are synthesized from certain derivatives of carbohydrates formed as a result of respiratory metabolism, there is no evidence available regarding the details of this process as it occurs in the higher plants. Investigations on bacteria and certain animal tissues indicate that fatty acids are built up stepwise out of two-carbon atom compounds. It seems probable that a similar mechanism of fatty acid synthesis occurs in the tissues of higher plants. Some of the possible two-carbon atom compounds which might serve as units in such reactions are acetaldehyde, ethanol, and acetic acid. This concept is in accord with the fact that naturally synthesized fatty acids always contain an even number of carbon atoms. Barker *et al.* (1945) have obtained direct evidence for the occurrence of such a process in the bacterium *Clostridium kluyveri*. Under anaerobic conditions this organism can accomplish synthesis of butyric and caproic acids from acetic acid and ethanol by reactions which proceed in overall effect as follows:

$$\text{C}_2\text{H}_5\text{OH} + \text{CH}_3\text{COOH} \longrightarrow \text{CH}_3(\text{CH}_2)_2\text{COOH} + \text{H}_2\text{O}$$
butyric acid

$$2\ \text{C}_2\text{H}_5\text{OH} + \text{CH}_3\text{COOH} \longrightarrow \text{CH}_3(\text{CH}_2)_4\text{COOH} + 2\text{H}_2\text{O}$$
caproic acid

By similar reactions it may be presumed that longer fatty acid chains could be built up, two carbon atoms at a time.

The conversion of carbohydrates to fatty acids, by whatever series of reactions this is accomplished, involves reduction of carbon atoms and requires energy. The energy for these chemical changes is furnished by the process of respiration.

3. *Condensation of Fatty Acids and Glycerol.*—The final stage in the process of fat synthesis consists in the esterification of glycerol with fatty acids. Using palmitic acid for purposes of illustration this reaction can be written as follows:

$$\begin{array}{ccc}
CH_2OH & C_{15}H_{31}COOH & C_{15}H_{31}COOCH_2 \\
| & & | \\
CHOH \; + & C_{15}H_{31}COOH \xrightarrow{\text{lipase}} & C_{15}H_{31}COOCH \; + \; 3\,H_2O \\
| & & | \\
CH_2OH & C_{15}H_{31}COOH \longleftarrow & C_{15}H_{31}COOCH_2 \\
\text{Glycerol} & \text{Three molecules of} & \text{Palmitin} \\
 & \text{palmitic acid} &
\end{array}$$

In the fat palmitin, represented in the above equation, the three fatty acid radicals are all of the same species. This is, however, the most infrequent type of fat structure. Most commonly each of the fatty acid radicals is different, and fats in which only two of the three fatty acid radicals are alike are of more frequent occurrence than those in which all three are alike. Naturally occurring fats are usually mixtures of a number of chemically different kinds of fats of which palmitin is simply one common example.

Evidence that this is the final step in the synthesis of fats may be regarded as conclusive. This is indicated on the one hand by the fact that when fats are hydrolyzed in the laboratory by the action of acids, alkalies, or extracts of the enzyme *lipase* the products of the reaction are fatty acids and glycerol, suggesting that these are also the compounds from which the fats are synthesized. Digestion of fats to fatty acids and glycerol in plant cells is also accomplished by lipase.

Furthermore, synthesis of fats from fatty acids and glycerol under the influence of lipase can actually be demonstrated in the laboratory. If glycerol, a fatty acid, and an extract of lipase be mixed in the proper proportions, precautions being taken to keep the mixture sterile, and incubated for a suitable period of time, the disappearance of fatty acids from the mixture can be demonstrated. Some of the fatty acid molecules are removed from the mixture under such conditions and tied up in the formation of fats.

The enzyme lipase is widely distributed in plants, but is found in greatest abundance in germinating seeds in which relatively large quantities of fats are present, such as those of castor bean, soybean, sunflower, flax, hemp, rape, and corn. This enzyme is also found in animals and in some species of bacteria.

The synthesis of fatty acids and glycerol appears to be so regulated in plant cells that neither of these compounds is present, ordinarily, in appreciable quantities. Furthermore, esters of glycerol with only one fatty acid molecule or with two fatty acid molecules are very rare. It would seem, therefore, that the rate of fatty acid synthesis is almost exactly three times the rate of glycerol production and that esterification of glycerol occurs promptly and completely. The synthesis of fats from fatty acids and glycerol involves only a negligible energy change.

The Phospholipids.—As the name implies the phospholipids are a highly complex group of fatty compounds which contain phosphorus. Nitrogenous groups are also present in many of these compounds. The best known of the phospholipids are lecithin and cephalin, which are believed to occur in all plant and animal cells. The structural formulas of these two compounds are as follows, R_1 and R_2 representing fatty acid radicals:

$$CH_2O—R_1$$
$$CHO—R_2 \quad O$$
$$CH_2—O—\overset{\overset{O}{\|}}{P}—O—CH_2—CH_2—N^+(CH_3)_3 \qquad \alpha\text{-lecithin}$$
$$OH$$

$$CH_2O—R_1$$
$$CHO—R_2 \quad O$$
$$CH_2—O—\overset{\overset{O}{\|}}{P}—O—CH_2—CH_2—NH_2 \qquad \alpha\text{-cephalin}$$
$$OH$$

The molecules of these two compounds are similar to fat molecules, the essential difference being that one fatty acid molecule is replaced by another group containing phosphorous and nitrogen. Since various kinds of fatty acids can be combined in the R_1 and R_2 positions as shown in the foregoing structural formulas, a number of different kinds of lecithins and cephalins are possible.

The physiological role of these compounds in cell metabolism is uncertain. They are believed to influence the permeability of the protoplasmic membranes and to be important, because of their emulsifying properties, in maintaining the structure of the protoplasmic system.

The lipositols are another group of phospholipids. In these compounds inositol constitutes the alcohol rather than glycerol. Inositol is a cyclic compound containing 6 hydroxyl groups:

Inositol

Inositol has a widespread occurrence in plant tissues both in the free and combined forms. It appears to be one of the essential vitamins (Table 44).

Sterols.—These are complex, cyclic (*i.e.*, containing ring groupings) alcohols of high molecular weight. Cholesterol ($C_{27}H_{45}OH$) is the best known of these compounds and is apparently present in all animal cells, being especially abundant in the brain and nervous tissue. Cholesterol is not known to occur in the higher plants, but a number of similar compounds, known as the *phytosterols*, have been isolated from plant tissues. One of the most interesting of the sterols is ergosterol ($C_{28}H_{43}OH$). This was first discovered in ergot but is now known to be widely distributed in plants and animals. It is abundant in yeast which serves as its commercial source. Especial interest attaches to this compound, since it is a precursor of the anti-rachitic vitamin D (Chap. XXVIII). Upon irradiation ergosterol is converted through a series of intermediate compounds into this vitamin.

Waxes.—These compounds are usually fatty acid esters of saturated monohydroxy (rarely dihydroxy) alcohols such as cetyl alcohol ($C_{16}H_{33}$-OH), ceryl alcohol ($C_{26}H_{53}OH$), and myricyl alcohol ($C_{31}H_{63}OH$). Some waxes, however, are fatty acid esters of the sterols. Waxes are of widespread occurrence in both plants and animals. Examples are beeswax, poppy wax, and the wax of the bayberry from which candles are made.

Physiologically waxes are important as constituents of the coatings which cover the outer surface of epidermal cell walls. The presence of these waxy coatings greatly reduces the loss of water from exposed plant tissues (Chap. IX). Waxes are very rarely found within living plant cells.

Cutin and Suberin.—The chemistry of both of these substances is very imperfectly known, although it has long been recognized that their chemical affinities are with the lipids.

Cutin apparently is a mixture composed principally of free fatty acids (often in oxidized form) and condensation products of the fatty acids such as waxes and soaps. The fatty acids present appear to be preponderantly hydroxy-fatty acids, *i.e.*, those which contain one or more hydroxyl groups in the molecule.

Suberin appears to be a mixture of substances consisting principally of condensation products and other modification of phellonic $(CH_3 \cdot (CH_2)_{19} \cdot CHOH \cdot COOH)$, phloionic $(C_{18}H_{34}O_6)$, and other similar acids. The principal chemical distinction between cutin and suberin is that the constituent fatty acids are different in the two materials, and that glycerol is one of the hydrolytic products of suberin, but not of cutin. Suberin is found in the walls of cork cells; cutin occurs on the outer surfaces of epidermal cell walls.

Soaps.—Fats react with inorganic bases as illustrated in the following representative reaction:

$$C_{15}H_{31}COO \diagdown$$
$$C_{15}H_{31}COO-C_3H_5 + 3\ NaOH \rightarrow 3\ C_{15}H_{31}COONa + C_3H_5(OH)_3$$
$$C_{15}H_{31}COO \diagup$$

palmitin   sodium palmitate   glycerol

This reaction is called *saponification* and the resulting salt of the fatty acid, in this example sodium palmitate, a *soap*. Soaps are of common occurrence in plant cells. They are excellent emulsifiers and probably serve in this role in the protoplasm.

Roles of the Lipids in Plants.—Protoplasm always contains lipids in finely emulsified form. They are especially abundant in the protoplasm of meristematic cells. It is impossible to determine just what proportion of the lipid material dispersed in this way represents storage food which may ultimately be used as such, and how much represents indispensable constituents of the protoplasm. In some cells, particularly those of seeds which are rich in stored fats, relatively large droplets of oil may occur as inclusions in the protoplasm.

Fats serve as storage forms of food in plants, and this is undoubtedly one of their principal roles. The fats which accumulate in most plants are liquid within the usually prevailing range of temperatures in temperate zones.

Fats are especially abundant as reserve foods in the seeds of many species. Those varieties of seeds in which oils occur in abundance usually

contain relatively small quantities of carbohydrates and *vice versa.*
Species which produce seeds rich in fats include cotton, corn, peanut,
sunflower, rape, flax, and castor bean. All of these species are important
commercial sources of vegetable oils. Olive oil, a staple food product
in many countries, is extracted from the fruits of the olive. Oils frequently occur in abundance in many other plant organs, as for example
in the rhizomes of potato and iris, and in the aerial organs of many woody
species, especially during the winter months.

Until recently fat storage tissues in both plants and animals have
been considered to be areas of low physiological activity. The use of
radioactive isotopes and other tracer techniques have shown that the
fat deposits in animal tissues are actually centers of great metabolic
activity. Fats are constantly being digested and resynthesized. Fatty
acids of one kind are rapidly converted into other fatty acids and built
back into other fat molecules. Whether the fats in storage tissues of
plants are similarly reactive is not known, but it is a reasonable presumption that continuous utilization and resynthesis of fat molecules
occurs in such tissues also.

During the germination of fatty seeds the oils present gradually disappear. This is shown for sunflower seeds in Table 34, in which the "ether

TABLE 34—CHANGES IN THE CHEMICAL COMPOSITION OF GERMINATING SUNFLOWER SEEDS, IN
TERMS OF GRAMS PER 100 SEEDS OR SEEDLINGS (DATA OF MILLER, 1910)

		Seeds	Seedlings				
			4 days	5 days	7 days	10 days	14 days
Ether extract......	Cotyledons	3.79	3.00	2.53	1.30	0.50	0.32
	Hyp. and roots	0.22	0.19	0.12	0.21	0.27	0.24
Total sugars.......	Cotyledons	0.28	0.06	0.09	0.12	0.09	0.05
	Hyp. and roots	0.02	0.07	0.30	0.43	0.35	0.16
Reducing sugars....	Cotyledons	....	....	....	0.05	0.09	0.02
	Hyp. and roots	....	0.07	0.27	0.38	0.35	0.16
Protein...........	Cotyledons	1.66	1.18	1.03	0.76	0.63	0.48
	Hyp. and roots	0.12	0.11	0.12	0.20	0.20	0.14
Cellulose.........	Cotyledons	0.15	0.12	0.13	0.18	0.20	0.21
	Hyp. and roots	0.01	0.05	0.10	0.24	0.40	0.32

extract" is taken as a composite measure of the oily constituents present. Concurrently with the disappearance of fats there is a temporary increase in the quantity of soluble carbohydrates present as well as a progressive increase in the amount of cellulose. The carbohydrates are undoubtedly formed from fatty acids and glycerol resulting from the digestion of fats. It can be shown that fatty acids accumulate temporarily in oily seeds during germination. This cannot be demonstrated for glycerol; apparently this compound is transformed into other substances as rapidly as it is made. The simpler carbohydrates are undoubtedly formed first and cellulose then synthesized by the condensation of glucose molecules. The protein content of the seeds also decreases during germination, but this is probably chiefly because of their conversion into amino acids and acid amides. Subsequently most of the hydrolytic products of the proteins are probably used in the construction of new protoplasm. A part of the carbohydrates resulting from chemical transformations of fats is utilized in the synthesis of cellulose and other cell wall constituents; another portion of them is used in respiration.

Essential Oils.—These substances are chemically quite different from the true fats and oils but can be discussed conveniently at this point. Most of the compounds classified as essential oils are pungent aromatic compounds. They are responsible for many of the distinctive odors and flavors of plants. Synthesis of essential oils is confined to a relatively small number of plants. They are especially characteristic of plants belonging to certain families such as the Pinaceae, Labiatae, Compositae, Lauraceae, Myrtaceae, and Umbelliferae. Essential oils are usually found only in certain cells of the plant body. In many kinds of plants they are synthesized in glandular cells or hairs of stems or leaves. In various species of pine the oleoresin, an essential oil from which turpentine is obtained, is synthesized in cells lining the resin ducts.

A rather heterogeneous group of compounds is often lumped together under the classification of the essential oils but most of them are _terpenes_. Chemically the terpenes can be regarded as derivatives of the C_5H_8 compound isoprene, which has the following structural formula:

$$CH_2\!=\!\overset{\overset{\textstyle CH_3}{\textstyle |}}{C}\!-\!CH\!=\!CH_2 \qquad C_5H_8$$

Terpene molecules are constructed from multiples of isoprene molecules, having molecular formulas of $C_{10}H_{16}$, $C_{15}H_{24}$, $C_{20}H_{32}$, or $C_{30}H_{48}$. The bulk of the essential oils is composed of the two simpler types of terpenes. The isoprene units in the terpenes may be linked together as straight chains or in the form of rings, some of which may be quite complex. Further modifications in structure may occur as a result of oxidation or reduction of certain groups, resulting in the frequent presence in the molecule of aldehyde, ketone, or alcohol groups.

Such oils as peppermint, lemon, rose, pennyroyal, bergamot, lavender, and sassafras consist largely or entirely of terpenes. The principal constituent of turpentine is pinene, a $C_{10}H_{16}$ terpene. Camphor is a pure terpene of this same molecular formula. Most of the essential oils are highly volatile and evaporate readily from plants.

The essential oils have no known role in plants. They are probably to be regarded as metabolic by-products.

Rubber.—This well-known product of plant metabolism is also an isoprene derivative. A rubber molecule consists of a long chain (500-5000) of isoprene units linked together end to end.

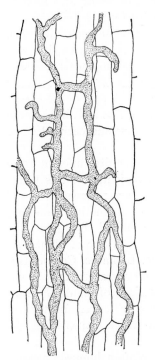

FIG. 115. Longitudinal section through portion of the cortex of a dandelion root showing lactiferous system.

Although by no means a universal metabolic product in plants, rubber is known to be present in more than 2000 species. The principal families in which rubber plants occur are the Euphorbiaceae, Moraceae, Compositae, Asclepidaceae, and Apocynaceae. Practically all of the natural rubber of commerce comes from the tree species *Hevea brasiliensis*. Minor quantities of rubber are harvested from certain other tropical species and from two temperate zone species, guayule (*Parthenium argentatum*) and Russian dandelion (*Taraxacum kok-saghyz*).

Rubber occurs as microscopic particles (0.01-50 μ in diameter) suspended in the latex. The stability of the suspended rubber particles is maintained by proteins of the latex, some of which become adsorbed on the surface of the particles. Latex is a usually milky appearing liquid that is confined in those plants in which it occurs to the latex ducts (Fig. 115). The latex tubes commonly ramify to all parts of those plants in which they are present. In the trunks of *Hevea* and other woody species they are confined to the bark. Rubber is not present in the latex of all latex containing plants, and is only one constituent of the latex when it does occur. Other constituents, in addition to water, include amino acids, proteins, mineral salts, lipids, sugars, terpene derivatives, and enzymes. The rubber is actually synthesized within the cytoplasm of the latex ducts. The percentage of rubber in latex varies greatly from species to species and from plant to plant within a species. *Hevea* latex is 20-60 per cent rubber by weight.

There is no evidence that rubber plays any essential metabolic role in plants. As far as is known it is merely a metabolic by-product.

SUGGESTED FOR COLLATERAL READING

Bloor, W. R. Biochemistry of the Fatty Acids and Their Compounds, the Lipids. Reinhold Publishing Corp. New York. 1943.

Guenther, E., and others. *The Essential Oils.* Vol. I-VI. D. Van Nostrand Co., Inc. New York. 1948-1952.

Hilditch, T. P. *The Chemical Constitution of Natural Fats.* 2nd Ed. John Wiley & Sons, Inc. New York. 1947.

Markley, K. S. *Fatty Acids, Their Chemistry and Physical Properties.* Interscience Publishers, Inc. New York. 1947.

SELECTED BIBLIOGRAPHY

Barker, H. A., M. D. Kamen, and B. T. Bornstein. The synthesis of butyric and caproic acids from ethanol and acetic acid by *Clostridium kluyveri. Proc. Nat. Acad. Sci. (U.S.A.)* **31**: 373-381. 1945.

Burr, G. O., and E. S. Miller. Synthesis of fats by green plants. *Bot. Gaz.* **99**: 773-785. 1938.

Jordan, R. C., and A. C. Chibnall. Observations on the fat metabolism of leaves. II. Fats and phosphatides of the runner bean. (*Phaseolus multiflorus*). *Ann. Bot.* **47**: 163-186. 1933.

Kleinzeller, A. Synthesis of lipides. *Advances in Enzymol.* **8**: 299-341. 1948.

Leclerc du Sablon, M. Sur la formation des réserves non azotées de la noix et de l'amande. *Compt. Rend. Acad. Sci. (Paris)* **123**: 1084-1086. 1896.

McNair, J. B. Plant fats in relation to environment and evolution. *Bot. Rev.* **11**: 1-59. 1945.

Medes, Grace. Fat metabolism. *Ann. Rev. Biochem.* **19**: 215-234. 1950.

Miller, E. C. A physiological study of the germination of *Helianthus annuus. Ann. Bot.* **24**: 693-726. 1910.

XXIV

ABSORPTION OF MINERAL SALTS

The dry-matter content of any plant tissue can be determined with a fair degree of accuracy by drying a sample of that tissue in a suitable oven at a temperature of 100°C. The residue remaining after evaporation of the water represents the nonaqueous constituents of the tissue. The percentage dry-matter content of plant tissues varies greatly, ranging from 90 per cent or even more in dormant structures such as seeds to 5 per cent or sometimes less in very succulent tissues. That the dry matter fraction of any plant tissue is composed principally of organic compounds can be demonstrated by subjecting it to combustion. This is accomplished by transferring a sample of the dry matter to a crucible and heating it over a flame or in a muffle furnace at a temperature of about 600°C. The small grayish residue resulting from this treatment is called the *ash*. Almost all of the dry matter is oxidized at this temperature and the decomposition products pass off in the form of gases. Practically all of the dry matter that disappears during combustion represents organic compounds which are decomposed as a result of subjection to high temperatures.

The ash corresponds roughly to the mineral salts that have been absorbed from the soil, but does not include any nitrogen since this element passes off in the combustion process along with carbon, hydrogen, and oxygen. The mineral elements do not occur in the ash in the pure state, but mostly as oxides. The actual values obtained for the ash content of a plant tissue depend upon the ignition temperature used. A portion of some of the mineral elements present is often lost by sublimation or vaporization. This is especially likely to happen to chlorine and sulfur, but potassium, calcium, phosphorus, and perhaps other elements are sometimes

456

lost in this way. Hence the ash content of a tissue furnishes only a rather crude measure of the mineral element content of that tissue.

The role of nitrogen in the metabolism of plants is discussed in Chap. XXVI, but from the standpoint of the mechanism of absorption of mineral salts, nitrogen will be included among the mineral elements.

The total ash content of plant tissues and organs varies from a fraction of 1 per cent to 15 per cent or even more of the dry weight of the plant material. Fleshy fruits and woody tissues are usually low in ash content, often containing less than 1 per cent, while the ash content of leaves is usually relatively high, often exceeding 10 per cent. Tobacco leaves, for example, contain on the average about 12 per cent of ash on a dry-weight basis. The ash content of other plant organs usually lies somewhere between these two extremes.

Elements Found in Plants.—It is probable that there is not a single one of the chemical elements that is not found at least in traces in some species of plant, under certain conditions. Actually about forty of the known elements have been identified as occurring in plants by chemical analysis. The list of these elements includes aluminum, arsenic, barium, boron, bromine, caesium, calcium, carbon, chlorine, chromium, cobalt, copper, fluorine, hydrogen, iron, lead, lithium, magnesium, manganese, mercury, molybdenum, nitrogen, oxygen, phosphorus, potassium, rubidium, selenium, silicon, silver, sodium, strontium, sulfur, thallium, titanium, tin, vanadium, and zinc.

TABLE 35—ELEMENTAL ANALYSIS OF THE STEM, LEAVES, COB, AND GRAIN OF A MATURE CORN PLANT ("PRIDE OF SALINE"), BASED ON AVERAGE VALUES FOR FIVE PLANTS (DATA OF LATSHAW AND MILLER, 1924)

Element	Weight in grams	Percentage of total dry weight
Carbon.............	364.19	43.569
Oxygen............	371.42	44.431
Hydrogen.........	52.17	6.244
Nitrogen..........	12.19	1.459
Sulfur.............	1.416	0.167
Phosphorus........	1.697	0.203
Calcium...........	1.893	0.227
Potassium.........	7.679	0.921
Magnesium........	1.525	0.179
Iron..............	0.714	0.083
Manganese........	0.269	0.035
Silicon............	9.756	1.172
Aluminum.........	0.894	0.107
Chlorine..........	1.216	0.143
Undetermined......	7.8	0.933

Only fourteen of the elements listed above are found regularly in plants in appreciable quantities (Table 35) and not all of these appear to be essential. The question of which are the essential plant elements is considered in the next chapter.

The composition of plant ash varies both with the species and the environmental conditions under which the plant has developed. Comparative figures on the percentages of five of the more important mineral elements in several different species of plants growing in the same soil are given in Table 36.

The data in Table 36 show that, even if they develop under soil and climatic conditions as nearly identical as possible in a greenhouse, different species of plants contain very different proportions of the various elements obtained from the soil. Until the mechanism of the absorption and translocation of mineral salts into and through plants is better understood, it is doubtful if any even partially adequate explanation of this fundamentally important fact can be formulated.

TABLE 36—PERCENTAGE OF CALCIUM, POTASSIUM, MAGNESIUM, NITROGEN, AND PHOSPHORUS IN THE TOPS OF SEVERAL SPECIES OF PLANTS GROWN IN A GREENHOUSE IN AN ALBERTA "BLACK BELT" LOAM SOIL (DATA OF NEWTON, 1928)

Species	Percentage of dry weight				
	Ca	K	Mg	N	P
Sunflower...........	1.68	3.47	0.730	1.47	0.080
Bean................	1.46	1.19	0.570	1.48	0.053
Wheat..............	0.46	4.16	0.225	2.26	0.058
Barley.............	0.68	4.04	0.292	1.94	0.125

The composition and other properties of the soil in which a plant is rooted will also have an effect on the proportion of each of the various elements absorbed by that plant. Innumerable examples of this fact can be cited from the practice of fertilizing. Addition to the soil of a compound which can be absorbed by plants usually results in an increased absorption of that substance by the plants although the increase in the amount of the element within the plant tissues is usually not proportionate to the increase in the amount of that element in the soil. Plants often absorb from the soil mineral salts far in excess of their actual metabolic requirements. Potassium, phosphate, sulfate, and other ions often accumulate in plant cells in excess of the quantities actually utilized by the cells.

The Soil as a Source of Mineral Elements.—With only minor exceptions, all of the mineral elements which enter into the composition of terrestrial plants come from the soil. For a long time in discussions of the absorption of mineral salts by plants, attention was focused on the soil solution. Recent advances in soil science have made it increasingly clear, however, that the mineral salts dissolved in the soil solution are not the only ones which must be considered in any evaluation of the mineral salt relations of soils as they influence the entrance of such solutes into plants.

The fundamental physicochemical properties of soils result largely from components present in the colloidal state. In most soils the colloidal fraction is made up principally of clay micelles, but organic matter, when present in any considerable quantities, is also an important constituent of the colloidal fraction of the soil. The clay particles of the soil are composed principally of alumino-silicates and, although mostly of colloidal dimensions, have a definite crystalline structure.

The micelles of colloidal clay are usually negatively charged and have associated with them certain cations which may be regarded as occupying a position analogous to the ions in the outer layer of an electrical double layer (Chap. III). Such ions may be located, not only at the surfaces of the particles, but also within the spaces of the crystal lattice itself. The cations most commonly associated with the clay particles of natural soils in this manner are Ca^{++}, Mg^{++}, K^+, Na^+ and H^+. Cations are also similarly associated with soil colloidal particles of organic origin.

Under certain conditions cations of one kind can be displaced from clay particles and replaced by cations of another kind. For example, if an acidic soil be treated with a calcium chloride solution, some of the introduced Ca^{++} ions replace H^+ ions, an equivalent quantity of H^+ ions being displaced into the solution where they pair with the residual Cl^- ions. This reaction may be represented as follows:

$$\boxed{\text{Clay}}\begin{array}{l}H^+\\[4pt]H^+\end{array} + Ca^{++} + 2\,Cl^- \rightarrow \boxed{\text{Clay}}\ Ca^{++} + 2\,H^+ + 2\,Cl^-$$

Actually each clay micelle usually has many cations, of like or unlike species, associated with it, but, in the interests of simplicity, this equation has been written in terms of only two adsorbed H^+ ions. Other cations associated with micelles can be replaced in similar reactions, but the proportion of any kind of adsorbed ion entering into such reactions will vary greatly depending upon the conditions under which the interchange of cations takes place.

The phenomenon which has just been described is called *cation exchange*. Such interchanges of cations often occur very rapidly and are reversible. In most neutral and slightly alkaline soils Ca^{++} is the principal replaceable cation, although appreciable quantities of Mg^{++} are also often present. The H^+ ion is the principal replaceable cation in acidic soils. In alkali soils Na^+ ions constitute a considerable proportion of the replaceable cations. All of the exchangeable cations are not retained by the micelles with equal effectiveness. The usual order of the retentive capacity of the micelles for cations is $H^+ \rangle Ca^{++} \rangle Mg^{++} \rangle K^+ \rangle NH_4^+ \rangle Na^+$. In other words, of all the cations in the above series, the H^+ ions are the most tenaciously bound to the colloidal particles and are the most difficult to displace, whereas the opposite is true of the Na^+ ions.

The addition of inorganic fertilizers to soils often induces exchanges of cations between the clay particles and the soil solution. If lime, for example, be applied to a soil, some of the introduced Ca^{++} ions will participate in exchanges with some of the cations already adsorbed on the micelles. H^+ ions will be among the ones which are displaced by Ca^{++} ions (*cf.* equation given above). In fact one of the principal objectives in liming a soil is to replace some of the H^+ ions which have been adsorbed on the micelles as a result of continuous cropping of the land (see later) with Ca^{++} ions.

The principal anions found in soils are Cl^-, SO_4^{--}, HCO_3^-, $H_2PO_4^-$, NO_3^- and OH^-. Most anions leach out of soils rather readily, although phosphate is an important exception to this statement. Even in soils which have received heavy applications of phosphates, it is usual to find only small quantities of phosphates in the drainage waters. Evidently the $H_2PO_4^-$ ions are tied up by the soil particles in some manner. The mechanism by which such an immobilization of phosphate is accomplished is not the same in all kinds of soils.

In neutral and alkaline soils most phosphate fixation apparently results from precipitation by calcium or magnesium. In acidic soils hydrated oxides of iron and aluminum and the mineral kaolinite are largely responsible for phosphate fixation. $H_2PO_4^-$ ions substitute for OH^- ions of such compounds. This may be regarded as a type of anion exchange roughly analogous to the cation exchange previously described, although the exact mechanism is somewhat different. Arsenate, fluoride, molybdate, and hydroxyl anions may also be fixed in soils in a manner similar to that by which phosphate ions are fixed.

Micro-organisms utilize nitrates, sulfates, and phosphates in the synthesis of organic compounds and these anions may thus become fixed in the soil in the form of such compounds. This is an entirely different kind of phenomenon, however, than the retention of anions in the soil by purely physicochemical mechanisms.

The Penetration of Electrolytes into Plant Cells.—It is not known with certainty whether electrolytes penetrate into cells as molecules or as ions. Osterhout (1936) favors the former view. Although electrolytes are largely or entirely dissociated when dissolved in water, considerable evidence indicates that the plasma layers of the cytoplasm are of a lipoidal constitution and electrolytes can dissociate only very slightly when dissolved in such solvents. Other workers, however, believe that electrolytes pass into cells in the form of ions.

Because of electrostatic attraction between oppositely charged ions passage of a cation into a plant cell must be accompanied by passage of an anion or anions of equal electrostatic charge, and *vice versa*, unless the unbalanced electrical forces which would develop as the result of such a situation are compensated for in some other manner. For example, the K^+ ions of K_2SO_4 might move into cells of roots immersed in a solution unaccompanied by SO_4^{--} ions, provided each were attended in its passage by an OH^- ion. Each SO_4^{--} ion would then pair with two H^+ ions resulting from the dissociation of the water. Similarly, NO_3^- ions from $Ca(NO_3)_2$ might enter the cell, accompanied by H^+ ions originating from water, the anions of the water pairing with the Ca^{++} ion. Such a mechanism permits the more rapid absorption of the one ion than of its original partner, and commonly brings about a change in the hydrogen ion concentration of the solution in which the roots are immersed. In the first example cited, the solution would become more acid because of the formation of H_2SO_4, and in the second example the solution would increase in alkalinity as a result of the formation of $Ca(OH)_2$. Such changes in the pH of culture solutions as a result of the differential adsorption of ions are very common.

The H^+ and HCO_3^- ions of carbonic acid, which is almost invariably present in solutions, may act in a manner analogous to the H^+ and OH^- ions of water in facilitating the entry of anions and cations into plant cells.

Mechanisms of Mineral Salt Absorption.—For many years it was commonly stated or implied that the entrance of mineral salts into the peripheral cells of roots or of submerged aquatics occurred by diffusion. Although it is undoubtedly true that limited quantities of mineral salts do pass into some kinds of cells, under some conditions, by diffusion, in general this is a relatively unimportant mechanism of electrolyte absorption compared with certain others. Two other and much more important mechanisms of mineral salt absorption have been recognized to be operative in plant cells: the salt accumulation mechanism, and the ionic exchange mechanism.

As shown in the later discussion, roots not only absorb freely diffusible ions in the soil solution, but can also liberate cations (and perhaps anions) adsorbed on colloidal soil particles. The rate of root growth through the soil is in itself not only an important factor in the absorption of water (Chap. XIV) but also in the absorption of mineral salts. The growth of roots through the soil constantly brings them into contact with additional micelles and with additional increments of soil solution, from both of which ions can be absorbed.

Accumulation of Salts by Plant Cells.—This process is so named because it results in the building up of concentrations of salts in plant cells which are greater, often many times greater, than the concentration of the same salts in the surrounding medium. It is probably the most important single mechanism of salt absorption. This process is also called "primary salt absorption."

General Aspects of Salt Accumulation.—The fact that ions may attain a higher concentration within living cells than in the circumambient solution was first clearly demonstrated in the large cells of certain species of algae. Sap from the cells of the fresh water alga *Nitella*, for example, can be obtained in sufficient quantities to permit its accurate analysis (Table 37). In this analysis, and in other similar ones, it has been found that anions and cations accumulate within the cells in concentrations which greatly exceed those in the bathing medium. Furthermore the electrical conductivity of the sap has been found to be approximately equal to that of a solution of electrolytes of the same concentration, indicating that the accumulated salts are present within the cell sap in the dissolved state. Both cations and anions are accumulated in cells by the operation of this mechanism, and often in approximately equivalent quantities. An increase

TABLE 37—ANALYSIS OF THE VACUOLAR SAP OF *Nitella clavata* AND OF THE POND WATER IN WHICH IT WAS GROWING (DATA OF HOAGLAND AND DAVIS, 1929)

Ion	Sap concentration (Milliequivalents[1] per L.)	Pond water concentration (Milliequivalents per L.)
Ca^{++}	13.0	1.3
Mg^{++}	10.8	3.0
Na^+	49.9	1.2
K^+	49.3	0.51
Sum cations	123.0	
Cl^-	101.1	1.0
SO_4^{--}	13.0	0.67
$H_2PO_4^-$	1.7	0.008
Sum anions	115.8	

[1] A milliequivalent of an ion is one-thousandth its gram ionic weight divided by its valence.

in the concentration of free ions in the cell sap to a value many times greater than their concentration in the external solution can only be attained as a result of the diffusion of those ions against a concentration gradient, *i.e.,* from a region of lesser concentration to region of greater concentration for each ion that accumulates.

The cells near the tips of roots also have the capacity of accumulating ions (Hoagland and Broyer 1936). If the initial salt content of the root cells is low and if other conditions are favorable (see later), the concentration of ions in the absorbing cells may soon greatly exceed that of the

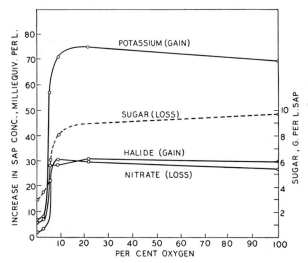

Fig. 116.   Relation between oxygen concentration of aeration stream, uptake of ions, and consumption of sugar in excised barley roots. Data of Hoagland and Broyer (1936).

same ions in the soil solution. Rapid accumulation of ions does not occur, however, if the cells already contain a relatively high concentration of the same ions. The rate of salt accumulation is often influenced, therefore, by the previous metabolic history of the absorbing cells.

The phenomenon of salt accumulation seems confined largely to cells which have the capacity for cell division and growth (Steward, 1935). Meristematic cells and cells in the early stages of enlargement are particularly active in absorbing ions. As cells lose their capacity for growth they also lose their capacity for mineral salt accumulation. The parenchyma cells of an apple fruit, for example, are fully mature and are not able to accumulate ions from dilute solutions, while the cells in potato tubers and some other storage organs are capable of renewed growth and salt accumulation occurs in such cells under favorable conditions. It is probable that all or most plant cells are able to accumulate mineral salts when in a meristematic condition, but that this capacity decreases as the cells become mature.

Necessity of Aerobic Respiration for Salt Accumulation.—When excised roots of barley are immersed in dilute solutions of certain salts, accumulation of salts within the root cells occurs readily if air is bubbled through the system, but little or no accumulation occurs if nitrogen is bubbled through the solution (Hoagland and Broyer, 1936). In the absence of

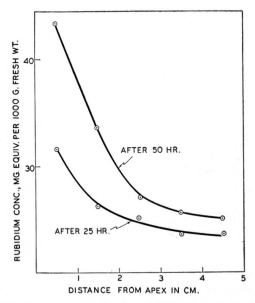

Fig. 117. Distribution of accumulated rubidium in excised roots of barley in relation to distance from root apex. Data of Steward *et al.* (1942).

oxygen aerobic respiration is checked and the accumulation of electrolytes in the root cells virtually ceases (Fig. 116). A similar relation between aerobic respiration and accumulation of salts has also been demonstrated in other plant tissues. It is pertinent to recall in this connection that absorption of water by most kinds of plants also requires adequate aeration of the roots.

In addition to adequate aeration, other conditions conducive to respiration must prevail if accumulation of salts is to occur at physiologically significant rates. In particular there must be present in the cells a supply of respiratory substrate (*cf.* Fig. 116) and the prevailing temperature must be within a favorable range (see later).

The rate of salt accumulation in roots is highest close to the apex and decreases with distance from the root tip (Fig. 117). This is true of both attached and excised roots. Dividing and enlarging cells such as are found in the younger parts of all growing regions have an especially high capacity for the accumulation of ions. The gradient in the accumulative capacity of the root cells is correlated with a progressive diminution in their respiratory activity with increasing distance from the apex (Machlis, 1944). As previously discussed in Chap. IX there is not commonly any close correlation between the rate of absorption of water by roots and the rate of absorption of mineral salts. Most accumulation of salts occurs in the young cells close to the apex of the root, while the bulk of the absorption of water appears to occur in the root-hair zone.

Roots capable of rapid salt accumulation do not absorb salts at an appreciable rate from a culture solution even when the concentration of ions in the solution greatly exceeds that of the root cells unless aerobic respiration is taking place (Hoagland and Broyer, 1942). In the absence of aerobic respiration the membranes of cells otherwise capable of salt accumulation behave as if they were relatively impermeable to salts.

The accumulation of ions in root cells to concentrations exceeding those of the same ions in the external solution requires a continuous expenditure of energy. Likewise the retention of free ions within cells in greater concentration than in the external medium also requires a continuous expenditure of energy. The necessary energy undoubtedly comes from the process of respiration, but the exact manner in which it is utilized in the accumulation mechanism is not known.

Effects of the Environment of the Aerial Organs on Salt Accumulation. —Aerobic respiration in the root cells is dependent upon carbohydrates and other organic compounds which are translocated to the roots from the leaves and other aerial organs. Any conditions which markedly reduce the rate of photosynthesis in the leaves or the rate of downward translocation of foods may therefore also bring about a diminution in the rate of salt accumulation. The salt absorbing capacity of roots of barley plants, for example, has been observed to vary appreciably at different seasons of the year (Broyer and Hoagland, 1943). During winter months when light intensities are low and the days are relatively short, barley plants absorbed much less salt from culture solutions in the greenhouse than during the summer months. The reduction in the salt-absorbing capacity of roots grown during the winter is attributed to the decrease in the quantity of photosynthetic products (carbohydrates, growth substances, and other organic materials) reaching the root system.

The rate of transpiration may also exert an indirect effect on salt accumulation. Upward movement of mineral salts appears to occur chiefly in the xylem ducts in which they are carried along in the transpiration stream (Chap. XXVII). Crafts and Broyer (1938) suggest that, since the cortical cells of the roots are progressively less well aerated toward the center, there is in such cells a corresponding gradient of decreasing capacity to accumulate or hold solutes. As a result a concentration gradient may be established from peripheral cells to the xylem elements along which solutes move by diffusion, perhaps supplemented by protoplasmic streaming. Solute movement from cell to cell is probably at least in part through plasmodesms. Rapid transpiration, in general, results in accelerating the rate of movement of salts from the xylem elements of the roots to the leaves. Indirectly transpiration rates may also influence the rate of movement of salts across the root, since a high rate of transpiration presumably would favor the establishment of a steeper gradient of mineral salt concentrations across the root.

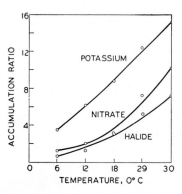

Fig. 118. Relation between temperature and accumulation of ions by excised barley roots. "Accumulation ratio" is the concentration in the sap divided by the final concentration in the external solution. Data of Hoagland and Broyer (1936).

Permeability and Salt Accumulation. —Most investigations of the permeability of the cytoplasmic membranes indicate that electrolytes enter plant cells relatively slowly. Nevertheless, when conditions favorable to salt accumulation prevail, the salt content of root cells may increase several hundred per cent within a few hours. The apparent discrepancy between the rapid accumulation of salts under some conditions and the low measured permeabilities of cytoplasmic membranes to electrolytes are probably to be explained on the grounds that most measurements of permeability have been made with cells in which metabolic conditions favorable to the rapid penetration of electrolytes did not prevail. The relative amounts of different cations which accumulate in plant cells appear to bear no relation to the permeability of cytoplasmic membranes to them as measured by usual methods. Ca^{++} and Mg^{++} ions, for example, commonly accumulate in cells to greater concentrations than Na^+ ions, yet most studies indicate that protoplasmic membranes are more permeable to Na^+ ions. The relative quantities of the various cations found in plant cells cannot be correlated with their lipoid solubility, kinetic activity, or physical dimensions (Collander, 1941).

The Influence of Temperature upon Salt Accumulation.—The fact that salt accumulation by root cells is dependent upon respiration suggests that temperature may have a marked effect on the process, a supposition which has been confirmed experimentally (Fig. 118). As indicated in this figure the Q_{10} of the process of ion accumulation is in the range of two to three.

Salt Accumulation and Organic Acid Metabolism.—The number of cations and anions in the cell sap must be maintained in such a balance that the solution remains electrostatically neutral. It is common, however, to find that the cell sap contains a large excess of inorganic cations (Pierce and Appleman, 1943). The excess of inorganic cations is electrically balanced by organic anions synthesized in the cells. The high ratio of inorganic cations to inorganic anions in the cell sap may arise in at least two ways: (1) the cation may be accompanied into the cell by an OH^- ion or an HCO_3^- ion instead of its original inorganic partner in the external medium, or (2) certain inorganic anions may enter more rapidly into organic combinations and be removed from the cell sap by the metabolic activities of the protoplasm. Nitrate anions, for example, are often quickly reduced in the cells of the roots and synthesized into organic nitrogenous compounds (Chap. XXVI) leaving behind in the cell sap the inorganic cations with which they were paired upon entering the cell. There is, therefore, a close correlation between the excess absorption of inorganic cations and the increased organic acid content of plant tissues. Whenever surplus inorganic cations accumulate in the cells organic acid anions also accumulate and whenever the content of anions exceeds that of cations the organic acid content of the cells is correspondingly decreased (Ulrich, 1942).

The Influence of Ions of One Species upon the Absorption of Ions of Other Species.—The rate at which specific ions are absorbed by living cells appears to be influenced by the particular species of ions that are present in the culture solution. There is good evidence, for example, that the rate at which KBr is absorbed from a culture solution by excised barley roots may be increased by the presence, within certain limits of concentration, of Ca^{++}, Mg^{++} and other polyvalent cations in the solution (Viets, 1944). The favorable effect of the polyvalent cations upon the inward movement of K^+ and Br^- ions occurs only when the absorbing cells are actively carrying on aerobic respiration and is therefore, in part at least, related to the effect of the polyvalent cations upon the respiratory mechanism of the cells. It is probable, however, that the polyvalent cations influence the absorption of monovalent ions in ways other than their effect upon the oxidative mechanism of the cell. Previous accumulation of Ca^{++} ions by absorbing cells does not increase the intake of K^+ or Br^- ions. To be effective the Ca^{++} or other polyvalent cations must be present in the culture solution at the time the monovalent ions are being absorbed, a circumstance which indicates that the more important effect may be some change in the structure of the protoplasmic membranes affecting their permeability, brought about, however, only in connection with aerobic respiration.

Ionic Exchange Mechanisms.—Fundamentally these mechanisms consist in the exchange of anions or cations from within cells for ions of the same sign and equivalent charge in the environment of the absorbing cell.

If excised barley roots in which radioactive K^+ ions have been allowed to accumulate from a solution are transferred to distilled water, almost none of the radioactive ions are lost from the roots into the water (Jenny and Overstreet, 1938). The cytoplasmic membranes of the root cells behave as if completely impermeable to the ions which entered the cells readily before their transfer to distilled water. When similar excised roots are transferred to a dilute solution of nonradioactive KBr, some of the radioactive K^+ ions move out of the root cells into the solution at the same time that nonradioactive K^+ ions are moving into the cells from the solution. Under these conditions the cytoplasmic membranes are permeable to K^+ ions moving in both directions. Since analysis of the solution around the roots does not show any gain in total potassium, it is evident that radioactive K^+ ions have, in effect, exchanged places with nonradioactive K^+ ions in the solution.

This exchange process between two isotopes of potassium is not materially influenced by temperature or by the rate of aerobic respiration. Furthermore, very little loss of radioactive K^+ occurs from roots into solutions of a calcium salt (Broyer and Overstreet, 1940).

The process of *cation exchange*, in which cations adsorbed on clay micelles exchange with cations in the soil solution, has already been described. Similar exchange mechanisms operate between the root and the soil. Root tips are, under favorable conditions, not only rapidly growing organs, but centers of high metabolic activity. Carbon dioxide is continually being released in respiration, most of which reacts with water, forming carbonic acid, a large part of which escapes into the soil. Around each root tip, therefore, there will usually be a localized zone of relatively high carbonic acid content, and hydrogen ions from this acid become adsorbed on the root surfaces. Such hydrogen ions presumably may exchange places with other cations in the soil solution, some of the latter having previously been released from clay micelles by cation exchange. A possible alternative explanation is that organic acids, released by roots, function in exchange mechanisms in an analogous manner to that postulated for carbonic acid.

A similar exchange of cations can also take place directly between roots and clay micelles, without the operation of the soil solution as an intermediate in the transaction. This process is called *contact exchange* (Jenny and Overstreet, 1939). The cations adsorbed on the root and clay surfaces are not held rigidly in position, but oscillate within a range controlled by the attractive forces between them and the adsorbing surface. The orbits of the ions adsorbed on the surfaces of a root which is in intimate contact with a clay micelle may overlap with the orbits of the ions adsorbed on the micelle. When this occurs the adsorbed ions may exchange places. A H^+ ion adsorbed on the root surface may, for example, move into the orbit occupied by a K^+ ion adsorbed on a clay particle, the K^+ ion replacing the H^+ ion on the root surface.

Any cation adsorbed on a root surface, whether acquired by exchange from the soil solution or directly from a soil colloid, may move across the cell wall, probably by further exchanges with other H^+ ions. Once in contact with the protoplasm further movement of the ion into the cell may occur by the accumulation mechanism.

Various experimental results indicate it to be very likely that the first step in the absorption of cations by the peripheral cells of roots is an ionic exchange process. This is possibly also true of anions. It is probable that both the ionic exchange mechanism and the accumulation mechanism are involved in most absorption of mineral salts by the cells of roots.

Absorption of Mineral Salts by Aerial Organs.—Under natural conditions absorption of mineral salts through the aerial organs of a plant rarely occurs in appreciable quantities. Plants are sometimes "fertilized," however, by spraying the aerial organs with dilute solutions, a practice which involves the absorption of the solutes directly through the leaves or stems. This practice has been followed most successfully as a means of supplying certain micrometabolic elements (Chap. XXV) to plants. Iron deficiency in pineapple plants, for example, may be rectified by spraying the plants with a dilute solution of ferrous sulfate. In similar fashion copper, manganese, and zinc are often supplied to citrus and other crops by spraying the foliage with a dilute solution of a salt of the metal which is to be supplied.

Mycorrhizas.—The roots of many species of plants are regularly infected with the mycelium of fungi. Such a root, together with its associated fungal hyphae, is called a *mycorrhiza* (literally "fungous-root"). In the *ectotrophic* mycorrhizas the mycelium is chiefly external to the root, investing it with a web-like mantle of hyphae. Some hyphae also penetrate into the root, infecting principally the cortex. In the *endotrophic* mycorrhizas the hyphae are intracellular, being found principally within the cells of the epidermis and the cortex. Roots which become infected with mycorrhizal fungi stop elongating and often branch extensively. Mycorrhizas are therefore usually short and stubby as compared with uninfected roots on the same plant. Many authorities believe that mycorrhizas are present on the roots of the majority of vascular species.

Ectotrophic mycorrhizas are found on many forest tree species such as beeches, oaks, hickories, and many conifers. They are particularly abundant on trees growing in soils rich in humus. The fungal associates in forest tree mycorrhizas are mostly members of the group of *Basidiomycetes*, many of them apparently being common woodland species of mushrooms.

Endotrophic mycorrhizas are found on many species of orchid, heath, and gentian families, and also on some trees, such as the red maple and walnut. The fungous associates in such mycorrhizas are apparently mostly microscopic molds.

Diverse opinions have been advanced regarding the significance of these root-fungus associations. Apparently, the relationships between fungus and host may range all the way from true parasitism to genuine symbiosis. There can be no doubt that many conifers often grow better when mycorrhizas are present and some species even appear to be dependent upon mycorrhizas. Although many suggestions have been advanced to explain the beneficial effects of mycorrhizas on the vascular plant associate (increase in water, mineral salt, carbohydrate, and nitrogen supply, synthesis of growth regulators and enzymes; "stimulation" of metabolic processes of roots, especially respiration, etc.), there is very little experimental support for most of these views.

Substantial evidence is accumulating, however, that mycorrhizas may play a significant role in the absorption of mineral salts. The rate of respiration of mycorrhizas of short-leaf pine (*Pinus echinata*) has been shown to be considerably greater than that of uninfected roots suggesting that the former may have greater capacity for the absorption of mineral salts (Routien and Dawson, 1943). Similarly the influence of mycorrhizas upon seedlings of white pine (*Pinus strobus*) and Douglas fir (*Pseudotsuga douglasi*) has been interpreted as resulting from effects upon respiration and phosphorus metabolism (McComb and Griffith, 1946). Experiments with radioactive phosphorus have shown that the mycorrhizal portions of the roots of two species of pine accumulate much larger quantities of phosphate than nonmycorrhizal portions (Kramer and Wilbur, 1949). It has further been shown by Melin and Nilsson (1950) that mycorrhizal fungi can absorb phosphate ions and transfer them to the roots of *Pinus silvestris*.

SUGGESTED FOR COLLATERAL READING

Hoagland, D. R. *Lectures on the Inorganic Nutrition of Plants.* Chronica Botanica Co. Waltham, Mass. 1944.

Marshall, C. E. *The Colloid Chemistry of the Silicate Minerals.* Academic Press, Inc. New York. 1949.

Russell, E. J. *Soil Conditions and Plant Growth.* 8th Ed. Revised by E. W. Russell. Longmans, Green and Co. London. 1950.

Truog, E., Editor. Mineral nutrition of plants. University of Wisconsin Press. Madison. 1951.

SELECTED BIBLIOGRAPHY

Broyer, T. C. The movement of materials into plants. Part II. The nature of solute movement into plants. *Bot. Rev.* **13:** 125-167. 1947.

Broyer, T. C., and D. R. Hoagland. Metabolic activities of roots and their bearing on the relation of upward movement of salts and water in plants. *Amer. Jour. Bot.* **30:** 261-273. 1943.

Broyer, T. C., and R. Overstreet. Cation exchange in plant roots in relation to metabolic factors. *Amer. Jour. Bot.* **27:** 425-430. 1940.

Burström, H. Mineral nutrition of plants. *Ann. Rev. Biochem.* **17:** 579-600. 1948.

Collander, R. Selective absorption of cations by higher plants. *Plant Physiol.* **16:** 691-720. 1941.

Crafts, A. S., and T. C. Broyer. Migration of salts and water into xylem of the roots of higher plants. *Amer. Jour. Bot.* **25:** 529-535. 1938.

Hoagland, D. R., and T. C. Broyer. General nature of the process of salt accumulation by roots with description of experimental methods. *Plant Physiol.* **11:** 471-507. 1936.

Hoagland, D. R., and T. C. Broyer. Hydrogen-ion effects and the accumulation of salt by barley roots as influenced by metabolism. *Amer. Jour. Bot.* **27:** 173-185. 1940.

Hoagland, D. R., and T. C. Broyer. Accumulation of salt and permeability in plant cells. *Jour. Gen. Physiol.* **25:** 865-880. 1942.

Hoagland, D. R., and A. R. Davis. The intake and accumulation of electrolytes by plant cells. *Protoplasma* **6:** 610-626. 1929.

Jenny, H., and R. Overstreet. Contact effects between plant roots and soil colloids. *Proc. Nat. Acad. Sci. (U.S.A.)* **24:** 384-392. 1938.

Jenny, H., and R. Overstreet. Cation interchange between plant roots and soil colloids. *Soil Sci.* **47:** 257-272. 1939.

Kramer, P. J., and K. M. Wilbur. Absorption of radioactive phosphorus by mycorrhizal roots of pine. *Science* **110:** 8-9. 1949.

Latshaw, W. L., and E. C. Miller. Elemental composition of the corn plant. *Jour. Agric. Res.* **27:** 845-859. 1924.

Lundegårdh, H. Mineral nutrition of plants. *Ann. Rev. Biochem.* **16:** 503-528. 1947.

Machlis, L. The influence of some respiratory inhibitors and intermediates on respiration and salt accumulation of excised barley roots. *Amer. Jour. Bot.* **31:** 183-192. 1944.

Machlis, L. The respiratory gradient in barley roots. *Amer. Jour. Bot.* **31:** 281-282. 1944.

McComb, A. L., and J. E. Griffith. Growth stimulation and phosphorus absorption of mycorrhizal and non-mycorrhizal northern white pine and Douglas fir seedlings in relation to fertilizer treatments. *Plant Physiol.* **21**: 11-17. 1946.

Melin, E., and H. Nilsson. Transfer of radioactive phosphorus to pine seedlings by means of mycorrhizal hyphae. *Physiol. Plantarum* **3**: 88-92. 1950.

Newton, J. D. The selective absorption of inorganic elements by various crop plants. *Soil Sci.* **26**: 85-91. 1928.

Osterhout, W. J. V. The absorption of electrolytes in large plant cells. *Bot. Rev.* **2**: 283-315. 1936.

Pierce, E. C., and C. O. Appleman. Role of ether soluble organic acids in the cation-anion balance in plants. *Plant Physiol.* **18**: 224-238. 1943.

Routien, J. B., and R. F. Dawson. Some interrelationships of growth, salt absorption, respiration, and mycorrhizal development in *Pinus echinata. Amer. Jour. Bot.* **30**: 440-451. 1943.

Steward, F. C. Mineral nutrition of plants. *Ann. Rev. Biochem.* **4**: 519-544. 1935.

Steward, F. C., P. Prevot, and J. A. Harrison. Absorption and accumulation of rubidium bromide by barley plants. Localization in the root of cation accumulation and of transfer to the shoot. *Plant Physiol.* **17**: 411-421. 1942.

Stout, P. R., and R. Overstreet. Soil chemistry in relation to inorganic nutrition of plants. *Ann. Rev. Plant Physiol.* **1**: 305-342. 1950.

Ulrich, A. Metabolism of organic acids in excised barley roots as influenced by temperatures, oxygen tension and salt concentration. *Amer. Jour. Bot.* **29**: 220-226. 1942.

Viets, F. G., Jr. Calcium and other polyvalent cations as accelerators of ion accumulation by excised barley roots. *Plant Physiol.* **19**: 466-480. 1944.

Wadleigh, C. H. Mineral nutrition of plants. *Ann. Rev. Biochem.* **18**: 655-678. 1949.

DISCUSSION QUESTIONS

1. Suggest as many explanations as you can for the fact that different kinds of plants, growing in the same soil and under the same climatic conditions, absorb various ions in different proportions.

2. Can the mineral element requirements of a plant be judged from a chemical analysis of the plant?

3. When plants are grown in a solution containing calcium nitrate the H-ion concentration of the solution usually shows a gradual decrease. If ammonium sulfate is used as a source of nitrogen, however, the solution usually increases in H-ion concentration. Explain.

4. How would you undertake to obtain the maximum possible rate of absorption of potassium ions by the root system of a young herbaceous plant from a solution culture? From a soil?

5. How would you attempt to show experimentally whether or not absorption of water and mineral salts by plants are largely independent processes?

6. A group of healthy barley plants, with their roots in tap water, are exposed to sunlight for 12 hr. under conditions which insure rapid transpiration. The tap water is then replaced with a well-aerated solution culture and the plants placed in the dark. By means of two curves, plot probable rates of water and salt absorption during the next 12 hr. in the dark, and during a subsequent 12 hr. in bright sunlight.

XXV

UTILIZATION OF MINERAL SALTS

A clear distinction should be drawn between the *absorption* of a salt and the subsequent *utilization* of it or its component ions. The term utilization is employed in a loose sense to refer to the incorporation of mineral elements into the relatively permanent constituents of the cell walls and protoplasm, or to their participation in fundamental metabolic reactions. Absorption of the ions or molecules of salts does not necessarily mean that they will be utilized. Many of the ions absorbed by a plant remain for more or less indefinite periods in the ionic state in the cells. Sooner or later many of these ions are usually incorporated either into the structure of more complex but unassimilated molecules synthesized by the plant such as storage proteins, calcium oxalate, glycosides, etc., or into the protoplasm or cell walls. There may, therefore, be a considerable time lag between the absorption of an ion and its utilization, while some of the absorbed ions may remain indefinitely as such within the cells. Furthermore, some mineral elements may be utilized in one organ of a plant, subsequently released by disintegration of cell constituents, translocated to other organs of the plant, and there re-utilized. Redistribution of minerals which have accumulated in cells but have not actually been utilized is also of common occurrence in plants (Chap. XXVII).

General Roles of the Mineral Elements in Plants.—Strictly speaking mineral elements as such do not influence the physiological processes of plants. It is only when present in ionic form or as constituents of organic molecules that they assume important roles in plants. For the convenience of brevity, however, the term mineral elements is in common use to refer to these substances regardless of the exact form or combination in which they exert their effects in plants.

Considered as one group or class of substances found in plants, mineral elements function in a number of different ways:

1. _Constituents of Protoplasm and Cell Walls._—A number of the mineral elements become permanent constituents of molecules which are integral parts of the protoplasm and cell walls. As examples we may cite the sulfur in proteins, the phosphorus in nucleoproteins and lecithins, the magnesium in chlorophyll, and the calcium in calcium pectate. A considerable proportion of the mineral elements in plants, however, acts in some way other than as material from which essential parts of plant cells are constructed, or else are of no apparent consequence in the metabolism of the plant whatsoever.

2. _Influence on the Osmotic Pressure of Plant Cells._—In Chap. VIII it was shown that a portion of the osmotic pressure of the cell sap of any plant cell results from the dissolved mineral salts which it contains. While in most plant cells the absolute concentration of mineral salts in the plant sap is so low that only a small proportion of the osmotic pressure can be ascribed to their presence, there are some important exceptions to this statement as discussed previously.

3. _Influence on Acidity and Buffer Action._—The mineral salts absorbed from the soil often have an influence on the pH of the cell sap and other parts of plant cells, although usually not a very great one, as organic acids and other compounds resulting from the metabolic activities of plants ordinarily exert the predominant influence in determining pH values within cells. As shown in Chap. IV, two of the important buffer systems found in plants—the phosphate and the carbonate systems—have their origin in substances absorbed by the plant from its environment. The phosphate system, however, is the only one found in plants which may be classed as a mineral element buffer system. The cation components of plant buffer systems, other than H^+, are mostly such mineral elements as potassium, calcium, sodium, and magnesium.

4. _Influence on the Permeability of Cytoplasmic Membranes._—The permeability of the cytoplasmic membranes is influenced by the cations and anions in the medium with which they are in contact. Calcium and other di- and trivalent cations usually have a decreasing effect on the permeability of the cytoplasmic membranes of many cells, at least initially, while monovalent cations commonly have an increasing effect. Not only is the permeability of the cytoplasmic membranes in the static sense influenced by ions, but operation of the physiological mechanism by which ions accumulate in plant cells is also influenced by the specific ions in contact with the cell, as described in the preceding chapter.

5. _Toxic Effects of Mineral Elements._—Many mineral elements in their ionic form have a marked toxic effect upon protoplasm, often resulting in

its disorganization and death, even when present in very low concentrations. Among the elements which are known to be highly toxic to plants, at least under certain conditions, are aluminum, arsenic, boron, copper, lead, magnesium, manganese, mercury, molybedenum, nickel, selenium, silver, and zinc. Included in this list are certain of the elements essential in plant metabolism which exert toxic effects when present within the tissues in concentrations exceeding physiological requirements. Toxic effects of some of these elements are discussed more fully later in the chapter.

6. *Antagonistic Effects.*—The effect of one ion or salt in offsetting or even reversing the usual effect of another ion or salt is called *antagonism*. Some degree of antagonism exists between almost any pair of salts. Sodium chloride, for example, results in an increase in the permeability of the cytoplasmic membranes to various solutes under certain conditions. If calcium chloride is introduced into the medium, however, this increasing effect is diminished, or may even be replaced by a decreasing effect.

Similar antagonistic effects are evident in toxicity phenomena. For example in one experiment it was found that the roots of lupines would elongate only about 3.5 mm. per day in a solution of about 0.000015 M $CuCl_2$, but if sufficient $CaCl_2$ were added to make its concentration in the solution about 0.0078 M the roots elongated at a rate of 10.5 mm. per day. The antagonism between the Cu^{++} and Ca^{++} ions was sufficient to reduce greatly the toxicity of the Cu^{++} ions.

7. *Catalytic Effects.*—Certain effects of mineral elements in plants result from their participation in one way or another in catalytic systems. Iron, copper, and zinc are known to be prosthetic groups of certain enzymes and this may also be true of certain other mineral elements. Iron is also a constituent of the cytochromes. Other mineral elements such as magnesium, manganese, and cobalt act as activators or inhibitors in one or more enzymatic systems.

Essential and Nonessential Elements.—Of the large number of elements that have been identified as occurring in plant tissues, only a limited number have been found to be indispensable. Beginning about 1860 a number of extensive investigations were undertaken to determine specifically which elements are essential for green plants and which are not. Some of the earliest workers on this problem were the German botanists, Sachs and Knop. Their investigations, conducted by the method of solution cultures (see later) and subsequently confirmed by a number of other workers, indicated that in addition to the elements carbon, hydrogen, and oxygen, obtained by plants from water or from atmospheric gases, the only essential elements were nitrogen, phosphorus, sulfur, calcium, magnesium, potassium, and iron, all of which enter the plant from the soil.

From the work of these investigators and others developed the almost classical precept that ten elements, and ten only, were essential for the existence of green plants. This viewpoint was first seriously challenged by Mazé (1915), who considered that at least several other elements are essential for the continued development of green plants. The older concept of the "ten essential elements" was so strongly entrenched, however, that Mazé's contentions evoked very little immediate interest, but more recently extensive studies have been undertaken on the problem of the possible roles of other elements in plant metabolism.

It is now realized that there were certain unrecognized sources of error in the experiments upon which the conclusions of earlier investigators were based. Almost all of their investigations were pursued by the method of solution cultures, in which "pure" chemicals in certain proportions were dissolved in distilled water, and these solutions were used as the medium in which the plants were rooted. Many of the "pure" chemicals used, however, contained at least traces of other compounds which might be sufficient in amount to supply plants with an adequate quota of certain necessary elements, especially if they were required only in minute quantities. Similarly, the elements stored in the seed were not usually considered in such experiments. The amounts of some elements available to a plant from this source might suffice for its entire life history if they were required in only small quantities. Furthermore, it is now more generally realized that small amounts of certain elements often dissolve in solution cultures from the walls of the containers and thus become available for utilization by plants. Traces of silicon and zinc, for example, may dissolve out of the walls of ordinary glass vessels into solutions contained within them. Even distilled water, of the grade generally used in such experiments, may contain amounts of certain elements, required only in traces, sufficient to supply the needs of the plants. For these reasons, therefore, it is clear that in practically all of the earlier experiments designed to determine which elements are essential for plants, small quantities of various elements other than those deliberately supplied were usually present in the solution cultures. The failure of earlier investigators to recognize the possibility of the presence of such contaminating substances makes it impossible to accept the results of their investigations as the final word on the mineral salt requirements of plants.

Recognition of these sources of contamination in solution culture techniques has led, more recently, to refinements in such methods, which eliminate or at least enormously reduce the possibility of introducing unknown solutes into solutions used in plant culture work. By repeated crystallizations or other procedures it is possible to obtain chemicals of a much higher degree of purity than those used by the earlier workers. The water used may be distilled from special stills and redistilled a number of times to remove even traces of most solutes. Containers can be used which are inert when in contact with the culture solutions employed. By removal of the cotyledons at a very early stage in germination, or by other procedures, the supply of elements obtained by the plant from the seed can be largely eliminated.

Various more or less critical observations have led to claims that many other elements are essential for normal plant development in addition to the ten which have long been accepted as essential to plants. Among these are arsenic, aluminum, barium, boron, bromine, caesium, chromium, chlorine, cobalt, copper, iodine, lithium, manganese, molybdenum, nickel, selenium, silicon, strontium, tin, titanium, vanadium, and zinc. Most of these elements are considered to be necessary for plants only in traces. With few exceptions each is toxic to plants when present in any appreciable concentration.

In the face of this rather overwhelming array of possibly essential elements it appears desirable to adopt criteria by which the indispensability of an element can be judged. While it is undoubtedly true that any one of these elements, at least when supplied to certain species of plants, under certain cultural conditions, will result in beneficial effects upon growth, this is far from indubitable evidence of its indispensability. Necessity of an element in plant metabolism is demonstrated only if lack of it can be shown to result in injury, aberrant development, or death of plants when grown in sand or solution cultures by a technique including the refinements of method described above. Complete proof of the necessity of an element also requires demonstration that no other element of similar properties can be substituted for it. Furthermore, before it can be considered to be proved that a given element is essential for green plants generally, its indispensability must have been demonstrated for a wide variety of species, representing a number of different families of plants.

It is now quite generally agreed that five other elements—boron, manganese, copper, zinc, and molybdenum—must be added to the group recognized to be essential in the metabolism of green plants. A total of fifteen elements are therefore now considered to be essential. All of the five elements just listed are required in only minute quantities, hence they may be termed *micrometabolic* elements in contrast with those necessary in relatively large amounts, which may be termed *macrometabolic* elements. All of the ten elements long recognized as being essential for plants, except iron, belong in the latter group. It is possible that future investigations may result in the addition of other elements to the list of those considered indispensable in the metabolism of green plants generally, but it seems certain that any such additions will fall into the category of micrometabolic elements.

The question is often asked whether or not the same elements are essential for all kinds of plants. On theoretical grounds it might be argued that, for a group of metabolically similar organisms such as the vascular green plants, it is unlikely that there would be differences from one species to another in the kinds of elements required. In spite of the plausibility of this viewpoint, considerable experimental evidence exists, some of which is mentioned later in the chapter, that certain vascular plants may require elements in addition to the fifteen listed above. There is also evidence that the list of essential elements for at least some species of algae and fungi is not exactly the same as that for the higher green plants.

Specific Roles of the Essential Elements in Plants.—The roles of carbon, hydrogen, and oxygen in the synthesis of carbohydrates, fats, and related compounds have already been discussed in preceding chapters. There are only a few physiologically significant compounds in either plants or animals which do not contain all three of these elements. The roles of these three elements and of nitrogen in the synthesis of proteins and other important nitrogen-containing compounds are considered in the following chapter. The remaining essential elements are usually lumped together under the classification of "mineral elements."

The parts played by the mineral elements in plant metabolism are incompletely understood and it is probable that each of them is involved in metabolic processes occurring in plant cells in ways which are not at present recognized. When an element is a constituent of some important plant compound—such as the sulfur in proteins or the magnesium in chlorophyll—that particular role of the element is relatively easy to identify. When, however, an element plays some less conspicuous role, such as that of a constituent of an enzyme system or carrier in some metabolically important reaction, its significance in such a capacity is often more difficult to recognize.

Some of the known specific roles of each of the essential mineral elements are discussed below. The effects of certain other elements not definitely known to be necessary for plants in general, but which sometimes have important effects on plants, will also be discussed.

Sulfur.—As a rule this element is fairly well distributed throughout the tissues and organs of plants. Sulfur is a constituent of the amino acid *cystine*, which is one of the compounds from which plant proteins are made (Chap. XXVI), and of thiamine and biotin, which are important hormones in plants (Chap. XXVIII). It is also a constituent of the mustard oil glycosides (Chap. XX) such as *sinigrin*, which impart character-istic odors and flavors to such species as mustards, onions, and garlic.

Sulfur is usually absorbed by roots as the SO_4^{--} ion, but may also enter the leaves as SO_2 when that gas is present in the atmosphere (Thomas *et al.*, 1944). It should be noted, however, that SO_2 gas becomes toxic to plants at very low concentrations (Chap. XXX). Although sulfur enters the plant in oxidized form, it is reduced, usually to the sulfhydryl (—SH) group in the formation of amino acids or other organic sulfur-containing molecules. The sulfur of organic molecules in living cells ap-parently may be reconverted into inorganic sulfur, usually the sulfate ion, in which form it may be redistributed within the plant and re-utilized in the formation of organic sulfur compounds in other tissues. Relatively large amounts of sulfur may be moved in this way from the leaves to ripening seeds and fruits.

The symptoms of sulfur deficiency in plants are similar in general to those characteristic of insufficient nitrogen. Amino acids and other nitro-gen-containing compounds accumulate in the tissues of sulfur deficient plants, probably because protein synthesis is not maintained at a rate comparable with that in plants receiving adequate sulfur (Eaton, 1942).

Phosphorus.—Phosphorus is absorbed by plants principally as the $H_2PO_4^-$ ion. Unlike nitrogen and sulfur, however, phosphorus is not re-duced in plant tissues but is linked into organic combinations in highly oxidized form. Phosphorus enters into the composition of phospholipids and of nucleic acids (Chap. XXVI). Chemical combinations of the nucleic acids with proteins result in the formation of the nucleoproteins which, as the name suggests, are important constituents of the nuclei of plant cells. The significance of phosphate carriers, phosphorylation, and of the energy of phosphate bonds in metabolic processes has already been discussed (Chaps. XX, XXII). Participation in such reactions is one of the primary metabolic roles of phosphorus in the cells of both plants and animals.

A very large proportion of the phosphorus in a mature plant is located in the seeds and fruits, accumulating there during the period of their de-velopment. In growing plants, phosphorus is most abundant in meriste-matic tissues where it is utilized in the synthesis of nucleoproteins and other phosphorus containing compounds, some of which operate in the respiration mechanism.

The roles of phosphorus and nitrogen in plant metabolism appear to be interrelated in a number of ways. Inorganic nitrogen compounds are rapidly absorbed and accumulate in plant tissues when the available phos-phates are low. When available phosphates are abundant in the rooting medium, on the other hand, the absorption of inorganic nitrogen compounds is depressed (Nightingale, 1942). The application of phosphate fertilizers, therefore, may alter the nitrogen balance of the plant. Illustrations of this effect are the earlier maturation of plants that often occurs when available phosphorus is high and the delay in reaching maturity occasioned by phosphorus deficiency. Synthesis of proteins (Chap. XXVI) apparently does not occur at usual rates in phosphorus deficient plants (Eckerson, 1931; Richards and Templeman, 1936). Correlated with this decrease in protein synthesis there is often an accumulation of sugars in the vegetative organs of the plant. The purple coloration of leaves associated with phosphorus deficiency in certain varieties of corn, tomatoes, and other species reflects the relatively high concentration of sugars in the leaf tissues which often favors anthocyanin synthesis (Chap. XX). There is also good evidence that phosphates are more rapidly absorbed and accumulated in plants when nitrogen is supplied in organic form (urea) than when nitrate is being absorbed (Breon et al., 1944).

Phosphorus is readily redistributed in plants from one organ to another. Such redistributions probably occur largely in the form of phosphates. During periods of phosphorus deficiency a large proportion of the phosphorus in older leaves may move into other tissues (MacGillivray, 1927) and developing fruits of tomatoes may obtain phosphorus from even the youngest leaves when phosphorus is unavailable in the rooting medium (Arnon and Hoagland, 1943). Studies with radioactive phosphorus have contributed additional evidence of the high mobility of phosphorus and of the rapid rate with which it may move out of leaves and into growing tissues when the external supply is deficient (Arnon et al., 1940; Biddulph, 1941).

Calcium.—A large part of the calcium in most plants is located in the leaves, and, in contrast to phosphorus and potassium, more calcium is present in the older than in the younger leaves. An analysis of strawberry plants, for example, showed more than twice as much calcium in the leaves as in the crowns and roots together (Lineberry and Burkhart, 1943). Much of the calcium in plant tissues may be permanently fixed in the cell walls as a calcium salt of the pectic compounds of the middle lamella. Leaves of squash were found to have as much as 70 per cent of their calcium immobilized in the walls of the cells (Smith, 1944). In many plant species calcium is present in the form of insoluble crystals of calcium oxalate. Calcium also forms salts with other organic acids and probably enters into chemical combination with protein molecules. It is of widespread occurrence in plants in the form of calcium soaps, and calcium ions are generally present as one constituent of the vacuolar sap. Calcium is necessary for the continued growth of apical meristems. In the absence of calcium mitotic divisions become aberrant or suppressed (Sorokin and

Sommer, 1940). Formerly it was considered that the formation of calcium salts of organic acids prevented accumulation of toxic quantities of organic acids within the cells. More recent work, however, suggests that the organic acids are synthesized as a result of the absorption of calcium and other cations (Chap. XXIV). Calcium is also known to have a role in the nitrogen metabolism of plants. In the absence of calcium, some species, at least, are unable to absorb or assimilate nitrates (Nightingale, 1937). Organic forms of nitrogen such as urea, however, seem to serve as sources of nitrogen when calcium is absent (Skok, 1941). These observations are interpreted to mean that calcium is important in the reduction of nitrates in plant tissues (Chap. XXVI).

Calcium is relatively immobile and is not readily redistributed in plant tissues when it becomes deficient in the rooting medium. Older leaves of a plant may have large calcium reserves at the same time that younger leaves on the same plant are deficient in calcium. However, crystals of calcium oxalate in old leaves of peanut plants disappear at times of severe calcium deficiency and are reformed in very young leaves indicating that some degree of redistribution is taking place (Burkhart and Collins, 1942). Similar observations have been reported for other species, but the redistribution of calcium does not appear to be sufficiently rapid or complete to meet the metabolic requirements of the younger tissues.

Magnesium.—This element is the one and only mineral constituent of the chlorophyll molecule. A large proportion of the magnesium present in plants is therefore in the chlorophyll-bearing organs, although seeds are also relatively rich in this element. Magnesium generally occurs in soils in sufficient abundance to supply the needs of plants, although occasional exceptions to this statement are found. Deficiency of magnesium usually results in the development of a characteristic chlorosis and in some species in the appearance of a purple coloration in the foliage. Redistribution of magnesium from older to younger organs of plants occurs readily.

Magnesium plays a role in the phosphate metabolism of plants and, indirectly, therefore, in the respiratory mechanism. Magnesium ions appear to be specific activators for a number of enzymes, including certain transphosphorylases, dehydrogenases, and carboxylases.

Excess quantities of magnesium may prove toxic in solution cultures, an effect which may be offset by the presence of sufficient amounts of calcium. Magnesium toxicity in soils is not common but may occasionally occur in alkali or serpentine soils.

Potassium.—Unlike all of the other macrometabolic mineral elements required by plants potassium is not definitely known to be built into organic compounds essential for the continued existence of the plant. It occurs in plants principally as soluble inorganic salts, although potassium salts of organic acids also are found in plant cells. In spite of these facts potassium is an indispensable element and cannot be completely replaced even by such chemically similar elements as sodium or lithium. The young and actively growing regions of plants, especially buds, young leaves, and root tips, are always rich in potassium while as a rule the proportion of potassium is relatively low in seeds and mature tissues. The fundamental roles of this element in plant metabolism are undoubtedly regulatory or catalytic.

The specific roles of potassium in plants are obscure. However a large number of experimental studies involving many species of plants have given considerable information about what happens to plants when potassium is deficient. Plants deficient in potassium usually contain a higher percentage of soluble organic nitrogen compounds (amino acids and amides) than plants supplied with adequate potassium (Wall, 1940). The protein content of the potassium deficient plants, on the other hand, is relatively low. These facts suggest that potassium is in some way involved in the synthesis of proteins from amino acids. Further support for this hypothesis is furnished by the very different behavior of potassium deficient plants when grown with ammonium compounds as compared with those grown with nitrates as sources of nitrogen. Plants supplied with ammonium nitrogen soon develop signs of serious injury, apparently resulting from the rapid accumulation of ammonia in the tissues. The reduced nitrogen compounds are not synthesized into proteins and so accumulate in toxic quantities in the leaves and stems (Wall and Tiedjens, 1940).

The carbohydrate metabolism is also disturbed by inadequate supplies of potassium. There is evidence that photosynthesis is checked and that respiration is increased by severe potassium deficiency. The effects of low potassium are usually first apparent in the disturbed nitrogen metabolism which, because of the failure of protein synthesis, may lead to an initial increase of carbohydrates in the tissue. As potassium deficiency continues, carbohydrates rapidly decrease in quantity probably as a result of decreased photosynthesis and increased respiration.

Potassium is highly mobile in plants. Internal redistributions of this element occur readily and more or less continuously during the life history of the plant. Older leaves and other organs frequently lose potassium which is translocated to growing regions. Those tissues of the plant that are undergoing the most active growth appear to have the greatest capacity for accumulating potassium in contrast with cells that are physiologically less active (Arnon and Hoagland, 1943).

The potassium ion is usually the most abundant monovalent cation in plant cells. Although it cannot be replaced entirely by any other element, symptoms of potassium deficiency may appear much sooner and are more severe in barley in the absence of sodium ions than when these are present in the culture solution (Mullison and Mullison, 1942). It is probable, therefore, that during the early stages of growth, potassium may be partially replaced by sodium, at least in some species of plants.

Iron.—A deficiency of available iron in soils is seldom a limiting factor in plant development, although occasional exceptions to this statement are encountered. Deficiency of iron in soils is usually a consequence of its insolubility rather than its actual absence. In general, a larger proportion of the iron is in a soluble state in relatively acid soils than in approximately neutral or alkaline soils. One of the most common causes of iron deficiency is an excess of lime in the soil. Even in alkaline soils, however, some iron may be absorbed by plants as a result of the intimate contact between the root surface and the soil particles (Chapman, 1939).

Iron is indispensable for the synthesis of chlorophyll in green plants. Deficiency of this element results in the development of a characteristic chlorosis. Iron does not, however, enter into the constitution of the chlorophyll molecule. The *state* of the iron in plant tissues is also often a factor determining its influence in chlorophyll synthesis. Chlorosis, as a result of iron deficiency, is sometimes found in leaves which contain as much iron as green leaves, the iron being present in an unavailable form in the chlorotic tissue. Iron is physiologically active in the ferrous state and, Fe^{++} although often absorbed as the ferric ion, much of it is rapidly reduced within the cells. The rate at which iron is reduced in the living cells seems to be influenced by the quantity of manganese in the cells as discussed later.

Some of the enzymes and carriers which operate in the respiratory mechanism of living cells are iron compounds. Specific examples are catalase, peroxidase, cytochrome oxidase (probably), and the cytochromes. The participation of iron in the form of such compounds in the oxidative mechanism of cells is undoubtedly one of its more important roles in cellular metabolism.

The proportionate amount of iron in plant tissues is very low; much of that present is a constituent of organic compounds. Iron is one of the most immobile of all elements in plants, little redistribution occurring from one tissue to another. If plants which have been supplied with iron are transferred to a solution culture lacking this element, the subsequently developing leaves exhibit a marked iron chlorosis, while the older leaves retain their normal green color. This is a graphic demonstration of the fact that no appreciable transfer of iron occurs from older to younger leaves.

Manganese.—Only small quantities of this element are required by plants, manganese compounds being distinctly toxic to plants except in very low concentrations. Manganese, as a rule, seems to be most abundant in the physiologically active parts of plants, especially leaves. It is a relatively immobile element, little redistribution occurring from one part of a plant to another.

The roles of manganese in plants are undoubtedly those of a primary or accessory catalyst. This element probably plays a direct part in oxidation-reduction phenomena, especially in relation to iron compounds. Iron is commonly absorbed as the ferric ion and reduced in cells to the ferrous condition unless some oxidizing agent is present which prevents this reaction. According to Somers and Shive (1942), manganese plays the role of such an oxidizing agent, and an excess of manganese may, therefore, induce symptoms of iron deficiency by converting the available iron into the physiologically inactive ferric condition.

Manganese is an activator of some enzyme systems including certain dehydrogenases and carboxylases. Some of the same enzymes activated by magnesium are also activated by manganese and, less commonly, by certain other metallic cations.

Manganese is also related in some way to chlorophyll synthesis as chloroplasts are soon affected by deficiency of this element. Chlorosis resulting from manganese deficiency is distinctive in appearance as compared with that resulting from inadequate iron or magnesium.

Certain "deficiency diseases" of plants have been traced to an inadequate amount of manganese within the tissues. Some of the better known of these are Grey Speck of oats, Speckled Yellows of sugar beet, and Frenching of tung. Manganese deficiency in soils is most likely to occur when the soil reaction is relatively alkaline. Manganese toxicity as a result of soil conditions is not common, but occurs occasionally, especially on acid soils.

Boron.—Although, in general, this element is necessary in only small quantities, the boron requirements of different plants vary over a considerable range. Investigations by solution or sand culture techniques (see later) show that only a trace (less than 1 p.p.m.) of boron is required for the best development of some species such as tomato and carrot, while others such as sugar beet and asparagus do not show maximum development unless boron is available in a concentration of 10-15 p.p.m. The range between the amount of boron necessary for the best development of a plant and that causing injury is often very narrow and may even overlap so that, when plants are provided with sufficient boron for maximum growth, they may at the same time exhibit some signs of boron toxicity (Eaton, 1944).

The exact role of boron in plants is unknown. In boron deficient plants a variety of physiological reactions and morphogenic changes are induced which differ with the species and the environmental conditions. The accumulation of carbohydrates, ammonium compounds, and other soluble nitrogenous compounds in boron deficient plants suggests a breakdown of protein synthesis (Briggs, 1943; Scripture and McHargue, 1945). The death or serious injury to cells of the apical meristems of the stem and root which is a usual symptom of boron deficiency may have a similar explanation. There is also considerable evidence of interrelationships between boron and the calcium and potassium metabolism of the plant.

In most plants boron is not a readily mobile element. It reaches its greatest concentration in the leaves and seems to be fixed in the leaf cells in some manner which precludes its translocation to other tissues. The boron concentration of meristems, roots, fruits, and storage tissues is much lower than that of leaves. Boron may be present in the lower leaves of a plant in such quantities as to cause them injury at the same time that cells of the apical meristems exhibit symptoms of boron deficiency (Eaton, 1944).

A number of "physiological diseases" of plants have been found to be caused by a deficiency of boron within the tissues. Among these are Heart Rot of sugar beet, Leaf Roll of potato, Brown Heart of turnip, and Browning of cauliflower. Injury as a result of boron toxicity is also a fairly common occurrence in field grown plants. Use of irrigation water containing compounds of boron in solution is a frequent cause of boron toxicity in plants.

Zinc.—This element is highly toxic to plants except in very dilute concentrations, but traces must be present if normal plant metabolism is to be maintained. Deficiency of zinc results in structural aberrancies in the root tips (Eltinge and Reed, 1940), dwarfing of vegetative growth, and failure of seed formation (Reed, 1942).

Zinc is known to be a constituent of the enzyme carbonic anhydrase (Table 18). This is a well-known enzyme in animals, and evidence is accumulating that it is also of widespread occurrence in plants. Whether or not it plays any important role in plant metabolism has not yet been ascertained. There is good evidence that zinc is also necessary in the synthesis of indoleacetic acid, an important growth hormone in plants (Chap. XXVIII).

A number of disease conditions, especially of tree species, have been recognized to result from zinc deficiency. Among these are Rosette of pecan, Little Leaf of various species of deciduous fruit trees, Bronzing of tung, and White Bud of maize. The abnormal growth behavior of fruit trees and other species when deficient in zinc may result at least in part from the necessity of zinc for the synthesis of indoleacetic acid or other auxins (Skoog, 1940).

Copper.—Like zinc this element is highly toxic to plants except in very dilute concentrations. Nevertheless there seems little doubt that traces of copper are essential in plant metabolism. Because of the fact that copper is a constituent of certain oxidizing-reducing enzymes, such as tyrosinase and ascorbic acid oxidase (Chap. XXII), it is certain that at least one of its roles in plant metabolism is participation in oxidation-reduction reactions. Apart from this catalytic role no definite relation has been recognized between copper and any other specific physiological process.

The Die-back disease of citrus and some other trees and the so-called "Reclamation Disease" have been found to have their origin in a deficiency of copper. The latter disease has been found in plants growing on reclaimed heath and moorland soils in some parts of northern Europe. Live stock grazing on such lands are also subject to a copper deficiency disease.

Molybdenum.—This is the latest element to be added to the list of those now generally considered indispensable for higher green plants. The first green plant for which this element was shown to be essential was the tomato (Arnon and Stout, 1939), although its necessity for certain bacteria and fungi had been shown previously. Necessity of this element for a number of other higher plant species has been clearly demonstrated (Hewitt, 1951). Of all the elements definitely considered to be essential, molybdenum is required in the smallest amounts. One part in 100,000,000 of a culture solution is sufficient to prevent the appearance of molybdenum deficiency symptoms in tomato plants. This element is usually supplied to plants as the molybdate ion. One of the roles of molybdenum in plants appears to be that of playing a part in the reduction of nitrates (Chap. XXVI).

Molybdenum-deficient soils have been found in regions as far apart as Australia, California, New Jersey, and central Europe. Applications of MoO_3 at the rate of an ounce an acre or even less have resulted in marked increases in the yield of certain crops on such soils. In any appreciable concentration molybdenum is highly toxic to plants. Excess molybdenum is also harmful to animals. The teart disease of livestock, which occurs in certain parts of England, has been found to result from excess of this element in the diet. Soils of areas in which this disease occurs are relatively rich in molybdenum, and unusually large amounts of molybdenum compounds accumulate in many of the forage plants from which it is obtained by the animals which browse on them.

Sodium.—Although there is no convincing evidence that sodium is actually essential in plant metabolism, it is almost invariably present in the ash, sometimes in relatively large amounts (Collander, 1941). Furthermore, addition of sodium compounds to the soil has been found to result in more vigorous development of many kinds of plants. This is true of some species only when potassium is deficient but is true for some other species when potassium is present in a sufficiency. Examples of some plants in the first category are barley, carrot, cotton, flax, and tomato; of plants in the second category, celery, table and sugar beet, turnip and Swiss chard (Harmer and Benne, 1945).

Silicon.—This element comprises a very large proportion of the ash of some species, particularly of the aerial portions of members of the grass and *Equisetum* families. It is also relatively abundant in the bark of trees. Earlier investigators believed, principally because of the large amounts present in the ash of many species, that silicon is essential for plants. Many years ago, however, it was shown that even those species in which silicon was most abundant could be grown to maturity in culture solutions to which no silicon was added. It is doubtful, however, if plants have ever grown in the complete absence of this element since, even in cultures to which it is not supplied, traces are probably present in the form of impurities from various sources. The results of Lipman (1938) with sunflower and barley, and Raleigh (1939) with beet, suggest very strongly that small amounts of this element are essential, at least for some species.

Formerly it was believed that silicon was important in contributing to the stiffness of the straw in cereal crops, but the experimental evidence does not support this view. Some investigators have also considered that the silicified cell walls of some species, such as the cereals, render them more resistant to fungous and insect parasites.

Silicon appears, however, to exert an important influence upon the phosphate metabolism of plants. Application of sodium silicate results in an increase in the yields of plants growing in plots inadequately supplied with phosphates. Some workers believe this effect of silicon to be upon the metabolism of the plant itself. They believe that the presence of this element in some way increases the efficiency of the plant in the utilization of phosphorus. Others believe that silicon increases the availability of the phosphates in the soil. It is possible that both such effects may occur.

Chlorine.—This element was earlier considered to be essential for plants, although in more recent times this view has not received much support. Chlorine seems, however, to be of universal occurrence in plants and is apparently present almost wholly in the form of soluble inorganic chlorides. The experimental results which have been obtained upon supplying chlorides to plants have been very variable. In some species a definite beneficial effect has been noticed; in others applications of chlorides have resulted in a retardation of plant growth; and in still others no apparent influence could be detected. The apparent results of supplying chlorides to plants may be caused largely, if not entirely, by effects on ionic relationships in the soil or solution culture rather than by direct effects of this element on the metabolism of the plant. As a result of critical experiments with buckwheat and peas, however, Lipman (1938) concluded that, if chlorine is not actually essential, it greatly influences plant development.

Plants indigenous to salt marshes and saline soils can endure the presence of relatively large quantities of chlorides, usually sodium chloride, in the soil. Asparagus is an example of a crop plant which not only tolerates but actually requires treatment with sodium chloride for its best development.

Aluminum.—This element is one of the most abundant of those present in the soil, although it occurs chiefly in insoluble forms. A larger proportion of soluble aluminum is generally present in relatively acid soils (below pH 5.0) than in soils of higher pH.

Aluminum is probably universally present in plants, although in terms of percentage composition the amount in the ash of most species is very small. Aluminum is not usually considered to be one of the essential elements, but the results of Sommer (1926), Lipman (1938), and Tauböck (1942) suggest strongly that traces may be necessary, at least for some species.

Except in very dilute concentrations, aluminum is distinctly toxic to plants. Its toxicity to such species as corn and barley may become evident in concentrations as low as 1 part per million in culture solutions. The detrimental effect of soils with a pH of 5 or less upon the growth of some species undoubtedly results, at least in part, from the toxic effect of the relatively high concentration of aluminum ions in such soils. In acid soils aluminum may precipitate phosphorus and so decrease its availability to plants. The beneficial effect upon the growth of some species of adding lime or phosphates to acid soils results at least partly from a reduction in the solubility of the aluminum compounds present as well as from an increase in the availability of phosphorus.

The color of the flowers of *Hydrangea macrophylla* is related to aluminum content of the floral tissues (Allen, 1943). Blue flowers always contain more aluminum than pink flowers. Addition of soluble aluminum compounds to the soil in which hydrangea plants are growing induces a shift in flower color from pink to blue.

Selenium.—For many years a serious and often fatal disease of livestock, usually called "alkali disease," has been known to occur in certain regions of the great plains of western North America. The cause of this disease was long unknown but was finally recognized to be a result of selenium poisoning. The distribution of this disease was found to correspond closely with that of seleniferous soils. Such soils are of common occurrence in a belt extending from Alberta and Saskatchewan to Arizona and New Mexico and doubtless also occur in many other parts of the world (Trelease and Beath, 1949). Some of the plants native to such seleniferous soils, notably certain species of *Astragalus*, a kind of vetch, accumulate selenium in relatively large quantities. Selenium poisoning is a common outcome of the browsing upon such plants by cattle, sheep, or horses. On the other hand, very little selenium accumulates in many kinds of plants, including most crop plants, even when growing on highly seleniferous soils. Plants in this latter category exhibit symptoms of selenium toxicity at relatively low concentrations in solution cultures. Selenium-accumulating species, on the contrary, may acquire a selenium content as high as a hundred times that of nonaccumulating species without injury. and there are indications that selenium may even be a necessary element for such species (Trelease and Trelease, 1939).

Iodine, Fluorine, and Cobalt.—These elements are included in the discussion, not because they are known to be essential to plants, but because of the critical roles they play in the metabolism of higher animals.

Iodine is a constituent of the essential animal hormone, thyroxin, and deficiency of iodine leads to the development of goiter in man and higher animals. When iodides are present in the soil they are absorbed by plants; hence in some regions vegetable foods may be an important dietary source of iodine for animals.

Lewis and Powers (1941), in a critical study, were unable to find any evidence of the essentiality of iodine in several kinds of plants. Marked toxicity effects were exhibited by tomato plants growing in sand culture to which 16 p.p.m. of iodine were added as potassium iodide, but not by plants at a concentration of 4 p.p.m. (Hageman et al., 1942).

Fluorine has attracted much attention in recent years because of its apparent role in preventing dental caries in humans. Fluoride ions are readily absorbed by plants, especially from the more acid types of soils, but in any appreciable concentration they are highly toxic. Concentrations as low as 10 p.p.m. of fluorine (in the form of NaF) in solution cultures were found to be toxic to several species of plants (Leone et al., 1948). Fluorine gas is an effulgent waste in certain industrial processes, and fluorine from this source has been suspected of having detrimental effects on plants in some localities.

Although not definitely known to be an essential element, cobalt may exert marked effects on plant metabolism and development. Cobalt ions are known to activate some plant enzymes, such as certain carboxylases and peptidases. Cobalt also has an enhancing effect upon the enlargement phase of growth in etiolated leaves and certain other plant tissues (Miller, 1951). Cobalt deficiency leads to the development of a diseased condition in cattle and sheep which has been called by a number of names (Pining, Bush Sickness, Morton Mains Disease) and which has been recognized in such widely separated parts of the world as Scotland, New Zealand, and Australia. This disease can be combated by soil treatments with a cobalt salt, resulting in an increased content of cobalt in the forage plants on which the animals browse. The fact that cobalt has been found to be a constituent of vitamin B_{12} (Chap. XXVIII) is probably significant in relation to such deficiency diseases.

Symptoms of Mineral Element Deficiency.—Absence or deficiency of any of the necessary mineral elements in the soil or other substratum in which a plant is rooted will sooner or later become apparent in the development of the plant by the appearance of growth aberrations of one kind or another. Symptoms of mineral element deficiency may also occur when the element is present in the tissues of the plant if for some reason or another it cannot be used in plant metabolism. Plants may exhibit symptoms of

Fig. 119. Symptoms of mineral element deficiencies as shown by tobacco plants. The deficient elements are: (1) nitrogen, (2) phosphorus, (3) potassium, (4) calcium, (5) magnesium, (7) boron, (8) sulfur, (9) manganese, and (10) iron. All of the elements were supplied to (6). Photograph, U. S. Department of Agriculture.

nitrogen deficiency, for example, even when the tissues contain an abundant supply of nitrates if the reduction of nitrates is prevented for some reason or another.

In a general way the symptoms of the deficiency of a given mineral element are similar in all species of plants. Certain deficiency symptoms assume, however, more or less distinctive aspects in some species. For example, manganese deficiency results in the development of a characteristic mottled chlorosis in the leaves of many species. In maize and other cereals, however, chlorosis resulting from manganese deficiency assumes the pattern of an alternate yellow and green striping running lengthwise of the leaves. Symptoms of the deficiency of a given element also frequently differ somewhat in woody plants from herbaceous plants. It is therefore important that the symptoms of mineral element deficiency be studied for each economic species of plants individually. Once such symptoms have been distinguished for a species they are of assistance in diagnosing abnormal development of plants of that species under natural or cultural conditions.

Keys to the symptoms of various elemental deficiencies have been devised for a number of species of plants. The following key for tobacco is taken, with slight modifications, from McMurtrey (1938). The effects of such deficiencies upon tobacco plants are depicted in Fig. 119. Keys for other kinds of plants, as well as colored illustrations of mineral deficiency symptoms for a number of species are given by Hambidge (1949).

KEY TO MINERAL ELEMENT DEFICIENCY SYMPTOMS IN TOBACCO

A. Effects localized on older leaves or more or less general on the whole plant.
  B. Local, occurring as mottling or chlorosis with or without necrotic spotting of lower leaves, little or no drying of lower leaves.
    C. Lower leaves curved or cupped under with yellowish mottling at tips and margins. Necrotic spots at tips and margins.
                                                                    Potassium.
    C. Lower leaves chlorotic between the principal veins at tips and margins of a light-green to white color. Typically no necrotic spots.   *Magnesium.*
  B. General; also yellowing and drying or "firing" of lower leaves.
    C. Plant light green, lower leaves yellow, drying to light-brown color.   *Nitrogen.*
    C. Plants dark green, leaves narrow in proportion to length; plants immature.   *Phosphorus.*
A. Effects localized on terminal growth, consisting of upper and bud leaves.

B. Dieback involving the terminal bud, which is preceded by peculiar distortions and necrosis at the tips or base of young leaves making up the terminal growth.

    C. Young leaves making up the terminal bud first light green followed by a typical hooking downward at tips, followed by necrosis, so that if later growth takes place tips and margins of the upper leaves are missing.   *Calcium*.

    C. Young leaves constricted and light green at base, followed by more or less decomposition at leaf base; if later growth takes place leaves show a twisted or distorted development; broken leaves show blackening of vascular tissue.   *Boron*.

B. Terminal bud remains alive, chlorosis of upper or bud leaves, with or without necrotic spots, veins light or dark green.

    C. Young leaves with necrotic spots scattered over chlorotic leaf, smallest veins tend to remain green, producing a checkered effect.   *Manganese*.

    C. Young leaves without necrotic spots, chlorosis does or does not involve veins so as to make them dark or light green in color.

        D. Young leaves with veins of a light-green color or of the same shade as interveinal tissue. Color light green, never white or yellow. Lower leaves do not dry up.   *Sulfur*.

        D. Young leaves chlorotic, principal veins characteristically darker green than tissue between the veins. When veins lose their color, all the leaf tissue is white or yellow.   *Iron*.

Solution and Sand Cultures.—Much of our knowledge regarding the roles of mineral elements in plants has been obtained by means of solution culture experiments. The growing of plants in solution and sand cultures is today one of the most widely used experimental techniques employed by plant physiologists. The necessary solutions, often rather inappropriately called "nutrient solutions," are prepared by dissolving salts in certain definite proportions in distilled water. A multitude of combinations and concentrations of salts have been suggested for use in solution culture work. In general, however, it has been found that most species of plants, under a given set of climatic conditions, grow almost equally well over a considerable range of variations in the mineral salt complex of a solution culture, a sand culture, or a soil.

Shive (1915) pointed out that the six principal elements obtained by plants from the soil—nitrogen, sulfur, phosphorus, calcium, potassium and magnesium—could be supplied by a solution containing only three salts. He proposed a "three-salt" solution containing $Ca(NO_3)_2$, KH_2PO_4, and $MgSO_4$ to which was added a trace of iron salt. Such three-salt solutions were widely used for some years but for various reasons have been almost entirely replaced by solutions in which four or more salts are used to provide the six macrometabolic elements obtained by plants from the soil. Two solutions which have been widely used are those described by Hoagland and Arnon (1938) and by Shive and Robbins (1938). The former of these has the following composition: 0.001 M KH_2PO_4, 0.005 M KNO_3, 0.005 M $Ca(NO_3)_2$, and 0.002 M $MgSO_4$; the latter has the following composition: 0.0023 M KH_2PO_4, 0.0045 M $Ca(NO_3)_2$, 0.0023 M $MgSO_4$, and 0.0007 M $(NH_4)_2SO_4$.

In order to make either of the above solutions, or any of a number of similar ones which have been devised, "complete," it is also necessary to introduce into it the necessary micrometabolic elements. A solution of ferric tartrate is often used as the source of iron. One milliliter of a 0.5 per cent solution of this salt per liter of the culture solution is usually sufficient, although supplementary additions of iron salt are necessary under some conditions as indicated in the later discussion. The other micrometabolic elements are usually supplied to the culture solution in the form of a supplementary solution of which a number have been described. One such solution is prepared as follows: 2.5 g. H_3BO_3, 1.5 g. $MnCl_2 \cdot 4H_2O$, 0.10 g. $ZnCl_2$, 0.05 g. $CuCl_2 \cdot 2H_2O$, and 0.05 g. MoO_3. One milliliter of this solution is usually added to each liter of the culture solution.

A number of schemes have been devised whereby a series of closely comparable solutions can be prepared, each of which is lacking in one macrometabolic element. One such relatively simple scheme is described by Meyer (1945). Such series of solutions are used in studying symptoms of the deficiency of the various elements. More elaborate systems of solutions in which the proportions of the cations and anions present can be varied systematically have been described by Hamner et al. (1942) and others. In solution culture experiments the solution is transferred to suitable vessels, the size and shape of which depend upon the purpose of the investigation, and the kind and size of the experimental plants. Jars, crocks, trays, and tanks of various kinds have been used as the containers in solution culture investigations. It is usually desirable, and in some kinds of experiments essential, that the containers be made of some relatively inert material such as Pyrex glass or well-glazed porcelain. Seedling plants are fastened into position on the containers in such a way that their root systems are immersed in the solution.

Many precautions must be observed if reliable results are to be obtained in work with solution cultures, only a few of the most important of which can be summarized in a brief discussion: (1) All of the solutions used in any series must have essentially the same osmotic pressure, except in experiments in which the effects of different osmotic pressures of the solutions themselves are being investigated. In general, however, with the one exception just noted, solutions with an osmotic pressure of more than 2 atm. are not employed in solution culture experiments. (2) The possible effects of differences in pH from one solution to another in any given series should be evaluated. It is probable, however, that the effects of pH as such in solution cultures are not as significant as they were at one time supposed to be. Arnon and Johnson (1942) have shown that several species of plants develop almost equally well in solution cultures at any pH between 4 and 8 if precautions are taken to assure that all of the necessary elements remain available at all pH values. (3) Most species of plants grow better in aerated than in unaerated solution cultures. A solution is an unnatural environment for the roots of most species of plants. The oxygen concentration of such aqueous media is relatively low, and carbon dioxide may accumulate as a result of root respiration. Aeration of solution cultures is therefore often necessary and almost always desirable. If aeration is to be efficient the air forced through the solution must be broken into very fine bubbles. This is usually accomplished by forcing air under pressure through tubes of porous carbon or some similar material which are immersed in the solutions. (4) In many types of experiments provision must be made for at least approximate maintenance of the ionic concentrations and proportions within the solution. The various ions in a solution are not absorbed at the same rate. Neither is the rate of absorption of water proportional to the rate of absorption of ions. Furthermore, various ions, and perhaps also organic compounds, diffuse from the roots into the solution. The modifying effects of these processes on the composition and concentration of the solution may be minimized in several ways. If the initial proportion of volume of solution to the size of the root system is relatively large, ionic proportions and total concentration of the solution will usually be maintained longer than if the opposite is true. In some solution culture installations, provision is made for a slow constant renewal of the solution. In large-scale work, especially, analyses are made at frequent intervals for the various ions, and the concentration of any one found to be deficient in the solution is restored to its initial value. The most commonly followed procedure, however, is to replace the solution at relatively frequent intervals with fresh solution. (5) Considerable difficulty is often experienced in keeping certain elements in soluble form in culture solutions under certain conditions. This is particularly true of iron. In general, the more alkaline the solution the more likely is the iron to be precipitated. In solutions with a pH of 6.0 or higher, special precautions must be taken to prevent iron deficiency from becoming a limiting factor in plant growth.

A procedure commonly used to prevent the development of iron deficiency is to add fresh portions of a dilute solution of an iron salt to a culture solution from time to time. Another procedure is to supply the iron as iron humate (Horner et al., 1934). In this form iron is not readily precipitated from the kinds of solutions used in culture work with plants. Still another procedure is to supply iron in an "insoluble" form such as magnetite. Iron from such a compound slowly passes into solution thus maintaining the supply of this element over an extended period. The same considerations which apply to the solubility of iron in solution cultures also apply to manganese. Phosphates also are highly insoluble in alkaline solutions, and special precautions must be taken if availability of phosphates is to be maintained in solutions above a pH of about 7.

For many types of investigations "sand cultures" are preferred to solution cultures. Suitable vessels are filled with a pure quartz sand or some similar inert granular material in which the plants are rooted. The sand must not be too fine, else difficulties will be encountered in insuring adequate drainage and aeration. For this reason a fine-textured gravel is often used instead of a sand. The sand is kept moistened with the solution by one or another of several techniques. "Drip cultures" have often been used, in which the solution falls from an overhead reservoir, usually drop by drop, on the surface of the sand, provision being made for the drainage of any excess solution from the vessels. Another commonly used procedure is that of subirrigation. The bottom of the sand container is con-

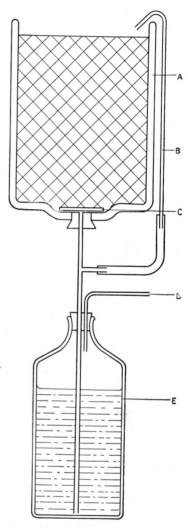

Fig. 120. Diagram (shown in sectional view) of apparatus for sand culture of plants by the sub-irrigation method. (A) Two-gallon urn-shaped porcelain vessel filled with sand. (B) Overflow tube. (C) Fiber glass or glass wool pad. (D) Connection to compressed air line or air pump. (E) Reservoir bottle (one gallon) containing solution.

nected by means of suitable tubing with a reservoir of solution (Fig. 120). By placing the solution in the reservoir under pressure, the solution is forced up through the sand in the vessel to its surface. The pressure on the solution in the reservoir is then turned off, and the excess solution drains from the sand back into the reservoir. From one to several irrigations per day are necessary, depending upon the plant, volume and particle size of the sand, and the prevailing environmental conditions. Automatic subirrigation installations have been devised and used by a number of investigators.

An important advantage of sand over solution cultures is that, in the former, the roots grow in a much more nearly natural environment, particularly as regards aeration. A sand medium, however, is a much simpler environment for roots than most naturally occurring soils. For some purposes solution cultures have definite advantages over sand cultures. This is especially true in experimental work with micrometabolic elements, because it is simpler to eliminate sources of contamination with unwanted elements when the additional complexity of a sand medium is not present in the system.

Employment of the techniques of sand and solution cultures has led to many advancements in knowledge of the mineral salt relations of plants. Most of the available information regarding the essentiality of various elements for plants has resulted from investigations in which such techniques have been used. The symptoms of the deficiency of the various essential elements in many species of plants have also been ascertained by such techniques. Sand and solution cultures have also been used in the investigation of such other problems as the relative proportions of different ions most favorable to the development of different plants, the toxicity of various ions to plants, the mechanism of the absorption of ions, and the tolerance of different plants to different total concentrations of salts in the substratum.

The fact that it has been found possible to grow many species of plants to maturity in sand or solution cultures has led to the advocacy of this method for the production of crops on a commercial scale. The terms _hydroponics_ and _soilless growth_ of plants, among others, have been applied to such procedures. Much publicity was given to this possibility for a while, and many extravagant claims were made for these methods which by-pass the time-hallowed procedure of using soil as the substratum of plant growth. There is a moderate measure of truth in the claims of the proponents of such methods, but it is unlikely that soilless methods of culturing plants will make any appreciable inroads on conventional agriculture in the foreseeable future. Actually such procedures are entirely feasible, and the techniques of large-scale soilless culture of plants have been worked out in considerable detail (Ellis and Swaney, 1947). There is little evidence, however, that the yield of a crop plant rooted in sand or solution cultures will exceed that for the same plant when rooted in a good agricultural soil. Critical comparison of soil-grown and solution-grown plants under similar conditions of light, temperature, and spacing show no significant difference in yield between the two methods of culture (Hoagland and Arnon, 1938). The methods of sand and solution culture have been adapted, with apparent success, to the culture of certain greenhouse crops. Such techniques have also been employed for the raising of certain crops in isolated, barren regions such as remote oceanic islands. A number of large-scale solution culture installations were operated in such places during World War II for military purposes. The extent to which such methods will be employed commercially in the future is largely a matter of economics.

SUGGESTED FOR COLLATERAL READING

Ellis, C., and M. W. Swaney. *Soilless Growth of Plants*. 2nd Ed. Revised by T. Eastwood. Reinhold Publishing Corp. New York. 1947.

Hambidge, G., Editor. *Hunger Signs in Crops*. 2nd Ed. Judd and Detweiler. Washington. 1949.

Hoagland, D. R. *Lectures on the Inorganic Nutrition of Plants*. Chronica Botanica Co. Waltham, Mass. 1944.

Russell, E. J. *Soil Conditions and Plant Growth*. 8th Ed. Revised by E. W. Russell. Longmans, Green and Co. London. 1950.

Stiles, W. *Trace Elements in Plants and Animals*. The Macmillan Co. New York. 1946.

Truog, E., Editor. *Mineral Nutrition of Plants*. University of Wisconsin Press. Madison. 1951.

Wallace, T. A., *et al. Rothampsted International Symposium on Trace Elements in Plant Physiology*. Chronica Botanica Co. Waltham, Mass. 1951.

Bibliography of the literature on the minor elements and their relation to plant and animal nutrition. 4th Ed. Vol. I, II. Chilean Nitrate Educational Bureau, Inc. New York. 1948, 1951.

SELECTED BIBLIOGRAPHY

Allen, R. C. Influence of aluminum on the flower color of *Hydrangea macrophylla*. *Contr. Boyce Thompson Inst.* **13:** 221-242. 1943.

Arnon, D. I., and D. R. Hoagland. Composition of the tomato plant as influenced by nutrient supply, in relation to fruiting. *Bot. Gaz.* **104:** 576-590. 1943.

Arnon, D. I., and C. M. Johnson. Influence of hydrogen ion concentration on the growth of higher plants under controlled conditions. *Plant Physiol.* **17:** 525-539. 1942.

Arnon, D. I., and P. R. Stout. Molybdenum as an essential element for higher plants. *Plant Physiol.* **14:** 599-602. 1939.

Arnon, D. I., P. R. Stout, and F. Sipos. Radioactive phosphorus as an indicator of phosphorus absorption of tomato fruits at various stages of development. *Amer. Jour. Bot.* **27**: 791-798. 1940.

Biddulph, O. Diurnal migration of injected radiophosphorus from bean leaves. *Amer. Jour. Bot.* **28**: 348-352. 1941.

Brenchley, Winifred E. The essential nature of certain minor elements for plant nutrition. *Bot. Rev.* **2**: 173-196. 1936. **13**: 169-193. 1947.

Breon, W. S., W. S. Gillam, and D. J. Tendam. Influence of phosphorus supply and the form of available nitrogen on the absorption and the distribution of phosphorus by the tomato plant. *Plant Physiol.* **19**: 495-506. 1944.

Briggs, G. B. Effect of boron in the substrate on the rate of nitrate absorption and on nitrogen distribution in nasturtium. *Plant Physiol.* **18**: 415-432. 1943.

Burkhart, L., and E. R. Collins. Mineral nutrients in peanut plant growth. *Proc. Soil Sci. Soc. Amer.* **6**: 272-280. 1941.

Chapman, H. D. Absorption of iron from finely ground magnetite by citrus seedlings. *Soil Sci.* **49**: 309-314. 1939.

Collander, R. Selective absorption of cations by higher plants. *Plant Physiol.* **16**: 691-720. 1941.

Eaton, F. M. Deficiency, toxicity and accumulation of boron in planets. *Jour. Agric. Res.* **69**: 237-277. 1944.

Eaton, S. V. Influence of sulphur deficiency on metabolism of black mustard. *Bot. Gaz.* **104**: 306-315. 1942.

Eckerson, Sophia H. Influence of phosphorus deficiency on metabolism of the tomato. *Contr. Boyce Thompson Inst.* **3**: 197-217. 1931.

Eltinge, Ethel T., and H. S. Reed. The effect of zinc deficiency upon the root of *Lycopersicum esculentum. Amer. Jour. Bot.* **27**: 331-335. 1940.

Hageman, R. H., E. S. Hodge, and J. S. McHargue. Effect of potassium iodide on the ascorbic acid content and growth of tomato plants. *Plant Physiol.* **17**: 465-472. 1942.

Hamner, K. C., C. B. Lyon, and C. L. Hamner. Effect of mineral nutrition on the ascorbic-acid content of the tomato. *Bot. Gaz.* **103**: 586-616. 1942.

Harmer, P. M., and E. J. Benne. Sodium as a crop nutrient. *Soil Sci.* **60**: 137-148. 1945.

Hewitt, E. J. The role of the mineral elements in plant nutrition. *Ann. Rev. Plant Physiol.* **2**: 25-52. 1951.

Hoagland, D. R., and D. I. Arnon. The water-culture method for growing plants without soil. *Univ. Calif. Agric. Expt. Sta. Circ. 347.* 1938.

Horner, C. K., D. Buck, and S. R. Hoover. Preparation of humate iron and other humate metals. *Plant Physiol.* **9**: 663-669. 1934.

Leone, I. A., E. G. Brennan, R. H. Daines, and W. R. Robbins. Some effects of fluorine on peach, tomato, and buckwheat when absorbed through roots. *Soil Sci.* **66**: 259-266. 1948.

Lewis, J. C., and W. L. Powers. Iodine in relation to plant nutrition. *Jour. Agric. Res.* **63**: 623-637. 1941.

Lineberry, R. A., and L. Burkhart. Nutrient deficiencies in the strawberry leaf and fruit. *Plant Physiol.* **18**: 324-333. 1943.

Lipman, C. B. Importance of silicon, aluminum and chlorine for higher plants. *Soil Sci.* **45**: 189-198. 1938.

MacGillivray, J. H. Effect of phosphorus on the composition of the tomato plant. *Jour. Agric. Res.* **34**: 97-127. 1927.

Mazé, P. Déterminations des éléments minéreaux rares nécessaires au développement du mais. *Compt. Rend. Acad. Sci.* (*Paris*) **160**: 211-214. 1915.

McMurtrey, J. E., Jr. Symptoms on field-grown tobacco characteristic of the deficient supply of each of several essential chemical elements. *U. S. Dept. Agric. Tech. Bull. 612*. 1938.

Meyer, B. S. Effects of deficiencies of certain mineral elements on the development of *Taraxacum kok-saghyz. Amer. Jour. Bot.* **32**: 523-528. 1945.

Miller, C. O. Promoting effect of cobaltous and nickelous ions on expansion of etiolated bean leaf disks. *Arch. Biochem. and Biophys.* **32**: 216-218. 1951.

Mullison, W. R., and Ethel Mullison. Growth responses of barley seedlings in relation to potassium and sodium nutrition. *Plant Physiol.* **17**: 632-644. 1942.

Nightingale, G. T. Potassium and calcium in relation to nitrogen metabolism. *Bot. Gaz.* **98**: 725-734. 1937.

Nightingale, G. T. Nitrate and carbohydrate reserves in relation to nitrogen nutrition of pineapple. *Bot. Gaz.* **103**: 409-456. 1942.

Raleigh, G. J. Evidence for the essentiality of silicon for growth of the beet plant. *Plant Physiol.* **14**: 823-828. 1939.

Reed, H. S. The relation of zinc to seed production. *Jour. Agric. Res.* **64**: 635-644. 1942.

Richards, F. J., and W. G. Templeman. Physiological studies in plant nutrition. IV. Nitrogen metabolism in relation to nutrient deficiency and age in leaves of barley. *Ann. Bot.* **50**: 367-402. 1936.

Scripture, P. N., and J. S. McHargue. Boron supply in relation to carbohydrate metabolism and distribution in the radish. *Jour. Amer. Soc. Agron.* **37**: 360-364. 1945.

Shive, J. W. A three-salt nutrient solution for plants. *Amer. Jour. Bot.* **2**: 157-160. 1915.

Shive, J. W., and W. R. Robbins. Methods of growing plants in solution and sand cultures. *N. J. Agric. Expt. Sta. Bull. No. 636*. 1938.

Skok, J. Effect of the form of the available nitrogen on the calcium deficiency symptoms in the bean plant. *Plant Physiol.* **16**: 145-158. 1941.

Skoog, F. Relationships between zinc and auxin in the growth of higher plants. *Amer. Jour. Bot.* **27**: 939-951. 1940.

Smith, M. A. The role of boron in plant metabolism. I. Boron in relation to the absorption and solubility of calcium. *Austral. Jour. Expt. Biol. and Med. Sci.* **22**: 257-263. 1944.

Somers, I. I., and J. W. Shive. The iron-manganese relation in plant metabolism. *Plant Physiol.* **17**: 582-602. 1942.

Sommer, Anna L. Studies concerning the essential nature of aluminum and silicon for plant growth. *Univ. Calif. Publ. Agric. Sci.* **5**: 57-81. 1926.

Sorokin, Helen, and Anna L. Sommer. Effect of calcium deficiency upon the roots of *Pisum sativum. Amer. Jour. Bot.* **27**: 308-318. 1940.

Tauböck, K. Über die Lebendsnotwendigkeit des Aluminums für Pteridophyten. *Bot. Arch.* **43**: 291-304. 1942.

Thomas, M. D., R. H. Henricks, L. C. Bryner, and G. R. Hill. A study of the sulfur metabolism of wheat, barley and corn using radioactive sulfur. *Plant Physiol.* **19**: 227-244. 1944.

Trelease, S. F., and O. A. Beath. *Selenium*. Published by Authors. New York. 1949.

Trelease, S. F., and Helen M. Trelease. Physiological differentiation in *Astragalus* with reference to selenium. *Amer. Jour. Bot.* **26:** 530-535. 1939.

Wadleigh, C. H. Mineral nutrition of plants. *Ann. Rev. Biochem.* **18:** 655-678. 1949.

Wall, M. E. The role of potassium in plants. III. Nitrogen and carbohydrate metabolism in potassium deficient plants supplied with either nitrate or ammonium nitrogen. *Soil Sci.* **49:** 393-408. 1940.

Wall, M. E., and V. A. Tiedjens. Potassium deficiency in ammonium and nitrate-fed tomato plants. *Science* **91:** 221-222. 1940.

DISCUSSION QUESTIONS

1. The addition of inorganic nitrogen to a soil in which both legumes and grasses are growing together often results in the disappearance of the legumes. What is a probable explanation of this result?

2. The growing of sorghums has frequently been found to be injurious to crops planted later on the same soil. What are possible explanations of this effect?

3. Why are some crops such as tobacco "hard on the soil"?

4. What is a "fertilizer"? What elements are most commonly supplied to plants as fertilizers? List several reasons for the addition of fertilizers to soils.

5. Is it scientifically permissible to use the term "plant food" as synonymous with fertilizer? Discuss.

6. How does the list of essential elements for plants compare with that for animals?

7. Why are salts of copper and other heavy metals more toxic to plants in lower concentrations in solution cultures than in soils?

8. Why does nitrogen deficiency become evident in plants more quickly than sulfur deficiency?

9. In which above ground parts of a plant would you expect "salt injury" (injury resulting from over-fertilization) to appear first? Why?

10. Would an overdose of fertilizer be more injurious to plants growing in the bright light or to similar plants growing in the shade? Explain.

11. Can the mineral salt deficiencies of a soil be determined by analyzing the leaves of plants growing on that soil?

12. When planted in certain kinds of soils, leaves of oak trees often show chlorosis. How would you proceed to ascertain the cause of such a chlorosis in the shortest possible time?

13. Given a species of plant which had not been experimented with before, how would you proceed to devise a suitable solution for the growth of this plant in sand cultures?

14. Which would be more useful in indicating whether or not a given soil was deficient in some essential elements, an analysis of the soil or an analysis of the leaves of plants growing on that soil? Explain.

XXVI

NITROGEN METABOLISM

All of the many physiological reactions characteristic of living cells appear to center around the physical and chemical properties of protein molecules and related compounds. Proteins are nitrogen-containing molecules relatively huge in size and of enormous complexity of structure. Together with water they are the principal constituents of protoplasm. The protein molecules of protoplasmic systems possess the inherent capacity of reproducing themselves exactly from simpler units, thus maintaining and enlarging the system of which they form so essential a part.

In addition to their fundamental role in protoplasmic systems, proteins also often occur in plant cells in the form of stored foods, especially in the seeds of many species. Such "reserve" or storage proteins differ in their physical and chemical properties from the protoplasmic proteins. The latter are more complex than the former and cannot be extracted from tissues by the same methods used in extracting storage proteins. The structural organization of both kinds of proteins is believed to be essentially similar, however.

In addition to the proteins a number of other kinds of nitrogenous organic compounds occur in plants, some of which play important parts in plant metabolism.

The Proteins.—All proteins contain carbon (50-54 per cent), hydrogen (about 7 per cent), nitrogen (16-18 per cent), and oxygen (20-25 per cent). Although some animal proteins do not contain sulfur, this element is apparently present in all plant proteins. The percentage of sulfur in protein molecules never exceeds 2 per cent, however. Phosphorus is also a constituent of certain important types of plant proteins.

The percentage composition of proteins gives no idea of the structure of protein molecules nor of their tremendous size relative to that of most molecules. Even the smallest protein molecules have molecular weights of about 17,600, whereas the more complex proteins have molecular weights of many millions. Determinations made by the ultracentrifuge method indicate that proteins may be classified, on the basis of their molecular weights, into certain groups or classes. One group appears to have molecular weights of about 17,600, a second group, $2 \times 17,600$ or 35,200, a third, $4 \times 17,600$ or 70,400, a fourth, $6 \times 17,600$ or 105,600, etc. (Svedberg and Pederson, 1940).

Results obtained when molecular weights of proteins were determined by chemical analysis also suggest a grouping of proteins into certain classes. Bergmann and Niemann (1938) concluded that protein molecules are made up of 288, or some multiple thereof, simpler units, the amino acid residues. Proteins fall into groups according to the number of basic units making up the molecule rather than according to their molecular weights. This concept of protein structure is not inconsistent, however, with the theory of weight classes mentioned above.

Although the assumption that protein molecules have molecular weights which fall naturally into certain groups has met with wide acceptance, it has also received serious criticism (Bull, 1941). All of the evidence indicates, however, that the molecular weights of proteins are very high and that they are distributed over a wide range of values.

The relatively enormous size of protein molecules should not be taken as an indication that they are aggregations of atoms and atomic groups without definite structural organization. The evidence from X-ray studies, as well as that from many other lines of work, points to a high degree of structural individuality in protein molecules. Each kind of protein molecule is built upon an architectural pattern in which every atom is essential for the completion of its structure. The many remarkable properties of proteins owe their existence to the presence of these definite structural patterns within their molecules.

Although some proteins can exist in true solution or in the form of crystals, most of them occur in living organisms in the colloidal state. The individual molecules of some proteins are so large as to bring them within the size range of colloidal micelles. The colloidal micelles of other protein sols are probably aggregates of a number of molecules. The significant point, however, is not whether the micelles are composed of one molecule or many, but that they are micelles. Protein sols are hydrophilic, and many of them form gels under suitable conditions. They also possess amphoteric properties (Chap. III).

Most of our knowledge of the structure of protein molecules has been gained by studying their hydrolytic products. Proteins can be hydrolyzed by treating them with acids, alkalies, or suitable enzymes. The end product of the complete hydrolysis of any protein is always a mixture of amino acids. During the course of protein hydrolysis a number of types of compounds are formed which are intermediate in complexity between the proteins and the amino acids:

Proteins ⟶ Proteoses ⟶ Peptones ⟶ Polypeptides
⟶ Dipeptides ⟶ Amino Acids

It seems virtually certain, therefore, that amino acids are the structural units from which the proteins and intermediate products of protein hydrolysis are synthesized in living cells. A consideration of the chemical nature and synthesis of the amino acids is therefore necessary before discussing the proteins further.

The Amino Acids.—Amino acids are, as the name suggests, compounds with the properties of both acids and amines. Every amino acid contains at least one carboxyl (—COOH) group and one or more amino (—NH_2) groups. The simplest amino acid is glycine. Glycine may be considered as acetic acid in which one of the hydrogen atoms of the methyl group has been replaced by an amino group:

$$CH_3COOH$$
Acetic acid

$$CH_2COOH$$
$$|$$
$$NH_2$$
Glycine

In naturally occurring amino acids the amino group, or one amino group if several occur in the molecule, is always attached to the α carbon atom, which is the one next to the —COOH group. About twenty amino acids are definitely known to be constituents of protein molecules, and a number of others are believed to be, by at least some investigators. Still other amino acids probably remain to be discovered. The names and chemical formulas of the better known amino acids are listed in Table 38. All of the amino acids listed in this table are known to be constituents of plant proteins.

It should be noted that, although proline is a product of protein hydrolysis and is usually classed as an amino acid, it contains only an NH group and no NH_2 group.

Absorption of Nitrogen Compounds from the Soil.—No reliable evidence has been obtained that higher green plants can utilize directly the gaseous nitrogen of the atmosphere in the synthesis of nitrogen-containing organic compounds. Nitrogenous compounds absorbed from the soil serve as the sole source of nitrogen for all rooted green plants. Such plants can utilize four kinds of compounds as sources of nitrogen: (1) nitrates, (2) nitrites,

(3) ammonium salts, and (4) organic nitrogen compounds. The mechanism of the absorption of ionic forms of nitrogen is believed to be essentially similar to that involved in the intake of other ions (Chap. XXIV). Nitrates apparently can be absorbed by many kinds of plant cells against a concentration gradient.

Many plants absorb most of their nitrogen in the form of nitrates. Normally metabolizing plants usually contain only relatively small quantities of nitrate, because the nitrogen of nitrate ions is reduced to other forms almost as rapidly as it enters the plant. Under certain conditions, however, plants accumulate relatively large quantities of nitrates in their

TABLE 38—THE PRINCIPAL AMINO ACIDS

Glycine	$CH_2(NH_2) \cdot COOH$
Alanine	$CH_3 \cdot CH(NH_2) \cdot COOH$
Serine	$CH_2OH \cdot CH(NH_2) \cdot COOH$
Threonine	$CH_3 \cdot CH(OH)CH(NH_2) \cdot COOH$
Valine	$(CH_3)_2 \cdot CH \cdot CH(NH_2) \cdot COOH$
Leucine	$(CH_3)_2 \cdot CH \cdot CH_2 \cdot CH(NH_2) \cdot COOH$
Isoleucine	$\begin{array}{c} CH_3 \\ \end{array}\!\!>CH \cdot CH(NH_2) \cdot COOH$ C_2H_5
Aspartic acid	$HOOC \cdot CH_2 \cdot CH(NH_2) \cdot COOH$
Glutamic Acid	$HOOC \cdot CH_2 \cdot CH_2 \cdot CH(NH_2) \cdot COOH$
Arginine	$HN{=}C(NH_2) \cdot NH \cdot CH_2 \cdot CH_2 \cdot CH_2 \cdot CH(NH_2) \cdot COOH$
Lysine	$CH_2(NH_2) \cdot CH_2 \cdot CH_2 \cdot CH_2 \cdot CH(NH_2) \cdot COOH$
Cystine	$S \cdot CH_2 \cdot CH(NH_2) \cdot COOH$ $\mid$ $S \cdot CH_2 \cdot CH(NH_2) \cdot COOH$
Methionine	$\begin{array}{c} \\ CH_2 \end{array}\!\!<^{\textstyle S \cdot CH_3}_{\textstyle CH_2 \cdot CH(NH_2) \cdot COOH}$
Phenylalanine	$C_6H_5 \cdot CH_2 \cdot CH(NH_2) \cdot COOH$
Tyrosine	$HO \cdot C_6H_4 \cdot CH_2CH(NH_2) \cdot COOH$
Histidine	$HC{=\!\!=}C \cdot CH_2 \cdot CH(NH_2) \cdot COOH$ $\mid\mid$ NNH $\searrow_{\!\!C}\!\!\swarrow$ H
Tryptophane	
Proline	

tissues without any toxic effects. Subsequently such accumulated nitrates may be utilized in the nitrogen metabolism of the plant. Plants sometimes exhibit acute symptoms of nitrogen deficiency while they still contain considerable quantities of nitrates. Although such plants have been able to absorb nitrates, metabolic conditions within the plant have been such that they have been unable to utilize them in the formation of nitrogenous organic compounds.

As shown in the next section the first step in the utilization of nitrates by plants is their reduction to nitrites. It seems probable, therefore, that plants can utilize nitrites as a source of nitrogen, and this supposition has been confirmed by solution culture experiments. However, nitrites are rarely if ever an important source of nitrogen for plants in nature.

Many species of plants, when grown in sand or solution cultures under suitable conditions, develop as well or better when supplied with ammonium salts as when supplied with nitrates. This is not surprising since the nitrogen in ammonium compounds is in a highly reduced form similar to that found in amino acids and related compounds. In certain types of soils it is probable that ammonium compounds are the chief form in which nitrogen is available to plants. This is apparently true of the acid podsolic soils of northern latitudes and of many uncultivated soils in the southern United States. Such soils contain little nitrate, but considerable quantities of ammonium compounds and plants growing in them apparently obtain their nitrogen in the latter form. Unlike nitrate ions, plants seldom accumulate appreciable concentrations of ammonium ions.

Even when ammonium fertilizers are applied to agricultural soils, much, if not most, of the absorption of nitrogen by plants occurs in the form of nitrates. In such soils nitrification (see later) often occurs very effectively, resulting in rapid conversion of ammonium compounds to nitrates.

As a result of the decay of organic remains there are present in most soils at least small quantities of amino acids and other organic nitrogenous compounds. There is considerable evidence that plants can absorb and utilize such compounds in the synthesis of proteins. Under some conditions a considerable proportion of the nitrogen used may be absorbed by plants in the form of such compounds.

Reduction of Nitrates in Plant Tissues.—Since in nitrates the nitrogen is in a highly oxidized state ($-NO_3$) while in amino acids and other organic compounds it is usually in a highly reduced state, it is evident that reduction of nitrogen is one of the steps in the synthesis of amino acids and other organic nitrogenous compounds whenever nitrates are the source of nitrogen.

There is considerable evidence for the existence of two principal mechanisms of nitrate reduction. One appears to operate principally in roots or other non-green organs, the energy required in the reduction process being supplied by the aerobic respiration of carbohydrates. Nitrites appear to be an intermediate stage in such reductions of nitrates. The latter are further reduced to NH_3, perhaps through intermediate steps of hyponitrous acid and hydroxylamine (Chibnall, 1939). The NH_3 is ultimately incorporated into the molecules of amino acids or related kinds of molecules.

In leaves, especially when young, nitrate reduction appears to be accomplished by a light activated mechanism. Experimental studies by Burström (1943, 1945) of the reduction of nitrate in the leaves of young wheat plants indicate that the process is closely linked with the simultaneous reduction of CO_2 in the process of photosynthesis and that light is the source of energy. No reduction of nitrates was found to take place in wheat leaves in the dark, even when conditions appeared to be favorable for the process. It seems probable that nitrate is reduced in the leaves to some transitory compound which combines with an intermediate product of photosynthesis, resulting in the formation of amino acids or related organic nitrogenous compounds. Respiratory energy is not utilized in this mechanism of nitrate reduction.

Eckerson (1924) followed some of the steps in the reduction of nitrates in the tomato plant by microchemical tests. Rapidly growing tomato plants were transplanted from soil to quartz sand when about 8 in. tall. The plants were watered with a solution lacking nitrogen compounds until the tissues showed no tests for nitrates, nitrites, ammonia, and amino acids, although they still contained an abundance of carbohydrates. Calcium nitrate was then added to the sand. The nitrate ions were rapidly absorbed and could be detected in all parts of the plant within 24 hr. In 36 hr. *nitrites* were present in considerable amounts at the tips of the stems and in certain other tissues. Traces of ammonia could also be detected. By the end of 48 hr. the quantity of nitrite had decreased, the amount of ammonium ion in the plants had increased, and a small quantity of asparagine was also found to be present. Three to five days after the addition of the nitrate to the sand around the roots amino acids were present in abundance in the plant tissues and they continued to increase in quantity for three weeks. During the synthesis of these amino acids the carbohydrate content of the cells decreased.

Temperature exerts a marked effect on the nitrate reducing capacity of plants. In the tomato plant, for example, although nitrates are quickly absorbed, their reduction and the synthesis of organic nitrogen compounds occur very slowly at 13°C. At 21°C., on the other hand, both absorption and reduction of nitrate ions occur very rapidly (Nightingale, 1933).

Synthesis of Amino Acids.—Reference to their chemical formulas (Table

38) shows that amino acid molecules contain considerably more carbon and hydrogen than nitrogen. On the average about 85 per cent of the weight of amino acid molecules represents nonnitrogenous components, chiefly carbon, hydrogen, and oxygen. It is evident, therefore, that amino acid synthesis cannot occur without an adequate supply of carbon compounds in addition to a source of nitrogen in suitable chemical combination. This process is also closely related to the process of reduction of nitrates just discussed.

Glutamic acid is an amino acid which appears to play a key role in the nitrogen metabolism of both plants and animals. When, for example, tomato plants were supplied with $(NH_4)_2SO_4$ containing the N^{15} isotope, much larger amounts of the heavy nitrogen were found within 12 hr. in glutamic acid than in any of the other amino acids (McVickar and Burris, 1948). This indicates the occurrence of either a rapid rate of synthesis of this amino acid, a rapid rate of exchange of ammonia between it and other compounds, or of both these processes.

Glutamic acid is probably synthesized in plant cells by a reaction between ammonia, often originating from the reduction of nitrates, and α-ketoglutaric acid, originating in the tricarboxylic cycle (Fig. 114), as follows:

$$
\begin{array}{ll}
\begin{array}{l}
\text{COOH} \\
| \\
\text{C=O} \\
| \\
\text{CH}_2 \\
| \\
\text{CH}_2 \\
| \\
\text{COOH} \\
\text{\small α-ketoglutaric acid}
\end{array}
+ \text{NH}_3 + \text{DPN} \cdot \text{H}_2 \rightleftarrows
\begin{array}{l}
\text{COOH} \\
| \\
\text{CHNH}_2 \\
| \\
\text{CH}_2 \\
| \\
\text{CH}_2 \\
| \\
\text{COOH} \\
\text{\small glutamic acid}
\end{array}
+ \text{H}_2\text{O} + \text{DPN}
\end{array}
$$

This reaction is catalyzed by the enzyme *glutamic dehydrogenase* with diphosphopyridine nucleotide (DPN) as the coenzyme. This enzyme is widely and probably universally present in plants. Although details of this reaction have been worked out only in animal tissues (von Euler *et al.*, 1938), there is little doubt that this reaction also occurs in plant tissues.

This reaction is of the type known as a *reductive amination*. As subsequent discussion shows, this reaction may represent the principal route of entry of ammonia into amino acids. It is also considered likely that aspartic acid may arise from oxalacetic acid, and alanine from pyruvic acid by analogous reactions, but actual evidence for the synthesis of these amino acids by reductive amination is not very strong. A close interrelation exists between the synthesis of certain amino acids, organic acid metabolism, and the process of aerobic respiration. The conversion of α-ketoglutaric acid to glutamic acid and other analogous reactions which may occur can be considered as side reactions of the tricarboxylic cycle.

There is considerable evidence that some of the amino acids may arise as a result of *transamination* reactions in which amino groups are transferred from one kind of a molecule to another. The following example of such a reaction has been shown to proceed very rapidly in oat seedlings (Albaum and Cohen, 1943):

$$
\begin{array}{cccc}
\text{COOH} & \text{COOH} & \text{COOH} & \text{COOH} \\
| & | & | & | \\
\text{CHNH}_2 & \text{C}{=}\text{O} & \text{C}{=}\text{O} & \text{CHNH}_2 \\
| & | \;\text{transaminase}\; & | & | \\
\text{CH}_2 \quad + & \text{CH}_2 & \text{CH}_2 \quad + & \text{CH}_2 \\
| & | & | & | \\
\text{CH}_2 & \text{COOH} & \text{CH}_2 & \text{COOH} \\
| & & | & \\
\text{COOH} & & \text{COOH} & \\
\text{glutamic} & \text{oxalacetic} & \text{α-ketoglutaric} & \text{aspartic} \\
\text{acid} & \text{acid} & \text{acid} & \text{acid}
\end{array}
$$

Reactions of this kind are catalyzed by an enzyme of the type called a *transaminase* (Table 18). Such enzymes are widely distributed in higher plants. The coenzyme or prosthetic group of at least some of the transaminases is pyridoxyl phosphate, a derivative of pyridoxine, one of the B group of vitamins (Chap. XXVIII). There is evidence that the amino acids alanine, phenylalanine, valine, leucine, and aspartic acid are formed in plants as a result of transamination reactions.

As discussed earlier, there is considerable evidence that nitrate reduction and amino acid synthesis, as they occur in green leaves, may be closely interrelated with photosynthesis. Experiments by Benson and Calvin (1950) and others, in which green plants were allowed to absorb carbon dioxide containing radioactive carbon in the light, have shown that some of the radioactive carbon appears in alanine and other amino acids after only very short periods of illumination. This is further evidence that a close interrelationship exists between photosynthesis and amino acid synthesis as it occurs in chlorophyllous organs.

Some of the amino acids present in plant cells are often of secondary origin, resulting from chemical transformations of acid amides (see later) or other nitrogenous compounds, or from the hydrolysis of proteins. A number of protein-digesting enzymes have been found to be present in plant cells (Table 18). Such enzymes hydrolyze proteins or peptides to amino acids or to intermediate products of protein hydrolysis. Two of the best known of the plant proteases are *papain*, from the latex of the tropical papaw (*Carica papaya*) and *bromelin* from fruit of the pineapple (*Ananas sativus*) and other members of the Bromeliaceae. The effectiveness of papain as a protein-digesting enzyme, in particular, has long been recognized. Natives of Central and South America, where the tropical papaw grows wild, have long known that its leaves have a digestive effect on meat. It is said that simply wrapping meat in crushed papaw leaves will increase its tenderness. Commercial preparations of papain are made from the latex of the papaw.

Cystine, cysteine, and methionine are the sulfur-containing amino acids. Chemically cysteine is derived by splitting a cystine molecule (Table 38) into two identical halves, with the addition of one atom of hydrogen to each half. These amino acids undoubtedly play an important role in the sulfur metabolism of plants. Sulfur always occurs in amino acids and other plant sulfur-containing compounds in reduced forms. Plants obtain most of their sulfur in the form of sulfates absorbed from the soil, but very little is known of the chemical mechanism whereby sulfate ions are reduced in plant tissues.

In some species of plants reduction of nitrates and amino acid synthesis appear to take place principally in the smaller roots, little if any occurring in the aerial organs of the plant. In other species reduction of nitrates and synthesis of amino acids appear to occur predominantly, although not entirely, in the leaves (Nightingale, 1937). Examples of plants belonging to the first group are apple, asparagus, and narcissus; examples of species belonging to the second group include tobacco, tomato, and cucurbits. As the previous discussion has indicated, the metabolic pathways followed by these fundamental processes are different in the two organs.

The Synthesis of Proteins.—The theory that proteins are formed by the condensation of numerous amino acid molecules was first suggested by Emil Fischer. He succeeded in linking together eighteen amino acid molecules (fifteen of glycine, three of leucine) and thus producing a synthetic polypeptide in which the amino acids were bound together by peptide linkages. A peptide linkage is one in which the amino group of one amino acid molecule is united with the carboxyl group of another amino acid molecule, water being split off in the process. The simplest dipeptide is that formed by condensation of two molecules of glycine:

$$
\begin{array}{c}
\underset{\underset{NH_2}{|}}{CH_2} - \overline{C\underset{}{O}OH} + \overline{H} - \underset{\underset{H}{|}}{N} \overset{\overset{CH_2-COOH}{|}}{} \longrightarrow \quad \underset{\underset{NH_2}{|}}{CH_2} - CO - \overset{\overset{CH_2-COOH}{|}}{NH} \quad + H_2O
\end{array}
$$

The dipeptide resulting from the condensation of the two amino acid molecules possesses an amino group and a carboxyl group to which other amino acids can be linked. The addition of amino acid molecules by peptide linkages to either or both of these groups still leaves amino and carboxyl groups present in the resulting molecule. According to the generally accepted view polypeptides, peptones, proteoses, and finally proteins are formed by the condensation of more and more amino acid molecules in this way, at least several hundred being required for the building up of a single protein molecule. Although the net effect of protein synthesis is that of a condensation of amino acids, the actual mechanism of the process is probably more complex. There is some indirect evidence that a phosphorylation mechanism may be involved in the synthesis of proteins, as it is in many carbohydrate transformations.

The arrangement of the amino acid residues in protein molecules is not entirely understood. It is clear, however, that protoplasmic proteins, in general, are long chain-like molecules. In some other proteins the chain of amino acid residues appears to be much folded giving rise to a compact, closely knit molecule. These latter are known as globular proteins because the molecules are believed to be roughly globular in shape. Both kinds of protein molecules are systems of polypeptide chains, the difference between them depending largely upon the degree to which the chains of amino acid residues are folded.

Every species of plant or animal produces characteristic and specific proteins which are not found in other species. Therefore a very large number of kinds of proteins must exist. It has generally been considered that the number of possible combinations of amino acids found in proteins is virtually innumerable. Random combinations of 19 different kinds of amino acid molecules in the formation of a polypeptide chain of only 50 molecular units could take place in the inconceivably large number of 10^{48} ways. There are good reasons for believing, however, that the structure of protein molecules is governed by general principles which greatly limit the number of possible combinations of amino acids (Bergmann and Niemann, 1938). According to these workers all protein molecules are built upon a recurring pattern so that every amino acid in the polypeptide chain recurs at constant intervals. For example, in silk fibroin (a protein), they find that every other amino acid residue is glycine, every fourth one is alanine, and every sixteenth one is tyrosine. This arrangement can be diagramed as follows, X representing other amino acid residues than those mentioned:

G-A-G-X-G-A-G-T-G-A-G-X-G-A-G-X-G-A-G-X-G-A-G-T-G-A-G-X

A similar recurrence of amino acid residues in a periodic manner was found in the molecules of other proteins. The various kinds of proteins differ from each other in the kinds and frequencies of the constituent amino acids.

X-ray analysis of silk fibroin, however, suggests that the periodic repetition of specific amino acid residues does not occur with the exactness and regularity described above (Astbury, 1943). It seems possible that protein molecules may contain definite proportions of specific amino acid residues without their occurring in a fixed and regular sequence.

Although the theory that protein synthesis is accomplished by the successive union of amino acids is widely accepted, it is not the only possible explanation of protein synthesis. The fact that certain protein molecules can exactly duplicate themselves, time after time, in the environment of living cells, suggests that the molecular pattern of an existing protein may serve as a model or template against which other molecules of the same protein may be constructed. If one protein molecule serves as the model upon which a second identical molecule is molded, it is possible that the units which are fitted together on the pattern are not solely amino acids but may include a wide variety of other atomic groupings (Steward and Street, 1947).

The intimate linkage of the mechanism of protein synthesis with other physiological activities of the cell is an important consideration in plant metabolism. Steward *et al.* (1940) have demonstrated experimentally that protein synthesis in aerated slices of potato is closely dependent upon the oxidative mechanisms of the cell. At times of rapid protein synthesis the respiration rate is also high. Low rates of protein synthesis are correlated with low rates of respiration. Similarly, growth is interrelated with both protein synthesis and respiration (Chap. XXIX). Growing cells always exhibit high rates of protein synthesis. Salt accumulation may also be correlated with protein synthesis since both are linked to respiratory energy. Protein synthesis, respiration, salt accumulation, growth, and other cellular processes are interdependent both in the energy transformations that occur and in the organic molecules which participate in the reactions.

The principal regions of protein synthesis in plants do not necessarily correspond to the principal regions of amino acid synthesis. In fact, a clear distinction should be made between these two processes. In some species of plants most amino acid synthesis occurs in the roots. In all plants most formation of proteins occurs in meristems or in storage tissues, although some protein synthesis can probably occur in most cells. Amino acids and closely related compounds are commonly translocated from the tissues in which they originate to other, often distant, tissues before being converted into proteins. Little or no translocation of proteins as such occurs in plants.

In meristems protoplasmic proteins are constructed from amino acids. This is one phase of the process of assimilation (Chap. XXIX). In many seeds and some other organs storage proteins are constructed from amino acids. This is a phase of the process of accumulation. Most such proteins are subsequently digested to amino acids which, usually after translocation to other tissues, are assimilated. Reutilization of assimilated proteins may also occur. In senescent leaves, for example, decomposition of protoplasmic proteins may take place and some of the resulting organic nitrogenous compounds, at least, may be translocated to meristems and there resynthesized into proteins.

The Nucleoproteins.—Previous discussion (Chap. XVI) has indicated that the genes of the chromosomes exert their influence upon the metabolic processes of cells through their controlling effect on the synthesis of enzymes. Although such a relation has long been postulated, it is only in comparatively recent years that experimental verification of this hypothesis has been forthcoming (Beadle, 1945).

The primary role of the genes in charting the metabolic pattern of a cell has focused the attention of many investigators upon their chemical composition. Evidence from various sources has led to the conclusion that genes are composed of proteins of the type known as nucleoproteins (Beadle, 1946). It is even possible that a given gene may be a single nucleoprotein molecule.

The nucleoproteins are molecules of relatively enormous size (some have molecular weights of many millions) in which a protein portion is linked to a nucleic acid. These latter compounds are themselves extremely complex. Upon hydrolysis they yield phosphoric acid, a pentose sugar, two purine bases, and two pyrimidine bases. Purine and pyrimidine bases are cyclical nitrogen-containing compounds. The only two purines known to occur naturally in nucleic acids are guanine and adenine. The pyrimidine bases which have been found in nucleic acids are cytosine, thymine, uracil, and methylcytosine. A nucleic acid unit appears to consist of four pentose sugar residues to each of which is attached a different cyclic nitrogen base and a molecule of phosphoric acid (Gulick, 1944).

Nucleoproteins, in spite of the name, are not restricted to the nuclei of cells but are also present in the cytoplasm. The cytoplasmic nucleoproteins are chemically different from those of the nucleus (Mirsky, 1943). Both the nucleic acid and the protein components of the two kinds of nucleoproteins are dissimilar. The sugar radical of the nucleic acids present in nuclei is the pentose, desoxyribose, while the sugar in the cytoplasmic nucleoproteins is D-ribose, another pentose. The proteins of the nuclear nucleoproteins are of the types known as histones and protamines, but the protein constituents of the cytoplasmic nucleoproteins have not been identified. The proportion of nucleic acid in each of the two kinds of nucleoproteins also appears to differ, being higher in the nuclear than in the cytoplasmic nucleoproteins.

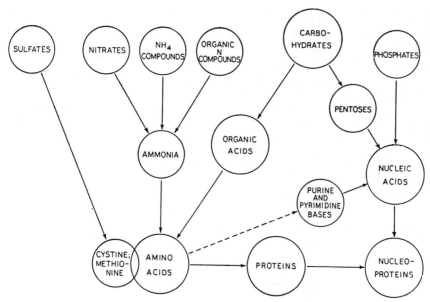

Fig. 121. Diagram illustrating stages in the process of protein synthesis in plants.

The recent discovery that the crystalline plant viruses are also nucleoproteins has led to much speculation regarding a possible relationship between viruses and genes. All of the crystalline viruses, however, have been shown to be nucleoproteins of the cytoplasmic type rather than of the nuclear kind (Mirsky, 1943).

The various steps in protein synthesis are indicated diagrammatically in Fig. 121.

Other Compounds Playing an Important Part in the Nitrogen Metabolism of Plants.—1. *Ammonia.*—This compound is believed to play a central role in the nitrogen metabolism of plants, although it does not occur in the free state in plant cells in more than traces. There are at least three important sources of ammonia in the higher plants: (1) absorption from the soil in the form of ammonium ions, (2) formation within cells as a result of the reduction of nitrates, and (3) liberation within cells in the oxidation of amino acids and related compounds.

Ammonium ions are readily absorbed from the soil and utilized in amino acid synthesis as long as the medium around the roots is well aerated and the supply of carbohydrates is adequate. If, on the other hand, the roots are inadequately supplied with oxygen, or if the tissues are low in carbohydrates, ammonia may accumulate in the cells and injury to the plant follows quickly (Arnon 1937, Burkhart 1938). Under conditions of carbohydrate starvation, ammonium ions are neither absorbed nor utilized in the roots. The accumulation of ammonia in the tissues under these conditions appears to be the result of the breakdown of proteins and the amides, asparagine and glutamine, as described later.

In spite of its prominent position in the reactions of nitrogen metabolism, ammonia is definitely toxic to plants if present in any appreciable quantity. Large amounts are involved in the various phases of nitrogen metabolism, but only traces are ordinarily present in the uncombined state in plant cells. Apparently ammonia is usually metabolized so rapidly that it rarely accumulates in plant cells.

2. *Asparagine and Glutamine.*—The compound resulting if one of the carboxyl groups of aspartic acid is replaced with an acid amide group is called *asparagine.* A similar substitution in the molecule of glutamic acid gives the compound *glutamine,* thus:

$$
\begin{array}{ll}
\mathrm{COOH} & \mathrm{COOH} \\
| & | \\
\mathrm{CH \cdot NH_2} & \mathrm{CH \cdot NH_2} \\
| & | \\
\mathrm{CH_2} & \mathrm{CH_2} \\
| & | \\
\mathrm{COOH} & \mathrm{CONH_2} \\
\text{Aspartic acid} & \text{Asparagine}
\end{array}
$$

$$
\begin{array}{ll}
\mathrm{COOH} & \mathrm{COOH} \\
| & | \\
\mathrm{CH \cdot NH_2} & \mathrm{CH \cdot NH_2} \\
| & | \\
\mathrm{CH_2} & \mathrm{CH_2} \\
| & | \\
\mathrm{CH_2} & \mathrm{CH_2} \\
| & | \\
\mathrm{COOH} & \mathrm{CONH_2} \\
\text{Glutamic acid} & \text{Glutamine}
\end{array}
$$

The exact modes of synthesis of asparagine and glutamine are not known. Both of these compounds are commonly present in plant tissues, although one of them is often present in larger amounts than the other. In beets, tomato plants, potato tubers and rye grass, for example. more glutamine accumulates than asparagine. On the other hand, asparagine predominates in many legume seedlings and in Sudan grass. Some species, such as corn, synthesize appreciable amounts of both amides, when metabolic conditions are favorable for their formation, although asparagine is usually more abundant than glutamine (Viets *et al.*, 1946).

The role of the amides in nitrogen metabolism has been extensively studied by many investigators (Robinson 1929, Murneek 1935, Chibnall 1939, Mothes 1940, Vickery *et al.*, 1946, Steward and Street, 1946). The appearance of asparagine and glutamine in plant tissues is closely linked with the presence of ammonia. The amides usually appear, for example, whenever large amounts of ammonium ions are being absorbed by the root system (Clark 1936, Viets *et al.*, 1946, Vickery *et al.*, 1936). Asparagine and glutamine are also formed in young seedlings when the protein of the food storage tissues of the seed are being utilized in growth. At times of carbohydrate starvation, amino acids and related compounds may be oxidized in respiration, releasing ammonia within the cells. Under such conditions the ammonia set free is rapidly used in amide synthesis, thus obviating any toxic effect it would otherwise exert. If carbohydrate deficiency becomes very severe, asparagine and glutamine may also be oxidized, resulting in the liberation of ammonia within the tissues. When this occurs the tissues are usually injured.

It has long been assumed that the amides are important in nitrogen metabolism largely because, as a result of their synthesis, the accumulation of free ammonia in plant tissues is prevented. The correlation known to exist between amide formation and metabolic or environmental conditions which favor the accumulation of ammonia (rapid absorption of ammonium ions, carbohydrate starvation leading to the oxidation of amino acids, and hydrolysis of proteins) is undoubtedly a consequence of the utilization of ammonia in amide synthesis.

Asparagine and especially glutamine, however, are very reactive and highly mobile components of metabolic systems. Their role in nitrogen metabolism is certainly not confined to the preventing of injury from the accumulation of ammonia in plant tissues. These amides undoubtedly participate extensively in transamination, reductive amination, and other reactions which are important in the nitrogen metabolism of plants.

Both of the amides are readily translocated in plant tissues; in fact asparagine and glutamine are probably among the most important vehicles of nitrogen transport in the higher green plants. The nitrogen found in amide synthesis in root systems, for example, may be transported rapidly as amides to expanding leaves, stem tips, or other growing organs where the amino groups are released and utilized in amino acid and protein synthesis.

Some plant species usually accumulate one of the amides in greater concentrations than the other. This fact has led to the suggestion that asparagine and glutamine may have different roles in the nitrogen metabolism
of such species (Vickery *et al.*, 1946). It is entirely possible, for example,
that in some plant species asparagine may be more important as a storage
form of soluble nitrogen, whereas glutamine may play a greater role in
amino acid and protein synthesis (Street *et al.*, 1946). In other species
asparagine may participate more actively in protein synthesis.

3. *Urea.*—Urea($(NH_2)_2 \cdot CO$) occurs abundantly (as much as 11 per
cent of the dry weight) in some fungi and is also present in small quantities in certain seed plants (Klein and Tauböck, 1930). Urea is one of the
products formed when the amino acid arginine is hydrolyzed by the enzyme
arginase (Table 18). Urea, like asparagine and glutamine, may also be
one of the products of the oxidation of amino acids in tissues with a low
carbohydrate content. Under the influence of the enzyme *urease* urea is
hydrolyzed to ammonia and carbon dioxide (Table 18). Some investigators believe that urea may serve as the starting point in the synthesis of
some of the complex cyclic nitrogen compounds which appear to be present in some proteins but there is no actual evidence in favor of this view.
The physiological role of urea in the seed plants is probably similar to
that of asparagine and glutamine.

4. *The Alkaloids.*—Alkaloids are complex cyclic compounds containing
nitrogen that are synthesized only in certain species of plants. They are
especially common in members of the Solanaceae, Papaveraceae, Leguminosae, Ranunculaceae, Rubiaceae, and Apocynaceae. Species of plants
which contain one alkaloid are very likely to contain others. More than
twenty different alkaloids have been isolated from opium, which is the
dried juice of the unripe fruits of certain species of poppies.

Some of the better known alkaloids are *nicotine* from tobacco, *quinine*
from the bark of the cinchona tree, *morphine* from poppy fruits, *strych-
nine* and *brucine* from the seeds of *Strychnos nuxvomica*, *atropine* from
the deadly nightshade (*Atropa belladonna*), and *colchicine* from meadow
saffron (*Colchicum autumnale*). *Caffein* from coffee and tea, and *theo-
bromine* from the cocoa bean are also often classed with the alkaloids.
The formula for nicotine, a representative alkaloid, gives some idea of the
chemical nature of these substances:

Most of the alkaloids are white solids, but nicotine is a liquid at ordinary temperatures. They are all basic in reaction as the name indicates, and only slightly soluble in water.

It is common for the alkaloids synthesized in a given plant species to accumulate in certain organs of a plant. About 85 per cent of the nicotine in a tobacco plant, for example, is located in the leaves. However, when a tobacco scion is grafted on the root system of a tomato plant, no nicotine is found in the leaves; when the reverse graft is made, the leaves of the tomato contain nicotine (Dawson, 1942). It appears, therefore, that the nicotine is synthesized in the roots whence it is translocated into the leaves and other aerial organs. Of especial interest is the fact that this upward translocation appears to occur in the xylem. The alkaloids in *Atropa belladonna* (Cromwell, 1943), and *Datura stramonium* (Peacock *et al.*, 1944) also appear to be synthesized largely, if not entirely, in the roots. Anabasine, however, another alkaloid of tobacco, appears to be synthesized in both the root and shoot (Dawson, 1944). The physiological role of the alkaloids in plants is unknown. Their restricted distribution indicates that they are not essential in any process of general importance. It is possible that many of them are physiologically unimportant by-products of the nitrogen metabolism of the species in which they are found. Extensive studies of the role of nicotine in tobacco (Dawson, 1946) suggest, however, that this alkaloid can be converted into other forms of nitrogen which may play a useful role in the nitrogen metabolism of the plant.

The Origin of Nitrogenous Compounds in the Soil.—The entire nitrogen supply of the higher plants is obtained from compounds in the soil that contain this element. Nitrogen compounds are continually being lost from the soil by the leaching action of rains and by the removal of the plant cover through fire or other agencies. Large quantities of nitrogen are lost every year from cultivated soils as constituents of crops harvested therefrom. The soils, however, show no equivalent depletion of their nitrogen supply. Since there is no nitrogen in the rocks from which the soils are derived, it is obvious that the supply of nitrogenous compounds in the soil must constantly be replenished in some way. Maintenance of a supply of nitrogenous compounds in the soil is accomplished principally by the activities of certain soil organisms, the *nitrogen-fixing* bacteria. The process of *nitrogen fixation* and other important phenomena influencing the soil nitrogen supply will be briefly discussed in the following paragraphs.

1. *Nitrogen Fixation.*—Two groups of bacteria are able to fix appreciable quantities of atmospheric nitrogen in organic combination: (1) certain saprophytic bacteria which obtain their energy from dead organic matter in the soil, and (2) symbiotic nitrogen-fixing bacteria which live

in the roots of leguminous plants. Other bacteria and fungi and some blue-green algae also appear to be able to combine atmospheric nitrogen with organic compounds but the amount of the nitrogen fixed by these organisms is probably not very significant.

Symbiotic nitrogen fixation is the result of the activities of species of *Rhizobium* which are rod-shaped bacteria that enter the roots of legumes by way of the root hairs and cause the formation of nodules on the young roots (Fig. 122). Each species of *Rhizobium* infects the roots of only certain leguminous species. These bacteria live inside the nodules and there synthesize organic nitrogen compounds from the carbohydrates of the host and gaseous nitrogen of the air.

Fig. 122. Nodules containing nitrogen-fixing bacteria on roots of soybean. Photograph, courtesy of Dr. H. W. Batchelor.

Most of the nitrogen fixed by the symbiotic bacteria in organic combination moves out of the nodules into the other tissues of the host plant where it is utilized in protein synthesis. Soybean plants, for example, are estimated to utilize about 90 per cent of the nitrogen fixed by the bacteria in the nodules on their roots. Under certain conditions some of the nitrogen-containing compounds in the nodules may move out into the surrounding soil where they can be absorbed by other species of plants. The quantity of nitrogenous compounds lost by nodules into the soil ordinarily is small and appears to be determined by the relative rates of photosynthesis and nitrogen fixation (Wilson, 1940). Loss of such compounds from the nodules into the soil apparently occurs only when photosynthesis in the legume is sufficient to induce a favorable rate of nitrogen fixation but insufficient to build up an excess of carbohydrate. When carbohydrates are present in amounts greater than necessary to insure favorable rates of nitrogen fixation, they combine with the nitrogen compounds released by the bacteria thus largely preventing loss of such compounds to the soil. Sloughing off and decay of root tissues of legumes is undoubtedly a more important source of nitrogen compounds to the soil than outward diffusion of soluble nitrogen compounds from their living roots.

Symbiotic nitrogen fixation is depressed if inorganic nitrogen compounds are present in abundance in the soil around the roots of the legume plants. Nevertheless, even with an abundance of such compounds in the soil it is not uncommon for the amount of nitrogen fixed by the bacteria in the nodules to exceed that absorbed from the soil.

Nitrogen fixation by symbiotic bacteria is, in general, favored by the same factors that promote good vegetative growth of the host plants. Surprising quantities of atmospheric nitrogen may be combined into organic compounds by these bacteria. Under very favorable conditions a good crop of alfalfa may add as much as 400 pounds of nitrogen per acre to the soil. The average, however, is much lower, being estimated by Giobel (1926) as roughly between 100 and 200 pounds per acre when common legumes are used as host plants.

Although the chemistry of nitrogen fixation has been the subject of intensive study in recent years, the details of the process are not yet fully understood. It seems probable, however, that ammonia is the key intermediate compound in nitrogen fixation as it is in the synthesis of amino acids and proteins in the higher plants (Wilson and Burris, 1947).

Most of the nitrogen fixation by saprophytic bacteria is brought about by two groups of organisms: (1) the *Azotobacter* group composed of coccus-like aerobic organisms, and (2) the *Clostridium* group which are rod-shaped anaerobic bacteria. Both types are common in well-aerated soils. The aerobic forms occur around the surface of the soil particles, whereas the anaerobic forms are found within aggregations of soil particles or in regions of the soil in which the oxygen content has been depleted by respiration. These bacteria combine the gaseous nitrogen of the air with carbohydrate compounds obtained from the soil. *Azotobacter* is usually absent from soils more acid than pH 6, but *Clostridium* can tolerate soil acidities as great as pH 5. Both groups can operate effectively in relatively dry soils.

It is conservatively estimated that the saprophytic nitrogen-fixing bacteria add, on the average, about 6 pounds of combined nitrogen to each acre of soil each year. This is much less than the amount produced by the symbiotic organisms, yet, because the latter are effective nitrogen fixers only when in the living roots of legumes, while the former are generally present in agricultural soils, the total amount of combined nitrogen added to the agricultural lands of the United States by saprophytic nitrogen-fixing bacteria is about equal to that fixed by the symbiotic bacteria (Wilson, 1940). Together they are credited with adding nearly 10 million tons of nitrogen annually to the agricultural areas of the United States (Lipman and Conybeare, 1936).

2. *Ammonification.*—In the process of decay the complex nitrogenous compounds present in dead plant and animal tissues are broken down into a number of simpler compounds, most of the nitrogen being released in the form of ammonia. This process is termed *ammonification* and the bacteria involved are called *ammonifying bacteria*. Ammonification is not the result of the activities of a single group of bacteria but may be brought about by a large number of different microorganisms, including the actinomyces and filamentous fungi in addition to numerous groups of bacteria. Probably most of the bacteria commonly present in soils participate in the formation of ammonia from one kind of nitrogenous material or another. The amount of ammonia formed in the decay of nitrogenous materials is influenced by (1) the available carbohydrate supply, (2) the chemical composition of the nitrogenous materials, (3) the organisms involved, and (4) the acidity, aeration, and moisture content of the soil. The ammonifying organisms utilize carbohydrates as a source of energy more readily than proteins so the amount of ammonia formed is markedly decreased when large amounts of carbohydrates are available.

3. *Nitrification.*—The ammonia formed in the decomposition of proteins and other organic nitrogenous compounds may be acted upon by the *nitrifying bacteria* and transformed in two steps to nitrates. The first step is the oxidation of ammonia to nitrites. This is accomplished by organisms belonging to the two genera: *Nitrosomonas* and *Nitrosococcus*. Neither of these organisms can oxidize the nitrite which they produce, but this compound is oxidized to nitrates by a different organism, *Nitrobacter*. All of these organisms differ from each other morphologically, but they are similar physiologically in that they use the energy obtained from the oxidation of ammonia or nitrites in the synthesis of carbohydrate compounds from carbon dioxide and water. All of these organisms are therefore chemosynthetic in their metabolism (Chap. XVIII). The soil conditions favoring nitrification are: (1) pH values on the alkaline side of neutrality, (2) the absence of large amounts of carbohydrates in the soil, and (3) good aeration.

4. *Denitrification.*—A large number of organisms are capable of reducing nitrates to nitrites and ammonia. This occurs commonly in the tissues of the higher plants as we have seen earlier. Certain soil organisms, however, can reduce nitrates all the way to molecular nitrogen. These organisms are known as *denitrifying bacteria* and include a number of species of which *Bacterium denitrificans* is probably the best known. Denitrification occurs only in the absence of atmospheric oxygen and most

effectively when an abundant supply of carbohydrates is present in the soil. It does not normally occur in well-cultivated soils.

5. *Rain as a Source of Nitrogen Compounds.*—Small amounts of inorganic nitrogen compounds reach the soil from the atmosphere. Oxides are formed during electrical storms, and these are brought into the soil by the rain. Ammonia also escapes from various sources into the atmosphere and may be returned to the soil in solution in raindrops. Measure-

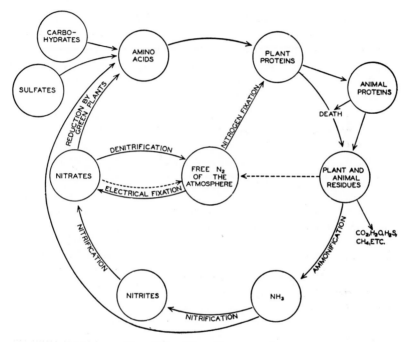

FIG. 123. The nitrogen cycle.

ments made at the Rothamsted Experiment Station in England over a five-year period showed that rain water brought down 4.4 pounds of nitrogen per acre per year. The amount of nitrogen added to the soils at Rothamsted in this way approximately equaled losses of nitrogen suffered by leaching.

The complete story of nitrogen in relation to plant life involves a whole series of events, some of which occur in the cells of micro-organisms of the soil and some in the tissues of the higher plants. This series of events is frequently referred to as the "nitrogen cycle" (Fig. 123).

SUGGESTED FOR COLLATERAL READING

Bonner, J. *Plant Biochemistry*. Academic Press, Inc. New York. 1950.

Chibnall, A. C. *Protein Metabolism in the Plant*. Yale University Press. New Haven. 1939.

Porter, J. R. *Bacterial Chemistry and Physiology*. John Wiley & Sons, Inc. New York. 1946.

Wilson, P. W. *The Biochemistry of Symbiotic Nitrogen Fixation*. University of Wisconsin Press. Madison. 1940.

SELECTED BIBLIOGRAPHY

Albaum, H. G., and P. P. Cohen. Transamination and protein synthesis in germinating oat seedlings. *Jour. Biol. Chem.* **149:** 19-27. 1943.

Arnon, D. I. Ammonium and nitrate nutrition of barley at different seasons in relation to hydrogen ion concentration, manganese, copper, and oxygen supply. *Soil Sci.* **44:** 91-113. 1937.

Astbury, W. T. X-rays and the stoichiometry of the proteins. *Advances in Enzymol.* **3:** 63-108. 1943.

Beadle, G. W. Genetics and metabolism in *Neurospora*. *Physiol. Rev.* **25:** 643-663. 1945.

Beadle, G. W. The gene and biochemistry. In *Currents in Biochemical Research*. D. E. Green, Editor. 1-12. Interscience Publishers, Inc. New York. 1946.

Benson, A. A., and M. Calvin. Carbon dioxide fixation by green plants. *Ann. Rev. Plant Physiol.* **1:** 25-42. 1950.

Bergmann, M., and C. Niemann. The chemistry of amino acids and proteins. *Ann. Rev. Biochem.* **7:** 99-124. 1938.

Bull, H. C. Protein structure. *Advances in Enzymol.* **1:** 1-42. 1941.

Burkhart, L. Ammonium nutrition and metabolism of etiolated seedlings. *Plant Physiol.* **13:** 265-293. 1938.

Burström, H. Photosynthesis and assimilation of nitrate by wheat leaves. *Ann. Agric. Coll. Sweden* **11:** 1-50. 1943.

Burström, H. The nitrate nutrition of plants. *Ann. Agric. Coll. Sweden* **13:** 1-86. 1945.

Clark, H. E. Effect of ammonium and of nitrate nitrogen on the composition of the tomato plant. *Plant Physiol.* **11:** 5-24. 1936.

Cromwell, B. T. Studies on the synthesis of hyoscyamine in *Atropa belladonna* L. and *Datura stramonium* L. *Biochem. Jour.* **37:** 717-726. 1943.

Dawson, R. F. Accumulation of nicotine in reciprocal grafts of tomato and tobacco. *Amer. Jour. Bot.* **29:** 66-71. 1942.

Dawson, R. F. Accumulation of anabasine in reciprocal grafts of *Nicotina glauca* and tomato. *Amer. Jour. Bot.* **31:** 351-355. 1944.

Dawson, R. F. Development of some recent concepts in the physiological chemistry of the tobacco alkaloids. *Plant Physiol.* **21:** 115-130. 1946.

Eckerson, Sophia H. Protein synthesis by plants. I. Nitrate reduction. *Bot. Gaz.* **77:** 377-390. 1924.

Euler, H. von, E. Adler, G. Günther, and N. B. Das. Über den enzymatischen Abbau und Aufbau der Glutaminsäure. II. *Zeitschr. Physiol. Chem.* **254:** 61-103. 1938.

Giobel, G. The relation of soil nitrogen to nodule development and fixation of nitrogen by certain legumes. *N. J. Agric. Expt. Sta. Bull. No. 436*. 1926.

Gulick, A. The chemical formulation of gene structure and gene action. *Advances in Enzymol.* **4**: 1-39. 1944.

Klein, G., and K. Tauböck. Harnstoff und Ureide bei den höheren Pflanzen I. Das Vorkommen von Harnstoff im Pflanzenreich und sein Wandel im laufe der Vegetationsperiode. *Jahrb. Wiss. Bot.* **73**: 193-225. 1930.

Lipman, J. G., and A. B. Conybeare. Preliminary note on the inventory and balance sheet of plant nutrients in the United States. *N. J. Agric. Expt. Sta. Bull. No. 607.* 1936.

MacVicar, R., and R. H. Burris. Studies on nitrogen metabolism in tomato with use of isotopically labelled ammonium sulfate. *Jour. Biol. Chem.* **176**: 511-516. 1948.

Mirsky, A. E. Chromosomes and nucleoproteins. *Advances in Enzymol.* **3**: 1-34. 1943.

Mothes, K. Zur Biosynthese der Säureamide Asparagin und Glutamin. *Planta* **30**: 726-756. 1940.

Murneek, A. E. Physiological role of asparagine and related substances in nitrogen metabolism of plants. *Plant Physiol.* **10**: 447-464. 1935.

Nightingale, G. T. Effects of temperature on metabolism in tomato. *Bot. Gaz.* **95**: 35-58. 1933.

Nightingale, G. T. The nitrogen nutrition of green plants. *Bot. Rev.* **3**: 85-174. 1937; **14**: 185-221. 1948.

Peacock, S. M., D. B. Leyerle, and R. F. Dawson. Alkaloid accumulation in reciprocal grafts of *Datura stramonium* with tobacco and tomato. *Amer. Jour. Bot.* **31**: 463-466. 1944.

Robinson, Muriel E. The protein metabolism of the green plant. *New Phytol.* **28**: 117-149. 1929.

Steward, F. C., and H. E. Street. The soluble nitrogen fractions of potato tubers; the amides. *Plant Physiol.* **21**: 155-193. 1946.

Steward, F. C., and H. E. Street. The nitrogenous constituents of plants. *Ann. Rev. Biochem.* **16**: 471-502. 1947.

Steward, F. C., P. R. Stout, and C. Preston. The balance sheet of metabolites for potato discs showing the effect of salts and dissolved oxygen on metabolism at 23°C. *Plant Physiol.* **15**: 409-447. 1940.

Street, H. E. Nitrogen metabolism of higher plants. *Advances in Enzymol.* **9**: 391-454. 1949.

Street, H. E., A. E. Kenyon, and C. M. Watson. The assimilation of ammonium and nitrate nitrogen by detached potato sprouts. *Ann. Applied Biol.* **33**: 369-381. 1946.

Svedberg T., and K. O. Pedersen. *The Ultracentrifuge.* Clarendon Press. Oxford. 1940.

Vickery, H. B. The metabolism of proteins of green leaves. *Cold Spring Harbor Symposia Quant. Biol.* **6**: 67-78. 1938.

Vickery, H. B., G. W. Pucher, and H. E. Clark. Glutamine metabolism of the beet. *Plant Physiol.* **11**: 413-420. 1936.

Vickery, H. B., G. W. Pucher, A. J. Wakeman, and C. S. Leavenworth. Chemical investigations of the metabolism of plants. I. The nitrogen nutrition of *Narcissus poeticus. Conn. Agric. Expt. Sta. Bull. No. 496.* 1946.

Viets, F. G., Jr., A. L. Moxon, and E. I. Whitehead. Nitrogen metabolism of corn (*Zea mays*) as influenced by ammonium nutrition. *Plant Physiol.* **21**: 271-289. 1946.

Wilson, P. W., and R. H. Burris. The mechanism of biological nitrogen fixation. *Bact. Rev.* **11**: 41-73. 1947.

DISCUSSION QUESTIONS

1. List the different kinds of chemical combination in which nitrogen is present in green plants.

2. Why does not the continuous occupancy of an uncultivated area by native plants eventually exhaust all the nitrogen in the soil?

3. Corn (maize) was planted on a field which was in alfalfa the preceding year. Trace the origin of the various kinds of nitrogenous compounds that would be available to the corn plants.

4. List the important known inter-relationships between respiration and the nitrogen metabolism of green plants.

5. How would you undertake to show experimentally whether or not green plants can use the nitrogen of the atmosphere?

6. Why does the presence of abundant nitrates in the soil usually result in decreased nodule formation on the roots of legumes growing in that soil?

7. Would nitrates or ammonium compounds be a more satisfactory source of nitrogen under conditions favoring their rapid absorption and slow utilization?

8. Sometimes plants exhibiting symptoms of nitrogen deficiency are found to contain abundant nitrates upon analysis. What are possible explanations?

9. Azaleas, blueberries, and some other species grow well only in acid soils. What kinds of nitrogenous compounds would you recommend for use on such plants if you wished such compounds to serve also a secondary role in helping maintain soil acidity? Explain.

10. Organic nitrogen compounds, such as urea, can be absorbed through the leaves of some species of plants. What advantages would there be in supplying nitrogen to such plants as foliar sprays?

11. At temperatures below about 15°C. and low light intensities, organic nitrogen compounds leach out of the nodules of legume roots into the surrounding soil. When soil temperatures are above 15°C. and light intensities are high no such leaching occurs. Explain.

XXVII

TRANSLOCATION OF SOLUTES

In most plants a large proportion of the living cells do not contain chloroplasts. All such non-green cells are dependent for essential carbohydrates upon the chlorophyllous cells of the plant. Many of the non-green cells are remote from the photosynthesizing cells. The cells in the root tips of trees, for example, are sometimes hundreds of feet distant from the nearest leaves. They, as well as all other non-green cells in the body of a plant, are dependent for their existence upon the carbohydrates which move to them through intervening tissues from the chlorenchyma. Such a movement of soluble carbohydrates is but one example of a number of kinds of solute transfer which occur in plants.

Movement of organic and inorganic solutes from one part of the plant to another is designated as the *translocation, transport,* or *conduction* of solutes. These terms are generally restricted to movements of solutes in the tissues of the phloem and xylem in which the distance through which they are transported is usually very great in proportion to the size of the individual cells. They are not ordinarily used to refer to the cell-to-cell movement of solutes which may occur in any part of the plant.

Anatomy of Phloem Tissues.—Of the various stem tissues only the xylem and phloem possess such a structure as to suggest that a relatively rapid longitudinal movement of solutes can occur through them. Both of these tissues are characterized by the presence of elongated cells and elements which are joined in such a way as to form essentially continuous ducts. Furthermore, it has been shown experimentally that the rate of movement of solutes through other stem tissues, such as the pith and cortex, is totally inadequate to account for known rates of translocation through stems.

The structure of the xylem tissues has already been discussed in Chap. XII. Discussion of the anatomy of the conductive tissues will now be

completed by a consideration of the structure of the phloem. Like the
xylem, the phloem is continuous from the top to the bottom of the plant,
the ultimate terminations of the phloem
system being in the tissues of the stem
tips or leaves and other lateral organs,
and in the root tips. Although in most
species solutes move for the greatest distance through stems, it is important to
realize that the conductive tissues of
plants constitute a complicated but unit
system which ramifies to all parts of the
plant body.

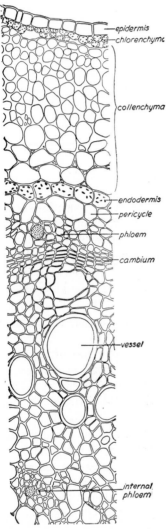

The general arrangement of the xylem
and phloem tissues in representative
types of stems has already been considered (Fig. 49, Fig. 50). In the majority
of dicot stems the phloem usually occurs
as a continuous cylinder of tissues just
external to the cambium layer. In a few
species some strands of internal phloem
are present inside of the xylem (Fig.
124). In roots the primary phloem and
xylem are present, as seen in cross section, in a radial arrangement, but the
secondary conductive tissues are oriented
in essentially the same pattern found in
stems (Fig. 68).

Five principal types of cells are found
in the phloem: (1) *sieve elements*, (2)
companion cells, (3) *phloem fibers*, (4)
phloem parenchyma, and (5) *phloem-ray
cells*. The proportions of these various
types of cells present are different in
every individual species and in some species not all are present.

FIG. 124. Cross section of a
small portion of a tomato stem
showing internal phloem.

Sieve elements are of two main types.
In most angiosperms *sieve tubes* are
present, each consisting of a linear series
of elongated, rather thick-walled cells
joined together end to end (Fig. 125). The individual cells are called
sieve-tube elements. Fine strands of cytoplasm pass from one sieve-tube
element to the next through pores in the end walls. These pores are

grouped into definite areas called *sieve plates*. Sieve plates may also be present in the side walls of sieve tubes. When the end wall of a sieve-tube element is transverse, it usually has only a single sieve plate, but if the end wall is oblique it commonly bears several sieve plates. In potato stolons the sieve-tube elements range up to 100 μ. in length; in cucurbits some of them attain lengths of 1000 μ., but in most species they are shorter.

In gymnosperms true sieve tubes are not present. The elongated cells in which conduction occurs are called *sieve cells* and resemble the sieve-tube elements in many ways. However, they are not regularly arranged end to end and do not possess such elaborate sieve plates as sieve-tube elements

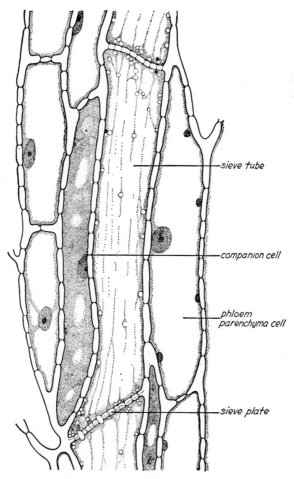

FIG. 125. Longitudinal section through a sieve tube element and associated cells from the stem of tobacco. Redrawn from Holman and Robbins (1938).

Sieve-tube elements usually develop by the longitudinal division of mother cells which have arisen as a result of the division of a cambium cell. The division of such mother cells results in a sieve-tube element and a companion cell (Fig. 125). Sometimes the mother cell may divide longitudinally more than once forming one sieve-tube element and two or more companion cells.

Young sieve elements are nucleate cells and contain actively streaming cytoplasm. The cytoplasmic membranes exhibit their usual property of differential permeability. A network of cytoplasmic strands commonly extends across the vacuole. Plastids and slime-bodies are usually present. The latter are small, usually more or less rounded masses, probably composed of proteinaceous materials. After reaching mature size, a sieve element undergoes a series of changes which are unique among plant cells (Crafts, 1951). A sieve element apparently does not enter upon the main period of its functional life until it has passed through this series of changes. The nucleus disintegrates, as do also the plastids and slime-bodies. Cytoplasm becomes confined largely to a thin layer lining the wall, and streaming of the cytoplasm ceases. There is considerable evidence that the cytoplasm of such mature sieve elements, and particularly that of the end walls, is in a highly permeable condition. Its appearance suggests a state of low metabolic activity. Cytoplasmic connections from element to element remain well developed during these later stages in the development of the sieve element.

The functional life of most sieve elements is relatively short. For protophloem elements it may be only a few days. In most woody species the cytoplasm disappears from most of the sieve elements by the end of the growing season in which they were formed. At about the time that the cytoplasm disintegrates the sieve plates become capped with plugs called *callus* composed of carbohydrate material. In a few woody species such as grape, rose, linden, and tulip tree, the cytoplasm of most sieve-tube elements does not disintegrate at the end of the first season. In such species temporary callus caps are deposited at the approach of the dormant season, which are dissolved at the advent of the next growing season. In such species sieve tubes may remain functional for two or even more years.

The *companion cells* are much smaller in cross section than the sieve-tube elements. They may have the same length as the sieve-tube elements or they may be half or even less than half the length. The protoplasm of each companion cell contains a prominent nucleus, and numerous small vacuoles, but no starch grains. The walls separating the companion cell or cells from the sieve-tube element are characterized by the presence of numerous small pits, but the walls between the companion cells and the parenchyma cells contain few or no pits. In some species some sieve-tube elements do not have companion cells adjacent to them, whereas in other species every sieve-tube element is accompanied by one or more companion cells. Gymnosperms and pteridophytes do not have companion cells.

Phloem parenchyma is composed of living cells which are somewhat elongate parallel to the long axis of the stem. This tissue does not occur in monocots and is also absent from the phloem of some dicots. The proportion of phloem-parenchyma cells in the phloem varies widely according to species. In most herbaceous dicots they constitute a smaller proportion of the phloem than do the sieve tubes and companion cells. The phloem of seedlings, however, may consist largely of phloem parenchyma. Woody species also differ greatly in the proportion of phloem-parenchyma cells present. The arrangement of phloem-parenchyma cells likewise exhibits a great variation. They may occur in definite clusters, in tangential bands, or in radial rows that are closely associated with the sieve tubes. Many of the phloem-parenchyma cells contain starch, and in certain species they often contain crystals.

Phloem fibers, found in the phloem of some plants, are elongated cells with thick, usually lignified walls. They are more common in woody than in herbaceous species and, like the companion cells, they do not occur in the gymosperms or in the pteridophytes. The phloem fiber cells have long, tapering ends which overlap, forming strong fibrous strands. They frequently occur in groups or as cylindrical sheaths surrounding the inner phloem tissues.

As discussed in Chap. XII, vascular rays are present in the stem tissues of most species. The vascular rays are initiated in the cambium and extend both into the xylem and into the phloem. The distribution of the *phloem rays*, as the portions of the vascular rays located in the phloem are called, varies greatly according to species. As a rule, they consist of bandlike bundles of transversely oriented living cells varying from one to many cells in width and from several to many cells in height. Certain types of phloem-ray structure are characteristic of each species. The cells of phloem rays are radially elongate, and parenchymatous. The phloem-ray cells of roots and stems contain considerable quantities of starch and probably other organic compounds as well.

Longitudinal conduction in the phloem undoubtedly occurs principally through the sieve elements since they alone are universally present and are constructed so that they offer less resistance to movement than other types of phloem cells. Nevertheless there is a distinct possibility that the parenchyma and companion cells also play a part in translocation processes. The phloem-ray cells undoubtedly serve as channels of lateral conduction. The phloem fibers probably play no part in conduction.

As a result of cambial growth there is a continued formation of new xylem and phloem cells during part or all of the growing season. This results in most species in crushing the older phloem tissues, including the sieve tubes. Other changes which occur as phloem grows older include lignification of fibers and sometimes also ray and parenchyma cells and, in certain species, modification of ray and parenchyma cells into hard, thick-walled, dead cells known as *stone cells*. Development or enlargement of lactiferous systems is also unusual in the older phloem of some species. In woody stems and roots further profound modifications occur in the aging phloem tissues as the result of the activity of secondary meristems called *cork cambiums*.

Developmental aspects of the phloem tissues are given further consideration in Chap. XXIX.

General Aspects of the Translocation of Solutes in Plants.—From the time that a young plant starts to grow until its death, a more or less continuous movement of solutes is in progress through the conducting elements of every organ of the plant. In a very young seedling, foods are usually translocated upward in the growing stems and downward in the developing roots from the storage tissues of the seed. As soon as the rate of photosynthesis in the developing seedling becomes sufficiently high, at least part of the photosynthate moves in a downward direction from the leaves toward the roots while some of it is often moving upward toward apical meristems. Furthermore, as soon as the developing roots make effective contact with the substrate, absorption of mineral salts begins, followed by translocation of a large part of them in a generally upward direction through the plant. At least some of the solutes absorbed from the soil, especially those containing nitrogen, phosphorus, or sulfur, often react within the root cells with organic compounds which have descended into the roots from the leaves. The resulting chemically more complex compounds, such as amino acids and acid amides, may then be translocated in the reverse direction from the roots into the aerial parts of the plant.

Mineral salts absorbed by the roots are mostly translocated to young leaves and other growing organs of the plant. All of them do not remain, however, in the organ into which they are first translocated. A considerable proportion of the mineral salts which move into a leaf or a flower petal, for example, may sooner or later move out of such a lateral organ back into the stem, and become redistributed to other, usually younger parts of the plant.

The translocation patterns within a plant often exert significant effects upon its behavior. At the time that young fruits and seeds are developing, for example, there appears to be a general migration of organic materials from all parts of the plant toward the enlarging fruits and seeds.

This movement may so nearly monopolize the food resources of the plant as to check severely the growth of vegetative organs. In cotton plants, for example, there is a conspicuous decrease in vegetative growth when the plant is fruiting heavily. A large part of the carbohydrate synthesized in photosynthesis and of the nitrogenous compounds in the above ground organs of the plant moves into the enlarging fruits. The supply of carbohydrates reaching the root system becomes insufficient to maintain rapid respiration and root elongation. As a result there is a decrease in the rate of absorption of mineral salts, which in turn results in checking or even stopping the vegetative growth of the plant (Eaton and Joham, 1944).

As the preceding discussion indicates, the patterns of translocation in plants are complex and may be different at different stages in the life history of the plant. Many kinds of solutes are being translocated in various directions within the plant. Nevertheless certain predominant translocation routes can be recognized as follows: (1) downward translocation of organic solutes from leaves to other parts of the plant, (2) upward translocation of organic solutes to growing or storage regions, (3) upward translocation of mineral salts from roots to aerial organs, (4) outward translocation of mineral salts from leaves and other lateral organs into stems, (5) lateral or cross transfer of solutes within stems.

Downward Translocation of Organic Solutes.—Downward translocation of organic compounds unquestionably occurs for the most part through the phloem tissues. Much of the evidence indicating that organic solutes move toward the basal portions of the plant in the phloem has been obtained by ringing experiments. "Ringing," when the term is employed without qualification, refers to the removal of a narrow continuous band of tissues external to the xylem. Since ringing entirely encircles the stem, all tissues external to the xylem are completely intercepted. This operation is also called "girdling."

In a girdled tree carbohydrates and other organic compounds slowly accumulate in the tissues above the ring and slowly decrease in quantity in the tissues below the ring as they are utilized in respiration and assimilation. Unless special conditions intervene, such, for example, as development of sprouts on the tree trunk below the ring, a girdled tree ultimately dies because of starvation of the roots, showing clearly that no appreciable amounts of foods are conducted downward through the xylem. Accumulation of organic compounds above a ring has also been demonstrated in certain herbaceous plants such as cotton (Mason and Maskell, 1928). Experimental results of this kind indicate that the downward translocation of carbohydrates and other organic compounds occurs through the phloem tissues.

Chemical analyses show that cells of the phloem are relatively rich in carbohydrates and organic nitrogenous compounds. This finding is consistent with the concept that translocation of organic compounds occurs through the phloem but is not proof, since storage tissues also contain relatively high concentrations of foods.

It has been shown earlier (Chap. XII) that the upward movement of water takes place in the xylem. For this reason it is difficult to conceive of the xylem as an important avenue of downward translocation of organic substances. Dyes injected into stems at times of rapid water movement usually move both upward and downward—sometimes to approximately equal distances. Such results have sometimes been cited as evidence of downward currents in the xylem. Downward movements of injected dyes probably result, however, from the effects of tension or from a subatmospheric pressure in vessels occupied only by gases (Chap. XII). They cannot be accepted as valid evidence that downward movements of solutes ordinarily occur in the xylem of intact stems.

Further evidence that the phloem is the tissue in which organic compounds are translocated has come from experiments in which short segments of the stem have been killed. Since the conducting elements of the xylem are nonliving, the passage of solutes through the xylem is not prevented by the death of the cells in the stem. The conducting elements of the phloem, on the other hand, are living, hence any phase of translocation which is interrupted by killing the cells in a stem segment can be assumed to be occurring in the phloem. Rabideau and Burr (1945) labeled the carbohydrate formed in bean plants by allowing one leaf on the plant to photosynthesize in an atmosphere containing carbon dioxide made with the identifiable C^{13} isotope (Chap. XVIII). They then showed that movement of carbohydrates occurred readily in the stem, both upward and downward, from the node at which the leaf petiole was attached. If short segments of the stem above and below the node at which the petiole was attached were killed by treatment with hot wax, however, no upward or downward movement of carbohydrates occurred. Phosphates, containing radioactive phosphorus (P^{32}), however, were readily conducted through such killed stem segments, indicating that their translocation occurred through the xylem (cf. later discussion of upward translocation of mineral salts.) Bonner (1944) and Went (1944) obtained similar results in investigations of the translocation of organic compounds through tomato stems, short segments of which had been killed with superheated steam.

Upward Translocation of Organic Solutes.—Under many conditions an upward [1] translocation of organic solutes takes place in plants. This oc-

[1] The terms "upward" and "downward" as applied to translocation phenomena should not be interpreted too literally. As a rule translocation in the general direction of roots to leaves or other apical regions is termed "upward translocation"; movement in the reverse direction, "downward translocation."

curs, for example, in the stems of woody species when the buds resume growth in the spring. The tissues of the new shoots are constructed largely out of foods which move in an upward direction from the storage tissues of the stems, as during the early stages in their expansion the leaves do not photosynthesize at a rate sufficient to supply all the carbohydrates used in the growth of the shoot which bears them. Upward translocation of foods from the older leaves on a given shoot to developing leaves situated closer to its apex also probably occurs. As the leaves mature there is a reversal in the direction of translocation of carbohydrates; they are then translocated from the leaves into the stems in which they move to other organs of the plant.

A number of other examples of the upward transport of foods in plants can be cited. Opening flowers and developing fruits are often attached to stems in such a position that some or all of the organic compounds translocated into them move through the stems in an upward direction. In the early stages of the development of seedlings, upward translocation occurs from the endosperm or cotyledons toward the apical portions of the plant in which rapid growth is taking place. Likewise upward transport of foods invariably occurs during the earlier stages of shoot growth from bulbs, tubers, rhizomes, and other types of underground organs.

The "classical" view that upward translocation in plants takes place in the xylem was long accepted as referring to mineral salts and organic compounds as well as to water. The concept that upward transport of carbohydrates occurs principally through the xylem is based largely on phenomena which have been observed in certain woody species. Large quantities of soluble and insoluble carbohydrates are present in the wood parenchyma, wood rays, and (in the younger stems) pith cells of many varieties of trees and shrubs. At certain seasons soluble carbohydrates are also found in the xylem conduits, as illustrated by data of Anderssen (1929, Fig. 126). As found by this investigator the concentrations of both sucrose and free reducing substances (probably largely hexoses) in the xylem sap of pear trees were highest in the winter and early spring. Both fell to a zero value during the summer months, and increased slowly during the autumn. The sugars found in the conducting elements undoubtedly come from the storage tissues of the pith or xylem. The relatively high soluble carbohydrate content of the xylem tissues in the winter and spring probably results largely from shifts in the starch $\rightleftharpoons$ sugar equilibrium toward the sugar side, as a result of the relatively low temperatures prevailing during these seasons (Chap. XX).

The fact that, in the early spring, the soluble carbohydrate content of the xylem sap is relatively high and by the time the shoots are well developed has dropped to a low or zero value seems to indicate that soluble

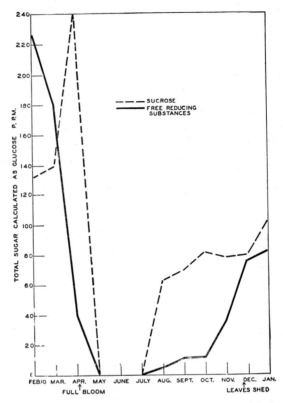

FIG. 126.   Seasonal variations in the carbohydrate content of the xylem sap of
pear trees. Data of Anderssen (1929).

carbohydrates have been conducted upward through the xylem to the
developing buds. Although this assumption appears to be superficially
plausible, there are good reasons for doubting if this phenomenon actually
is very strong evidence that upward translocation of organic solutes occurs
in the xylem. In the first place the concentration of organic solutes in the
xylem sap is always very low, seldom exceeding 2 or 3 per cent. Furthermore, the highest concentrations of sugar occur in the sap during the
winter when there is little or no upward translocation of water, and it is
not at all certain that these solutes do not largely disappear from the
xylem sap in the spring before its upward flow begins to take place at an
appreciable rate.

Investigations by Curtis, summarized in 1935, point to a conclusion
regarding the upward transport of organic solutes which is directly the
opposite of the long accepted view. His experiments all seem to indicate
that it is the phloem and not the xylem which is the principal tissue

through which such translocation occurs. In one investigation the contrasting effects of intercepting the xylem and intercepting the phloem of woody stems upon upward transport of organic solutes were studied (Curtis, 1925). In these experiments a number of growing shoots were first defoliated. Some received no further treatment, thus serving as checks. In others (Fig. 127) a ring of the tissues external to the xylem was removed, and in still others a segment of the xylem was excised, leaving the phloem and cortical tissues intact. Every stem which was cut into was enclosed in a glass cylinder as shown in the figure. This cylinder was filled with water in order to keep the exposed tissue surfaces moist and in order to supply water to the top of the stems in which the xylem was cut. The outcome of experiments in which the water jacket was rinsed out once

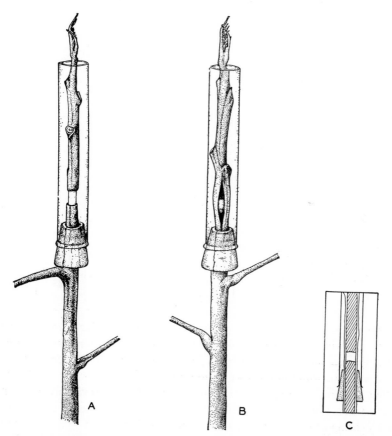

FIG. 127. Diagrams to show (A) stem with phloem removed, (B) with xylem removed, the cut portion of each stem being enclosed in a water jacket, (C) sectional view of (B). Redrawn from Curtis (1935).

each day with distilled water was essentially the same as in those experiments in which this was not done, indicating that translocation of solutes did not occur through the water.

The results of some of these experiments are presented in Table 39. Invariably the stems in which the xylem was cut showed greater elongation than those in which the phloem was cut, indicating greater upward translocation of foods in the former than in the latter.

Shoot elongation is a somewhat indirect measure of translocation, but the conclusions drawn from such observations were supported in a number

TABLE 39—COMPARATIVE EFFECTS OF CUTTING THE XYLEM OR PHLOEM ON GROWTH, DRY WEIGHT, AND SUGAR CONTENT OF DEFOLIATED SHOOTS (DATA OF CURTIS, 1925)

Species	Treatment	Ave. total growth, mm.	Dry weight, per cent of fresh growth	Total sugar per stem, mg.	Sugar, per cent fresh weight	Sugar, per cent dry weight
Mock Orange (*Philadelphus pubescens*) June 13–June 19	Check	63.6	10.8	3.08	0.12	1.12
	Phloem cut	7.8	9.0	0.08	0.03	0.35
	Xylem cut	49.2	10.8	5.32	0.22	2.03
Mock Orange (*Philadelphus pubescens*) June 25–July 1	Check	105.3	13.0	2.10	0.094	0.72
	Phloem cut	19.7	9.4	1.63	0.087	0.93
	Xylem cut	47.4	11.8	4.83	0.231	2.08
Sumac (*Rhus typhina*) June 26–July 1	Check	63.0	22.3	4.17	0.33	1.48
	Phloem cut	15.8	17.2	3.05	0.67	3.89
	Xylem cut	49.5	20.5	3.90	0.42	2.05

of experiments by dry weight determinations and analyses for sugar. As shown in Table 39, the dry weight and total sugar content per stem were invariably least in the ringed stems. This was also true for the percentage of sugar in terms of fresh weight or dry weight.

The experiments of Rabideau and Burr (1945), previously discussed, and of Chen (1951), discussed later, supply further evidence that upward translocation of organic solutes occurs in the phloem.

In general the evidence seems to warrant the conclusion that the phloem is the principal tissue in which upward translocation of organic solutes occurs, although it seems probable that small quantities of such compounds are, on occasion, translocated in an upward direction through the xylem.

Upward Translocation of Mineral Salts.—The term "mineral salts" is necessarily employed in this discussion somewhat loosely. For present purposes, nitrogen, which may be translocated upward in either inorganic or organic combination (Chap. XXVI) is included among mineral salts. Upward translocation of sulfur and phosphorus also probably occurs in both organic and inorganic combination.

For many years it was universally agreed that upward translocation of mineral salts occurred through the xylem, although it now appears that the situation is not quite this simple.

Studies of the sap from xylem vessels show that it usually contains at least traces of both organic and inorganic solutes. In proportion to the total quantities utilized, however, the concentration of inorganic constituents in the xylem sap is usually relatively higher than that of organic solutes. Furthermore, appreciable concentrations of mineral salts are commonly present in the sap of vessels at seasons when upward flow of water is occurring at its most rapid rates. At such times the xylem sap contains little or no organic material in solution. Presence of dissolved mineral salts at such seasons is presumptive evidence that at least some of them are translocated upward in the plant through the xylem.

Clements and Engard (1938), Phillis and Mason (1940), and others have shown that ringing stems of various species does not prevent upward movement of mineral salts through the plant. Results of such experiments show that upward translocation of mineral salts can occur in the xylem.

Curtis (see Curtis and Clark, 1950) employed the technique of intercepting the xylem versus intercepting the phloem (Fig. 127) in attempting to ascertain whether mineral salts moved into growing, defoliated stems of sumac through the xylem or through the phloem. Relative to the quantity which moved through check stems, a much larger proportion of mineral salts or nitrogenous compounds was translocated through the stems in which the xylem was intercepted than through those in which the phloem was intercepted. Movement of mineral salts into such woody shoots can therefore occur in the phloem. Somewhat similar experiments performed by Mason and Phillis (1940) on cotton plants also led to the conclusion that upward translocation of nitrogenous compounds can occur in the phloem.

Experiments on ringing often show that mineral salts can be conducted in the xylem, and experiments on intercepting wood often show that they can be conducted in the phloem, but no such experiments show conclusively which is the predominant pathway of such conduction in intact plants.

Stout and Hoagland (1939) were among the first to employ the radioactive tracer technique in experiments designed to ascertain the path of upward movement of mineral salts in plants. Small plants of cotton, geranium, and willow, rooted in sand or solution cultures, were used. Certain branches of each plant were "stripped" by cutting longitudinal slits 9 in. long on opposite sides of the stem, and then carefully pulling the bark away from the wood, but leaving it attached at the ends. A sheet of paraf-

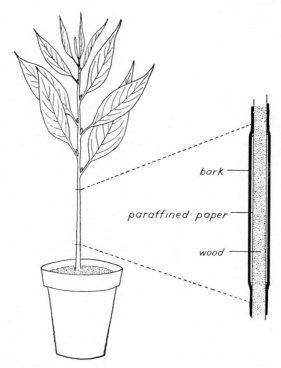

FIG. 128.   Diagram to illustrate technique employed in the experiment of Stout and Hoagland (see text).

fined paper was then introduced between the phloem and the xylem (Fig. 128). This treatment resulted in no visible signs of injury to the plants during the course of an experiment. Radioactive ions of potassium, sodium, phosphate, or bromide were introduced into the rooting medium. After a period of not more than a few hours, under conditions favorable to transpiration, distribution of the tracer ions in the stem was ascertained by measuring the quantity of radioactive elements in ashed segments of the xylem and phloem from the stem above, below, and in the region where the xylem and phloem were separated with paraffined paper.

TABLE 40—DISTRIBUTION OF RADIOACTIVE POTASSIUM IN THE STEM OF WILLOW AFTER AN ABSORPTION PERIOD OF 5 HOURS

		Branch stripped 1½ hr. before absorption period		Intact branch	
		ppm in bark	ppm in wood	ppm in bark	ppm in wood
Above strip	SA	53	47	64	56
	S6	11.6	119		
	S5	0.9	122		
Stripped section	S4	0.7	112	87	69
(see Fig. 128)	S3	<0.3	98		
	S2	<0.3	108		
	S1	20	113		
Below strip	SB	84	58	74	67

As shown by the results from a representative one of their experiments (Table 40), radioactive potassium (K^{42}) was found to be relatively abundant in both the bark and the wood above and below the section of the willow stem in which the xylem and phloem had been separated by paraffined paper. Within this latter segment of the stem, however, almost all of the tracer element was located in the xylem. In the intact branch there was no such marked difference in the distribution of the radioactive potassium.

Similar results were obtained with the other plants used, and with each of the radioactive elements employed as a tracer.

In these experiments it is obvious that mineral salts absorbed by the roots were transported upward at a relatively rapid rate through the xylem. During their upward passage some of the mineral salts moved laterally from the xylem into the phloem, thus accounting for the relatively large amounts of tracer element in the phloem. When, however, the lateral movement of salts from xylem to phloem was intercepted by interposing an impermeable barrier between these two tissues, practically all of the tracer element was found in the xylem.

These results demonstrate that upward movement of mineral salts occurs in the xylem, but the possibility of some such movement in the phloem also is not excluded even though it is clear that lateral movement from xylem to phloem takes place readily. The data in Table 40 furnish some evidence of upward and downward translocation in the phloem. Bark sections S1 and S6, adjacent to the unstripped portions of the stem, are both higher in radioactive potassium than sections S2 to S5. This can be accounted for only by assuming that a slow movement of radioactive potassium has occurred into these sections from adjacent unstripped portions of the bark. Somewhat similar experiments of Gustafson (1939) also indicate that a limited amount of upward translocation of radioactive phosphate may occur through the phloem.

There is no doubt that upward translocation of mineral salts occurs in the xylem, and it seems virtually certain that this is the main pathway along which their general upward movement from roots to leaves occurs. Conditions which are especially favorable to mineral salt translocation in the xylem include high rates of transpiration, high concentrations of mineral salts in the substrate, and the prevalence in the root cells of metabolic conditions which favor rapid movement of mineral salts from the absorbing cells to the xylem.

Some upward translocation of mineral salts also occurs in the phloem under certain circumstances. Such movement appears to occur at rates that are usually slower than in the xylem. As described in the next section, upward movement of mineral salts in the phloem of younger stems appears to be a usual occurrence when they are "exported" from leaves into the stem. There are some indications that mineral elements are more likely to move in the phloem when in organic than when in inorganic combination. Entrance of such elements as nitrogen, phosphorus, and sulfur into organic combinations in the root cells may favor their upward translocation in the phloem.

Outward Movement of Solutes Other Than Carbohydrates from Leaves and Other Lateral Organs.—As the previous discussion has indicated, movement of mineral salts to the leaves appears to occur principally, if not wholly, in the xylem. Not all of the mineral salts which enter a given leaf remain in that leaf, however, some of them being "exported" back into the stem, whence they are translocated to other parts of the plant. This is shown by the results of chemical analyses of leaves at different times of the day (Penston, 1935; Phillis and Mason, 1942) and also by results of periodic chemical analyses of leaf and stem tissues during the period just prior to leaf abscission (Denny, 1933; Deleano, 1936). Nitrogen, phosphorus, potassium, sulfur, magnesium, and chlorine may all be exported from leaves in one form or another, but calcium, boron, iron, and manganese appear to be virtually immobile. Nitrogen, phosphorus, and sulfur probably move out of leaves at least partly in organic combination, while potassium, magnesium, and chlorine probably move out mostly in the form of inorganic ions. Translocation of mineral elements out of flower petals just prior to their abscission also occurs (Phillis and Mason, 1936). In general, those mineral elements which are readily redistributed in plants (Chap. XXV) are the ones which are the most readily exported from leaves.

The earlier evidence of the export of substances other than carbohydrates from leaves and other lateral organs has been augmented and strengthened by more recent studies in which radioactive elements have been used. To study this phenomenon by means of tracer elements it is necessary to apply the tagged ions directly to the leaf tissues rather than to let them enter the plant in the usual way through the root system. The manner in which the radioactive elements are introduced into the leaf tissues may determine the channel through which they pass in moving from the leaf to the stem. If the solution containing the tagged compound is brought into contact with the open ends of severed xylem vessels it may be drawn rapidly into the stem by way of the xylem. This is particularly likely to happen if an internal water deficit exists in the leaf at the time the solution is applied. On the other hand, when the marked ions are allowed to reach the vascular system by cell-to-cell transfer in the mesophyll, the result obtained is very different.

Colwell (1942) found that radioactive phosphorus (P^{32}), introduced as phosphate into intact leaves of squash plants under suitable conditions, moved out of such leaves into the stem readily but did not move out of similar leaves if the petioles had first been scalded. This is evidence that outward movement of the phosphorus-containing compounds occurred in the phloem.

Biddulph and Markle (1944) introduced radioactive phosphorus as phosphate into the leaves of cotton plants in such a way as to insure that the tagged ions would move into the phloem tissue of the leaf. The xylem and phloem of the stem were separated by a membrane of waxed paper in a segment extending for 4 in. immediately below the point of leaf attachment. The phosphate ions were allowed to migrate through the tissues of the leaf and stem for from 1 to 3 hr. before their distribution in the stem was determined. Examination of the treated portion of the stem revealed that almost all of the radioactive phosphate was located in the bark. The phosphate had moved both up and down after reaching the stem, but only traces of the tagged element were found in the xylem where it was separated from the phloem by the waxed paper. It is evident from these results that the phosphate was translocated out of the leaf and longitudinally within the stem almost entirely in the tissues of the phloem.

When the radioactive phosphate was applied to leaves of plants with intact stems, the marked ions were found in both the xylem and the phloem of the stem and both above and below the point of leaf attachment. Again, much more of the radioactive element was present in the bark than in the wood which suggests that the tracer ions reached the latter by lateral diffusion from the phloem.

Studies of the outward movement of radioactive phosphate from the leaves of bean plants indicated that more such movement occurred during the daytime than at night (Biddulph, 1941). The direction of the movement of phosphate was principally downward, under the conditions of these experiments, but some lateral diffusion of the radioactive ions into the xylem took place with a consequent upward movement in the transpiration stream. Other evidence shows quite clearly that a diurnal alternation between a movement of mineral salts into leaves and a movement out of the leaves is of frequent occurrence. Phillis and Mason (1942) have shown by chemical analyses that the magnesium, potassium, chlorine, phosphorus, and nitrogen content of cotton leaves regularly increases during the daylight hours, and decreases at night.

The general picture of the movements of mineral salts in plants seems to be about as follows. After entering the roots from the soil most of the mineral salts move across the cells of the young roots to the xylem ducts in which they are carried upward into the leaves. Some of the molecules of which these elements are a part or of which they become a part as a result of chemical transformations in the leaf do not become immobilized in the leaves but move out of them *via* the phloem. Once in the stem such solutes move both upward and downward in the phloem, entering other leaves, and probably also reaching the apical growing regions of roots and stems. Some of the mineral compounds in the phloem also migrate laterally and enter the transpiration stream in which they are transported upward at a usually rapid rate. In a sense, therefore, we may speak of a "circulation" of mineral compounds within the various organs of a plant.

Lateral Translocation of Solutes.—As shown in Chap. XII, lateral translocation of water in a tangential direction readily occurs in woody stems. This does not appear to be true of many solutes. In straight-grained trees the sugars from the leaves on one side of the tree are translocated to the roots directly below them and, if nitrates are added to the soil on one side of a tree, increase in nitrogen occurs principally in the leaves and branches above the roots on that side (Auchter, 1923). A similar lack of lateral translocation of solutes has been shown in certain species of herbaceous plants (Caldwell, 1930; McMurtrey, 1937). On the other hand, radial transfer of solutes from xylem to phloem or *vice versa* appears to occur readily. Some of the radial movement of solutes probably occurs along the vascular rays.

In perennial woody plants, however, there is evidence that reorientation of conductive tissues may occur in such a way as to offset the effects of a lack of lateral translocation of solutes (MacDaniels and Curtis, 1930). If all branches on one side of a tree are removed or destroyed, for example, the effect of diminishing growth of trunk and roots on that side usually does not persist for more than one year. Subsequently developed conductive tissues are usually oriented in such a fashion as to permit translocation to the trunk and roots on the side of the tree which no longer bears branches.

Mechanism of Translocation of Solutes in the Xylem.—Dissolved mineral salts and organic solutes, when present, are carried along with the ascending streams of water in the xylem ducts which are pulled up through the plant according to the mechanism which has already been discussed in Chap. XII. During upward translocation some of the solutes are lost by lateral movement into living cells of the stem adjacent to the xylem conduits. In the leaves the solutes of the xylem vessels migrate into the living cells of the mesophyll. The rates at which solutes are translocated upward through the xylem of the stem will correspond with the rates of translocation of water.

Basic Considerations Regarding Mechanism of Translocation of Solutes in the Phloem.—Although several theories have been advanced to account for the mechanism of the movement of solutes in phloem tissues, no one theory has ever received general acceptance. As a background for considering the principal theories that have been proposed, it will be helpful to review briefly some of the pertinent facts regarding the problem of movement of solutes in the phloem.

1. *Living Cells Are Essential.*—Unlike movements of water and solutes in the xylem, translocation in the conducting elements of the phloem ceases when the cells are killed. Evidence for this fact is presented earlier in the discussion.

2. *The Movement May Be Bidirectional.*—There is no doubt that movement of solutes in the phloem can sometimes occur in one direction and sometimes in the other. The question of whether or not simultaneous bidirectional movement can occur through the same region of phloem has an important bearing on concepts of the mechanism. Experiments already discussed show that both carbohydrates (Rabideau and Burr, 1945) and phosphates (Biddulph and Markle, 1944) move both up and down in the phloem of a stem from the point at which they enter it from the petiole of a leaf. This phenomenon does not, however, involve bidirectional movement through the same phloem at the same time.

Indications that two different kinds of solutes—sugar and the dye fluorescein—could move simultaneously through the same phloem region in opposite directions were obtained by Palmquist (1938). Simultaneous movement of phosphate and carbohydrate, labeled with radioactive phosphorus (P^{32}) and radioactive carbon (C^{14}) respectively, in opposite directions through the phloem tissue of geranium stems has been shown to occur, at least over short distances and at relatively slow rates (Chen, 1951). It was further shown that phosphate could move up in the phloem while carbohydrate was moving down in the same phloem, and *vice versa*.

Although there is thus evidence that simultaneous bidirectional movement of solutes through a given region of the phloem many take place, no experiments have ever been devised which would show whether or not such bidirectional movement can occur through individual sieve tubes.

3. *Relatively Large Amounts of Material Are Transported.*—The amount of carbohydrate translocated through the phloem into such organs as fleshy roots, tubers, or fruits is almost incredibly great when considered in relation to the cross-sectional area of the conducting elements of the phloem.

For example, Crafts and Lorenz (1944a) calculated the gain in fresh weight of pumpkin fruits (Connecticut Field variety) to be about 5500 g. in a 33-day growing period. A large proportion of this increase represents water. However, when the average *hourly* increase in *dry weight* of the fruits was calculated, a value of 0.61 g. was obtained. On the average, therefore, something more than half a gram of organic matter was delivered to each fruit during each hour of the 33-day growing period. All such material entered the developing fruit through the one slender stem connecting it with the vine.

Similar calculations have been made for the developing fruits of the sausage tree (*Kigelia africana*) by Clements (1940). These fruits commonly develop as clusters of four, all hanging from the tree on one slender stem. As much as 32.6 g. of organic material (Table 41) must pass through this one slender stem per day in order to account for the measured gain in dry weight of one such cluster of fruits.

TABLE 41—INCREASE IN GREEN AND DRY WEIGHTS OF ONE CLUSTER OF FOUR *Kigelia* FRUITS
(DATA OF CLEMENTS, 1940)

Date, 1939	Total green weights of fruits in g.	Per cent dry matter	Total dry weight of fruits in g.	Increase in dry weight g.	Daily increase in dry weight g.
June 18..........	692	11.9	82.3	82.3	9.1
June 25..........	2207	11.9	262.8	180.5	25.8
July 2..........	4267	11.5	490.7	227.9	32.6
July 9..........	6073	11.3	686.3	195.6	27.9
July 15..........	7305	11.3	825.6	139.3	23.2
July 21..........	8086	11.3	913.8	88.2	14.7
July 29..........	8541	12.1	1033.5	119.7	14.9
August 9........	8648	14.1	1219.3	185.8	16.9
August 20.......	8716	15.4	1342.3	123.0	11.2
August 29.......	8824	17.4	1535.5	193.2	21.5
* Sept. 10.......	8771	18.7	1640.3	104.8	8.7

* Growth nearly completed on this date.

4. *Velocity of Movement Is Rapid.*—The velocities with which organic solutes must move through sieve tubes in order to account for a gain in dry weight of 0.61 g. per day (average) by a pumpkin fruit have been calculated by Crafts and Lorenz (1944a). The required rate would be about 11 cm. per hr. if the organic compounds move in the dry state (an obviously hypothetical assumption), about 55 cm. per hr. if they move as a 20 per cent solution, and about 110 cm. per hr. if they move as a 10 per cent solution. These calculations assume that transport occurs in the entire lumen of the sieve tubes. Since the cytoplasm of mature sieve tubes is essentially restricted to a thin layer lining the inner surface of the cell walls, if it is assumed that organic solutes are restricted in their movement to the cytoplasm, then the rate of solute movement would be of the order of 500 to 1000 cm. per hr. It should be noted that all these calculations are based on *average* and not on maximum rates of gain in dry weight.

Evidence from other sources also indicates relatively rapid rates of movement of solutes in the phloem. Biddulph and Markle (1944) found the rate of downward movement of radioactive phosphate in the phloem to be in excess of 21 cm. per hr. According to Huber (1941) the rates of downward translocation in the phloem of broad-leaved forest trees may range up to at least 100 cm. per hr.

5. *Periodicity of Movement.*—The movements of organic and inorganic solutes in the phloem do not appear to occur at a constant rate both day and night. The more rapid translocation of radioactive phosphate from leaves of bean plants during the day than during the night has already been discussed. Diurnal variations in the rate of movement of organic solutes also occur in plants and do not follow the same pattern in all species. Most of the carbohydrates which enter growing cotton bolls appear to move into them during the daytime rather than at night (Mason and Maskell, 1928). The rate of translocation of carbohydrates into date fruits in their preripe stage of development, on the other hand, appears to be more rapid at night than in the daytime (Curtis, 1947).

The Mass Flow Hypothesis.—This theory of translocation has been ad-

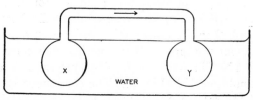

FIG. 129. Diagram of an osmotic system in which mass flow of solution will occur.

vocated by Münch (1927, 1930) and in modified forms also by Crafts (1933, 1938) and others. The principles involved in this hypothesis can most easily be clarified by reference to a simple physical system (Fig. 129).

As shown in this figure two membranes permeable only to water, both dipping in water, are connected by a tube to form a closed system. Membrane X is assumed to enclose a stronger solution of sucrose than membrane Y. Water will at first enter both membranes, but the greater turgor pressure developed in X will soon be transmitted throughout the system. This will result in a greater diffusion pressure in the water in Y than in the pure water in which the membranes are immersed. Water will therefore pass out of the membrane Y, and coincidentally there will be a flow of *solution* along the tube from X to Y. The mass movement of solution from X to Y will continue until the concentrations of the sugar solutions in both membranes are equal. At this point the flow of solution in the tube will stop and a dynamic equilibrium will be established between the solution in the closed system and the circumambient water.

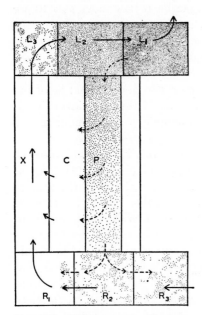

FIG. 130. Diagram to illustrate mechanism of solute translocation according to the Münch hypothesis. Redrawn from Crafts (1931).

If such an apparatus could be set up so that the sugar could be utilized or be converted into an insoluble form as fast as it was translocated into Y, and so that additional sugar could pass into solution in X as rapidly as it moved out of that membrane, flow of solution from X to Y would continue indefinitely.

The Münch hypothesis assumes that a system analogous to that just described accounts for translocation of solutes through the phloem. Fig. 130 (from Crafts, 1931) illustrates diagrammatically how it is supposed to operate as applied to the downward translocation of solutes. Cells L_1, L_2, and L_3 represent the green cells of the leaf and correspond to membrane X in Fig. 129. Similarly R_1, R_2, R_3 represent root cells which are analogous to membrane Y in Fig. 129. The continuous system of phloem connecting leaf and root cells is represented by P. Similarly X represents the xylem and C the cambium. The osmotic pressure of the leaf cells is maintained at a relatively high value as a result of photosynthesis. In the root cells the osmotic pressure is (usually) lower because most of the sugars translocated into them are used in metabolic activities or are converted into insoluble storage forms. Water is supplied continuously to the leaf cells through the xylem.

This hypothesis assumes that the higher turgor pressure of the leaf cells will cause a mass flow of solution downward in the phloem toward the roots. Plasmodesms connecting adjacent cells are supposed to permit mass movement of solution from leaf cell to leaf cell, and from leaf cells into the phloem elements. Movement from one sieve tube to another is supposed to be facilitated by the cytoplasmic strands in the communicating pores. Some of the solute molecules may be lost to the cambium and other living cells of the stem, but it is assumed that the greater proportion of them are translocated to the roots. The water component of the downward moving solution is supposed to be exuded back into the xylem from the cambium or other receiving cells.

If it is assumed that the entire phloem is acting as a unit system, this theory will account for translocation through the phloem in only one direction at a time. Transport might occur at times in one direction and at times in the other. Flow will occur from the end at which the turgor pressure is highest toward the other. In the spring, for example, if it is postulated that the turgor pressure of the supplying cells in the stem or root is greater than that of the growing stem tips, upward flow would usually occur. Later in the season, as the turgor pressure of the leaf cells increases, a reversal in the direction of flow would be expected. It is also possible, in terms of this theory, to conceive of diurnal variations in the rate of flow, and even of diurnal reversals in the direction of flow.

In favor of this hypothesis are the facts that it is based upon sound physical principles and that the structure and properties of mature sieve elements seem better adapted to the operation of such a mechanism than to others that have been proposed.

Almost the only tangible evidence in support of a mass-flow mechanism, however, is that sap, usually with an appreciable sugar content, will often exude from a cut made into the phloem of a stem. This has been shown to occur both from many woody (Münch, 1930; Dixon, 1933; Huber, 1941) and many herbaceous stems (Crafts, 1936, 1939a). The latter investigator, for example, has shown that a continued exudation of phloem sap occurs from stems of squash for periods of at least 24 hr. Because the exudate rapidly coagulates in contact with air, thus plugging the phloem, the flow is maintained only if a fresh cut is made at frequent intervals. Exudation occurs from the sieve elements (Crafts, 1939b) and takes place at rates varying from 0.01 to 0.1 cc. per minute. These observations suggest the occurrence of a mass flow under pressure in the phloem elements of intact stems. Some investigators have considered such exudations to be abnormal flows resulting from cutting open the phloem system, but it seems difficult to apply this interpretation to some of Crafts' results. In one of his experiments the sap exuded in 24 hr. was equivalent to the total phloem volume in 189.9 cm. of stem. Furthermore, phloem exudation still occurred in stems which were distinctly wilted, indicating it to be unlikely that the flow of sap from the phloem could result from pressure exerted by adjacent cells as has sometimes been suggested. Such a flow of exudate, representing sieve-tube contents of many centimeters of a stem, indicates that the sieve elements must be permeable to the constituents of the exudate.

The exudate from phloem is, however, often chemically unlike the contents of the storage tissues into which transport is occurring. The proportion of nitrogenous compounds in the phloem exudate of cucurbit stems, for example, is much higher than the proportion of nitrogenous compounds in the fruits of the same plant (Crafts and Lorenz, 1944b). A possible explanation of this discrepancy is that the abnormally high rates of flow which occur through sieve tubes when the phloem is cut into may result in tearing free certain loosely held nitrogenous compounds which are present in sieve elements as a result of the maturation process (Crafts, 1951).

Bennett (1940) and others have shown that translocation of certain viruses through the phloem is closely correlated with the translocation of foods. Translocation of certain chemicals such as 2,4-D (dichlorophenoxyacetic acid) which exert hormone-like effects on plants (Chap. XXVIII) also seems to be closely correlated with the movement of foods (Mitchell and Brown, 1946; Weintraub and Brown, 1950). This also appears to be true of certain vitamins (Chap. XXVIII) and "florigen" (Chap. XXXII). Although these facts have been cited as supporting the concept that a mass flow of solution occurs through the sieve elements, they are actually amenable to alternative and equally plausible interpretations.

There are a number of serious objections to the mass-flow hypothesis. (1) Resistance to a mass flow of solution through the end walls and cytoplasmic strands of the numerous sieve plates would undoubtedly be very great, and there is considerable doubt if turgor pressures of sufficient magnitude can develop to cause a mass flow over the distances which solutes are translocated in many plants. (2) This hypothesis requires that the supplying cells have a higher turgor pressure than the receiving cells. Measurements by some investigators (Curtis and Scofield, 1933; Tingley, 1944) indicate that this is not always true, and movement of solutes in the phloem appears to occur in the direction opposite to that required by the hypothesis. For various reasons that cannot be discussed in detail, measurements of the concentrations or osmotic pressures of different tissues may not accurately reflect the conditions affecting movement of solutes which prevail in those tissues. Hence there is some uncertainty as to just how serious an argument against the mass flow theory these findings are. (3) The mass-flow hypothesis accounts for the translocation through phloem in only one direction at a time, although there is some evidence that movement of solutes in phloem may take place both upward and downward simultaneously. (4) The calculated rates of movement of a solution through the phloem, discussed earlier, seem too great to be accounted for by such a mechanism. (5) The retarding effects of low temperatures and oxygen deficiency on translocation, discussed later, suggest an active participation of the cytoplasm in the transport of solutes, whereas the mass flow theory relegates the cytoplasm of the sieve elements to a relatively passive role. Proponents of the mass-flow theory, however, consider that the retarding effects of these conditions upon solute translocation may result from a lowering effect which they exert on the permeability of the cytoplasm.

The Streaming of Protoplasm Theory.—De Vries (1885) and other nineteenth century investigators postulated that streaming of the protoplasm in the cells of the phloem might explain the relatively rapid rate of transport of solutes. More recently this theory has been supported by Curtis (1935). The basic assumption is that rotational streaming of the protoplasm occurs in the sieve-tube elements, and that solute molecules, caught in the protoplasmic matrix, are carried by this protoplasmic movement from one end of the element to the other. The molecules are usually assumed to pass from one sieve-tube element to the next by diffusion, presumably largely through the cytoplasmic strands in the sieve plates. Diffusion over short distances can occur very rapidly even if the molecules are moving along a gradient which is not very steep. Some advocates of this theory have been postulated that streaming protoplasm may be continuous from sieve-tube element to sieve-tube element through the communicating pores. This theory would account for simultaneous movement of solutes in both upward and downward directions in the same sieve tube.

About the only positive evidence which can be cited in favor of this theory is that solute translocation through phloem is checked by conditions which are known to retard or inhibit protoplasmic streaming. Exposure of stems or petioles to temperatures of 15°C. or lower has been found by several investigators (Curtis and Herty, 1936; Hewitt and Curtis, 1948; Swanson and Böhning, 1951) to retard the rate of translocation of carbohydrates as compared with their rate of translocation at 20°-30°C. Oxygen deficiency in stem tissues has also been shown to retard translocation through them (Curtis, 1929; Mason and Phillis, 1936).

Shortage of oxygen would rarely be a factor influencing translocation of solutes through aerial organs of plants under natural conditions. Deficiency of oxygen in soils is not uncommon, however, and translocation of solutes through roots and underground stems is probably affected when such a condition obtains.

The effects of low temperatures and oxygen deficiency on solute translocation are consistent with the protoplasmic streaming theory but are not proof of its validity. Most metabolic activities of cells are retarded by exposure to such conditions, and the mechanism whereby they influence solute translocation may be a very different one from that envisaged by the streaming of protoplasm theory.

A serious argument against the protoplasmic streaming theory is that, although streaming of cytoplasm is usual in young sieve elements, many careful studies have failed to reveal its occurrence in mature elements. Unless it is assumed that most translocation in the phloem takes place in young elements, a postulation which ignores much anatomical and cytological evidence to the contrary, existence of the very mechanism upon which this theory is predicated seems improbable.

Another weakness of the protoplasmic streaming theory is the inadequacy of known rates of streaming to account for known rates of solute transfer through the phloem. Visible streaming of the larger granules in the cytoplasm occurs at rates up to about 15 cm. per hr. at temperatures of 20°-25°C., and the smaller granules appear to move several times faster than this. Calculations indicate, however, that these rates are inadequate by a considerable factor to account for the rates at which solutes sometimes move through phloem. While it seems impossible, therefore, that protoplasmic streaming in the usual sense of the word could account for known rates of solute transport, the possibility remains that streaming of cytoplasmic films or layers which are below the usual range of microscopic visibility might occur at rates which are sufficient to account for known rates of solute translocation.

Activated Diffusion Hypothesis.—This theory, first suggested by Mason and Phillis (1936) postulates that the protoplasm of the sieve elements is in some manner capable of hastening the diffusion of solutes either by "activating" the diffusing molecules, or by decreasing the resistance of the protoplasm to their diffusion. Beyond the fact that either of these modes of activation would require respiratory energy, no clear picture of how such a mechanism could work has been presented.

Polar Translocation.—As discussed in the next chapter, movement of auxins (one kind of plant hormone) through certain tissues is a *polar* phenomenon, *i.e.*, occurs in only one direction. Polar translocation seems not to be confined to the auxins, but is evident at certain stages in the translocation of carbohydrates in at least some kinds of plants. Leonard (1939) showed that sugars would move out of the blades of mature leaves of sugar beet in the dark into the petiole until the blade was depleted. This occurred in both attached and detached leaves. Reverse movement from the petiole into a mature blade already depleted of sugars would not occur; i.e., the movement was unidirectional or polar. Such polar movement did not occur in young leaves or in etiolated leaves. The polar movement was believed by this investigator to be localized in leaf parenchyma cells bordering sieve tubes. Further polar movement of sucrose apparently occurs in the roots of the sugar beet. Apparently the storage parenchyma cells of the root can accumulate sucrose relative to its concentration in the above ground parts. Loomis (1945) presents evidence for similar polar movements of sucrose through certain tissues of corn. The facts of polar movement of solutes must be taken into account in formulating any adequate explanation of the overall mechanism of solute translocation in plants.

SUGGESTED FOR COLLATERAL READING

Curtis, O. F. *The Translocation of Solutes in Plants.* McGraw-Hill Book Co., Inc. New York. 1935.

Curtis, O. F., and D. G. Clark. *An Introduction to Plant Physiology.* McGraw-Hill Book Co., Inc. New York. 1950.

Eames, A. J., and L. H. MacDaniels. *An Introduction to Plant Anatomy.* 2nd Ed. McGraw-Hill Book Co., Inc. New York. 1947.

Münch, E. *Die Stoffbewegungen in der Pflanze.* Gustav Fischer. Jena. 1930.

SELECTED BIBLIOGRAPHY

Anderssen, F. G. Some seasonal changes in the tracheal sap of pear and apricot trees. *Plant Physiol.* **4**: 459-476. 1929.

Auchter, E. C. Is there normally a cross transfer of foods, water and mineral nutrients in woody plants? *Md. Agric. Expt. Sta. Bull. No. 257.* 33-62. 1923.

Bennett, C. W. The relation of viruses to plant tissues. *Bot. Rev.* **6**: 427-473. 1940.

Biddulph, O. Diurnal migration of injected radiophosphorus from bean leaves. *Amer. Jour. Bot.* **28**: 348-352. 1941.

Biddulph, O., and Jane Markle. Translocation of radioactive phosphorus in the phloem of the cotton plant. *Amer. Jour. Bot.* **31**: 65-70. 1944.

Bonner, J. Accumulation of various substances in girdled stem of tomato plants. *Amer. Jour. Bot.* **31**: 551-555. 1944.

Caldwell, J. Studies in translocation. II. The movement of food materials in plants. *New Phytol.* **29**: 27-43. 1930.

Chen, S. L. Simultaneous movement of P^{32} and C^{14} in opposite directions in phloem tissue. *Amer. Jour. Bot.* **38**: 203-211. 1951.

Clements, H. F. Movement of organic solutes in the sausage tree, *Kigelia africana. Plant Physiol.* **15**: 689-700. 1940.

Clements, H. F., and C. J. Engard. Upward movement of inorganic solutes as affected by a girdle. *Plant Physiol.* **13**: 103-122. 1938.

Colwell, R. N. The use of radioactive phosphorus in translocation studies. *Amer. Jour. Bot.* **29**: 798-807. 1942.

Crafts, A. S. Movement of organic materials in plants. *Plant Physiol.* **6**: 1-41. 1931.

Crafts, A. S. Phloem anatomy, exudation, and transport of organic nutrients in cucurbits. *Plant Physiol.* **7**: 183-225. 1932.

Crafts, A. S. Sieve-tube structure and translocation in the potato. *Plant Physiol.* **8**: 81-104. 1933.

Crafts, A. S. Further studies on exudation in cucurbits. *Plant Physiol.* **11**: 63-79. 1936.

Crafts, A. S. Translocation in plants. *Plant Physiol.* **13**: 791-814. 1938.

Crafts, A. S. The relation between structure and function of the phloem. *Amer. Jour. Bot.* **26**: 172-177. 1939a.

Crafts, A. S. The protoplasmic properties of sieve tubes. *Protoplasma* **33**: 389-398. 1939b.

Crafts, A. S. Movement of viruses, auxins, and chemical indicators in plants. *Bot. Rev.* **5**: 471-504. 1939c.

Crafts, A. S. Movement of assimilates, viruses, growth regulators, and chemical indicators in plants. *Bot. Rev.* **17**: 203-284. 1951.

Crafts, A. S., and O. A. Lorenz. Fruit growth and food transport in cucurbits. *Plant Physiol.* **19**: 131-138. 1944a.

Crafts, A. S., and O. A. Lorenz. Composition of fruits and phloem exudate of cucurbits. *Plant Physiol.* **19**: 326-337. 1944b.

Curtis, O. F. Studies on the tissues concerned in the transfer of solutes in plants. The effect on the upward transfer of solutes of cutting the xylem as compared with that of cutting the phloem. *Ann. Bot.* **39**: 573-585. 1925.

Curtis, O. F. Studies on solute translocation in plants. Experiments indicating that translocation is dependent on the activity of living cells. *Amer. Jour. Bot.* **16**: 154-168. 1929.

Curtis, O. F., and S. Dorothea Herty. The effect of temperature on translocation from leaves. *Amer. Jour. Bot.* **23**: 528-532. 1936.

Curtis, O. F., and H. T. Scofield. A comparison of osmotic concentrations of supplying and receiving tissues and its bearing on the Münch hypothesis of the translocation mechanism. *Amer. Jour. Bot.* **20**: 502-512. 1933.

Curtis, O. F., Jr. Diurnal translocation of carbohydrates into date fruits. *Amer. Jour. Bot.* **34**: 388-391. 1947.

Deleano, N. T. The return of nitrogenous substances from the leaves and their accumulation in the stem and roots. *Beitr. Biol. Pflanzen* **24**: 19-49. 1936.

Denny, F. E. Changes in leaves during the period preceding frost. *Contr. Boyce Thompson Inst.* **5**: 297-312. 1933.

De Vries, H. Über die Bedeutung der Circulation und der Rotation des Protoplasmas für den Stofftransport in der Pflanze. *Bot. Zeit.* **43**: 1-6; 18-26. 1885.

Dixon, H. H. Bast sap. *Sci. Proc. Roy. Dublin Soc.* **20**: 487-494. 1933.

Eaton, F. M., and H. E. Joham. Sugar movement to roots, mineral uptake, and the growth cycle of the cotton plant. *Plant Physiol.* **19**: 507-518. 1944.

Esau, Katherine. Development and structure of the phloem tissue. *Bot. Rev.* **5**: 373-432. 1939, **16**: 67-114. 1950.

Gustafson, F. G. Upward transport of minerals through the phloem of stems. *Science* **90**: 306-307. 1939.

Hewitt, S. P., and O. F. Curtis. The effect of temperature on loss of dry matter and carbohydrate from leaves by respiration and translocation. *Amer. Jour. Bot.* **35**: 746-755. 1948.

Huber, B. Gesichertes und Problematisches in der Wanderung der Assimilate. *Ber. Deutsch. Bot. Ges.* **59**: 181-194. 1941.

Leonard, O. A. Translocation of carbohydrates in the sugar beet. *Plant Physiol.* **14**: 55-74. 1939.

Loomis, W. E. Translocation of carbohydrates in maize. *Science* **101**: 398-400. 1945.

MacDaniels, L. H., and O. F. Curtis. The effect of spiral ringing on solute translocation and the structure of the regenerated tissues of the apple. *Cornell Univ. Agric. Expt. Sta. Mem. 133.* 1930.

Mason, T. G., and E. J. Maskell. Studies on the transport of carbohydrates in the cotton plant. I. A study of diurnal variation in the carbohydrates of leaf, bark, and wood, and of the effects of ringing. *Ann. Bot.* **42**: 189-253. 1928.

Mason, T. G., and E. Phillis. Further studies on transport in the cotton plant. V. Oxygen supply and the activation of diffusion. *Ann. Bot.* **50**: 455-499. 1936.

Mason, T. G., and E. Phillis. Concerning the upward movement of soil solutes. *Ann. Bot.* **4**: 765-771. 1940.

Mason, T. G., and E. Phillis. Some comments on the mechanism of phloem transport. *Plant Physiol.* **16**: 399-404. 1941.

Mason, T. G., and E. Phillis. On diurnal variations in the mineral content of the leaf of the cotton plant. *Ann. Bot.* **6**: 437-442. 1942.

McMurtrey, P. E., Jr. Cross transfer of mineral nutrients in the tobacco plant. *Jour. Agric. Res.* **55**: 475-482. 1937.

Mitchell, J. W., and J. W. Brown. Movement of 2,4-dichlorophenoxyacetic acid stimulus and its relation to the translocation of organic food materials in plants. *Bot. Gaz.* **107**: 393-407. 1946.

Münch, E. Versuche über den Saftkreislauf. *Ber. Deutsch. Bot. Ges.* **45**: 340-356. 1927.

Palmquist, E. M. The simultaneous movement of carbohydrates and fluorescein in opposite directions in the phloem. *Amer. Jour. Bot.* **25**: 97-105. 1938.

Penston, N. L. Studies of the physiological importance of the mineral elements in plants. VIII. The variation in potassium content of potato leaves during the day. *New Phytol.* **34**: 296-309. 1935.

Phillis, E., and T. G. Mason. Further studies on transport in the cotton plant. VI. Interchange between the tissues of the corolla. *Ann. Bot.* **50**: 679-697. 1936.

Phillis, E., and T. G. Mason. The effect of ringing on the upward movement of solutes from the roots. *Ann. Bot.* **4**: 635-644. 1940.

Rabideau, G. S., and G. O. Burr. The use of the C^{13} isotope as a tracer for transport studies in plants. *Amer. Jour. Bot.* **32**: 349-356. 1945.

Stout, P. R., and D. R. Hoagland. Upward and lateral movement of salt in certain plants as indicated by radioactive isotopes of potassium, sodium and phosphorus absorbed by roots. *Amer. Jour. Bot.* **26**: 320-324. 1939.

Swanson, C. A., and R. H. Böhning. The effect of petiole temperature on the translocation of carbohydrates from bean leaves. *Plant Physiol.* **26:** 557-564. 1951.

Tingley, Mary A. Concentration gradients in plant exudates with reference to the mechanism of translocation. *Amer. Jour. Bot.* **31:** 30-38. 1944.

Weintraub, R. L., and J. W. Brown. Translocation of exogenous growth-regulators in the bean seedling. *Plant Physiol.* **25:** 140-149. 1950.

Went, F. W. Plant growth under controlled conditions. III. Correlation between various physiological processes and growth in the tomato plant. *Amer. Jour. Bot.* **31:** 597-618. 1944.

DISCUSSION QUESTIONS

1. Why does a tree which has been ringed to the xylem die eventually, but not immediately?

2. Occasionally a tree which has been ringed to the xylem has been found to live for many years after ringing. What are some possible explanations?

3. When a tree is ringed to the xylem, buds below the ring often begin to develop almost immediately. What are some possible explanations?

4. How would you determine from how far back in the stem system of a tree the food used by terminal buds in their spring development comes?

5. How would you demonstrate whether the translocation of foods away from the leaves occurs more rapidly in the daytime or at night?

6. Why does ringing a stem to the xylem, no matter how carefully it is done, usually result in a decrease in the rate of transpiration from leaves attached above the ring?

7. Measurements of the rate of apparent photosynthesis in a given plant by the dry weight method showed it to be 1.5 g. hexose per meter^2 per hr.; measurements by the carbon dioxide utilization method during the same period showed it to be 1.8 g. hexose per meter^2 per hr. Assuming that the methods are equally accurate, what was the rate of translocation of hexose out of the leaves?

8. Pioneers in certain middle western states made it a rule to ring trees which they wished to kill about August 1. Is there any scientific justification for this date?

9. Measurements sometimes show that the nitrogen content of leaves, expressed as a percentage of their fresh weight, is greater in the daytime than at night. Does this necessarily indicate that nitrogen compounds are translocated out of the leaves at night? Explain.

10. Cut stumps of certain species of tree on which there are no sprouts have sometimes been found to remain alive for years. What are some possible explanations?

XXVIII

PLANT HORMONES

Among the substances which markedly influence the reactions and metabolism of plants are those internally synthesized compounds called *hormones*. In general, the term "hormone" is used to designate certain organic compounds which exert important regulatory effects upon the metabolism of an organism when present in only minute quantities. In the animal body it is generally considered that a further characteristic of a hormone is that it exerts its effects at a site remote from the locus of its synthesis. Adrenalin, for example, secreted in higher animals by the adrenal gland, has pronounced effects upon the heart and vascular system. Many, but not all, plant hormones similarly exert their effects in cells at some distance from those in which they are synthesized, after translocation from the latter to the former. Included among the plant hormones are certain substances usually classified as vitamins in considerations of animal physiology. In the higher plants those vitamins which are essential exhibit essentially the same general type of behavior as hormones and may be regarded as falling into the same general category of substances.

In addition to the naturally occurring hormones in plants, a number of organic compounds are known which, when introduced into plants in relatively small quantities, induce effects which are similar to, and often apparently identical with, those induced by naturally occurring hormones. By an extension of the original concept, such substances are also often called plant hormones, although the more rigorous definition of the term would restrict it to naturally occurring compounds.

Other terms commonly used to designate plant hormones are *phytohormones, growth hormones, growth substances,* and *growth regulators* (a term which includes both *growth activators* and *growth inhibitors*).

555

Relation of Auxins to Growth of the Oat Coleoptile.—The *auxins* have been the most comprehensively investigated group of plant hormones.

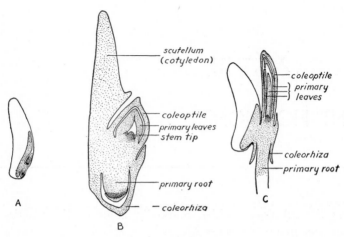

Fɪɢ. 131. Oats (*Avena sativa*). (*A*) Longitudinal section through grain, showing location of embryo. (*B*) Longitudinal section through embryo. (*C*) Early stage in germination, showing emergence of coleoptile. Redrawn with modifications from Avery (1930).

Their action was first clearly demonstrated in the leaf sheath or *coleoptile* of the oat plant (*Avena sativa*). This is a tubular, leaf-like structure, closed at the top, which is the first part of the plant to emerge from the soil (Fig. 131). Similar coleoptiles develop during early seedling growth of other members of the grass family. The coleoptile encloses the initial leaf and is eventually pierced at the tip as a result of the growth of this leaf, soon after which all growth in length of the coleoptile ceases. Oat coleoptiles are approximately 1.5 mm. in diameter, and when illuminated seldom attain lengths of more than 2 cm. In the dark they may attain heights ranging up to 6 cm. Cell divisions cease relatively early in the life history of an oat coleoptile, and during approximately

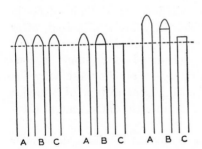

Fɪɢ. 132. Effect of removal of tip on elongation of oat coleoptile. (*A*) Check, (*B*) tip severed and replaced, (*C*) tip removed. The effects of the treatments are shown by differences in increase in length of coleoptiles at right.

the last three-fourths of its growth period all increase in its length results from cell elongation (Avery and Burkholder, 1936).

If the tip of a coleoptile is removed by a clean cut made several milli-meters below the apex, the rate of elongation of the stump is immediately retarded (Söding, 1925). If, however, the cut-off tip of the coleoptile or a similar tip from another coleoptile is affixed on the stump, its elongation will be resumed, and may nearly regain the original rate (Fig. 132). Re-tipping the coleoptile with a short segment cut out of another coleoptile somewhat below the apex results in little or no increase in elongation rate. Such experiments indicate that the elongation of a coleoptile, which occurs in the more basal regions, is maintained only under the influence of some sort of a "stimulus" originating in the tip, whence it is transmitted basi-petally (apex to base) through the coleoptile.

Went (1928, 1935) placed the cut-off tips of oat coleoptiles on a thin layer of 3 per cent agar and after 1 hr. removed them and sliced the agar into a number of equal-sized small blocks (Fig. 133). If one of these blocks was placed upon the stump of a detipped coleoptile, the rate of elongation was accelerated just as if the stump had been capped with a

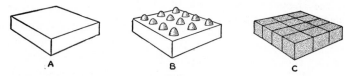

FIG. 133. Diagram illustrating stages in the collection of auxin in agar from coleoptile tips.

fresh coleoptile tip. On the other hand, retipping a coleoptile with a block of pure agar had no appreciable accelerating effect on elongation. It seems evident from these results that some substance or substances were trans-ported out of the cut-off tip into the agar block, and subsequently out of the block into the coleoptile stump, whence they were translocated down-ward to the elongating region of the coleoptile (Fig. 134). The substances which induce such a reaction now are classed as auxins.

Many other plant organs such as stems, petioles, flowerstalks, and coleoptiles of other species behave similarly upon removal of the apical region. Elongation is stopped or retarded by such a treatment but will be resumed if the excised apex of the organ is carefully relocated on the cut surface of the stump.

Biological Tests for Auxins.—Auxins are known to be of widespread distribution in plants. They occur in such small quantities, however, that detection of their presence in an organic material by chemical methods is usually impossible. Recourse is had, therefore, to sensitive biological tests in order to demonstrate the presence of these substances. Several such tests have been used rather widely.

The oat coleoptile test has been the most extensively employed method of determining the relative quantitics of auxins present in plant tissues or other materials. If an agar block containing auxin from one source or another is affixed one-sidedly on a detipped oat coleop-tile, elongation is found to be more rapid on the side of the coleoptile below the portion of the tip on which the block is perched, resulting in curvature of the coleoptile (Fig. 135). Translocation of the hormone is almost strictly longitudinal, the elongating cells on the side of the coleoptile under the block receiving much more auxin than cells on the opposite side, with a corresponding differential ef-fect on growth. When the block

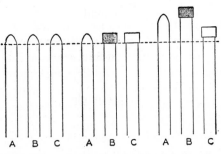

FIG. 134.   Effect of agar blocks contain-ing auxin on elongation of oat coleoptiles. (A) Check, (B) block containing auxin placed on decapitated tip, (C) block of pure agar placed on decapitated tip. The effects of the treatments are shown by relative increases in length of coleoptiles at right.

is centered on the coleoptile stump, as in the experiment described in the preceding section, all sides of the coleoptile receive approximately equal quantities of auxin, and growth proceeds in a vertical direction.

Furthermore, it has been found that the curvature resulting from the eccentric attachment of agar blocks to detipped oat coleoptiles is propor-tional, within the range of about 0 to 20 degrees, to the concentration of

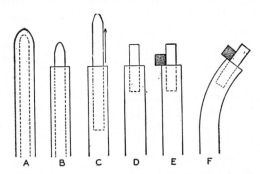

FIG. 135.   Diagram of method of determining auxin content of agar block quan-titatively. (A) Intact coleoptile enclosing primary leaf, (B) tip of coleoptile removed, (C) primary leaf pulled loose so its elongation will not dislocate agar block, (D) tip of primary leaf cut off, (E) agar block affixed unilaterally to coleoptile tip, (F) curvature resulting from movement of auxin into side of coleoptile below agar block. Redrawn from Went (1935).

the auxin in the agar block. It is this proportionality between hormone concentration and curvature that makes possible the use of oat coleoptiles as living test objects in the quantitative estimation of the auxin content of plant tissues or other materials (Went, 1928).

Quantitative measurements of auxins by the oat coleoptile technique must be carried out under carefully standardized conditions. The oat seedlings (usually from a genetically uniform variety) are grown in a dark room at a temperature of 25°C. and a relative humidity of 90 per cent. All manipulations are performed under phototropically inactive orange or red light (Chap. XXXVI). The coleoptiles are used when about 2.5 to 4 cm. in length. The extreme tip of the coleoptile is first cut off, and after 3 hr. the topmost 4 mm. of the stump is removed. For reasons which cannot be considered in a brief discussion, the coleoptiles are more sensitive when this method of double decapitation is employed than when the tip is cut off in one operation. The primary leaf, which is enclosed by the coleoptile, is then pulled loose so it will not interfere with the determination by its continued growth. If guttation water exudes at the cut surface it is carefully blotted off. An agar block (2 x 2 x 1 mm. is a commonly used size), containing the substance to be tested, is then affixed unilaterally to the cut tip. After a standard length of time (usually 90 min.), the resulting degree of curvature of the coleoptile is determined. The greater the degree of curvature, within limits, the greater the hormone concentration in the agar block.

Various methods of applying the material to be tested for auxins to detipped coleoptiles have been employed. Sometimes small plant organs or pieces of plant organs are affixed directly to the cut surface of the coleoptile. More commonly plant tissues are placed in contact with 3 per cent agar into which the hormone will move. The tissue is generally left in contact with the agar for about 2 hr. The agar is then cut into blocks of standard size each of which is then affixed unilaterally to a detipped coleoptile. The effects of pure chemicals or extracts can be tested by first dispersing them in agar, and then, after solidification, determining the influence of standard sized blocks of this agar on curvature of the coleoptiles. Or agar blocks can be soaked in a solution of the substances and then used in the coleoptile test for auxins.

Another commonly used biological test for auxins is to immerse sections of young oat coleoptiles in the solution to be tested and measure their increase in length over a certain period of time (commonly 6-24 hr.) as compared with increase in length of similar sections immersed in water or an auxin-free solution.

Chemical Constitution of the Naturally-occurring Auxins.—Kögl *et al.* (1934) isolated from biological sources three chemically pure crystalline substances which give the reactions of auxins when tested by the oat cole-optile technique. These substances have been called auxin a ($C_{18}H_{32}O_5$), auxin b ($C_{18}H_{30}O_4$), and heteroauxin ($C_{10}H_9O_2N$). The chemical names of these substances are auxentriolic acid, auxenolonic acid, and indole-3-acetic acid, respectively. Auxin a was isolated from urine, and both auxins a and b from malt and various vegetable oils. Indoleacetic acid was isolated from urine and from certain yeasts and molds. At one time it was considered possible that indoleacetic acid did not occur in the tissues of higher plants, but more recently it has been isolated from corn grains (Haagen-Smit et al., 1942, 1946; Berger and Avery, 1944), and there are numerous indications that it occurs in many other tissues of higher plants including oat coleoptiles (Wildman and Bonner, 1948). It seems probable that this will prove to be the principal naturally-occurring auxin.

The Occurrence and Synthesis of Naturally-occurring Auxins in Plants.— Auxins appear to be universally present in plants, and their occurrence has actually been demonstrated in a wide variety of species. Furthermore, the auxins are nonspecific in their action, i.e., the same auxin, chemically speaking, which influences growth phenomena in one species usually also influences the same or similar phenomena in other species.

Auxins are present in plant cells in several different forms: free auxins, auxin precursors, and bound auxins. Various methods of extracting the "total" auxins (all forms) from plant tissues have been devised and more or less successfully employed (Thimann et al., 1942; Haagen-Smit et al., 1942; Gordon and Wildman, 1943; Avery et al., 1941, 1945; and Gordon, 1946). Other investigators have devised methods which they believe extract only the free auxins from plant tissues (Gustafson, 1941; Van Overbeek et al., 1947; Wildman and Muir, 1949).

Only in the free form is an auxin readily diffusable, and only in this form is it effective in the oat coleoptile tests. Since, however, free auxins may be continuously formed from bound or precursor auxins, considerably more free auxin than originally present may diffuse into agar blocks from plant tissues (Van Overbeek, 1941). In most tissues thus far investigated the auxins present in inactive forms are many times greater than the free auxins present; the latter seldom constituting more than 10 per cent of the potentially available auxins.

The amino acid tryptophane (Chap. XXVI) has been shown to be a precursor of indoleacetic acid in plants (Wildman et al., 1947, and others). Conversion of the former compound into the latter apparently takes place through the intermediate step of indoleacetaldehyde, which is therefore an even more immediate precursor of indoleacetic acid (Larsen, 1949). The transformation of tryptophane to indoleacetic acid is catalyzed by a specific enzyme system which has been found in a number of plant tissues.

The presence of zinc is necessary for tryptophane synthesis, and one of the indirect effects of zinc deficiency is a reduction in the quantity of auxin present (Tsui, 1948). Following are the structural formulas for tryptophane and indoleacetic acid:

Tryptophane

Indoleacetic acid

Many, but not all, of the bound auxins are auxin-protein complexes. Since, by suitable treatments, active auxins can be released from bound auxins, the latter are sometimes referred to as "auxin precursors," although they would not be so regarded in the usual sense of the term.

The auxins naturally present in plants are synthetic products of plant metabolism. The principal centers of auxin synthesis are apical meristematic tissues of aerial organs such as opening buds, young leaves, and flowers or inflorescences on growing flowerstalks. Small quantities of auxins are also synthesized in apical root meristems (Van Overbeek and Bonner, 1938), although much of the auxin present in roots probably comes from aerial organs of the plants. The auxin synthesized in one tissue is frequently translocated to other organs of the plant. The concentration of auxin may vary greatly from one tissue to another; in general auxin is found in greatest concentrations in the tissues in which it is synthesized or stored. Temperature is a factor in auxin synthesis, but the optimum for this process probably is not the same in all plants and tissues. In coleoptile tips the auxin is apparently synthesized from a precursor which is translocated acropetally (base to apex) through the coleoptile from the grain (Skoog, 1937).

Auxins are not only synthesized in plant cells but are also inactivated in them. Inactivation may be brought about in various ways. Among other inactivation agents is a specific enzyme which breaks down indoleacetic acid; this enzyme has been isolated from the epicotyls of etiolated pea seedlings (Tang and Bonner, 1947, 1948). Light inactivation or destruction of auxin is also of widespread occurrence in plants and is discussed more fully in Chap. XXXVI.

The Role of Auxins in Cell Elongation.—Auxins play a role in the elongation phase of growth in many other plant organs similar to that described for the oat coleoptile. It is generally considered that cell elongation occurs only in the presence of auxins, and that with increase in auxin concentration there is an increase in the rate of elongation if no other factors are limiting. The optimum range of concentration for cell elongation varies greatly with different tissues, and relatively high concentrations usually exert an inhibiting effect upon this phase of growth.

If the extreme tip of a maize or lupine root is cut off, its rate of elongation increases, although not greatly (Cholodny, 1926). Replacement of the root tip in maize plants results in a retardation in elongation rate as compared with detipped roots. Furthermore, attachment of coleoptile tips of maize to detipped root tips of the same plant results in a retardation in the elongation rate of the root tip. These results suggest that the same

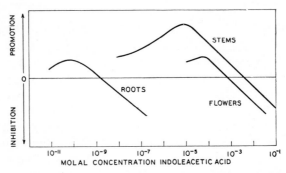

FIG. 136. Relation between auxin (indoleacetic acid) concentration and its promoting or inhibiting effect on the development of certain plant organs. Modified from Leopold and Thimann (1949).

concentrations of auxin which accelerate elongation in coleoptiles and other aerial organs retard elongation in roots.

This supposition has been confirmed by experiments in which the roots of oat seedlings were immersed in pure solutions of auxins. The growth of the roots was found to be retarded in proportion to the concentration of auxin used. However, when roots which contain either no auxin at all, or virtually none, are treated with auxin solutions of very low concentration, acceleration of growth as compared with similar but untreated roots often results.

The apparently contrasting effects of auxins upon elongation of roots and aerial organs may be explained by assuming that roots, buds, and stems all react in a comparable way to auxins (Fig. 136), their growth being inhibited by relatively high, and promoted by relatively low, auxin concentrations. Elongation of roots is favored only at very low concentrations; at all higher concentrations their growth is checked. Stems and coleoptiles show a similar behavior except that the optimum range of concentrations for elongation is much higher than for roots. The same concentrations of auxins which favor stem elongation result in retardation of root elongation. The effect of auxin on bud development is considered in Chap. XXXIII, and its effect on flower initiation in Chap. XXXII. Briefly, therefore, whether an auxin will exert an accelerating or an inhibiting effect upon growth seems to depend in part upon its concentration and in part upon the specific tissue involved.

Shortly after the discovery of the naturally-occurring auxins various investigators showed that certain compounds, not known to occur naturally in plants, induce reactions in plants similar to those evoked by the naturally-occurring auxins. The list of such "synthetic" auxins has become quite extensive (Zimmerman and Hitchcock, 1942; Thompson, et al., 1946). The best known of these substances are α-naphthalene acetic acid, indolebutyric acid, 2,4-dichlorophenoxyacetic acid, and α-naphthoxyacetic acid. Most of these compounds induce curvature of oat coleoptiles when tested by the standard technique, although many of them are not as effective in causing this reaction as the naturally-occurring auxins.

The term "auxin" has been used in different senses by different authorities. Most commonly, however, an auxin is considered to be any organic compound that promotes growth along a longitudinal axis when applied in low concentrations to organs which are initially low in their content of such growth-promoting substances but are under conditions which are otherwise favorable for elongation growth. The phrase "low concentrations" is a somewhat vague one, but in general can be taken to refer to concentrations of less than 10^{-3} molar.

In spite of the apparent diversity of the compounds which act as auxins, certain similarities in molecular structure are common to all of them. These are: a ring system with a side chain containing at least one carbon atom between a terminal carboxyl or potential carboxyl group and the ring, a double bond in the ring adjacent to the side chain, and a definite space relationship between the carboxyl group and the ring system (Koepfli et al., 1938). Cf. the structural formula for indoleacetic acid given earlier.

Translocation of Auxins.—If a block of agar containing auxin is affixed to the morphologically upper end of a segment of oat coleoptile, and a block of pure agar to the lower end, auxin will move into and accumulate in the lower block. The final concentration of auxin in the basally attached block may greatly exceed that in the one affixed to the apex (Fig. 137 A). If the agar block containing auxin is affixed to the morphologically basal end, no translocation of auxin will occur (Fig. 137 B). Translocation of auxin in oat coleoptiles apparently takes place through the parenchyma tissues. The results of such experiments show that transport of auxin in the oat coleoptile is *polar*, *i.e.*, occurs only basipetally, and that it can occur against a concentration gradient since the auxin accumulates in the lower block (Van der Weij, 1934; Went and White, 1939).

There is evidence that a similar basipetal translocation of auxin, either naturally-occurring or introduced, occurs in many other plant tissues or organs. Among these are coleoptiles of other species than oat, the veins and petioles of leaves, hypocotyls, herbaceous stems, and woody stems (Oserkowsky, 1942). In such organs the polarized downward movement occurs in parenchyma or phloem tissues. In roots, on the other hand,

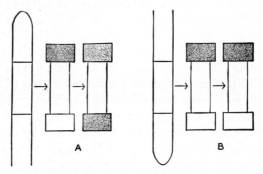

FIG. 137.   Diagram to illustrate basipetal movement of auxin. (*A*) Agar block containing auxin attached to apical end of segment of oat coleoptile. (*B*) Agar block containing auxin attached to basal end of segment of oat coleoptile. Redrawn from Went (1935).

movement of auxins appears to be nonpolar and there are undoubtedly other tissues in which this is also true.

The mechanism of the polar movement of auxins is unknown. Etherization stops the transport of auxin, except insofar as it can be accounted for by diffusion, and destroys its polarity. This indicates that living cells are involved in the process, but tells nothing of the manner in which they operate. It has been suggested that the polarity in the movement of auxins may result from differences of electrical potential in the tissues, but experiments designed to test this hypothesis have not yielded evidence in its support (Clark, 1938).

Upward translocation of auxins can occur in plants, at least under certain conditions. If an auxin is applied to the soil or to the basal parts of entire plants or to cuttings in adequate concentrations, their absorption and upward movement through the plant can be demonstrated (Hitchcock and Zimmerman, 1935, 1938; Ferri, 1945). Such upward transport apparently takes place only when the auxin molecules pass into the transpiration stream. As soon as the auxin molecules move back into the living tissues of the stem or leaf their polar basipetal movement is resumed (Skoog, 1938).

Role of Auxins in Root Formation.—It has been known for many years that the presence of buds on a cutting favors development of roots when the basal portion of the cutting is introduced into a suitable rooting medium. Developing buds are more effective in promoting root formation than quiescent buds. Leaves, especially if young, also often favor the production of roots on cuttings. These observations suggest that root initiation on cuttings is favored by hor-mones which are synthesized in the buds and young leaves and are subsequently translocated to the basal part of the cutting. Soon after the identification of them as na-turally-occurring auxins it was found that auxin *b* and indoleacetic acid are active in inducing root formation (Kögl, 1935; Thi-mann and Koepfli, 1935). There is good evidence (Chap. XXIX) that other hor-mones besides auxins are also necessary for root formation or at least for their con-tinued development, whether the roots are initiated on other roots, on stems, or on leaves.

The effect of auxins on root *formation* should be clearly distinguished from their effect on root *elongation*. In general, the concentrations required for the former proc-ess are much greater than for the latter.

A number of the "auxins" not known to occur naturally in plants have also been found to be effective in promoting root for-mation in many species (Fig. 138). Exten-

Fig. 138. Root formation on stem of tomato plant result-ing from treatment with lano-lin containing 2 per cent alpha naphthalene acetic acid. Pho-tograph from Zimmerman and Wilcoxon (1935).

sive experiments have been carried out on the suitability of treatments with various auxins as a practical method of aiding in the rooting of cut-tings. Such treatments are not effective with all kinds of plants, but with cuttings of many species they lead to a speeding up of the process of root formation and to the development of a greater number of roots per cut-ting. Hormones do not induce root formation, however, on cuttings of species on which at least some roots do not develop without their appli-cation.

Various techniques are used to introduce hormones into cuttings. For-merly the most favored procedure was to immerse the basal end of the cuttings in a dilute (10-200 p.p.m.) solution of the hormone for periods ranging up to 24 hr. before setting them in the rooting medium. Latterly this method has been largely superseded by two less time-consuming procedures. In one of these the hormone is applied in a dry form, being first mixed with an inert powder such as talc, most commonly in proportions of 500-2000 parts of the hormone to 1,000,000 parts of talc. The basal end of the cutting is first dipped in water, and then in the powder before insertion into the rooting medium. In the "quick dip" method the basal ends of the cuttings are dipped momentarily (for about 5 sec.) into a relatively concentrated solution of the hormone (4,000-10,000 p.p.m. in water or 50 per cent ethyl alcohol) before being set in the cutting bench. Auxins may also be applied to stems or cuttings in lanolin (Fig. 138) or as vapors.

The compounds most commonly employed in all of these methods, either singly or in mixtures, are α-napthaleneacetic acid, napthalene acetamide, and indolebutyric acid. The most effective treatment varies according to species; extensive tabulations of the effects of various compounds and methods of treatment on numerous species are given by Avery and Johnson (1947) and Mitchell and Marth (1947).

Other Effects of Auxins.—One of the most remarkable facts about the auxins is the multiplicity of the growth reactions in which they participate. Only a few of their roles are discussed in this chapter; other important growth phenomena in which they play a part include the development of fruits, abcission of leaves and fruits, activation of cambial cells, apical dominance, flower initiation, geotropism and phototropism. These various roles of the auxins will be discussed in subsequent chapters.

Toxic Effects of Auxins.—Reference has already been made to the inhibitory effect of relatively high concentrations of auxins on the process of cell elongation (Fig. 136). Applications of auxins in relatively high concentrations also result in various kinds of growth malformations in plants such as distortions of leaves, stems and roots, discolorations of leaves, inhibitions of stem or root elongation or flower opening, and the formation of tumors. It should be emphasized that the term "relatively high concentrations" as used in this discussion refers to concentrations which, in absolute terms, are very low, of the general order of magnitude of 1000 p.p.m. In somewhat higher concentrations, but in absolute terms still very low, these compounds often result in death of the plant.

Realization that auxins, when applied in relatively high but actually very low concentrations, exert toxic or lethal effects on plants led to the suggestion that they could be employed for the purpose of killing weeds or other noxious plants. The phenoxyacetic acids (Zimmerman *et al.*,

1942, 1944) have proved especially effective as herbicides. The most widely used of these has been 2,4-dichlorophenoxyacetic acid ("2,4-D"), although numerous other organic compounds with hormone-like effects on plants also show promise as herbicides. The results of tests on the growth-inhibiting activity of over a thousand different organic compounds are listed by Thompson et al. (1946), who also summarize previous work on the chemical control of plant growth. Most of the compounds which they list are not auxins in the usual sense of the word, but all of them may be classified, broadly speaking, as plant hormones or growth regulators.

The effects on plants of 2,4-dichlorophenoxyacetic acid may be taken as an example of the action of an auxin-like herbicide. This compound is readily absorbed from sprays or dusts when applied to leaves. It is quickly translocated to other parts of the plant and affects especially the meristems. The rapid distribution of this compound throughout the plant contributes greatly to its effectiveness as a toxicant. Death results from derangements of metabolism, especially in the meristems.

Different kinds of plants differ markedly in their reactions to applications of 2,4-dichlorophenoxyacetic acid. Cereal grains and most other grasses are less susceptible, for example, than most broad-leaved annuals, and most woody plants are less susceptible than most herbaceous species. This very selectivity of effect is one of the advantages of this compound, and of many similar ones, as herbicides. Broad-leaved weeds can be eliminated from sugar cane fields or from lawns, for example, by application of a spray in the proper concentration and at the proper volume per square foot.

Besides its selectivity of effect, 2,4-dichlorophenoxyacetic acid has certain other advantages when used as a herbicide. The absolute concentrations required are very low. Many plants can be killed, for example, by spraying with an 0.1 per cent solution at the rate of 5 gal. per 1000 ft^2. In the concentrations generally employed this compound is harmless to men and animals. Under most conditions, 2,4-dichlorophenoxyacetic acid disintegrates rapidly in soils. The possibility of detrimental effects on plants which subsequently grow on soils in which this compound was once present thus disappears rapidly. Great care must be exercised, however, in the use of this herbicide, that the spray does not drift to plants other than those being treated. Accidental damage or destruction of valuable plants as a result of careless application has been the chief disadvantage in the use of 2,4-dichlorophenoxyacetic acid as an herbicide.

The differential effects on various species of plants of some of the other compounds used as herbicides is unlike that of 2,4-dichlorophenoxyacetic acid. Isopropylphenylcarbamate, for example, in contrast with 2,4-dichlorophenoxyacetic acid is much more effective in killing certain grasses than broad-leaved annuals (Allard *et al.*, 1946).

It is convenient to mention several other growth inhibitors at this point, although whether or not they would be classed as hormones is a matter of definition. Coumarin favors cell enlargement in such plant tissue as oat coleoptiles and leaf blades at very low concentrations, but checks cell enlargement at all higher concentrations (Thimann and Bonner, 1949; Miller and Meyer, 1951). Similar checking effects upon root elongation have been found for certain coumarin derivatives (Goodwin and Taves, 1950). Another growth inhibitor which has attracted considerable attention is maleic hydrazide (Schoene and Hoffmann, 1949). Applied to plants in relatively low concentrations (about 0.4 per cent) this compound results in a general cessation of growth. At somewhat lower concentrations loss of apical dominance is evident, and axillary buds start to grow soon after treatment. At certain concentrations flowering appears to be largely suppressed without much suppression of vegetative development (Chap. XXXII). Plants of various species seem to be affected in essentially the same way by this compound (Naylor and Davis, 1950).

Mechanism of Auxin Action.—The earlier attempts to elucidate the mechanism of auxin action mostly centered around proposed explanations of the part played by such compounds in cell elongation. Auxins appear to have two main effects in this process: they cause an increase in the plasticity of the wall, and they participate, directly or indirectly, in the reactions whereby additional cellulose molecules are deposited within the wall. With the growing realization, however, of the large number of growth reactions conditioned by auxins, it has become obvious that these compounds must play a role in some pivotal metabolic process. The apparent necessity of specific chemical structure for a compound to act as an auxin, mentioned earlier, also suggests a particular metabolic role. The effect of auxins on cell wall development is, therefore, now generally considered to be, not a direct one, but only one possible end expression of fundamental auxin-conditioned or regulated metabolic processes.

There is considerable evidence that the auxins act primarily in a catalytic or regulatory capacity in some phase of the carbohydrate metabolism of plants. A suggestive finding in this connection is that introduction of auxins into leaves or cuttings induces a marked hydrolysis of starch (Mitchell and Whitehead, 1940; Bausor, 1942). Auxin also appears to participate in some part of the respiratory process (Commoner and Thimann, 1941; Berger *et al.*, 1946), but the exact nature of this relationship has not yet been traced. A significant fact in this connection is that auxins exert their effects only under aerobic conditions.

The discovery by Wildman and Bonner (1947), that certain auxin-protein complexes from spinach leaves possess phosphatase activity, may prove to be a significant one in allocating a specific role to the auxins. Although the question of the metabolic role of the naturally-occurring auxins as yet eludes a definite answer, it seems practically certain that they operate as carriers, coenzymes, or prosthetic groups in some fundamental enzyme system which plays a part in carbohydrate or organic acid metabolism.

The inhibiting as well as the accelerating effects of the auxins must be accounted for in any hypothesis of the mechanism of their action. If we accept the likely assumption that an auxin is active when it operates as the prosthetic group of an enzyme, it is reasonable to postulate that two fundamental properties of its molecules would be: (1) a specific group which reacts with the substrate molecules, and (2) the necessary structural configuration to combine in some manner with the protein portion of the enzyme (Skoog et al., 1942).

Viewed in the light of this hypothesis (which incidentally is also applicable to other enzyme systems), relatively high concentrations of an active auxin may result in inhibitory effects as a result of some of the auxin molecules preempting all free positions on the protein component of the enzyme, while others become chemically attached to substrate molecules. This effectively blocks the reaction which can occur only when the protein and auxin operate as a catalytic team, so that substrate molecules become linked temporarily to the protein through auxin bridges.

Inhibition of auxin-controlled reactions may also result from the presence in the metabolic system of growth-inhibitors with an auxin-like structure (Skoog, 1947) which possess strongly only one of the two properties listed above, and the other one only weakly or not at all. If such a compound possesses only the capacity of combining with the protein, it may act as an inhibitor by occupying positions in the protein complex which would otherwise be taken by more active auxins. On the other hand, if the auxin-like compound possesses only the property of reacting with the substrate, it may block the overall reaction which can only take place if the compound can act as a chemical bridge between the protein and substrate molecules.

Certain compounds, often called *antiauxins*, are known which offset or counteract the usual growth-enhancing effect of auxin in plants. Among these are coumarin (Veldstra and Havinga, 1945) and maleic hydrazide (Leopold and Klein, 1951), both mentioned earlier in this chapter as growth inhibitors. Another antiauxin is *trans*-cinnamic acid (Van Overbeek et al., 1951). The effect of this compound is of especial interest in view of the fact that its isomer *cis*-cinnamic acid has the properties of an auxin.

Other Plant Hormones.—The auxins are only one kind of a number of hormones occurring in plants. Some of the other compounds in this category have been isolated from plant tissues; the existence of others is inferred from the occurrence of various physiological reactions; other such substances doubtless are as yet undiscovered or unsuspected.

Traumatic Acid.—Haberlandt (1921) showed that if freshly cut plant tissue is immediately rinsed with water, very few cell divisions occur in the cells adjacent to the wound. However, if the wounded area is smeared with finely ground tissue of the same species cell division takes place. This result led him to postulate the existence of substances which he called "wound hormones" in injured tissues, which are required if cell division is to be engendered in the cells bordering a wound.

More recently English *et al.* (1939) have succeeded in extracting from bean pods and purifying a compound called traumatic acid which acts like a "wound hormone." This compound has the following formula:

$$HOOC \cdot CH{=}CH \cdot (CH_2)_8 \cdot COOH$$

Traumatic acid induces extensive wound periderm formation in washed disks of potato tuber. It is probable that there are also other "wound hormones" present in plants.

Calines.—Went (1938) has postulated the existence in plants of a group of hormones which he calls the *calines:* (1) rhizocaline, made in the leaves and necessary for root formation; (2) caulocaline, synthesized in roots, but necessary for elongation of stems; and (3) phyllocaline, made or at least stored in cotyledons, and necessary for leaf growth. It is also considered that rhizocaline and caulocaline may be stored in seeds. Most of the evidence for the existence of such hormones in plants is indirect and the effects attributed to these hypothetical hormones may actually turn out to result from the activity of substances already well known to have important influences on the growth or metabolism of plants. Galston and Hand (1949), for example, have obtained evidence that adenine (Chap. XX) has effects on plants analogous to those of the postulated calines. The calines are discussed further in the following chapter.

Hormones of Reproduction.—Several hormones are known or believed to play a role in the reproductive process of plants. Among these are the ubiquitous auxins, the "embryo growth factor," and the postulated "florigen" (Chap. XXXI, Chap. XXXII).

Vitamins.—From the standpoint of human physiology the vitamins constitute a group of specific organic substances which must be supplied in the diet, but which are required in relatively small, often only minute, quantities compared with carbohydrates, fats, and proteins. From the standpoint of living organisms in general, for reasons discussed later, vitamins must be regarded simply as one rather arbitrarily delimited group of growth and metabolism regulators which cannot be sharply distinguished from the hormones.

The principal substances recognized as vitamins in human and animal nutrition are listed in Table 42. Chemically they constitute a very heterogeneous group of compounds. All of the vitamins, or at least their immediate precursors, are synthesized in green plants. The human body, on the other hand, is dependent on sources outside its own metabolism for most essential vitamins and obtains a large proportion of them in green plants used as food. One partial exception is vitamin D which can be synthesized in the human body under irradiation from appropriate precursors which come from foods. Absence or deficiency of any one of the necessary vitamins in the human body results in physiological malfunctioning often evidenced as a specific disease. Some of the vitamin-deficiency diseases of man, such as scurvy, resulting from ascorbic acid deficiency, and beri-beri, resulting from thiamine deficiency, have been known for centuries, although only in comparatively recent years have their causes been recognized. Other higher animals appear to have vitamin requirements very similar to those of man.

The latest addition to the group of B vitamins, not included in Table 42 because its complete chemical formula is not yet known, is vitamin B_{12}. This vitamin is of especial interest because cobalt is a constituent of the molecule. Whether or not this vitamin plays any role in plant metabolism is not known.

Vitamin requirements differ from one kind of living organism to another, but no plant or animal is known for which at least some of them are not essential. The first fundamental question to be answered regarding the vitamin physiology of any organism is: Does the organism require this specific vitamin in its metabolism? Certain of the vitamins appear to be necessary in the metabolism of all plants and animals. This is true of many, if not all, of the vitamins of the so-called B complex. On the other hand, certain vitamins seem to be essential in the metabolism of only certain kinds of organisms.

A second fundamental question to be answered regarding any essential vitamin for a given organism is: Does the organism synthesize this vitamin in quantities adequate to meet its own metabolic requirements? The answer to this question for the human organism is essentially "no" for all of the vitamins known to be necessary. The answer to the corresponding question for green plants is "yes." For bacteria and fungi no categorical answer is possible since the vitamin-synthesizing capacities of such organisms vary greatly from one species to another, and even from one variety of a given species to another.

For many years it has been known that, in the culturing of bacteria or fungi on artificial media, it is necessary to introduce some organic material such as potatoes, peptone, oat or corn meal, yeast extract, dung, or wood into the medium in addition to sugar and other pure chemicals if growth of the organism is to occur. Only in comparatively recent years has it been recognized that these organic materials are sources of essential growth substances, some of which, at least, are identical with the known vitamins.

Direct experimentation has demonstrated that many bacteria and fungi cannot synthesize certain of the vitamins which they require, or at least cannot synthesize them in sufficient quantities to permit optimum growth even when all other growth conditions are favorable. If the substrate on which they are growing is deficient or lacking in one or more of the necessary vitamins, development of the organism will be retarded and may cease entirely. By systematic addition of the various vitamins

TABLE 42—THE VITAMINS

"Alphabetical" Designation	Name	Molecular Formula
Vitamin A	Hydrolytic product of carotene	$C_{20}H_{29}OH$
Vitamin B (Complex)	Thiamine chloride hydrochloride (B_1)	$C_{12}H_{18}N_4SOCl_2$
	Riboflavin (B_2, vitamin G)	$C_{17}H_{20}N_4O_6$
	Nicotinic acid (niacin)	$C_5H_4N \cdot COOH$
	Pyridoxine (B_6)	$C_8H_{11}NO_3$
	Pantothenic acid	$C_9H_{17}NO_5$
	Inositol	$C_6H_{12}O_6$
	Biotin (vitamin H)	$C_{10}H_{16}O_3N_2S$
	Folic acid	$C_{19}H_{19}N_7O_6$
	p-amino benzoic acid	$NH_2C_6H_4COOH$
Vitamin C	Ascorbic acid	$C_6H_8O_6$
Vitamin D	Derivatives of ergosterol, cholesterol, and other sterols	$C_{28}H_{43}OH$ (activated dehydrocholesterol)
Vitamin E	α-tocopherol (and others)	$C_{29}H_{50}O_2$
Vitamin K	K_1: 2-methyl, 3 phytyl, 1,4-naphthoquinone K_2: 2-methyl, 3-difarnesyl, 1,4-naphthoquinone	$C_{31}H_{46}O_2$

to a vitamin-free medium on which an organism is cultured it is possible to ascertain which of the essential vitamins that organism must obtain from its substrate.

It is probable that the vitamin requirements of all fungi are very similar; but different species differ greatly in their vitamin-synthesizing capacity. Many species, for example, cannot synthesize thiamine in adequate quantities (Robbins and Ma, 1943). Hence, unless this compound is present in the substrate, the fungus will be retarded in development as a result of the thiamine deficiency. Incapacity to synthesize adequate quantities of biotin, pyridoxine, pantothenic acid, inositol, and nicotinic acid have also been demonstrated for many species of the fungi (Burkholder and Moyer, 1943).

It has already been mentioned that all of the known vitamins, or at least their immediate precursors, are synthesized in higher green plants. Whether or not all such compounds are essential in the metabolism of green plants is an open question. The evidence regarding this point must of necessity be somewhat indirect. There are no good reasons, however, for believing this to be true of vitamins A, D, E, and K. On the other hand, thiamine, nicotinic acid, riboflavin and pyridoxine are known to be constituents of the prosthetic groups or coenzymes of important enzymes found in vascular green plants (Chap. XXII, Chap. XXVI) and are probably necessary in the metabolism of all living cells in such organisms. It is highly probable that some, and perhaps all, of the other B vitamins are required by green plants (Bonner and Bonner, 1948), and ascorbic acid may also be an essential green plant vitamin (Carroll, 1943). The structural formulas for several of the B vitamins known to be indispensable in plant metabolism are given in Table 43; that for ascorbic acid is given in Chap. XXII.

Although the higher green plants appear to be self-sufficing with regard to necessary vitamins, and such compounds are widely distributed through the organs of such plants, this does not necessarily mean that all cells of all tissues synthesize these compounds in adequate quantities. Some parts of a plant are dependent upon other parts for certain necessary vitamins. Experiments on excised roots of certain plants growing in sterile culture (Chap. XXIX) show, for example, that thiamine must be added to the culture medium if normal growth is to continue. Obviously roots, at least of some species, do not synthesize enough thiamine to meet their own needs, and intact plants are presumably dependent upon downward translocation of this substance from leaves in which it is synthesized. Such downward translocation of thiamine, and also of pantothenic acid and pyridoxine, has been demonstrated in the tomato (Bonner, 1944). This is probably also true of nicotinic acid. Upward translocation of thiamine from older to younger leaves also occurs. There is also evidence for a similar downward translocation of ascorbic acid in plants (Reid and Weintraub, 1939). On the other hand, roots of at least some species appear to synthesize certain other vitamins in such quantities as not to be dependent upon the tops for a supply of these compounds (Chap. XXIX).

The growing embryo and endosperm in the developing seeds of at least some kinds of plants appear, like roots, to be dependent upon transloca-tion from other parts of the plant for necessary thiamine. In wheat, for

TABLE 43—STRUCTURAL FORMULAS OF CERTAIN VITAMINS

Thiamine chloride hydrochloride (B₁)

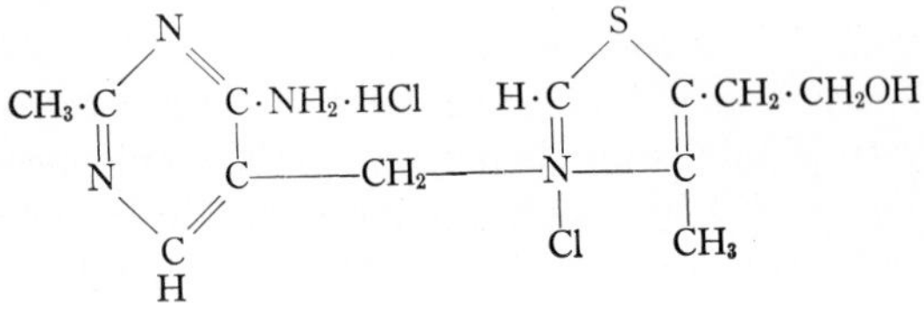

Riboflavin (B₂)

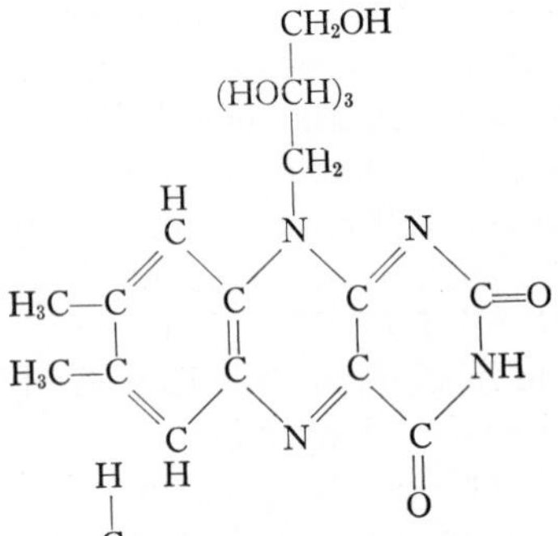

Nicotinic acid (Niacin)

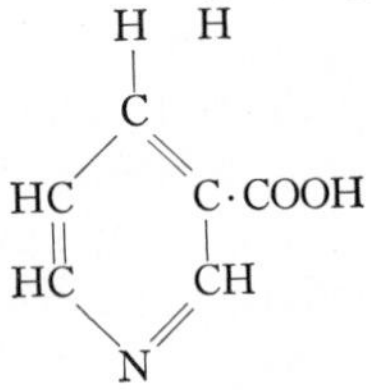

Pyridoxine (B₆)

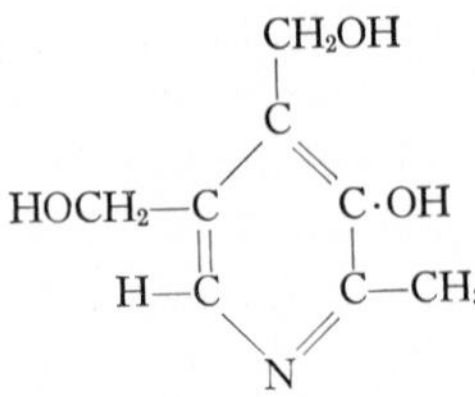

example, as the content of this hormone in the developing grains increases, there is a corresponding diminution in the thiamine content of vegetative parts (Geddes and Levine, 1942). It is possible that young developing embryos of some species may similarly be dependent upon vegetative tissues for other essential vitamins.

From the foregoing discussion it should be evident that no sharp distinction can be drawn between "vitamins" and "hormones" in considerations of the metabolism of higher plants. Some of the so-called hormones, such as traumatic acid, operate in or close to the cells in which they are synthesized; others, such as the auxins, are frequently translocated to other, often distant cells, in which they influence metabolic processes. Similarly, some of the so-called vitamins, such as riboflavin, appear to operate principally in cells in which they are synthesized, whereas others, such as thiamine, are often present in some tissues largely or entirely as a result of translocation from other organs of the plant. From the standpoint of plant metabolism, all such compounds fall into the one comprehensive category of "growth-regulating substances" or "hormones."

SUGGESTED FOR COLLATERAL READING

Avery, G. S., Jr., and Elizabeth Johnson. *Hormones and Horticulture.* McGraw-Hill Book Co., Inc. New York. 1947.

Boysen Jensen, P. *Growth Hormones in Plants.* Translated and revised by G. S. Avery, Jr., and P. R. Burkholder. McGraw-Hill Book Co., Inc. New York. 1936.

Mitchell, J. W., and P. C. Marth. *Growth Regulators.* University of Chicago Press. 1947.

Schopfer, W. H. *Plants and Vitamins.* Translated by N. L. Noecker. Chronica Botanica Co. Waltham, Mass. 1943.

Skoog, F., Editor. *Plant Growth Substances.* University of Wisconsin Press. Madison. 1951.

Went, F. W., and K. V. Thimann. *Phytohormones.* The Macmillan Co. New York. 1937.

SELECTED BIBLIOGRAPHY

Allard, R. W., W. B. Ennis, H. R. DeRose, and R. J. Weaver. The action of isopropylphenylcarbamate upon plants. *Bot. Gaz.* **107:** 589-596. 1946.

Avery, G. S., Jr. Comparative anatomy and morphology of embryos and seedlings of maize, oats, and wheat. *Bot. Gaz.* **39:** 1-39. 1930.

Avery, G. S., Jr., J. Berger, and R. O. White. Rapid total extraction of auxin from green plant tissue. *Amer. Jour. Bot.* **32:** 188-191. 1945.

Avery, G. S., Jr., and P. R. Burkholder. Polarized growth and cell studies on the *Avena* coleoptile, phytohormone test object. *Bull. Torrey Bot. Club* **63:** 1-15. 1936.

Avery, G. S., Jr., H. B. Creighton, and B. Shalucha. Expression of hormone yields in relation to different *Avena* test methods. *Amer. Jour. Bot.* **28**: 498-506. 1941.

Bausor, S. C. Efforts of growth substances on reserve starch. *Bot. Gaz.* **104**: 115-121. 1942.

Berger, J., and G. S. Avery, Jr. Isolation of an auxin precursor and an auxin (indoleacetic acid) from maize. Chemical and physiological properties of maize auxin precursor. *Amer. Jour. Bot.* **31**: 199-208. 1944.

Berger, J., Patricia Smith, and G. S. Avery, Jr. The influence of auxin on the respiration of the *Avena* coleoptile. *Amer. Jour. Bot.* **33**: 601-604. 1946.

Bonner, J. Accumulation of various substances in girdled stem of tomato plants. *Amer. Jour. Bot.* **31**: 551-555. 1944.

Bonner, J., and Harriet Bonner. The B vitamins as plant hormones. *Vitamins and Hormones* **6**: 225-275. 1948.

Burkholder, P. R., and Dorothy Moyer. Vitamin deficiencies of fifty yeasts and molds. *Bull. Torrey Bot. Club* **70**: 372-377. 1943.

Carroll, G. H. The role of ascorbic acid in plant nutrition. *Bot. Rev.* **9**: 41-48. 1943.

Cholodny, N. Beiträge zur Analyse der geotropischen Reaktion. *Jahrb. Wiss. Bot.* **65**: 447-459. 1926.

Clark, W. G. Electrical polarity and auxin transport. *Plant Physiol.* **13**: 529-552. 1938.

Commoner, B., and K. V. Thimann. On the relation between growth and respiration in the *Avena* coleoptile. *Jour. Gen. Physiol.* **24**: 279-296. 1941.

English, J., Jr., J. Bonner, and A. J. Haagen-Smit. Structure and synthesis of a plant wound hormone. *Science* **90**: 329. 1939.

Ferri, M. G. Perliminary observations on the translocation of synthetic growth substances. *Contr. Boyce Thompson Inst.* **14**: 51-68. 1945.

Galston, A. W., and Margery E. Hand. Adenine as a growth factor for etiolated peas and its relation to the thermal inactivation of growth. *Arch. Biochem.* **22**: 434-443. 1949.

Geddes, W. F., and M. N. Levine. The distribution of thiamin in the wheat plant at successive stages of kernel development. *Cereal Chem.* **19**: 547-552. 1942.

Goodwin, R. H., and Carolyn Taves. The effect of coumarin derivatives on the growth of *Avena* roots. *Amer. Jour. Bot.* **37**: 224-231. 1950.

Gordon, S. A. Auxin-protein complexes of the wheat grain. *Amer. Jour. Bot.* **33**: 160-169. 1946.

Gordon, S. A., and S. G. Wildman. The conversion of tryptophane to a plant growth substance by conditions of mild alkalinity. *Jour. Biol. Chem.* **147**: 389-398. 1943.

Gustafson, F. C. The extraction of growth hormones from plants. *Amer. Jour. Bot.* **28**: 947-951. 1941.

Haberlandt, G. Wundhormone als Erreger von Zellteilungen. *Betr. Allg. Bot.* **2**: 1-53. 1921.

Haagen-Smit, A. J., W. B. Dandliker, S. H. Wittwer, and A. E. Murneek. Isolation of 3-indole acetic acid from immature corn kernels. *Amer. Jour. Bot.* **33**: 118-120. 1946.

Haagen-Smit, A. J., W. D. Leech, and W. R. Bergren. The estimation, isolation, and identification of auxins in plant materials. *Amer. Jour. Bot.* **29**: 500-506. 1942.

Hitchcock, A. E., and P. W. Zimmerman. Absorption and movement of synthetic growth substances from soil as indicated by the responses of aerial parts. *Contr. Boyce Thompson Inst.* **7**: 447-476. 1935.

Hitchcock, A. E., and P. W. Zimmerman. The use of green tissue test objects for determining the physiological activity of growth substances. *Contr. Boyce Thompson Inst.* **9**: 463-518. 1938.

Koepfli, J. B., K. V. Thimann, and F. W. Went. Phytohormones: Structure and physiological activity. I. *Jour. Biol. Chem.* **122**: 763-780. 1938.

Kögl, F. Über Wuchstoffe der Auxin- und der Bios-Gruppe. *Ber. Deutsch. Chem. Ges.* **68**: 16-28. 1935.

Kögl, F., H. Erxleben, and A. J. Haagen-Smit. Über die Isolierung der Auxine *a* und *b* aus pflanzlichen Materialien. *Zeitschr. Physiol. Chem.* **225**: 215-229. 1934.

Kögl, F., and H. Erxleben. Über die Konstitution der Auxine *a* und *b*. *Zeitschr. Physiol. Chem.* **227**: 51-73. 1934.

Kögl, F., A. J. Haagen-Smit, and H. Erxleben. Über ein neues Auxin (Hetero-auxin) aus Harn. *Zeitschr. Physiol. Chem.* **228**: 90-103. 1934.

Larsen, P. Conversion of indole acetaldehyde to indole acetic acid in excised cole-optiles and in coleoptile juice. *Amer. Jour. Bot.* **36**: 32-41. 1949.

Leopold, A. C., and W. H. Klein. Maleic hydrazide as an antiauxin in plants. *Science* **114**: 9-10. 1951.

Leopold, A. C., and K. V. Thimann. The effect of auxin on flower initiation. *Amer. Jour. Bot.* **36**: 342-347. 1949.

Miller, C. O., and B. S. Meyer. Expansion of *Chenopodium album* leaf disks as affected by coumarin. *Plant Physiol.* **26**: 631-634. 1951.

Mitchell, J. W., and Muriel R. Whitehead. Starch hydrolysis in bean leaves as affected by application of growth-regulating substances. *Bot. Gaz.* **102**: 393-399. 1940.

Naylor, A. W., and E. A. Davis. Maleic hydrazide as a plant growth inhibitor. *Bot. Gaz.* **112**: 112-126. 1950.

Oserkowsky, J. Polar and apolar transport of auxin in woody stems. *Amer. Jour. Bot.* **29**: 858-866. 1942.

Reid, Mary E., and R. L. Weintraub. Synthesis of ascorbic acid in excised roots of the white moonflower. *Science* **89**: 587-588. 1939.

Robbins, W. J., and Roberta Ma. The relation of certain fungi to thiamine. *Bull. Torrey Bot. Club* **70**: 190-197. 1943.

Schoene, D. L., and O. L. Hoffmann. Maleic hydrazide, a unique growth regulant. *Science* **109**: 588-590. 1949.

Skoog, F. A deseeded *Avena* test method for small amounts of auxin and auxin precursors. *Jour. Gen. Physiol.* **20**: 311-334. 1937.

Skoog, F. Absorption and translocation of auxin. *Amer. Jour. Bot.* **25**: 361-372. 1938.

Skoog, F. Growth substances in higher plants. *Ann. Rev. Biochem.* **16**: 529-564. 1947.

Skoog, F., C. L. Schneider, and P. Malan. Interactions of auxins in growth and inhibition. *Amer. Jour. Bot.* **29**: 568-576. 1942.

Söding, H. Zur Kenntnis der Wuchshormone in der Haferkoleoptile. *Jahrb. Wiss. Bot.* **64**: 587-603. 1925.

Tang, Y. W., and J. Bonner. The enzymatic inactivation of indoleacetic acid. I. Some characteristics of the enzyme contained in pea seedlings. *Arch. Bio-*

chem. **13:** 11-25. 1947. II. The physiology of the enzyme. *Amer. Jour. Bot.* **35:** 570-578. 1948.

Thimann, K. V., and W. D. Bonner, Jr. Inhibition of plant growth by protoanemonin and coumarin, and its prevention by BAL. *Proc. Nat. Acad. Sci.* (*U. S. A.*) **35:** 272-276. 1949.

Thimann, K. V., and J. B. Koepfli. Identity of the growth-promoting and root-forming substances of plants. *Nature* **135:** 101-102. 1935.

Thimann, K. V., F. Skoog, and Ava C. Byer. The extraction of auxin from plant tissues. II. *Amer. Jour. Bot.* **29:** 598-606. 1942.

Thompson, H. E., C. P. Swanson, and A. G. Norman. New growth-regulating compounds. I. Summary of growth-inhibiting activities of some organic compounds as determined by three tests. *Bot. Gaz.* **107:** 476-507. 1946.

Tsui, C. The role of zinc in auxin synthesis in the tomato plant. *Amer. Jour. Bot.* **35:** 172-179. 1948.

Van Overbeek, J. A quantitative study of auxin and its precursor in coleoptiles. *Amer. Jour. Bot.* **28:** 1-10. 1941.

Van Overbeek, J. Growth-regulating substances in plants. *Ann. Rev. Biochem.* **13:** 631-666. 1944.

Van Overbeek, J., R. Blondeau, and V. Horne. Trans-cinnamic acid as an anti-auxin. *Amer. Jour. Bot.* **38:** 589-595. 1951.

Van Overbeek, J., and J. Bonner. Auxin in isolated roots growing *in vitro. Proc. Nat. Acad. Sci.* (*U. S. A.*) **24:** 260-264. 1938.

Van Overbeek, J., E. S. de Vasquez, and S. A. Gordon. Free and bound auxin in the vegetative pineapple plant. *Amer. Jour. Bot.* **34:** 266-270. 1947.

Veldstra, H., and E. Havinga. On the physiological activity of unsaturated lactones. *Enzymologia* **11:** 373-380. 1945.

Weij, H. G. van der. Der Mechanisms des Wuchstoff transportes. II. *Rec. Trav. Bot. Nèerland* **31:** 810-857. 1934.

Went, F. W. Wuchstoff und Wachstum. *Rec. Trav. Bot. Nèerland* **25:** 1-116. 1928.

Went, F. W. Auxin, the plant growth-hormone. *Bot. Rev.* **1:** 162-182. 1935; **11:** 487-496. 1945.

Went, F. W. Specific factors other than auxin affecting growth and root formation. *Plant Physiol.* **13:** 55-80. 1938.

Went, F. W., and R. White. Experiments on the transport of auxin. *Bot. Gaz.* **100:** 465-484. 1939.

Wildman, S. G., and J. Bonner. The proteins of green leaves. I. Isolation, enzymatic properties and auxin content of spinach cytoplasmic proteins. *Arch. Biochem.* **14:** 381-413. 1947.

Wildman, S. G., and J. Bonner. Observations on the chemical nature and formation of auxin in the *Avena* coleoptile. *Amer. Jour. Bot.* **35:** 740-746. 1948.

Wildman, S. G., M. G. Ferri, and J. Bonner. The enzymatic conversion of tryptophan to auxin by spinach leaves. *Arch. Biochem.* **13:** 131-144. 1947.

Wildman, S. G., and R. M. Muir. Observations on the mechanism of auxin formation in plant tissues. *Plant Physiol.* **24:** 84-92. 1949.

Zimmerman, P. W. Formation influences of growth substances on plants. *Cold Spring Harbor Symposia Quant. Biol.* **10:** 152-157. 1942.

Zimmerman, P. W., and A. E. Hitchcock. Substituted phenoxy and benzoic acid growth substances and the relation of structure to physiological activity. *Contr. Boyce Thompson Inst.* **12:** 321-343. 1942.

Zimmerman, P. W., and A. E. Hitchcock. Plant hormones. *Ann. Rev. Biochem.* **17:** 601-626. 1948.

Zimmerman, P. W., A. E. Hitchcock, and E. K. Harvill. Xylenoxy growth substances. *Contr. Boyce Thompson Inst.* **13:** 273-280. 1944.

Zimmerman, P. W., and F. Wilcoxon. Several chemical growth substances which cause initiation of roots and other responses in plants. *Contr. Boyce Thompson Inst.* **7:** 209-229. 1935.

XXIX

VEGETATIVE GROWTH

That plants more or less continuously increase in size and develop new organs at least intermittently throughout their life history is one of the most self-evident of natural phenomena. The term "growth" is popularly employed to designate this complex of processes and, in a loose sense, at least, is so employed by botanists. Growth is the one plant process with which few persons are unfamiliar, even if they have never observed it on any larger scale than a potted plant on a window sill. For farmers, horticulturists, foresters, and all others who depend upon the productivity of plants for their livelihood, the phenomenon of plant growth holds the center of the stage of interest.

In many discussions of plants as living organisms emphasis is laid upon the "structure" and "function" of various organs and tissues. Most such discussions overlook or at least fail to emphasize that structure is also a result of "function" if this latter term is considered to refer to physiological activity. The coordinated development or growth of plant organs and tissues is just as clearly a form of physiological activity as such relatively simpler processes as photosynthesis and respiration. However, because of the complexity of the process, the physiology of growth has been studied much less intensively than the end products—cells and tissues—of growth activity.

Assimilation.—The dry matter which is incorporated into the structure of both protoplasm and cell walls during growth comes almost entirely from foods. The process whereby foods are utilized in the building of protoplasm and cell walls is called *assimilation*. In the synthesis of protoplasm the foods assimilated are largely proteinaceous, whereas those assimilated in the fabrication of cell walls are almost entirely carbohydrates. The chemical reactions involved in assimilation are principally

580

of a kind in which relatively simple, soluble foods are converted into complex, insoluble constituents of cell systems. These reactions are catalyzed by enzymes. As a result of assimilation a growing region invariably increases in dry weight during growth.

Apparent exceptions to the principle of increase in dry weight during growth are sometimes cited. A seedling developing in the dark, as described in Chap. XXI, although obviously growing, continuously decreases in total dry weight. Even when seeds germinate in the light, the total dry weight of the plant decreases for a period prior to the initiation of photosynthesis in the developing seedling. Similarly, for a short time in the spring, after the buds of woody plants resume growth, a slight decrease occurs in the total dry weight of the plant. Likewise an actively growing plant steadily decreases in total dry weight during the night hours. Such examples, however, only obscure the crucial fact that the *growing region* invariably increases in dry weight during the process of growth. Such an increase in dry weight of growing regions is entirely possible, even when there is a simultaneous decrease in the total dry weight of the plant as a result of an excess of respiration over photosynthesis.

Growth as a Process.—Growth is by far the most complex of all physiological processes and, as such, is not susceptible to any precise definition. The simplest connotation of the word is merely that of an increase in size; in this sense a crystal or a rolling snowball grows. But increase in size, although the most obvious aspect of growth, is only one feature of the process, which is, in turn, a complex of sub-processes.

Differentiation, which is of several kinds, is another aspect of growth which precedes, accompanies, and follows cell division and enlargement. Physiological differentiation of the protoplasm in a cell precedes its division. Such physiological differentiation continues throughout the development of the cell, being supplemented at first by size and shape differentiation which occurs principally during the enlargement phase in the growth of a cell and still later in the ontogeny of the cell by structural and chemical differentiation of the cell walls.

Many authors restrict the term "growth" to the cell-division and cell-enlargement processes, and distinguish between growth thus defined, on the one hand, and differentiation (*i.e.*, structural differentiation), on the other, as separate phenomena. Whenever the term "differentiation" is used without qualification in reference to growth, it can be assumed to refer to structural differentiation. Some term is needed, however, to designate the overall process whereby new organs and their constituent tissues develop. "Growth" is the most natural and suitable term for this process and will be used in this sense in this book. Separate phases of the growth process are designated by the terms "cell division," "cell enlargement" (or elongation) and "cell differentiation." This latter phase of growth is called cell maturation by some authors.

The discussion in this chapter is restricted to the vegetative growth of vascular plants, *i.e.*, to the development of the roots, stems, and leaves. Reproductive growth—the formation of flowers, fruits, and seeds—is considered in Chap. XXXII.

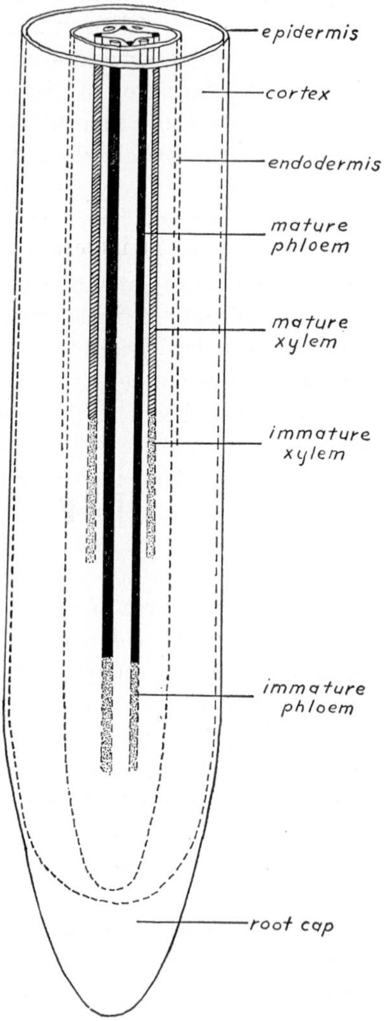

FIG. 139. Diagram of the root tip of a dicotyledon showing origin of first vascular elements. Redrawn with modifications from Esau (1943).

Meristems.—Growth does not occur indiscriminately in all parts of a plant but is initiated only in certain tissues of restricted distribution called *meristems*. A meristem is a tissue in which, under favorable conditions, new cells are more or less continually being formed as a result of repeated divisions of some or all of the cells. As a result of the subsequent further enlargement and structural differentiation of cells originating in a meristem, various tissues are developed according to a pattern which is more or less distinctive for each species.

The most important meristems in the body of the majority of vascular plants are the apical-root (Fig. 66) and apical-stem (Fig. 140) meristems, and the vascular cambium (Fig. 51). An apical-stem meristem is present at every stem tip including those of quiescent or dormant buds, an apical-root meristem is present at every root tip, and a vascular cambium is present in the stems and roots of gymnosperms and most dicotyledons. Differentiation of these three major meristems occurs very early in the ontogeny of an individual plant.

Intercalary meristems are also present in many kinds of plants. These are found in the stems of some species and also in the leaves of certain species, especially monocots. In stems, intercalary meristems are most commonly located just above the nodes, as in corn and other monocots; but in some species they occur just below the nodes, as in some mints; and in still other species they occur in the middle of the node. Leaves of grasses, iris, and some other kinds of monocots have basal intercalary meristems. This fact can be attested to by anyone who has ever pushed a lawnmower. An intercalary meristem can be regarded as a portion of an apical-stem meristem which has become separated from the latter by differentiation of tissues between it and the intercalary meristem. These meristems ultimately disappear, sooner or later in the life history of the plant becoming entirely converted into nonmeristematic tissues.

Whether or not a meristem will be active at a given time depends upon both environmental and internal conditions. Most apical-stem meristems of the woody plants of temperate zones, for example, are inactive during the winter months, largely because of unfavorable environmental conditions. This is particularly true during the latter part of the winter when the buds of most such species have passed out of the condition of dormancy (Chap. XXXIV). The contrary situation is illustrated by the many lateral-bud meristems on many kinds of plants which fail to develop even when environmental conditions are favorable as a result of the inhibiting effect of apical buds (Chap. XXXIII).

Growth which is initiated in apical-stem and -root meristems is called *primary growth*. Primary growth results in the construction of the *primary tissues* of a plant, accounts for all increase in length of the plant axis at both stem and root tips, results in the development of the branching system of the stems and roots, and is responsible for the formation of lateral appendages such as root hairs, leaves, and floral parts.

In many species the primary tissues constitute the entire plant. This is true of the pteridophytes and of many monocotyledons. In gymnosperms and most dicotyledons, however, stems and roots not only grow more or less continuously by a proliferation of the fundamental tissues of which these organs are composed, but also increase in diameter as a result of the activity of the vascular cambium.

Some increase in diameter may occur, however, even in stems and roots which do not possess a vascular cambium. Increase in the girth of a young stem as a result of primary growth may continue for some time after increase in length of that region of the stem has ceased, as a result of a slow continuance of cell division and enlargement in some of the tissues, particularly those near the periphery. In species in which the primary tissues constitute the entire body of the plant, this is the sole mode of growth in diameter.

Tissues which arise as a result of the growth activity of vascular or cork cambiums are called *secondary tissues* (see later).

Culture of Excised Plant Organs and Tissues on Synthetic Media.—*Culture of Root Tips.*—The idea that the cultivation of excised plant and animal tissues or organs on sterile media would be a valuable technique in investigations of certain aspects of growth and metabolism has been entertained by physiologists for many years. To date, however, only plant tissues have been successfully cultured on purely synthetic media. The development of plant tissue culture techniques is reviewed by White (1943).

Excised root tips were the first plant part to be successfully cultured as isolated organs on sterile synthetic media. Tips of very young roots are cut off and transferred aseptically to a sterile culture medium. If the latter has a suitable composition (see later) and environmental conditions are favorable, the root tips continue to grow and branch at rates approximating those of roots attached to the plant. After a week or longer one or more root tips on an original explant may be cut off and transferred as before. This procedure can be continued indefinitely, and tomato roots have been maintained in sterile culture, with weekly transfers, for more than seven years.

The fact that the roots can be subcultured repeatedly shows that the only requirements for their maintained growth are the substances in the culture medium, since calculations indicate that, after a year or more, the material of the original root tip has become so diluted that many of its progeny, after successive subculturing, could not contain even a single molecule from the original root tip. Considerable interest therefore attaches to the substances which must be present in the culture medium if potentially unlimited growth of roots is to occur. Earlier investigators soon found that the only necessary constituents which must be introduced into the medium (water or a dilute agar gel) were a carbohydrate (sucrose is generally used), essential mineral salts, and a trace of some organic material such as yeast extract. More recently it has been found that certain specific hormones or mixtures of hormones can be substituted for the yeast extract.

The hormones which must be present in the culture medium as substitutes for the yeast extract differ according to the species of root. Bonner and Devirian (1939) and Bonner (1940) list the necessary requirements for ten species. For all ten it was essential that thiamine be present in the medium if good growth was to be maintained; for flax roots no other growth substance was found necessary. For pea, radish, alfalfa, clover, and cotton roots nicotinic acid must also be present; for tomato and carrot roots, pyridoxine; for *Datura* and sunflower roots both nicotinic acid and pyridoxine. Slow rates of growth, however, could be obtained with some of these species without addition of any hormones to the medium.

Even roots from different varieties of the same species may react differently to the presence of hormones in a culture medium. Although apparently not required for the usual growth of tomato roots, some strains show a further increase in growth if nicotinic acid is also present in the medium while others do not (Bonner, 1943).

An important inference to be drawn from these results is that roots do not synthesize, or at least do not synthesize in adequate quantities, those hormones which must be present in the medium if excised roots are to maintain a good rate of growth. In intact plants these substances are translocated from aerial organs to the roots. Both inferential, and some direct, evidence indicates that other growth substances, presumably also required in root metabolism, are synthesized in adequate quantities in the roots of at least some species. Among these are auxin, biotin (Bonner, 1940), and riboflavin (Bonner, 1942).

It has not yet been found possible to obtain continued growth in sterile culture of excised roots of a number of species which have been tried. This has been particularly true of the roots of monocotyledons. Almestrand (1950), for example, in spite of extensive experimentation, was unable to obtain continued growth of excised barley or oat roots in sterile culture. It seems probable that unknown growth factors are required for continued growth of such roots, and that in intact plants these factors may be translocated to the roots from the aerial organs.

Culture of Excised Stem Tips.—The first fully successful attempts to culture excised stem tips on sterile media were those of Loo (1945, 1946) who used the stem tips of asparagus. The excised stem tips were cultured through a series of thirty-five transfers over a period of twenty-two months. Growth thus appeared to be potentially unlimited. The only constituents found to be essential in the agar or water medium were sucrose and mineral salts. These results were obtained only under diffuse light; in darkness growth of the excised stem tips soon stopped. Apparently some necessary, but unknown, growth substances in such stem tips are synthesized in the light but not in the dark. Roots did not ordinarily develop on the explants. The growth rate of the excised, rootless stem tips was considerably slower than that of the stem tips of intact plants under comparable conditions. Growth rates of the occasional stem tips on which roots developed were considerably greater than growth rates of rootless stem tips.

Galston (1948) discovered that roots will form on the base of excised asparagus stem tips in the dark but not in the light if indoleacetic acid is present in the medium. Stem tips subcultured in the dark continue to grow, but lose their capacity to root when later exposed to indoleacetic acid, although this capacity will be regained if the tips are first exposed to light for a week in the absence of indoleacetic acid. One implication of these results is that some substance other than auxin which is necessary for root initiation is made in the stems in the light, and is depleted by prolonged culture in the dark. This substance may correspond to the so-called "rhizocaline" (see later).

Stem tips of lupine and nasturtium have been cultured, but not sub-cultured, on sterile media containing only sucrose and mineral salts by Ball (1946). Roots regularly formed on the excised stem tips of these species with the end result that complete plantlets developed in the cultures. Somewhat similar results were obtained by de Ropp (1946) with excised stem tips of rye. Continued growth of stems and leaves in the dark occurred only on those isolated stem tips on which roots regenerated; when roots failed to form growth was confined to the first leaf.

Culture of Plant Tissues on Synthetic Media.—Cultures of excised stem and root tips can most appropriately be referred to as *organ cultures.* In contrast with such cultures are those in which individual *tissues* of plants have been used. As examples of such work may be cited the culture on sterile media of "callus" tissue developed from the procambium of tobacco stems (White, 1939a), of cambium (Gautheret, 1949), and of bacteria-free crown-gall tissue of sunflower (Riker and Gutsche, 1948).

The technique of tissue culture affords one important mode of approach to the problem of the conditions governing the differentiation of organs. Tobacco callus tissue continues to develop as an undifferentiated mass of cells on the surface of the medium, but if submerged in an aqueous medium develops stems and roots (White, 1939b, Skoog, 1944). Further investigations (Skoog and Tsui, 1948) have showed that auxins (indoleacetic acid, α-naphthalene acetic acid) favor root initiation on such callus tissues, but inhibit bud formation. Adenine (Chap. XX) and certain other chemically similar compounds were found to have a seemingly specific effect in inducing bud initiation on such tissues. Further development of buds into plantlets, however, required that roots also be present.

Dynamics of Primary Growth.—Most of our knowledge of the cellular dynamics of primary growth (growth initiated at apical meristems) has been gained from the study under the microscope of thin sections of tissue cut longitudinally through apical stem or root meristems or cut crosswise at different distances back from the tip of such meristems. Since the developmental stages through which the cells at any level of a stem or root axis pass can be found at any given moment in successive levels of the axis, each in turn further away from the apex, the progressive series of modifications which cells undergo during the growth process can be inferred from a study of such tissue sections under the microscope. This is an indirect approach to the problem of growth dynamics since such sections portray to us only the results of growth activity up to the moment the tissue was killed and cannot convey any impression of the cellular dynamics of the process. Another difficulty with this approach is that it does not permit observation of the behavior of any single cell and its progeny through the exact series of changes which they undergo during growth. In spite of the limitations of this method it has been possible to infer many important facts regarding the behavior of cells during growth by a study of thin sections of tissue cut through growing regions.

Primary Growth of Roots.—Examination of a median longitudinal section through a root tip (Fig. 66) shows that the region just back of the root cap is one of intense meristematic activity. The very youngest part of this meristematic region is called the *promeristem*. The central portion of the root promeristem becomes transformed, during growth, into the *procambium* from which develop, in turn, the vascular tissues.

The cells throughout the meristematic region are relatively small, thin-walled, and approximately isodiametric. The vacuoles are minute, and the nuclei are relatively large, although in absolute size they are smaller than in mature cells (Trombetta, 1939). Intercellular spaces are lacking. Cell divisions are of frequent occurrence in this region and are accompanied by some enlargement of the cells.

From certain of the apical cells of the promeristem, called *initials*, originate, directly or indirectly after intervening cell divisions, all new cells formed in the growth process at a root tip. One of the daughter cells resulting from each division of an initial retains its position and identity as an initial. From several to many generations of cell progeny may arise from the other, but ordinarily all of the ultimate offspring of this daughter cell become differentiated into cells characteristic of the tissue of which they become a part. The cells of the root cap are also formed from the initials. Cell divisions in an apical root meristem occur both longitudinally and in variously oriented lateral planes, thus giving rise to the typically cylindrical configuration of a root.

Just back of the meristematic zone is a short region—seldom more than a millimeter in length—in which elongation of cells continues, but in which cell divisions have ceased. Enlargement or elongation of cells is an integral part of the growth process. Some enlargement occurs during cell division, but usually the increase in the size of cells occurring during this phase of growth is small compared with that taking place subsequently. Increase in the volume of all cells does not occur equally, neither do they all enlarge symmetrically along all axes. Hence cells of very diverse sizes and configurations arise in plant tissues.

The fact that during enlargement cells acquire a wide assortment of sizes and configurations requires that each cell must in some manner become adjusted to the changes in size and shape which take place in adjacent cells. A given cell may, for example, be in contact with other cells which have very different rates of enlargement. Several methods by which such an adjustment in configuration can be accomplished have been suggested, but one of the most important appears to be that of different rates of expansion in different parts of the wall of a given cell (Sinnott and Bloch, 1939), the rate in each area of the wall corresponding to that of the area of the wall of the adjacent cell with which it is in contact.

Since many of the cells originating at an apical-root meristem enlarge principally in a direction parallel to the long axis of the root, this phase of growth is often called *cell elongation*. The continued formation of new cells by division and their elongation result in projecting the root tip forward, which is one of the most obvious manifestations of its apical growth.

Differentiation of some of the kinds of cells in a growing root axis occurs much closer to the apex than others. Particular interest attaches to the stage in the growth of a root at which the vascular tissues develop, because of the part played by them in translocation processes. In roots both xylem and phloem differentiate only acropetally and as continuations of the older xylem and phloem in the more basal part of the root. In general, phloem tissues differentiate much closer to the apex of the root than xylem tissues. In tobacco root tips developing sieve tubes are present within less than 200 μ of the apex of the meristem, which is well within the region in which cell divisions are occurring (Esau, 1941). First differentiation of xylem tissues in this species, on the other hand, occurs at least twice as far back of the apical initials as first differentiation of phloem tissues (Fig. 139); this is within the region in which elongation of many cells is still in progress.

Techniques by which the dynamics of the growth process in living root tips can be observed while actually in progress have been devised and used by Brumfield (1942) and Goodwin and Stepka (1945). In the root tips of timothy (*Phleum pratense*), used in these investigations, two rather distinct regions can be recognized in the meristematic zone. One of these, about 300 μ long, lies immediately adjacent to the root cap and is characterized by a relatively slow rate of cell division accompanied by a limited amount of cell elongation. Just back of this region is a shorter zone—about 125 μ long—in which cell division and cell elongation are both relatively rapid. Cells in this region are simultaneously dividing and vacuolating. Back of the meristematic region is a zone about 600 μ long in which cell divisions have ceased, but in which cell elongation continues slowly.

As previously described for the tobacco root, differentiation of sieve tubes occurs in the roots of timothy well in advance of differentiation of xylary elements. Fully differentiated sieve tubes are present within 230 μ of the base of the root cap. The youngest xylary elements to show characteristic secondary wall thickenings were not found to be present closer to the root tip than a point 740 μ back of that at which fully differentiated sieve tubes are present. As in the tobacco root, differentiation of sieve tubes is completed well within the region in which many cells are still dividing; differentiation of vessels begins in the upper part of the region of cell elongation. The first phloem elements to form in a root tip are usually crushed or distorted by the continued division and elongation of surrounding cells. Likewise, the first vessels to form are usually stretched and often torn or destroyed as a result of the continued elongation of surrounding cells.

Primary Growth of Stems.—The meristematic region at a stem tip is fundamentally similar to that at a root tip, but its behavior is more complicated since growth at a stem tip involves not only proliferation of the stem axis, but also the formation of leaves and other lateral organs. The youngest and most apical portion of a stem tip is called the *promeristem;* this is not more than a few hundred microns in length (Fig. 140). During growth a part of the promeristem is gradually transformed into a procambium from which the primary vascular tissues develop.

The cells in a stem tip meristem have thin, delicate walls and are approximately isodiametric. During active growth cell divisions are of frequent occurrence throughout this region. The mass of cells in the meristematic region appears to be in a highly plastic condition, and its continuity is not interrupted even by minute intercellular spaces. The nuclei are relatively prominent, although actually they are smaller than in mature cells (Trombetta, 1939). The cells in the younger portions of apical-stem and other meristems contain only minute vacuoles (Zirkle, 1937). The cells in older portions of an apical-stem meristem show evidence of the simultaneous occurrence of division and vacuolation (Priestley, 1929).

As in the promeristem of roots there is present at or near the apex of the promeristem of stems one or more initials. All new cells formed at any growing stem tip originate from these persistently meristematic cells.

Cell divisions in apical-stem meristems occur both longitudinally and in various lateral planes, thus giving rise to the more or less cylindrical configuration of the typical stem.

As in root-tip meristems some enlargement of cells occurs during the cell division phase of growth, but in the development of many kinds of cells most enlargement or elongation occurs after cell division. As in roots, cells of very different shapes and sizes arise as a result of differential en-

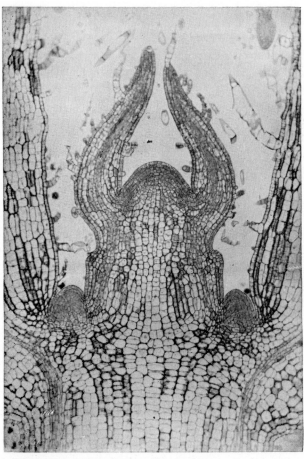

FIG. 140. Longitudinal section of the apical-stem tip of coleus. The apical meristem appears between the two first, only partly developed, leaves. Just below, appearing as shoulders on the sides of the stem, are bases of the second pair of leaves, which are borne oppositely to the first pair. Farther below is the third pair of leaves in the axils of each of which is a young lateral bud. Distance from the top of the apical meristem to the base of the section is 0.86 mm. Photomicrograph by Tillman Johnson.

largement. Many cells become distinctly elongate in shape during this phase of growth. During enlargement of cells in an apical-stem meristem intercellular spaces may be formed. Both the continued formation of new cells by division and their elongation contribute toward the lengthening of a stem, which is one of the most obvious aspects of apical stem growth.

Cell division in stems is generally restricted to the uppermost internodes, but the elongation of cells often extends over a long series of internodes. The rate of elongation becomes progressively slower, however, with increasing distance of the internode from the stem tip. The elongation region back of a stem tip is sometimes as much as 10 cm. in length, and in twining plants even longer.

Investigators of the differentiation phase of growth in apical-stem meristems have focused most of their attention on the development of the vascular tissues. The first vascular strands to appear in stem apices originate in connection with the developing leaf primordia. The details of

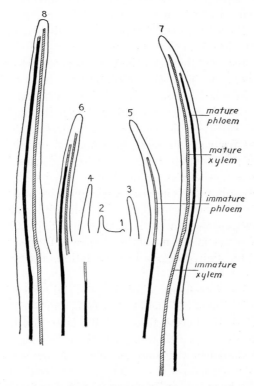

FIG. 141. Diagram of an apical meristem of tobacco, showing order of development of leaves and position of first sieve tube and first xylem vessel in each leaf. Redrawn from Esau (1943).

this differentiation process have been studied by Esau (1938, 1943a, 1943b, 1945) in tobacco, flax, sunflower, and elder. Differentiation of procambium, in continuity with the procambium of the older bundles in the axis, and acropetally into the leaves, precedes differentiation of the vascular tissues. As in roots phloem tissues differentiate earlier in the ontogeny of a stem than the xylary elements of the same strand (Fig. 141). The first xylem generally appears at the base of the leaf primordium or in the primordium itself, whence it differentiates both acropetally into the leaf primordium and basipetally into the stem axis until it unites with older strands of xylem. Differentiation of the phloem, on the other hand, appears to occur only acropetally into each leaf primordium as a continuation of the older phloem in the stem axis. Crushing, or distortion, or stretching of the first phloem or xylem elements formed in a stem tip may occur in much the same manner as in a root tip as previously described.

Physiological Aspects of Cell Division.—The portion of a meristem in which cell divisions are of frequent occurrence is a center of intense assimilatory activity. Since every cell formed as a result of mitosis contains its own complement of protoplasm, and since every cell division involves the formation of a cross wall between the two daughter cells as well as some extension of existing walls, both carbohydrates and proteinaceous foods are assimilated in relatively large quantities during cell division. Cellulose, pectic compounds, and other cell-wall constituents are synthesized from the molecules of simple soluble carbohydrates. Protoplasmic proteins are formed from amino acids, acid amides, or related compounds. Such substances are probably transported to meristems from the tissues in which they are synthesized, although it is possible that some of them may be synthesized in meristems from carbohydrates or derivatives therefrom, and from nitrogenous compounds. The close interrelation of growth, protein synthesis, and respiration is stressed in Chap. XXVI.

Utilization of water in the hydration of newly formed protoplasm and cell walls, and to a limited degree in vacuolation, also occurs during cell division.

Certainly most and probably all of the essential mineral elements must be present, as constituents of one kind of compound or another, in meristematic cells if their physiological activity is to continue unimpaired. Some of these are translocated to meristematic cells as simple inorganic salts, others as components of more complex organic compounds.

During mitosis, therefore, a continuous translocation of water and various kinds of solutes is in progress toward the dividing cells. Significant in this connection is the fact that the sieve tubes, through which at least part of the solutes are presumably transported into a meristem, differentiate well into the zone of dividing cells. Translocation of solutes beyond the limits of the vascular elements must be by cell-to-cell movement. Since the rate of movement of solutes into such cells is usually too rapid to be accounted for by diffusion, it seems likely that such cells possess the capacity of accumulating solutes or of accelerating the rate at which they are translocated as a result of metabolic activity. Much cell-to-cell movement of water obviously also occurs in meristems. Such passage of water from one meristematic cell to another is probably accomplished by osmotic and imbibitional mechanisms, although the possibility of a metabolically activated movement of water through such cells cannot be entirely disregarded (Chap. VIII).

Regions of dividing cells are invariably centers of intense respiratory as well as assimilatory activity, and considerable quantities of carbohydrates are oxidized in such cells. A direct correlation has been demonstrated between the mitotic rate and rate of oxygen consumption in young leaves (Beatty, 1946). Cell for cell the respiratory rate in meristematic regions is higher than in fully differentiated tissues. Dividing cells utilize energy in various ways, a number of which are mentioned in Chap. XXI.

Maintenance of the process of cell division requires the presence in the cells of numerous growth-regulating substances. Many of these belong in the category of enzymes or coenzymes; others would ordinarily be classed as hormones or vitamins; all of them participate in essential reactions of the metabolic mechanism.

As shown in the previous discussion, all species of roots that have been experimented with by the technique of sterile culture of excised root tips require that thiamine must be present in the medium if continued elongation of roots is to occur. In addition, many kinds of roots require the presence of one or both of the compounds pyridoxine and nicotinic acid. There is good evidence that in intact plants these substances are translocated from the aerial parts to the root meristems (Chap. XXVIII). As mentioned earlier other important hormones such as riboflavin, biotin, and auxin appear to be synthesized in adequate quantities in the roots of at least some species.

Apical-stem meristems appear to be more nearly self-sufficient in synthesizing essential growth substances than apical-root meristems. As mentioned earlier, excised stem tips of asparagus, for example, on which roots ordinarily do not develop, continue to grow in diffuse light for long periods in sterile culture media to which no growth substances have been added. Apical-stem meristems appear therefore to synthesize all necessary growth-regulating substances, although not necessarily in optimal quantities. Nevertheless, formation of roots on such excised stem tips usually favors an enhanced rate of elongation of the stem, and there is evidence that this effect is not principally a result of the presence of a better absorptive system. A more probable explanation is that one or more hormones, synthesized in the roots, are translocated into the stems, favoring their more rapid elongation. This substance or complex of substances may correspond to the postulated "caulocaline" (Chap. XXVIII). Went and Bonner (1943) have presented strong circumstantial evidence for the existence of such a hormone in plants. That it need not come directly from the roots is shown by the fact that application of a diffusate from pea cotyledons or coconut milk has an effect on the growth of stems from which roots have been removed similar to that of attached roots. Aeration of roots appears to be an important factor in "caulocaline" synthesis, at least in the roots of many species (Went, 1943), and one cause of the injurious effects on plants of inadequate aeration of roots may be interference with caulocaline synthesis.

Physiological Aspects of Cell Enlargement.—The increase in size of plant cells involves an increase—often manyfold—in the volume of the vacuoles, and an areal extension of the cell walls. Some increase in the thickness of the cell walls also often occurs during this phase of growth. During the enlargement of a cell additional protoplasm is usually synthesized, but the increase in quantity of cell-wall material—principally cellulose and pectic compounds—is proportionately greater than the increase in quantity of protoplasm. Hence the proportion of carbohydrate to proteinaceous foods assimilated during cell enlargement is greater than during cell division.

As cells increase in volume there is a movement of water into the enlarging vacuoles. Water is also used in the hydration of the protoplasm and cell walls which are constructed during cell enlargement. Relatively large quantities of water therefore become integral parts of each cell system during this stage of growth. In most kinds of plant cells, as they increase in size, the cytoplasm gradually becomes attenuated into a thin layer which lines the inside of the cell wall, against which it is held by the turgor pressure of the water in the vacuole.

Regions in which enlargement of most or all of the cells is proceeding rapidly are centers of relatively high respiratory activity. Cell for cell, the rate of respiration of enlarging cells is probably not much less than that of dividing cells.

Rapid translocation of both water and solutes is continuously in progress into any region of enlarging cells.

Despite the presence of differentiated vascular elements, considerable cell-to-cell movement of water and solutes must occur in meristematic zones in which cell enlargement is prevalent. The same mechanisms of water and solute movement are doubtless operative in this part of a meristem as in the younger portion in which cell division is the predominant phase of growth.

As discussed in the preceding chapter, areal extension of cell walls occurs only in the presence of specific substances called auxins.

Two main views regarding the mechanism of cell enlargement have been advanced. One of these holds that the cell wall must first be subjected to elastic (reversible) or plastic (irreversible) stretching as a result of a turgor pressure developed by the cell sap. The latter view is supported especially by Heyn (1940). While in the stretched condition it is assumed that the material substance of the wall is increased, either by the intercalation of additional molecules in the wall (*intussusception*), by the deposition of additional molecules on the cell-wall layers already present (*apposition*), or by a combination of these two processes. Plastic extension of a wall alone would also result in an increase in its area, but if this occurs unaccompanied by the incorporation of new material the wall necessarily becomes thinner.

A second hypothesis holds that active growth of the cell wall is the primary step in cell enlargement. Growth of the wall is believed to result from the intercalation of additional molecules between those already present. Entrance of water into the cell is considered to be a result of the increase in the volume of the cell rather than its cause. Ursprung and Blum's (1918) finding that, although the diffusion-pressure deficit of dividing cells is relatively high, because of the appreciable concentration of solutes present, their turgor pressure is low, is considered to be evidence in support of this hypothesis. Continued areal extension of the wall would keep the wall pressure and hence the turgor pressure of the cell at a low value.

Physiological Aspects of Cell Differentiation.—Size differentiation of a given type of cell is usually completed during the enlargement phase of its growth. The cells of various tissues differ, however, not only in spatial dimensions, but also in various structural features, most of which do not develop until enlargement of the cell is nearly or entirely complete. Such structural differentiation begins earlier in the ontogeny of some kinds of cells than others.

The cells which develop into pith, cortex, and certain other tissues do not elongate greatly along the axis of growth in length, although their elongation in this direction is usually greater than radially. Other kinds of cells, such as fibers and tracheids, elongate greatly parallel to the long axis of the stem or root, and only slightly in other directions. Differentiation of cell walls ensues at about the time that cell enlargement ceases. During this phase of growth the walls of practically all cells become thicker, although usually not uniformly so. The walls of many kinds of cells and tissue elements become pitted while in others distinctive structural features are developed, the most striking of which are the spiral and other characteristic thickenings of the walls of the xylem vessels.

Chemical differentiation of cell walls often accompanies their structural differentiation. The walls of some cells, such as those of the pith, the living cells of the phloem, and most of the cells in the cortex, retain their original cellulose-pectic composition indefinitely. The walls of other cells, such as those of most of the xylem tissues, become lignified. Similarly suberin lamellae develop in the walls of cork cells and some others.

In general the protoplasm soon disappears from those cells in which the walls become lignified, while those in which such a chemical modification of the wall does not occur retain their protoplasm in an unimpaired condition for a much longer period. Further structural differentiation of the walls of cells in which the protoplast dies, such as vessels, tracheids, and fibers, occurs only by such purely physicochemical processes as continue in them, or under the influence of the activities of adjacent living cells. The changes occurring in the heartwood of trees, for example, are a result of such processes. Disintegration of certain parts of some kinds of cells may also occur while structural modifications are proceeding in other parts of the same cell. The most familiar example of this is the disappearance of the cross walls between the xylem elements in the formation of vessels.

Assimilation of carbohydrates occurs in all types of cell differentiation involving a thickening of the cell walls, but little or no formation of protoplasmic proteins occurs during this phase of the growth process. The respiratory activity of even those fully differentiated cells which retain their protoplasm is generally less than that of dividing or enlarging cells.

Development of Lateral Organs.—Leaves originate from the *leaf primordia* which are small protuberances which develop laterally from an apical-stem meristem close to its apex (Fig. 140). The histogenic development of a leaf from its primordium does not follow the same pattern in all species (Foster, 1936), although there are many points of similarity in the development of most kinds of leaves. As an example we may consider the development of the tobacco leaf (Avery, 1933). A single apical cell of the leaf primordium continues to form new cells until the leaf is 2-3 mm. long; then its activity ceases. A midrib primordium develops as a result of subsequent divisions of these newly-formed cells, no lamina being present until the leaf is about 0.6 mm. long. The lamina originates from two rows of subepidermal meristematic cells, one on each side of the midrib primordium. Subsequent divisions, enlargement, and differentiation of these cells result in the development of all of the mesophyll tissues, including the lateral veins. The epidermis increases in area as a result of continued division and enlargement of the epidermal cells. Cell divisions cease first in the epidermis, followed in order by the middle and lower mesophyll, and the palisade layers. The tissues of the lateral veins may continue to develop long after cell division has stopped in other parts of the leaf. Although cessation of cell division occurs first in the epidermis, enlargement of the cells in this layer continues longer than in any other tissue of the leaf. Intercellular spaces do not develop markedly until the leaf has attained one-fourth to one-third its final size.

Evidence from various sources indicates that auxins play an essential role in the elongation of the petiole, midrib, and larger lateral veins of leaves, but growth substances other than auxin seem to be required for expansion of the leaf blade. When seedlings of dicotyledonous species develop in total darkness, little or no expansion of the leaf blade occurs. A very brief exposure to light of relatively low irradiance is sufficient to induce a considerable increase in area of the leaf blade (Chap. XXX). The expansion of such leaves appears to be dependent upon a photo-chemical reaction which presumably is an essential step in the synthesis of some necessary growth substance. In a search for clues to the physio-logical mechanism of leaf expansion several investigators have attempted to discover compounds which will induce this phenomenon independently of light. Adenine (Bonner *et al.*, 1939) has been found to favor enlarge-ment growth in detached radish and pea leaves, but other investigators have found this compound not to be effective with some other kinds of leaves. Coumarin has been found to promote leaf expansion in leaves of some species (Chap. XXVIII), and cobalt and nickel salts apparently have a similar effect on etiolated bean leaves (Chap. XXV). The sig-nificance of these various findings and their relation to the light-activated enlargement of leaf blades is not yet clear.

The origin of lateral roots has already been discussed from an anatom-ical standpoint in Chap. XIV. Auxins (Chap. XXVIII) appear to be specifically required for root initiation to occur, whether on roots, stems, or other organs. At least one growth substance, tentatively named "rhizo-caline," has also been considered to be necessary if initiation of roots is to occur (Chap. XXVIII). Evidence in favor of such a view is presented by Galston (1948); evidence opposed to it by Van Overbeek *et al.* (1946).

In addition to the terminal bud present on most stem axes, lateral buds —which are essentially rudimentary side branches—develop in the axils of leaves. These first appear as mound-like meristems in the axils of the embryonic leaves (Fig. 140). In temperate zone woody plants both ter-minal and lateral buds are encased in bud scales which are shed only when, and if, growth of the stem tip is resumed. The buds of most herba-ceous plants are devoid of bud scales. A great many more axillary buds form on most plants than ever develop into lateral branches. Whether or not one of the rudimentary stem tips which is an essential part of a bud will ever resume growth depends in part on environmental, and in part on internal conditions.

Lateral Growth of Stems and Roots.—Growth in diameter of roots and stems results principally from the activities of lateral meristems called cambiums. Such meristems are responsible for the *secondary growth* of plants, *i.e.*, the formation of secondary tissues. The most important of these meristems is the vascular cambium (commonly referred to simply as "cambium") which is present in the stems and roots of gymnosperms and most dicotyledons. The vascular cambium consists typically of a uniseriate layer of cells that is located between the xylem and phloem. In most plants in which it occurs this cambium constitutes an almost continuous sheath of cells extending from just back of every root tip to just below every stem apex. This continuous lamina of cambium is broken, in most species, only at the leaf gaps and branch gaps (Fig. 142) which occur just above the strands of vascular tissue which lead to the leaves and stems. Usually, however, even such gaps are found only in the young parts of the axis, since they are gradually bridged by extensions of the cambium layer as the stem grows older.

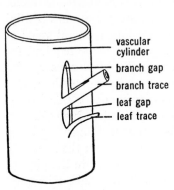

vascular cylinder
branch gap
branch trace
leaf gap
leaf trace

FIG. 142. Diagram of a portion of the vascular cylinder of a stem illustrating leaf and branch gaps. Redrawn from Eames and MacDaniels (1947).

Structurally cambium cells are of two distinct types. The vascular ray initials from which the vascular rays develop are more or less isodiametric. The vertically elongated elements of the xylem and phloem develop from a second and more abundant type of cambium initial. As viewed in cross section the tangential width of cambium cells of this *fusiform* type is usually several times as great as their radial width. The length of such a cambium cell usually exceeds even the greatest of its cross-sectional dimensions by many times (Fig. 143). The cambium initials of a tulip tree, for example, are about 600 μ. long, 25 μ. in tangential width, and 8 μ. in radial width. Much longer cambium cells have been reported in the stems of some conifers. In the white pine they may attain lengths up to 4000 μ.. In the Scotch pine (*Pinus sylvestris*) the fusiform cambial cells have, on an average, 18 faces (Dodd, 1948). Cambium cells are vacuolated and often prominently so (Bailey, 1930), and often show protoplasmic streaming.

The cambium usually becomes active in the formation of new cells before primary growth has entirely ceased in all of the tissues at the corresponding level of the stem. Successive divisions of cambium cells at right angles to their radial axis result in the development of *secondary xylem* on its inner face and *secondary phloem* on its outer face and cause an increase in the diameter of the axis. Increase in length of the vascular rays also occurs as a result of cambial activity. The secondary xylem and secondary phloem lie between the *primary xylem* and *primary phloem,* as the conductive tissues formed during primary growth are termed. All increase in the diameter of stems resulting from cambial activity is caused by the formation of additional layers of phloem and xylem within the body of the stem. In annual plants, or in perennial species in which the stems die down to the ground at the end of each growing season, secondary growth never continues beyond the current season. In species with woody stems new layers of both xylem and phloem are developed during each period of cambial activity, so that such species exhibit an annual increase in diameter. In some woody perennials the vascular cambium may continue to develop secondary tissues for hundreds of years, cambial activity being resumed periodically with the advent of each growing season. Since in such species the older phloem is first converted into bark and is eventually sloughed off, the bulk of the structure of all older stems and roots is composed of secondary xylem.

Cells originating from the cambium pass through the same three morphological stages of growth as do those developed from apical meristems. Formation of a new cell in the xylem is initiated by division of one of the cells of the cambium layer, the new cell wall developing midway of the cell in the tangential plane (Fig. 51). The outer one of the two daughter cells remains a cambium cell, but the inner one enlarges, usually in length as well as in cross-sectional area, and generally develops directly into one of the xylem elements. Often, however, the inner of the two cambium derivatives may divide one or more times before maturation of the cells ensues. This usu-

Fig. 143. Perspective view of typical fusiform cambium cell.

ally happens in the formation of wood parenchyma cells during which
the xylem mother cell is cut into a vertical series of cells by transverse
divisions. Tracheids, fibers, vessels, wood parenchyma, and wood-ray cells
are developed in the xylem from the cambial derivatives (Chap. XII).

A new phloem cell is initiated in a similar manner from the outer of
the two daughter cells after division of a cambium cell (Fig. 51). These
outer cells may develop directly into mature phloem elements, or may
first divide before maturation ensues. In general, division of the phloem
mother cells before maturation appears to be of more frequent occurrence than division of the corresponding xylem mother cells. Maturation
of the cambial derivatives formed on the outer face of the cambium
results in the development of sieve tubes, companion cells, phloem parenchyma, phloem-ray cells, and phloem-fiber cells (Chap. XXVII).

Continuation of secondary growth from the cambium results during
each growing season in the development of a zone of secondary xylem
cells inside of the cambium, and a zone of secondary phloem exterior to

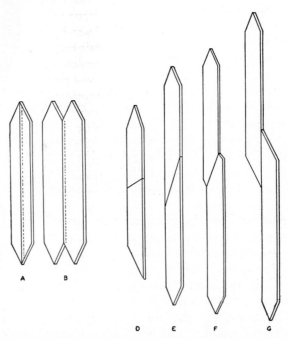

A   B

D   E   F   G

Fig. 144.   Diagram illustrating two methods by which cambium cells divide
resulting in the formation of additional cambium cells. (A) and (B) two stages
in the radial division of a cambium cell. (D) to (G) four stages in the "pseudo-
transverse" division of a cambium cell followed by a sliding of the two derivative cambium cells past each other.

it. The enlargement of the xylem cells originating from the cambium initials results in outward movement of the cambium and all of the cells lying outside of this layer, necessarily resulting in an increase in the girth of the cambium cylinder. Enlargement of the immature phloem cells developed from the cambium, on the other hand, results in outward movement only of the phloem and tissues external to it. Generally several times as many new xylem elements as phloem elements are formed from the cambium during a period of growth activity.

Division of the cambium cells results not only in the formation of secondary phloem and xylem, but also, as the stem grows in diameter, in an increase of the girth of the cambium layer. Some increase in the circumference of the cambium cylinder results from a lengthening of the cambium initials along their tangential axis as seen in cross section, but mostly this is brought about by an increase in the number of cells around the cylinder as the stem grows older. According to Bailey (1923) two principal methods by which this occurs can be recognized. New cambium cells may result from radial divisions of older cambium initials (Fig. 144 A-B), or by "pseudo-transverse" divisions followed by a sliding of the derivatives past each other (Fig. 144 D-G). Each of these methods of multiplication of cambium cells is characteristic of certain species.

Vascular cambiums, in the usual sense of the term, are not present in the monocotyledons, although traces of cambial-like activity often occur in the vascular bundles. In some tree-like species of monocotyledons, however, secondary thickening of the stem results from the operation of a special kind of lateral meristem which is usually considered to be a type of cambium. This meristem occurs as a cylinder of tissue near the periphery of the stem. Unlike the cambium of dicotyledons and gymnosperms, it does not produce phloem on the outside and xylem on the inside but forms complete vascular bundles and intervening parenchyma tissue toward the interior of the stem. These secondary vascular bundles are thus present in stems in a cylinder of tissues outside of the primary tissues in which the primary bundles are located. A limited amount of parenchyma tissue is also formed by such cambiums toward the exterior.

Still another kind of lateral meristem is the cork cambium or *phellogen*, present in most woody stems and roots (Chap. XIV). In young twigs the first cork cambium usually develops as a continuous uniseriate cylinder of tissue, either from the epidermis or from the layer of cells just beneath the epidermis. The operation of a cork cambium as a meristem is analogous to that of a vascular cambium. As a result of tangential divisions of cork cambium cells, layers of cork cells (*phellum*) are formed externally, and layers of *phelloderm* cells are formed internally (Fig. 145). In most species more phellum cells than phelloderm cells are formed as the result of cork cambium activity, but in a few the opposite is true, and in some no phelloderm cells are formed. Mature cells of the cork or phellum layer are nonliving and are characterized by the presence of suberin lamellae in the walls which renders them highly impermeable to water. Phellogen cells are living cells, more or less loosely arranged, and

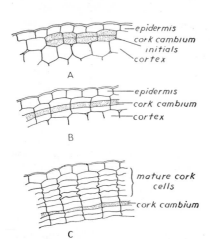

FIG. 145. D.agrams showing formation of cork in stem of geranium (*Pelargonium*). (*A*) Division of outer cortex cells, forming a cork cambium. (*B*) First layer of cork cells has formed. (*C*) Several layers of mature cork cells have formed.

often resemble cortical cells. The entire system of phellum, phellogen, and phelloderm is often called the *periderm*.

In some species, such as birch, iron-wood (*Carpinus*), and beech, the initial cork cambium persists for many years or even for the entire life of the tree. In the majority of woody species, however, the first cork cambium ceases activity after a relatively brief time, and is replaced by other relatively short-lived cork cambiums which arise progressively more and more deeply in the tissues of the stem or root. Each such cork cambium is a uniseriate layer of cells; as a rule relatively small in area. Such secondary cork cambiums usually arise first in the cortex, still later in the pericycle, and finally in the secondary phloem. They operate as meristems in essentially the same manner as the initial cork cambium. The various layers of cork cells formed overlap or join each other in one way or another so that a continuous corky layer, except for lenticels, completely encloses all woody parts of stems and roots. In older tree trunks of many species all periderm layers have developed in the secondary phloem. The older bark of such trees thus consists of alternating layers of cork and dead phloem cells (Fig. 146).

The same, or at least very similar, physiological processes undoubtedly accompany the different stages in the growth of cells originating from the various kinds of cambial initials as accompany the corresponding stages in the growth of cells arising from apical initials.

Measures or Indices of Growth.—It is frequently desirable to give some sort of a quantitative expression to the amount of growth which is accomplished by a plant or a group of plants during a given period of time.

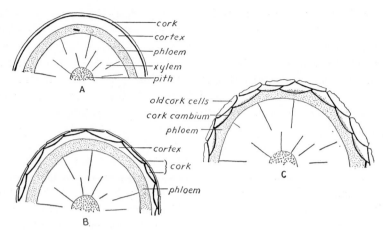

Fig. 146. Diagrams showing development of cork in woody stems. (A) Cork cambium developing in the outer cortex of a young stem. (B) Later stage. Cork cambiums forming deeper in the cortex. Epidermis ruptured. (C) Still later stage. Cork cambiums forming in the old phloem. Older cork being shed as the stem enlarges. Redrawn from Eames and MacDaniels (1947).

The principal indices which have been employed for this purpose are (1) increase in the length of the stem, root, or other organ of the plant, (2) increase in the area of the leaves, (3) increase in the diameter of the stem (or other organ), (4) increase in volume (especially of fruits), (5) dry weight increment, and (6) fresh weight increment.

All of these indices have at least a limited value as measures of growth, especially from various practical standpoints. Determinations of the height and diameter growth of forest trees, for example, are standard forestry practices as indices of the productivity of forests and have considerable practical value for such purposes. Similarly, the number of tons of dry hay or the fresh weight of cabbage or spinach produced per acre would usually be an adequate measure of growth to the mind of the practical farmer.

Each of the indices listed above, however, measures only certain quantitative phases of growth. A yardstick can measure only length, a balance only weight, but growth phenomena generally involve not only such quantitative changes as expansion in length and girth and increase in weight, but qualitative aspects as well. How, for example, could the relative development of the vegetative and reproductive phases of growth be expressed in terms of any of the units listed above? Yet qualitative differences in growth are often of as great or greater scientific significance or practical importance as quantitative differences. The floriculturist is not primarily interested in the pounds of plant substance produced nor the height to which his plants grow, if they bear flowers which will be attractive to his customers. Likewise, the orchardist is much more interested in the development of the fruits on his tree than in the increase in the height or weight of their vegetative organs. Evidence of this difficulty in giving adequate expression to the results of growth phenomena is seen in the common expedient of investigators in relying upon photographs as a means of recording the results of their experiments upon the growth of plants.

Rates of Growth.—The absolute growth rates recorded in the botanical literature are mostly for increase in height of stems. A number of measurements have also been made of the fresh and dry weight increments of fruits, examples of which are given in Chap. XXVII.

The rate of height growth varies enormously with different species of plants and with the same species under different environmental conditions. Only a few examples of the most rapid known rates of height growth will be cited. Young bamboo shoots sometimes grow as rapidly as 2 ft. in 24 hr. and asparagus shoots as much as 1 ft. in the same period of time. When a flower stalk develops on a century plant (*Agave* spp.) it often elongates as much as 6 in. in a single day. Under favorable growing conditions corn plants sometimes add visibly to their stature during a single night.

The rates of elongation of the fastest growing stems are just a shade too slow for detection with the naked eye. By observing rapidly growing stem tips under a horizontally placed microscope, the externally visible aspects of growth can often be observed and measured directly.

The rate of growth of stem or root tips can also be measured by the very simple method of marking the organ with short horizontal lines spaced equidistantly. The marks are generally made with India ink applied with a fine brush. The rate of elongation is determined by observing the position of the marks after the lapse of a definite period of time. A similar method can be used for measuring the rate of increase in the area of a leaf by ruling a cross-sectional pattern of lines on the leaf. Such methods are of value in indicating in what part of the organ enlargement is occurring most rapidly.

Accumulation of Foods.—Although the simple carbohydrates synthesized in photosynthesis may undergo many transformations, the sum total of the food available to a green plant, except under special experimental conditions, where carbohydrates or other foods are artificially supplied, can never exceed the quantity synthesized in photosynthesis. A large proportion of the photosynthate is normally used in the processes of assimilation and respiration. Any surplus which remains accumulates in one or more tissues or organs of the plant. Accumulation of foods, however, does not occur continuously. For considerable periods in the life cycle of most plants not only is no accumulation of food occurring, but a more or less rapid consumption of accumulated food is in progress. In woody plants during the dormant season slow utilization of food in the processes of respiration and assimilation continues. When growth is resumed in the meristematic tissues of such species in the spring there is always a considerable drain on the foods stored in the plants since much of this growth is accomplished before the photosynthetic rate is rapid enough to compensate for the necessarily speedy utilization of food which occurs. Similarly the sprouting of bulbs, corms, tubers, and rhizomes always occurs at the expense of accumulated foods in such organs. The same is true of seeds when germination occurs. Much of the food which accumulates in plants during periods when photosynthesis exceeds the food-consuming processes is utilized by the plant sooner or later in its life history.

The organs in which most accumulation or "storage" of food occurs are different in different species. In annuals food storage occurs predominantly in the seeds. Foods also accumulate in the seeds of most biennial and perennial species. During the process of germination the embryo uses food that was made by the preceding sporophyte generation.

Most of the accumulation of food in typical biennials such as beet, carrot, parsnip, and turnip occurs in fleshy roots or root-like structures. This accumulation of food by biennial species occurs mostly during their first season's growth.

In perennial species considerable storage of food often occurs in seeds and fruits, but the principal organs of food accumulation in many species which live for a number of years are the stems and roots. In woody species the pith, cortex, vascular rays, and wood parenchyma are the stem and root tissues in which most of the accumulation of surplus foods occurs. Modified stems such as rhizomes (iris, many ferns, Solomon's seal), tubers (potato, Jerusalem artichoke), corms (crocus, gladiolus, jack-in-the-pulpit), and bulbs (onion, tulip, hyacinth) are almost invariably regions of food storage in species which possess such organs.

The great bulk of all foods which accumulate in plants can be classified into the familiar categories of carbohydrates, fats, and proteins.

The principal storage carbohydrates are starch, sucrose, "hemicelluloses," and inulin (Chap. XX). Accumulation of oils (fats) in abundance occurs most commonly in seeds, although such compounds are stored in at least small quantities in the cells of many tissues. Proteins, like fats, accumulate principally in seeds.

The cells of "storage" tissues are not merely passive reservoirs in which excess foods pile up. Foods move into the cells in which they accumulate only in the soluble form, yet with few exceptions, sucrose being the most familiar example, the foods amassed in storage cells are converted into an insoluble form. Upon translocation into storage cells, glucose is converted into starch, amino acids into proteins, fructose into inulin, fatty acids and glycerol into fats, etc. All of these chemical transformations are catalyzed by enzymes occurring in the living cells in which the foods accumulate.

Conversely, insoluble stored foods cannot be utilized by any part of a plant until they have first been digested into soluble forms as a result of enzymatic activity. Until such a transformation has occurred they cannot be translocated out of the cells in which they are situated into the cells in which they are utilized in assimilation or respiration.

SUGGESTED FOR COLLATERAL READING

Benecke, W., and L. Jost. *Pflanzenphysiologie*. Vol. II. G. Fischer. Jena. 1924.
Eames, A., and L. H. MacDaniels. *An Introduction to Plant Anatomy*. 2nd Ed. McGraw-Hill Book Co., Inc. New York. 1947.
Gautheret, R. *La Culture des Tissues*. Gallimard. Paris. 1945.
White, P. R. *A Handbook of Plant Tissue Culture*. Jaques Cattell Press. Lancaster, Penn. 1943.

SELECTED BIBLIOGRAPHY

Almestrand, A. Further studies on the growth of isolated roots of barley and oats. *Physiol. Plantarum* **3:** 205-224. 1950.
Avery, G. S., Jr. Structure and development of the tobacco leaf. *Amer. Jour. Bot.* **20:** 565-592. 1933.
Bailey, I. W. The cambium and its derivative tissues. IV. The increase in girth of the cambium. *Amer. Jour. Bot.* **10:** 499-508. 1923.
Bailey, I. W. The cambium and its derivative tissues. V. A reconnaissance of the vacuome in living cells. *Zeitschr. Zellf. Mikr. Anat.* **10:** 651-682. 1930.
Ball, E. Development in sterile culture of stem tips and subjacent regions of *Tropaeolum majus* L. and *Lupinus alba* L. *Amer. Jour. Bot.* **33:** 301-318. 1946.
Beatty, A. V. Respiration and cell division in plants. I. Oxygen consumption and cell division in the leaves of *Ligustrum lucidum* and *Hedera helix*. *Amer. Jour. Bot.* **33:** 145-148. 1946.
Bonner, D. M., A. J. Haagen-Smit, and F. W. Went. Leaf growth hormones. I. A bio-assay and source for leaf growth factors. *Bot. Gaz.* **101:** 128-144. 1939a.
Bonner, D. M., and A. J. Haagen-Smit. Leaf growth factors. II. The activity of pure substances in leaf growth. *Proc. Nat. Acad. Sci. (U. S. A.)* **25:** 184-188. 1939b.
Bonner, J. On the growth factor requirements of isolated roots. *Amer. Jour. Bot.* **27:** 692-701. 1940.
Bonner, J. Riboflavin in isolated roots. *Bot. Gaz.* **103:** 581-585. 1942.
Bonner, J. Further experiments on the nutrition of isolated tomato roots. *Bull. Torrey Bot. Club* **70:** 184-189. 1943.
Bonner, J., and P. Devirian. Growth factor requirements of four species of isolated roots. *Amer. Jour. Bot.* **26:** 661-665. 1939.

Brumfield, R. T. Cell growth and division in living root meristems. *Amer. Jour. Bot.* **29:** 533-543. 1942.

de Ropp, R. S. Studies in the physiology of leaf growth. *Ann. Bot.* **9:** 369-381. 1945. **10:** 31-40, 353-359. 1946. **11:** 439-447. 1947.

Dodd, J. D. On the shapes of cells in the cambial zone of *Pinus silvestris* L. *Amer. Jour. Bot.* **35:** 666-682. 1948.

Esau, Katherine. Ontogeny and structure of the phloem of tobacco. *Hilgardia* **11:** 343-424. 1938.

Esau, Katherine. Phloem anatomy of tobacco affected with curley top and mosaic. *Hilgardia* **13:** 437-490. 1941.

Esau, Katherine. Vascular differentiation in the vegetative shoot of *Linum*. *Amer. Jour. Bot.* **29:** 738-747. 1942. **30:** 248-255. 1943a.

Esau, Katherine. Origin and development of primary vascular tissues in seed plants. *Bot. Rev.* **9:** 125-206. 1943b.

Esau, Katherine. Vascularization of the vegetative shoots of *Helianthus* and *Sambucus*. *Amer. Jour. Bot.* **32:** 18-29. 1945.

Foster, A. S. Leaf differentiation in angiosperms. *Bot. Rev.* **2:** 349-372. 1936.

Galston, A. W. On the physiology of root initiation in excised asparagus stem tips. *Amer. Jour. Bot.* **35:** 281-287. 1948.

Gautheret, R. Sur la culture du tissu cambial de carrotte. *Compt. Rend. Sci. Biol. (Paris)* **134:** 398-399. 1940.

Goodwin, R. H., and W. Stepka. Growth and differentiation in the root tip of *Phleum pratense*. *Amer. Jour. Bot.* **32:** 36-46. 1945.

Heyn, A. N. J. The physiology of cell elongation. *Bot. Rev.* **6:** 515-574. 1940.

Loo, S. Cultivation of excised stem tips of asparagus *in vitro*. *Amer. Jour. Bot.* **32:** 13-17. 1945.

Loo, S. Further experiments on the culture of excised asparagus stem tips *in vitro*. *Amer. Jour. Bot.* **33:** 156-159. 1946.

Priestley, J. H. Cell growth and cell division in the shoot of the flowering plant. *New Phytol.* **28:** 54-81. 1929.

Priestley, J. H. Studies in the physiology of cambial activity. *New Phytol.* **29:** 56-73, 96-140, 316-354. 1930.

Riker, A. J., and Alice E. Gutsche. The growth of sunflower tissue *in vitro* on synthetic media with various organic and inorganic sources of nitrogen. *Amer. Jour. Bot.* **35:** 227-238. 1948.

Sinnott, E. W. Structural problems at the meristem. *Bot. Gaz.* **99:** 803-813. 1938.

Sinnott, E. W., and R. Bloch. Changes in intercellular relationships during the growth and differentiation of living plant tissues. *Amer. Jour. Bot.* **26:** 625-634. 1939.

Skoog, F. Growth and organ formation in tobacco tissue cultures. *Amer. Jour. Bot.* **31:** 19-24. 1944.

Skoog, F., and C. Tsui. Chemical control of growth and bud formation in tobacco stem segments and callus cultured *in vitro*. *Amer. Jour. Bot.* **35:** 782-787. 1948.

Trombetta, Vivian B. The cytonuclear ratio in developing plant cells. *Amer. Jour. Bot.* **26:** 519-529. 1939.

Ursprung, A., and G. Blum. Besprechung unserer bisherigen Saugkraftmessungen. *Ber. Deutsch. Bot. Ges.* **36:** 599-618. 1918.

Van Overbeek, J., S. A. Gordon, and L. E. Gregory. An analysis of the function of the leaf in the process of root formation in cuttings. *Amer. Jour. Bot.* **33:** 100-107. 1946.

Went, F. W. Effect of the root system on tomato stem growth. *Plant Physiol.* **18:** 51-65. 1943.

Went, F. W., and D. M. Bonner. Growth factors controlling tomato stem growth in darkness. *Arch. Biochem.* **1:** 439-452. 1943.

White, P. R. Potentially unlimited growth of excised plant callus in an artificial nutrient. *Amer. Jour. Bot.* **26:** 59-64. 1939a.

White, P. R. Controlled differentiation in a plant tissue culture. *Bull. Torrey Bot. Club* **66:** 507-513. 1939b.

Zirkle, C. The plant vacuole. *Bot. Rev.* **3:** 1-30. 1937.

XXX

ENVIRONMENTAL FACTORS AFFECTING VEGETATIVE GROWTH

Regardless of the habitat in which it is growing, whether a greenhouse, cultivated field, forest, prairie, mountain top, or lake bottom, a plant is continuously subjected to the variabilities of a complex, more or less interdependent set of environmental factors. The environment is the foster parent of every plant and animal and plays as indispensable a role in its development as do hereditary factors which have been transmitted to it from its biological parents.

The development and reactions of an organism are the result of the coordinated interplay of the hereditary factors and environmental conditions upon the internal physiological processes of that organism:

Genetic Constitution
\
↘ Internal Processes → Organic Development
↗ and Conditions   and Behavior
Environment /

Under the term "internal processes and conditions" is included all of the manifold variations possible in the physicochemical conditions within cells and tissues, as well as the relative rates of the various physiological processes. In our present state of knowledge we are able to visualize only some of the grosser aspects of these processes with any great clarity. Most of the preceding chapters of this book have been devoted to a discussion of the internal processes and conditions in plants. The intermediate stages between genetic constitution and environmental factors on the one hand, and the development or reaction of the organism on the other, are large

609

and intricate ones and are far from being bridged in terms of present-day knowledge.

As a specific example of this principle we will recall the process of chlorophyll synthesis as it occurs in corn (maize). The usual varieties of this species contain the genetic factors which ordinarily induce chlorophyll formation. Certain environmental conditions, including light, are also necessary for its synthesis in this species. A corn seedling developing in a dark room is devoid of chlorophyll, even if all the other environmental conditions necessary for chlorophyll formation are present. In a seedling growing in the light, however, interaction of the environmental factors with the hereditary mechanism will occur in such a way as to induce the process of chlorophyll synthesis in the leaf cells. While environmental conditions only rarely have a direct influence upon the genetic make-up of an organism, they do exert a profound influence upon the expression of its heredity. As discussed earlier (Chap. XVI), it is now a widely accepted hypothesis that the genes of the chromosomes exert their influence upon physiological processes through a controlling effect on the synthesis of enzymes.

So far, however, we have considered only one side of the story. Certain varieties of maize do not carry all of the genetic factors necessary for the development of chlorophyll. This trait is inherited in such strains of corn as a Mendelian recessive and hence is apparent only in plants homozygous for this factor. Even if all the environmental factors necessary for chlorophyll synthesis are present, such seedlings cannot make chlorophyll, and they develop as "albinos." As soon as the food stored in the seed is exhausted, such albino seedlings die.

The genetic constitution of a given organism sets definite ultimate limits to the types of development and the reactions of which that organism is capable, beyond which no environmental conditions can carry it. Potato plants, for example, may vary greatly in their morphogenic development. Under some environmental conditions the plants may be large; under others, small. Under some they will flower; under others they will not. Under still others tubers will develop; under others they will not. Nevertheless, all of these plants will remain unmistakably potato plants.

The specific environment to which a plant is subjected also sets limits upon its development. For example, under "short-day" conditions, as discussed in Chap. XXXII, a radish plant continues to grow vegetatively for an indefinite period of time. Although radish plants possess the hereditary capacity for reproductive development, such an environment imposes a barrier to the expression of this particular potentiality. On the other hand, under long day-lengths, if other environmental conditions are favorable, a radish plant will flower and fruit within the course of a few weeks. Innumerable other examples of the environmental limitation of the expression of hereditary factors can be cited.

The full gamut of the hereditary potentialities of a species can never be realized until individuals of that species have been observed growing in each of a wide range of environmental complexes. Since most observations of the behavior of plants are made while they are growing under natural or cultural conditions which represent only a rather narrow range of variations in the environmental complex, the many possible developmental reactions of a given species of plant are not always appreciated.

Environmental Factors Influencing Plant Growth.—The environment of living organisms is so complex as to defy any completely logical analysis. However, the principal physical factors of the environment which ordinarily exert a more or less *direct* effect upon the growth and development of terrestrial plants can be recognized and are enumerated in the following list:

1. Temperature (soil and air)
2. Radiant energy
3. Soil water
4. Water vapor (in soil and atmosphere)
5. Solutes in the soil solution
6. Gases of the soil atmosphere
7. Exchangeable ions in the soil
8. Gases of the atmosphere
9. Gravity
10. Atmospheric pressure
11. Wind

The environment to which the roots are exposed is usually very different from that which the aerial organs of plants encounter. Because of reciprocal influences between the roots and tops of a plant, effects of any environmental factor upon the development or physiological processes of the roots almost invariably will be indirectly reflected in the behavior of the aerial organs, and *vice versa* (Chap. XXXIII).

Some important environmental factors, such as precipitation (rain, snow, and hail), are usually indirect in their influence on plants, operating through their effects on one or more of the direct factors listed above. Precipitation, for example, influences not only the soil-water content, but also soil aeration and atmospheric humidity. Many of the factors listed above which exert direct effects upon growth also exert important indirect effects on growth.

Many of the environmental conditions to which plants growing under out-of-door conditions are subjected are in turn influenced by more remote factors. The intensity and quality of impinging sunlight, for example, are functions of the angle of the earth's inclination to the sun (which varies with the hour of the day, the latitude and the season), the pitch of the slope upon which the light falls, and the direction toward which the slope faces. The soil-water content is controlled not only by the precipitation, but by the surface runoff (which in turn is largely a function of the slope and the porosity of the soil), and by factors which influence the rate of evaporation such as air temperature, humidity, wind, and insolation. Similarly, with increase in altitude differences in such physical factors as the irradiance, quality, and duration of radiant energy, soil and air temperature, and atmospheric pressure are encountered.

Furthermore, complex interrelationships exist among the medley of environmental factors which exert direct effects upon plants. Changes in the magnitude or duration of one factor seldom occur without inducing subsidiary changes in other factors. Increase in the intensity of radiant energy in any habitat results in an increase in soil and air temperatures; increase in soil-water content diminishes soil aeration, and so forth.

In addition to the physical factors discussed above, plants are subject to the influence of another entirely different group of factors—the other living organisms in their environment. Among these are bacteria, fungi, green plants, and animals. Man himself, from the standpoint of a plant, is merely one of the factors in its environment. The influence of such *biotic factors* is not generally considered to come within the scope of a discussion of plant physiology, but their effects upon growth and development of plants are often as pronounced as the effects of physical factors. Biotic factors often operate as limiting factors in the survival or distribution of plants. The elimination of that once prominent tree species—the chestnut—from eastern North America by the chestnut blight disease is an example of the profound effects sometimes wrought by biotic factors.

In order to interpret the effect of changes in the magnitude of any one of the various factors influencing a process, such as growth, it is necessary to formulate certain guiding principles. In 1843 Liebig proposed his well-known "law of the minimum," which was the first attempt at such a formulation. Liebig was thinking primarily of the effect of fertilizers upon the yield of crop plants when he suggested this "law," which states in essence that the yield is limited by the factor which is present in relative minimum. Blackman's "principle of limiting factors" as applied to photosynthesis (Chap. XIX) is essentially an extension of Liebig's principle.

Mitscherlich (1909) proposed a somewhat different concept of the law of the minimum. His conception of the operation of a "limiting factor" may be stated as follows: "the increase in any crop produced by a unit increment of a deficient factor is proportional to the decrement of that factor from the maximum."

Both of these interpretations of the effect of minimal factors can be illustrated by a diagram (Fig. 147), in which it is supposed that five factors are affecting growth, but that each is present in a different relative intensity as compared with its maximum effectiveness.

According to Liebig's law of the minimum, only an increase in factor A will cause an increase in the yield of a crop. According to Mitscherlich, increase in any one of these factors will cause an increase in yield. A unit increase in A will have the greatest effect, a unit increase in B the next greatest effect, and so forth. Factor E is so close to its maximum that a unit increase in it will have an almost negligible influence on yield. Mitscherlich's interpretation of the law of the minimum seems to be more nearly in accord with the results obtained in experiments on plants than Liebig's simpler formulation of this same principle.

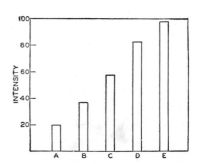

Fig. 147. Diagram to illustrate two interpretations of the law of the minimum.

The discussion in this chapter will be restricted to the effects of environmental factors on the vegetative growth of plants; their effects on reproductive growth are considered in Chap. XXXII.

Effects of Temperature upon Vegetative Growth.—The rate of every physiological process occurring in plants, including growth, is markedly influenced by the all-pervading factor of temperature. Temperature, however, exerts qualitative as well as quantitative effects upon the development of plants. In other words, the structural development and physiological reactions of a plant may vary greatly, depending upon the temperature pattern of that plant's environment. Finally, whether or not a plant can survive in a given habitat often depends upon the temperature extremes which occur in that habitat.

1. *Effect of Temperature on the Rate of Growth.*—It has been customary to consider that there are three "cardinal" temperatures for growth, a *minimum,* an *optimum,* and a *maximum,* although these so-called cardinal points on the temperature scale may vary greatly with different species. While in a loose sense this is true, and such temperatures can be approximately determined by experimentation, they are by no means immutable. All three of these "critical" temperatures have been found to vary considerably with the stage in the development and the physiological

condition of the plant, the time and rate of exposure, and other environmental conditions.

In general, the range of temperatures within which growth will take place varies considerably with the species. Arctic and alpine species may grow at the freezing point or even at temperatures slightly below, and their optimum growth temperature is often no higher than 10°C. Most species of temperate zone origin do not grow appreciably at temperatures below 5°C. Their optimum growth temperature is usually about 25°-30°C., and their maximum about 35°-40°C. The cardinal growth temperatures of most tropical and subtropical species are still higher. For maize, a crop plant of subtropical origin, the minimum growth temperature is about 10°C., the optimum about 30°-35°C., and the maximum about 45°C.

Leitch (1916) has made one of the few comprehensive studies of the effect of temperature upon the quantitative aspects of growth. She found that the rate of elongation of the roots of pea seedlings increased consistently with rise in temperature in the range of −2° to 29°C., and further that the rates within this range of temperatures, once established, showed little or no diminution with time. Above about 30°C., the higher the temperature, the lower the initial rate of growth and the more rapidly the rate decreased with time. Elongation ceased entirely at temperatures of 45°C. or higher. In other words, in the temperature range of 30°-45°C., a distinct time factor effect was evident in the relation between temperature and growth. A similar time factor effect has been demonstrated for the growth of maize seedlings (Lehenbauer, 1914).

In an elaborate study of the effects of temperature upon developing cotton seedlings, Arndt (1945) found the optimum for germination, initial elongation of the primary root, and initial elongation of the hypocotyl to be about 33°C. After a few days, however, the optimum for root elongation had fallen to 27°C., whereas that for hypocotyl elongation had risen to 36°C. Such shifts in temperature optima for various phases of growth are probably characteristic of many plant organs.

Each stage in the development of a plant may and often does have a different optimal temperature. The relationship between temperature and stage of development has been investigated most thoroughly in certain species of bulbs, such as the tulip (Hartsema et al., 1930). In this species, at the time bulbs are usually lifted from the ground, the next season's stem apex has differentiated to the extent of three or four leaf primordia. The next stage in development within the stored bulb is initiation of the flower primordia, a process which requires about 3 weeks. The optimal temperature for this process is 20°C. For a subsequent period of about 3 months, during which flower parts develop into a complete flower, the optimal temperature is 8°-9°C. As leaves begin to emerge from the bulb, the optimal temperature gradually rises to 23°C., the latter value being reached when the leaves are about 6 cm. long. Similar differences in optimal temperature at different stages of development are found in other temperate climate bulbs, but such differences are lacking in bulbs native to tropical regions.

Such differences in the optimal temperatures for different stages of growth are not confined to bulbs. In many temperate zone species the optimum temperature for the germination of seeds is less than for vegetative growth, which in turn is often lower than the most suitable temperature for flowering and fruiting.

2. *Temperature Limitations upon Plant Survival.*—A clear distinction should be drawn between the extremes of temperature at which the growth of a plant ceases, and the extremes of temperature which that plant can endure without death resulting. The minimum temperature which a plant can tolerate without injury is almost invariably below that at which growth ceases; likewise plants can usually endure without lethal effects, at least temporarily, temperatures considerably in excess of the maximum at which growth occurs. A given plant, for example, may cease to grow when the temperature to which it is exposed rises to 40°C. Death, however, occurs only if the temperature of the plant is raised to some still higher temperature, perhaps 55° or 60°C. Within this intervening range of temperatures the plant passes into a state of *heat rigor* in which it neither grows nor exhibits growth movements. Similarly there is a range of temperatures between the lowest temperature at which a plant will grow and its death point as a result of cold. Within this zone of temperatures the plant passes into a corresponding condition of *cold rigor.*

The upper and lower extremes of temperature which plants or plant organs can endure vary greatly according to species and depend upon their capacity for heat resistance and cold resistance, respectively, as discussed later.

3. *Morphogenic Effects of Temperature.*—No two of the many and varied physiological processes occurring in a plant are equally influenced by a change in temperature. Hence the morphogenic development of a plant, which is controlled by the pattern of its physiological activity, is often markedly different under one set of temperature conditions than under another. Such effects upon the structural development of plants are the most complex and most striking of the many influences of temperature upon plants.

Numerous examples of morphogenic effects of temperature upon the vegetative development of plants can be cited. Some such effects are clearly related to the differential influences of temperature upon the processes of photosynthesis and respiration. The net daily gain in photosynthate by any plant is the difference between the quantity of carbohydrate synthesized during the photoperiod and the quantity of carbohydrate consumed per 24 hr. in respiration. In a maize plant, for example, under favorable conditions, the average quantity of hexose synthesized per photoperiod during its life history is about 9 g. while the average quantity of hexose consumed in respiration is about 2 g. per 24 hr. (Table 25). The average net daily gain in photosynthate by a corn plant is therefore about 7 g.

Only the net daily increment of photosynthate can be used by a plant in the assimilatory phases of growth or can accumulate as unused food in one or more organs of the plant. If its total daily respiration consistently exceeds its total daily photosynthesis, a plant can often survive for a while at the expense of previously accumulated foods, but eventually it will starve to death.

The rate of photosynthesis ordinarily does not change much in many species under favorable field conditions over a temperature range of 15°-30°C., mainly, it appears, because of the limiting effect of carbon dioxide at atmospheric concentration on the process (Chap. XIX). The temperature coefficient of respiration, on the other hand, over a similar temperature range, is approximately two (Chap. XXI). With rise in temperature the rate of respiration therefore increases more rapidly than the rate of photosynthesis, and the net daily gain in photosynthate by the plant is curtailed. Respiration is not, of course, confined to the photosynthetic tissues, but occurs in all non-green parts of the plant including the underground organs. Also significant is the fact that photosynthesis is restricted to the daylight hours while respiration goes on every hour of the twenty-four. Hence prevailing night temperatures markedly influence the daily net gain of photosynthate by a plant. Approximately twice as much food would disappear per hour as a result of respiration at 25°C., for example, as at 15°C. A daily alternation between relatively cool night temperatures and moderately high daytime temperatures will therefore usually result in a greater net gain of photosynthate by a plant than if night temperatures are also relatively high.

Translation of differential effects of temperature upon photosynthesis and respiration into morphogenic effects on growth can be illustrated by the process of tuberization in the potato. When tuberization occurs foods are used in the construction of the cellular framework of the tubers and accumulate within the cells. The optimum rate of photosynthesis is apparently attained in the potato at about 20°C. The higher the daytime temperature above this value and the higher the night temperature, the greater the proportion of the photosynthate which will be consumed in respiration and the smaller the proportion which can be used in assimilation or which can accumulate as stored food. Higher temperatures also favor development of the aerial vegetative organs of a potato plant (Werner, 1934), which further reduces the quantity of photosynthate which can be used in tuberization. Hence yields of potatoes are usually higher in a relatively cool climate, other conditions being favorable, than in a relatively warm climate.

A low net daily gain in photosynthate will not only retard accumulation of foods but may also check assimilation and growth of a plant. The results of Nightingale (1933) on the effect of temperature on the development of the tomato plant are largely explainable in terms of its effect on the net daily increment of photosynthate. This investigator grew tomato plants under continuous temperatures of 55°F. (13°C.), 70°F. (21°C.), and 95°F. (35°C.). The plants survived, developed and accumulated carbohydrates at both the lower temperatures, indicating that in these two groups of plants daily photosynthesis exceeded daily respiration. At 35°C., however, the carbohydrate content of the plants decreased rapidly, indicating that daily respiration exceeded daily photosynthesis, and many of these plants died within a relatively short time.

Soil temperature, as considered apart from air temperature, also has morphogenic effects on plants. Maximum vegetative development of Marquis wheat under greenhouse conditions (air temperature range about 20°-35°C.), for example, occurred at a soil temperature of 22°C., as compared with a number of higher soil temperatures (Wort, 1940).

Among the most pronounced of the morphogenic effects of temperature are those upon reproductive growth which will be discussed in Chap. XXXII.

4. *Thermoperiodicity.*—Temperature is one of the characteristically cyclical factors of the environment. Both rates of growth and the morphogenic development of plants are markedly influenced by the pattern of the temperature cycle to which they are subjected. For example, Went (1944) found that, when grown under a constant temperature, the maximum rate of elongation of the stems of tomato plants more than 40 cm. high occurred at 26.5°C., but that elongation was still more rapid if the plants were exposed to a 26.5°C. daytime temperature alternating with a 17°-20°C. night temperature. Approximately the same temperature relation was found for fruit development. This favorable effect of a lower night temperature was eliminated, however, if the plants were artificially illuminated during the night.

The term *thermoperiodicity* has been proposed to designate the effects of an alteration of temperature between the day and night periods upon the reactions of plants. Other species of plants besides the tomato are known to exhibit the phenomenon of thermoperiodicity, but the critical temperatures differ from one species or even one variety to another, and from one stage of development to another (Went, 1945).

Cold Injury and Cold Resistance.—1. *Causes of Injury to Plants upon Exposure to Low Temperatures.*—Several types of injury may occur in plants as a result of exposure to relatively low temperatures:

(1) Desiccation.—Relatively high winter transpiration rates in evergreens during a period when absorption of water can proceed only at a relatively slow rate often lead to a type of injury frequently called *winter-killing* (Chap. XI). Injury under such circumstances results from desiccation of the tissues. A similar type of injury may result to some plants, especially herbaceous species, as a result of frost heaving of the soil. Such heaving often tears the roots loose from the soil or, in extreme cases, may even result in breaking them. If environmental conditions favoring high transpiration rates intervene before the root system can be securely re-established in the soil, the plant may be so severely desiccated that death or marked injury results. This is often a serious source of injury to winter wheat during "open" winters. One of the advantages of mulching plants with straw, leaves, or other materials during the winter months is that it greatly reduces frost heaving of the soil.

(2) Chilling Injury.—Many species of plants, particularly those which are native to tropical or subtropical regions, are killed or seriously injured by relatively low temperatures *above* their freezing point. This type of low temperature injury is often called *chilling injury.* For example, Sellschop and Salmon (1928) found that exposure to a temperature of 0.5° to 5.0°C. for 24 to 36 hr. was fatal or markedly injurious to rice, velvet beans, cotton, peanuts, and Sudan grass. Species which were only slightly injured included maize, sorghums, watermelons, and pumpkins, while soybeans, buckwheat, tomatoes, and flax showed no evidence of injury from such a chilling. The cause of such pronounced effects of low but not freezing temperatures undoubtedly lies in disturbances which are induced in the metabolic activities and physiological conditions within the cells. In general, the longer the exposure of such plants to chilling temperatures, the greater the resulting injury.

(3) Freezing Injury.—Many plant tissues are killed or irreparably injured when they are exposed to temperatures which are low enough to cause ice formation within them. This is the most frequent and fundamental type of low-temperature injury in temperate climates, and most of the remainder of the discussion will be devoted to it.

2. *Ice Formation in Plant Tissues.*—As their temperature falls below 0°C., ice crystals sooner or later form in the majority of plant tissues. Dry tissues, such as dormant or quiescent seeds, constitute the only im-

portant exception to this statement. When liquid water gradually cools, freezing usually does not begin at 0°C., but only after its temperature has dropped from a fraction to several degrees below its freezing point. In other words, the water first *undercools* before freezing begins. Similarly the water in plant tissues usually does not freeze until after the tissues have first undercooled. Some plant tissues can undercool as much as 15°C. below their true freezing point before crystallization of water occurs, although this is uncommon. The actual freezing points of plant tissues, however, are seldom below −5°C.

Because of their considerable capacity for undercooling some plant tissues, normally susceptible to frost injury, can survive short exposures to freezing temperatures without injury. This is true, for example, of certain species of cacti, which often can undercool 10°-15°C. Once such tissues actually freeze, however, they are killed or seriously injured.

When tissues of higher plants freeze, crystallization of water most commonly takes place in the intercellular spaces. The ice crystals enlarge at the expense of water which moves toward them, not only from the cells immediately bordering the intercelluar spaces, but also from more distant cells by passage through intervening cells. The lower the temperature, in general, the greater the proportion of the water which freezes in the tissues.

When freezing occurs very rapidly, and sometimes under other conditions, crystallization of water takes place within the cells instead of in the intercellular spaces. When intracellular crystallization of water occurs ice may form in the cytoplasm or in the vacuole, or both, or it may form between the cell wall and the protoplasm. Ice formation within cells is often accompanied by ice formation in the intercellular spaces.

3. *Causes of Freezing Injury in Plants.*—Living plant cells are usually killed when water freezes within them, and this is probably the most usual mechanism of freezing injury. In intracellular freezing small crystals of ice ramify throughout the cytoplasm (Stuckey and Curtis, 1938; Simonovitch and Scarth, 1938) and their lacerating effect is apparently so effective in disorganizing the protoplasmic structure that death of the cell results.

When ice formation occurs in the intercellular spaces of a plant tissue, death of the cells may or may not result, depending upon the *hardiness* (see later) of the tissue. One explanation of freezing injury under these conditions is that the withdrawal of water from the cells results in a dehydration of the protoplasm which in turn induces various disorganizing effects, of which a coagulation of certain layers of the protoplasm appears to be the most destructive. A second is that the formation of ice crystals in the intercellular spaces results in mechanical deformations of the protoplasm, either as a result of direct pressure, or by a withdrawal of water from the cell, or a combination of both, which in turn causes death of the cells. Freezing injury under some conditions appears to result, not at the time of ice formation in the intercellular spaces, but during the subsequent thawing. This is especially prone to occur when the thawing is rapid (Iljin, 1933). Death under these conditions apparently results from various mechanical distortions of the protoplasm attendent upon the too-rapid re-entry of water into the cells from the intercellular spaces.

4. *Frost Resistance and Hardening.*—Many plant tissues can survive the formation of ice crystals within them, a property called *frost resistance* or *hardiness*. Furthermore, the degree of frost resistance is not a fixed quantity but can be modified in many plants as a result of the natural or artificial conditions to which they are subjected. On the other hand, there are many plants which are never frost resistant under any conditions. Increase in the frost resistance of a plant tissue is called *hardening;* a decrease in its frost resistance, *dehardening.* Temperature is the principal, although not the only, environmental factor inducing changes in the hardiness of plants. Exposure of many kinds of plants to temperatures just above the freezing point results in a marked increase in their frost resistance. Crop plants such as cabbage which are to be planted early in the spring are often hardened artificially before being set out in the field. This is usually done by transferring the cabbage seedlings from the greenhouse to a cold-frame for a few days before they are transplanted into the field. Harvey (1930) found that exposure of cabbage plants to a temperature of 0°C. for 2 to 4 hr. per day kept the plants in a hardy condition even if they were exposed to temperatures of 20°C. during the remainder of the day. Continuous exposure of hardened plant tissues to relatively warm temperatures, on the other hand, sooner or later results in dehardening.

Seasonal variations in hardiness are of normal occurrence in the organs of temperate zone species which are exposed to freezing temperatures during the winter months. The leaves of temperate zone evergreens and the buds and stems of temperate zone deciduous trees and shrubs have little or no frost resistance during the summer, but pass into a hardened condition during the autumn, remain relatively frost resistant during the winter months, and undergo a dehardening process in the spring (Winkler, 1913; Meyer, 1932).

Not all of the organs on a plant are equally frost resistant at a given time. In deciduous woody plants mature leaves are commonly more hardy than young leaves, mature stems commonly more hardy than young stems, and stems in general more hardy than leaves. Floral organs may be more or less hardy than leaves, depending upon the species. In temperate zone woody species on which the flower buds open earlier in the season than leaf buds, such as elms, maples, and witch hazel, the floral parts are more frost resistant than the leaves. On the other hand, floral parts of apple and some other fruit trees, at a certain stage in their development, are notoriously more sensitive to frost injury than the young leaves which are present on the tree at the same time.

Complete immunity of any plant tissue to frost injury requires prevention of intracellular freezing and also either prevention of intercellular freezing or else a capacity of the cells to survive its effects. The fundamental basis of frost resistance undoubtedly lies in certain properties of the protoplasm. The changes in protoplasmic properties which are known to be closely correlated with the hardening of plant tissues are an increased permeability of the protoplasmic membranes to water and other polar compounds, a decreased structural viscosity of the cytoplasm, and a reduced liability to coagulation as a result of dehydration of certain layers of the cytoplasm (Levitt, 1941; Scarth, 1944). An increased hydrophily of the protoplasmic colloids—largely proteins—could account for all of these shifts in the properties of the protoplasm. The increased permeability of the protoplasmic membranes favors outward movement of water during freezing and reduces the likelihood of intracellular ice formation. The structural changes which occur in the protoplasm presumably make it better able to withstand mechanical stresses resulting from withdrawal of water when ice forms extracellularly.

Certain grosser features of plant tissues are frequently, although not invariably, correlated with frost resistance. Among these are the three interrelated properties of relatively low cell-water content, relatively high sugar content of the cells, and relatively high osmotic pressure of the cells. It is also noteworthy that many tissues in which the cells are relatively small in size are potentially capable of marked resistance to freezing. All of these factors, however, appear to be of only secondary significance in frost resistance as compared with the protoplasmic factors previously mentioned. They appear to be accessory factors in frost resistance because they lessen the amount of cell shrinkage upon freezing and hence decrease the severity of the resulting deformations of the protoplasm.

It is also worthy of mention that a high correlation between frost resistance and drought resistance (Chap. XV) has been found in many kinds of plants.

5. *Survival of Extremely Low Temperatures by Plant Tissues.*—In apparent contradiction to some of the preceding discussion is the fact that various kinds of seeds, spores, algae, bacteria, fungi, and other plants or plant parts can be cooled to the temperature of liquid air (about $-192°C.$), or even lower, without injury. Relatively dry plant tissues or organs such as seeds or spores survive such treatments unharmed largely

because the quantity of water present in them is so small that freezing cannot occur. However, even relatively moist plant tissues can be exposed to liquid air temperatures under certain conditions without injury. For example, moss plants (*Mnium* sp.), with a water content of more than 65 per cent, survived exposure to liquid air if they were warmed up rapidly when removed, but were killed if warmed up slowly (Luyet and Gehenio, 1940). The explanation for the tolerance without injury of such low temperatures by tissues of relatively high water content, as given by these authors, is as follows. Below a temperature of about −20°C. the mechanism of crystallization in water operates very feebly. It is not possible to cool pure water fast enough to prevent its freezing, but many aqueous solutions and colloidal systems, if cooled very rapidly, as by immersion in liquid air, fail to freeze, but pass instead into a vitreous (glasslike) condition. This is also true of the cellular constituents of many plant and animal tissues. If such vitrified tissues are warmed up very rapidly no crystallization of water ever occurs in them and they survive the low temperature treatment without injury. If, on the other hand, their temperature is raised gradually after vitrification, ice crystals form when the zone of freezing temperatures is reached, and the tissues will be killed or damaged.

Heat Injury and Heat Resistance.—1. *Causes of Injury to Plants at Relatively High Temperatures.*—Several types of injury result to plant cells either directly or indirectly from relatively high temperatures:

(1) Desiccation Injury.—High leaf temperatures resulting either from intense insolation or high air temperatures, or both, may result in excessive rates of transpiration. A relatively high rate of water loss, particularly at times when the rate of absorption of water is sluggish, often leads to death of some or all of the leaves or branches on a plant as a result of desiccation. In extreme cases entire plants are killed in this way.

(2) Injury Resulting from Metabolic Disturbances.—Relatively high temperatures often induce various types of metabolic disturbances which are detrimental or even fatal to plants. One important example of such an effect has been described earlier in the chapter. With rise in temperature, increase in the daily photosynthesis in a plant usually fails to keep pace with increase in its daily respiration. Relatively high temperatures therefore frequently cause a stunting of plants because a disproportionate amount of the foods manufactured is consumed in respiration. Maintenance of such a condition for extended periods may result in the death of plants.

(3) Direct Thermal Effects upon the Protoplasm.—The thermal death point of most active living plant cells is in the approximate range of 50°- 60°C. The exact temperature at which death of the protoplasm will occur

depends upon the length of the period during which the cells are warming up to the lethal temperature. For example, according to Lepeschkin (1912), if the leaf epidermal cells of *Rhoeo discolor* were heated at such a rate that death occurred in 4 min., the lethal temperature was 72.1°C. If the rate of warming was so slow that death did not take place until 150 min. had elapsed, the thermal death point was only 52.0°C.

Air temperatures in temperate regions seldom exceed 40°C., and, although the temperature of an insolated plant organ often exceeds that of the atmosphere, lethal temperatures are seldom attained for reasons discussed in Chap. IX. The surface temperatures of some soils, however, may attain values of 70°C., or even higher, when exposed to intense insolation. Attempts to reforest denuded areas in certain regions have sometimes failed because of such high soil-surface temperatures. The living cells of the stems of the young trees which had been set out were killed at the soil line by contact with soil at a temperature above their thermal death point, thus causing death of the entire transplant. On the other hand, many woody species are habitants of semi-desert regions in which high soil temperatures often prevail. The stems of such species are obviously more heat resistant than those which are injured or killed by contact with hot soils.

Another example of direct heat injury to plants is often evident after a "ground" forest fire sweeps through a woods. Such fires burn fallen leaves and branches on the forest floor and are often without any apparent immediate effects upon living trees and saplings. Subsequently the tops of many of the trees in an area burned over by such a fire die as a result of the killing of an encircling zone of living cells at the base of the trunk by the high temperatures to which they have been exposed.

2. *Cause of Heat Injury.*—The most generally advocated theory of the cause of direct heat injury to plant cells is that it results largely, if not entirely, from a coagulation of protein components of the protoplasm (Lepeschkin, 1935).

3. *Heat Resistance.*—Certain types of tissues are more resistant to heat injury than others. Tissues low in water content generally can endure relatively high temperatures better than those of which the contrary is true. Dry seeds and spores of some species have endured exposure to temperatures of 125°C. and even higher without loss of germinative capacity.

In some plants otherwise susceptible tissues are protected against heat injury because they are enclosed within tissues which have a low thermal conductivity. The bark of many trees is so thick that it insulates the inner, living tissues against the destructive effects of forest fires. The bark of the well-known Big Tree (*Sequoia gigantea*) of California, for example, is almost as resistant to fire as asbestos, has a very low thermal conductivity, and may be two feet in thickness. Many other species of coniferous trees have a thick, incombustible bark of low thermal conductivity. Another well-known example of such a tree is the long-leaved pine (*Pinus palustris*) of the southern United States.

Effects of Radiant Energy on Vegetative Growth.—The spectrum of radiant energy (Fig. 86) ranges from the very long electric waves to the infinitesimally short cosmic waves. All kinds of radiant energy, including light, vary in several different ways, the most important of which are: (1) irradiance ("intensity"), (2) quality, and (3) duration (Chap. XVII). Light is essential to all green plants because of its primary role in photosynthesis. Numerous other effects of light upon physiological conditions and processes in plants have been discussed in previous chapters. Among these are: (1) chlorophyll synthesis, (2) stomatal action, (3) anthocyanin formation, (4) temperature of aerial organs, (5) absorption of electrolytes, (6) permeability, (7) rate of transpiration, and (8) protoplasmic streaming. Several of the most important effects of light on plants remain to be discussed in this and the following chapters.

In this chapter the discussion will be restricted to a few of the more striking examples of the effects of differences in the irradiance, quality, and duration of light and other forms of radiant energy upon the vegetative development of plants.

1. *Irradiance.*—Variations in irradiance, especially of sunlight, are almost invariably accompanied by at least minor variations in the *quality* of light. This fact must frequently be considered in evaluating the effects of different irradiances upon growth or other plant processes. Generally speaking, however, under natural conditions, differences in irradiance have more significant effects upon the growth of plants than differences in light quality.

For a picture of the overall effect of differences in irradiance ("intensity") upon growth, we must consider the results of investigations such as those of Popp (1926) on soybeans. The plants were grown under six different irradiances equivalent on the average to illumination values of 4285, 1536, 560, 390, and 26 foot-candles, respectively. While during the initial period of growth the rate of stem elongation varied inversely with the irradiance, when growth was considered for a 7 weeks' period, a somewhat different relation was found to hold. For such periods the greatest height was attained at intermediate values, in this particular experiment at 560 foot-candles. The thickness of the stems was found to vary directly with the irradiance, while the best general development of leaves, flowers, and fruits occurred at the highest irradiance used, which was approximately half that at noon on a clear summer's day (Chap. XVII).

Somewhat similar results were obtained by Shirley (1929, 1935), who studied the effects of differences in irradiance upon the development of a number of species. In general, the absolute dry weight, percentage of dry matter in the tops, rigidity of the stem, and leaf thickness all increased with increase in irradiance up to full sunlight, providing other factors were not limiting growth. Maximum height of the plants and maximum leaf area were attained, on the other hand, at irradiances considerably below that of full summer sunlight. Low irradiances also resulted in a considerable delay in the time of maximum flowering and fruiting.

In general the results of these and other similar investigations indicate that maximum height and leaf area were attained at irradiances which are considerably less than full summer sunlight. Relatively high irradiances result in most species in shorter internodes, plants of lower stature and smaller leaves, but the dry weight, number and size of the root system, and production of flowers and fruits is greater than in weaker irradiances. Many species show increased growth in terms of dry weight increment with increased irradiance up to 100 per cent of summer sunlight, if no other factor is limiting. All phases of the growth of typical shade species are usually retarded, however, by high irradiances. Many tropical species, for example, are shade plants, and attain their maximum development at irradiances considerably less than that of full sunlight.

Effects on growth such as those described in the preceding several paragraphs actually represent the integrated influences of many processes occurring within the plant, a number of which are conditioned directly or indirectly by light. Some of these effects of light are directly on one phase or another of growth, but others are indirect effects on growth resulting in turn from direct effects of light on some other process or processes. For example, high irradiances may result in high rates of transpiration which are likely to lead to internal deficiencies of water within the plant and a consequent retardation or cessation of cell division or cell enlargement. Low irradiances, on the other hand, may lead to a retarded development of a plant because of the resulting low rate of photosynthesis.

Direct effects of light on different phases of the growth process have often been studied in comparison with the kind of growth exhibited by similar plants which have developed in complete absence of light. Growth of plants under such a condition can be maintained only if a supply of food is available to the growing parts from a storage organ such as a seed or tuber (MacDougal, 1903) or if the plant is artificially fed with soluble carbohydrates.

Seedlings of dicotyledons which have developed in the absence of light have whitish or yellowish, elongate, spindling stems on which the leaves fail to expand (Fig. 148) and have relatively poorly developed root sys-

FIG. 148. Seedlings of bean (*Phaseolus vulgaris*) about two weeks old grown in light (left) and total darkness (right).

tems. When seedlings of monocotyledonous species develop in the absence of light the chlorophyll-free leaves are relatively narrow and more attenuated than the leaves of similar plants which have developed in the light (Fig. 149). The distinctive development of plants in the complete absence of light is called *etiolation*.

Exposure of a plant to light of a very low irradiance is sufficient to prevent the development of any pronounced earmarks of etiolation. When seedlings develop in weak light, expansion of leaves and synthesis of chlorophyll occurs much as in strong light, and the internodes do not elongate as much as in similar plants growing in the dark, although the plant will usually present a more attenuated appearance than in strong light. Even short temporary exposures to light result in the development of a much more nearly normal configuration in plants which are otherwise kept in the dark (Priestley, 1925, 1926; Biebel, 1942; and others).

The attenuated structure of leaves (monocotyledons) and of hypocotyls and stems (dicotyledons) of etiolated plants as compared with similar organs developed in the light appears to result chiefly from an increase in the length of their component cells, but is also in part a result of a greater number of cell divisions in the etiolated plants (Avery *et al.*, 1937). Light thus has two distinctly different retarding effects upon growth in length of plant organs, one on cell division and one on cell elongation. In the first internode of oats, inhibitory effects of light on cell division can be induced at much lower irradiances than inhibitory effects on cell enlargement (Goodwin, 1941). Within limits the magnitude of the retarding effect of light upon increase in length of plant organs becomes greater with increased irradiance or with increased exposure time at the same irradiance (Biebel, 1942).

Thomson (1950) has shown that light has an accelerating effect on the rate of elongation of the coleoptile and internodes of oats but that the duration of this phase of growth is sufficiently shortened by exposure to

Fig. 149. Seedlings of maize (*Zea mais*) about two weeks old grown in light (left) and in total darkness (right).

light that the net effect is that of a lessened elongation of these organs. On the other hand, light was found to increase the rate of elongation of the leaf, but had little or no effect on the duration of the elongation period in this organ, so that the net effect of illumination is to increase the length of the leaf.

In contrast with its retarding effects on elongation and enlargement of many plant cells, exposure to light generally favors structural differentiation of cells.

2. *Light Quality.*—Different qualities of light are obtained in two principal ways for experimental work with plants. The most commonly used method is to interpose a filter of colored glass, gelatin, or other trans-

parent material between a light source and the plant or plant part to be irradiated. The light source may be the sun but is more commonly an artificial one such as a tungsten filament, fluorescent, carbon arc, or mercury-vapor arc lamp. The wave-length composition ("quality") of the light falling on the plant will be in part a function of the emission spectrum of the source, and in part a function of the transmissive properties of the filter, and can be determined with a spectrophotometer. By following such a technique it is possible to separate out from the visible spectrum a number of bands of wave lengths each corresponding approximately to a known color or narrow range of colors. In the simplest experiments upon the effect of light quality on growth as few as three wavebands may be used, corresponding roughly, for example, to the blue, green, and orange-red regions of the spectrum.

A second method which has been employed to obtain different qualities of light in plant experimentation is that of dispersion of a beam of "white light" through a system of prisms and exposing the plant material to different regions of the resulting spectrum. This method can be used only when the plant parts to be irradiated are relatively small, as even with the largest prisms available only narrow bands of light of a given color can be isolated by this method.

Most qualitatively different lights which have been available for experimental use are relatively low in irradiance, and this fact has imposed definite limitations on the scope of investigations into the relation between light quality and various plant processes. Comparisons between the effects of one quality of light and another one on a given reaction in plants are valid only when their irradiances at the plant surface are equal. When such comparisons are made in the following discussion such an equality of irradiance is to be assumed.

All experiments upon the effect of limited ranges of wave lengths of light upon growth lead to the not surprising conclusion that overall development of a plant and increase in its dry weight take place more effectively in the full spectrum of visible light than in any spectral portion thereof. Overall growth of plants in the green is much less than in either the blue-violet or orange-red portions of the spectrum (Rohrbaugh, 1942). The lesser growth in the green undoubtedly results largely, if not entirely, from the restricted expansion of leaves (see later) and the lower efficiency of photosynthesis in the green per unit of incident light as compared with other parts of the spectrum.

The growth reactions to a given spectral band of visible light differ from one organ of a plant to another. Light from the orange-red region generally results in a lesser elongation of stems and hypocotyls than light from other parts of the spectrum. The first internode of oats and other grasses (Weintraub and Price, 1947; Goodwin and Owens, 1948), the hypocotyl and first internode of bean (Withrow, 1941; Rohrbaugh, 1942), and the internodes of pea (Went, 1941) all elongate less in the orange-red region of the visible spectrum than in the other regions. Elongation of such organs appears to be greatest in the blue-violet, less in the green, still less in the orange-red, and least in the complete spectrum of visible light (Fig. 150). There is also evidence that ultraviolet radiation has a marked inhibitory effect upon the elongation of plant organs (Popp and McIlvaine, 1937).

The order of effect of different regions of the spectrum on leaf growth differs from that on the elongation of stems. Expansion of the leaf blades

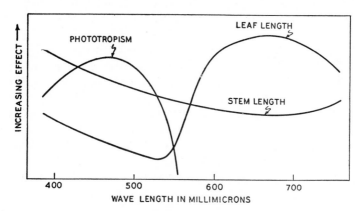

Fɪɢ. 150. Relation between wave length of light and stem and leaf growth. A curve for phototropism is also included for purposes of comparison. Modified from Went (1941).

of pea (Went, 1941) and bean (Rohrbaugh, 1942) is much retarded in the green portion of the spectrum as compared with the orange-red or blue-violet regions (Fig. 150). Maximum expansion occurs in the full spectrum of visible light, next greatest in the blue-violet, and least in the green. Parker *et al.* (1949), in a more precise study of the "action spectrum" of this phenomenon, have shown that the spectral region of maximum effectiveness in promoting elongation of pea leaves lies in the orange-red between wave length limits of 610 and 710 mμ.

All wave lengths of ultraviolet shorter than those found in the sunlight which reaches the earth's surface have a retarding effect on growth and often a destructive influence on seed plants. The longer wave lengths of ultraviolet which are components of the solar radiation falling on the earth's surface are apparently not essential for plants. Such wave lengths of ultraviolet do not penetrate ordinary greenhouse glass, but many kinds of plants readily complete their life cycle from seed to seed when grown in greenhouses. It is highly probable that the effects of such relatively long wave-length ultraviolet radiation on plants do not differ greatly from those of the relatively short wave-length visible radiation at the violet end of the visible spectrum.

Although nearly half of the solar radiant energy which reaches the earth's surface is in the infrared, there is no evidence that radiations in this part of the spectrum are in any way essential to plants. Although much of the infrared falling on plants is reflected or transmitted by leaves or other organs, some is absorbed, and may have effects on growth and other plant processes. Tomato plants exposed to a relatively high irradiance of infrared plus visible radiation had longer internodes, larger leaves, and less chlorophyll than similar plants receiving the same quantity of visible radiation, but no infrared (Johnston, 1932).

3. *Duration of the Light Period.*—In all parts of the world except the tropics and subtropics, marked seasonal variations occur in the length of the daylight period. At 39° N. latitude (approximately that of Washington, D. C.), for example, on the shortest day (December 21) the period from sunrise to sunset is only about 9½ hr.; on the longest day (June 21) it is about 15 hr. At higher latitudes the annual variation in day length is greater; at lower altitudes less (Table 44). In the southern hemisphere the annual variation in day length is the same as that at corresponding latitudes in the northern hemisphere, but the season of short days north of the equator is the season of long days south of the equator, and *vice versa*.

TABLE 44—APPROXIMATE NUMBER OF HOURS OF SUNSHINE POSSIBLE AT VARIOUS
DEGREES OF NORTH LATITUDE

Degrees N. latitude	Approximate latitude of	Hours of sunshine possible			
		Dec. 21	Mar. 21	June 21	Sept. 21
25	Key West, Fla................	10.6	12.2	13.7	12.2
27	Palm Beach, Fla..............	10.4	12.2	13.9	12.2
29	San Antonio, Tex.............	10.3	12.2	14.0	12.2
31	Mobile, Ala..................	10.1	12.2	14.1	12.2
33	Charleston, S. C..............	10.0	12.2	14.3	12.2
35	Memphis, Tenn...............	9.8	12.2	14.5	12.2
37	San Francisco, Cal............	9.6	12.2	14.7	12.2
39	Washington, D. C.............	9.4	12.2	14.9	12.2
41	Omaha, Neb.................	9.2	12.2	15.1	12.2
43	Milwaukee, Wis..............	9.0	12.2	15.4	12.2
45	Portland, Ore...............	8.8	12.2	15.6	12.2
47	Duluth, Minn................	8.5	12.2	15.9	12.3
49	Vancouver, B. C..............	8.2	12.2	16.2	12.3

The development of plants as conditioned by the daily length of the light period, a phenomenon called *photoperiodism*, is one of the most notable of all reactions of plants to their environment. The length of the natural *photoperiod* is somewhat longer (on clear days about 1 hr.) than the period from sunrise to sunset, because light intensity during a portion of the morning and evening twilights is sufficient to induce photoperiodic effects.

Fig. 151.   Maryland Mammoth tobacco plants from Garner and Allard's experiments. Plant on left kept under natural winter daylight (short day); plant on right kept under natural winter daylight plus artificial light from sunset to midnight (long day). Photograph from U. S. Department of Agriculture.

The foundations of our knowledge of photoperiodism were laid when Garner and Allard (1920) observed the behavior of plants of the "Maryland Mammoth" variety of tobacco while growing in a greenhouse during the winter months. This variety of tobacco grows to a height of 10-15 feet but does not ordinarily blossom in the summer while growing outdoors in the vicinity of Washington, D. C. Plants grown in a greenhouse during the winter, on the other hand, did not exceed a few feet in height, but blossomed profusely and bore excellent crops of seed (Fig. 151). These observations led to the hypothesis that the dissimilar development of the tobacco plants during the two seasons resulted from the difference in length of day, and subsequent more critically performed experiments confirmed this hypothesis.

Further experimentation on a variety of species soon resulted in the discovery that different kinds of plants react differently to a given length of photoperiod and that the most conspicuous effect of day length is on the reproductive growth of plants. Flowering in some kinds of plants, such as Maryland Mammoth tobacco, is favored by short days, in other kinds by long days, and in still other kinds by a wide range of day lengths (Chap. XXXII).

In this chapter discussion of this topic will be restricted to a consideration of certain effects of day length upon vegetative growth. A number of such effects have been recognized. Photoperiodic effects upon reproductive growth may indirectly induce effects upon vegetative growth. Many short-day plants, exposed to long days, grow in height indeterminately, but if exposed to short days vegetative growth in height is soon checked as a result of the differentiation of a terminal inflorescence. Many long-day plants, on the other hand, develop only as leaf rosettes when exposed to short days, elongation of flower-bearing stems occurring only under long-day conditions. The length of the photoperiod also has direct effects upon certain phases of vegetative growth; examples of two such effects are discussed below.

Tuberization in a number of species is markedly influenced by the length of the photoperiod. In the McCormick variety of potato, for example, no tubers form when the plants are exposed to an 18-hour photoperiod, but there is a good yield of tubers when the photoperiod is 10 hr. long (Garner and Allard, 1923). Similarly, tubers form abundantly on the underground stolons of the Jerusalem artichoke (*Helianthus tuberosus*) when the plants are exposed to 9-hr. photoperiods, but do not form when the plants are exposed to 18-hr. photoperiods. Furthermore, exposure of only one leaf of a plant of this species to a 9-hr. photoperiod while the rest of the plant is at an 18-hr. photoperiod induces tuber formation just as if the entire plant were exposed to the short photoperiod, but exposure of the terminal bud to a 9-hr. photoperiod while the rest of the plant is at an 18-hr. photoperiod has no such an effect (Hamner and Long, 1939). Obviously the leaves are the locus of a photoperiodic reaction, the effects of which are communicated in some manner or another to the underground organs of the plant and influence their development. Such an effect can be visualized most easily in terms of a hormonal mechanism.

The development of bulbs by certain species of plants is markedly influenced by the length of the photoperiod to which the plant is exposed. Bulb formation in most varieties of onions, for example, is favored by relatively long photoperiods, the minimum effective photoperiod varying from about 12 to 16 hr. according to the variety (Magruder and Allard 1937).

Water.—The dynamic condition of the water in a plant is largely controlled by the opposing effects of the processes of transpiration and water absorption (Chap. XV). Whenever the rate of the former process exceeds the latter for any appreciable period of time the volume of water within the plant shrinks. This results in a diminution in cell turgidity, an increase in the diffusion-pressure deficit of the water in the cells, and a decrease in the hydration of the protoplasm and cell walls. A decrease in the hydration of the protoplasm in the cells of any meristematic tissue usually results in a cessation or checking of cell division or cell enlargement or both. Contrariwise, a shift in environmental conditions which brings about, directly or indirectly, an increase in the hydration of the protoplasm of a meristem usually results in an increase in the rate of these two phases of growth if no other factors are limiting.

Not all phases of growth are equally affected by a diminution in the volume of water within a plant. Both cell division and cell enlargement are adversely influenced by even a moderate deficiency of water. It should be recalled, however, that when an internal deficiency of water exists within a plant, water often moves from other organs toward the meristematic tissues (Chap. XV). The enlargement phase of growth is seemingly checked more by an internal shortage of water than the cell division phase. Maximum enlargement of cells during growth apparently can be attained only when the water supply to them is not appreciably restricted. If a shortage of water prevails within the plant the enlargement of cells terminates earlier than when water is present in abundance, and structural differentiation of the cells ensues sooner. Deficiency of water, in general, favors structural differentiation of cells over the cell division and enlargement phases of growth.

Water, as it affects growth processes, operates primarily as an internal factor but, as such an internal factor, is influenced by a galaxy of environmental conditions. Any external factor which affects the rate of transpiration or the rate of intake of water will therefore have an influence on the rate of growth. While temporary periods of internal-water deficiency may result from the effects of other environmental factors, principally those influencing transpiration rates, prolonged periods of internal dearth of water in plants mostly result from an inadequate supply of available soil water.

In many habitats periods during which available water is present in the soil may alternate with periods during which there is virtually no available water present. Most kinds of plants can survive such intermittent periods of soil drought if none of them is too prolonged. In general, however, the more frequent and longer such periods of drought are during a growing season, the less the overall growth of a plant.

For most kinds of plants, a soil-water content in the vicinity of the field capacity is the most favorable to continued growth. With a decrease in the soil-water content, marked effects on growth do not appear until the permanent wilting percentage is approached (cf., effects on absorption of water, Chap. XIV). At the permanent wilting percentage all growth ceases (Wadleigh and Gauch, 1948). As the soil-water content increases above the field capacity, the growth of most species will sooner or later be retarded as a result of the concomittant decreased aeration of the soil.

While the roots of plants are usually in contact with liquid water in the soil, the aerial parts of plants are continuously bathed in a gaseous medium in which water-vapor molecules are present. The humidity of the atmosphere is thus another water factor which affects growth and other processes in plants. In this connection it should be recalled that the significant index of atmospheric humidity is the vapor pressure and not the relative humidity (Chap. XI). In general, small variations in the vapor pressure of the atmosphere have very little influence on the water content of plants, and hence no appreciable effect on growth rates. This is especially true whenever the soil-water supply is adequate. When the differences in vapor pressure are considerable, however, marked effects on growth result. This is exemplified in the work of Nightingale and Mitchell (1934) who exposed two groups of tomato plants, both at 70°C. and provided with adequate supplies of soil water, to relative humidities of 35 per cent and 95 per cent, respectively. The plants at the higher humidity grew much faster and developed thin-walled, succulent tissues. Those at the lower humidity, in which there was undoubtedly a more marked internal deficiency of water, grew relatively slowly, developed thick-walled cells, and in general lacked succulence. At the higher humidity, cell division and enlargement, resulting in the development of succulent tissues, were obviously favored more than structural differentiation. At the lower humidity, structural differentiation, principally in the form of a thickening of the walls, predominated rather than cell division and enlargement.

In general, plants which have developed under adverse soil-water conditions are dwarfed or stunted. Excellent naturally occurring examples of the effect of soil drought on the development of plants are always evident during years of deficient precipitation in normally mesic habitats. Wheat, maize, and other cereal crops, for example, never attain their usual stature during a drought season. Similarly the annual shoots of woody species do not increase as much in length during droughts as during seasons when water is present in abundance. Diameter growth of woody stems is also often retarded during drought years. On the basis of this fact, numerous attempts have been made to trace past climatic cycles in regions in which trees that have attained a considerable age are found by a study of the growth rings in the trunks. Considerable caution must be exercised, however, in interpreting such data (Glock, 1941).

An inadequate soil-water supply may check the growth of a plant more at certain stages in its development than others. In many species vegetative growth is more likely to be retarded by soil-water deficiency than the development of reproductive organs. In some species there are certain critical periods during which the water supply must be adequate else pronounced modifications in the morphogenic development of the plant will occur. This is true of wheat and the other small grains in which elongation of the inflorescence-bearing stem does not occur until the internodes and inflorescence have been differentiated. Deficiency of water during this elongation or "shooting" period exerts a marked retarding effect upon the height growth of such species, and also upon their yield.

Concentration of the Soil Solution.—Although the concentration of solutes in the soil solutions of most soils is so low that their osmotic pressures do not exceed a fraction of an atmosphere, certain noteworthy exceptions to this statement exist. Among these are salt marsh, saline and alkali soils, in which soil solution osmotic pressures of tens or even hundreds of atmospheres may be attained. Soil solution osmotic pressures ranging up to at least ten atmospheres may also exist under certain cultural conditions. Examples are soils which have been irrigated with water containing relatively high concentrations of salts, or soils which have been injudiciously overfertilized. This latter situation is quite commonly encountered in greenhouses.

Increase in the osmotic pressure of the soil solution leads to a decrease in the rate of absorption of water and, hence, would also be expected to result in a retardation in growth. The reality of such an effect has been demonstrated by a number of investigators. The results of Hayward and Long (1943), for example, show that the higher the osmotic pressure of the solution in a sand culture, as brought about by increased concentrations of sodium salts, the less the growth, measured as dry weight increment, of tomato plants (Fig. 152). Similarly Gauch and Wadleigh (1944) showed that dry-weight increment of bean plants decreased proportionately with increase in osmotic pressure of aerated solution cultures up to 4.5 atm. if NaCl, Na_2SO_4, or $CaCl_2$ was the salt used to bring about the increase in osmotic pressure. If the osmotic pressure was increased by the addition of $MgCl_2$ or $MgSO_4$, however, growth was retarded more in solutions above 1.5 atm. osmotic pressure than in isosmotic solutions in which sodium or calcium salts were the principal solutes present. Although the

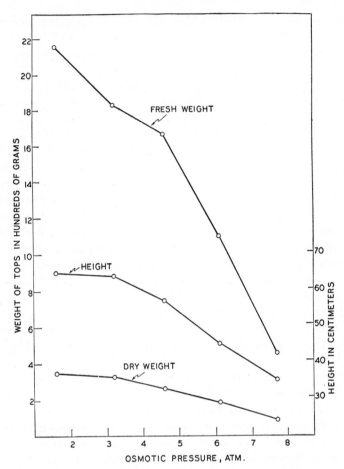

FIG. 152.   Relation between osmotic pressure of substrate and vegetative growth
of tomato. Data of Hayward and Long (1943).

primary cause of the retarding effect of an increased concentration of
solutes in the soil solution is undoubtedly an osmotic one, some kinds of
solutes, such as magnesium salts, when present above a certain concentration, exert secondary toxicity effects which further retard growth. In
naturally occurring alkali soils still other conditions are present which
have a depressing effect on growth (Magistad, 1945).

The relation between concentration of solutes in the aqueous medium
and the rate of growth is also an important consideration in sand and
solution culture techniques (Chap. XXV).

Concentration of Gases in the Soil Atmosphere.—Except in very well-
aerated soils, such as sands or sandy loams, the concentration of carbon

dioxide in the soil atmosphere is usually higher, and the concentration of oxygen usually lower, than in the aerial atmosphere (Chap. XIV). Marked deficiencies in soil aeration exist most commonly in over-wet soils, but such a condition may also be present in fine-pored, tightly packed soils even when they are relatively dry.

In general, indequate aeration results in a retardation in the growth of most kinds of plants. The principal exceptions to this statement are plants which are native to marshy or boggy terrains. As an example of such an effect we may consider the growth of sunflower and soybean plants which developed in unaerated sand and loam as contrasted with other plants of the same species grown in similar but aerated soils (Loehwing, 1934). Aerated plants were taller and heavier, had larger and more fibrous root systems, and a smaller shoot-root ratio (Chap. XXXIII) than the unaerated plants. The ash, calcium, potassium, and phosphorus contents per plant were greater in terms of absolute weight in aerated as contrasted with unaerated plants. Similarly the total weights per plant of starch, total sugars, and nitrogen were greater in the aerated plants than in the unaerated plants.

The retarded growth of plants in poorly aerated soils undoubtedly results largely from the reduced absorption of water (Chap. XIV) and from the reduced absorption of mineral salts (Chap. XXIV) which occur under such conditions. Another possibility is that of diminished caulocaline synthesis (Chap. XXIX). Although when carbon dioxide concentrations in soils are sufficiently high that they exert a retarding effect on growth, such concentrations are not often obtained even in poorly aerated soils. Leonard and Pinckard (1946), for example, found that a carbon dioxide concentration of at least 30 per cent was necessary in the gas mixture saturating a solution culture to result in even a small inhibiting effect on the growth of cotton roots. Concentrations of carbon dioxide in the soil atmosphere apparently do not often exceed 15 per cent. On the other hand, concentrations of oxygen low enough to exert a retarding effect on growth are frequently attained in poorly aerated soils. Growth is retarded in the roots of many species when the oxygen concentration of the soil drops below 10 per cent (Cannon, 1925, and others). In poorly aerated soils oxygen concentrations are frequently less than this and often approach a zero value. A deficiency of oxygen therefore appears to be the more important factor in causing diminished growth of both roots and plants as a whole in poorly aerated soils than an excess of carbon dioxide.

Mineral Elements.—Although it is conventional to speak of the effects of mineral elements on plant growth, strictly speaking they do not have effects as such, but only when present in the form of ions, or as constituents of molecules. The many and complex relations of the various essential and some nonessential mineral elements to the growth and metabolism of plants have already been discussed in Chap. XXV.

Nitrogen.—In the literal sense nitrogen *per se* has no effects on the metabolism or growth of the higher green plants. The word is conventionally used, however, for brevity, as a blanket designation for the various nitrogenous compounds which participate in the physiological processes of plants.

Both carbohydrate and nitrogenous foods are necessary for the development of any plant. Deficiency of either soon results in the appearance of characteristic and recognizable peculiarities of growth. The supply of carbohydrate and nitrogenous foods within a plant is influenced by many factors. Among these are the reciprocal relationships which exist between these two kinds of foods. Primary synthesis of amino acids and similar compounds occurs only at the expense of carbohydrates or their derivatives which serve both as building material (together with nitrates, or other nitrogen-containing compounds) and as a source of energy (Chap. XXVI). Rapid amino-acid synthesis therefore results in a diminution in the proportion of carbohydrate foods in a plant, while plants in which amino acid synthesis occurs slowly will often be proportionately rich in carbohydrates.

As described in the preceding chapter, continued growth of any meristem requires that there be maintained to it a supply of both carbohydrate and nitrogenous foods. Both of these kinds of compounds are assimilated in relatively large quantities, especially during the cell division and enlargement phases of growth, and, next to water, these two classes of substances are utilized in greatest quantities during growth. Considerable quantities of carbohydrates are also used up in any actively growing meristem in the process of respiration.

If the supply of nitrogenous foods to any actively growing vegetative meristem is abundant relative to the supply of carbohydrate foods, a large quantity of protoplasm will be formed relative to the amount of cell-wall material constructed. The resulting cells will usually be large, thin-walled, and will contain an abundance of protoplasm. Tissues composed mostly or entirely of such cells are usually soft and succulent. The proportion of mechanical tissue developing under such metabolic conditions is ordinarily small.

As a direct outcome of its influence on the development of organs and tissues from meristems, a relatively high proportion of nitrogenous to carbohydrate foods within a plant results in distinctive morphogenic effects on plants (Kraus and Kraybill, 1918, and others). Such plants are usually vigorously vegetative. The tops are generally large, both in absolute size, and relative to the size of the root system. Leaves are usually large, soft in texture, and dark green in color. The stems are generally thick, pithy, and succulent. In common parlance the plants "go to tops" under these metabolic conditions, which are most commonly engendered by an excess of nitrogenous compounds in the soil. Plants exhibiting this luxuriant type of vegetative development usually are comparatively unfruitful (Chap. XXXII).

If the opposite metabolic situation prevails within a plant, and carbohydrate foods are relatively more abundant than nitrogenous foods, proportionately more cell-wall structure and less protoplasm will be fabricated. The resulting cells will be small and thick-walled and will contain comparatively little protoplasm. Tissues composed largely or entirely of such cells are usually compact and more or less woody. The development of fibers and of mechanical tissues generally is also favored by an excess of carbohydrate relative to nitrogenous foods.

Under metabolic conditions such as those described in the preceding paragraph the overall morphogenic development of a plant is different from that which results when nitrogenous foods are relatively more abundant (Kraus and Kraybill, 1918, and others). If the proportion of nitrogenous foods available is not too low, the vegetative development of the plant will be good but not luxuriant. Stems will be thick and relatively woody; leaves will be well developed and a normal green in color. In size and stature such plants are smaller than those developed when nitrogenous foods are present in greater abundance, and the proportion of tops to roots is smaller. Generally speaking, however, flowering and fruiting occur much more abundantly in such plants than in those in which the proportion of nitrogenous to carbohydrate foods is greater.

An extreme deficiency of nitrogenous foods, which rarely occurs unless nitrogen compounds are deficient in the soil, results in a stunting of plants, and development of the characteristic symptoms of nitrogen deficiency (Chap. XXV). On the other hand, an extreme deficiency of carbohydrate foods also results in a stunting of plants. Such *carbohydrate deficient* plants are likely to be succulent in growth in contrast to nitrogen-deficient plants which are usually woody. Dearth of nitrogenous foods limits growth because little or no new protoplasm can be formed; dearth of carbohydrate foods limits growth largely because it checks synthesis of new cell-wall materials, although indirectly synthesis of protoplasm may also be limited because carbohydrates are also required in amino-acid synthesis.

In the practical growing of plants more or less control over their development is often exercised by employing cultural practices which influence the proportionate quantities of carbohydrate and nitrogenous foods within the plant. One of the more obvious ways in which this can be done is by varying the quantity of nitrogenous fertilizer applied to a soil. Many other cultural practices also influence the relative quantities of these two major kinds of foods as well as other metabolic conditions in a plant, and hence its morphogenic development. The more important of these are watering, shading, pruning, controlling of temperature in greenhouses, fertilizing, crop rotation, and the interplanting of one crop with another.

Atmospheric Gases.—In the aerial atmosphere, unlike the soil atmosphere, the concentration of oxygen is virtually constant, and does not need to be considered as a variable influencing the development of plants under natural conditions. Variations in the carbon dioxide concentration, although occurring over a much narrower range in the aerial than in the soil atmosphere, are often sufficient to have considerable effect on the rate of photosynthesis (Chap. XIX). The water-vapor content of the air varies considerably and the pronounced influences of this factor upon transpiration, the internal water relations of plants, and indirectly upon growth, have already been considered.

Sometimes gases other than those normally present in the atmosphere become a part of the environment of plants. Smelters, for example, release considerable quantities of sulfur dioxide into the atmosphere. This gas, in any appreciable concentration, is highly toxic to plants; hence the countryside in the vicinity of smelters is often virtually denuded of vegetation. Most species of plants are injured by an exposure of only one hour to an atmosphere containing as little as one part of this gas in a million (Zimmerman and Crocker, 1934).

Escaping illuminating gas often has injurious or lethal effects upon plants. Leaky gas mains sometimes cause the death or injury of shade trees along city streets. Similarly injury or death of house or greenhouse plants has sometimes been found to result from leakage of gas. Manufactured illuminating gas contains both carbon monoxide and ethylene, the former being present in much larger proportions than the second. Ethylene, however, is the chief toxic constituent of such gas. Prolonged exposure to even very small concentrations of manufactured illuminating gas in the atmosphere results in death or profound physiological disturbances in most species of plants. Natural gas is much less injurious to plants than manufactured illuminating gas (Gustafson, 1944), and probably never accumulates in houses or greenhouses in harmful concentrations. Natural gas is composed principally of methane and ethane, and contains no carbon monoxide or ethylene.

Some species, of which the tomato is an example, are exceedingly sensitive to ethylene. The leaves of tomato plants soon show epinasty (Chap. XXXVI) at concentrations as low as 0.1 part of ethylene to a million of air. A few species are even more sensitive to ethylene (Crocker *et al.*, 1932). Since such minute concentrations of ethylene are far less than can be detected by odor, or even by chemical tests, the simplest method of detecting this gas when present only in traces is to stand several young potted tomato plants in the room to be tested for several days. If traces of ethylene are present epinasty of the leaves will soon appear (Fig. 153).

A comparison between the toxicity of certain gases to animals (rats, mice, house flies) and the toxicity of the same gases to green plants

Fig. 153. Epinasty in tomato resulting from exposure to ethylene. Plant on right exposed to 0.1 part per million of ethylene for 48 hr.; plant on left kept under same conditions in an ethylene-free atmosphere. Photograph from Crocker *et al.*, (1932).

(tomato, buckwheat, tobacco) is afforded by the work of Thornton and Setterstrom (1940) and Weedon *et al.* (1940). The order of decreasing toxicity of the several gases to animals was HCN: H_2S: Cl_2: SO_2: NH_3. The order of their decreasing toxicity to green plants was notably different: Cl_2: SO_2: NH_3: HCN: H_2S.

Gaseous emanations from certain woods, oils, and varnishes have been shown by Weintraub and Price (1948) to have marked inhibitory effects on the growth of plants.

Mercury vapor is present in the atmosphere of any room in which liquid mercury is exposed to the air and is highly toxic to many kinds of plants. Mercury spilled in a greenhouse, for example, has been known to result in complete defoliation of certain species, such as roses.

Another aerial, although not gaseous, factor in the environment of many plants is salt-water spray, droplets of which may be carried a mile or two inland by only moderately strong winds, and under hurricane conditions much farther. Ocean-water spray is highly toxic to many land plants, young leaves and twigs being the most susceptible, but some species are much more liable to injury from such spray than others. The sheared off configuration of many species of seaside trees and shrubs results at least in part from salt-spray injury. The distribution of plants in coastal areas is also controlled in part by their tolerance to ocean-water spray (Wells and Shunk, 1938).

Physiological Preconditioning.—The growth performance of a plant at any stage of its development is not only continuously influenced by its hereditary make-up and by the prevailing environmental conditions, but often shows a lingering effect of the environmental conditions to which it has been exposed during some previous stage in its life history. The induction within a plant of internal metabolic conditions which carry over into and influence its growth or reactions during a later stage in its life history is called *physiological preconditioning*. The phenomena of hardening, already discussed, and of photoperiodic and thermal induction (Chap. XXXII) are excellent examples of physiological preconditioning. Another example is the phenomenon called *vernalization*. This term usually designates a low temperature (usually just above freezing) treatment given slightly germinated seeds before sowing which shortens the time to flowering of plants which develop from them. Less commonly the term is applied to the treatment of seeds at relatively high temperatures, or to treatment of other plant organs than seeds (McKinney, 1940). Vernalization of the grains of a winter wheat variety, for example, so speeds up the completion of its life cycle that it can be grown as a spring wheat. The fundamental physiological effect of vernalization appears to be an earlier induction of flowering. The physiological mechanism involved is probably akin to those of thermal and photoperiodic induction. Vernalization of seeds sometimes occurs while they are still attached to the parent plant, so that the environmental conditions prevailing while seeds are developing within the ovulary may have a delayed influence upon the subsequent development of plants from them. "Devernalization" of seeds may also occur. A temporary period of high temperatures may largely or entirely offset any vernalization already achieved during a preceding period of low temperatures. For further information on this topic the works of Whyte (1946) and Murneek and Whyte (1948) should be consulted.

SUGGESTED FOR COLLATERAL READING

Crocker, W. *Growth of Plants*. Reinhold Publishing Corp. New York. 1948.
Duggar, B. M., Editor. *Biological Effects of Radiation*. McGraw-Hill Book Co., Inc. New York. 1936.
Levitt, J. *Frost Killing and Hardiness of Plants*. Burgess Publishing Co. Minneapolis. 1941.
Lundegårdh, H. *Environment and Plant Development*. Translated and edited by E. Ashby. Edward Arnold and Co. London. 1931.
Murneek, A. E., R. O. Whyte, and others. *Vernalization and Photoperiodism*. Chronica Botanica Co. Waltham, Mass. 1948.
Whyte, R. O. *Crop Production and Environment*. Faber and Faber. London. 1946.

SELECTED BIBLIOGRAPHY

Arndt, C. H. Temperature growth-relations of the roots and hypocotyls of cotton seedlings. *Plant Physiol.* **20**: 200-220. 1945.
Avery, G. S., Jr., P. R. Burkholder, and Harriet B. Creighton. Polarized growth and cell studies in the first internode and coleptile of *Avena* in relation to light and darkness. *Bot. Gaz.* **99**: 125-143. 1937.
Biebel, J. P. Some effects of radiant energy in relation to etiolation. *Plant Physiol.* **17**: 377-396. 1942.
Burkholder, P. R. The role of light in the life of plants. *Bot. Rev.* **2**: 1-52, 97-172. 1936.
Cannon, W. A. Physiological features of roots, with especial reference to the relation of roots to aeration of the soil. *Carnegie Inst. Washington Publ. No. 368.* 1925.
Chase, Florence M. Increased stimulation of the alga *Stichococcus bacilarus* by successive exposures to short wave lengths of the ultraviolet. *Smithsonian Misc. Coll.* **99**. No. 17. 1941.
Crocker, W., P. W. Zimmerman, and A. E. Hitchcock. Ethylene-induced epinasty of leaves and the relation of gravity to it. *Contr. Boyce Thompson Inst.* **4**: 177-218. 1932.
Garner, W. W., and H. A. Allard. Effect of the relative length of day and night and other factors of the environment on growth and reproduction in plants. *Jour. Agric. Res.* **18**: 553-606. 1920.
Garner, W. W., and H. A. Allard. Further studies in photoperiodism, the response of the plant to relative length of day and night. *Jour. Agric. Res.* **23**: 871-920. 1923.
Gauch, H. G., and C. H. Wadleigh. Effects of high salt concentration on growth of bean plants. *Bot. Gaz.* **105**: 379-387. 1944.
Glock, W. Growth rings and climate. *Bot. Rev.* **7**: 649-713. 1941.
Goodwin, R. H. On the inhibition of the first internode of *Avena* by light. *Amer. Jour. Bot.* **28**: 325-332. 1941.
Goodwin, R. H., and Olga v. H. Owens. An action spectrum for inhibition of the first internode of *Avena* by light. *Bull. Torrey Bot. Club* **75**: 18-21. 1948.
Gustafson, F. G. Is natural gas injurious to flowering plants? *Plant Physiol.* **19**: 551-558. 1944.

Hamner, K. C., and E. M. Long. Localization of photoperiodic perception in *Helianthus tuberosus*. *Bot. Gaz.* **101:** 81-90. 1939.

Hartsema, A. M., I. Luyten, and A. H. Blauuw. The optimal temperatures from flower-formation to flowering. *Verh. Kon. Akad. Wentsch. Amsterdam* II, **27:** 1-46. 1930.

Harvey, R. B. Time and temperature factors in hardening plants. *Amer. Jour. Bot.* **17:** 212-217. 1930.

Hayward, H. E., and E. M. Long. Some effects of sodium salts on the growth of the tomato. *Plant Physiol.* **18:** 556-569. 1943.

Iljin, W. S. Über den Kältetod der Pflanzen und seine Ursachen. *Protoplasma* **20:** 105-124. 1933.

Johnston, E. S. The functions of radiation in the physiology of plants. II. Some effects of near infra-red radiation on plants. *Smithsonian Misc. Coll.* **87.** No. 14. 1932.

Kraus, E. J., and H. R. Kraybill. Vegetation and reproduction with special reference to the tomato. *Oregon Agric. Expt. Sta. Bull. No. 149*. 1918.

Lehenbauer, P. A. Growth of maize seedlings in relation to temperature. *Physiol. Res.* **1:** 247-288. 1914.

Leitch, I. Some experiments on the influence of temperature on the rate of growth in *Pisum sativum*. *Ann. Bot.* **30:** 25-46. 1916.

Leonard, O. A., and J. A. Pinckard. Effect of various oxygen and carbon dioxide concentrations on cotton root development. *Plant Physiol.* **21:** 18-36. 1946.

Lepeschkin, W. W. Zur Kenntnis der Einwerkung supramaximaler Temperaturen auf die Pflanze. *Ber. Deutsch. Bot. Ges.* **30:** 703-714. 1912.

Lepeschkin, W. W. Zur Kenntnis des Hitzetodes des Protoplasmas. *Protoplasma* **23:** 349-366. 1935.

Loehwing, W. F. Physiological aspects of the effect of continuous soil aeration on plant growth. *Plant Physiol.* **9:** 567-583. 1934.

Luyet, B. J., and P. M. Gehenio. Life and death at low temperature. *Biodynamica.* Normandy, Mo. 1940.

MacDougal, D. T. The influence of light and darkness upon growth and development. *Mem. N. Y. Bot. Gard.* **2:** 1-319. 1903.

Magistad, O. C. Plant growth relations on saline and alkali soils. *Bot. Rev.* **11:** 181-230. 1945.

Magruder, R., and H. A. Allard. Bulb formation in some American and European varieties of onions as affected by length of day. *Jour. Agric. Res.* **54:** 719-752. 1937.

McKinney, H. H. Vernalization and the growth-phase concept. *Bot. Rev.* **6:** 25-47. 1940.

Meyer, B. S. Further studies on cold resistance in evergreens, with special reference to the possible role of bound water. *Bot. Gaz.* **94:** 297-321. 1932.

Mitscherlich, E. A. Des Gesetz des Minimums und das Gesetz des abnehmenden Bodenertrags. *Landw. Jahrb.* **38:** 537-552. 1909.

Nightingale, G. T. Effects of temperature on metabolism in tomato. *Bot. Gaz.* **95:** 35-58. 1933.

Nightingale, G. T., and J. W. Mitchell. Effects of humidity on metabolism in tomato and apple. *Plant Physiol.* **9:** 217-236. 1934.

Parker, M. W., S. B. Hendricks, H. A. Borthwick, and F. W. Went. Spectral sensitivities for leaf and stem growth of etiolated pea seedlings and their similarity to action spectra for photoperiodism. *Amer. Jour. Bot.* **36:** 194-204. 1949.

Popp, H. W. Effect of light intensity on growth of soy beans and its relation to the autocatalyst theory of growth. *Bot. Gaz.* **82:** 306-319. 1926.

Popp, H. W., and H. R. C. McIlvaine. Growth substances in relation to the mechanism of action of radiation on plants. *Jour. Agric. Res.* **55:** 931-936. 1937.

Priestley, J. H. Light and growth. I, II. *New Phytol.* **24:** 271-283. 1925. **25:** 145-169. 1926.

Rohrbaugh, L. M. Effects of light quality on growth and mineral nutrition of bean. *Bot. Gaz.* **104:** 133-151. 1942.

Scarth, G. W. Cell physiological studies of frost resistance: a review. *New Phytol.* **43:** 1-12. 1944.

Sellschop, J. P. F., and S. C. Salmon. The influence of chilling, above the freezing point, on certain crop plants. *Jour. Agric. Res.* **37:** 315-338. 1928.

Shirley, H. L. The influence of light intensity and light quality upon the growth of plants. *Amer. Jour. Bot.* **16:** 354-390. 1929.

Shirley, H. L. Light as an ecological factor and its measurement. I, II. *Bot. Rev.* **1:** 355-381. 1935. **11:** 497-532. 1945.

Siminovitch, D., and G. W. Scarth. A study of the mechanism of frost injury to plants. *Canadian Jour. Res.* **C 16:** 467-481. 1938.

Stuckey, Irene H., and O. F. Curtis. Ice formation and the death of plant cells by freezing. *Plant Physiol.* **13:** 815-833. 1938.

Thomson, Betty F. The effect of light on the rate of development of *Avena* seedlings. *Amer. Jour. Bot.* **37:** 284-291. 1950.

Thornton, N. C., and C. Setterstrom. Toxicity of ammonia, chlorine, hydrogen cyanide, hydrogen sulphide and sulphur dioxide gases. III. Green plants. *Contr. Boyce Thompson Inst.* **11:** 343-356. 1940.

Wadleigh, C. H., and H. C. Gauch. Rate of leaf elongation as affected by the intensity of the total soil moisture stress. *Plant Physiol.* **23:** 485-495. 1948.

Weedon, F. R., A. Hartzell, and C. Setterstrom. Toxicity of ammonia, chlorine, hydrogen cyanide, hydrogen sulfide, and sulphur dioxide gases. V. Animals. *Contr. Boyce Thompson Inst.* **11:** 365-385. 1940.

Weintraub, R. L., and L. Price. Developmental physiology of the grass seedling. II. Inhibition of mesocotyl elongation in various grasses by red and violet light. *Smithsonian Misc. Coll.* **106.** No. 21. 1947.

Weintraub, R. L., and L. Price. Inhibition of plant growth by emanations from oils, varnishes and woods. *Smithsonian Misc. Coll.* **107.** No. 17. 1948.

Wells, B. W., and I. V. Shunk. Salt spray: an important factor in coastal ecology. *Bull. Torrey Bot. Club* **65:** 485-492. 1938.

Went, F. W. Effects of light on stem and leaf growth. *Amer. Jour. Bot.* **28:** 83-95. 1941.

Went, F. W. Plant growth under controlled conditions. II. Thermoperiodicity in growth and fruiting of the tomato. *Amer. Jour. Bot.* **31:** 135-150. 1944. V. The relation between age, light, variety, and thermoperiodicity of tomatoes. *Amer. Jour. Bot.* **32:** 469-479. 1945.

Werner, H. O. The effect of controlled nitrogen supply with different temperatures and photoperiods upon the development of the potato plant. *Univ. Neb. Agric. Expt. Sta. Bull. No. 75.* 1934.

Winkler, A. Über den Einfluss der Aussenbedingungen auf die Kälteresistenz ausdauernder Gewächse. *Jahrb. Wiss. Bot.* **52:** 467-506. 1913.

Withrow, R. B. Response of seedlings to various wavebands of low light intensity. *Plant Physiol.* **16:** 241-256. 1941.

Wort, D. J. Soil temperature and the growth of Marquis wheat. *Plant Physiol.* **15:** 335-342. 1940.

Zimmerman, P. W., and W. Crocker. Toxicity of air containing sulphur dioxide gas. *Contr. Boyce Thompson Inst.* **6:** 455-470. 1934.

DISCUSSION QUESTIONS

1. In critical physiological experiments it is often desirable to work with a number of plants of identical physiological constitution. Suggest several ways in which this can be accomplished.

2. Why are hilltops usually better locations for apple orchards than nearby valleys?

3. Peach trees often show winter injury on the side of the trunk with a southern exposure. The north side of the trunk seldom shows such injury. Explain.

4. Some of the largest yields of hay per acre have been obtained in Alaska. Suggest possible explanations.

5. In regrading lawns, the depth of the soil is often increased by one or more feet above the original level. Trees of some species are killed by such a treatment. Why? If a relatively small area around the tree trunk is kept free from soil the tree may survive. Why?

6. What type of low temperature injury is probably most effective in preventing the spread of subtropical species into temperate regions?

7. Suggest reasons why northern species of plants often fail to survive when transplanted to more southern latitudes.

8. List the important physiological processes occurring in a leaf-bearing meristematic shoot of an herbaceous plant that will usually show a change in rate when a cloud obscures the sun after a period of direct exposure to sunlight under "standard day" conditions. Explain, for each process, whether you would expect an increase or a decrease in rate and why.

9. Why are greenhouses often operated at lower night temperatures than day temperatures?

10. In general, would you expect soil nitrogen conditions which are favorable to the development of good crops of lettuce or celery to be equally favorable to the development of good crops of Irish potatoes? Explain.

11. What are some of the ways in which the proportion of carbohydrate to nitrogenous foods in plants can be increased? Decreased?

12. Why do not apple or peach trees grow well in Florida?

13. To insure maximum hardiness of young plants, to what combination of light, temperature, and water supply conditions would you expose them for a period before exposure to freezing temperatures?

XXXI

REPRODUCTIVE GROWTH

As applied to the seed plants, to which this discussion is restricted, "reproductive growth" refers, in general, to the formation of flowers, fruits, and seeds. This term therefore embraces a complex of closely interrelated processes and phenomena, some of which occur sequentially, while others overlap in time.

The principal events which usually occur during the reproductive growth of a seed plant are: initiation of flower primordia, maturation of floral parts, development of the pollen grains within the anthers, development of an embryo sac with an egg and a fusion nucleus in each ovule in the ovulary, pollination, formation of two sperms from the generative nucleus in the pollen grain or tube, growth of the pollen tube from the stigma into the ovule, fertilization (fusion of one sperm with the egg) and triple fusion (fusion of the other sperm with the fusion nucleus), development of the embryo from the fertilized egg, development of the endosperm from the endosperm nucleus, development of the seed from the ovule, and development of the fruit from the ovulary or from the ovulary and adjacent tissues.

Although all of the processes and phenomena listed above are phases of reproductive growth, two main stages, the flowering stage and the fruiting stage, can be clearly distinguished. The latter can be considered usually to begin with pollination. Not only are these two stages morphologically distinct, but they are physiologically even more distinct. Flowering, despite its morphological and physiological complexity, is a relatively transitory phase in growth. Vegetative growth and fruit growth, on the other hand, are usually processes of considerable duration and physiologically resemble each other more closely than either resembles flowering. These former two kinds of growth are usually conditioned much more by the general nutritive conditions of the plant than is flowering which appears to be predominantly under hormonal control (see later).

Initiation and Development of Flowers.—Some vegetative apical stem meristems continue to grow as such indefinitely but sooner or later, in the life history of most plants, some of them become transformed into reproductive meristems. The vegetative state may be regarded as a basic one, less differentiated physiologically and morphologically than the reproductive state. A shift from the vegetative into the reproductive state may occur, however, whenever environmental conditions become such that the requisite internal conditions leading to flower induction are established within the meristem. The phrase "sooner or later" as used above may cover a range in time from a few days to many years. The length of time which a given apical meristem remains in the vegetative state before undergoing transformation into a reproductive meristem differs greatly from one kind of plant to another and from one meristem to another on a given plant, being conditioned in part by genetic and in part by environmental factors. Under certain environmental conditions, not exactly the same for any two kinds of plants, a plant may remain indefinitely in the vegetative condition (Chap. XXXII).

Some meristems start differentiating as reproductive meristems almost from the moment of their inception. This is true, for example, of the apical meristems of the lateral flower buds of many woody plants such as peach, redbud, elm, and some species of maples. Among temperate zone woody plants such floral meristems usually differentiate during one growing season but the flowers do not open until the next.

Examples of delayed transformation of a vegetative into a reproductive meristem can be seen in any herbaceous plant which bears a terminal inflorescence at the end of a leafy shoot which has first elongated for some weeks or months before the initiation of flower primordia begins. Examples include tobacco, mints, asters, goldenrods, phloxes, and grains. Similar growth behavior is exhibited by many woody plants such as dogwood, magnolias, rhododendrons, spiraeas, sumacs, and aralias. In many such woody species conversion of apical vegetative meristems to reproductive meristems occurs toward the end of a period of shoot growth, resulting in the formation of terminal flower buds, which do not open until the next growing season.

The first steps in the transformation of a vegetative to a reproductive meristem are invisible physiological changes resulting in metabolic conditions within the meristematic cells which completely alter the differentiation pattern of the meristem.

In some species of plants the transformed meristem becomes in effect an inflorescence primordium from which an inflorescence bearing a number of flowers develops; whereas in the other species only a single flower becomes differentiated from the transformed meristem. Fig. 154 shows the morphological stages in the transformation of a vegetative into a reproductive meristem, as it occurs in one species. The first microscopically visible change in the transformation of a vegetative into a reproductive meristem is one in its configuration. Growth of the central portion seemingly is inhibited, and the meristem becomes flattened on top instead of more or less conical. Small protuberances develop from this modified

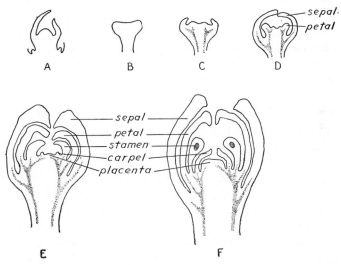

Fig. 154. Stages in the transformation of a vegetative to a floral meristem in pepper, as seen in longitudinal section. (A) Vegetative stem tip (cf. Fig. 140). (B) Apical meristem has become flattened. (C) Initiation of first floral parts (sepals) has begun. (D) Later stage showing initiation of petals. (E) Still later stage showing initiation of stamens and carpels. (F) Well differentiated flower bud showing an early stage of carpel formation. Redrawn from Cochran (1938).

meristem in a regular spiral or whorled arrangement. These mound-like protuberances are the primordia from which flower parts develop in a manner analogous to that by which leaves develop from similar protuberances on a vegetative meristem. A marked difference in the development of the two meristems, however, is that there is no elongation of the axis between successive floral primordia such as usually occurs between successive leaf primordia. Although details of flower development differ considerably from one species to another the fundamental pattern followed is similar in all species.

At first the floral parts of most flowers are tightly enclosed within the overlapping sepals, constituting a flower bud. Subsequently expansion of the flower bud into the opened flower occurs, a stage in flower development called *anthesis*. While sepals, or both sepals and petals, are present in the majority of flowers, the only essential parts are the stamens and the pistils. The majority of plants are bisporangiate species and have both of these structures present in each flower. In some plants (monoecious species), however, some flowers are staminate and others pistillate, but both kinds are borne on the same plant. In others (dioecious species) some plants bear only staminate, other plants only pistillate flowers.

The most pronounced physiological and developmental changes in the plant's existence occur in the brief period of floral differentiation. The whole pattern of structural differentiation changes profoundly during the transformation of a vegetative to a reproductive meristem, reflecting equally deep-seated changes in metabolism. The rapid change from the male physiological state (stamens, etc.) to the female physiological state (carpels, etc.) over a very short distance is another striking feature of the differentiation of most flowers. Physiologically these two states may differ from each other as much as either of them differs from the vegetative state.

Young developing flowers are centers of a myriad of metabolic changes. The metabolic complexity within the cells of developing flower parts is probably greater than within any other plant tissue. Very little is actually known, however, of the specific metabolic conditions which are associated with the reproductive state in general as contrasted with the vegetative state, or of the physiological differences between the male and female states. That hormones play a role in the initiation of flowers does, however, seem clearly indicated (Chap. XXXII). Respiratory activity, an indirect index of metabolic activity, is always high in young floral meristems, but this is also true of other meristems. Assimilatory rates are also high, and there is a continuous translocation toward a developing flower of foods, water, compounds containing mineral elements, and hormones.

Pollen and Pollination.—Pollen grains differ greatly in size, ranging from about 5-200 μ in diameter, and also in configuration (Fig. 155) from one plant to another, but their physiological role is similar in all species. The quantity of pollen produced also differs greatly from one kind of plant to another. Some plants produce pollen only sparingly; others, with great prodigality. A single corn plant, for example, is estimated to release 50,000,000 pollen grains. Only about 1000 pollen grains are required if fertilization of all of the egg cells in all of the ovules of one corn plant is to be accomplished.

Ontogenetically the pollen grain and the pollen tube that develops from it represent the male gametophyte. When first formed a pollen grain contains two nuclei, the *tube nucleus,* and the *generative nucleus.* The latter subsequently divides, either in the pollen grain or in the pollen tube, resulting in the formation of two sperms which are male gametes.

Pollination, or transfer of pollen from the anther to the stigma of the same or another flower, is effected principally by wind and insects. Some species are entirely wind-pollinated, some are entirely insect-pollinated, while in some both modes of pollen transfer may occur. Other less common agents of pollen dispersal are gravity, water, and certain animals, including man.

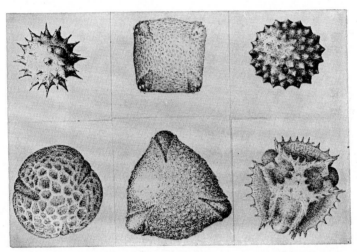

Fig. 155. Pollen grains. Top row, left to right: sunflower (*Helianthus annuus*), ash (*Fraxinus americana*), ragweed (*Ambrosia trifida*). Bottom row, left to right: privet (*Ligustrum ibota*), white oak (*Quercus alba*), dandelion (*Taraxacum officinale*). From Wodehouse (1935).

Self-pollination is the transfer of pollen to the stigma of the same flower, or of another flower on the same plant. *Cross-pollination* is the transfer of pollen from the anthers on one plant to the stigmas of another plant of the same kind. When the two plants involved in cross-pollination carry identical chromosome complements, however, the genetic effect of the "cross-pollination" is the same as self-pollination. Self-pollination is the usual occurrence in a number of species, such as wheat, oats, barley and tobacco, in which the pollen is shed before the flowers open. In some species both self- and cross-pollination may occur. Cross-pollination is obligatory in *self-sterile* plants, if normal fertilization is to occur.

Numerous pollen grains may alight on or be deposited on a single stigma. Under conditions of abundant pollination from 600 to 900 pollen grains may be present, for example, on a single stigma of jimsonweed (Buchholz, 1931). Even "foreign" pollen grains sometimes germinate on a stigma, but growth of the pollen tube usually fails to occur or takes place very slowly. If a pollen grain from one plant falls on a stigma of the same plant, germination usually occurs, although not always. Pollen from a given plant often fails to germinate on the same individual plant; or, if germination occurs, the pollen tube grows sluggishly. This is one cause of self-sterility in plants. On the other hand, pollen from a given plant usually germinates on the stigma of another plant of the same species, provided the stigma has reached an appropriate stage of development and environmental conditions are favorable.

Germination of a pollen grain, under favorable environmental conditions, commonly occurs within a few minutes of its making contact with the stigmatic surface. Usually only one pollen tube elongates from a pollen grain, but in some species more than one develops. When a plural number of tubes forms, however, ordinarily all except one soon cease growing. Even branching of pollen tubes may occur in some species.

The pollen tube serves as the mode of transport of the sperms from the stigma into the embryo sac. The distance which the pollen tube must grow if this transfer is to be accomplished is very short in some species, but may be as much as 30 cm. in other kinds of plants, such as maize, with long styles.

The time interval between germination of a pollen grain and fertilization differs greatly from one kind of plant to another, but for many lies within the range of 12 to 48 hr. In a few plants, however, such as barley, this time interval is less than an hour and in some, such as certain oaks and pines, it may be months, even exceeding a year in a few species. The absolute rate of elongation of pollen tubes ranges up to about 34 mm. per hr.

The rate of growth of the pollen tube is markedly influenced by environmental conditions, especially temperature. In tomato, for example, their maximum rate of growth occurs at about 20°C., being less at higher and lower temperatures (Smith and Cochran, 1935).

Apart from environmental conditions, the rate of pollen-tube growth is markedly influenced by the degree of physiological "compatibility" between the pollen tube and the tissues of the pistil. Incompatibility usually exists between the pollen of one species and the stigma of another. Incompatibility between pollen and pistillary tissues is also common in many species when self-pollination occurs. Although germination of the pollen grains may occur, the pollen tubes grow very slowly, and fertilization seldom results. When cross-pollination occurs in the same species, however, rapid growth of the pollen tubes is the usual occurrence. The exact physiological basis of such incompatibilities is unknown.

Even when a high degree of physiological compatibility exists between the pollen tube and pistillar tissues, some pollen tubes elongate through the tissues of the style and ovulary much more rapidly than others. The tube which enters a given embryo sac first is usually the one from which the sperms come which accomplish fertilization and triple fusion. If an ovulary contains but one ovule, only one pollen tube is required if fertilization of the egg in the enclosed embryo sac is to be accomplished; if it contains more than one ovule one pollen tube is required for each, if all egg cells in all the embryo sacs are to be fertilized.

The growing pollen tube is largely parasitic upon the tissues of the pistil, from which it undoubtedly obtains water, mineral salts, foods, and probably also hormones. The growing tube probably releases enzymes which aid in the digestion of foods. There is also much indirect evidence (see later) that it releases enzymes or hormones which have marked effects upon the development of the pistil and organs enclosed within it.

Pollen grains germinate under artificial conditions if strewn on the surface of a sucrose-water, or sucrose-agar (about 1.5 per cent)—water medium (Brink, 1924; Blair and Loomis, 1941; Sartoris, 1942; and others). The most favorable concentration of sucrose for germination differs considerably according to the kind of pollen, but is usually in the range of 5-25 per cent. Germination of at least some kinds of pollen on such media occurs within a few minutes, and elongation of the pollen tube may be very rapid.

Various extracts and compounds have been shown to influence the germinative capacity of pollen grains and rate of growth of pollen tubes in artificial media (Brink, 1924; Smith, 1942; Addicott, 1943). Of possibly especial significance is the fact that boron has a markedly enhancing effect upon the percentage germination of some kinds of pollen (Schmucker, 1934; and others).

The length of time for which pollen grains of different species remain viable under ordinary air dry conditions ranges from a few hours to several months (Holman and Brubaker, 1926). The pollen of grasses, including corn, rye, barley, and wheat is notoriously short-lived, often retaining its germinative capacity for only a few hours and seldom for more than a few days even under the most favorable conditions.

The life duration of many kinds of pollen can be extended, in some species up to at least a year, by storage at low humidities in conjunction with relatively low temperatures. Prolongation of the life of pollen is often an important consideration in certain plant breeding problems—

for example, when it is desired to cross two varieties which bloom at different seasons.

Wholly apart from its role in reproduction, pollen is of considerable medical interest because it is the causal agent in the well-known ailment of hayfever. This disease is induced in many persons when the free-floating pollen of the atmosphere comes in contact with the mucous membranes of the eyes, nose, throat, bronchial tubes, and lungs. The number of kinds of pollen which cause hayfever is relatively small. Only pollens which are liberated in abundance and which are wind-borne are causal agents in this malady, and of them only those pollens which possess allergenic toxicity to at least some humans actually do cause hayfever. Pines and other conifers, for example, are extravagant producers of pollen, but with the exception of the junipers, none of the North American species is known to be a hayfever plant. Some plants such as roses and goldenrods, which are popularly supposed to be major culprits, actually play only minor or negligible roles as causal agents in hayfever.

In much of temperate North America three main hayfever seasons can be distinguished (Wodehouse, 1945). An early spring season, usually the least severe and of shortest duration, results from the presence of certain tree pollens in the atmosphere, especially those from elms, maples, willows, poplars, birches, and oaks. Early summer hayfever is caused principally by the pollens of a number of species of grasses, especially June grass, orchard grass, timothy, and redtop. The incidence of early summer hayfever is much greater than that of spring hayfever, and the season is considerably longer. Late summer hayfever, which accounts for more victims of this affliction than the other two seasons combined, is caused principally by the pollen of the ragweeds, sagebrushes, cockleburs, false ragweeds, and salt bushes.

A sufferer from hayfever may be allergic to the pollen of only a few, or even of only one, species of plants. Only a competent allergist can determine, by means of suitable skin tests, the kinds of pollen which actually cause hayfever in a given person. Complete relief from the malady can usually be obtained only if the victim moves, during the pollination season of the causative plants, into a region in which they do not grow. At least partial relief can usually be obtained from injections of extracts prepared from the causative pollen.

Initiation of Embryo and Endosperm Growth.—*Fertilization and Triple Fusion.*—The essential feature of sexual reproduction is the union of an egg and a sperm, the process called *fertilization*. In the angiosperms the egg cell is an integral part of the embryo sac, which is enclosed within an ovule. In the majority of angiosperm species, the fully developed embryo sac is a seven-celled, eight-nucleate structure (Fig. 156). In some species, however, the embryo sac is four-nucleate; in others sixteen-nucleate. Ontogenetically the embryo sac represents the female gametophyte in the angiosperms.

Access of the pollen tube into the ovule is commonly, although not always, achieved through the micropyle. The tube then penetrates the nucellus and passes into the embryo sac between the egg and an adjacent cell. Fertilization usually occurs shortly after the tube enters the embryo sac.

In addition to the egg cell, especial significance attaches to the polar nuclei in the large central cell (Fig. 156) of the embryo sac. These two nuclei join, forming a *fusion nucleus,* with which the second sperm from the pollen tube unites, resulting in a triploid *endosperm nucleus.* In a few species only one polar nucleus is present which unites with the male gamete in forming the endosperm nucleus, and in some species more than two polar nuclei are formed during embryo sac development, all of which fuse with a sperm in the formation of the endosperm nucleus. Ordinarily only one pollen tube penetrates an embryo sac, one sperm uniting with the egg, the other with the fusion nucleus. Occasionally more than one pollen tube may enter, and the sperm which unites with the egg may come from a different pollen tube than the sperm which unites with the fusion nucleus.

Apomixis.—The reproductive apparatus does not operate identically in all plants, and many deviations from the most common mechanism as described above are known. Modes of asexual reproduction (*i.e.,* reproduction without fertilization) which outwardly appear to be sexual reproduction are of regular occurrence in some species and occasional in others (Stebbins, 1941). The generic term for this kind of reproduction is *apomixis,* of which three main types are recognized.

In one kind of apomixis the haploid egg cell develops into an embryo sporophyte without

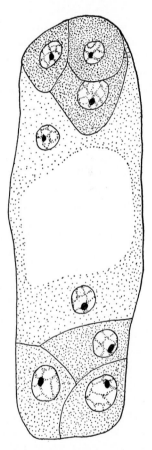

FIG. 156. Embryo sac (eight-cell stage) of *Epipactis.* Egg cell and two synergids at upper end; three antipodals at lower end. Subsequent union of the two nuclei nearest center (polar nuclei) results in formation of the fusion nucleus. Redrawn from Brown and Sharp (1911).

fertilization, either autonomously (*haploid parthenogenesis*), or under the influence of a promotive influence from the growing pollen tube or the process of triple fusion (*haploid pseudogamy*). Less commonly an embryo may develop without fertilization from another cell of the embryo sac (*haploid apogamety*). Plants resulting from this kind of apomixis have the haploid number of chromosomes and are usually sterile.

In a second type of apomixis the cells of the embryo sac, because of some deviation or other from the usual course in their development, all contain the diploid number of chromosomes. Development of the embryo may proceed according to methods analogous to those occurring in haploid apomixis, *i.e.*, by *diploid parthenogenesis, diploid pseudogamy*, or *diploid apogamety*.

In a third type of apomixis (*adventitious embryony*) the embryo develops directly from an ovular tissue of the parental sporophyte, usually the integument or the nucellus. Such embryos are diploid and genetically identical with the parent sporophyte.

Polyembryony.—This term refers to the development of more than one embryo within a single ovule. Polyembryony is of frequent or regular occurrence in some species, and of sporadic occurrence in others (Webber, 1940). The causes of polyembryony are complex, and only the main mechanisms can be mentioned in this discussion. In many gymnosperms there are regularly two or more egg cells in each female gametophyte, each of which, upon fertilization, develops into an embryo. An analogous situation occurs in some angiosperms, in which other cells of the embryo sac in addition to the egg may develop into supernumerary embryos, either with or without previous fertilization. Cleavage of the fertilized egg or young embryo into two or more units, and subsequent development of each into a genetically identical embryo, occurs in a number of species, especially among the gymnosperms. Another cause of polyembryony is the development of two embryo sacs within the same ovule, as in alder (*Alnus rugosa*), the egg in each of which gives rise to an embryo. Still another and common cause of a plurality of embryos within an ovule is the apomictic development of one or more embryos from ovular tissue as previously described. In some species one or more embryos of this origin may occur side by side in an ovule with an embryo derived from a fertilized egg; in other species only apomictic embryos are formed.

Development of the Seed.—The processes of fertilization and triple fusion not only set in motion the development of the embryo and the endosperm, respectively, but also exert a promotive influence on the development of the ovule into the seed and frequently also on the development of the fruit (see later).

The fertilized egg cell does not usually divide at once, but only after a short delay. Once cell divisions start, however, they usually continue without interruption until a fully differentiated embryo has been developed. The foods used by the developing embryo come from the plant on which the flowers were borne, usually through the endosperm as an intermediary. The specific nutritive requirements of plant embryos are discussed later.

The endosperm, which in most species is a short-lived tissue, develops from the endosperm nucleus. The endosperm usually becomes an actively growing tissue shortly after the occurrence of triple fusion. In most species considerable development of the endosperm has already taken place before cell division starts in the fertilized egg.

The extent to which the endosperm develops as an organized tissue differs greatly from one kind of plant to another (Brink and Cooper, 1947). In some species, such as orchids, little or no growth of this tissue occurs. In the majority of species the endosperm grows rapidly during the early stages of seed development, but is later digested and used as a source of food by the growing embryo. The endosperm matrix appears to be an especially suitable medium for the growth of embryos, particularly in the early stages of their development. In such species the endosperm cells adjacent to the embryo disintegrate and disappear, and by the time the seed is mature, little if any of the endosperm remains. During the latter stages of embryo development in such species considerable quantities of foods usually accumulate in the cotyledons. In a smaller number of species, such as the cereals, date, coconut, and castor bean, the endosperm persists as a storage tissue in the mature seed. In such plants the cotyledons are less well developed than in most other plants, and the foods in the endosperm are utilized by the developing seedling during germination (*cf.* Fig. 167).

In the developing ovules of some plants the nucellus grows and becomes much enlarged, resulting in the presence in the mature seed of a tissue called the *perisperm*. Foods accumulate in this tissue much as they do in the endosperm. Representative species in which a perisperm is present include spinach, black pepper, beet, water lily, and coffee. In a few species both the endosperm and the perisperm persist as storage tissues in the mature seed.

Another major transformation which occurs during the morphogenesis of seeds is the development of the seed coats from the ovule coats (integuments). The latter are usually soft and fleshy, while most seed coats are hard and dry.

Although the development of seeds is a usual outcome of the process of pollination it is by no means an invariable one. Failure of seeds to form within the fruit is especially common when a usually cross-pollinated species is self-pollinated, or when cross-pollination occurs between different species or different varieties of the same species. The principal causes of a failure of seeds to develop are: (1) failure of pollen to germinate after pollination, (2) pollen tubes may grow too slowly for fertilization to be accomplished or the tubes may burst before reaching the embryo sac, (3) fertilization fails to take place, (4) fertilization occurs but abortion follows before more than a few divisions of the fertilized egg occur, (5) fertilization occurs and embryo growth proceeds but is arrested at a later stage in its development. Failure of the embryo to develop to maturity appears to result from physiological conditions inherent in the young embryo or in the surrounding endosperm. The first four conditions listed above commonly lead to the development of "empty" seeds; the last one usually results in the formation of shrunken and usually nonviable seeds.

Development of Fruits.—The diversity in sizes, shapes, colors, textures, and arrangements of fruits is as great as that of the flowers which are their forerunners. Fundamentally, however, the morphogenic development of all fruits is similar. The simpler kinds of fruits develop solely from pistils. Such gradual transformations of pistils to fruits can easily be observed in many kinds of plants. Examples of simple fruits, which are in essence only modified pistils, include the bean, pea, tomato, cotton, grape, avocado, orange, maple, elm, basswood, peach, cherry, and olive. In the development of some kinds of fruits, however, other parts, most commonly the receptacle or floral cup, ripen along with the pistil and are incorporated into the final structure of the fruit. Examples of such fruits include apple, pear, rose, cucumber, blueberry, and sunflower.

In general, development of a fruit and its enclosed seed or seeds occurs concomitantly and in a reciprocally coordinated fashion. During the transformation of some pistils, or pistils plus adjacent parts, into fruits a considerable enlargement may occur, as much as several hundred fold in some. The resulting mature fruit tissues may be soft and fleshy as in tomato, or hard and dry as in nut fruits. In other plants development of floral organs into fruits may occur with relatively little enlargement of the tissues; the resulting fruits more frequently being dry and hard than soft and fleshy.

The processes of pollination and fertilization exert marked influences on the development of most fruits. Failure of pollination to occur usually results in abscission of the pistil and a consequent failure of fruit to form. The influence of pollination upon the development of fruits is probably mediated at least in part through auxins. Pollen grains and tubes are known to contain auxins in considerable quantities. It seems unlikely however, that the quantity of auxins furnished by the pollen tubes is sufficient to be the sole cause of fruit development (Van Overbeek *et al.*, 1941). Ovularies contain very little active auxin, but considerable quantities of bound auxin. The results of Muir (1947) indicate that bound auxin in the pistils of several species is converted into active auxin under the influence of some substance, probably an enzyme, which comes from the pollen tubes thus further increasing the auxin content of the pistils. A primary effect of its increased auxin content is the prevention of abscission of the pistil (Chap. XXXV). Soon after pollination, but before fertilization, the ovules and ovularies start to grow. Enlargement of these organs, at least during the early stages of fruit development, is presumably induced by auxin set free as described above.

However, most fruits do not develop normally unless pollination is followed by fertilization and resulting development of the embryo or embryos. The young seeds within developing fruits contain relatively high concentrations of auxins (Gustafson, 1939a, and others). Furthermore, if the central part of a fruit including the ovules is removed, the fruit ceases to grow, but if the eviscerated cavity is packed with lanolin containing auxin its growth continues (Dollfus, 1936). Auxin derived from developing seeds therefore appears to be necessary for the continued growth of most fruits.

Fruits usually contain seeds but this is not invariably true. Seedless fruits are of regular occurrence in some kinds of plants such as certain varieties of banana, orange, grape, cucumber, and sunflower. Such fruits are also of sporadic occurrence in many other kinds of plants (Gustafson, 1942). This condition of seedlessness is termed *parthenocarpy*. The designation "seedless" as applied in this connection refers to a lack of viable seeds; many parthenocarpic fruits contain partially developed seeds which are empty, *i.e.*, lacking an embryo.

The sequence of events leading to the development of parthenocarpic fruits is different in different kinds of plants. In some species development of fruits proceeds in the absence of pollination, and hence of fertilization, although the more usual consequence of a failure of pollination is for the pistil to abscise. In other plants the physiological effect of pollination not followed by fertilization is adequate to induce fruit development. Failure of fertilization to follow pollination is most commonly caused by such a slow rate of growth of the pollen tubes that they either never reach the egg, or reach it after it is no longer viable. Even alien pollen has been found to induce parthenocarpic fruit development in some species, and other kinds of "stimulation" such as infestation with aphids sometimes leads to fruit development in the absence of pollination. Unless apomixis occurs, all fruits developing in the absence of fertilization will be devoid of viable seeds.

Even when pollination is followed by fertilization, development of the embryo from the fertilized egg may be arrested at an early stage as previously mentioned and seedless fruits or fruits with imperfect seeds result unless apomixis occurs.

The auxins required in the development of parthenocarpic fruits obviously cannot come from the seeds although some auxins may become available in the ovulary as a direct or indirect effect of pollination as previously described. Varieties on which parthenocarpic fruits commonly form have a higher auxin content in the ovularies than other varieties of the same species which produce fruits only following pollination and fertilization (Gustafson, 1939b).

When both parthenocarpic and seeded fruits occur on the same plant the former often fail to develop if the supply of foods within the plant is limited. Apparently the presence of developing seeds in a fruit aids in some way in promoting the translocation of foods into the fruit. Hence parthenocarpic fruits are more likely to develop to maturity if none of the fruits on the same plant are seeded. When both seedless and seeded fruits are borne on the same plant, the former are more likely to develop if the general nutritional status of the plant is high.

Not only does pollination usually have a determinative effect on whether or not fruits will develop, but the genetic constitution of the pollen may have differential effects upon the growth of fruits. When, for example, date palms of the Deglet Noor variety are crossed with the Mosque variety as the pollen parent, the weights of the resulting seeds and fruits are considerably greater than when the Deglet Noor variety is crossed with the Ford No. 4 variety as the pollen parent (Nixon, 1928). Such an effect of the source of the pollen upon the development of the fruit is called *metaxenia*. Examples of this phenomenon are known in apple, cotton, oak, and other species. The phenomenon of metaxenia is almost certainly to be interpreted in terms of a hormonal mechanism.

Gustafson (1936) showed that application of certain hormones in lanolin to the styles of young flowers of several species from which the stamens had been removed induced the development of parthenocarpic fruits. A number of other plants are now known in which formation of parthenocarpic fruits can be induced by treatment with suitable chemicals in the absence of pollination. Among them are pepper, watermelon, jimsonweed, holly, tomato, egg plant, petunia, tobacco, strawberry, and pumpkin. The principal compounds known to be effective in the induction of parthenocarpic fruit formation are indoleacetic, indoleproprionic, indolebutyric, phenylacetic, α-naphthaleneacetic, α-naphthoxyacetic, and phenoxyacetic acids. Most of the compounds having this effect upon plants fall into the category of auxins. The effective concentrations of those compounds which induce parthenocarpic fruiting vary considerably depending upon the kind of plant treated and the specific compound used, but commonly lie, for aqueous solutions, in the range of 50 to 3000 p.p.m.

Certain practical applications of the effect of specific compounds in inducing the formation of parthenocarpic fruits have been made. The usually inadequate natural pollination of tomato plants in greenhouses during the winter, for example, has been supplemented by hormone treatment, resulting in a better set of fruits, which are largely or entirely seedless. Treatment of the flowers on carpellate holly trees induces the development of berries in the absence of any nearby staminate trees (Gardner and Marth, 1937). For large-scale treatment of plants, hormones can be applied as sprays, emulsions, or dusts, or can be vaporized into the air surrounding the plants, as in a greenhouse (Avery and Johnson, 1947).

A developing fruit is a complex system of meristematic tissues. Simultaneously, each fertilized egg cell is developing into an embryo, each endosperm nucleus into an endosperm, each nucellus (in some plants) into a perisperm, and the ovulary or ovulary and adjacent parts into a pericarp. Physiologically the growth of fruits, particularly those of the fleshy type, is closely akin to vegetative growth. Formation of the component parts of a fruit involves the same three morphological phases of growth as the development of vegetative organs, i.e., cell division, cell enlargement, and cell differentiation. Growth of the embryo, however, is largely limited to the cell division phase of growth. Water, carbohydrates, nitrogenous compounds, mineral salts, and probably certain growth substances must all be transported into the fruit from other parts of the plant. If the supply of any one of these substances to a growing fruit becomes deficient the rate of growth is retarded. The proportions of these various kinds of substances which are required vary with the kind of fruit, being different, for example, in a fleshy, succulent fruit from those in a hard, dry fruit. Within any given fruit the proportions of these various substances moving toward each of the several meristematic regions also differ considerably. During active growth of the fruits on a plant there is often a curtailment in the growth of other organs and also a drain on accumulated foods within the plant (Chap. XXXIII).

Furthermore, the different growing regions which are integral parts of the complex system of tissues called a fruit, exert reciprocal correlative influences on the growth of one another. Several such effects, such as the necessity of an endosperm for the early development of the embryo, and the necessity of developing seeds for fruit growth in most species, have been referred to previously. The development of the lint hairs appendent to a cotton seed afford another example of such a growth correlation.

These hairs go through two distinctly separate stages of development: (1) a period during which the hairs grow in length without appreciable wall thickening, and (2) a period during which wall thickening occurs without increase in length of the hairs. The first period coincides with the growth of the endosperm in the seed. As soon as endosperm growth ceases, elongation of the lint hairs also stops. Secondary thickening of the walls of the hairs coincides with the active growth of the young embryo.

An emanation of ethylene gas has been found to occur during ripening from a number of kinds of fruits, including apple (Gane, 1934), pear (Hansen, 1942), banana (Niederl *et al.*, 1938), and avocado (Pratt *et al.*, 1948). Ethylene synthesis is not confined to fruits but also occurs in at least some other organs of plants (Denny and Miller, 1935). Ethylene is known to have a number of marked physiological effects on plants (Crocker *et al.*, 1935), even in very low concentrations. One of these is its effect in inducing epinasty of leaves (Chap. XXX). Also well-known is the effect of ethylene in hastening the coloring and ripening of some kinds of fruits, a process which involves chlorophyll decomposition. Treatment of green-picked citrus fruits and bananas with ethylene gas has been a widely-used commercial practice. Naturally-synthesized ethylene appears to promote the ripening process in a number of kinds of fruits.

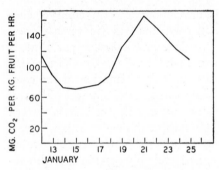

FIG. 157. Respiration rates of avocado fruits at 15°C. for a period of 2 weeks after picking, illustrating occurrence of climacteric. Data of Biale (1946).

The course of respiration in many kinds of developing fruits follows a characteristic cycle. The rate per unit fresh weight of very young fruits is relatively high and gradually declines to a minimum at about the time the fruits reach maturity. In apples and at least some other kinds of fruits there is a secondary rise in rate of respiration often beginning about the time the fruits are usually picked, followed by a secondary decline. The peak of this secondary rise is called the "climacteric" (Kidd and West, 1945) and occurs, in apples at least, whether the fruits are picked or whether they remain on the tree. The climacteric cycle in picked, mature avocado fruits is illustrated in Fig. 157.

Embryo Culture.—White, 1932; Tukey, 1934; La Rue, 1936, and others have shown that partially developed plant embryos can be cultured on sterile media according to techniques very similar to those employed in the culture of other parts of plants. Mature or nearly mature embryos usually grow when the medium contains only inorganic salts and a sugar; such embryos soon develop into seedlings with roots and epicotyl.

Although mature embryos appear to be autotrophic with respect to hormones this does not seem to be true of immature embryos. Young embryos (about one-fourth mature size) of *Datura* (jimsonweed), for example, do not develop on a medium containing dextrose, mineral salts, and several physiologically active organic compounds, but do develop rapidly to many times their initial volume (Fig. 158) if a small amount of coconut milk be added to the medium (Van Overbeek *et al.*, 1942). Further investigation indicated the presence in coconut milk of at least three substances or complexes, one of which appears to be auxin, which affect the growth of embryos. The one promoting growth of the embryo has been tentatively called the *embryo factor*. This factor exerts its growth-promoting effect principally on cell division and may be present, not only in embryos but in meristems generally. The capacity of the embryo to synthesize this factor or complex probably increases with age; apparently only in very early stages of development is it required from an outside source. Embryo factor activity has also been shown to be present in extracts from malt (Blakeslee and Satina, 1944), *Datura* ovules, yeast, wheat germ and almond meal (Van Overbeek *et al.*, 1944). Small maize embryos (less than 0.3 mm. in length), however, have been found not to develop in sterile culture, even when coconut milk was added (Haagen-Smit *et al.*, 1945). Mixtures of certain amino acids have also been found to enhance the growth of young

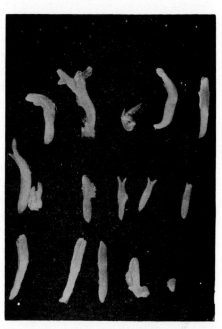

FIG. 158. Effect of coconut milk on development of *Datura* embryos isolated 10 days after pollination. Top row, embryos after 8 days on medium containing sugar, mineral salts, and vitamins. Note that almost no growth has occurred. Bottom three rows, embryos after 8 days on same kind of medium plus coconut milk. From Van Overbeek *et al.* (1942).

Datura embryos (Sanders and Burkholder, 1948), and at least a part of
the promotive effect of plant extracts on embryo growth probably can be
ascribed to amino acids.

A practical application of embryo culture is that it provides a method
of preserving genetically desirable embryos when the seeds formed are,
for one reason or another, nongerminable. Hybrid embryos in some species, for example, become arrested in development before they are mature
and the seeds fail to germinate. It is often possible to dissect out the
embryos from such seeds, grow them for a while in culture, and eventually
transplant them into soil. Embryos can also be excised from some kinds
of dormant seeds and successfully grown in culture. Iris seed, for example, shows a pronounced dormancy (Chap. XXXIV), but seedlings
can be obtained in a short time if the embryos are removed from the
seed and cultured artificially (Randolph and Cox, 1943).

Development of Fruits in Sterile Culture.—La Rue (1942) and Nitsch
(1951) have shown that fruits will develop from detached flowers cultured sterilely *in vitro* under suitable conditions. The latter investigator
found, for example, that if tomato flowers in which pollination had recently occurred were cultured in this manner, fruits developed from the
ovularies when the flowers were implanted on a medium containing only
sucrose and mineral salts as solutes. Fruits developed from excised, un-
pollinated flowers of tomato, on the other hand, only if the culture medium
also contained certain hormones such as 2,4-dichlorophenoxyacetic acid.

SUGGESTED FOR COLLATERAL READING

Avery, G. S., Jr., and Elizabeth B. Johnson. *Hormones and Horticulture.* Mc-
   Graw-Hill Book Co., Inc. New York. 1947.
Maheshwari, P. *An Introduction to the Embryology of Angiosperms.* McGraw-
   Hill Book Co., Inc. New York. 1950.
Wodehouse, R. P. *Pollen Grains.* McGraw-Hill Book Co., Inc. New York. 1935.
Wodehouse, R. P. *Hayfever Plants.* Chronica Botanica Co. Waltham, Mass. 1945.

SELECTED BIBLIOGRAPHY

Addicott, F. T. Pollen germination and pollen tube growth, as influenced by pure
   growth substances. *Plant Physiol.* **18:** 270-279. 1943.
Biale, J. B. Effect of oxygen concentration on respiration of the Fuerte avocado
   fruit. *Amer. Jour. Bot.* **33:** 363-373. 1946.
Blair, R. A., and W. E. Loomis. The germination of maize pollen. *Science* **94:**
   168-169. 1941.
Blakeslee, A. F., and Sophie Satina. New hybrids from incompatible crosses in
   Datura through cultures of excised embryos on malt media. *Science* **99:** 331-
   334. 1944.
Brink, R. A. The physiology of pollen. *Amer. Jour. Bot.* **11:** 218-228, 283-294,
   351-264, 417-436. 1924.

Brink, R. A., and D. C. Cooper. The endosperm in seed development. *Bot. Rev.* **13:** 423-541. 1947.

Brown, W. H., and L. W. Sharp. The embryo sac of *Epipactis*. *Bot. Gaz.* 439-452. 1911.

Buchholz, J. T. The dissection, staining, and mounting of styles in the study of pollen-tube distribution. *Stain Tech.* **6:** 13-24. 1931.

Cochran, H. L. A morphological study of flower and seed development in pepper. *Jour. Agric. Res.* **56:** 395-419. 1938.

Crocker, W., A. E. Hitchcock, and P. W. Zimmerman. Similarities in the effects of ethylene and the plant auxins. *Contr. Boyce Thompson Inst.* **7:** 231-248. 1935.

Denny, F. E., and L. P. Miller. Production of ethylene by plant tissue as indicated by the epinastic response of leaves. *Contr. Boyce Thompson Inst.* **7:** 97-102. 1935.

Dollfus, H. Wuchsstoffstudien. *Planta* **25:** 1-21. 1936.

Gane, R. Production of ethylene by some ripening fruits. *Nature* **134:** 1008. 1934.

Gardner, F. E., and P. C. Marth. Parthenocarpic fruits induced by spraying with growth promoting compounds. *Bot. Gaz.* **99:** 184-195. 1937.

Gustafson, F. G. Inducement of fruit development by growth promoting chemicals. *Proc. Nat. Acad. Sci. (U. S. A.)* **22:** 628-636. 1936.

Gustafson, F. G. The cause of natural parthenocarpy. *Amer. Jour. Bot.* **26:** 135-138. 1939a.

Gustafson, F. G. Auxin distribution in fruits and its significance in fruit development. *Amer. Jour. Bot.* **26:** 189-194. 1939b.

Gustafson, F. G. Parthenocarpy: natural and artificial. *Bot. Rev.* **8:** 599-654. 1942.

Haagen-Smit, A. J., R. Siu, and Gertrude Wilson. A method for the culturing of excised, immature corn embryos *in vitro*. *Science* **101:** 234. 1945.

Hansen, E. Quantitative study of ethylene production in relation to respiration of peas. *Bot. Gaz.* **103:** 543-558. 1942.

Holman, R. M., and Florence Brubaker. On the longevity of pollen. *Univ. Calif. Publ. in Botany* **13:** 179-204. 1926.

Kidd, F., and G. West. Respiratory activity and duration of life of apples gathered at different stages of development and subsequently maintained at a constant temperature. *Plant Physiol.* **20:** 467-504. 1945.

La Rue, C. D. The growth of plant embryos in culture. *Bull. Torrey Bot. Club* **63:** 365-382. 1936.

La Rue, C. D. The rooting of flowers in sterile culture. *Bull. Torrey Bot. Club* **69:** 332-341. 1942.

Muir, R. M. The relationship of growth hormones and fruit development. *Proc. Nat. Acad. Sci. (U. S. A.)* **33:** 303-312. 1947.

Niederl, J. B., M. W. Brenner, and J. N. Kelly. The identification and estimation of ethylene in the volatile products of ripening bananas. *Amer. Jour. Bot.* **25:** 357-361. 1938.

Nitsch, J. P. Growth and development *in vitro* of excised ovaries. *Amer. Jour. Bot.* **38:** 566-576. 1951.

Nixon, R. W. Immediate influence of pollen in determining the size and time of ripening of the fruit of the date palm. *Jour. Hered.* **19:** 241-255. 1928.

Pratt, H. K., R. E. Young, and J. B. Biale. The identification of ethylene as a volatile product of ripening avocados. *Plant Physiol.* **23:** 526-531. 1948.

Randolph, L. F., and L. G. Cox. Factors influencing the germination of *Iris* seed and the relation of inhibiting substances to embryo dormancy. *Proc. Amer. Soc. Hort. Sci.* **43**: 284-300. 1943.

Sanders, Mary E., and P. R. Burkholder. Influence of amino acids on growth of *Datura* embryos in culture. *Proc. Nat. Acad. Sci. (U. S. A.)* **34**: 516-526. 1948.

Sartoris, G. B. Longevity of sugar cane and corn pollen. *Amer. Jour. Bot.* **29**: 395-400. 1942.

Schmucker, T. Über den Einfluss von Borsäure auf Pflanzen, insbesondere keimende Pollenkörner. *Planta* **23**: 264-283. 1934.

Smith, O., and H. L. Cochran. Effect of temperature on pollen germination and tube growth in the tomato. *Cornell Univ. Agric. Expt. Sta. Mem.* *175*. 1935.

Smith, P. F. Studies of the growth of pollen with respect to temperature, auxins, colchicine, and vitamin B_1. *Amer. Jour. Bot.* **29**: 56-66. 1942.

Stebbins, G. L., Jr. Apomixis in the angiosperms. *Bot. Rev.* **7**: 507-542. 1941.

Tukey, H. B. Artificial culture methods for isolated embryos of deciduous fruits. *Proc. Amer. Soc. Hort. Sci.* **32**: 313-322. 1934.

Van Overbeek, J., Marie E. Conklin, and A. F. Blakeslee. Chemical stimulation of ovule development and its possible relation to parthenogenesis. *Amer. Jour. Bot.* **28**: 647-656. 1941.

Van Overbeek, J., Marie E. Conklin, and A. F. Blakeslee. Cultivation *in vitro* of small *Datura* embryos. *Amer. Jour. Bot.* **29**: 472-477. 1942.

Van Overbeek, J., R. Siu, and A. J. Haagen-Smit. Factors affecting the growth of *Datura* embryos *in vitro. Amer. Jour. Bot.* **31**: 219-224. 1944.

Webber, J. M. Polyembryony. *Bot. Rev.* **6**: 575-598. 1940.

White, P. R. Plant tissue culture. *Arch. Exp. Zellforsch.* **12**: 602-620. 1932.

XXXII

ENVIRONMENTAL FACTORS INFLUENCING REPRODUCTIVE GROWTH

Initiation of the internal physiological conditions which lead to the conversion of vegetative to reproductive meristems is brought about, as are all other growth phenomena, by interactions between the genetic constitution of a plant and the factors which impinge upon it from its environment. In this chapter the effects of those environmental factors which exert major effects upon reproductive growth will be discussed.

Irradiance.—That the flowering and fruiting of many kinds of plants are less abundant in the shade than in full light is a common observation. The relation between irradiance and flowering for any given species is not a simple one, because it is complicated by the influence of the photoperiod (see later). The effect of an irradiance which is adequate for flower induction can be completely nullified, in some species, if the photoperiod is too long; in other species, if it is too short. In general, however, assuming day length, temperature, and other conditions to be favorable for flowering, there is a minimum irradiance for each species below which no blooming occurs. The minimum varies considerably from one species to another, usually being lower, for example, in woodland shade species than in sun species. At irradiances only slightly greater than the minimum, flowering usually occurs only sparsely; at still higher irradiances this factor ceases to be the limiting one in the initiation of flower primordia.

Light Quality.—The effects of variations in the quality of light upon reproductive growth are principally of theoretical interest, since naturally occurring variations in the wave-length composition of light are seldom, if ever, great enough to have any very significant effects upon the flowering and fruiting of plants. Although all wave lengths of the visible spectrum appear to influence blooming, results of several investigators indicate that the orange-short red portion of the spectrum has the most pronounced effect upon initiation of flowers. The influence of light quality upon this process can be profitably considered only in relation to the effects of light duration and is discussed later in the chapter.

Duration of the Light Period.—*Classification of Plants According to Photoperiodic Reaction.*—The fundamental discovery of Garner and Allard (1920, 1923) that the length of the daily photoperiod has a marked effect on the reproductive development of plants (Chap. XXX) has been confirmed by many subsequent workers. The experimental procedure followed by most pioneer investigators of photoperiodism was a relatively

| 5 HOUR DAY | 7 HOUR DAY | 12 HOUR DAY | 17 HOUR DAY | 19 HOUR DAY | 24 HOUR DAY |

FIG. 159.   Effect of the length of the photoperiod upon flowering of salvia, a short-day species. Photograph from Arthur *et al.* (1930).

simple one. "Short-day" conditions were provided, during the summer months, by transferring the plants to a dark house or cabinet after exposure to the desired number of hours of daylight, while exposure to the usual summer day length provided "long-day" conditions. Long photoperiods were obtained during the winter months by supplementing the natural day length with the necessary number of hours of artificial illumination, relatively low intensities of supplemental light having been found adequate to induce photoperiodic reactions in plants.

The following classification of plants according to the effect of the length of the natural photoperiod upon their reproductive development is essentially that of Allard and Garner (1940).

(1) "Short-day" plants flower only within a range of relatively short photoperiods. Blooming may occur, although more slowly, or less profusely, within a range of photoperiods somewhat longer than the most

FIG. 160. Effect of the length of the photoperiod upon flowering of lettuce, a long-day species. Photograph from Arthur *et al.* (1930).

FIG. 161. Effect of length of the photoperiod upon flowering of buckwheat, an indeterminate species. Photograph from Arthur *et al.* (1930).

favorable ones. Under still longer photoperiods or under continuous illumination, short-day plants do not bloom and remain in the vegetative state indefinitely (Fig. 159). Examples of short-day plants are cosmos, strawberry, aster, ragweed, cocklebur, poinsettia, chrysanthemum, sweet potato, violet, and most early spring or late summer blooming garden or wild flowers of the temperate zone. Differentiation of the flower buds of many early spring-blooming plants occurs during the shortening days of the latter part of the preceding season.

(2) "Long-day" plants flower readily only under a range of relatively long photoperiods, up to and including continuous illumination. Blooming is usually induced most rapidly under continuous illumination or very long photoperiods, but may occur, although more slowly or less profusely, under shorter photoperiods. Under still shorter photoperiods the plants remain in the vegetative state indefinitely (Fig. 160). Examples of long-day plants are spinach, beet, radish, lettuce, English plantain, most grains, timothy, clover, hibiscus, potato, and most late spring or early summer blooming garden or wild flowers of the temperate zone.

(3) "Indeterminate" plants flower readily over a wide range of day lengths from relatively short photoperiods to continuous illumination (Fig. 161). Examples of indeterminate plants are zinnia, dandelion, chickweed, tomato, cotton, buckwheat, and most varieties of tobacco.

(4) "Intermediate" plants bloom only under day lengths within a certain range, and fail to flower under either longer or shorter photoperiods. Examples of intermediate plants are climbing hempweed (*Mikania scandens*), wild kidney bean (*Phaseolus polystachyus*), boneset (*Eupatorium torreyanum*) (Allard, 1938), Indian grass (*Sorghastrum nutans*) (Allard and Evans, 1941), some varieties of side-oats grama grass (*Bouteloua curtipendula*) (Olmsted, 1945), and some varieties of broom grass (*Andropogon furcatus*) (Larsen, 1947).

For many short-day plants the range of photoperiods under which initiation of flowers occurs is sharply delimited, and a definite *critical photoperiod* can be recognized. Such plants flower only in a range of photoperiods *shorter* than the critical. The critical photoperiod for cocklebur, for example, is about 15.5 hr.; and for Biloxi soybean, about 13.5 hr. A critical photoperiod can likewise be distinguished for many long-day plants, such plants flowering only in a range of photoperiods *longer* than the critical. At an irradiance of 1000-1400 foot-candles the critical photoperiod for dill, for example, is between 11 and 14 hr.; and for annual beet, between about 13 and 14 hr. (Naylor, 1941). Indeterminate plants, like long-day plants, flower only in a range of day lengths longer than a critical, but their critical photoperiods are, in general, shorter than those for long-day plants. Intermediate species have two critical photoperiods, blooming neither under day lengths which are longer than the upper, nor at day lengths which are shorter than the lower critical photoperiod.

From the above discussion it should be clear that there are certain day lengths which may induce flowering both in many short-day and in many long-day species. At a day length of 13 hr., for example, both short-day plants with a critical photoperiod greater than this, and long-day plants with a critical photoperiod less than this, will bloom.

Different varieties of the same species may differ in photoperiodic reactions. Of thirteen varieties of soybeans investigated by Borthwick and Parker (1939), eight behaved essentially as indeterminate plants, and five essentially as short-day plants. Because of such varietal differences in photoperiodic reaction, the examples of short-day, long-day, indeterminate, and intermediate plants as given above may not hold strictly for every single variety of every species mentioned.

The fact that reproductive growth is a complex of integrated processes was emphasized in the preceding chapter. Different stages in reproductive growth may be affected differently by the length of the photoperiod. For example, in the Biloxi soybean *initiation* of flower primordia occurs over a range of photoperiods from about 2 to about 13.5 hr. Subsequent development of the flower buds into macroscopic flowers, once primordia are present, occurs most rapidly under 8- to 13-hr. photoperiods, more slowly under 14- and 15-hr. photoperiods, and not at all under 16-hr. photoperiods. No development of fruits takes place when photoperiods are longer than 13 hr. (Parker and Borthwick, 1939a).

The season of the year at which a plant blooms is largely controlled, at least in temperate regions, by its type of reaction to day-length conditions. The natural blooming period of long-day plants is in the late spring and early summer. Short-day species which can grow at relatively low temperatures bloom in the early spring, the flower buds in many such species being formed during the preceding growing season. The majority of the members of this group do not develop flowers until the advent of the shortening days of late summer or early autumn. This latter type of behavior is invariably found in short-day annual species and is characteristic of many short-day perennial species as well. Indeterminate species, on the other hand, may flower at almost any season during which other environmental conditions are favorable.

The geographic distribution of plants is also governed in part by their photoperiodic reactions. Species requiring photoperiods appreciably longer than 12 hr. obviously cannot accomplish sexual reproduction in tropical regions. Pronounced short-day species are for the most part excluded from the high latitudes (60° and farther north or south) unless they can be propagated vegetatively, because the growing season in such regions is restricted largely to the period during which very long photoperiods prevail. In temperate zones, long-day, short-day, indeterminate, and intermediate species all flourish, but bloom at different seasons as already described. Indeterminate species can bloom over such a wide range of day lengths that their geographic distribution is controlled by factors other than the length of the photoperiod.

A complication to be considered in any analysis of photoperiodism is that the length of the daylight period is constantly changing over large portions of the earth's surface. In the north temperate zone, for example, the photoperiod lengthens from day to day between December 21 and June 21, and shortens from day to day between June 21 and December 21. Many herbaceous plants in such regions start life under relatively short photoperiods, pass through a period of lengthening photoperiods, and then in turn through a period of shortening photoperiods. Many perennials, especially of the herbaceous type, pass through similar seasonal changes in length of photoperiod during their annual growth cycle. This situation has important implications both for the development of plants in nature and for the development of crop plants. If, for example, a series of plantings be made of a distinctly short-day plant, such as the Biloxi soybean, during the spring and early summer, none of the plants will flower until the day length has decreased to the critical photoperiod in late summer. In other words, the crops sown late in the season will bloom at about the same time as those sown early in the season. The late-sown plants, however, will have had very little time in which to develop vegetatively; hence they will bear fewer flowers and yield a smaller crop of fruits than the early-sown plants.

Photoperiodic Induction.—If a short-day plant which has been growing under long days is transferred temporarily to short days and then returned to a long-day environment, flowering will often be initiated, even though the plant remains exposed to long photoperiods thereafter. This phenomenon is referred to as *photoperiodic induction.* The number of photoperiodic cycles required to induce flowering differs from one species to another. In the cocklebur, exposure to one short day followed by one long night is sufficient to induce the formation of flowers on plants which are kept both before and after such a treatment under long-day conditions (see later). Similarly, initiation of flower primordia occurs in Biloxi soybean upon exposure of the plants to a minimum of two consecutive short-day cycles (Hamner, 1940).

The phenomenon of photoperiodic induction is also exhibited by long-day plants. From one to four long-day cycles, depending upon irradiance and length of the photoperiod, are sufficient to induce flower formation in dill [1] (Naylor, 1941). Annual beet, on the other hand, requires a minimum of 15 to 20 long-day cycles (Hamner, 1940), and English plantain (*Plantago lanceolata*), a minimum of 15-25 long days (Snyder, 1948), for the induction of flowers.

Both of these latter two plants exhibit the phenomenon of "partial induction," which is distinctive to some species. English plantain, for example, can be exposed to 10 long days, then to as many as 20 short days, then to 15 long days, and finally returned to short days under which flowering will take place. Apparently the "partial induction" which occurs during the first series of long-day cycles carries over a period of short-day cycles and operates essentially as if it were a part of the second series of long-day cycles.

Any photoperiodic cycle which induces initiation of flowers on plants is called a *photoinductive cycle;* one which does not is called a *non-photoinductive cycle.* An 8-hr. photoperiod alternating with a 16-hr. dark period is one possible photoinductive cycle for short-day cocklebur plants; a 16-hr. photoperiod alternating with an 8-hr. dark period is one possible non-photoinductive cycle for this plant.

In general, the number of flower primordia initiated, the subsequent development of the flowers, time of blooming, and development of fruits will be influenced by the number of induction photoperiods, as well as by their exact length. For example, although one photoinductive cycle is sufficient to induce flowering in cocklebur, the flowers require about 64 days to mature, whereas continuous exposure to photoinductive cycles results in an increase in the number of flowers initiated and in the maturation of flowers within about 13 days (Naylor, 1941).

Locus of the Photoperiodic Reaction and Transmission of the Effect. —Knott (1934) showed that induction of flowering in spinach (a long-day plant) occurred only when the leaves were exposed to long photoperiods. Exposure of the meristem to long photoperiods while the leaves were under short photoperiods resulted in maintenance of the vegetative condition. Similar results have been obtained with a number of other plants. Among these are long-day dill (Hamner and Naylor, 1939), and short-day chrysanthemum (Cajlachjan, 1936), Biloxi soybean (Borthwick and Parker, 1938a), and cocklebur (Hamner and Bonner, 1938). In both the cocklebur and Biloxi soybean the young, just fully expanded leaves have been shown to be most effective in inducing flower formation, and this is probably true of plants in general.

---

[1] Dill is commonly considered a long-day plant but, if given sufficient time (three months), will flower under photoperiods as short as 7 hr. (Murneek, 1940). Its exact status, therefore, appears to be that of an indeterminate plant.

That the leaves are the locus of the photoperiodic reaction has also been shown by grafting experiments. When the short-day Biloxi variety of soybean is kept under a 17-hr. photoperiod no flowers are initiated. If, however, leaves of the Agate variety, which flowers over a wide range of day lengths, are grafted on Biloxi plants exposed to a 17-hr. photoperiod, the latter will soon initiate flowers (Heinze et al., 1942). Similar results have been obtained in analogous grafting experiments with other species.

Since the photoperiodic reactions occur in the leaves, the influence of such reactions must in some manner be transmitted to meristems if their transformation from a vegetative to a reproductive state is to be accomplished. The distance over which transmission of the effect occurs varies with the kind of plant and other conditions.

In experiments with short-day cosmos, Garner and Allard (1923, 1925) showed that flowering occurred only on the portion of the stem, be it top, middle, or bottom, that was exposed to short days if the remainder of the plant was exposed to long days. With a two-branched cosmos plant, one branch of which was exposed to short, the other to long, days, only the branch exposed to short days flowered. In this plant the influence of the photoperiodic reaction appears to be highly localized.

In the cocklebur, on the other hand, exposure of one leaf to short days, while the rest of the plant is exposed to long days, causes initiation of flowers at meristems throughout the plant. The effect in cocklebur is thus systemic and is transmitted both in the upward and downward directions through the plant. Furthermore, unlike cosmos, both branches of a two-stemmed cocklebur flower if only one of them is exposed to a short day (Hamner and Bonner, 1938). The "floral stimulus" in cocklebur is transmitted through the bark, most likely in the phloem (Withrow and Withrow, 1943), and this is doubtless also true in other species. Furthermore, if one leaf of a cocklebur is exposed to a photoinductive cycle and this leaf be removed within 24 hr. after cessation of the cycle, no induction of flowers occurs. This indicates that the rate of transmission of the floral-inducing effect is relatively slow. In the Biloxi soybean, the effect of the exposure of one leaf to photoinductive cycles is also transmitted in both the upward and downward directions through the plant, but inception of flowering takes place only in buds relatively close to the exposed leaves.

The facts just discussed have led to the postulation that some substance or complex of substances is synthesized in leaves under photoinductive cycles, whence it is translocated to apical meristems, inducing their conversion from the vegetative to the reproductive condition. The name "florigen" has been proposed for this postulated flower-inducing hormone by Cajlachjan (1936).

Role of the Light and Dark Periods in Photoperiodism.—In nature the photoperiodic cycle is 24 hr. in length, a long photoperiod being auto-

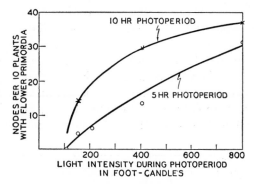

FIG. 162. Relation between irradiance and initiation of flower primordia in Biloxi soybean. Data of Hamner (1942).

matically accompanied by a short dark period and *vice versa*. Experimenters, however, are not restricted by the inflexibilities of solar time tables. One important technique of evaluating the relative roles of the light and dark periods has been the use of photoperiodic cycles other than those which occur under natural conditions. In the laboratory, for example, a 10-hr. photoperiod need not be accompanied, as in nature, by a 14-hr. dark period, but may be made to alternate with an 8, 10, 12, 16, 20-hr. or any length of dark period.

An induction technique was employed by Hamner (1940) in an investigation of the roles of the light and dark periods in the initiation of flowering in short-day Biloxi soybean. Plants were first allowed to develop to a suitable size under long days, then subjected to seven consecutive experimental cycles, the pattern of which differed from one experiment to another, and finally returned to long days. The quantitative effect of each treatment

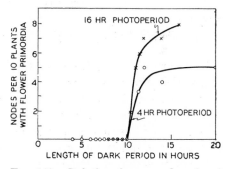

FIG. 163. Relation between length of the dark period and initiation of flower primordia in Biloxi soybean. Data of Hamner (1942).

was measured as the number of nodes per ten plants at which flower primordia were initiated.

In one experiment the effect of variations in irradiance during the photoperiods of the seven experimental cycles upon the initiation of flowers was investigated (Fig. 162). With photoperiods of either a 5-hr. or 10-hr. duration in a 24-hr. cycle, no initiation of floral primordia occurred at illumination values of less than about 100 foot-candles; and, under 10-hr. photoperiods, approximately maximum effectiveness was attained at about 800 foot-candles. The irradiance during the photoperiods is therefore not without influence in inducing photoperiodic reactions, but in general a maximum effect is obtained in this species at irradiances which are relatively low compared with full sunlight.

In other experiments the length of the dark period was varied from

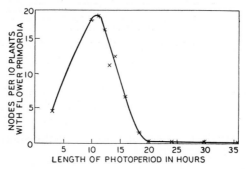

Fig. 164. Relation between length of photoperiod and initiation of flower primordia in Biloxi soybean (dark period 16 hr.). Data of Hamner (1942).

4 to 20 hr., while the length of the photoperiod (irradiance about 1200 foot-candles) was kept constant, in one experiment at 16 hr., in another at 4 hr., during the seven experimental cycles. The results showed (Fig. 163) that a certain minimum length of dark period (about 10.5 hr.) is necessary if induction of any floral primordia is to occur and that the length of the minimum dark period required is the same within a wide range of photoperiods. Furthermore, under 16-hr. photoperiods, the longer the dark period, up to 16 hr., the greater its effectiveness.

In still other experiments the length of the dark period was kept constant at 16 hr., while the length of the photoperiod (irradiance about 1200 foot-candles) was varied from 4 to 36 hr. during the seven experimental cycles. Maximum initiation of floral primordia occurred under a photoperiod about 11 hr. long, but any photoperiod between about 1 hr. (estimated) and about 19 hr. in length was effective in inducing the formation of some primordia (Fig. 164). No primordia were initiated, however, in photoperiods which were 20 hr. or more in duration. Although the *number* of flower primordia initiated is thus influenced markedly by the length of the photoperiod, the length of the dark period, as previously indicated, determines whether the plant will bloom or not.

Similar photoperiodic requirements for flowering have been demonstrated in other kinds of short-day plants, but the effective lengths of the photoperiods and the dark periods differ from one species to another. In the cocklebur the photoperiod of the single necessary photoinductive cycle need be only 0.5 hr. at 2000-3000 foot-candles and a temperature of 30°C. At lower irradiances, with increasing length of the photoperiod up to a certain point, the effect on initiation of flower primordia and their rate of development increases (Mann, 1940). The minimum effective dark period for this species is about 8.5 hr. (Hamner, 1940).

In general, if flowering is to occur, short-day plants require cyclical alternations of continuous dark periods of a minimum duration with photoperiods of adequate irradiance within a certain range of lengths. Minimum effective photoperiods may be very short—less than an hour in some species—but photoperiods may also be too long to induce blooming. Minimum effective dark periods, on the contrary, are never very short. Short-day plants do not bloom under alternating cycles of relatively short dark periods and photoperiods, as do long-day and indeterminate plants (see later).

The so-called "intermediate" plants appear to be fundamentally similar to short-day plants in that both dark and light periods are necessary if they are to flower. "Intermediates" appear to differ from short-day plants only in that the minimum length of photoperiod required for flowering is considerably longer in the former than in the latter.

The cyclical requirements of long-day plants are quite different from those of short-day plants. Dill blooms in about 40 days after sowing under continuous illumination of 1000-1400 foot-candles (Naylor, 1941). This plant flowers sooner under continuous illumination than under any of a number of kinds of cycles of alternating dark and light periods (Allard and Garner, 1941). Similarly, annual beet, another long-day plant, flowers in 4-7 weeks after sowing under continuous illumination of 1000-1400 foot-candles, but does not flower at all at 500 foot-candles. (Naylor, 1941). In general, long-day species flower under continuous illumination, provided other environmental conditions, especially irradiance and temperature, are suitable.

In general, long-day plants, unlike short-day plants, do not require an alternating cycle of light and dark periods, but flower without exposure to any dark intervals whatsoever. The only requirement of such plants, if flowering is to occur, is that they be exposed to a photoperiod of minimum irradiance which must not be less than a certain minimum duration out of each 24-hr. day. The exact length of this minimum (critical) photoperiod differs from one long-day species to another, and for a given species varies somewhat depending upon irradiance and temperature.

Failure of long-day species to bloom under short photoperiods results from the dark periods being too long, rather than from the photoperiods being too short. This is shown by the fact that such species bloom under short photoperiods if they alternate with dark periods which are also short. Dill, for example, flowers on alternating cycles of 0.5-hr. light: 0.5-hr. dark, and also on 1:1, 2:2, 12:12, 24:24, and 30:30-hr. cycles (Allard and Garner, 1941).

Like long-day plants, all indeterminate species which have been tested flower under continuous illumination. *Zinnia angustifolia*, for example, blooms under continuous illumination, under a cycle of 12-hr. light, 12-hr. dark, but not under a cycle of 6-hr. light, 18-hr. dark (Allard and Garner, 1941). Indeterminate plants, like long-day plants, require only that they be exposed to a photoperiod of minimum irradiance and of not less than a certain duration out of each 24-hr. day if flowering is to be induced. The distinction between long-day and indeterminate plants thus appears to be an arbitrary one, the only important difference between the two types being that indeterminate plants have a lower critical photoperiod than long-day plants. As in long-day plants the light period need not be continuous for indeterminate species to bloom. *Zinnia angustifolia*, for example, flowers under alternating cycles similar to those under which dill flowers (Allard and Garner, 1941).

Mechanism of Photoperiodism.—There can be little doubt that flower-inducing substances of a hormonal nature exist in plants, that the rates of synthesis and destruction of such compounds are markedly influenced by the photoperiodic cycle and temperature (see later), and that the environmental conditions under which synthesis of such substances occurs differ from one kind of plant to another. However, present evidence for the existence of such substances is purely inferential, since all attempts to extract from plants and identify such compounds have failed to date.

Although earlier workers recognized four types of plants on the basis of their photoperiodic reactions, later work has indicated that the only fundamentally distinct categories are those of long-day plants and short-day plants. In spite of the often diametrically opposite reactions of plants of these two types to a given photoperiodic cycle, there are many indications that the photoperiodic mechanism of both long-day and short-day plants is basically similar.

One such line of evidence is that grafting of a long-day or indeterminate plant to a short-day plant induces the latter to flower if the "donor" part of the graft is kept under photoinductive cycles (Moshkov, 1937; Heinze *et al.*, 1942 and others). Such experiments show that compounds synthesized in one kind of plant are effective in inducing flower formation in other kinds.

Another line of evidence which indicates that the photoperiodic mechanism in all plants is basically similar is that within a single species there often exist varieties which differ in the pattern of their photoperiodic reaction. This is true of soybeans, as already discussed. Another example is side-oats grama grass (*Bouteloua curtipendula*), some strains of which consist almost entirely of short-day or intermediate plants, while others consist of a mixture of long-day and intermediate plants (Olmsted, 1945).

A similarity in photoperiodic mechanism is also suggested by the fact that both flowering of short-day plants under short natural photoperiods, and inhibition of flowering of long-day plants under the same conditions occur because the dark periods in such 24-hr. cycles are long—not because the photoperiods are short. This is shown by the results of experiments in which the dark period of such cycles is interrupted at approximately its midpoint by exposure of the plants to a short period of illumination, which need not be of a very high irradiance. The photoperiodic reaction of both types of plants is reversed by such a treatment. In other words, flowering of short-day plants (cocklebur, Biloxi soybean) is inhibited (Hamner and Bonner, 1938), while flowering of long-day plants (Wintex barley, *Hyocyamus niger*) is promoted (Borthwick *et al.*, 1948a; Parker *et al.*, 1950). The effect of interrupting the dark period is the same as is obtained with each type of plant by extending the length of the photoperiod with weak supplemental illumination as described earlier.

Furthermore, the same spectral regions which most effectively inhibit flowering of short-day plants (Parker *et al.*, 1946) are also the ones which most effectively promote flowering of long-day plants (Borthwick *et al.*, 1948b) when used to interrupt the dark period. Although all wave lengths of visible light are active in inducing such reactions, there is a region of maximum effectiveness in the orange-short red and a region of minimum effectiveness in the blue-green. This "action spectrum" closely resembles that for the elongation of pea leaves (Chap. XXX), suggesting the likelihood of a similarity in the basic mechanism of the two processes.

Although more attention has been devoted to investigations of the role of the dark period in photoperiodism, the role of the photoperiod is at least equally significant. In typical long-day and indeterminate plants, a dark period is not even necessary for induction of flowering. Furthermore there is some experimental evidence of a close relation between photoperiodism and photosynthesis (or at least CO_2 consumption). No flower primordia developed on Biloxi soybeans when no CO_2 was supplied during the 8-hr. photoperiods, and plants that received CO_2 at atmospheric concentration during 2, 4, 6, and 8 hr. of each photoperiod formed flower primordia in numbers which were proportional to the length of the period during which CO_2-containing air was supplied (Parker and Borthwick, 1940).

However, Leopold (1949) and others have shown that potato, pea, bean, and some other species initiate flower primordia if grown from tubers or seed in total darkness. Such etiolated plants apparently can synthesize flower-inducing compounds when stored substances are available in tubers or cotyledons. On the other hand, green leafy plants, transferred to continuous darkness while still in a vegetative state, fail to initiate flower primordia. This suggests the existence of an inhibitory effect in the dark of the green leafy condition on flowering, and that an effect of exposure to the photoperiod is the elimination of this inhibition.

Hypotheses regarding the exact mechanism of the hormonal regulation of flowering in plants are too much in the realm of speculation to warrant detailed consideration in an introductory discussion. Possible physiological mechanisms of photoperiodism are discussed by Melchers (1939), Cholodny (1939), Hamner (1940), Borthwick et al., (1948b), and Snyder (1948).

The relative lengths of the photoperiod and dark period not only have an influence on whether or not flowers develop, but may also effect the sexual expression of plants. In corn (Zea mays), a monoecious species, short photoperiods favor production of carpellate and suppression of staminate flowers (Schaffner, 1930), the "tassels" becoming more or less completely converted into carpellate flowers. Several other species, including cocklebur and ragweeds, are known to react in similar fashion to short photoperiods. Hemp, however, a dioecious species, reacts somewhat differently. Usually about half the plants in a field of hemp are carpellate and about half staminate. The shorter the day length under about 14 hr. the greater the proportion of carpellate plants on which some staminate flowers develop and the greater the proportion of staminate plants on which some carpellate flowers develop (Schaffner, 1923).

Temperature.—The influence of temperature upon reproductive growth of plants is closely interrelated with photoperiodic effects. Depending upon the particular combination of temperature cycle and photoperiod, the influence of this factor may be to reinforce the effect of the photoperiod in inducing or inhibiting reproductive development, or to act in opposition to it. In the latter situation the effect of either temperature or the photoperiod may predominate, depending upon the plant and other conditions.

It is obvious that temperature may affect any hormonal mechanism of flowering in various ways. Temperature may influence the rates of synthesis, or of destruction of the compounds involved, the rate of their translocation from leaves to meristems, and the effectiveness of the hormone or hormones in inducing morphogenic changes in the meristems.

The influence of temperature upon the photoperiodic reactions of Biloxi soybean has been investigated in considerable detail. Initiation of flower primordia in this species was found to be influenced much more by the temperature of the dark period than by the temperature of the photoperiod (Parker and Borthwick, 1939b). At 13°C., during the dark period, the number of flower primordia-containing buds initiated was much smaller than at dark period temperatures of 18° or 24°C. Fewer primordia were initiated at a 29°C. dark-period temperature than at 18° or 24°C., but more than at 13°C. The effect of dark-period temperatures upon the initiation of flower primordia was much the same, whether the photoperiod temperature was 13°, 18°, 24°, or 29°C., although photoperiod temperatures of 24° and 29°C. were more favorable to initiation than 13° or 18°C.

The effects of a localized cooling of the leaves, petioles, and of the terminal buds on initiation of flower primordia (Borthwick, Parker, and Heinze, 1941; Parker and Borthwick, 1943) were studied in order to find out whether the principal effect of low temperature was upon synthesis of hormone within the leaves, its translocation from leaves to meristems, or its effect on differentiation of flower primordia at apical meristems. Although low temperatures applied at any of these points exert a retarding effect on initiation of flowers, lower temperatures must be applied to the petioles or buds (about 2°-7°C.) than to leaves during the dark period (about 7°-13°C.) if marked inhibition of the flowering reactions is to occur. The checking effect of low night temperatures on flower initiation in this species appears therefore to result primarily from their influence on reactions which occur in the leaf blades, since, as temperature is lowered, such processes are suppressed sooner than translocation of flower-inducing substances or differentiation of floral parts.

There are other indications that the temperature of the dark period has an important influence on the photoperiodic reactions of plants. Roberts and Struckmeyer (1938, 1939) have shown that the reactions of a number of kinds of plants to length of day may be altered under greenhouse conditions as a result of the night temperature which prevails. For example, the well-known Maryland Mammoth tobacco bloomed under a short photoperiod (about 9-10 hr.) if the night temperature was 18°C., but not under a long photoperiod (about 16-18 hr.); whereas under a night temperature of 13°C. this plant bloomed under both of these photoperiods. Similarly morning glory (Heavenly Blue variety) bloomed only under long days (about 16-18 hr.) at a night temperature of 13°C., only under short days (about 9-10 hr.) at a night temperature of 21°C., but under both of these photoperiods at a night temperature of 18°C. Similar illustrations can also be given for long-day plants. Beet, for example, ordinarily flowers only under a relatively long day but, in the relatively low temperature range of 10°-16°C., flowers under an 8-hr. photoperiod, although not as abundantly as under a 15-hr. photoperiod (Chroboczek, 1934).

The fact that the temperature of the dark period is much more critical in its influence on the reproductive growth of many plants than the temperature of the photoperiod has important implications for growers of greenhouse crops. The patterns of plant behavior in relation to temperature as described above come largely under the heading of thermoperiodic reactions. It is often not merely a matter of temperatures within a certain range being conducive to reproductive development, but that cyclical patterns of alternation between certain day and certain night temperatures are required.

Considered primarily from the standpoint of temperature, some plants require relatively low temperatures for flowering, some require relatively high temperatures, and others flower over a wide range of temperatures (Thompson, 1939). Flowering of plants in the first category is adversely affected in warm climates, flowering of those in the second is adversely affected in cool climates.

Lettuce is an example of a species in which flowering is favored by relatively high temperatures. If the white Boston variety is grown at 21°-27°C., no heads form and the plants soon begin to develop flowerstalks; at 16°-21°C., heads develop first and flowerstalks later; whereas at 10°-16°C., heads develop more slowly and flowerstalks either very slowly or not at all. Other species in which relatively high temperatures are conducive to flowering include cleome, phlox, pepper, and some varieties of chrysanthemum.

Celery, beet, onion, cabbage, carrot, cosmos, and stocks are examples of plants in which flowering is favored by relatively low temperatures. Celery plants, exposed for 10-15 days to 4°-10°C. or 10°-16°C., develop flowerstalks and seed if grown subsequently at 16°-21°C., but if grown continuously under the latter range of temperatures remain vegetative. Exposure to relatively low temperatures also favors reproductive growth of a number of biennial plants, such as the garden and sugar beet. Such plants ordinarily do not flower the first growing season, but usually bloom and set fruit the second. However, flower, fruit, and seed development fails to take place in these plants during the second season unless they are exposed to relatively low temperatures between their first and second growing seasons. Furthermore, by suitable temperature treatments it is possible to induce flowering and seed development of biennial beets the first season, thus modifying their growth habit from that of a biennial to that of an annual. Beet plants (Crosby Egyptian variety), for example, maintained at 10°-16°C., all fruited the first season; maintained at 16°-21°C., only a few fruited; maintained at a still higher temperature, none fruited (Chroboczek, 1934).

As several of the examples given above illustrate, the influence of a certain temperature treatment at one stage in the life history of a plant may influence its development during a later stage. In other words, a plant can undergo a *thermal induction*, which is closely analogous to photoperiodic induction. The efficacy of thermal induction may depend upon the subsequent temperature treatment of the plant. Celery, beet, or cabbage plants, thermally induced to initiate flowers by exposure to 10°-16°C., develop flowers and seed more quickly if subsequently maintained at 16°-21°C. than at 10°-16°C., and remain vegetative indefinitely at 21°-27°C. In other words, the effect of the low temperature thermal induction can be reversed by subsequent exposure to too high a temperature.

Temperature has complicated effects upon the fruiting as well as the flowering phases of reproductive growth. Among these are thermoperiodic effects. In tomato, for example, fruit set is abundant only when night temperatures are between 15° and 20°C., being less prevalent or even absent at higher or lower night temperatures (Went, 1944). More or less similar relationships doubtless hold for many other kinds of plants.

Carbohydrate and Nitrogen Metabolism.—The flowering phase of reproductive growth is a relatively transitory one and is controlled predominantly by a hormonal mechanism rather than by nutritive conditions within the plant. Nevertheless, the construction of floral parts proceeds at the expense of foods translocated to the floral meristems, and some effects of the nutritional status of the plant are exerted even on this phase of growth since no organ of a plant grows well unless adequately supplied with both carbohydrates and nitrogenous foods.

High nitrogen appears to favor development of carpellate rather than staminate flowers in a number of dioecious species (Loehwing, 1938). In the tomato, deficiency of carbohydrates induces microspore degeneration and pollen sterility, whereas nitrogen deficiency has no such effect. Development of the female organs, on the contrary, is not greatly influenced by carbohydrate deficiency but is markedly repressed by nitrogen deficiency (Howlett, 1936).

Development of fruits, particularly those of a fleshy type, is physiologically very similar to vegetative growth. The effects of different proportions of carbohydrates and nitrogenous foods on the development of fleshy fruits is, in general, similar to their effects upon the development of vegetative organs. In tomato, even when all other conditions are favorable for fruit development, deficiency of nitrogen results in the formation of small, tough, woody fruits. When nitrogenous foods are present in adequate quantities and if other growth conditions are also favorable, large, juicy, succulent fruits develop. An adequate supply of water is also an obvious requisite for the maximum development of fruits of the fleshy type.

Specific Chemical Compounds.—As the previous discussion has shown, there are many indications that flowering in plants is induced by naturally synthesized hormones. Flowering can also be promoted, at least in some species, by the external application of certain chemical compounds. Blooming of pineapple, for example, can be induced by treatment of the plants with acetylene or ethylene (Rodriguez, 1932; Cooper and Reece, 1942).

Certain auxins (α-naphthaleneacetic acid, 2,4-dichlorophenoxyacetic acid) also elicit the flowering reaction in pineapples under certain conditions when applied in suitable concentrations (Clark and Kerns, 1942; Van Overbeek, 1946). On the other hand, certain auxins such as α-naphthaleneacetic acid and indoleacetic acid have been found to exert an inhibitory effect on flowering in some species of plants (Bonner and Thurlow, 1949, and others).

A more complete analysis of the relation of auxins to flowering is afforded by the results of Leopold and Thimann (1949), who found that relatively low concentrations of α-naphthaleneacetic acid or indoleacetic acid promote flowering in barley or teosinte, while relatively high concentrations inhibit it (Fig. 136).

Various other chemicals have been found to have rather specific effects on the flowering of plants; 2,3,5-triiodobenzoic acid, for example, results in an enhanced production of flowers on tomato and some other plants when it is sprayed on them in certain concentrations (Zimmerman and Hitchcock, 1949). Maleic hydrazide, on the other hand, is an example of a compound which inhibits flower initiation when applied in any appreciable concentration (Naylor, 1950).

Known and probable roles of naturally occurring hormones in the ripening of fruits are discussed in the preceding chapter. External application of certain compounds, largely of the auxin type, has various effects upon fruit development. Among these are prevention of abscission (Chap. XXXV), induction of parthenocarpy, already discussed, and accelerated ripening of fruits. This latter effect can be induced in some kinds of fruits by treatment with 2,4-dichlorophenoxyacetic acid. H. stened ripening of fruits of apple, banana, and pear has been obtained by treatment with this compound (Mitchell and Marth, 1944). The effect is somewhat similar to that of ethylene, previously discussed.

SUGGESTED FOR COLLATERAL READING

Murneek, A. E., R. O. Whyte, and others. Vernalization and photoperiodism. Chronica Botanica Co. Waltham, Mass. 1948.

SELECTED BIBLIOGRAPHY

Allard, H. A. Complete or partial inhibition of flowering in certain plants when days are too long or too short. *Jour. Agric. Res.* **57**: 775-789. 1938.

Allard, H. A., and M. W. Evans. Growth and flowering of some tame and wild grasses in response to different photoperiods. *Jour. Agric. Res.* **62**: 193-228. 1941.

Allard, H. A., and W. W. Garner. Further observations on the response of various species of plants to length of day. *U. S. Dept. Agric. Tech. Bull. 727*. 1940.

Allard, H. A., and W. W. Garner. Responses of some plants to equal and unequal ratios of light and darkness in cycles ranging from 1 hour to 72 hours. *Jour. Agric. Res.* **63**: 305-330. 1941.

Arthur, J. M., J. D. Guthrie, and J. M. Newell. Some effects of artificial climates on the growth and chemical composition of plants. *Contr. Boyce Thompson Inst.* **2**: 445-511. 1930.

Bonner, J., and J. Thurlow. Inhibition of photoperiodic induction in *Xanthium* by applied auxin. *Bot. Gaz.* **110**: 613-624. 1949.

Borthwick, H. A., S. B. Hendricks, and M. W. Parker. Action spectrum for photoperiodic control of floral initiation of a long-day plant, Wintex barley (*Hordeum vulgare*). *Bot. Gaz.* **110**: 103-118. 1948a.

Borthwick, H. A., and M. W. Parker. Photoperiodic perception in Biloxi soybean. *Bot. Gaz.* **100**: 374-387. 1938a.

Borthwick, H. A., and M. W. Parker. Influence of photoperiods upon the differentiation of meristems and the blossoming of Biloxi soybeans. *Bot. Gaz.* **99**: 825-839. 1938b.

Borthwick, H. A., and M. W. Parker. Photoperiodic responses of several varieties of soybeans. *Bot. Gaz.* **101**: 341-365. 1939.

Borthwick, H. A., M. W. Parker, and P. H. Heinze. Influence of localized low temperature on Biloxi soybean during photoperiodic induction. *Bot. Gaz.* **102**: 792-800. 1941.

Borthwick, H. A., M. W. Parker, and S. B. Hendricks. Wave length dependence and the nature of photoperiodism. *Lotsya* **1**: 71-78. 1948b.

Cajlachjan, M. C. On the mechanism of photoperiodic reaction. *Comp. Rend. (Doklady) Acad. Sci. U.S.S.R.* **1**: 89-93. 1936.

Cajlachjan, M. C. On the hormonal theory of plant development. *Comp. Rend. (Doklady) Acad. Sci. U.S.S.R.* **3**: 443-447. 1936.

Cholodny, N. G. The internal factors of flowering. *Herbage Rev.* **7**: 223-247. 1939.

Chroboczek, E. A study of some ecological factors influencing seed stalk development in beets (*Beta vulgaris* L.) *Cornell Univ. Agric. Exp. Sta. Mem.* 154. 1934.

Clark, H. E., and K. R. Kerns. Control of flowering with phytohormones. *Science* **95**: 536-537. 1942.

Cooper, W. C., and P. R. Reece. Induced flowering of pineapples under Florida conditions. *Proc. Florida State Hort. Soc.* **54**: 132-138. 1942.

Garner, W. W., and H. A. Allard. Effect of the relative length of the day and night and other factors of the environment on growth and reproduction in plants. *Jour. Agric. Res.* **18**: 553-606. 1920.

Garner, W. W., and H. A. Allard. Further studies in photoperiodism, the response of the plant to relative length of day and night. *Jour. Agric. Res.* **23**: 871-920. 1923.

Garner, W. W., and H. A. Allard. Localization of the response in plants to relative length of day and night. *Jour. Agric. Res.* **31**: 555-566. 1925.

Hamner, K. C. Interrelation of light and darkness in photoperiodic induction. *Bot. Gaz.* **101**: 658-687. 1940.

Hamner, K. C., and J. Bonner. Photoperiodism in relation to hormones as factors in floral initiation and development. *Bot. Gaz.* **100**: 388-431. 1938.

Hamner, K. C., and A. W. Naylor. Photoperiodic responses of dill, a very sensitive long day plant. *Bot. Gaz.* **100**: 853-861. 1939.

Heinze, P. H., M. W. Parker, and H. A. Borthwick. Floral initiation in Biloxi soybean as influenced by grafting. *Bot. Gaz.* **103**: 518-530. 1942.

Howlett, F. S. The effect of carbohydrate and nitrogen deficiency upon microsporogenesis and the development of the male gametophyte in the tomato, *Lycopersicum esculentum* Mill. *Ann. Bot.* **50**: 767-803. 1936.

Knott, J. E. Effect of localized photoperiod on spinach. *Proc. Amer. Soc. Hort. Sci.* **31**: 152-154. 1934.

Larsen, E. C. Photoperiodic responses of geographical strains of *Andropogon scoparius*. *Bot. Gaz.* **109**: 132-149. 1947.

Leopold, A. C. Flower initiation in total darkness. *Plant Physiol.* **24**: 530-533. 1949.

Leopold, A. C., and K. V. Thimann. The effect of auxin on flower initiation. *Amer. Jour. Bot.* **36**: 342-347. 1949.

Loehwing, W. F. Physiological aspects of sex in angiosperms. *Bot. Rev.* **4**: 581-625. 1938.

Mann, L. K. Effect of some enviromental factors on floral initiation in *Xanthium*. *Bot. Gaz.* **102**: 339-356. 1940.

Melchers, G. Die Blühhormone. *Ber. Deutsch. Bot. Ges.* **57**: 29-48. 1939.

Mitchell, J. W., and P. C. Marth. Effects of 2,4-dichlorophenoxyacetic acid on the ripening of detached fruit. *Bot. Gaz.* **106**: 199-207. 1944.

Moshkov, B. S. Flowering of short day plants under continuous day as a result of grafting. *Bull. Appl. Bot., Genetics, and Plant Breed.* **21**: 145-156. 1937.

Murneek, A. E. Length of day and temperature effects in *Rudbeckia*. *Bot. Gaz.* **102**: 269-279. 1940.

Naylor, A. W. Effects of some environmental factors on photoperiodic induction of beet and dill. *Bot. Gaz.* **102**: 557-575. 1941.

Naylor, A. W. Observations on the effects of maleic hydrazide on flowering of tobacco, maize and cocklebur. *Proc. Nat. Acad. Sci.* (*U.S.A.*) **36**: 230-232. 1950.

Naylor, Frances L. Effect of length of induction period on floral development of *Xanthium pennsylvanicum*. *Bot. Gaz.* **103**: 146-154. 1941.

Olmsted, C. E. Growth and development of range grasses. IV, V. *Bot. Gaz.* **106**: 46-74. 1944. 382-401. 1945.

Parker, M. W., and H. A. Borthwick. Effect of photoperiod on development and metabolism of the Biloxi soybean. *Bot. Gaz.* 100: 651-689. 1939a.

Parker, M. W., and H. A. Borthwick. Effect of variation in temperature during photoperiodic induction upon initiation of flower primordia in Biloxi soybean. *Bot. Gaz.* 101: 145-167. 1939b.

Parker, M. W., and H. A. Borthwick. Floral initiation in Biloxi soybeans as influenced by photosynthetic activity during the induction period. *Bot. Gaz.* 102: 256-268. 1940.

Parker, M. W., and H. A. Borthwick. Influence of temperature on photoperiodic reactions in leaf blades of Biloxi soybean. *Bot. Gaz.* 104: 612-619. 1943.

Parker, M. W., S. B. Hendricks, and H. A. Borthwick. Action spectrum for the photoperiodic control of floral initiation of the long-day plant *Hyoscyamus niger. Bot. Gaz.* 111: 242-252. 1950.

Parker, M. W., S. B. Hendricks, H. A. Borthwick, and N. J. Scully. Action spectrum for photoperiodic control of floral initiation of short-day plants. *Bot. Gaz.* 108: 1-26. 1946.

Rodriguez, A. G. Influence of smoke and ethylene on the fruiting of the pineapple. *Jour. Dept. Agric. Puerto Rico* 16: 5-18. 1932.

Roberts, R. H., and B. Esther Struckmeyer. The effects of temperature and other enviromental factors upon the photoperiodic responses of some of the higher plants. *Jour. Agric. Res.* 56: 633-677. 1938.

Roberts, R. H., and B. Esther Struckmeyer. Further studies of the effects of temperature and other environmental factors upon the photoperiodic responses of plants. *Jour. Agric. Res.* 59: 699-709. 1939.

Schaffner, J. H. The influence of relative length of daylight on the reversal of sex in hemp. *Ecology* 4: 323-334. 1923.

Schaffner, J. H. Sex reversal and the experimental production of neutral tassels in *Zea mays. Bot. Gaz.* 90: 279-298. 1930.

Snyder, W. E. Mechanism of the photoperiodic response of *Plantago lanceolata* L., a long-day plant. *Amer. Jour. Bot.* 35: 520-525. 1948.

Thompson, H. C. Temperature in relation to vegetative and reproductive development in plants. *Proc. Amer. Soc. Hort. Sci.* 37: 672-679. 1939.

Van Overbeek, J. Control of flower formation and fruit size in the pineapple. *Bot. Gaz.* 108: 64-73. 1946.

Went, F. W. Plant growth under controlled conditions. II. Thermoperiodicity in growth and fruiting of the tomato. *Amer. Jour. Bot.* 31: 135-150. 1944.

Withrow, Alice P., and R. B. Withrow. Translocation of the floral stimulus in *Xanthium. Bot. Gaz.* 104: 409-416. 1943.

Zimmerman, P. W., and A. E. Hitchcock. Triiodobenzoic acid influences flower formation of tomatoes. *Contr. Boyce Thompson Inst.* 15: 353-361. 1949.

DISCUSSION QUESTIONS

1. With most floricultural plants which is the more practical way of increasing flowering during the winter months—increasing the intensity of light or its daily duration?

2. Why do radishes rapidly "go to seed" if planted in the late spring?

3. What would be the probable photoperiodic classification of each of the following plants: One that flowers only at day lengths longer than 10 hr.? One that flowers only at day lengths longer than 8 and less than 14 hr.? One that flowers under alternating 5-min. intervals of light and dark and on a photoperiod

of 6 hr.? One that flowers when exposed to continuous illumination but not at a photoperiod which is less than 12 hr.? One that flowers at a 9-hr. photoperiod, 15-hr. dark period; but not on a cycle consisting of 9-hr. photoperiod, 7-hr. dark period, 1-hr. photoperiod, and 7-hr. dark period? One that does not flower on a 9-hr. photoperiod, 15-hr. dark period; but does on a cycle of a 9-hr. photoperiod, 7-hr. dark period, 1-hr. photoperiod, and 7-hr. dark period? One that does not flower under a continuous illumination of 100 foot-candles, but does under a continuous illumination of 1000 foot-candles?

4. What would be the probable photoperiodic classification of each of the following plants: One that flowers in far northern latitudes? One that flowers in the tropics? One that flowers in a greenhouse in winter in north central United States? One that flowers in January in Argentina? One that flowers in late summer or early autumn in north central United States?

5. The climate at certain altitudes on high mountains in tropical regions is similar in most respects to that of temperate regions. Plants transplanted from such mountain habitats to temperate regions often fail to grow and bloom. Explain.

XXXIII

GROWTH CORRELATIONS

The development of every organ of a growing plant is influenced to some degree by the physiological processes or physicochemical conditions prevailing in some other organ or organs. Thus, the vegetative growth of many plants is sharply checked during the period of fruiting because the presence of developing fruits strongly influences processes occurring in the root system. Similarly, the size and vigor of root systems are influenced by photosynthetic activities of the leaves, and the formation of flower buds and flowers may be controlled by processes taking place in leaves. Such relationships, often reciprocal, existing among the organs of a plant, are termed *growth correlations* or often simply *correlations*.

Growth correlations are not only exerted by one organ on another but also occur among tissues and even among cells. The harmonious development of the plant body as a whole is a result of correlative influences operating from organ to organ, tissue to tissue and cell to cell. Hundreds of correlative influences are operating more or less continuously in the tissues of a growing plant. The discussion in this chapter will be restricted almost entirely, however, to some of the better known examples of the correlative influences of one plant organ on another.

Not all growth correlations result from operation of the same internal mechanism. Some result from the effect of one organ upon the supply and distribution of foods to other organs. One of the effects of leaves upon the root system is a correlation of this kind. Other correlations may be caused by the greater use of water or mineral salts in one organ than in another. A large number of growth correlations apparently result from the influence of hormones or hormone-like substances. Examples of such correlations have been described in the preceding chapters. It is also possible that differences in electrical potential from one part of the plant to another may play a role in the correlative development of plants.

Correlations Between Reproductive and Vegetative Development.—A study of the correlation between vegetative development and fruiting in the tomato plant has been made by Murneek (1925). When tomato plants were deflorated or the fruits were removed as rapidly as they set, the plants continued to grow vegetatively. If, however, the fruits were allowed to remain on the plant and enlarge, vegetative development and the formation of flowers gradually slowed down as more and more fruits began to develop. The steps in the inhibition of the development of such plants proceeded in approximately the following order: (1) loss of fecundity by the blossoms, (2) decrease in the size of the floral clusters, (3) abscission of the flower buds, (4) checking and later cessation of terminal growth of the stem, and (5) eventual death of all parts of the plant except the fruit.

The checking effect of the enlargement of fruits upon continued vegetative development and the development of flowers resulted, according to this investigator, from the virtually complete monopolization of all of the nitrogenous compounds in the plants by the fruits. Carbohydrates, on the other hand, were found to be stored in considerable quantities in both the fruits and vegetative organs. In general, the more nitrogenous compounds available, the more fruits that set and started to develop before inhibition of flowering and vegetative growth began. Removal of the fruits at any time before the vegetative parts died resulted in a renewal of vegetative growth, and, ultimately, in another cycle of reproductive development.

The interrelationships between vegetative and reproductive growth have also been studied in cotton plants (Eaton and Rigler, 1945; Eaton and Joham, 1944). The reduction in vegetative growth which was found to accompany the formation of bolls was attributed to the small quantity of carbohydrate reaching the root system. Most of the carbohydrate synthesized in the leaves found its way into the developing fruits with the result that the root systems received relatively small amounts of food. The effect of the low carbohydrate supply to the roots was to reduce markedly the absorption of mineral salts which in turn restricted vegetative growth. Removal of the fruits resulted in tripling the sugar content of the root system and greatly increased the absorption of mineral salts.

Correlative effects between fruiting and flowering can be observed in most species which develop flower primordia over a considerable period of time, as is true of many summer-blooming species. If the blossoms of the sweet pea (*Lathyrus odoratus*) are allowed to develop, for example, flowering soon ceases, but if they are picked from time to time flower primordia and blossoms develop continually throughout the growing season. All experienced flower gardeners know that, if continued flowering is to be maintained in many species, especially annuals, the flowers must be cut as rapidly as they open, and that allowing fruit development to proceed soon results in a checking or even complete cessation of flowering.

The most satisfactory explanation of the growth correlations just described is that they result from modifications in the internal food relations of the plants. In general, they are believed to be caused by a diversion of such a large proportion of the available foods to developing flowers or fruits that other organs suffer a deficiency and hence are checked in growth. Both developing flowers and fruits are organs of high assimilatory and respiratory activity and hence their maturation may result in a considerable drain on the available food supply. Some such correlative effects seem to result from a virtual monopolization of nitrogenous foods by the growing fruits (*cf*. Murneek's results on tomato) ; others appear to result mainly from the diversion of carbohydrate foods to the developing flowers or fruits (*cf*. Eaton and Joham's studies on cotton).

The Shoot-Root Ratio.—A number of investigations have been made of the so-called shoot-root ratios in crop plants. Such ratios are usually calculated by dividing the dry weight of shoots formed by the dry weight of the roots formed during the growth period under consideration. The shoot-root ratio is influenced by reciprocal correlative influences between the aerial parts of a plant and its roots. The kind and magnitude of these correlative effects depend largely upon the environmental conditions to which the plant is exposed. For example, the nitrate concentration of the substratum has been shown to have a marked influence upon the shoot-root ratios of plants (Table 45).

The results of this experiment indicate a consistent increase in the shoot-root ratio with increase in the nitrate concentration of the solution culture. In this particular experiment there was also an absolute reduction in the dry weight of the roots developed with increase in nitrate concentration, but this was not found to be true in all the experiments performed by this investigator. Similar results have been obtained with a number of other species and by plants rooted in the soil as well as in solution cultures.

The effect of nitrates upon the shoot-root ratio can be interpreted in

TABLE 45—INFLUENCE OF NITRATE CONCENTRATION UPON THE SHOOT-ROOT RATIO OF BARLEY PLANTS. DURATION OF THE EXPERIMENT 49 DAYS (DATA OF TURNER, 1922)

	Dry weight of shoot in grams	Dry weight of roots in grams	S/R ratio
Low nitrate	9.64	1.81	5.33
Medium nitrate	11.81	1.43	8.28
High nitrate	10.55	1.17	9.08

terms of their influence upon the internal food relations of plants. If the nitrate concentration of the substratum in which the plant is rooted is low, most of the nitrates absorbed are utilized in the synthesis of amino acids in the roots, the carbohydrates necessary for this process being translocated downward from the leaves. Most of these amino acids are used in the synthesis of protoplasmic proteins during the growth of the roots. Only a small proportion of the available nitrogenous compounds escapes utilization in the roots and is translocated (either as nitrates or as amino acids and related compounds) to the aerial portions of the plant. The tops are, therefore, relatively deficient in proteins. Hence the growth rate of the aerial portions of the plant will be relatively slow and the shoot-root ratio relatively low.

When the supply of nitrates is more abundant, however, a smaller proportion of the total quantity absorbed is utilized in the roots. A larger proportion of the nitrogen, as a constituent of one kind of compound or another, is translocated into the aerial portions of the plant, where much or all of it is usually utilized in the synthesis of protoplasmic proteins. The enhanced vegetative development of the aerial organs of the plant which is favored by such metabolic conditions results in the utilization of more carbohydrates as well as more proteinaceous foods by the aerial meristems. Because of the vigorous vegetative development of the shoot system the proportion of the carbohydrate foods which are translocated to the roots may be relatively small. Hence, relative to the shoots, the roots are likely to be deficient in both carbohydrates and proteins, since synthesis of the latter requires carbohydrates as well as nitrates, and grow at a relatively slower rate than the tops. The net result is a higher shoot-root ratio than when the plants are grown in a soil which is deficient in nitrates.

Similarly, a decrease in the supply of carbohydrates within the plant, as a result of a diminution in the rate of photosynthesis, or any other cause, influences the shoot-root ratio of plants. In general, diminution in the quantity of carbohydrate foods available in the tops results in an increased shoot-root ratio, and *vice versa*. Plants grown in the shade, for example, have higher shoot-root ratios than other plants of the same species grown in full sunlight. Pruning commonly results in increasing the shoot-root ratio of woody plants, since the new growth following pruning is usually especially vigorous, resulting in monopolization of most of the available carbohydrates by the shoots. For similar reasons, defoliation from any cause, or cutting of leaves or tops (grasses, alfalfa, etc.) usually has the effect of increasing the shoot-root ratio. Removal of flowers, developing fruits, or developing buds, on the other hand, often favors root growth and may result in a decrease in the shoot-root ratio. The explanation of such effects follows a line of reasoning similar to that just presented in explanation of the relative influence of high and low nitrate supply on the shoot-root ratios of plants.

The shoot-root ratio is also influenced by the available soil-water content. In general, a relatively low soil-water content and adequate soil aeration favor relatively low shoot-root ratios, while the opposite conditions favor relatively high ones (Table 46). The shoot-root ratios as shown in this table are computed on a fresh weight basis but undoubtedly would show essentially the same relations if expressed on a dry weight basis. The results indicate clearly that the shoot-root ratio increases with increase in the percentage of water in the soil. The absolute weight of the shoots increases consistently with increase in soil-water content, while the absolute weight of the roots increases to a maximum at a soil water content of 20 per cent, after which it diminishes. The lesser development of roots at the higher soil water contents is undoubtedly a result of the poorer aeration of the wetter soils (cf. Table 47).

TABLE 46—SHOOT-ROOT RATIOS OF CORN SEEDLINGS GROWN FOR 17 DAYS IN SAND AT VARIOUS WATER CONTENTS (DATA OF HARRIS, 1914)

Per cent water in terms of dry weight of sand	Fresh weight in grams		S/R ratio
	Shoots	Roots	
38	3.63	4.05	0.90
30	3.54	4.21	0.84
20	3.36	5.18	0.65
15	2.35	4.90	0.48
11	1.56	4.30	0.36

The relationship between photoperiodism and the shoot-root ratio has also received some study (Roberts and Struckmeyer, 1946). In general, long-day plants have higher shoot-root ratios under long photoperiods, and short-day plants have higher shoot-root ratios under short photoperiods. These generalizations are in agreement with the observation that plants blossoming or with young fruits have higher shoot-root ratios than vegetative plants. The explanation probably lies in the monopolization of food materials by flowers and developing fruits. It is also possible that the decreased formation of phloem tissues associated with flowering plays a role in restricting the flow of foods into the root system.

Inadequate soil aeration results in a reduction in root growth in most species and commonly leads to an increased shoot-root ratio (Table 47).

Concentration of oxygen, milliequivalents per liter	Dry weight in grams		S/R ratio
	Shoots	Roots	
0.05	1.31	0.23	5.88
0.15	2.44	0.53	4.47
0.25	2.68	0.70	3.86
0.5	2.78	0.74	3.77
* 1.0	3.11	0.78	4.05

* Approximate equilibrium with oxygen at atmospheric concentration.

Increase in temperature within the physiological range for plants usually results in an increase in shoot-root ratio (Table 48).

Temperature °F.	Fresh weight in grams		S/R ratio
	Shoots	Roots	
50–60	13.6	58.1	0.234
60–70	22.1	76.1	0.290
70–80	14.2	29.5	0.481

In addition to the effects of environmental factors it is highly probable that the shoot-root ratio is also influenced by the movement of hormones such as the postulated rhizocaline and caulocaline (Chap. XXVIII) from shoot to root and *vice versa*.

Apical Dominance.—In many herbaceous plants which produce aerial stems growth in length takes place principally or entirely at the apex of the main axis of the plant. Although a lateral bud is present in the axil of every leaf, side branches do not often develop from these buds as long as the terminal bud retains its vigor and continues to grow. If, however, the terminal bud is destroyed or injured in any way, or is artificially removed, development of one or more of the lateral buds usually starts at once. This inhibiting effect of a terminal bud upon lateral bud development is called *apical dominance* and is much more pronounced in some species than in others.

The phenomenon of apical dominance is usually also in evidence in all woody plants on which true terminal buds form. The lateral buds on current shoots usually do not develop unless the terminal bud is destroyed or injured. Development of the lateral buds on older shoot segments is of more frequent occurrence, indicating that the inhibitory effect of the apical bud diminishes with greater distance of the lateral buds from the apex of the stem. In many woody species most of the axillary buds regularly develop into lateral branches the next growing season after the one during which they formed.

The controlling effect of the apical bud in apical dominance apparently results from its auxin content. When agar blocks containing either auxin *b* or indoleacetic acid were applied to broad bean (*Vicia faba*) plants in place of the terminal buds which had been removed, the blocks being replaced with fresh ones from time to time in order to maintain the supply of auxin, inhibition of lateral bud development occurred just as if the terminal bud were intact (Skoog and Thimann, 1934). The lateral buds on check plants, to which only plain agar blocks were applied, developed rapidly.

A number of growth regulating compounds have similar effects upon the growth of lateral buds if applied in proper concentrations to the cut surface of a detipped stem. Lateral buds on vigorous field grown tobacco plants, for example, can be kept from growing for three weeks after removal of the terminal bud by the application of a lanolin paste containing 5 per cent α-naphthaleneacetic acid to the upper end of the decapitated stem. Lateral buds on similar detipped to-

FIG. 165. Plants in the left foreground treated with α-napthaleneacetic acid. Plants on the right and in the central background are untreated.

bacco plants to which no growth regulator was applied grew to a length of 3 or 4 feet in the same interval of time (Fig. 165).

When potato tubers begin to sprout, the apical buds grow rapidly but the lateral buds usually fail to elongate. If, however, the apical and lateral buds are cut out of the parent tuber, both grow at similar rates (Michener, 1942). Treatment of the tubers with ethylene chlorohydrin, which causes the destruction of auxin, results in the rapid growth of both lateral and apical buds. As in the other examples cited above, the evidence clearly supports the thesis that the growth of lateral buds is checked by auxins formed in the apical buds.

Although there is no doubt that auxins play a key role in the phenomenon of apical dominance, the exact mechanism of their operation in this kind of growth correlation is not known with certainty. The original suggestion of Skoog and Thimann (1934) was that the auxin exerted a direct retarding effect on the development of lateral buds. According to this theory, as long as the auxin concentration in the adjacent tissue exceeds a given threshold, concentration growth of the lateral buds is inhibited; if the auxin concentration falls below this value, lateral buds begin to grow if no other factors are limiting (Skoog, 1939). *Cf.* Fig. 136.

Other more elaborate interpretations of the mechanism whereby auxins inhibit lateral bud development have been made. It has been postulated that certain other substances necessary for bud growth are diverted to regions of relatively high auxin concentration such as terminal buds and that lateral buds fail to develop because of their lack of these substances in adequate quantities. One such suggestion is that caulocaline (Chap. XXVIII)—considered to be necessary for stem elongation—moves primarily to regions of maximum auxin synthesis, *i.e.*, in intact stems to the apical buds (Went, 1938).

Another postulated mechanism, one for which there is considerable supporting evidence (Snow, 1939, 1940), is that, under the influence of auxin, a growth inhibitor is formed that is responsible for the inhibition of lateral bud growth. The auxin, moving in its usual downward direction through the stem, is considered to engender in some manner the synthesis of a growth inhibitor which, upon movement into lateral buds, prevents their growth. Since it is known that some growth inhibitors have a chemical structure not greatly different from that of the auxins it is possible that such an inhibitor may actually be made from auxin.

Another aspect of apical dominance is illustrated by the growth habit of many trees. Most coniferous trees and some broad-leaved trees as well have a single main stem which grows vertically upward. The lateral branches, however, assume an obliquely upright or almost horizontal position. If the apex of the main stem is destroyed or seriously injured, one or more (often all) of the lateral branches originating at the node or nodes immediately below the apex gradually turn upward as a result of greater growth on their lower than on their upper sides. Eventually these branches assume an approximately vertical position often giving a candelabrum-shaped top to the tree. Subsequent vertical growth of the tree is accomplished by means of these reoriented branches. Maintenance of the more or less horizontal growth of the lateral branches in uninjured trees is obviously a result of some kind of control exerted by the apical growing region. Although no concrete evidence exists in support of such a theory, the probability seems very great that this type of growth correlation is also to be explained in terms of a hormonal mechanism.

Cambial Activity and Tissue Differentiation.—The first sign of growth in trees in the spring of the year is the swelling of the buds. This is quickly followed by the opening of the buds and the rapid elongation of the young stems. The resumption of growth by cambium cells in the older stems occurs much more slowly, however, and many days may elapse after the opening of the buds before cambium cells in the older stems begin to divide and enlarge. The division and enlargement of cambium cells first begins near the tips of the stems. A wave of cambial activity moves slowly from this region down the stems and branches and into the roots. Accompanying this basipetal migration of cambial activity is the differentiation of secondary xylem and phloem tissues. This progressive march of tissue differentiation from opening buds toward the roots has been known for many years, but until the discovery of hormones no satisfactory explanation of the phenomenon had been advanced.

There is considerable evidence that resumption of cambial activity is activated by auxins which move in a basipetal direction in stems from developing buds. Snow (1935) showed that, if solutions of certain auxins were applied to the cut surface of detipped sunflower seedlings, activation of cambial growth was induced just as in intact plants, but no such activation occurred in detipped plants to which no auxin was applied. Similarly introduction of a crystal of indoleacetic acid into the cambium of willow and other woody species leads to rapid cambial growth below the point of insertion of the crystal (Söding, 1936). Avery et al. (1937) showed that the auxin concentration of buds of apple and horse-chestnut increases at the time of their enlargement and reaches a peak value just prior to the most rapid elongation of the current season's shoots. Movement of the hormone takes place from the current season's growth basipetally into older portions of the stem, paralleling the downward migration of cambial activity.

In herbaceous plants a growth correlation also appears to exist between cambial activity and flower production (Wilton, 1938). Cambium cells divide rapidly throughout the entire length of the stem in plants that are strongly vegetative and growing vigorously. When flowering begins, the activity of the cambium cells is sharply checked. Cambial activity continues to decline as flowering progresses until, in profusely flowering plants, all of the cambium cells appear to have been differentiated into xylem and phloem tissues. The check to cambial activity first occurs in the region of the stem closest to the inflorescence and progresses basipetally from this region. The correlations between flower formation and cambial activity suggest the operation of a hormonal mechanism. Since transformation of a large proportion of vegetative to reproductive meristems would greatly reduce auxin output, it seems likely that this may be another auxin-controlled growth correlation.

Growth Correlations Between Leaves and Buds.—Examination of a leafy shoot will show that a bud is present in the axil of every leaf. This same relationship between the position of leaves and the location of buds also holds at the shoot apex where embryonic buds develop above the center of each leaf primordium. When leaves are caused to form in unusual positions, buds also arise above the center of the point where the leaf joins the stem. The constancy of this relationship between leaves and buds suggests some controlling influence of the former organ over the development of latter. Very soon after the leaf primordium begins its development the first signs of bud formation also can be detected. However, if the young leaf primordium is carefully excised no bud will develop. Furthermore partial separation of a very young leaf primordium from the stem apex by a vertical incision results in the formation of the bud upon the isolated portion of the leaf primordium—never upon the stem axis itself (Snow and Snow, 1942). Experiments of this kind demonstrate that the development of buds is controlled by the leaf and not by factors in the stem axis. The mechanism of this control is unknown, but it is probably of a hormonal type.

Polarity.—Many growth correlations are polar; that is, the two ends of a growing axis exhibit a marked dimorphism in development. The most familiar example of polarity in plants is that shown by cuttings, in which roots develop from the basal end and shoots from the apical end. Even if such cuttings are inverted and kept in a moist atmosphere roots will usually develop only from the morphologically basal end and shoots only from the morphologically apical end. It is not difficult, however, to induce the formation of roots at the upper end of a stem by the application of relatively high concentrations of growth regulators (Fig. 165).

While the obvious manifestations of polarity are morphological, basically all such phenomena depend upon a physiological mechanism. Many of the polar phenomena of plants probably result from the polar transport of auxins or other hormones. The polarity of cuttings, for example, can be explained largely, if not entirely, on a hormonal basis.

The movement of auxins in stems is usually polar in the basipetal direction (Chap. XXVIII). This polarity of movement appears to be associated with some fundamental organizational pattern of the protoplasm and cannot be changed easily. Segments of a stem with roots induced to form at the morphologically upper end of the stem axis can be inverted and grown for weeks in the inverted position without altering the original apex-to-base polarity of auxin transport (Went, 1941). After 3 or 4 weeks in the inverted position a new polarity appears. The stem segments now transport auxin from the original base to the morphological apex as well as in the original direction. The inherent apex to base polarity of the stem persists, but a new polarity in the reverse direction is also present. Presumably the new polarity is limited to cells formed during growth in the inverted position.

In addition to morphological polarities and polarities in the distribution of certain compounds, plants also exhibit electrical polarities. The apexes of the stems, hypocotyls, and coleoptiles of a number of herbaceous species have been shown to be electronegative relative to more basal portions (Clark, 1937). In larger plants, such as trees, the distribution of gradients of electrical potential is more complex (Lund, 1931). Apparently each individual cell in a plant is electrically polarized and acts like a tiny battery. The electrical potentials occurring in plant tissues are summation effects of the potentials of individual cells which may act either in series or in parallel (Rosene, 1935).

As a result of differences in electrical potential from one part of a plant to another electric currents flow continuously along certain circuits in the plant, and it has been suggested that these may serve as a mechanism of correlation. Electrical energy may thus be transferred from one cell to another, influencing the processes or development of the recipient cell. Although there is no doubt that polarity potentials exist in plants, the evidence that they are the basis of a correlation mechanism is as yet very insubstantial. On the other hand, it is possible that the differences in electrical potentials known to exist in plants are purely secondary phenomena which bear no causal relation to the correlative behavior of plants.

Plant Galls.—Growth correlations are not restricted to the influence one plant organ exerts over the growth of another plant organ. Remarkable control over the growth and structural differentiation of plant cells may also be exerted by insect larvae. When the eggs of certain dipterous insects are deposited on the surface of young hickory leaves, for example, the leaf tissue begins a rapid growth around the egg and develops a distinctive and often extremely complicated structure, the anatomical features of which are determined by the species of the insect laying the egg. These intricate and beautifully symmetrical structures are known as galls (Fig. 166). So complete is the control exerted by the growing insect larvae over the architecture of the plant tissue constituting the gall that the species of insect larvae present can be identified by an examination of the structure of the gall. It is possible for twenty or thirty different insect galls to grow side by side on the same hickory leaf. The same kind of plant

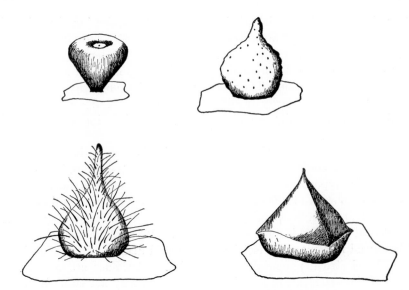

FIG. 166.   Plant galls on leaves of hickory. All of these kinds of galls and others may be formed on a single hickory leaf. Redrawn from Wells (1915).

tissue thus develops into a wide variety of architectural forms under some mechanism of control determined wholly by the particular species of insect larva present. The mechanism of control is not known but probably represents another example of the influence of growth regulating substances on the physiological activities of plant cells.

SUGGESTED FOR COLLATERAL READING

Pincus, G., and K. V. Thimann, Editors. *The Hormones.* Vol. I. Academic Press, Inc. New York. 1948.

Went, F. W., and K. V. Thimann. *Phytohormones.* The Macmillan Co. New York. 1937.

SELECTED BIBLIOGRAPHY

Avery, G. S., Jr., P. R. Burkholder and Harriet B. Creighton. Production and distribution of growth hormone in shoots of *Aesculus* and *Malus* and its probable role in stimulating cambial activity. *Amer. Jour. Bot.* **24:** 51-58. 1937.

Barnes, W. C. Effects of some environmental factors on growth and color of carrots. *Cornell Agric. Expt. Sta. Mem. 186.* 1936.

Bloch, R. Polarity in plants. *Bot. Rev.* **9:** 261-310. 1943.

Clark, W. G. Polar transport of auxin and electrical polarity in coleoptile of *Avena. Plant Physiol.* **12:** 737-754. 1937.

Eaton, F. M., and H. E. Joham. Sugar movement to roots, mineral uptake, and the growth cycle of the cotton plant. *Plant Physiol.* **19:** 507-518. 1944.

Eaton, F. M., and N. E. Rigler. Effects of light intensity, nitrogen supply and fruiting on carbohydrate utilization by the cotton plant. *Plant Physiol.* **20:** 380-411. 1945.

Erickson, L. C. Growth of tomato roots as influenced by oxygen in the nutrient solution. *Amer. Jour. Bot.* **33:** 551-561. 1946.

Harris, F. S. The effect of soil moisture, plant food, and age on the ratio of tops to roots in plants. *Jour. Amer. Soc. Agron.* **6:** 65-75. 1914.

Lund, E. J. Electric correlation between living cells in cortex and wood in the Douglas fir. *Plant Physiol.* **6:** 631-652. 1931.

Michener, H. D. Dormancy and apical dominance in potato tubers. *Amer. Jour. Bot.* **29:** 558-568. 1942.

Murneek, A. E. Correlation and cyclic growth in plants. *Bot. Gaz.* **79:** 329-333. 1925.

Roberts, R. H. and B. Esther Struckmeyer. The effect of top environment and flowering upon top-root ratios. *Plant Physiol.* **21:** 332-344. 1946.

Rosene, Hilda F. Proof of the principle of summation of cell E. M. F's. *Plant Physiol.* **10:** 209-224. 1935.

Skoog, F. Experiments on bud inhibition with indole-3-acetic acid. *Amer. Jour. Bot.* **26:** 702-707. 1939.

Skoog, F. Growth substances in higher plants. *Ann. Rev. Biochem.* **16:** 529-564. 1947.

Skoog, F., and K. V. Thimann. Further experiments on the inhibition of the development of lateral buds by growth hormone. *Proc. Nat. Acad. Sci. (U.S.A.)* **20:** 480-485. 1934.

Snow, R. Activation of cambial growth by pure hormones. *New Phytol.* **34:** 347-360. 1935.

Snow, R. A second factor involved in inhibition by auxin in shoots. *New Phytol.* **38:** 210-223. 1939.

Snow, R. A hormone for correlative inhibition. *New Phytol.* **39:** 177-184. 1940.

Snow, Mary, and R. Snow. The determination of axillary buds. *New Phytol.* **41:** 13-22. 1942.

Söding, F. Über den Einfluss von Wuchstoff auf das Dickenwachstum der Bäume. *Ber. Deutsch. Bot. Ges.* **54:** 291-304. 1936.

Turner, T. W. Studies of the mechanism of the physiological effects of certain mineral salts in altering the ratio of top growth to root growth in seed plants. *Amer. Jour. Bot.* **9:** 415-445. 1922.

Wells, B. W. A survey of the zoocecidia on species of *Hicoria* caused by parasites belonging to the *Eriophydiae* and the *Itonididae. Ohio Jour. Sci.* **16:** 37-59. 1915.

Went, F. W. Specific factors other than auxin affecting growth and root formation. *Plant Physiol.* **13:** 55-80. 1938.

Went, F. W. Polarity of auxin transport in inverted *Tagetes* cuttings. *Bot. Gaz.* **103:** 386-390. 1941.

Wilton, O. C. Correlation of cambial activity with flowering and regeneration. *Bot. Gaz.* **99:** 854-864. 1938.

XXXIV

GERMINATION AND DORMANCY

The Structure of Seeds.—The development of seeds is discussed in some detail in Chap. XXXI. All seeds contain an embryo plant which is enclosed by one, or more commonly by two, seed coats.[1] The seed coats originate from the integuments of the ovule and often exhibit external structural evidences of this origin even in the mature seed. Among these are the *hilum,* which represents the place where the seed was attached to the ovule stalk (*funiculus*), and *micropyle,* which frequently persists in the mature seed, and the *raphe,* a remnant of ovule stalk which in certain kinds of seeds is adherent to the seed coats. When a single seed coat is present it is usually hard and woody, but when there are two seed coats the inner is almost invariably thin and membranous.

The embryos in seeds of different species of plants differ markedly in size and appearance, but all mature embryos are composed of one or more *cotyledons,* a *plumule,* and a *hypocotyl* (Fig. 167). The cotyledons are the seed leaves and vary in number from one in the monocotyledons to as many as fifteen in the embryos of some conifers. The embryos of dicotyledons have two cotyledons, as the name implies. Structurally the cotyledons are modified leaves, but usually they differ greatly in appearance from the foliage leaves of the same species. The cotyledons (or cotyledon) are attached near the upper end of the short thick stem-like axis of the embryo, the hypocotyl. The plumule or bud of the embryo is usually located just above the point at which the cotyledon or cotyledons are attached to the hypocotyl. The plumule consists of a meristem with several rudimentary foliage leaves. The primary root of the plant develops from the lower end of the hypocotyl. The rudimentary root at the lower end of the hypocotyl is often called the *radicle.*

---

[1] In the skunk cabbage (*Spathyema foetida*) and possibly in a few other species, the seed consists only of a naked embryo (Rosendahl, 1909).

An *endosperm* is also present in the seeds of many species (Fig. 167*D*). This tissue develops from the endosperm nucleus and usually contains considerable quantities of accumulated foods. In the seeds of those species which contain no endosperm, such as the legumes, the cotyledons are usually enlarged and contain considerable quantities of reserve foods (Fig. 167*B*). Some seeds contain a *perisperm* which represents remnants of the nucellus. The so-called "endosperm" in the seeds of gymnosperms is not a true endosperm but represents the female gametophyte (Fig. 167*E*).

Germination of Seeds.—The resumption of active growth on the part of the embryo resulting in the rupture of the seed coats and the emergence of the young plant is known as *germination*. The seeds of many plants will germinate as soon as ripe if environmental conditions are suitable. Pea seeds, for example, sometimes germinate within the pod, corn grains may sprout while still attached to the parent plant, and the seeds of some citrus species frequently germinate while still within the fleshy fruits. Seeds of many other species, however, will not sprout until after an interval of weeks, months, or years, even if environmental conditions are favorable for germination. The causes of this condition of *dormancy* in seeds will be discussed later.

In nature, germination of seeds usually occurs either at or just below the surface of the soil. The latter is more apt to happen in forests where seeds, especially smaller varieties, often fall into

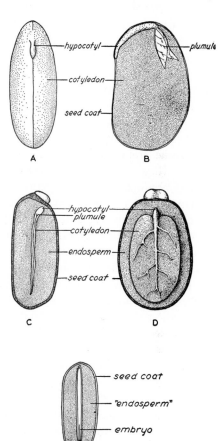

FIG. 167. Structure of seeds. (*A*) Seed of lima bean with seed coat removed, (*B*) seed of lima bean with one cotyledon removed, (*C*) seed of castor bean as seen in longitudinal median section, (*D*) seed of castor bean with endosperm removed down to the first cotyledon, (*E*) seed of pinyon (*Pinus edulis*) as seen in longitudinal median section.

interstices in the decaying detritus which composes the top layer of many forest soils and are later covered by falling leaves. In the laboratory, nondormant seeds will usually sprout if they are brought into contact with any moist substratum or even simply exposed to a saturated atmosphere, provided other environmental conditions are also suitable.

The initial step in germination is the imbibition of water by the various tissues within the seed. This generally results in an increase in its volume. The increase in the hydration of the seed coats usually causes a pronounced increase in their permeability to oxygen and carbon dioxide, which is very low in the dry seed coats. The swelling of the seed often ruptures the seed coat, but in some species this does not occur until the emergence of the primary root.

With an increase in the hydration of the cells, enzymes become activated. In seeds possessing an endosperm, enzymes apparently move into that tissue from the embryo as described in Chap. XVI. Stored foods, whether they occur in the endosperm or cotyledons, are digested and the soluble products of the digestion process are translocated toward the growing points of the embryo. If chemical analyses are made of samples of seeds at successive stages during their germination, it is found that the quantity of starches, oils, and proteins in the seed decreases markedly (Table 34). A large proportion of the fats present are usually converted, after digestion, into soluble carbohydrates. The soluble carbohydrates are not present during the later stages of germination in amounts quantitatively equivalent to the starch or other storage carbohydrates digested during the process, indicating that a large proportion of these compounds is consumed in respiration or assimilated in the construction of the carbohydrate constituents of cell walls. In oily seeds the soluble carbohydrates utilized in respiration result largely from chemical transformations of the products of the digestion of fats. Digested proteins are usually represented in the seeds by quantitatively equivalent amounts of amino acids, asparagine, etc. This indicates that proteins are not consumed in respiration but are utilized in the synthesis of the organic nitrogenous compounds of the growing embryo.

Insofar as the actual mechanics of seed germination are concerned two principal groups of seeds may be recognized: (1) those in which the cotyledons emerge from the seed and (2) those in which the cotyledons remain permanently within the seed. Most seeds of dicotyledons and seeds of some monocotyledons such as onion belong to the first group while the seeds of grasses and of some dicotyledons such as peas and oaks belong in the second.

1. *Seeds in Which the Cotyledons Emerge.*—The sequence of events that takes place during the germination of the seed of the lima bean

(*Phaseolus lunatus*) will be described as a type example in this group (Fig. 168). Germination is initiated by a marked swelling of the seed which usually ruptures the seed coat. This is followed by the emergence of the primary root which develops from the lower end of the hypocotyl and is the first structure of the embryo to make contact with the external environment. The primary root grows downward in the soil producing lateral roots and root hairs. The hypocotyl then elongates rapidly, pulling the cotyledons upward out of the soil into the air where they separate into an approximately horizontal position on either side of the plumule. The

Fig. 168. Stages in the germination of a seed of lima bean (*Phaseolus lunatus*).

plumule then begins active growth giving rise to the stem and foliage leaves of the seedling. Since the bean is a seed without an endosperm, the food used during germination is largely derived from the accumulations in the thick cotyledons.

2. *Seeds in Which the Cotyledons Do Not Emerge.*—The seed of the pea is structurally very similar to that of the bean, but its germination behavior is very different. Elongation of the hypocotyl does not occur, and the cotyledons remain in the seed. The primary root elongates early in the process of germination much as in the bean. The plumule is elevated through the soil by rapid elongation of the *epicotyl*, which is the stem region between the cotyledons and the first true leaves—in other words, the first internode.

This type of germination is also exhibited by oak acorns (Fig. 169).

Many monocotyledons also show this type of germination behavior. In the germination of the corn grain, for example, the primary root develops from the lower end of the axis of the embryo, growing through the *coleorhiza* (Fig. 84) and the wall of the grain (pericarp). As the primary root elongates, lateral roots soon appear and root hairs begin to develop just back of the elongating regions on all of the roots. The single cotyledon (*scutellum*) remains within the seed and acts as an absorbing organ

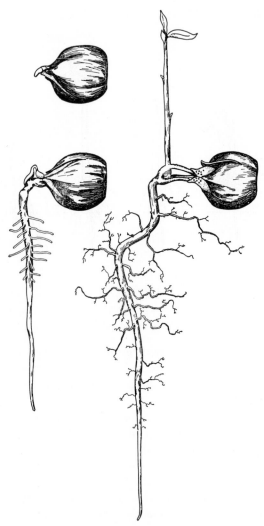

FIG. 169. Stages in the germination of a red oak (*Quercus borealis*) acorn. Redrawn from Korstian (1927).

through which soluble foods in the endosperm move into the tissues of the rapidly enlarging embryo. Soon after the appearance of the primary root the plumule and the *coleoptile,* which completely encloses it, grow out through the walls of the grain and upward as a result of elongation of the region of the axis just below the plumule. About the time the coleoptile breaks through the surface of the soil, or soon thereafter, the first foliage leaf grows through the tip of the coleoptile and emerges into the light and air.

Environmental Conditions Necessary for Germination.—The seeds of all species of plants require at least three external conditions before germination can occur: (1) water, (2) a suitable temperature, and (3) oxygen. A fourth factor, light, is of importance in the germination of the seeds of some species.

1. *Water.*—A low water content is one of the prominent characteristics of the dormant seeds of most plant species, although some seeds become injured and lose the capacity to germinate if their water content falls to low levels (Jones, 1920). The germination of grapefruit seeds, for example, was reduced 30 per cent by drying at room temperature to 52 per cent moisture, although much lower moisture contents did not reduce germination if the temperatures were reduced to 5°C. (Barton, 1943).

The physiological processes of living cells occur largely in an aqueous medium, and germination cannot occur unless the seed can absorb water from its environment. The absorption of water initiates a series of physical and chemical processes which, in the absence of any limiting factor, results in the emergence of the embryo from the seed. Soil-moisture contents need not be high, however, for germination to occur. When soil moisture levels are at or slightly below field capacity, germination of seeds is usually most rapid, but good germination of many species of seeds and subsequent emergence of the young seedlings may occur when the soil moisture level is at the permanent wilting percentage or even slightly lower (Doneen and MacGillivray, 1943).

The quantity of water absorbed during germination by seeds of different species or even by varieties of the same species varies within wide limits. Seeds of a drought resistant variety of cotton, for example, have been found to absorb only about one-half as much water during germination as seeds of a variety less resistant to dry weather (Stiles, 1948).

Water-vapor as well as liquid water can be imbibed by seeds. Most seeds, therefore, will pass through the earlier stages of germination in an atmosphere which is saturated, or nearly so, but if the vapor pressure of the atmosphere is appreciably below the saturation value germination will be checked or inhibited.

2. *Oxygen.*—The respiration of germinating seeds proceeds at a rapid

rate especially during the early stages of germination. The partial pressure of oxygen in the atmosphere can be reduced considerably, however, without greatly interfering with the rate of respiration (Chap. XXI). In fact, the seeds of some water plants such as cattail (*Typha latifolia*) germinate better under low oxygen pressures than in air. Seeds of many terrestrial plants can germinate under water where the concentration of oxygen often corresponds to a partial pressure of oxygen very much less than that of the atmosphere (Morinaga, 1926). Seeds of many common weeds may lie buried in the soil for years without germinating; yet when the soil is plowed or otherwise disturbed so that these seeds are brought to the surface germination usually occurs promptly. The cause for this delay in germination of viable seeds appears to be the low oxygen content or high carbon dioxide content, or both, of the soil in which they are buried. Exposure to the air, which occurs as a result of plowing, so increases the oxygen supply in the environment of the seeds that germination usually takes place within a few days if other conditions are not limiting (Bibbey, 1948).

During the early stages of germination of seeds of pea and some other species, respiration is largely or almost entirely of the anaerobic type because of the relative impermeability of even hydrated seed coats of such species to oxygen (Chap. XXII). As soon as the seed coats are ruptured, however, aerobic respiration replaces anaerobic oxidative processes even in seeds of this type.

3. *Suitable Temperature.*—In the absence of other limiting factors the seeds of any species will germinate within a certain range of temperatures, but at temperatures above or below this range no germination will occur. As a rule, the seeds of species indigenous to temperate regions germinate in a lower range of temperatures than seeds of species whose native habitat is in tropical or subtropical regions. Wheat seeds, for example, germinate at temperatures only slightly above 0°C. and at temperatures as high as 35°C., whereas the range of temperatures for germination of seeds of maize (a species of subtropical origin) lies between a lower value of 5°-10°C. and an upper limit of about 45°C. The optimum temperature is usually about midway between the two extremes of temperature at which germination will occur. It is not possible to designate any exact temperature as the optimum for germination, because this varies with the other prevailing environmental conditions and also with the exact criterion selected as an index of germination. The most favorable temperature for the elongation of the primary root, for example, does not always correspond to the most suitable temperature for the development of the plumule.

4. *Light.*—A few species of plants including the strangling fig (*Ficus*

aurea), mistletoe (*Viscum album*), and some other epiphytes have seeds which fail to germinate unless exposed to the light. Many kinds of seeds germinate better when exposed to the light than when kept in total darkness. Examples of these light-favored seeds are those of many grasses, especially species of *Poa*, the evening primrose (*Oenethera biennis*), and mullein (*Verbascum thapsus*). On the other hand, the germination of the seeds of some species appears to be retarded or even prevented by exposure to light. Seeds of the onion and many other members of the lily family belong in this group (Crocker, 1936). The effect of light upon the germination of seeds is profoundly influenced by other environmental factors. For example, the germination of the seeds of some species of grass (*Poa* sp.) is ordinarily influenced by light, but after a period of dry storage this effect disappears. Similarly the ordinarily light sensitive seeds of the pampas grass (*Chloris ciliata*) will germinate readily in complete darkness in an atmosphere of pure oxygen. Freshly harvested lettuce seeds germinate much better in diffuse light than in total darkness. The beneficial effects of light disappear, however, if the seeds are placed in an atmosphere containing 5-20 per cent of CO_2 (Thornton, 1936) or if the seeds are treated with thiourea (Raleigh, 1943).

Dormancy of Seeds.—Many kinds of seeds, apparently ripe, fail to germinate even if placed under such conditions that all environmental factors are favorable. In such seeds resumption of growth by the embryo is arrested by conditions within the seeds themselves. The state of inhibited growth of seeds or other plant organs as a result of internal causes is usually called *dormancy* but is sometimes referred to as the "rest period."

Failure of seeds to sprout does not necessarily mean that they are dormant. Environmental conditions may be unfavorable for germination. The water supply may be inadequate, or the temperature may be unfavorable. Deeply buried seeds are often prevented from germinating by an inadequate oxygen supply, or certain kinds of light-sensitive seeds may fail to germinate because of unfavorable light conditions. The term "dormancy" as applied to seeds is generally restricted to those which fail to germinate as a result of internal causes. For convenience we shall use the term *quiescence* as a designation for the situation in which failure of a plant organ to grow is a result of environmental conditions. In practice, it is often difficult to determine whether seeds or other plant organs under natural conditions are actually dormant or merely quiescent without resorting to an experimental test.

Dormancy of seeds results from one or a combination of several different factors:

1. *Seed Coats Impermeable to Water.*—The seed coats of many species are completely impermeable to water (and probably also to oxygen) at

the time the seeds are ripe. This condition is very common in the seeds of many legumes (clovers, alfalfa, black locust, honey locust, etc.), of the water lotus, and of the morning glory. Germination fails to occur until water penetrates through the seed coats. In many such seeds the permeability of the coats to water increases slowly in dry storage, but it occurs more rapidly when they are exposed to the fluctuations of temperature and moisture that are present in soils under natural conditions. The action of bacteria and fungi also increases the permeability of the seed coats to water and so shortens the dormant period of seeds of this kind that are buried in the surface layers of soil.

It is probable that the cause of the impermeability of seeds to water will be traced to some feature of the structure or the chemical composition of the walls of the cells in the seed coats. Comparative studies, however, of the cellular anatomy of seed coats of legume species with impermeable seed coats and of legume species with seeds that are permeable to water have failed to reveal the presence of any structural characteristics associated only with the impermeable condition (Watson, 1948).

2. *Mechanically Resistant Seed Coats.*—The seeds of some of the commonest weeds, such as mustard (*Brassica*), pigweed (*Amaranthus*), water plantain (*Alisma*), shepherd's purse (*Capsella*), and peppergrass (*Lepidium*), remain in the dormant condition because the seed coats are strong enough to prevent any appreciable expansion of the embryo. In the seeds of the pigweed (*Amaranthus retroflexus*), for example, water and oxygen penetrate through the seed coats readily, but the enlargement of the embryo is limited by the mechanical strength of the seed coats. As long as the seed coats remain saturated with water, dormancy persists, and may last for a period of 30 years or even longer. If the seed coats become dry, however, certain changes occur in the colloidal compounds that make up the walls of the cells of the seed coats so that, upon being again saturated with water, they are no longer able to resist the pressures developed by the imbibitional forces in the embryo. The coats are ruptured and germination occurs. High temperatures (above 40°C.) may also induce some germination of pigweed seeds at the time of ripening because the seed coats are less resistant at these temperatures. As the seeds age, the minimum temperature for germination becomes lower. The embryos of these seeds have no dormant periods and will grow readily if the seed coats are removed. Likewise any treatment which weakens the seed coats increases the percentage of seeds that germinate. In general, other seeds with mechanically resistant seed coats exhibit similar behavior.

3. *Seed Coats Impermeable to Oxygen.*—The two seeds in a fruit of cocklebur (*Xanthium*) are not equally dormant. Under natural conditions the lower seed usually germinates in the spring following maturity while

the upper seed remains dormant until the next year. The dormancy of these seeds has been demonstrated to result from the impermeability of the seed coats to oxygen (Shull, 1911). If the seed coats are ruptured, or if the oxygen pressure is increased around intact seeds, germination occurs. The oxygen requirements for germination are greater in the upper seed than in the lower, and this explains the more pronounced dormancy of the former. During dry storage or under natural conditions the seed coats gradually become more permeable to oxygen, and the oxygen requirements of the embryo decrease. Hence the intensity of the dormant condition gradually diminishes. The seeds of a number of grasses and of many Compositae also have dormant periods that seem to result from the impermeability of the seed coats to oxygen.

4. *Rudimentary Embryos.*—Many species of plants have seeds in which the embryo does not develop as rapidly as the surrounding tissues, so that when the seeds are shed the embryos are still imperfectly developed. In some species the ripened seeds contain embryos that have grown little beyond the fertilized egg stage, whereas in other species development of the embryos may be nearly complete when the seeds are shed. The germination of such seeds is necessarily delayed until formation of the embryo is complete. Examples of species in which dormancy of seeds is a consequence of incompletely developed embryos include ginkgo (*Ginkgo biloba*), European ash (*Fraxinus excelsior*), holly (*Ilex opaca*), and many orchids.

5. *Dormant Embryos.*—In many species, although the embryos are completely developed when the seed is ripe, the seeds fail to germinate even when environmental conditions are favorable. Dormancy of such seeds is a result of the physiological condition of the embryo. The embryos of such seeds will not grow when the seeds first ripen even if the seed coats are removed. Among the many species whose seeds exhibit dormancy of this type are apple, peach, hawthorne, iris, lily-of-the-valley, basswood, ashes, tulip poplar, dogwood, hemlock, and pines. Germination of such seeds occurs only after a period of "after-ripening." In many wild species after-ripening occurs during the winter while the seeds lie on the ground or just under the soil surface. Such seeds will not germinate in the fall just after they are shed, but will germinate the following spring if environmental conditions are favorable. In some species after-ripening occurs over a period of years, some germination occurring each year. After-ripening involves principally a series of changes in the physiological condition of the embryo which gradually converts a dormant embryo into one that can resume growth. The nature of these physiological changes is not clearly understood at the present time. In some species after-ripening also involves changes in the properties of the seed coats. The length of

time required for completion of the after-ripening process can be greatly modified by environmental conditions as subsequent discussion will show.

6. *Germination Inhibitors.*—Germination of seeds is sometimes checked or prevented by the presence of compounds known as inhibitors. These are often substances produced in one or more plant organs. The juice of tomato fruits, for example, inhibits the germination of tomato seeds and many other seeds as well. Even when tomato juice is diluted in a proportion of 1:25 it completely inhibits the germination of seeds of *Lepidium sativum* (Evenari, 1949). Germination inhibitors are known to be present within the seeds of some species such as those of iris (Randolph and Cox, 1943) and of at least some varieties of cabbage (Cox *et al.*, 1945). It is probable that such germination inhibitors are present in the seeds of many other species and that they represent a widespread mechanism of dormancy. Certain compounds having the structure of unsaturated lactones appear to be widely distributed in plants and to possess the property of inhibiting seed germination and other growth phenomena (Veldstra and Havinga, 1945). Among the compounds in this category are coumarin (Chap. XXVIII) and parasorbic acid. There are indications that at least some of the naturally occurring inhibitors are compounds of this type.

Secondary Dormancy.—Some seeds which are capable of germinating as soon as they are harvested lose this capacity after being kept in an unfavorable environment for a while. This induced dormant period is known as *secondary dormancy.* Usually secondary dormancy can develop only when at least one of the conditions essential for germination is unfavorable. For example, if seeds of white mustard (*Brassica alba*) are exposed to high concentrations of carbon dioxide they fail to germinate, even under favorable conditions, for a long period after the removal of the carbon dioxide (Kidd and West, 1917). Light-sensitive seeds may pass into secondary dormancy if kept in the dark, and seeds that germinate only in the dark may become dormant if exposed to light. Likewise, secondary dormancy may be induced in some kinds of seeds by exposures to low temperatures and in others by high temperatures (Davis, 1930).

Secondary dormancy is often caused by changes in the seed coat since, in some species, the embryos are able to grow immediately if the seed coats are removed. In other kinds of seeds, however, the dormancy is produced by physiological changes that occur within the embryo itself. Secondary dormancy, like primary dormancy, may be interrupted by various treatments.

Special Types of Dormancy.—The failure of seedlings to develop from seeds is not always traceable to dormancy of the seed itself. In many of the spring wild flowers, for example, germination of the seed may occur, but growth is restricted to the establishment of the young root system, the epicotyl failing to grow. In some species the epicotyls may push through the seed coat but remain dormant after this has been accomplished (Barton, 1944). Epicotyl dormancy is usually broken by exposure to low temperatures (1°-10°C.).

Young root systems also may exhibit dormancy after emerging from the seed and becoming established in the soil. In some species of *Trillium*, for example, there is present a double dormancy—that of the seed and that of the young root after emerging from the seed (Barton, 1944), Root dormancy, like dormancy of the epicotyl, is usually broken by exposure to low temperatures.

Methods of Breaking the Dormancy of Seeds.—The dormancy of seeds presents a practical problem of considerable economic importance. Plant growers are often interested in securing seed that will germinate soon after it is harvested. Ordinarily this would be possible only with seeds that have a short dormant period or none at all. Methods have been devised, however, whereby the dormancy of many kinds of seeds can be broken, and whereby the length of the dormant period in many other kinds can be shortened. The methods employed for the breaking of dormancy vary depending upon its cause. Methods which can be used for breaking the dormancy of one species may be totally ineffective when used with seeds of another species, and sometimes may even prolong dormancy.

1. *Scarification.*—Whenever dormancy is a consequence of any of the causes inherent in the seed coats it can be interrupted by scarification. We shall use this term to apply to any treatment—mechanical or otherwise—which results in rupturing or weakening the seed coats sufficiently to permit germination. For example, machine-threshed legume seeds usually show a higher percentage of germination than those that have been harvested by hand. The mechanical treatment is sufficiently severe to scratch or crack many of the seed coats, and this permits ready ingress of water. Various types of mechanical treatments have been devised for breaking the dormancy of seeds of this kind. Strong mineral acids have likewise been used successfully to interrupt seed dormancy caused by resistant or impermeable seed coats. It is essential, however, that any method used to interrupt seed-coat dormancy should not be injurious to the embryo. Under natural conditions dormancy of such seeds is broken by the slow decay of the seed coats or by the action of alternate freezing and thawing.

2. *Low Temperatures.*—After-ripening of many seeds occurs more rapidly when they are stratified in moist peat at low temperatures than when stored at higher temperatures. Temperatures between 5° and 10°C. for 2 or 3 months are effective with conifer seeds (Barton, 1930) and greatly increase the percentage of germination. Similarly, low temperatures com-

bined with moisture have been found to reduce the period of after-ripening in seeds of mountain ash, basswood, elder, bayberry, and many other species. The effectiveness of low temperatures in breaking dormancy appears to be associated in some species at least with a favorable relation between respiration rates and the rate of oxygen absorption or carbon dioxide liberation. Permeability changes in the seed coats may also be an important factor.

3. *Alternating Temperatures.*—In some seed testing laboratories it is common practice to subject seeds alternately to relatively low and high temperatures. The temperature extremes of such treatments may not differ by more than 10° or 20°C., and both are commonly well above the freezing point. The germination of seeds of Kentucky blue grass (*Poa pratensis*), for example, is greatly improved by subjecting the seeds alternately to temperatures of 20°C. for 16-18 hr. and 30°C. for 6-8 hr.; and the percentage germination of Johnson grass (*Holcus halepensis*) seeds is increased by alternate treatments at 30°C. for 18-22 hr. and 45°C. for 2-8 hr. (Harrington, 1923). The dormancy of some seeds may be interrupted by alternate freezing and thawing, although this is decidedly harmful to other species. The action of the alternating temperatures upon the seeds is not understood. It is entirely ineffective with seeds of some species. Seeds of carrot and timothy, for example, germinate just as well at constant temperatures as when temperatures are varied. In general, this method of treatment is used principally with seeds in which dormancy is inherent in the embryo.

4. *Light.*—In the previous discussion light was mentioned as one of the conditions essential for the germination of certain species of seeds. Light may be considered, therefore, as a means of breaking dormancy of such species. In some of the species other environmental factors can be substituted for light. In seeds of *Veronica longifolia* (one of the commonly cultivated speedwells), for example, light improves germination at low temperatures, but the seeds germinate equally well in total darkness at high temperatures. In seeds of Kentucky blue grass exposure to light is effective in improving germination at both variable and constant temperatures.

5. *Pressures.*—Seeds of sweet clover (*Melilotus alba*) and alfalfa (*Medicago sativa*) showed greatly improved germination after being subjected to hydraulic pressures of 2000 atm. at 18°C. (Davies, 1928). When the pressure was applied for periods of from 5-20 min. the germination of the seeds was increased by 50-200 per cent. The effect of the pressures persists after the seeds have been dried and stored and undoubtedly results from changes in the permeability of the seed coats to water.

6. *Growth Regulators.*—Growth regulators are widely used to hasten

the development of roots on cuttings and to increase the number of roots produced (Chap. XXVIII). The success obtained by these treatments has suggested the possibility of interrupting the dormancy of seeds or improving their germination by similar means. Considerable study has been devoted to this problem but with very few exceptions neither dormant nor quiescent seeds appear to react to treatments with growth regulators.

Longevity of Seeds.—The life-span of seeds varies from a few weeks to many years, depending upon the species and the environmental conditions to which the seeds are subjected. The silver maple (*Acer saccharinum*) may be cited as an example of a species which has short-lived seeds. When the seeds of this species are shed in June their water content is about 58 per cent. Once their moisture content drops below 30 to 34 per cent, the seeds die (Jones, 1920). Since this often happens within a few weeks in nature, seeds of this species soon perish. The seeds of the majority of crop plants are relatively short-lived under the usual storage conditions, generally remaining viable for only one to three years. The life-span of such seeds can often be increased several fold by keeping them under suitable storage conditions.

At the other extreme there are a few authentic records of seeds which have lived for more than a hundred years. Bequerel (1934) succeeded in germinating in 1934 seeds of *Cassia bicapsularis* which had been collected in 1819, and seeds of *Cassia multijuga* which had been collected in 1776. These are both South American species of legumes. Viable seeds of the Indian lotus (*Nelumbo nucifera*) have been found buried under layers of peat and soil in Manchuria of such depth that they must have been at least 120 years old and may have been 200 to 400 years old (Ohga, 1927). With this one exception all the authentic records of seeds living for 75 years or longer are of legumes. Further data on the longevity of seeds are given by Crocker (1938).

At least some of the seeds of a number of species of wild plants will remain viable for 50 years or more. This is especially true of hard-coated species. As a general rule only seeds with a pronounced dormancy remain viable very many years in nature. The seeds of many weed species are notoriously long-lived as compared with the seeds of most crop plants. This is illustrated by an experiment initiated by Beal at East Lansing, Michigan, in 1879. Seeds of twenty herbaceous species were mixed with sand and buried in pint bottles. Twenty such bottles were prepared. Once every five or ten years one of the bottles was excavated and the enclosed seeds tested for their percentage of germination. Fifty years later seeds of five species remained alive and showed the following percentages of germination: yellow dock (*Rumex crispus*), 52 per cent; evening primrose (*Oenethera biennis*), 38 per cent; moth mullein (*Verbascum blattaria*),

62 per cent; black mustard (*Brassica nigra*), 8 per cent; and water smartweed (*Polygonum hydropiper*), 4 per cent (Darlington, 1931). The 70-year period for this experiment is now past and the results in 1950 showed that seeds of three species (*Oenethera biennis, Rumex crispus,* and *Verbascum blattaria*) were still viable. The germination percentage of the *Verbascum* seeds was still high, 72 per cent, while the percentages for the seeds of *Rumex* and *Oenethera* were 8 and 14, respectively (Darlington, 1951).

Similar results were obtained from the buried seed experiment of Duvel which was terminated in 1945. In this experiment seeds of sixteen species were still capable of germination and growth after about 40 years. (Toole and Brown, 1946).

Methods of Detecting Seed Viability.—It is often important to know whether seeds are merely dormant and capable of germination under suitable conditions or whether they are dead. Since dormancy may be prolonged and since the causes of dormancy are sometimes difficult to ascertain, the existence of some reliable method of measuring the viability of seeds is highly desirable. Three of the many methods proposed have received considerable experimental study: (1) the behavior of excised embryos, (2) the use of certain dyes, and (3) the activity of specific enzyme systems. Of these the first two seem more reliable indices of viability than the last named. Enzyme activity is not closely correlated with seed viability in all species and cannot be used successfully as a general method to distinguish between living and nonliving seeds (Porter, 1947).

The excised embryo test is based upon the behavior of embryos when removed from the surrounding tissues of the seed. If carefully separated from the seed and placed upon moist filter paper at room temperature, embryos of viable seeds will show various types of growth behavior, whereas nonviable embryos deteriorate rapidly. This method of determining the germinating capacity of seeds seems widely applicable and has a high reliability (Flemion, 1938).

Methods involving dyes are of two kinds. One depends upon the impermeability of living cells to certain stains which readily enter and stain dead tissues. The second method depends upon the reduction by living cells of certain colorless compounds which are strongly colored in their reduced states. With this method the living cells become strongly colored and the nonliving tissues remain unstained. This method has in general proved to be more satisfactory than the use of dyes which enter and stain only the dead tissue. The two compounds most widely used are 2,3-diphenyl-5-methyl-tetrazolium chloride and 2,3,5-triphenyl-tetrazolium chloride. The latter is commonly preferred to the former. Dilute solutions of these salts (0.05-2.0 per cent) are used as solutions in which sections of the seeds are soaked for several hours. The embryos of living seeds become stained a deep red or orange while dead embryos remain unstained. The tetrazolium methods are highly successful with many species of seeds, especially so with seeds of the grasses (maize, wheat, etc.), but must be used with caution with some seed species (Porter et al., 1947; Flemion and Poole, 1948; Bennett and Loomis, 1949).

Methods of Prolonging Seed Viability.—Seeds of many species rapidly loose their capacity to germinate if stored in an unfavorable environment. The critical factors in determining the viable period of most seeds are moisture and temperature, although the oxygen and carbon dioxide content of the surrounding atmosphere are also of importance. In general, seeds remain viable for longer periods of time at low temperatures (5°C.) than at room temperature, and low relative humidities are usually more favorable for prolonging the life of seeds than high ones. Neither factor can be considered independently of the other, however, since the effect of one commonly depends upon the magnitude of the other (Barton, 1949). Marked fluctuations of temperature or relative humidity in storage rooms are not conducive to prolonging the viability of seeds. Similarly the packaging of vegetable or flower seeds in paper envelopes when displayed for sale frequently exposes the seeds to variations in temperature and humidity which shorten significantly the period in which good germination can be obtained.

Longevity of many seeds seems correlated with respiration rates of the embryo, and it is for this reason that low temperatures and low seed moisture content are usually essential if viability is to be maintained for long periods of time. There are exceptions to this general rule, citrus seeds and coffee seeds, for example, remaining alive longest in a humid atmosphere (Porter, 1949). It is nevertheless generally true that environmental conditions which reduce the rate of respiration in seeds are also conditions which are most favorable for seed storage.

In addition to the environmental factors just discussed a number of internal factors are known to influence the longevity of seeds in storage. The stage of maturity at the time the seed is harvested, the moisture content of the seed when placed in storage, and genetic factors all play a role, sometimes a decisive role, in determining the viability of the seeds. These factors vary so widely in different species of seeds that any general statement of their relative importance would be difficult or impossible.

Dormancy of Buds.—Lateral and terminal buds ordinarily develop on the newly elongated shoots of temperate zone woody plants during the spring and early summer months. Such buds are not commonly in the dormant state during this period. Defoliation of the tree or shrub from any cause, for example, often results in the development of new shoots from buds formed during the current season. By the time of, or somewhat prior to, leaf-fall, however, such buds have passed into a state of dormancy. In nature dormancy of buds borne on woody stems is broken by exposure to relatively low winter temperatures. The length of time for which such buds retain their dormancy, however, differs considerably according to species.

Howard (1910) made a comprehensive study of bud dormancy in a large number of species of woody plants, some of American, some of European, and some of Asiatic, origin. This investigation was conducted in Missouri. Of 234 species collected, buds of 125 species developed when branches were brought into a greenhouse between October 28 and November 4. Most of these were European or Asiatic species. In other words, the buds of more than half of the species experimented with were no longer in a dormant state on this date. A second collection of branches from 283 species was brought into the greenhouse on January 8-10. Of these, buds developed on 244 species. On February 23 a third collection of 63 species was made composed largely of kinds on which the buds failed to develop in the preceding two tests. On this date buds developed on all but five of the species collected. The results of this study indicate that the buds of some woody species retain their dormancy much longer into the fall or winter than others and that the buds of many such species are in a quiescent rather than a dormant state during much of the winter.

Dormancy of buds is sometimes a result of correlative effects, many of which probably have a hormonal mechanism. A familiar example is the phenomenon of apical dominance in which lateral buds remain dormant as long as the terminal growing region remains intact, but usually resume growth upon its injury or removal.

Likewise the buds of many kinds of tubers, rhizomes, corms, and bulbs often remain dormant for periods of greater or less duration while environmental conditions are favorable for their development.

Methods of Breaking the Dormancy of Buds.—As the previous discussion has shown the buds on many species of woody plants remain dormant through the autumn and at least the forepart of the winter. This dormancy is not caused by low temperatures, because it is also exhibited by such species when kept in a greenhouse where the temperature is continuously maintained at levels typical of midsummer weather. The dormant condition often persists as long as the temperatures are high but may be broken by subjecting the plants to temperatures near the freezing point (Coville, 1920). The buds of some species such as peach will begin to grow, if environmental conditions are favorable, after only a few days of chilling, but the buds of other kinds of plants such as the blueberry (*Vaccinium* *corymbosum*) fail to grow well unless exposed to temperatures near the freezing point for several weeks. Coville demonstrated that the effect of the low temperatures is restricted to the tissues exposed. When single branches are chilled while the rest of the plant is kept warm, only the buds on the chilled branch are able to grow, all of the others remaining dormant (Fig. 170).

Early in the twentieth century Johannsen discovered that dormant buds of many kinds of plants will begin to grow after being exposed to vapors of ether or chloroform for a day or two. The interval of time be-

FIG. 170. Breaking dormancy of buds of blueberry by low temperatures. The branch on the right was exposed to low temperatures by allowing it to project through a small hole in a greenhouse during the winter. The branch on the left remained within the greenhouse. Figure shows appearance of the plant on April 18. Photograph from Coville (1920).

tween the ether treatment and the beginning of growth differs widely
with the time of the year at which the vapor is applied. In late summer
or early fall, several weeks may elapse between the exposure to ether
vapor and the active growth of the buds. Late in the winter, however,
the interval is shortened to a day or two.

More recently a number of other chemical treatments have been discovered that are successful in breaking the dormancy of buds. Denny
(1926) found that dormant potato tubers sprouted freely when exposed to

FIG. 171.   Effect of ethylene dichlorid in breaking dormancy of lilac buds. Plant
on right received no treatment. Plant on left exposed 48 hr. to ethylene dichlorid, 2.5 cc. of liquid per 100 liters of space on December 10. Both plants kept in
greenhouse and photographed early in January. Photograph from Denny and
Stanton (1928).

ethylene chlorhydrin vapor. Sodium and potassium thiocyanate, thiourea,
dichloroethylene, carbon bisulfide, xylol, ethyl bromide, and a number of
other compounds were also effective. Vapors of ethylene chlorhydrin so
hastened the growth of tubers of the Irish cobbler variety that vines
2 feet high bearing young tubers 1 cm. in diameter grew from the treated
tubers before the sprouts of the untreated tubers appeared above the surface of the ground. Solutions of sodium and potassium thiocyanate gave
almost equally striking results. Thiourea solutions differed somewhat from

the other compounds used in that they overcame the inhibiting effect of the terminal bud upon the growth of lateral buds and caused the development of several shoots from each eye on the tuber.

Combinations of two or more compounds, each effective in overcoming the dormancy of buds in potato tubers, will give better results than any single treatment (Denny, 1945a). A mixture of ethylene chlorhydrin, ethylene, and carbon tetrachloride was more effective in breaking the dormancy of potato tubers than the sum of the effects of each compound used separately. These so-called "synergistic effects" are attributed to the increased penetration of the compounds as a result of changes in cellular permeability induced by one component of the mixture.

The vapors of ethylene chlorhydrin and ethylene dichloride also induce the growth of dormant buds of lilac (*Syringa vulgaris*), flowering almond (*Prunus triloba*), and some other species of woody plants (Fig. 171). The effect of the vapors was so restricted that when one of two paired buds of a lilac was exposed to the vapor, growth occurred only in the treated bud. The untreated bud remained as fully dormant as other buds more distant from the treated area. Apparently the factors causing the dormancy of the buds of these plants reside within the buds themselves and not in the adjacent tissues.

The dormancy of the buds of fruit trees is usually broken in nature by the low temperatures of the winter months. It is not uncommon, however, for entire winters to pass in southern United States without sufficient cold weather to interrupt the dormancy of buds of fruit trees. When this happens flowering is irregular and uncertain and yields of fruit suffer correspondingly. The discovery of some method of breaking the dormancy of fruit trees is a matter of great practical importance, and the problem has been given much study. The dormancy of the buds of some fruit and nut trees can be broken by the use of certain chemical compounds sprayed upon the trees during the dormant period, but results are not equally successful with different species (Avery and Johnson, 1947). Methods of treatment have not been sufficiently well developed as yet to warrant their extensive use in commercial orchards.

Methods of Prolonging Dormancy of Buds.—Often it becomes important to prolong, rather than to shorten, the dormancy of buds. The warm weather of an early spring may cause the buds to open before danger from frost is past. Under such conditions a severe frost can cause enormous damage. The prolongation of dormancy of buds of nursery stock held in storage or prepared for shipment is also very desirable. Dormancy of buds may be prolonged by spraying with certain chemical compounds —some of the growth regulators being particularly effective in this respect. The results of experimental studies of orchard grown fruit trees have not always been consistent, but greater success has been obtained in the treatment of nursery stock (Avery and Johnson, 1947).

Probably the most complete and satisfactory control of dormancy through the use of chemical agents is that obtained over the buds of potato tubers. The sprouting of potato tubers in storage may be prevented almost completely by treatment with certain growth regulators. The methyl ester of naphthalene acetic acid is now widely used for this purpose. When shredded paper impregnated with small amounts of this ester is scattered among potato tubers in a storage bin, sprouting of the buds is inhibited. The tubers remain completely dormant and are firm and sound after overwinter storage (Denny, 1945b). The dormancy induced in this way may be interrupted at any time by the treatments described earlier in this chapter.

SUGGESTED FOR COLLATERAL READING

Avery, G. S., Jr., and Elizabeth Johnson. *Hormones and Horticulture.* McGraw-Hill Book Co., Inc. New York. 1947.

Crocker, W., and Lela V. Barton. *Physiology of Seeds.* Chronica Botanica Co. Waltham, Mass. 1953.

Mitchell, J. W., and P. C. Marth. *Growth Regulators.* University of Chicago Press. Chicago. 1947.

Forest Service, U. S. Dept. of Agriculture. *Woody-plant Seed Manual. Misc. Publ. No. 654.* U. S. Government Printing Office. Washington. 1948.

SELECTED BIBLIOGRAPHY

Barton, Lela V. Hastening the germination of some coniferous seeds. *Contr. Boyce Thompson Inst.* **2:** 315-342. 1930.

Barton, Lela V. Effect of moisture fluctuations on the viability of seeds in storage. *Contr. Boyce Thompson Inst.* **13:** 35-45. 1943.

Barton, Lela V. Some seeds showing special dormancy. *Contr. Boyce Thompson Inst.* **13:** 259-271. 1944.

Barton, Lela V. Seed packets and onion seed viability. *Contr. Boyce Thompson Inst.* **15:** 341-352. 1949.

Bennett, Norah, and W. E. Loomis. Tetrazolium chloride as a test reagent for freezing injury of seed corn. *Plant Physiol.* **24:** 162-174. 1949.

Bequerel, P. La longévité des graines macrobiotiques. *Compt. Rend. Acad. Sci. (Paris)* **199:** 1662-1664. 1934.

Bibbey, R. O. Physiological studies of weed seed germination. *Plant Physiol.* **23:** 467-484. 1948.

Coville, F. V. The influence of cold in stimulating the growth of plants. *Jour. Agric. Res.* **20:** 151-160. 1920.

Cox, L. G., H. M. Munger, and E. A. Smith. A germination inhibitor in the seed coats of certain varieties of cabbage. *Plant Physiol.* **20:** 289-294. 1945.

Crocker, W. Mechanics of dormancy in seeds. *Amer. Jour. Bot.* **3:** 99-120. 1916.

Crocker, W. Effects of the visible spectrum upon the germination of seeds and fruits. In *Biological Effects of Radiation*. II. B. M. Duggar, Editor. 791-827. McGraw-Hill Book Co., Inc. 1936.

Crocker, W. Life-span of seeds. *Bot. Rev.* **4**: 235-274. 1938.

Darlington, H. T. The 50-year period for Dr. Beal's seed viability experiment. *Amer. Jour. Bot.* **18**: 262-265. 1931.

Darlington, H. T. The seventy-year period for Dr. Beal's seed viability experiment. *Amer. Jour. Bot.* **38**: 379-381. 1951.

Davies, P. A. High pressure and seed germination. *Amer. Jour. Bot.* **15**: 149-156, 1928.

Davis, W. E. Primary dormancy, after-ripening, and the development of secondary dormancy in embryos of *Ambrosia trifida*. *Contr. Boyce Thompson Inst.* **2**: 285-303. 1930.

Denny, F. E. Hastening the sprouting of dormant potato tubers. *Contr. Boyce Thompson Inst.* **1**: 59-66. 1926.

Denny, F. E. Synergistic effects of three chemicals in the treatment of dormant potato tubers to hasten germination. *Contr. Boyce Thompson Inst.* **14**: 1-14. 1945a.

Denny, F. E. Further tests of the use of the methyl ester of alpha-naphthalene acetic acid for inhibiting the sprouting of potato tubers. *Contr. Boyce Thompson Inst.* **14**: 15-20. 1945b.

Denny, F. E., and E. N. Stanton. Chemical treatments for shortening the rest period of pot-grown woody plants. *Amer. Jour. Bot.* **15**: 327-336. 1928.

Doneen, L. D., and J. H. MacGillivray. Germination (emergence) of vegetable seed as affected by different soil moisture conditions. *Plant Physiol.* **18**: 524-529. 1943.

Evenari, M. Germination inhibitors. *Bot. Rev.* **15**: 153-194. 1949.

Flemion, Florence. A rapid method for determining the viability of dormant seeds. *Contr. Boyce Thompson Inst.* **9**: 339-351. 1938.

Flemion, Florence, and Harriet Poole. Seed viability tests with 2,3,5-triphenyltetrazolium chloride. *Contr. Boyce Thompson Inst.* **15**: 243-258. 1948.

Harrington, G. T. Use of alternating temperatures in the germination of seeds. *Jour. Agric. Res.* **23**: 295-332. 1923.

Howard, W. L. An experimental study of the rest period in plants. *Mo. Agric. Expt. Sta. Res. Bull. No. 1*. 1910.

Jones, H. A. Physiological study of maple seeds. *Bot. Gaz.* **69**: 127-152. 1920.

Kidd, F., and C. West. The controlling influence of carbon dioxide IV. On the production of secondary dormancy in seeds of *Brassica alba* following treatment with carbon dioxide, and the relation of this phenomenon to the question of stimuli in growth processes. *Ann. Bot.* **31**: 457-487. 1917.

Korstian, C. F. Factors controlling germination and early survival in oaks. *Yale Univ. School of Forestry Bull. No. 19*. 1927.

Morinaga, T. Germination of seeds under water. *Contr. Boyce Thompson Inst.* **1**: 67-81. 1926.

Ohga, I. On the age of the ancient fruit of the Indian lotus, etc. *Bot. Mag. (Tokyo)* **41**: 1-6. 1927.

Porter, R. H. Recent developments in seed technology. *Bot. Rev.* **15**: 221-344. 1949.

Porter, R. H., Mary Durrell, and H. J. Romm. The use of 2,3,5-triphenyltetrazolium chloride as a measure of seed germinability. *Plant Physiol.* **22**: 149-159. 1947.

Raleigh, G. J. The germination of dormant lettuce seed. *Science* **98**: 538. 1943.

Randolph, L. F., and L. G. Cox. Factors influencing the germination of iris seed and the relation of inhibiting substances to embryo dormancy. *Proc. Amer. Soc. Hort. Sci.* **43**: 284-300. 1943.

Rosendahl, C. O. Embryo-sac development and embryology of *Symplocarpus foetidus. Minn. Bot. Studies* **4**: 1-9. 1909.

Shull, C. A. The oxygen minimum and the germination of *Xanthium* seeds. *Bot. Gaz.* **52**: 453-477. 1911.

Stiles, Isabel E. Relation of water to the germination of corn and cotton seeds. *Plant Physiol.* **23**: 201-222. 1948.

Thornton, N. C. Carbon dioxide storage. IX. Germination of lettuce seeds at high temperatures in both light and darkness. *Contr. Boyce Thompson Inst.* **8**: 25-40. 1936.

Toole, H. E., and E. Brown. Final results of the Duvel buried seed experiment. *Jour. Agric. Res.* **72**: 201-210. 1946.

Veldstra, H., and E. Havinga. On the physiological activity of unsaturated lactones. *Enzymologia* **11**: 373-380. 1945.

Watson, D. P. Structure of the testa and its relation to germination in the Papilionaceae tribes Trifoliae and Loteae. *Ann. Bot.* **12**: 386-409. 1948.

XXXV

GROWTH PERIODICITY

The growth of a plant or plant organ never proceeds steadily hour after hour or day after day, but is subject to more or less regularly recurring, often rhythmical, daily and seasonal variations in rate. Seasonal variations in growth phenomena involve qualitative as well as quantitative differences in development during different stages of the growth cycle. Most plants, for example, produce flowers only at certain stages in their life history and either grow only vegetatively or not at all at other times. The more obvious examples of growth periodicity often correlate very closely with cyclical daily or seasonal variations in environmental conditions, but internal factors also play an important role in many periodic growth phenomena.

Daily Periodicity of Growth.—All actively growing plant organs characteristically exhibit a daily periodicity in growth rate. A number of studies have been made of daily variations in the rate of increase in the length of stems, the areal expansion or elongation of young leaves, and the diameters of growing fruits. Such measurements reveal that marked differences in the growth rates at different times of the day are of common occurrence in plants.

Cyclical variations in the rate of elongation of plant organs during the course of a day can be interpreted in terms of the principle of limiting factors. During the progress of the day first one factor and then another is limiting. The rate of growth at any particular moment will be largely limited by the factor in relative minimum at that time. The three principal environmental factors influencing the daily periodicity in the rate of elongation of plant organs are temperature, the internal water relations of the plant, and light.

As an example of the daily periodicity of growth the results of Thut and Loomis (1944) on growth (elongation) of the leaves plus stem axis

of maize plants growing under field conditions in Iowa will be considered
(Fig. 172). Similar results were obtained with several other herbaceous
species. In general, rate of elongation was most closely correlated with
temperature. Growth during the daylight hours was therefore usually
greater than during the night hours, and growth during warm nights was
greater than during cool nights whenever the internal water supply of
the plants was not seriously deficient. Excessive temperatures (above
about 35°C.), however, apparently had a retarding effect on growth.

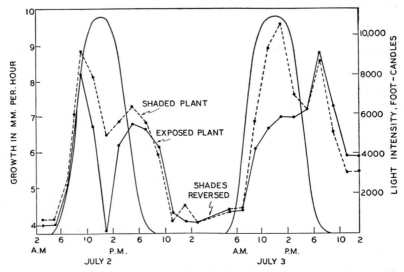

FIG. 172. Daily cycle of growth in height of two corn plants; one shaded, the
other not, in relation to the daily cycle of light intensity. The plant which was
shaded the first day was fully exposed to light the second, and *vice versa*. Data
of Thut and Loomis (1944).

Moderate internal water deficits reduced growth rates during the midday
hours. Hence a double peak in growth rate, with one maximum in the
early morning and the other in the evening, was common. Only when
internal water deficits became relatively severe did the greatest growth
occur at night. No evidence was found of a direct inhibiting effect of
light on growth.

Numerous patterns of daily growth periodicity may occur in plants
depending upon the particular cyclical combination of environmental and
internal factors which prevail. Maximum growth (elongation or enlargement) rates may take place at different times of the night, at midday,
in the early morning, in the late afternoon, or in the early evening. Examples of conditions under which several of these different patterns of

growth periodicity occur are given in the preceding paragraph. In some species, including maize (Loomis, 1934), even transit of a cloud across the sun permits a temporary acceleration in growth rate. Under some conditions internal factors such as the supply of foods may play a determining role in shaping the daily periodicity of growth.

The preceding discussion has dealt with the influence on growth of variations in temperature and internal-water deficit within ordinary limits. In addition, it should be recognized that excessive internal-water deficits, such as are engendered by drought conditions, or extremes of temperature, either high or low, may lead to a complete cessation of growth.

The factor of light must also be considered in relation to the phenomenon of growth periodicity. Although light is known to have direct effects on growth (Chap. XXIX), in plants growing under field conditions these appear to be relatively unimportant in comparison with its indirect effects. The influence of light on growth is exerted principally through its effects on the temperature of plant organs, rates of transpiration, and rates of photosynthesis. Plants exposed to intense light usually develop more severe internal water deficits than similar plants growing in the shade, because of the usually enhancing effect of light upon temperature and upon the rate of transpiration. Growth is slackened as a result of the greater water deficit within the plant. Low light intensities, on the other hand, may exert a retarding effect on growth because of a diminution in the total photosynthesis accomplished by the plant.

Measurements of the rate of growth (elongation or enlargement) of plant organs are sometimes complicated by the fact that there may be present in the organ mature cells which undergo reversible shifts in turgor and volume with changes in the intensity of the internal-water deficit in the plant. The effect of shifts in the turgidity of cells on apparent rates of growth is well illustrated by the results of Wilson (1948). When growth in length of entire tomato stems was measured, elongation during the night apparently exceeded elongation during the daylight hours. Elongation of the meristematic stem tip (above the first node), however, was approximately the same for both day and night periods. Growth of such meristems continues even when a considerable internal-water deficit exists in the plant (Chap. XV). During the day smaller than actual rates for the entire stem were recorded, because growth in length at the meristem was partially offset by shrinkage in volume of cells in older parts of the stem. During the night greater than actual growth rates for the entire stem were recorded, since, in addition to growth in length at the meristem, there was an increase in the volume of cells in older parts of the stem. Similar effects of reversible changes in cell turgidity on the apparent growth of cotton bolls (Fig. 78) and other fruits (Chap. XV) have been recorded.

Seasonal Periodicity of Vegetative Growth.—All plants exhibit more or less clearly marked seasonal variations in the rate of vegetative growth. In temperate regions the periodic resumption of growth by woody perennials every spring is one of the most spectacular biological accompaniments of the march of the seasons. This topic will be discussed almost entirely in terms of such woody plants.

The seasonal periodicity of vegetative growth of any species, like the daily periodicity, is conditioned by both environmental and internal factors. Among the former, water and temperature are especially important. Some of the internal conditions which are known to play a significant part in such phenomena are the genetic constitution of the species, dormancy, correlative effects among organs, and the internal water relations. One of the most striking features of the seasonal growth of trees is its relative independence of fluctuations in the environmental factors. Trees growing in dry habitats may exhibit growth patterns very similar

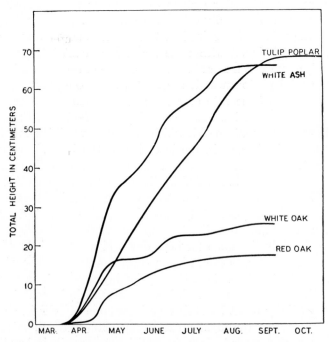

Fig. 173.   Growth in height of several species of tree seedlings in relation to season. Data of Kramer (1943).

to trees of the same species growing near by in locations where soil moisture is adequate (Avery et al., 1940). Although growth may be checked by low temperatures many tree species initiate their growth in the spring before the close of the frost season, and elongation of shoots ceases long before the onset of frosts in the fall and winter (Kramer, 1943). Similarly cambial activity of many coniferous and deciduous species decreases markedly long before environmental conditions become unfavorable (Daubenmire and Deters, 1947). The evidence clearly suggests that the seasonal growth patterns of many woody species are determined basically by the organism itself rather than by the vagaries of the environment.

The characteristic seasonal patterns of stem elongation in several tree species are illustrated in Fig. 173. Growth begins slowly with the appearance of the warmer days of early spring, accelerates rapidly during spring and early summer, and levels off by late summer or early fall. The shape of the growth curve cannot be correlated with environmental factors, nor is it appreciably modified by variations in rainfall unless these are exceptionally prolonged and severe.

In many species of woody plants buds do not ordinarily develop into shoots or flowers during the season in which they develop but remain in a dormant state. The length of time that buds remain dormant varies greatly according to the species (Chap. XXXIV). Some lose their dormancy early in autumn, others retain it until late in the winter. The buds of temperate zone woody plants seldom open as soon as they lose their dormancy but remain in a quiescent state until the favorable environmental conditions of spring. Low temperature is probably the principal factor preventing the development of quiescent buds in late winter and early spring, although a deficient water supply may also be involved, at least in some species. Photoperiodic and thermoperiodic effects may also play a part in the vernal resumption of vegetative growth by plants.

The development of new shoots from the buds on woody stems in the spring is not always a continuous process. In species such as cherries and willows which "leaf out" relatively early, the growth process is often intermittent. During this season periods of warm weather often alternate with colder spells. Hence elongation of the developing shoots may take place in a series of short spurts, each terminated upon the advent of unfavorably cool weather. Apical growth is much more likely to proceed uninterruptedly in species such as beech and the hickories in which it is initiated later in the spring. Under favorable conditions practically all stem elongation and development of the new crop of leaves may occur in such species during a growth period lasting only two or three weeks. Termination of the spring burst of growth in such species, like that of the coniferous species described earlier, is evidently a result of internal causes, since environmental conditions usually remain favorable for growth during much or all of the summer.

The stems of some ligneous species (sumac, dogwood, ailanthus, etc.) do not grow in the definite manner described above, but continue to elongate, producing leaf after leaf, for most or all of the summer, quiescent intermissions occurring only when environmental conditions are unfavorable. In some such species growth is not terminated until the advent of frost.

Under some conditions the buds on woody stems open the same season they are formed. This is a commoner occurrence in some species than in others and is more likely to happen on young trees or shrubs than on old ones. Defoliation of a tree relatively early in the season as a result of disease, insect ravages, late frost, or any other cause usually results in a resumption of growth from buds developed during the current season. During wet summers development of the current crop of buds into shoots occurs frequently in many species of woody plants. Among the oaks, especially when young, the development of two or even more successive shoots during a growing season is a common occurrence. When the terminal bud on the stem of an oak resumes growth during the season it is formed, lateral buds on that same segment also usually resume growth and develop into side branches. In the willow oak (*Quercus phellos*) three or even more prolongations of the same woody axis may take place during a single growing season. Almost always, however, when buds of the current crop on woody stems resume growth, there is a short dormant period between the time formation of the bud is completed and the time its active growth is resumed.

Cambial growth in trees commonly begins near the opening buds and moves basipetally toward the roots (Chap. XXXIII). Weeks may elapse between the initiation of cambial activity in the young twigs and the resumption of cambium growth in the oldest region of the tree. Secondary thickening of the stems of most woody species generally continues later in the summer than elongation of the current shoots, although usually at a diminishing rate. Cambial activity usually ceases in the young twigs by midsummer but may continue until late summer or early fall in the older stems and sometimes until winter in the roots.

Less is known regarding the seasonal periodicity of the growth of roots than of the aerial organs of plants. The existence of an inherent dormancy in roots appears to be uncommon. Seasonal periodicity of root growth is probably largely controlled by environmental conditions. In colder climates little or no root growth occurs during the winter months. No growth of white pine roots, for example, took place in New England between the middle of November and the first of April (Stevens, 1931). In milder climates elongation of roots through the winter months occurs in at least some species. Harris (1926), for example, records continued growth of apple and filbert roots in Oregon during the winter months.

Cyclical Periodicity of Vegetative and Reproductive Growth.—The examples of seasonal periodicity which have already been described involve principally variations in growth rates. Growth periodicity is expressed not only in terms of seasonal variations in the quantitative aspects of growth, but also in the development of certain organs at one stage in the life cycle and other organs at another stage. The most prominent periodicity in the qualitative aspects of plant growth is the cyclical development of vegetative and reproductive organs which is exhibited by most species of plants.

The seasonal periodicity of all annual species is similar and involves in sequence: (1) seed germination, (2) vegetative development, (3) flowering and fruiting, usually accompanied, at least during the later stages, by slowly diminishing vegetative growth, (4) senescence, and (5) death of all organs except the seeds. All such species are perennial only by their seeds.

The seasonal periodicity of annual species is by no means immutable, however, but can be altered in various ways. Removal of flowers or fruits or both often leads to an acceleration or renewal of vegetative growth (Chap. XXXIII). Similarly a change in the length of the photoperiod at the onset of senescence often causes a rejuvenation of vegetative growth.

The cyclical development of vegetative and reproductive organs is similar in all biennial species. Plants of this type develop only vegetatively during their first growing season, forming underground organs which live over winter. In many biennials the leaves are cold resistant and survive the colder months of the year without injury. During their second growing season vegetative development is often renewed, but before long is largely or entirely superseded by reproductive growth. Death of the plant follows closely after the formation of seeds and fruits. As with annuals the usual life cycle of biennials can be modified by various circumstances. For example, many biennials become annuals when growing in warmer or longer-season climates than those in which they normally behave as biennials.

A greater diversity of cyclical patterns of reproductive and vegetative development is found in perennial species than in those which live for only one or two growing seasons. The following discussion refers primarily to plants of temperate regions. In many woody perennials flowers develop in the spring before vegetative growth is resumed or concurrently with the early stages in the development of the new leaf-bearing shoots.

Examples of species which exhibit this type of periodicity include many fruit trees (peach, cherry, apple, etc.) and many forest tree species (elms, maples, oaks, chestnut, cottonwood, etc.). In some woody species such as the mulberry, in which flowers develop from axillary meristems on the current season's shoot, blooming occurs at the height of the season of vegetative growth. Flowers do not develop on many woody perennials until after the season's vegetative growth is nearly or entirely completed. This is true of many species which bear terminal inflorescences at the end of the current season's shoots such as lilac, buckeye, and horse chestnut.

As in woody species, development of flowers in herbaceous perennials may take place before vegetative growth occurs during the same growing season, concurrently with the development of stems and leaves, or only toward the end of a period of vegetative development. The first of these types of growth periodicity, which is the least common, is found in certain spring blooming species. The second is also characteristic of many spring blooming herbaceous plants but is by no means confined to such species. The third type of growth periodicity is especially common among summer and fall blooming species and is characteristic of all species which produce terminal inflorescences on foliage-bearing stems.

Abscission.—Leaf-fall, particularly as it occurs from the stems of deciduous trees and shrubs in the autumn, is a distinctive phenomenon of periodic occurrence in plants. The *abscission* of leaves occurs at their point of attachment to the stem. The phenomenon of leaf abscission is especially characteristic of woody dicotyledons but also occurs in some herbaceous species such as coleus, begonia, and fuchsia. In most herbaceous species, however, the leaves are retained even after they die, and only disappear by decay or by mechanical disruption from the plant. In many herbaceous species most or all of the leaves are retained until after the death of the entire shoot system.

The abscission of leaves is associated with the so-called "abscission layer." The abscission layer is made up of one or more layers of cells that undergo transverse division in a zone extending across the petiole near its base (Fig. 174). This zone of cells is often formed in the petiole before the leaf has reached its full size. The name "abscission layer" (absciss layer, abscission zone) has been applied to this region of the petiole because the separation of the cells of the petiole at the time of leaf-fall occurs between the cells of this zone. Separation of the cells of the abscission layer results from the dissolution of the middle lamella and sometimes also the cellulose wall of these parenchymatous cells. After separation of the cells of the abscission layer the petiole remains attached only by the vascular elements. These soon snap off under the pull of gravity or the pressure of the wind, and the leaf falls from the plant. The fractured elements of the vascular bundle usually become plugged with gums or tyloses.

Although the mechanism of abscission has never been clearly understood, it has been widely assumed that the abscission layer had a role of importance in the phenomenon of leaf-fall. There are at least three lines of evidence, however, which cast some doubt upon the validity of this assumption (Gawadi and Avery, 1950) : (1) abscission occurs readily in species where no abscission layer is present; (2) abscission may not occur in species where abscission layers are present; (3) leaves of species in which an abscission layer usually develops can be induced to abscise before the abscission layer is formed. It is possible that the abscission layer may be of greater importance in the formation of the cork layer which covers the leaf scar after leaf-fall than in bringing about abscission itself. Whatever may be the role of the abscission layer it is, when present, invariably the site of the separation of the leaf from the stem at the time of leaf-fall.

In species in which abscission occurs it may be brought about by altering the environmental conditions under which the plant is growing. Abscission of leaves, for example, is known to result from: (1) a water deficit in the plant usually developed as a result of drought conditions, (2) low temperatures, (3) reduced light intensity, and (4) change in the length of the photoperiod. Abscission also may be induced by destroying or removing all or most of the leaf blade, by dusting the leaves with ammonium thiocyanide, or exposing the leaves to certain gases such as ethylene or the vapors of ethylene chlorhydrin or carbon tetrachloride.

The abscission of leaves can be delayed or inhibited by the application of certain growth regulators to the leaf blade or to the surface of a debladed petiole (LaRue, 1935; Myers, 1940; Gardner and Cooper, 1943;

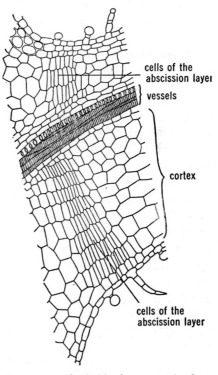

FIG. 174. Abscission layer at the base of the petiole of a leaf of coleus (*Coleus blumei*) as shown in vertical section.

Gawadi and Avery, 1950). Naphthaleneacetic acid and indoleacetic acid
are among the more effective growth regulators in checking abscission.
When applied before the development of the abscission layer the growth
regulators delay or inhibit its formation. The effectiveness of growth
regulators in checking abscission suggests that leaf-fall is another of the
many physiological processes controlled by hormones. It is quite possible
that abscission of leaves is retarded by the migration of a hormone from
the blade to the base of the petiole. Destruction or removal of the blade
eliminates the supply of this substance to the abscission zone and hence
induces leaf-fall.

Leaves, however, are not the only organs or parts of plants which abscise. In compound leaves the individual leaflets usually drop off one by
one, leaving the petioles attached to the otherwise defoliated plant. Usually abscission of the petioles follows within a relatively short time. Similarly bud scales, inflorescences, petals, and fruits may be detached from
the parent plant by abscission. Segments of the woody stems of some
species also abscise. In many species of woody plants (examples are elm,
cherry, birch, linden) abscission of the leafy stem tips occurs at the termination of the spring growing period. In such species elongation of the
stem continues the next season from the lateral bud just below the point
of abscission, such lateral buds functioning essentially as terminal buds.
Many species of conifers bear their needle-like leaves in fascicles, each
fascicle being attached to a dwarf branch. In the pines and other such
species leaves are shed in bundles by the abscission of the dwarf branches
rather than by detachment of the individual needles. In certain other
woody species (oaks, cottonwood) segments of woody stems of considerable age and diameter are often shed by abscission. In bald cypress and
coast redwood individual leaves do not fall from the tree, but branches
bearing numerous leaves abscise.

The phenomenon of the abscission of fruits presents certain practical
problems to the horticulturist. If apple fruits, for example, drop from the
tree before they can be picked, their quality is greatly impaired. The fact
that the application of certain auxins and auxin-like compounds to leaves
delays their abscission suggested that they would have a similar effect on
fruits. Gardner et al. (1940) showed that spraying of apples just before
harvest appreciably delayed the natural fall of the fruits. Naphthaleneacetic acid and naphthalene acetamide are two growth regulators that
have proved especially effective when used for this purpose. Postponement of fruit abscission as a result of such treatments is commonly a
week and sometimes longer. The length of time for which abscission is
delayed differs considerably with the variety of apple and with the prevailing environmental conditions. Postponement of fruit-fall allows a

longer period for picking and often permits the fruits to ripen to a higher quality on the tree before picking. It is possible that similar treatments may also prove feasible in delaying abscission of other horticultural fruits.

SUGGESTED FOR COLLATERAL READING

Avery, G. S., Jr., and Elizabeth Johnson. *Hormones and Horticulture.* McGraw-Hill Book Co., Inc. New York. 1947.
Benecke, W., and L. Jost. *Pflanzenphysiologie.* Vol. II. G. Fischer. Jena. 1924.
Went, F. W., and K. V. Thimann. *Phytohormones.* The Macmillan Co. New York. 1937.

SELECTED BIBLIOGRAPHY

Avery, G. S., Jr., H. B. Creighton and C. W. Hock. Annual rings in hemlocks and their relation to environmental factors. *Amer. Jour. Bot.* **27**: 825-831. 1940.
Brown, H. S., and F. T. Addicott. The anatomy of experimental leaflet abscission in *Phaseolus vulgaris. Amer. Jour. Bot.* **37**: 650-656. 1950.
Daubenmire, R. F., and M. E. Deters. Comparative studies of growth in deciduous and evergreen trees. *Bot. Gaz.* **109**: 1-12. 1947.
Gardner, F. E., and W. C. Cooper. Effectiveness of growth substances in delaying abscission of *Coleus* petioles. *Bot. Gaz.* **105**: 80-89. 1943.
Gardner, F. E., P. C. Marth, and L. P. Batjer. Spraying with plant growth substances for control of the pre-harvest drop of apples. *Proc. Amer. Soc. Hort. Sci.* **37**: 415-428. 1940.
Gawadi, A. G., and G. S. Avery, Jr. Leaf abscission and the so-called "abscission layer." *Amer. Jour. Bot.* **37**: 172-180. 1950.
Harris, G. H. The activity of apple and filbert roots, especially during the winter months. *Proc. Amer. Soc. Hort. Sci.* **23**: 414-422. 1926.
Kienholz, R. Leader, needle, cambial, and root growth of certain conifers and their interrelations. *Bot. Gaz.* **96**: 73-92. 1934.
Kramer, P. J. Amount and duration of growth of various species of tree seedlings. *Plant Physiol.* **18**: 239-251. 1943.
LaRue, C. D. The role of auxin in the development of intumescences on poplar leaves; in the production of cell outgrowths in the tunnels of leaf-miners; and in the leaf-fall in Coleus. *Amer. Jour. Bot.* **22**: 908. 1935.
Lee, E. The morphology of leaf-fall. *Ann. Bot.* **25**: 51-106. 1911.
Loomis, W. E. Daily growth of maize. *Amer. Jour. Bot.* **21**: 1-6. 1934.
McCown, M. Anatomical and chemical aspects of abscission of fruits of the apple. *Bot. Gaz.* **105**: 212-220. 1943.
Myers, R. M. Effect of growth substances on the absciss layer in leaves of *Coleus. Bot. Gaz.* **102**: 323-338. 1940.
Sampson, H. C. Chemical changes accompanying abscission in *Coleus blumei. Bot. Gaz.* **66**: 32-53. 1918.
Stevens, C. L. Root growth of white pine (*Pinus strobus* L.). *Yale Univ. School Forestry Bull. No. 32.* 1931.
Thut, H. F., and W. E. Loomis. Relation of light to growth of plants. *Plant Physiol.* **19**: 117-130. 1944.
Wilson, C. C. Diurnal fluctuations of growth in length of tomato stem. *Plant Physiol.* **23**: 156-157. 1948.

XXXVI

PLANT MOVEMENTS

The wide variety of movements which occur in the organs of the higher plants usually escape notice because of the slowness with which they take place. By employing the technique of motion picture photography, however, it is possible to demonstrate the movements of plant organs in a spectacular manner. If a growing plant is photographed at regular and frequent intervals for a period of several weeks with a motion picture camera and the resulting film run through a projecting machine, all the movements which occurred during several weeks of growth take place within a period of a few minutes. In this way the vigor and reality of the autonomous movements of leaves and stems can be demonstrated in a striking manner. The large leaves of tobacco plants, for example, appear to rise and fall almost like the wings of a bird in flight. Likewise the stem tip is seen to participate in more or less regular spiral movements, and the several types of movements associated with the expansion of young leaves are vividly portrayed. The movements that occur during the opening of flower and leaf buds can also be demonstrated by this technique. Anyone who has seen such pictures cannot fail to be impressed with the many kinds of movements which occur in the aerial organs of plants and with the magnitude of such movements.

Classification of Plant Movements.—Most of the movements exhibited by the organs of the higher plants may be classified as: (1) growth movements, (2) turgor movements, and (3) hydration movements.

1. *Growth Movements.*—Growth movements are changes in the position of organs resulting from an enlargement of cells, or from an increase in the number of cells, or both. Curvatures or other changes in position result from growth movements when the increase in size or number of cells is not uniform at all points in the region undergoing growth. Growth

movements are usually divided into three sub-groups: (1) tropic (or tropistic) movements, (2) nastic movements, and (3) nutations.

Tropic movements are those which occur under the influence of environmental factors that act with a greater intensity from one direction than from another. The direction of the curvatures resulting from such movements often bears a relation to the direction from which the initiating factor acts with greatest intensity. The curvatures of growing stems and roots induced by differences in the intensity or quality of incident light (*phototropic* curvatures) and those resulting under the influence of gravity (*geotropic* curvatures) are the most familiar tropic movements. Similarly changes in the position of organs which are evoked by differences in the water content of the soil, by physical contact, and by specific chemical compounds are known as *hydrotropic, thigmotropic,* and *chemotropic* movements, respectively. The movement is considered to be *positive* when the organ bends toward the direction from which the factor is acting and *negative* when it is in the opposite direction.

Nastic movements are those that occur in plant organs when the initiating factor affects all parts of the growing organ uniformly, or when the initiating factor, although acting entirely or principally from one direction, evokes a reaction which occurs in the same manner and in the same direction regardless of the direction from which the factor acts. The growth movements of very young leaves, bud scales, and flower petals are examples of nastic movements. At first the morphologically lower side of these structures grows more rapidly than the upper side so that they are bent upward and enclose the stem tip. This more rapid growth of the lower side is known as *hyponasty* (*hypo* = lower). The opening of the bud is brought about by a more rapid growth of the morphologically upper side of these structures, a phenomenon known as *epinasty* (*epi* = upper).

Although the main stem of most herbaceous plants appears to grow straight upward careful measurements demonstrate that the stem tip actually traces an irregular spiral pathway in space as it elongates. This approximately spiral movement of growing stem tips is known as *nutation*. Nutation results from unequal rates of growth in different vertical segments around the stem axis and often seems to occur independently of environmental factors. The term "nutation" is sometimes used to include all movements which result from unequal rates of growth. In this book, however, the term will be used only in the more limited sense just specified.

2. *Turgor Movements.*—Movements of plant organs caused by reversible changes in cell volume are known as *turgor movements.* Many of these movements are initiated in compact groups of relatively large, thin-

walled cells that constitute the so-called "motor organs" or *pulvini*, but they may also occur in any tissue that is largely composed of living, thin-walled cells. Examples of turgor movements associated with pulvini are the spectacular reactions of the sensitive plant (*Mimosa pudica*) to slight shocks or other "stimuli," and the so-called "sleep" movements of the leaves and leaflets of many other legumes. The opening and closing of stomates and the movements of leaves caused by wilting and recovery illustrate turgor movements that are not associated with pulvini.

3. *Hydration Movements.*—Movements may occur in nonliving plant tissues or organs as a result of the hydration or dehydration of the cell walls. These movements are illustrated by the splitting of pods, the opening of capsules, and the rapid movements of mature fern sporangia. Movements of these kinds are not caused by the physiological activities of living cells and will not be considered further in this discussion.

Phototropism.—Phototropic curvatures are familiar to all close observers of plants. They are particularly conspicuous in plants growing in situations in which they are exposed to unequal illumination on opposite sides. Under such circumstances the growing stems usually bend toward the direction of the more intense light and the leaves also become definitely oriented with relation to the light source, regardless of the position of their attachment to the stem. When vines such as the English ivy (*Hedera helix*) are growing on a wall so that light strikes the plants mainly from one direction, the leaf blades occupy practically the entire exposed surface with a minimum of overlapping. The leaf blades appear to fit together so exactly that the resulting patterns are known as "leaf mosaics." Similar, although less accurately formed, "leaf mosaics" are present in most plants bearing large numbers of leaves. Anyone standing beneath a large maple or oak tree, for example, cannot fail to be impressed by the completeness with which the sky is obscured by the leaf pattern. The leaves of some herbaceous plants (*Lactuca, Silphium,* etc.) are often so oriented that the blade surfaces face the east and west and only the edge of the blade receives the full intensity of the midday sun. This orientation is so conspicuous that these plants are commonly known as "compass plants." The leaf blades of the turkey oak (*Quercus catesbei*) also have a characteristic vertical orientation under conditions of intense sunlight.

Still another kind of phototropic movement occurs in some species (example: *Malva neglecta*) in which the surface of the blade is continuously oriented at right angles to the incident radiation of the sun. Such leaves follow the sun during the day, facing east in the morning and west in the afternoon (Yin, 1938). Similar movements, although caused by a different mechanism, occur during the development of the flower heads of some composites. The sunflower, for example, owes its name to the fact that the young flower head is oriented approximately at right angles to the sun's rays throughout the day.

The growth habits of some species of plants apparently are determined by their phototropic reaction. A number of species, including Bermuda and some other grasses, which are prostrate under usual field conditions of high light intensity, grow upright in light of low intensity. Such species are apparently negatively phototropic at high light intensities and positively phototropic at low light intensities (Langham, 1941).

Although many vines have numerous aerial roots, in general the root systems of the higher plants grow in total darkness. Nevertheless when exposed to unilateral illumination, many, but by no means all, roots exhibit phototropic curvatures. The usual reaction is negative, i.e., the root tip bends away from the direction of the incident light. Positive phototropic curvatures of roots are known but they are rare.

The movements which bring the leaves and stems into the oriented positions just described are caused either by differences in the growth rates on the illuminated and shaded portions of stems and petioles or by variations in the turgor of cells in specific tissues. Most of the phototropic movements result from differences in growth rates. Turgor changes in cells of the petiole, however, are known to account for the movements of those leaves which follow the path of the sun during the day. Although the "sleep movements" of many leaves and leaflets also are caused by turgor changes, these are photonastic (see later) rather than phototropic movements.

Most of our knowledge of the mechanism of phototropic movements has been derived from a study of the behavior of the coleoptile of the oat plant (*Avena sativa*) when subjected to one-sided illumination. Because of its reactivity, its structural simplicity, its uniformity of behavior under similar conditions, and its general suitability for such work, this structure has been widely used in experimental studies of phototropism, geotropism, and some other tropic movements (Chap. XXVIII).

It has been known since the time of Darwin that curvature of a coleoptile will occur if only the extreme tip of the coleoptile is exposed to unilateral illumination. The region in which the cell enlargement responsible for this curvature occurs, however, is some distance below the tip (Chap. XXVIII). If the tip of the coleoptile is shaded by means of a tin-foil cap and the entire coleoptile is illuminated unilaterally, little or no curvature results. Likewise, detipped coleoptiles react feebly to one-sided illumination, but if coleoptile tips which have been subjected to one-sided illumination are placed upon unilluminated coleoptile stumps, marked phototropic curvature of the stump results. Experiments like these indicate clearly that the tip of the coleoptile profoundly influences the enlargement phase of growth in cells below the tip of the coleoptile.

The positive phototropic curvature of oat coleoptiles is caused principally by greater elongation of the cells on the shaded side of the coleoptile than of the cells on the illuminated side. Since cell elongation is known to be influenced by the quantity of auxin present, it is logical to seek an explanation of such phototropic reactions by studying the effect of light upon the distribution of auxin in the coleoptiles. Extensive investigations have shown that, in oat coleoptiles at least, unilateral exposure to light increases the quantity of the auxin reaching the shaded side of the coleoptile from the tip and decreases the quantity on the illuminated side. The phototropic curvature of oat coleoptiles and presumably of many other plant structures apparently results from the presence of unequal quantities of auxin on the two sides of the coleoptile.

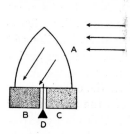

FIG. 175. Diagram to show method of demonstrating results of unilateral illumination upon auxin distribution in coleoptile tips. (A) Coleoptile tip, (B) and (C) agar blocks, (D) metal plate. Horizontal arrows indicate direction of illumination. Auxin is displaced toward side of coleoptile away from light.

The unequal distribution of auxin on the illuminated and shaded sides of coleoptiles could arise in several different ways (Galston and Hand, 1949). It is possible, for example, that the auxin on the illuminated side is inactivated more or less completely by the incident radiation while that on the shaded side remains active. A second possibility is that auxin migrates from the illuminated to the shaded side when the coleoptile is exposed to light from one direction. Another possibility is that the synthesis of auxin from its precursor in the coleoptile tip is checked by exposure to light resulting in the synthesis of larger amounts of auxin in the shaded sides than in the illuminated portion. No one of these possibilities can account satisfactorily for all light-induced growth movements. It seems probable, however, that the unequal distribution of auxin in oat coleoptiles is caused mainly by the migration of auxin from the illuminated side of the coleoptile tip to the shaded side. Some of the evidence upon which this conclusion is based will be reviewed briefly.

Went (1928) removed the tip of a coleoptile that had been exposed unilaterally to light of suitable intensity and placed it upon two small blocks of agar, separated from each other by a thin metal plate, in such a way that the auxin from the shaded and illuminated sides diffused into different agar blocks (Fig. 175). The blocks were then tested for auxin content by the oat coleoptile technique. The resulting curvatures indicated that more auxin diffused out of the shaded half of the coleoptile tip than out of the illuminated half. Furthermore, the quantity of auxin from the shaded half was appreciably more than the amount from half of an unilluminated tip. Went concluded, therefore, that one-sided exposure to light had caused some of the auxin to migrate from the illuminated to the shaded side of the coleoptile.

Boysen-Jensen (1928) came to a similar conclusion from a different kind of an experiment. The tip of a coleoptile was split longitudinally, a thin glass plate was inserted between the split halves, and the coleoptile was exposed to unilateral illumination of suitable intensity. When the glass plate was parallel to the light beam, normal phototropic curvatures occurred, but when the glass plate was at right angles to the direction of the light very little curvature resulted. When at right angles to the light beam, the glass plate apparently prevented the lateral migration of auxin from the lighted to the shaded side of the coleoptile so that the quantity of auxin was approximately the same on both sides. When the glass plate was parallel to the light beam, however, movement of auxin from the lighted side was not prevented. This experiment also indicates that under conditions of one-sided illumination, auxin, or its precursor, migrates from the illuminated to the shaded side of the oat coleoptile and that positive phototropic curvature is correlated with the greater auxin content of the cells on the darker side of the coleoptile.

Although the evidence supporting the hypothesis that auxin moves from the illuminated to the shaded side of the coleoptile when it is exposed to unilateral illumination is impressive, it has not been shown to be the only mechanism involved. It is probable that light-induced destruction of auxin also occurs. Riboflavin, which is abundant in the coleoptile, is known to bring about the photo-oxidation of auxin (Galston and Baker, 1949). The wave lengths of light absorbed by riboflavin are the same as the wave lengths most effective in producing curvature of the coleoptile, a fact which further supports the assumption that photo-inactivation of auxin is a factor in producing phototropic response in this structure.

All wave lengths of the visible spectrum are not equally effective in inducing phototropic curvatures. The shorter wave lengths are most effective, and the longer wave lengths at the red end of the spectrum evoke practically no phototropic reaction in etiolated oat coleoptiles or seedlings (Fig. 176). Light cannot bring about phototropic curvatures unless absorbed by the tissues. The effectiveness of the shorter wave lengths suggests the presence of some pigment in the sensitive tissues which absorbs these wave lengths and not others. The absorption spectrum of β carotene

(Fig. 91) corresponds very closely to the action spectrum of phototropic curvature in etiolated coleoptiles and seedlings. This correlation suggests that β carotene is responsible for the absorption of the light waves which are effective in inducing phototropic curvatures. It is also possible, however, that riboflavin, the absorption spectrum of which closely approaches that of β carotene, may be the sensitizing pigment (Galston and Baker, 1949).

In the early years of the present century Blaauw demonstrated that a certain minimum quantity of light was essential for a perceptible phototropic curvature of an oat coleoptile. Since quantity is a product of intensity and duration, low intensities are effective only upon long exposures but, with high intensities, extremely short exposures are sufficient. With a

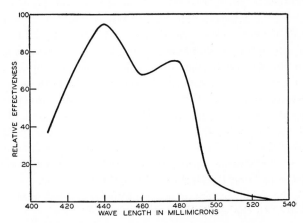

Fig. 176.   Relation between wave length of light and phototropic curvature of oat coleoptiles. Data of Johnston (1934).

light intensity of only 0.00017 meter-candles, an exposure of 43 hr. was required to induce phototropic curvature; but, with a light intensity of 26,520 meter-candles, an exposure of only 0.001 sec. resulted in phototropic curvature.

The minimum quantity of light required for phototropic movement, the so-called "threshold value," varies greatly with the portion of the coleoptile tip that is illuminated. The terminal 0.2 mm. of the coleoptile, for example, is nearly 6000 times as sensitive to illumination as a zone only 3 mm. below the tip (Lange, 1927).

Experimental results of a number of investigators have shown that the degree of phototropic curvature is controlled by the quantity of unilateral light. The curvature is not directly proportional to the amount of light but varies periodically as the quantity of light is increased (Fig. 177).

As the data in Fig. 177 indicate, once the threshold value is passed the coleoptiles curve toward the source of light and over a certain relatively low range of light intensities the degree of their curvature is proportional to the quantity of illumination. With further increase in the quantity of light, however, this relationship changes and the degree of phototropic curvature decreases until negative curvatures are evoked. Still greater quantities of light induce a second series of positive curvatures. On increasing the quantity of light still more the coleoptiles react with decreasing curvatures until a point is reached at which the light induces no visible end-reaction. Further increases in light quantity beyond this point evoke a third set of positive curvatures.

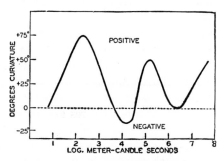

FIG. 177. Relation between phototropic curvature and quantity of light received unilaterally. Data of duBuy and Nuernbergk (1934).

A correlation exists between these variations in the magnitude of phototropic curvatures and the quantity of auxin diffusing from the illuminated and shaded sides of coleoptile tips (Table 49).

Auxin concentration is not the only factor involved in phototropic movements. The quantity of this hormone can only control the extent of cell elongation when it acts as a limiting factor. We have seen (Chap. XXVIII) that auxins are produced in the coleoptile tip and move basipetally into other parts of the structure. It is not probable, therefore, that

TABLE 49—THE RELATION BETWEEN THE AUXIN CONTENT OF COLEOPTILE TIPS SUBJECTED TO UNILATERAL ILLUMINATION OF DIFFERENT INTENSITIES AND THE DEGREES OF PHOTOTROPIC CURVATURES (FROM DATA COMPILED BY WENT AND THIMANN, 1937)

Amount of light, meter candle seconds	Type of curvature	Extent of curvature	Auxin distribution in per cent	
			Lighted side	Shaded side
0	Control	0°	49.9	50.1
20	First positive	+ (10°)	41	59
100	First positive	++	26	74
500	First positive	++	36	64
1,000	First positive	++(48°)	32	68
10,000	Indifferent	About 0°	49	51
?	First negative	....	58	42

curvatures of the upper portions of the coleoptile result from differences in auxin content since the hormones are present in excess in these regions. Photographic measurements have shown that, in the upper zone of the coleoptile, curvatures are not caused by increases in the rate of elongation of cells on the shaded side but by a decrease in the amount of cell elongation on the illuminated side. Likewise uniformly illuminated coleoptiles grow more slowly than coleoptiles kept in the dark. Numerous other experiments also indicate that light has a direct effect upon growth independent of its influence upon the auxin distributing mechanism of the plant (Van Overbeek, 1936a, 1936b).

The relative importance of this "light-growth" reaction in phototropic movements is somewhat uncertain. It seems clear that phototropic curvatures are not simple light-growth reactions as was widely believed at one time, for it has been demonstrated that the light-growth effect is inadequate to account for the differences in growth rates that are responsible for most phototropic curvatures. The effect of unilateral illumination upon the distribution or the inactivation of auxin appears to be the primary cause of phototropic curvatures and the direct influence of light upon the growth of cells seems to be of secondary importance.

Geotropism.—If a potted plant be placed in a horizontal position for a few days, the stems no longer lie prostrate but begin to turn upward away from the direction of gravitational attraction. This change in position first appears in the region of elongation just back of the stem tip and with time may extend backward toward the older portions of the stem. If the primary root tips of the plant are examined they will also be found to have

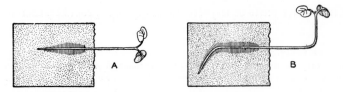

Fig. 178.   Diagram illustrating geotropic curvature of root and hypocotyl of a mustard plant. (A) Plant just after having been placed horizontally, (B) same plant one day later.

altered their position, but in exactly the opposite direction, by growing downward toward the center of the earth. The behavior of roots can be more easily observed in germinating seeds and as in stems the change in position first appears in the region of elongation just back of the root tip (Fig. 178).

If horizontally placed potted plants are rotated slowly around the stem as an axis, so that every vertical segment of the stem becomes successively the upper and then the lower side, no geotropic curvatures appear. No segment of the stem or root remains long enough in any one position for growth curvatures to occur. Similarly the roots fail to curve when germinating seeds are fastened to the rim of a wheel which is rotated rapidly in a horizontal plane. Growth is more strongly influenced by the centrifugal force generated by the rapid rotation than by the force of gravity. The roots react positively and grow toward the direction of the force (*i.e.,* outward) while the stems grow away from the direction of the force (*i.e.,* inward toward the hub of the wheel). If the rotation of the wheel is stopped or slowed down to a point where the centrifugal force is less than the pull of gravity, the usual geotropic curvatures of both root and stem soon appear.

Decapitated primary roots usually fail to exhibit geotropic curvatures when placed in a horizontal position even though the amputation of the root tip does not prevent the enlargement of cells below the tip. If tops from vertically oriented roots are placed upon such decapitated horizontal roots, positive geotropic curvatures appear. Such experiments indicate that the tip of the root exerts a predominating influence upon its geotropic movements, a relation comparable to that of the coleoptile tip in phototropic reactions of the coleoptile.

In stems, however, geotropic reactions are not prevented by amputation of the stem tip. In general, the stem tip is more "sensitive" to the force of gravity than zones at some distance below the tip, but this "sensitivity" to gravity is usually present throughout the growing region. In many grasses geotropic reactions occur in mature nodes independently of the stem tip (*cf.* later discussion of sugar cane).

The quantitative measurements of auxins made possible by the oat coleoptile technique have been utilized successfully in studying the role of auxins in geotropic curvatures. Coleoptiles which are slowly rotated around their own vertical axis while in a horizontal position do not differ from vertically oriented coleoptiles in their rate of growth. Tips of the horizontally placed coleoptiles produce the same amount of auxin as vertically oriented tips. The negative (upward) curvatures of the coleoptiles induced by gravity are not the result, therefore, of any total increase in the amount of hormones formed on the lower side of the coleoptile tip. When the amount of auxin diffusing out of the upper and lower halves of horizontally placed coleoptile tips is determined by the agar block method it is found that more than half of the auxin diffuses out of the lower half of the tip (Navez and Robinson, 1932). Apparently, gravity, like light, influences the distribution of the auxin in the coleoptile, and the upward curvatures obtained as a consequence of the force of gravity result from the greater concentrations of the hormone on the lower side of a horizontally placed coleoptile. Unlike the effect of light, however, the influence of gravity upon the distribution of the auxin within the coleoptile does not persist for very long after the organ has been returned to its original position. The effect of gravity upon curvature is lost within 40 min. after the removal of the "stimulus" but the effect of light upon the distribution of auxin in the cells of the coleoptile may persist as long as 6 hr. after removal of the light.

The same concentrations of auxin which favor the elongation of stems and coleoptiles retard the elongation of roots (Chap. XXVIII). This fact suggests that the positive (downward) geotropic reaction of root tips may be caused by the same mechanism which invokes the negative (upward) curvature of stems or coleoptiles. A greater concentration of auxin in the lower half of horizontally placed roots would check elongation rather than increase it, and the growth of the upper side of the root would exceed that of the lower, resulting in its downward curvature. Experimental tests have confirmed this explanation. The lower halves of tips of horizontal roots have been found to contain higher concentrations of auxins than the upper halves (Hawker, 1932). Since the growth rate of primary roots which are slowly rotated about their own axis in a horizontal plane does not exceed that of vertical roots (*i.e.*, auxin concentrations are equal in the root tips in both positions), the greater quantity of auxin in the lower half of the tips of horizontal primary roots indicates that the auxin migrates to this region under the action of gravity. The downward curvature of root tips is therefore found to be correlated with the auxin concentration.

The role of auxins in the geotropism of stems has also been demonstrated in quite a different manner. Sugar-cane stems fail to exhibit the usual geotropic curvatures if they have been immersed in water at 52°C. for about 20 min. The warm water treatment reduced concentration of free auxin in the stem by about 50 per cent (Brandes and Van Overbeek, 1948). If, however, the lower half of a horizontal sugar-cane stem is soaked in a very dilute solution of indoleacetic acid following the warm-water treatment the usual geotropic curvature occurs. The geotropic curvatures of sugar-cane stems occur at the nodes and result both from an increase in the size of cells and from the formation of new cells on the lower side of the stem (Brandes and McGuire, 1951). These processes are checked by treatments which reduce the auxin content of the stem appreciably in this region and are restored, at least in part, by supplying the lower half of the stem artificially with indoleacetic acid. It seems probable, therefore, that the geotropic curvatures of sugar-cane stems, like those of oat coleoptiles and root tips, result from the accumulation of auxin on the lower side of the organ in which the reaction occurs.

The unequal distribution of auxin in horizontal stems may have con-sequences quite apart from growth curvatures. In certain varieties of pineapple plants, for example, stems placed in a horizontal position develop flowers, whereas stems kept in a vertical position remain vegetative (Van Overbeek and Cruzado, 1948). The initiation of flowering was found to result from the accumulation of auxin on the lower side of the horizontal stem tip. In pineapple plants flower formation can be induced artificially by the application of growth regulators (Chap. XXXII). When plants are uprooted and placed in a horizontal position enough auxin migrates to the lower portion of the stem tip under the force of gravity to initiate the development of an inflorescence. In vertical stems the auxin concentration fails to reach the threshold value essential for flower induction until a much later period in the plant's development.

Thigmotropism.—The growth movements made by plants as a consequence of contact with solid objects are known as thigmotropic reactions. These movements are best illustrated in the growth of tendrils, although they are also exhibited by petioles, stems and other organs of some plants. Tendrils are slender cylindrical organs that structurally represent modified stems, leaves, or leaflets. Some common tendril-bearing species of plants are the grape vine, greenbriers (*Smilax*), sweet pea, and cucumber. As a result of unequal rates of growth the tips of young tendrils exhibit the phenomenon of nutation (see later) and make slow circular movements in space during their elongation. As soon as a tendril comes in contact with a solid object, rapid growth reactions are initiated. The cells on the side that makes contact with the solid object shorten somewhat and the cells on the opposite side quickly elongate with the result that the tendril is bent around the support. This movement usually occurs within a few minutes, and in the tendrils of some species may take place in less than a minute. The speed of the reaction is such as to suggest turgor changes in the cells rather than growth. However, since the resulting changes in cell size are irreversible the movement is classed as a tropism. Once the tendril becomes attached to some object further growth in length ceases. As a result of inequalities in growth in the basal region the tendril becomes spirally coiled so that it resembles a coil spring. Secondary wall formation then follows, transforming the delicate thin-walled tendril into a firm supporting organ.

A young tendril reacts readily to contacts with very light solids provided the solid surface is not perfectly smooth and that contact with the tendril is made at more than one place. No growth movements occur in tendrils as a result of contacts with liquids or perfectly smooth solids. If a very light thread weighing a small fraction of a milligram be moved along the surface of the tendril, curvature will result, but drops of mercury many thousand times heavier or raindrops bring about no reaction. The mechanism of thigmotropic movements cannot be satisfactorily explained at the present time.

Hydrotropism.—The roots of plants do not grow into soils in which the water content is at or below the permanent wilting percentage but usually do grow into soils of higher water content. When the soil in small pots containing growing plants is watered by means of porous clay irrigators the roots of plants are often matted heavily around the surface of the irrigators and are more sparsely distributed in the surrounding soil (Hendrickson and Veihmeyer, 1931). Such observations have often been cited as examples of positive hydrotropism in roots.

The work of Loomis and Ewan (1936) suggests, however, that curvatures of growing root tips toward regions of higher water content are not as common as was once supposed. These investigators filled shallow boxes half full of moist soil, placed the seeds to be observed upon the surface of the moist soil, and then filled the box with dry soil. The moist soil was near its field capacity, and the dry soil had a moisture content below the permanent wilting percentage (Chap. XIII). The soil was held firmly in position with paraffined paper and the box placed in a moist chamber in such a way that the boundary between the moist and dry soil made an angle of 45° to the vertical and so that the dry soil was on the lower side of this boundary. These conditions made it possible to determine the relative influence of soil moisture and gravity upon the direction of root growth. A positive hydrotropic reaction would result in a bending of the primary roots toward the moist soil. Examination of the root growth of thousands of seedlings representing twenty-six species revealed that few species exhibited positive hydrotropism. In most species the roots that started to grow downward as a consequence of gravitational attraction soon ceased to grow because of insufficient water. Roots that happened to develop in the moist soil grew normally. Positive hydrotropism was found to be present in a few species of the Cucurbitaceae and Leguminosae, because the roots of seedlings of these species curved away from the dry soil toward the moist soil and grew along the boundary between the moist and dry soil. The experiments demonstrate that hydrotropic curvatures do occur in the soil-grown roots of some species but also indicate that such curvatures are probably not a common phenomenon under field conditions.

Hydrotropic curvatures are caused by differences in the rate of enlargement of the cells on the opposite sides of the root, but no satisfactory explanation of the cause of this unequal growth has been suggested.

Traumatotropism.—Injury to the tissues of plants, especially to stems and roots, often results in curvatures caused by unequal growth. Such curvatures are examples of traumatotropic reactions. Transverse incisions in oat coleoptiles commonly result in positive curvatures, but detipped coleoptiles usually fail to react to injury inflicted near the upper end. Incisions made near the base of decapitated coleoptiles may induce positive curvatures, however. From the evidence available it seems probable that injuries influence either the distribution of auxin in the tissue (Keeble and Nelson, 1935) or interfere with the transport of foods or other substances into the growing regions from other parts of the plant, but no more detailed analysis of the mechanism of these reactions is possible in terms of currently available information.

Nastic Movements.—The essential distinction between nastic and tropic movements has already been described. With few exceptions, nastic movements are evoked by environmental factors such as temperature or diffuse light which influence the organ with equal intensity from all directions, while tropic movements are induced by factors which act with greater intensity from one direction than others. Equal illumination of all parts of a plant organ, for example, may result in *photonastic* movement, causing the organ to assume a different position in the light than in the dark. *Phototropic* movement of a plant organ occurs, however, only when the organ is illuminated unequally from different directions. Furthermore, nastic movements are chiefly restricted to organs such as leaves and petals, the structure of which largely or entirely prevents their movement except in certain directions.

The leaves of a number of different species of plants undergo marked changes in position during the day and night. In some species the leaves droop at night and become oriented more or less horizontally during the day. The common jewel-weed (*Impatiens*) and some other members of this family react in this way. The leaves of other species, notably the pigweeds (*Amaranthus*), move upward into a more nearly vertical position at night from the approximately horizontal position occupied during the day. Both of these kinds of movements are caused by differences in the rate of growth on the two sides of the leaf. The downward movement of leaves in the dark is the result of a more rapid growth upon the upper than upon the lower surface of the petiole while in those species in which the leaves move upward in the dark the growth rate is more rapid upon the lower side of the petiole. The movements just described are growth movements and cease entirely when the leaf reaches its full size.

Many of the movements of leaves and leaflets, however, are turgor movements rather than growth movements. Such movements are discussed later in the chapter.

Some flowers also exhibit such photonastic movements. *Oxalis* flowers, for instance, close at night while those of the evening primrose (*Oenothera*) open during the evening and night and close early on the following day as a consequence of photonastic reactions (Goldsmith and Hafen-richter, 1932).

Temperature changes may likewise bring about nastic movements of the flower petals of some species. In *Crocus* flowers, for example, an increase in temperature induces a more rapid growth of the inner surface of the petals than of the outer side resulting in the partial or complete opening of the flower. A decrease in temperature has the opposite effect, increasing the growth rate on the lower side more than that of the upper surface.

Nastic movements are growth movements and might, therefore, be expected to have some relation to the distribution of auxins in the tissues affected. Zimmerman and Wilcoxon (1935) were able to produce epinasty in the leaves of several species of plants by the application of different growth promoting substances. Avery (1935) demonstrated that typical nastic responses can be induced by the application of small amounts of auxins to the base of the petiole of tobacco leaves.

Nutation.—All growing stem tips describe an irregular spiral path in space as they elongate. This phenomenon, as previously mentioned, is known as *nutation* and appears to be caused, in most plants at least, by internal factors that affect the growth rate of vertical segments of the stem in the region of elongation.

The most striking examples of nutation are found among twining plants. The nutation of the stem tips of such species is at least partly a consequence of the influence of gravity. The stem tips of twiners are usually long and slender and devoid of leaves. Their mechanical tissues are not well developed so that the tip of the stem usually droops over into a more or less horizontal position. More rapid growth on the lower and outermost sides of the stem results in the upward swinging movements of the tip. This growth is associated with a twisting of the stem which follows as a result of the unequal growth rates so that different segments of the tip become successively placed on the lower side of the stem. It has been pointed out earlier that growth substances are known to accumulate in the lower half of horizontally placed stem tips. It seems probable that similar accumulations of auxin may influence the nutational movements of the stem tips of twining plants.

Turgor Movements.—In contrast to the growth movements which always involve a permanent increase in the size or number of cells in the tissues concerned, there are many movements which result from reversible changes in cell size. These are caused by variations, sometimes very rapid, of the turgor pressure in the cells concerned. Because of their dependence upon changes in turgor pressure, movements of this kind are known as *turgor movements.*

Turgor movements are responsible for the folding or rolling of the leaves of many grasses during wilting, for the so-called "sleep movements" that occur at night in the leaves of a number of species and for the sudden and spectacular movements that occur in the "sensitive plant" (*Mimosa pudica*) under the influence of various "stimuli."

Many turgor movements are caused by variations in the turgor of special cells or organs. The folding and rolling movements of blue grass leaves, for example, result from turgor changes in large, thin-walled cells that are located on the upper leaf surface at the base of two grooves that run parallel with the principal veins (Fig. 179). When turgor is high the

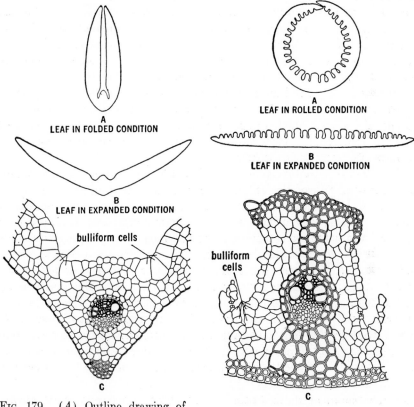

FIG. 179. (*A*) Outline drawing of blue grass (*Poa pratensis*) leaf in folded condition, (*B*) in expanded condition, (*C*) detailed drawing of mid-portion of the leaf showing the "bulliform cells," changes in the turgor of which control the folding and opening of the leaf.

FIG. 180. (*A*) Outline drawing of sand reed (*Amophila*) leaf in rolled condition, (*B*) in expanded condition, (*C*) detailed drawing of mid-portion of the leaf showing a few of the "bulliform cells," changes in the turgor of which are responsible for the rolling and opening of the leaf.

distention of these cells holds the leaf blade expanded and relatively flat, but when the turgor pressure of these cells decreases the pressure of the cells on the opposite side of the leaf forces the leaf blade to fold.

In the sand reed (*Ammophila*) such cells occur at the base of a number of grooves in the upper surface of the leaf, and upon the loss of turgor of these cells the leaf rolls up (Fig. 180).

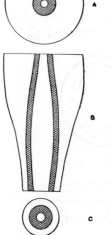

FIG. 181. Diagrams showing the distribution of the vascular tissue (shaded) in (*A*) cross section of a pulvinus, (*B*) the transition zone between a pulvinus and a petiole (longitudinal section), and (*C*) cross section of a petiole.

In some species of plants movements result from turgor changes in the cells of *pulvini*. These structures are found in many species of the Leguminosae. Pulvini are commonly located at the base of the petiole and at the point of attachment of the leaf blade to the petiole. Externally they appear as short, more or less swollen portions of the petiole. When pulvini are present in compound leaves there is usually one at the point of attachment of each leaflet to the petiole as well as one at the base of the petiole. A pulvinus is composed of a compact mass of large, thin-walled cells which surround a central vascular strand (Fig. 181).

When all of the cells in a pulvinus are distended by their turgor pressure the leaf is firmly supported. Movements result from sudden changes in the turgor of the cells in one portion of the pulvinus, while the turgor of cells on the opposite side is maintained or even increased. The unequal pressures thus arising on the two sides of the pulvinus cause the petiole to move toward the side having the reduced pressure. As the flaccid cells of the pulvinus regain their turgor the petiole is pushed slowly back into the position occupied before the movement occurred. Frequently the loss of turgor occurs very rapidly. In the sensitive plant detectable turgor movements have been reported to occur within 0.075 sec. after "stimulation," and the reaction may be complete in little more than a second. Recovery of turgor commonly occurs in from 8 to 20 min. The speed of the reaction and the time of recovery vary greatly with the intensity of the causal factor, the resulting movement being more rapid and recovery slower when the initiating factor is intense than when it is weak. In many species, however, pulvinal movements are too slow to be noticed without measurement.

The mechanism causing the sudden changes in turgor of the cells in one part of the pulvinus is not clearly understood. Water moves out of the cells into the adjacent intercellular spaces, and some probably enters other nearby cells of the petiole or stem. This outward movement of water from the cells into the intercellular spaces appears to be accompanied by an increase in the permeability of their cytoplasmic membranes and also by a decrease in the osmotically active contents of these cells (Blackman and Paine, 1918). All of these changes are reversible, since turgor may be

FIG. 182. A sensitive plant (*Mimosa pudica*). Left: leaves in expanded condition; right: leaves in a collapsed condition as a result of turgor movements.

regained by the flaccid cells of the pulvinus within a short period of time.

Turgor movements may be initiated in many different ways. In the sensitive plant (Fig. 182), movements result from physical contact, injury, exposure to various gases, electrical shock, jarring, insufficient water supply, the change from light to darkness or *vice versa*, and from other factors as well.

The sensitive plant also exhibits a difference in reactivity to the various wave lengths of light. Turgor movements result when darkened plants are illuminated by wave lengths of light of suitable intensity in the blue, the long ultraviolet, and the long red. No movements occur from exposure to wave lengths in the orange, yellow green, or infrared (Burkholder and Pratt, 1936).

The environmental factors initiating the movements may be received

FIG. 183.   Venus fly-trap (*Dionea muscipula*). Photograph by L. A. Whitford.

by organs at considerable distance from the pulvinus in which the turgor changes causing the movement actually take place. If a terminal leaflet of one leaf of a large sensitive plant is burned by a flame, all of the leaves on the entire plant may react with vigorous turgor movements. The conspicuous turgor movements that may easily be evoked in this plant have interested many students and the phenomenon has been exhaustively studied, especially with reference to the mechanism of "stimulus" transmission (Houwink, 1935). When the "stimulus" is mild (cool drops of water applied to the leaflets), it appears to be transmitted only through living cells, and the rate of transmission is controlled by the temperature. When a leaflet is injured by burning or cutting, substances appear to be formed at the point of injury, and the transmission of these compounds through the nonliving vessels of the vascular system apparently causes the reaction of pulvini located at some distance from the point at which the injury occurred. Whatever may be the mechanism by which reactions are induced at some distance from the point at which the initiating factor acted, the effect is the same: a rapid loss of turgor in the cells on one side of the pulvinus coupled with a maintenance or even an increase in turgor in the cells on the opposite side of the organ.

Movements in Carnivorous Plants.—Some of the most rapid movements known to occur in plants are those associated with the mechanisms by which insects and other small animals are captured by certain of the so-called "carnivorous" plants. The two halves of the leaf blade of the Venus fly-trap (*Dionea muscipula*), for example, spring together like the jaws of a steel trap when the trigger hairs on the leaf surface are given gentle pressure (Fig. 183). The whole process of closure may take place in less than 0.5 sec. so that small insects on the leaf surface are often imprisoned between the appressed halves of the leaf blade. The rapid movements of the leaf appear to result from tensions produced by differences in the growth of the upper and lower surfaces of the leaf blade. The way in which these tensions are suddenly released causing the movement of the leaf blade is not known.

Even more rapid movements are known to occur in other species of carnivorous plants, but, because of the variety of mechanisms involved and the complexity of the physiological processes responsible for these movements, it is not possible to give them adequate treatment here. For detailed descriptions of these unusual plants and their movements the student is referred to the monograph of Lloyd (1942).

SUGGESTED FOR COLLATERAL READING

Benecke, W., and L. Jost. *Pflanzenphysiologie*, Vol. II. G. Fischer. Jena. 1924.
Boysen-Jensen, P. *Growth Hormones in Plants*. Translated and revised by G. S.

Avery, Jr., and P. R. Burkholder. McGraw-Hill Book Co., Inc. New York. 1936.

Goldsmith, G. W., and A. L. Hafenrichter. Anthokinetics. *Carnegie Inst. Wash. Publ. No. 420.* Washington. 1932.

Lloyd, F. E. *The Carnivorous Plants.* Chronica Botanica Co. Waltham, Mass. 1942.

Pfeffer, W. *The Physiology of Plants.* 2nd Ed. Translated and edited by A. J. Ewart. Vol. III. Clarendon Press. Oxford. 1906.

Went, F. W., and K. V. Thimann. *Phytohormones.* The Macmillan Co. New York. 1937.

SELECTED BIBLIOGRAPHY

Avery, G. S., Jr. Differential distribution of a phytohormone in the developing leaf of *Nicotiana* and its relation to polarized growth. *Bull. Torrey Bot. Club* **62:** 313-330. 1935.

Blackman, V. H., and S. G. Paine. Studies in the permeability of the pulvinus of *Mimosa pudica. Ann. Bot.* **32:** 69-85. 1918.

Boysen-Jensen, P. Die phototropische Induktion in der Spitze der *Avena*-koleoptile. *Planta* **5:** 464-477. 1928.

Brandes, E. W., and Ruth C. McGuire. Auxin-thermal relations in cell growth and geotropic reaction of sugar cane. *Amer. Jour. Bot.* **38:** 381-389. 1951.

Brandes, E. W., and J. Van Overbeek. Auxin relations in hot-water-treated sugarcane stems. *Jour. Agric. Res.* **77:** 223-238. 1948.

Burkholder, P. R., and E. S. Johnston. Inactivation of plant growth substance by light. *Smithsonian Misc. Coll.* **95.** No. 20. 1937.

Burkholder, P. R., and R. Pratt. Leaf-movements of *Mimosa pudica* in relation to the intensity and wave length of the incident radiation. *Amer. Jour. Bot.* **23:** 212-220. 1936.

Buy, H. G. du, and E. Nuernbergk. Phototropismus und Wachstum der Pflanzen. II. *Ergeb. Biol.* **10:** 207-322. 1934.

Galston, A. W. Phototropism II. *Bot. Rev.* **16:** 361-378. 1950.

Galston, A. W., and Margery E. Hand. Studies on the physiology of light action I. Auxin and the light inhibition of growth. *Amer. Jour. Bot.* **36:** 85-94. 1949.

Galston, A. W., and Rosamond S. Baker. Studies on the physiology of light action II. The photodynamic action of riboflavin. *Amer. Jour. Bot.* **36:** 773-780. 1949.

Hawker, L. E. Experiments on the perception of gravity by roots. *New Phytol.* **31:** 321-328. 1932.

Hendrickson, A. H., and F. J. Veihmeyer. Influence of dry soil on root extension. *Plant Physiol.* **6:** 567-576. 1931.

Houwink, A. L. The conduction of excitation in *Mimosa pudica. Rec. Trav. Bot. Nèerland* **32:** 51-91. 1935.

Johnston, E. S. Phototropic sensitivity in relation to wave length. *Smithsonian Misc. Coll.* **92.** No. 11. 1934.

Keeble, F., and M. G. Nelson. The integration of plant behavior. V. Growth substance and traumatic curvature of the root. *Proc. Roy. Soc. (London).* B 117: 92-119. 1935.

Lange, S. Die Verteilung der Lichtempfindlichkeit in der Spitze der Haferkole-optile. *Jahrb. Wiss. Bot.* **67:** 1-51. 1927.

Langham, D. G. The effect of light on growth habit of plants. *Amer. Jour. Bot.* **28:** 951-956. 1941.

Loomis, W. E., and L. M. Ewan. Hydrotropic responses of roots in soil. *Bot. Gaz.* **97:** 728-743. 1936.

Navez, A. E., and T. W. Robinson. Geotropic curvature of *Avena* coleoptiles. *Jour. Gen. Physiol.* **16:** 133-145. 1932.

Rawitscher, F. Geotropism in plants. *Bot. Rev.* **3:** 175-194. 1937.

Schrank, A. R. Plant tropisms. *Ann. Rev. Plant Physiol.* **1:** 59-74. 1950.

Van Overbeek, J. Growth hormone and mesocotyl growth. *Rec. Trav. Bot. Nèerland* **33:** 333-340. 1936a.

Van Overbeek, J. Light growth response and auxin curvatures of *Avena*. *Proc. Nat. Acad. Sci. (U. S. A.)* **22:** 187-190. 1936b.

Van Overbeek, J. Phototropism. *Bot. Rev.* **5:** 655-681. 1939.

Van Overbeek, J., and H. J. Cruzado. Flower formation in the pineapple plant by geotropic stimulation. *Amer. Jour. Bot.* **35:** 410-412. 1948.

Went, F. W. Wuchstoff und Wachstum. *Rec. Trav. Bot. Nèerland* **25:** 1-116. 1928.

Yin, H. C. Diaphototropic movements of the leaves of *Malva neglecta*. *Amer. Jour. Bot.* **25:** 1-6. 1938.

Zimmerman, P. W., and F. Wilcoxon. Several chemical growth substances which cause initiation of roots and other responses in plants. *Contr. Boyce Thompson Inst.* **7:** 209-229. 1935.

AUTHOR INDEX

(Boldface type indicates bibliographic reference; asterisk indicates tabulated data, curves, or illustrations from the work of the author cited.)

SUBJECT INDEX

ABSCISSION, 732-734
Absorption of light by leaves, 345-346
Absorption of mineral salts,
mechanism of, 461-469
relation to transpiration, 133-134, 455-466
Absorption of nitrogenous compounds, 503-504
Absorption of water,
by aerial organs, 246-247
daily periodicity of, 255-257
effect of concentration of soil solution on, 246
effect of soil aeration on, 244-246
effect of soil temperature on, 243-244
effect of soil water content on, 243
mechanism of, 239-242
relation to absorption of mineral salts, 133
relation of growth of roots to, 237-239
relation to transpiration, 133, 239-240, 255-257
Absorption spectra,
of chlorophyll, 299
of carotene, 305
Accessory cells, 141
Accumulation of carbohydrates, effect of, on photosynthesis, 361
Accumulation of foods, 451-453, 501, 604-606
Accumulation of mineral salts, 462-468
Acetaldehyde, 426
Acetic acid, 20, 443, 447
Acetylene, 684
Acidity, total, 15
Acids, 14-15
Aconitic acid, 427-428, 429, 432
Activated diffusion, 550
Activation energy, 288
Activators, enzymatic, 284
Active absorption, 240-242

Adenine, 586, 597
Adenosine phosphates, 381, 382, 384, 424, 426, 430-431
Adsorption, 25-27
of water, 96-97
Adventitious embryony, 656
Aeration of soil, 210-211
Aeration of soil, effect of,
on absorption of water, 244-246
on growth, 636-637
After-ripening, 710-711
Alanine, 325, 504, 507, 508
Aldolase, 384, 424, 425, 446
Alkaloids, 516-517
Aluminum, role of, 488
Amino acids, 59, 503, 504
role in growth, 592, 594, 596, 638-639
synthesis of, 315, 506-509
Ammonia, 513-514
Ammonification, 520
Ammonium compounds,
absorption of, 514
in plants, 513-514
Amphoteric properties of protein sols, 41-42
Amygdalin, 280, 387-388
Amylases, 271, 272, 280, 383, 384
Amylopectin, 376-377, 383
Amylose, 376-377, 383
Anabasine, 517
Anatomy of leaves, 124-126
Anatomy of roots, 229-234, 525-530
Anatomy of stems, 180-191, 525-530
Anions, 12
in the soil, 460
Annual rings, 183, 635
Anode, 12
Antagonism, 475
Anthesis, 650
Anthocyanins, 388-389
Anthoxanthins, 389-390